INDIANA to 1816
The
COLONIAL PERIOD

THE HISTORY OF INDIANA

VOL. I

Published in observance of the ses-quicentennial of Indiana's statehood in 1971 by the Indiana Historical Society and the Indiana Historical Bureau with the aid of a grant from Lilly Endow-ment, Inc.

INDIANA to 1816
The COLONIAL
PERIOD

by John D. Barnhart
& Dorothy L. Riker

INDIANA HISTORICAL BUREAU & INDIANA HISTORICAL SOCIETY

Indianapolis 1971

FOREWORD

Plans for the publication of a five-volume history of Indiana by the Indiana Historical Society and the Indiana Historical Bureau in observance of the state's sesquicentennial were formulated more than a decade ago. One of the most enthusiastic advocates of the project was the late R. C. Buley, Pulitzer prize-winning historian, who proposed the idea in a breakfast conference in 1955. The Society's participation was supported by a grant from Lilly Endowment, Inc. The Indiana Sesquicentennial Commission provided funds to supply copies to the school libraries of the state.

Dr. John D. Barnhart, who made major contributions to Indiana history as president of the Indiana Historical Society, editor of the *Indiana Magazine of History,* chairman of the History Department at Indiana University and an individual scholar, played a major role in planning the history. He also agreed to prepare Volume I covering the period up to 1816. Other authors selected were: Donald F. Carmony, Indiana University, Volume II, 1816-1850; Emma Lou Thornbrough, Butler University, Volume III, 1850-1880; Clifton J. Phillips, DePauw University, Volume IV, 1880-1920; and Richard Gemmecke, Indiana State University, Volume V, 1920-1966.

Dr. Thornbrough was the first to finish her assignment and Volume III, *Indiana in the Civil War Era,* was published in 1965. Dr. Phillips' manuscript, Volume IV, was published in 1969 under the title, *Indiana in Transition: The Emergence of an Industrial Commonwealth.* Both volumes received Awards of Merit from the American Association for State and Local History and were honored at Indiana Authors' Days at Indiana University. Editorial responsibility has been principally shared thus far among Miss Gayle Thornbrough,

Director of Publications, Indiana Historical Society, and Miss Dorothy Riker and Mrs. Shirley McCord of the Indiana Historical Bureau.

Dr. Barnhart's work on Volume I was delayed by illness and following his death in December, 1967, Miss Dorothy Riker, senior editor of the Indiana Historical Bureau, accepted the task of completing its preparation. The publishers feel a special sense of gratitude to Miss Riker for accepting this assignment as an overload in addition to her normal duties. Miss Riker has produced several volumes in the "colonial period" and edited many others. She has an exceptional grasp of her subject materials.

It is hoped that the project may be completed in the near future with the publication of the remaining two volumes.

HUBERT H. HAWKINS
Director, Indiana Historical Bureau
Secretary, Indiana Historical Society

PREFACE

Professor John D. Barnhart's research in connection with the editing of Lieutenant Governor Henry Hamilton's Journal of 1778-79 and the writing of *Valley of Democracy. The Frontier versus the Plantation in the Ohio Valley*, plus his study of the constitutional conventions of Ohio and Indiana for publication in the *Indiana Magazine of History*, made it especially fitting that he should have been chosen to write Volume I of the sesquicentennial *History of Indiana*. His teaching and administrative duties at Indiana University and then illness slowed the work but it remained his principal interest up until his death in December, 1967. I accepted the invitation to complete the volume because of my deep interest in this phase of Indiana history.

Chapter I, "The Land," is taken in part from Dr. Barnhart's chapter on the same subject prepared for *Indiana. From Frontier to Industrial Commonwealth*, written in cooperation with Donald F. Carmony and published by the Lewis Historical Publishing Company in 1954. Chapter II, "Indiana's Prehistory," was written by Dr. James H. Kellar, archaeologist for the Indiana Historical Society.

Dr. Barnhart had asked Miss Frances Krauskopf, who had written on the French in Indiana for her doctoral thesis, to write the portion of Volume I dealing with the French period. Her very detailed account based on her study of French documents forms the basis for Chapters II and III.

The map of the Western Country and the one showing Indian Land Cessions were drawn especially for this volume by John T. McCord of Indianapolis.

Inasmuch as there were no garrisoned posts in the Indiana area during the British period of occupation, it has been passed over as uneventful, yet the authors found it to be a very interesting period.

For the Revolution in the West there is an abundance of source material, both British and American, as well as numerous secondary accounts and biographies. Following the war the new nation was faced with a multitude of problems and decisions concerning some of them would greatly affect the future of the Northwest, including the region of Indiana. Foremost among these were the problem of Indian ownership and occupation of the land, the manner in which the land was to be surveyed and transferred to individuals, and the type of government which was to be adopted for the West. Again, there is no lack of primary and secondary materials upon which to draw.

For the period of the Indiana Territory, 1800-1816, the previous publication of the *Laws* and the *Journals* of the General Assembly, the *Messages and Letters* of Governors Harrison and Posey, and the official papers of the territory found in the archives in Washington, D. C., provide an abundance of source material on the governmental aspects, while such volumes as the *Moravian Indian Mission on White River,* the *Letter Book of the Indian Agency at Fort Wayne,* and *The Correspondence of John Badollet and Albert Gallatin* throw additional light on the period.

I am especially indebted to Miss Gayle Thornbrough, Director of Publications, Indiana Historical Society, and Hubert H. Hawkins, Director of the Historical Bureau, who have read my revision of Dr. Barnhart's manuscript and made many helpful suggestions. Mrs. Hazel Hopper and Mrs. Frances Macdonald of the Indiana Division of the State Library and Miss Caroline Dunn of the Indiana Historical Society Library have been most helpful in various research problems and in obtaining manuscript material from other libraries for my use. To Mrs. Shirley McCord of the Historical Bureau staff I owe a special debt of gratitude for her assistance in all phases of the preparation of the volume and of seeing it through the press. The constant encouragement of the above individuals and their continuing interest in the volume have been invaluable.

February, 1971   D.L.R.

CONTENTS

Policy of Continental Congress—Treaties with Indians—
Indian Confederacy—Nonacceptance of Treaties by In-
dians—Strength of United States Army—Surrender of
Western Lands by States—Development of Govern-
mental and Land Policies for Western Territory—Land
Surveys—Virginia's Land Grant to Clark's Soldiers—
Chaotic Conditions at Vincennes—Expedition against
Wabash Indians—Clark's Plan for Indian Council—
Trouble with Spain—Establishment of Military Post at
Vincennes—Ordinance of 1787

Inauguration of American Government in Northwest
Territory—Formation of Knox County—Development
of a Penal Code—Vincennes Land Titles—Formulation
of a New Indian Policy—Treaty of Fort Harmar—
Failure of Peace Mission to Wabash Indians—Harmar's
Expedition against the Miami and Other Tribes—Ham-
tramck's Expedition up the Wabash—Scott's Expedition
against the Wabash Tribes—Wilkinson's Expedition
against Little Turtle's Village—St. Clair's Plan to
Erect a Chain of Forts in Indian Country—Defeat of
St. Clair's Army—Failure of New Peace Missions to
Ohio Tribes—Treaty Negotiations with Wabash Tribes
at Vincennes—Senate Rejection of Vincennes Treaty
—Repudiation of Earlier Treaties by Indian Council—
Failure of Proposed Peace Conference between United
States and Indians—British Preparation for War—Jay's
Mission to London—Wayne's Expedition—Battle of
Fallen Timbers—British Denial of Aid to Defeated
Tribesmen—Construction of Fort Wayne at Headwaters
of Maumee—Jay's Treaty with Great Britain—Green-
ville Treaty with Indians—Transfer of British Posts—
Settlements in Ohio—Advance to Representative Gov-
ernment—Revision of Land Act—Division of Northwest
Territory

Appointment of Governor, Secretary, and Judges for the
Indiana Territory—Census of 1800—Americans and

ILLUSTRATIONS

MAPS, CHART, AND DRAWING

CHAPTER I

THE LAND OF INDIANA[1]

Before man came to Indiana, great ice sheets that came down from what is now Canada divided the land of the present state into three major geographical divisions in which living conditions differ more than is generally realized. The glaciers changed the surface of the land, redirected the flow of the rivers, created lakes, and covered much of the land with a deep rich soil. The Wisconsin Glacier, which was the last and most effective of the ice sheets, covered approximately two thirds of the state, but left the southern third, which may be called the hill country, much less affected in comparison with the central and northern parts. An earlier ice sheet, the Illinois Glacier, had covered all of the state except the central portion of the southern third, which is known as the Driftless Area because it was not covered by any of the glaciers. It experienced less topographical change and missed particularly the beneficial effects so important in central Indiana. The Illinois ice sheet, however, did not obliterate the older surface and consequently the southern part of the state is separated into subdivisions which extend from the Ohio River northward to or beyond the Shelbyville Moraine, which marks the southern edge of the Wisconsin Glacier and the northern boundary of the hill country. These subdivisions, which are only a few miles from east to west, give to southern Indiana considerable variations in scenery, economic resources, and living conditions.

---

[1] The greater part of the chapter was originally prepared by Dr. Barnhart for an earlier publication, *Indiana. From Frontier to Industrial Commonwealth*, of which he was the co-author with Donald F. Carmony (5 volumes [3-5 biographical], Lewis Publishing Company, New York, 1954).

The Dearborn Upland, a relatively high, rough tableland, includes part or all of the eleven southeastern counties of Indiana.[2] Because most of the valley of the Whitewater River is north of the Shelbyville Moraine, the better soil is in the central rather than the southern part of the state. The part of this section which lies south of the moraine is characterized by "elevated, prolonged divides flanked by smooth, steep slopes and ending in rounded spurs overlooking relatively narrow valley lands often hundreds of feet below. Distant from the main valleys the elevated upland tongues merge into rather flat upland tracts of considerable extent."[3]

On the western border of the Dearborn Upland lies the Muscatatuck Regional Slope, which contains parts of ten counties. The better soil of the section is north of the Shelbyville Moraine. The southern part is marked by deeply entrenched valleys and steep slopes with higher elevations in between. Whether the visitor to southeastern Indiana who does not possess technical training can distinguish the differences between the Upland and the Slope is doubtful.

If, however, the visitor crosses to the west and enters the Scottsburg Lowland, which includes part of the remaining counties of the southeastern part of the state, he will note the characteristics of this third section easily and quickly: broad flat valleys, gentle slopes, low elevations, and agricultural production which exceeds that of much of the southern part of the state. Although it is not a large area it contains

[2] See map, page 6, showing the various physiographic units. For an extensive discussion of the physiography of Indiana, see Clyde A. Malott, "The Physiography of Indiana," *Handbook of Indiana Geology* (Indiana Department of Conservation, *Publication No. 21,* Indianapolis, 1922), Part II, 59-256. The subject is discussed in brief in Allan F. Schneider, "Physiography," *Natural Features of Indiana* (Indiana Academy of Science, 1966), pp. 40-56. The map is from *ibid.,* p. 41, and is a modification of one prepared for the Indiana Geological Survey, *Report of Progress No. 7,* issued in 1956. It is reproduced here by permission of the Geological Survey and Dr. Schneider.

[3] Malott, "The Physiography of Indiana," *Handbook of Indiana Geology,* p. 86.

the cities of Jeffersonville, Charlestown, Scottsburg, Seymour, and Columbus.

Some of the finest scenery of southern Indiana is to be found along the western edge of the Scottsburg Lowland, where the Knobstone Escarpment divides southeastern Indiana from the Driftless Area. The Knobs of Kentucky, which cross the Ohio River and pass northward to Brown County, are the most prominent topographic feature in Indiana. They tower hundreds of feet over the lowland to the east.

The Driftless Area includes three subdivisions, the Norman Upland, the Mitchell Plain, and the Crawford Upland. The first of these is an old and maturely dissected region of rugged hills with sharp slopes and deep stream valleys. The picturesqueness of Brown County is due to those features. Lovely panoramic views are to be had from the tops of the knobs and ridges. The soil is comparatively poor.

The Mitchell Plain is a region of sinkholes, lost streams, underground drainage, and a mixture of plains and hills created by dissection. The few surface streams that flow across the section are deeply entrenched. This part of the state is one of the poorer agricultural areas. From Bedford to Gosport, however, the outcropping of the Oolitic or Salem limestone has given the inhabitants a natural resource of great value.

The westernmost subdivision of the Driftless Area, the Crawford Upland, is one of great diversity: high and low hills; sharp, round and flat-topped ridges; trenchlike and flat-bottomed valleys; sinkholes, waterfalls, canyon-like gorges, a natural bridge, caves, and generally irregular topography. The variety and unevenness add to the natural beauty of the section, but only the Muscatatuck Slope equals it in the low average value of the land.

The southwestern part of Indiana is made up of the Wabash Lowland, most of which was covered by the Illinois Glacier. The lowland has a general, plainlike structure with stream valleys filled with silt and glacial deposits. It contains the best lands in the southern part of the state and is underlaid with valuable coal deposits. The wealth of natural resources, particularly coal and soil combined with adequate transportation, has produced a rich agricultural section, numerous mining centers, and the important cities of Evansville, Vincennes, and Terre Haute.

From this brief review of the physical properties of the hill country of southern Indiana, it is evident that the region is not rich agriculturally, and with the exception of the coal and Oolitic limestone districts there are few mineral resources. The topography is so rough and uneven as to have made the building of railroads expensive, and for this and other reasons the region is less well supplied than the rest of the state. With a few exceptions the largest cities of the area are located on the Ohio and Wabash rivers. The inland towns are generally small except where stone or coal have provided unusual stimuli.

Although the Shelbyville Moraine, which marks the southern limit of the Wisconsin Glacier, does not coincide all the way across Indiana with the southern boundary of the Tipton Till Plain, it seems to be the better demarcation between the hill country of southern Indiana and the plains region of central Indiana. The glacier came as far south as Terre Haute, Montezuma, Rockville, Greencastle, Monrovia, Martinsville, Morgantown, and Nineveh, and therefore the moraine is found near these communities.[4] Thus far it is also the boundary of the Till Plain, but at this point the two separate. The Shelbyville Moraine turns to the southeast, passes east of Columbus to the nearest corner of Jennings County, where it moves east and northeast into the valley of the West Fork of the Whitewater River. From there it turns

---

[4] Described in detail, the moraine begins at the state line west of Terre Haute, passes northward to the vicinity of Montezuma where it turns eastward and passes south of Rockville, southeastward across Putnam County a little to the southwest of Greencastle. It then turns eastward to the neighborhood of Monrovia, where it turns sharply to the south, missing Martinsville on the east, and then turns to Morgantown and Nineveh.

southeastwardly and passes through the vicinity of Brookville into Ohio. The southern limit of the Till Plain, however, turns sharply north at Nineveh and passes around Franklin, and moves northeastwardly past Richmond on the north and into Ohio. The latter is an important geological boundary, but the good soil and the large crops of the area between the two lines, both largely due to the thickness of the glacial deposits, seem to indicate that this area should be considered as a part of central rather than southern Indiana.

Central Indiana, the largest division of the state, possesses very fertile soil, which the glaciers deposited to a great depth. The surface of the land is generally level, but variation is found along the Wabash River, where the Vermilion and Tippecanoe rivers and other tributaries have cut deep valleys considerably below the glacial plain. Sugar Creek has produced some rugged scenery which has been preserved in the Shades and Turkey Run state parks. Elsewhere in the area morainal deposits have produced hills and ridges which attain their greatest altitude in Randolph County along the Ohio-Indiana boundary.[5]

The northern limit of the plains region crosses the Indiana-Ohio boundary southeast of Fort Wayne along the former beach of the glacial Lake Maumee which it follows to Fort Wayne, where it turns southwest along the valley of Little River to Huntington. From this city it passes westward along the Wabash River to a point ten miles west of Logansport and then pursues a straight line westward through Monticello and Kentland into Illinois.

The northern part of the state is a portion of the Eastern Lake Section of the Central Lowlands which may be called the moraine and lake region of Indiana. It is divided into five subregions, most of which are small. When the present outlet of Lake Michigan was dammed by the ice of the glaciers, its waters extended southward a few miles beyond its

[5] The highest point above sea level in Indiana, 1,285 feet, is near Lynn in Randolph County.

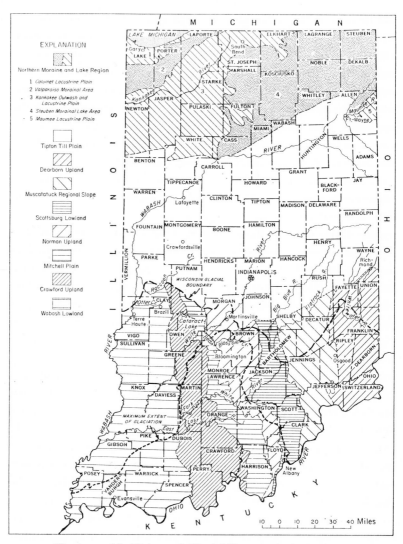

EXPLANATION

Northern Moraine and Lake Region

1 Calumet Lacustrine Plain
2 Valparaiso Morainal Area
3 Kankakee Outwash and Lacustrine Plain
4 Steuben Morainal Lake Area
5 Maumee Lacustrine Plain

Tipton Till Plain

Dearborn Upland

Muscatatuck Regional Slope

Scottsburg Lowland

Norman Upland

Mitchell Plain

Crawford Upland

Wabash Lowland

Physiographic Units and Glacial Boundaries in Indiana

present shore. The area which is no longer covered by the lake and of which the sand dunes are the most prominent feature is now known as the Calumet Lake Section. It is a small region and was not developed until manufacturing plants late in the nineteenth century began to be located along the lake shore where they could take advantage of water transportation. Now a highly industrialized section, it contains the cities of Hammond, Whiting, East Chicago, Gary, and Michigan City. The portion of the section in Illinois includes the lake shore from the Indiana boundary to the north of Chicago.

An even smaller but similar area east of Fort Wayne was once covered by the glacial Lake Maumee and is therefore called the Maumee Lake Section. It is today a rich agricultural area similar to northwest Ohio which was also covered by the glacial lake.

Another subdivision of northern Indiana is the Valparaiso Moraine Section which curves around the southern end of Lake Michigan just beyond the Calumet Lake area. It is formed by three moraines near the Illinois border, which shortly become one as the section extends across Indiana into Michigan.

Parts of the valleys of the Kankakee, Iroquois, Tippecanoe, and St. Joseph rivers form the area known as the Kankakee Lake Section. For a long time the Kankakee Valley, which is the heart of the region, drained so poorly that it was known as a marsh where wild life thrived in great quantity long after being driven out of the rest of the state.[6] Today, with better drainage the muck soils of the region are wonderfully productive. The valley of the Iroquois is not so marshy. Quite a number of small lakes are found in St. Joseph and Elkhart counties in the valleys of the Kankakee and St. Joseph rivers.

The Steuben Morainal and Lake Section, which includes most of northeastern Indiana, is the largest of the northern

6 Charles H. Bartlett in his *Tales of Kankakee Land* (New York, 1904) has preserved in his retelling of the legends of the Kankakee and St. Joseph rivers glimpses of the wild life that remained at the time of his boyhood. It is also interesting that three of the five state game preserves are in the Kankakee Lake Section.

subdivisions. The ice sheets remained in this part of the state longer than in the central and southern parts and left a large number of morainal deposits in the form of hills and ridges. Scattered throughout the area are also numerous small lakes and marshy places of poor drainage. The soil is much the same as in central Indiana, but the productiveness of this part of the state does not equal the plains region because of the moraines, lakes, and marshes. Modern drainage systems have done much to eliminate the marshy areas in contrast to conditions prevailing seventy-five years ago. When the country was first settled, Indiana was the subject of unfavorable comment because of its dampness and the prevalence of malarial fevers.[7] This may have discouraged Yankee migration and thus influenced the composition of the population.

As the glaciers retreated, the rivers and lakes that form the drainage system of Indiana came into being; rain and snow falling on Indiana flows in all directions. The Wabash River and its tributaries drain water from about two thirds of the state into the Ohio River, while the Kankakee and its tributaries flow into the Illinois River and on to the Mississippi. The Maumee River, formed by the confluence of the St. Joseph and St. Marys rivers, drains to the east through Ohio into Lake Erie.

The Great Lakes gave to the Middle West a vital highway to the Atlantic Ocean and Europe by way of the St. Lawrence River. By this route came the first white men who explored the river systems and found the portages connecting the streams. Four of Indiana's rivers, the St. Joseph of Lake Michigan, the Kankakee, the Maumee, and the Wabash were located where they were naturally used by the early explorers, missionaries, and traders. Two of them, the Wabash and the Maumee, were later utilized with temporary success in an attempt to join the waters of the Great Lakes with the Ohio.

[7] See Richard L. Power, "Wet Lands and the Hoosier Stereotype," *Mississippi Valley Historical Review*, XXII (1935-36), 33-48.

The St. Joseph of Lake Michigan rises in central southern Michigan, flows southward into Indiana where today the cities of Elkhart, Mishawaka, and South Bend occupy its banks, and then turns northwestward to enter Lake Michigan at St. Joseph. About four miles southwest of South Bend rise two small tributaries of the Kankakee, but the sluggish, meandering character of this stream made it difficult to follow so this route was not used extensively.

Of greater importance were the Maumee and Wabash rivers. The source of the St. Joseph of the Maumee is in southern Michigan, from which it flows southwestward to the site of Fort Wayne, where it is joined by the St. Marys, which rises in western Ohio and flows northwestward; the waters of the two streams form the Maumee, which after a northeasterly course empties into Lake Erie. The strategic location at the head of the Maumee was recognized by both Indians and whites, and became the site of an Indian village, a French trading post, an American fort, and then an important town and city. A few miles west of this point, the traveler comes to the Little River, which is wide and deep enough to float a canoe. Twenty-two miles south of Fort Wayne the Little River joins the Wabash, which rises in Ohio and flows northwestward to this point and then continues westward and southwestward to the mouth of the Tippecanoe River near the present city of Lafayette, receiving on the way the waters of the Salamonie, Mississinewa, and Eel. Below Lafayette it turns southward and is enlarged by the Vermilion, Sugar, Raccoon, Busseron, Embarrass, White, Patoka, and Little Wabash streams before it joins the Ohio. Along its banks in early days lived the Miami, Wea, Kickapoo, and Piankashaw Indians. The Maumee-Wabash route was sufficiently usable and important to bring considerable travel and business this way and to cause the French to build forts at the head of the Maumee, below the mouth of the Tippecanoe, and at Vincennes.

The Ohio River replaced the St. Lawrence as a significant highway for the people of the Middle West when American frontiersmen began to float down its waters. Its tributaries rose far to the east along the watershed of the Appalachians beginning with the Allegheny near the boundary of New York and Pennsylvania and continuing southward with the Youghiogheny, Monongahela, New, Licking, and Kentucky. These rivers served to direct prospective settlers from the older states and especially from the South Atlantic states into the Ohio Valley. Frequently the sources of these streams were near the beginning of rivers which flowed eastward to the Atlantic and near the passes through the mountains. Indian trails and hunters' paths used these passes and furnished routes through the Appalachians to the land of the western waters. The principal roads which grew out of these paths were the Genesee Road in New York from the Mohawk River to Lake Erie or to the Allegheny; the Forbes Road from the Susquehanna to the forks of the Ohio; Braddock's Road from the Potomac to the Monongahela; Zane's Trace from Wheeling to Maysville and on to central Kentucky; the Quaker Trace by way of the Great Kanawha River to the Ohio at Point Pleasant; and Boone's Wilderness Trail from the upper Tennessee Valley to the Kentucky bluegrass country and on to the Ohio at Louisville.

After using the waterways to reach Indiana, the pioneers used them to ship their surplus products to market. Rafts, flatboats, and finally steamboats carried the exportable surplus down stream, while keelboats and steamboats struggled with the current of the Mississippi and Ohio to bring to Indiana and the Middle West the manufactures and luxuries which the people desired. Though transportation by water was in time supplanted by the railroad, the waterways of the Great Lakes and the Ohio have enjoyed a revival in recent years.

The state as a whole, with minor variations from north to south, enjoys a stimulating climate which is favorable to agricultural production and human activity. The summer seasons are not ideal, but they are neither long nor hot enough to be seriously depressing, while the average winter temperatures are invigorating but not benumbing. Snowfall is not generally deep enough to be a serious handicap to outdoor activity. In the opinion of Stephen S. Visher, Indiana climatologist, the temperature in Indiana during about nine months in the year is more favorable than in most of the world.[8]

The warm summer days and nights are very suitable for raising corn. This crop requires temperatures of 48° and above for growth. The long growing seasons between killing frosts are also a favorable factor in the production of corn, tomatoes, and beans. The season, however, is not long enough for cotton, although some of the pioneers from southern states tried to raise cotton in Indiana as well as in Illinois. The growing season averages about 170 days, within which are several consecutive weeks of "corn weather," when the nights as well as the days are warm. The precipitation in the state is quite generally adequate for agricultural purposes, partly because a considerable portion of it falls during the growing season and is quite dependable year after year. The number of sunny days is sufficient for agriculture and the number of destructive storms is relatively small.[9]

Although the natural resources of Indiana do not compare in value with the coal, oil, and natural gas of Pennsylvania and West Virginia, the iron of Minnesota, the oil of Oklahoma, Texas, and California, or the precious minerals of the Rocky Mountain states, they are important to the people of this commonwealth and are basic in particular communities. Coal deposits under the southwestern part of Indiana have been extensively exploited, although much remains for future generations. Limited quantities of petroleum and natural gas have been found, and their use has aided in the development

8 Stephen S. Visher, *Climate of Indiana* (Bloomington, Ind., 1944), p. 21.
9 *Ibid.*, pp. 18, 22.

of manufactures. The presence of limestone in central southern Indiana has been mentioned as the basis of the building industry. Gravel and sand, gypsum, clays suitable for pottery making, and mineral waters are among the lesser resources.

Before the days of improved modern transportation, local iron ore was mined, but today the lake steamers bring Minnesota's ore to Indiana's mills. The relative nearness of the great deposits of iron ore near the shores of Lake Superior is one of the advantages which Indiana enjoys. Local coal is made into coke, and waste limestone is used as flux for steel furnaces and for other purposes. The exploitation of natural resources has constituted an important phase of Indiana's history.

Until the American frontiersman occupied Indiana, much of the land was covered with forests, and lumber became one of the most important natural resources. The pioneers were at first unwilling to venture on the prairies. They were unfamiliar with them and thought the soil was not fertile. Those who did try to cultivate the dry prairie land found the task of breaking the soil very difficult.[10] In preparing the timbered land for farming the settlers destroyed great quantities of trees, many of which were burned, but actually much of the timber was used. The business of clearing the land was gradual, a process which extended over many years.

By and large the physical features of Indiana constitute a substantial foundation for the development of a society which has achieved a generally high standard of living; a diversified economy supported by agriculture, industry, transportation, and the development of natural resources; and a great political commonwealth in which the citizens possess the means of governing themselves.

---

[10] Solon Robinson, a Vermonter who settled in Lake County, Indiana, did much to acquaint emigrants with the prairies by his articles in agricultural periodicals. See Volume I of *Solon Robinson, Pioneer and Agriculturist, 1825-1845,* edited by Herbert A. Kellar (*Indiana Historical Collections,* XXI, Indianapolis, 1936).

CHAPTER II

INDIANA'S PREHISTORY[1]

All too frequently in an understandable but ethnocentric concern for our own lives and time and their immediate antecedents, it is often forgotten that what is presently Indiana had been occupied for many millenniums prior to the appearance of Europeans. The contributions of these earlier occupants, the American Indian, are inescapable to even the most casual observer, although their cultures have long since been obliterated.

The name of the state and its capital city are obvious reminders of Indian occupation, as are the names of four of the immediately adjacent states. Other examples are Miami, Wabash, and Tippecanoe counties; the Mississinewa, Salamonie, Wabash, Kankakee, Tippecanoe, Patoka, and, of course, Ohio rivers; a host of lakes including Wawasee, Maxinkuckee, Manitou, and Winona; innumerable small communities and larger ones among which are Wabash, Elkhart, and Mishawaka. The briefest reference to an Indiana map can enlarge this list many times.

The native people also made incalculable contributions to the economy of Indiana. The millions of acres of field corn, the leadership in the production of popcorn, the contract

[1] The bibliographical information will permit the reader to pursue selected topics in greater detail, but it is not intended to be more than a sampling of the available literature. A useful source for additional references is Ronald L. Michael, *Bibliography of Literature on Indiana Archaeology* (Ball State University, *Archaeology Reports, No. 5*, 1969). Eli Lilly, *Prehistoric Antiquities of Indiana* (Indiana Historical Society, Indianapolis, 1937) describes some of the larger prehistoric sites in detail and discusses many of the classes of artifacts found in the state. Howard Winters, *An Archaeological Survey of the Wabash Valley in Illinois* (Illinois State Museum, *Reports of Investigations,* 1963) provides a tentative overview of a portion of the region.

tomato crop in the north, and the tobacco harvest in the south all involve plants originally domesticated by the Indian. The same is true of the turkey, the raising of which contributes to the agricultural wealth of the state. Pumpkins, squash, beans, and peppers are other common plant products first utilized by the native inhabitants.

American Indian themes recur in our music and literature and television programming. The last, unfortunately, relies upon the Indian-European conflict for some of its story line with the result that the contrived events rarely have much real relationship to actual happenings. And the early documentary history, as well as some of the recent, would have been markedly different had there been no human antecedents to contest the European claim to what we have erroneously called a "virgin wilderness."

Unlike the historical record for nearly five centuries of European-derived influence there are no coexistent written sources to document the several thousand years of Indian occupation. Therefore, it is generally impossible to obtain an understanding of individual lives and specific events, or to identify ethnic groups and the languages spoken. It is possible, however, to reconstruct something of the broad picture of cultural change and development through time and comprehend some of the conditions which produced these by reference to the surviving unintentional prehistoric record. This record includes a great variety of manufactured objects (artifacts), remains of plants and animals used by man, human burials, and the man-induced changes in the natural landscape. Careful archaeological excavations in contexts where these occur and the systematic study of the results provide the data whereby an otherwise silent past is permitted to speak.

There are literally thousands of such localities in Indiana and it is a rare river terrace that provides no such evidence. The most common items are the ubiquitous projectile points manufactured from chalcedony or chert. These are often found in association with other materials, such as animal bone, fire-cracked rock, and sometimes bits of pottery, all of which serve to identify the camps and villages of early peoples. Burial mounds are widely distributed, and there are a few hilltop "forts," some geometric earthworks, Indian cemeteries, and "workshops."

Archaeologists working with such materials in the eastern United States have developed a number of generally understood interpretive frameworks; one of these emphasizes what presently appears to be the dominant prehistoric cultural continuities.[2] These continuities are perceived of in terms of four broadly defined cultural *traditions*.

The *Big Game Hunting Tradition* (to about 8000 B.C.) has reference to the earliest well-documented New World populations whose distinctive projectile points have been found in direct association with some of the large Late Pleistocene mammals which are now extinct.

The *Archaic Tradition* (8000 B.C. to 1000 B.C.) makes reference to early groups small in size and seasonally mobile who depended upon hunting, fishing, and plant collecting as the basis for subsistence. There is evidence to suggest that this tradition represents a continuation from the preceding with changes resulting from an increasing ability to utilize a variety of natural resources. This ability was undoubtedly given impetus by the slow changes in the environment as the effect of the "ice age" (Pleistocene) was superseded by conditions approximating those of the present.

The *Woodland Tradition* (1000 B.C. to A.D. 900) is generally defined by the presence of pottery, the surface of which has been impressed with cords and/or fabrics, and the development of burial ritualism as exemplified by burial mounds and other earthwork features.

The *Mississippian Tradition* (A.D. 800 to Historic Period) ultimately led to settled "town" life in some areas and greater

[2] Gordon R. Willey, *An Introduction to American Archaeology. Volume I* (New York, 1966), pp. 454-479. Additionally, it is a well-documented summary source for North and Middle American prehistory.

residential stability in others based upon the intensive utilization of domesticated plants. The presence in the South of
flat-topped mounds upon the surfaces of which were erected
important structures and a distinctive ceramic complex are
definitive characteristics for this tradition.

These are commonly subdivided into time *periods* defined
by the presence of distinctive cultural patterns and artifact
styles. Additional differentiation is obtained by recognizing
highly localized cultural expressions which are variously referred to as *phases, foci,* or *complexes.* These will not be
utilized extensively in this discussion.

This interpretive framework applies generally to the whole
of eastern North America, of which Indiana is a small and,
from the perspective of natural areas, an artificially defined
part. Since human populations do move and it takes time for
ideas to be transmitted from one group to another, it is to
be expected that developments in one area need not occur at
the same time as in another or, for that matter, be expressed
in precisely the same way once they are present. For example,
in Indiana, the "classic" *Mississippian Tradition* sites appear
considerably later than in other areas to the west and, even
then, only in a very restricted area. Also, cultural expressions in northern Indiana consistently differ from those in the
south at every time period. Such situations are undoubtedly
accentuated by obvious and subtle differences in the natural
conditions encountered by prehistoric man.

§

There is considerable ambiguity in the use of the term,
"Big Game Hunter," to describe the earliest of the presently
recognized traditions, since there is almost no direct evidence
from eastern North America that man was in any way
dependent upon the large Late Pleistocene animals which
formerly roamed the region. The inference that he did is
based upon an assumed analogy with western areas where
such associations were present.

There is widely distributed in North America a distinctive projectile point form made from cherts and chalcedony. The distinguishing characteristics include its lanceolate shape, concave base, and basal edges which have been blunted and ground smooth to insure that the hafting material used to bind the point to a spear shaft would not be severed. Additionally, a distinctive narrow vertical flake was removed from both faces of the blade to produce grooves or "flutes." This latter characteristic is the basis for referring to such artifacts as *fluted points*. These occur with some variation and there is good evidence that some of this variability has time-space implication.

In a few areas of North America, particularly the High Plains region, fluted points have been recovered in direct association with extinct forms of bison, mammoth, mastodon, and, possibly, other animal forms. There is clear indication in the position in which the points are found and cutting marks on the bone that man was responsible for killing and butchering the animals. Carbon 14 has been used to date these associations and they are consistently placed between about thirteen thousand and nine thousand five hundred years ago. In the eastern United States, similar fluted points are found in considerable number, but these have only rarely been recovered from a good, dated context and, to the present at least, never in association with animal remains. They are customarily found on eroded terraces or other old landforms where few if any other artifacts are present; hence it is not possible to say whether or not they were employed in the same fashion as in the West.

There are a few possible exceptions to this presently negative picture. In southern Michigan, a mammoth skeleton was found associated with some piles of brush preserved in a bog. Careful excavation of the site has led to a proposal that the brush was intentionally structured to permit early man to butcher a mired animal. No flint tools were recovered. Two fluted point-producing sites have been dated using the Carbon

14 method. The earliest of these, the Debert Site in Nova Scotia, dates to about 9000 B.C. and Bull Brook, Massachusetts, to 7500 B.C. Though not as old as the maximum date obtained from sites in the West, both of these reflect the same order of time.

The fact that good datable contexts for fluted points are uncommon in the East has led to other approaches in the effort to perceive their time of production and use. Many lines of evidence suggest they were being employed by man during a time when the Pleistocene ice sheets were retreating northwards. As a consequence, some areas would have been open for human occupation while others would be inaccessible, either because of the actual presence of ice or the marshy conditions resulting from its melting. The absence of fluted points in particular areas might then be related to such glacially derived conditions and, therefore, their period of use would be suggested.

John T Dorwin studied 195 documented fluted points from Indiana.[3] More than a third of these were from the Ohio Valley and most of the remainder were associated with the other major river valleys. However, none of these had originally been found in the relatively recent floodplain deposits of these streams. Rather, they were generally encountered on older landforms or, as in one case, in the deepest level beneath a large *Archaic Tradition* deposit. One of the more interesting associations occurred in northeastern Indiana, where in the Allen, Huntington, Wells, and Adams County area, no fluted points were reported. Natural features in that region suggest that about fourteen thousand years ago an ice lobe melted in place producing a series of bogs and marshes. The presence of fluted points on the moraines and eskers around the margins of this region but not in it is suggestive of their time of use. Such associations provide no actual calendrical

3 John T Dorwin, *Fluted Points and Late Pleistocene Geochronology in Indiana* (*Prehistory Research Series,* IV, No. 3, Indiana Historical Society, 1966).

date but they are indicative in all probability of the general temporal order of these artifacts.

As of the date of this writing the fluted-point horizon constitutes the earliest well-documented material evidencing the presence of man in the New World. However, there are some logical arguments suggesting yet earlier levels remain to be recognized. One of the more persuasive of these arguments is that manufacture of fluted points involved considerable technical sophistication and, since there seem to be no recognized antecedents in northeast Asia, the probable place of origin for the first migrants, the development must have taken place in the New World. There are a few C14 dates available which more than double the generally accepted thirteen thousand years or so for man, but most of these are based upon questionable associations or, upon further investigation, have been found actually to be in error.

Periodically it has been proposed that migrants from Europe, North Africa, Japan, or some "lost" continent played a determinative role in New World prehistoric cultural development. Almost all of these have little to recommend them to the attention of the serious reader at the present time.

In sum, man was present in North America at least as early as 11,000 B.C. with technological resources sufficient to survive and permit his spread over much of the New World. There are some data from Indiana reflecting upon this early cultural level.

§ §

It is difficult to characterize briefly all of the Indian cultures comprising the *Archaic Tradition* since the dominant feature is change, both as regards the natural conditions faced by man and the nature of his response to these imposed conditions. Groups tended to be relatively small in size and mobile. Food gathering, hunting, and fishing provided the subsistence base; technology was generally simple. The practice of cultivating domesticated plants, though seemingly present in Mexico as early as 5000 B.C., made no substantial impact at this time in eastern North America. And the manufacture of pottery and the use of the bow and arrow were substantially later innovations.

The time of the *Archaic Tradition* is one in which the harsh environmental conditions and limited resources of the "ice age" were ameliorated and were finally superseded by a climate, fauna, and flora approximating that first encountered by Europeans upon entrance into the New World. Average yearly temperatures increased; the tundra-like aspect of portions of Indiana moved northward and was initially replaced by coniferous forests and, subsequently, by deciduous hardwoods. Rivers which served as major sluiceways for glacial meltwater diminished in size exposing broad flat aggraded valleys, and the large Pleistocene mammals became extinct. It has been suggested that man may have played a part in this extinction.

Man, in order to survive in an altered and changing world, found it necessary to modify his way of life and as a consequence discovered new opportunities. That portion of the record preserved for archaeological study indicates that culture changes were initially slow. Originating in what was a common cultural base, judged by the widespread occurrence of the antecedent fluted points, the early Archaic continues the dominant hunting pattern. However, projectile point styles occur with greater variety. Some of these retain the leaf shape and basal grinding of the earlier form but consistently lack the fluted characteristic; others are large and stemmed. Many of the points are extremely well made and indicate a substantial skill in flint chipping techniques. Dated sequences of such artifacts have been obtained from deeply stratified rock shelters and alluvial deposits in Missouri, Illinois, West Virginia, North Carolina, and Alabama and a plethora of named types have been described in the archaeological literature.

No systematic study of the earlier *Archaic* artifacts has been undertaken in Indiana, yet their presence has been confirmed. At least two ground concave-base, lanceolate points lacking only the fluting characteristic have been recovered from deep levels in a Perry County rock shelter. A number of similar points and flint end scrapers have been recovered from an open site situated on an old eroded Ohio River terrace in the same area. Unfortunately, materials are confined to the plow zone and excavation would produce no definitive results. A recent study of surface collections from west-central Indiana succeeded in identifying a series of points having formal similarities to named and dated types in nearby states, i.e., Quad, Dalton, Kirk Serrated, Le Croy, Cache Diagonal Notched.[4] The numerous artifact collections in private hands, though usually lacking contextual data, customarily contain a few projectile points attributable to this early occupation.

If the prehistoric way of life had remained at the foregoing level, the archaeological record would have been meager, indeed. However, an increasing familiarity with environmental resources and such technological innovations as the manufacture of more efficient stone tools by grinding, in addition to those made by chipping, resulted in more diversified and productive subsistence practices. As a result there would appear to have been an increase in population judged by the size of some of the remaining sites and, inferentially, the intensity with which they were occupied. Also, in contrast with the material uniformity of earlier periods, some marked regional variability can be perceived.

These changes are accentuated beginning about 4000 B.C. Interestingly, this is also the time of the Altithermal, an interval during which the average temperatures were higher and average rainfall lower than at present. Though there is substantial disagreement among specialists as to the geographic areas affected by these phenomena and their conse-

---

[4] Curtis H. Tomak, Aboriginal Occupations in the Vicinity of Greene County, Indiana (Unpublished M. A. thesis, Indiana University, 1970).

quences for the flora and fauna, one position is that a predominant hunting dependency was no longer as productive
as before and other food sources needed to be more fully
exploited. A related hypothesis is that areas such as the
northern plains were most adversely affected by the heat and
dryness and populations were forced to migrate to other
regions, some to the east. All of these could have materially
contributed to the developing diversity, though single-minded
environmental explanations rarely prove successful in explaining the diversity of human culture.

There are in Indiana literally hundreds of late *Archaic
Tradition* sites. They are, however, not all identical in nature
but reflect somewhat differing adaptations to the various
environmental zones.

Perhaps the most obvious and interesting of these adaptations are the numerous mussel shell middens found in the
southwestern portion of the state.[5] They occur along the
Ohio down river from Clark County to the mouth of the
Wabash, northward to Sullivan County, and east into Owen,
Lawrence, and Orange counties. The mussel, an oysterlike
bivalve, was once abundantly common in the streams of the
region before pollution and raised water levels destroyed
their beds. Man learned that they could provide an easily
accessible and reliable source of food. The shells, once the
meat was removed, were discarded with the result that the
slowly accumulating piles provided a well-drained elevation
upon which man could live and these sites were apparently
occupied for a considerable portion of each year. As a consequence, the shell mounds, in common with our so-called
sanitary landfills, contain not only garbage but provide considerable data regarding the way of life of those responsible
for the accumulation.

[5] Rex K. Miller, *McCain Site, Dubois County, Indiana* (*Prehistory Research
Series,* II, No. 1, Indiana Historical Society, 1941) ; Winters, *An Archaeological
Survey of the Wabash Valley in Illinois.*

None of the shell mounds present in Indiana compare in size and depth with some reported in Kentucky, Tennessee, and Alabama. However, a few represent an accumulation of nearly fifteen feet and those larger than an acre are common. Substantial data regarding size is difficult to obtain since many of the sites are hidden beneath several feet of Ohio River alluvium. Only a caving river bank, cultivation, or mechanical earthmoving equipment have succeeded in uncovering many of these in recent years and many more remain to be discovered. Along the smaller tributaries of the Ohio the shell middens tend to be located on high bordering bluffs rather than in the flood plain.

Though the mussel provided a reliable food source, and they must have been consumed in tremendous, albeit monotonous, quantities, other edibles were also utilized. Deer were killed in substantial numbers as were some elk and smaller mammals. Within the shell heaps are the remains of fish, turtles, water fowl, and, where conditions permit, the charred remnants of nuts and other native plant foods.

The major hunting weapon was the spear used in combination with the spear thrower. The latter in its simplest form is no more than a short wood shaft fifteen to eighteen inches in length, one end of which is held in the hand and the other with hook attached provides a temporary rest for the end of the spear. This simple mechanical device provides greater length for the arm and imparts significantly more force to the projectile when it is cast than would otherwise be the case. At least some of the spear throwers found in the shell mounds are composite in nature, consisting of a round wood shaft to which were attached a handle and hook carved of bone or antler. Perforated weights made of shell or stone were also sometimes added. Some of the latter, the so-called "bannerstones," were extremely well made; often manufactured from rose quartz, they were prismoidal in cross section and the surfaces were smoothed to a high polish.

Most of the material remains of the shell-mound people are simple, utilitarian, and unembellished. There are a variety of stemmed and notched projectile points, end and side scrapers, grooved stone axes, bell-shaped stone pestles, and disk shell beads. A few tubular stone pipes suggest the occurrence of smoking. The bone and antler artifact inventory is particularly rich and includes projectile points, bodkins, drills which are sometimes engraved with stylized designs, flint-flaking tools, long polished pins, needles, and fishhooks. Fire-cracked stone in great quantities is often associated with these sites and it is concluded that, lacking pottery, liquids were heated by placing them in skins and dropping in heated rocks (stone boiling). Little is known of the types of artificial shelter employed. Occasional scattered post molds in the shell middens suggest the use of a simple windbreak or brush hut. Prepared clay floors and fire hearths occur in these areas.

Human burials may be found in substantial numbers; one excavated site in Kentucky has produced in excess of one thousand individuals. Commonly, shallow circular pits were dug into shell middens and the dead were placed therein usually in a tightly flexed position. Artifact accompaniments, though present, are not the rule; the graves of children appear to have been given greater attention judged by the presence of shell beads and other artifacts. The domesticated dog was sometimes buried with the human dead or was given a separate burial.

While the general cultural picture which emerges is one which emphasizes utilitarian pursuits, there are indications of developing specialization and the breakdown of insularity. Some copper was obtained from the upper Great Lakes area and a few artifacts made from marine shells have been recovered.

Though the shell midden, as indicated, is the most apparent of the late *Archaic Tradition* settlements, life most certainly was not confined to these localities alone. The subsistence remains indicate that a wide range of native products were exploited and these would have required a somewhat mobile existence. It is also doubtful that shellfish could have been obtained at all seasons of the year due to high water levels and the flooding of alluvial flood plains. Throughout the area where shell mounds occur, there are small sites situated on higher terraces and along smaller streams which, except for the quantities of shell debris, produce identical materials and undoubtedly represent seasonal encampments. And the numerous rock shelters present in the rough Crawford Upland of south-central Indiana often contain deep deposits representing the same groups.

Northward from where mussels were present in abundance a related cultural pattern is present. For example, the Archaic occupation at the McKinley Site, located in Hamilton County in central Indiana, has some material similarities to that farther to the south: elements of the projectile point complex, a spear thrower hook, a bell pestle, and bannerstone fragments.[6]

The late *Archaic Tradition* in northern Indiana is quite different from that in the south and is less well understood. Few habitation sites are known, undoubtedly because they were small, not intensively occupied, and scattered; most of the present knowledge is derived from a number of accidentally discovered cemeteries. Thus a picture of day-to-day activities is presently impossible to obtain. However, what is known, including the fact that there is no single consistently available food source, suggests that migratory hunters and collectors are represented.

Glacial Kame is the most widespread of the northern late Archaic cultural manifestations. It derives the name from the fact that cemeteries were customarily made in sand and gravel ridges formed by glacial outwash to which the descriptive geological term "kame" has been given. Though

6 Robert M. Little, The McKinley Site (Unpublished M. A. thesis, Indiana University, 1970).

not all human burials encountered in such contexts were nec-
essarily in the same time interval, many of them do reflect
similar methods of disposal and are associated with a recurrent material complex indicative of some degree of cultural
integrity.

Glacial Kame cemeteries are unmarked, hence discovery is
usually a matter of accident.[7] They are often found during
the course of sand and gravel mining with the result that
information obtained is often secondhand. For example, it
was suggested at one time that some of these burials were
placed ten feet or more below the present surface, the inference being that they had been made before the development
of the kame itself, with all that this would imply for the
great age of the burial. However, it is now clear that the
cemeteries were intruded into an already-existent natural feature and the false assumption of great depth usually results
from the fact that surfaces are already removed and depth
reference is related to a high point on a ridge, rather than
to the original downward sloping surface.

Glacial Kame cemeteries contain from only a few to several dozen burials. The tightly flexed human remains, usually
singly but sometimes paired, were placed in circular pits
barely large enough to permit placement of the body. If a
stratum of hard silt overlay the more easily removed sands
and gravels, only the narrowest possible entrance way was
intruded through the former. Males and females representing all age groups were placed in these cemeteries.

Powdered ocher, an earthy clay material containing iron
oxides and ranging in color from bright yellow to a rich
orange-red, was often placed in the graves. Large drilled
sandal-sole-shaped and circular gorgets were cut from wall
sections of marine molluscans. A particularly distinctive artifact is the so-called "birdstone." Commonly carved from
slate and well made, it derives its name from a profile resem-

---

[7] Eli Lilly, "A Cedar Point 'Glacial Kame' Burial," Indiana Academy of
Science, *Proceedings*, LI (1941), 31-33.

bling the head, body, and tail of a stylized bird. A suggested function is that of a spear-thrower weight comparable to that of the bannerstone, but there are no clear associations confirming this interpretation. Other artifacts include copper and shell beads, some made from the columnella of marine shells, long bone pins, and bone awls.

Glacial Kame artifacts, some from burial associations, are found in northern Indiana and southward into Shelby County. The latter example, though somewhat outside the expected area of occurrence, is based upon the accidental discovery of a flexed human burial in a sandy knoll together with a sandle-sole gorget and copper beads; the whole was literally buried in a deposit of red ocher.

A related mortuary complex in the western part of the state bears the somewhat ambiguous title, Red Ocher. Small low artificial mounds were constructed and quantities of ocher were often placed with the burials. The distinctive artifact is a narrow bi-pointed blade with shallow side notches at one end; these are commonly referred to as "turkey-tails." They were frequently manufactured from a good quality blue-gray hornstone obtained from the numerous prehistoric quarries in south-central Indiana, particularly the Harrison County region. These blades have been found singly as well as in buried caches of upward of a hundred or more. There is some suggestion that an early form of heavy pottery, *Marion Thick,* may be coeval with Red Ocher. A recent salvage excavation of a low Red Ocher mound in Terre Haute, though hindered by premature bulldozing of a school construction site, succeeded in recovering a human cremation contained in a clay basin with which were associated flint blades, including a "turkey tail," an expanded end bar gorget made of stone, and scattered deposits of red ocher.[8]

A third late *Archaic Tradition* expression, the Old Copper Culture, is present in Wisconsin by at least 3000 B.C. In

[8] Personal communication with E. V. McMichael, Indiana State University.

addition to its mass burial deposits, a great variety of tools were manufactured from copper which was readily obtained in the upper Great Lakes area. Produced by hammering, not smelting, tools included tanged and socketed projectile points, harpoons, knives, and awls, as well as more conventional items. Though no Old Copper sites are known in Indiana, a few typologically similar tools have been found on the surface, one as far south as Jay County.

Because there are some general similarities in Glacial Kame, Red Ocher, and Old Copper burials, as well as others farther to the east, it has been proposed that they be grouped into a "northern" or "boreal" archaic. A further hypothesis is that they represent the beginnings of the mortuary cere-monialism which reaches a climax in the subsequent *Wood-land Tradition*. However, it should be kept in mind that burial practices are the only evidence perceived in the north, while in the south, if only mortuary customs were revealed instead of the broad view of technology, the same conclusion might be conceived for that area. For example, the Crib Mound, a shell midden in Spencer County, has produced a surprising number of non-utilitarian copper artifacts and, ap-parently, thousands of flint blades in a cache deposit.

By way of summary, then, the *Archaic Tradition* is char-acterized by change, slow in its earliest stages but with the end result of an increasingly efficient adaptation to local sit-uations. Though technology is relatively simple, the wide-spread if not abundant occurrence of copper from the north and marine shells from the warm salt waters to the south is indicative of an incipient trade network. Human groups have traversed a considerable distance from the unitary hunting pattern of an earlier time.

§   §   §

The beginning of the *Woodland Tradition* is marked by the appearance of fire-hardened pottery containers. This in-troduction constitutes a technical achievement of no small

importance, not only for the vessels produced but also as regards the intellectual endeavor represented. Ceramics are one
of the very few native products in which there is a transforma-
tion of raw materials into something totally different. Selected
clays, tempering, and water are combined and, after drying,
sufficient heat is applied to induce a physical reaction with the
result being a hard insoluble substance.

Ceramics are also important for the prehistoric archaeologist. Each step of the pottery-making process is susceptible
to considerable variation: the choice of clays and the tempering medium, the methods used to form the container, the
shape of the vessel itself, types of surface decorations, the
presence of handles or other appendages, the temperature
of the firing process. All of the foregoing separately and
in combination can produce an almost unending variability.
However, as with ourselves, what was produced was controlled by group style preferences; these were not universal but differed at particular times and places. Pottery
sherds are the most frequently recovered artifact on many
sites. This, combined with their systematic variability, permits the establishment of a ceramic chronology to which other
associated cultural materials can be related. Wherever pottery has been produced almost invariably archaeologists have
used it to establish time scales and, initially at least, to differ-
entiate cultures of the past.

The origin of pottery in northeastern North America is
presently unclear. Three hypotheses have been proposed.
The oldest pottery in North America was produced in the
Georgia-Florida area by 2000 B.C. It is thick and heavy,
tempered with vegetable fibres, and the shape is reminiscent
of yet earlier containers made from steatite, or soapstone.
Fibre-tempered pottery is also present in northwestern South
America at an earlier date. The substantial distance between
the two occurrences poses difficult problems for deriving one
from the other. In any case, it is a moot point whether the
southeastern fibre-tempered material provided the stimulus

for the subsequent developments in the north, since there are substantial technical differences between the two.

Because the presence of surface cord impressions is a common Woodland feature and the same is also present on earlier ceramics in the Old World, it has been proposed that the ultimate source was the latter region by way of northeast Asia. Logical as this might appear, the plain fact is that literally thousands of miles intervene between the two distributional areas with no direct evidence to connect them.

A third alternative is that this important innovation was arrived at independently in its area of occurrence. Until recently, the earliest dated pottery occurred in New York state about 3,000 years ago. However, a recent dated context in an Ohio rock shelter adds more than 500 years to this time depth. This, of course, does not resolve any of the problems, but it does suggest that much critical evidence is not yet in and the wisest choice may be to avoid the question of "origin" for the time being.

The *Early Woodland Tradition* groups, in common with their immediate predecessors, were fundamentally reliant upon hunting, fishing, and collecting for their means of subsistence. The major differences are in the presence of pottery and, in southwestern Indiana, a markedly decreased reliance upon the river mussel as a source of food.

The earliest pottery recognized is a type referred to as *Marion Thick*. It or related material is present in southern Indiana and northward in the Wabash drainage into the lake region. As the name indicates, it is very heavy, often being over an inch in thickness. The outer surface, sometimes the inner, too, is impressed with heavy cords patterned to suggest that a woven fabric might have been used. Since basketry and weaving antedate pottery, one interpretation is that this heavy pottery may have been molded in a woven form. Whether this is true or not, the application of a roughened surface of one type or another tends to compact the ceramic paste, removing captured air bubbles the presence of which would produce disastrous results upon firing. Vessel shape was similar to the common modern earthenware flower pot.

The sites upon which *Marion Thick* is found are small in size and reflect only seasonal or short-term occupation. In southwestern Indiana it is present in the upper levels of some of the shell middens. Though the presence there may be fortuitous, stemming from the suitability of the elevation for subsequent occupation, the recurrent pattern is suggestive of some degree of continuity.

The decline in the dependence upon the mussel is largely unexplained. Where once there was great reliance upon them, they later appear to represent only a small part of the diet. Perhaps they were no longer available in quantity, or changes in dietary preferences may have been a factor. Also, there is some evidence, as yet not overwhelming, that plant cultivation provided alternative food choices.

Recent excavations in deep alluvial deposits near Yankeetown in Warrick County, though providing only a small fragment of the total Early Woodland picture, suggest subsistence practices during the period. There were at depths in excess of seven feet irregularly shaped heavily burned areas. In addition to a few which contained some stone, many were filled with quantities of charred nut shells, mostly walnut and hickory. These date to about 790 B.C. This portion of the site (there were later materials at higher levels) was undoubtedly only a temporary camp reoccupied for short intervals, probably during the fall.

This same pattern of transiency involving the utilization of seasonally available resources was undoubtedly the practice over much of Indiana in the first millennium before Christ.

It is during the Early Woodland period that the first of the complex burial mounds were constructed, the widespread occurrence of which continues to exert an unfortunate influence on the popular notions concerning the prehistory of the eastern United States. It is unfortunate in the sense that the mound contents, burials and associated artifacts, were thought to represent, when compared with practices of the historic Indians encountered by European settlers, an infinitely superior level of culture. The presence of earthwork complexes, some containing structures geometric in shape, indications of a far-flung trade network, and artifacts exhibiting aesthetic sophistication all contributed to the creation of the "myth of the mound builders."[9] The responsible group was said to be intellectually superior, to possess advanced technological knowledge, have a political system able to control vast areas, and to be racially different from the American Indians, who were thought to be ultimately responsible for their downfall. A variety of hypotheses were offered to explain the superiority of the mound-builder "race," including its derivation from the Lost Tribes of Israel, Egyptians, Welsh, etc. Systematic archaeological work has long since laid to rest such interpretations, yet the notion persists, often in the most unanticipated places, e.g., public school textbooks.

As indicated above, the roots of burial ceremonialism seem to be present in the mortuary practices of the late *Archaic Tradition*. The practices apparent there underwent change and development during a 1500-year period and vary in time and place as they are reinterpreted in different cultural contexts. Though mound burial persists in some areas to late prehistoric cultures, it had largely run its course by about A.D. 500 or before.

The earliest of the burial-mound complexes, called Adena after the Ohio estate on which was located the type site which is widely distributed in the Ohio Valley from Pennsylvania and West Virginia into southeastern Indiana.[10] The mounds vary greatly in size from a maximum of seventy feet in height to others which are presently almost imperceptible. The larger mounds are frequently complex structures involving

9 Robert Silverberg, *Mound Builders of Ancient America: The Archaeology of a Myth* (New York Graphic Society, 1968).

10 Don W. Dragoo, *Mounds for the Dead* (*Annals* of the Carnegie Museum, Pittsburgh, 1963).

several sizeable building phases. The predominant inclusions are well-constructed tombs, often defined by large logs in which the dead were placed. Most of these contain a single extended burial, but multiple burials sometimes occur and cremation was also practiced. Because the number of burials may be small compared to the size of the mound, the elaborateness of the tombs, and the presence of numerous artifacts in the graves, it has been concluded that only socially prestigious individuals were given such burial.

Few Adena villages have been located because mounds were often constructed over them and the camp debris was gathered up for inclusion in the earth fill, along with any earlier cultural material. However, segments of the settlements have been preserved under the mounds. These contain little debris, suggesting that occupancy was of short duration. A few large structures suitable as extended family dwellings have been noted. They are circular in ground plan, had outward sloping walls, and the log frame was covered with bark. Some of the dwellings served as charnel houses, were subsequently burned, and mounds were constructed over them. Recent excavations in central Ohio, though not fully reported, indicate that these communities were small and dispersed over the countryside. Groups from several such settlements probably maintained a special social relationship and co-operated in the construction of the mounds.

Reference to two excavated Adena mounds in Indiana will provide some idea of contents and the variability of such structures. The Nowlin Mound was located in Dearborn County on an upland formation near the Whitewater River but adjacent to a small stream which drains into the Ohio.[11] Elliptical in ground plan, it was one of the largest burial mounds in Indiana, measuring 165 feet in length and 15 feet high. Structurally, it was made up of two adjacent mounds,

11 Glenn A. Black, *Excavation of the Nowlin Mound* (*Indiana History Bulletin*, XIII [1936]), 197-305.

each of which had had multiple additions, and these were subsequently covered by a single mantle of earth to bring it to its final form.

Seven log tombs were contained in the mound. Several of these were relatively simple and were defined by multiple logs up to eight feet in length placed on the ground so as to delimit a rectangular area. One was nearly 20 feet in length and 14 feet wide; not only did logs define the periphery but others had been placed laterally to form a roofed structure. Earlier excavations had removed some of the evidence but seven extended burials and four reburials were recovered. Those found in the tomb areas were customarily placed on a heavy layer of wood bark. Red ocher was also employed.

Associated artifacts tended to be few in number. Those in the tombs and with burials included: disk-shaped shell beads, *Marginella* beads, and others made from the columnella of marine mollusks, corner and side-notched projectile points, bone awls, bone handles, and a plain sandstone "tablet." A C-shaped copper bracelet, among other artifacts, was recovered but out of context.

The C. L. Lewis Stone Mound, located on a bluff overlooking the Flat Rock River in Shelby County, was also identified as Adena, though it differed considerably from Nowlin.[12] It was a low dome-shaped structure measuring approximately 55 by 50 feet, and 4 feet high. Three major building stages were identified. Temporally, the first of these had been the construction of a low embankment of earth which defined a circular area approximately 25 feet in diameter. A mantle of limestone slabs covered the above area, and subsequently, additional slabs were added.

Thirty-six human burials were directly associated with these several structural steps. A mass burial of at least fourteen individuals, both adults and children, had been placed within

---

[12] James H. Kellar, *The C. L. Lewis Stone Mound and the Stone Mound Problem* (*Prehistory Research Series,* III, No. 4, Indiana Historical Society, 1960).

the central area; these had been covered with an extensive layer of grass and twigs which had been burned. Directly above and within a large depression defined by the limestone slabs an intensive crematory fire had been kindled and at least two partial cremations were encountered during excavation. A second mass burial had been made peripheral to the central structure, and human skeletons and portions thereof were encountered at various locations beneath and among the slabs. Many of these burials were fully extended but there was great variety represented: slightly flexed reburials, disarticulated skeletal parts, and individual human crania.

Artifacts in burial association include four C-shaped copper bracelets, 26 copper beads, a copper ear ring, three bone combs, a bone handle, a flint hammerstone, a large corner-notched blade, an antler flaker, a stone chisel, beaver incisors, and an "expanded center" slate gorget.

Though these two mounds are obviously quite different in many details, the Adena affiliation has been indicated because of traits shared with other mounds so identified in the Ohio Valley, e.g., the log tombs at Nowlin and several of the artifacts at Lewis. However, there is a growing suspicion among archaeologists that the Adena concept as it has been employed and extended over an ever larger area tends to gloss over a considerable amount of potentially meaningful cultural variations and that a fruitful line for future research is the effort to gain some greater understanding of these regional and temporal variations.

The middle period of the *Woodland Tradition* is typically the time during which ritualism as perceived through burial practices reaches a climax. It, in a sense, constitutes the culmination of trends begun in the Archaic and given additional impetus during the early Woodland period. This is reflected in many ways. Burial mounds are widely dispersed over eastern North America from southern Canada to the Gulf of Mexico and the Appalachians to the Plains. Even more widely spread trade patterns are apparent: obsidian from Wyoming, grizzly bear teeth from the Rocky Mountains, copper from the upper Great Lakes region, pipestone and flint from Ohio, hornstone from Indiana, mica from the southern Appalachians, and marine shells from the Gulf of Mexico region. Also, a few distinctive artifacts and decorative styles occur sporadically in distant sites: copper "pan pipes," bicymbal-shaped copper ear spools, "monitor" type stone pipes, clay human figurines, and some techniques of pottery decoration, i.e., dentate stamping, as well as vessel form. All of these contribute to a picture of considerable social interaction at about the beginning of the Christian Era.

The area where this cultural patterning is most accentuated is central Ohio, particularly in the Scioto River Valley. Here great mounds were built, often in combination with geometric earthworks, and these were sometimes joined together by thousands of feet of earthen embankment to form prehistoric centers of unusual size and complexity. All of these highly visible surface features attracted some of the earliest archaeological work undertaken in North America.[13] And the discovery of artifacts in burial associations which were relatively elaborate, made from exotic raw materials, and sometimes occurring in impressive numbers, gave impetus for even more excavation. The results of this work with the inferred notions of vast cultural superiority succeeded in coloring interpretations of North American prehistory to the present moment. Hopewell, the name given to this Ohio cultural expression, became the epitome of "mound-builder culture" and it was supposed that it was to this unique center that all else could ultimately be tied.

While there can be little doubt that the central Ohio region was of real consequence during Middle Woodland, the emerging interpretation is suggestive of significantly greater complexity than was originally supposed. For many years it has

13 Ephraim G. Squier and Edwin H. Davis, *Ancient Monuments of the Mississippi Valley* . . . (Smithsonian Institution, *Contributions to Knowledge,* Vol. I, Washington, D. C., 1847).

been recognized that Ohio Hopewell was related to the earlier resident Adena. This relationship was evident in aspects both of the burial practices and artifacts and some of the differences could ultimately be attributable to cultural developments occurring through time. However, there were other features, such as elements of the ceramic complex, which seemed to have no antecedents in the Ohio area and, therefore, must have represented external influences. It has since been determined that some of the features characteristic of Middle Woodland were present at an earlier time in the cultural sequences determined for the Illinois River valley and this has led to the conclusion that influences derived from there stimulated the resident Adena populations in Ohio. Giving added credence to this hypothesis is the presence of items of almost certain Ohio manufacture in Illinois sites.

Some archaeologists, particularly those working farther to the south, believe that some of the cultural antecedents will be found in the lower Mississippi Valley and these, in turn, will ultimately have a Middle American base. There is presently no direct evidence to support this position and the few C14 dates of relevance suggest that the related southern cultures are actually later than those in the north.

There is no single cultural expression present during the middle period. There are many richly varied local groups, each of which reflects in some measure its own material tradition and environmental circumstance. Even the ceremonialism associated with burial disposal exhibits a considerable degree of the same variability.

The food-producing activities utilized to support the trade, craft specialization, and earthwork construction, and the socially defined status differences which can be inferred from these, involve the old hunting-fishing-collecting triad. However, there is growing evidence that plant cultivation, specifically maize, contributed to the subsistence base.

In Indiana, Middle Woodland sites have a widespread distribution, though these presently seem to cluster into a number of localized expressions, each of which is partially separable from the others. These undoubtedly reflect time differences as well as geographic ones, but further work is necessary before this can be determined in detail.

The earliest materials in the state datable to Middle Woodland come from the previously mentioned site near Yankeetown. These have been dated at 300 B.C. and consist of pottery tempered with clay, flint, and/or quartzite and with both plain and heavy cord-impressed surfaces. The pottery is associated with burial features which contain many charred nuts and some animal bone. None of the decorative ceramic features definitive for the period in other areas have been found, however, nor is it known whether mound building is associated with this horizon in the area. It seems likely that this is representative of a localized cultural expression which was ultimately influenced by the later ceremonialism.

In the Ohio and lower Wabash valleys many of the burial mounds are attributable to the Crab Orchard tradition, a basically ceramic development defined by the presence of fabric or corded dowel-impressed pottery. Mounds sometimes occur in groups and large central log tombs containing multiple burials are common inclusions. It was possible to demonstrate in one instance that several individuals had been killed at the time of mound construction, probably to serve as retainers in the afterworld for an individual buried in a central subfloor pit. In addition to marine and turtle shell containers, antler flaking tools, a copper celt and beads, several distinctive platform pipes with bowls carved in animal form were recovered.[14]

There were many other burial mounds in the Wabash Valley at least as far north as Tippecanoe County; others occurred up the White River in Greene County and the adjacent areas. The past tense is employed because most of

[14] Georg K. Neumann and Melvin L. Fowler, "Hopewellian Sites in the Wabash Valley," *Hopewellian Communities in Illinois,* edited by Thorne Deuel (Illinois State Museum, *Scientific Papers,* V, 1952), 175-248.

these have been destroyed or badly disturbed by indiscriminate, senseless excavation and changes in land usage. However, casual reports of contents indicate a Middle Woodland relationship, though some considerable time span is suggested.

There is in Posey County in the extreme southwestern part of Indiana one of the largest Middle Woodland settlements present anywhere in the Ohio Valley. This village, more properly a series of overlapping occupations, encompasses an undetermined area, but it is in excess of two hundred acres. Many burial mounds were formerly present and several are still visible. Excavation of several of these in the 1870s produced many burials and artifacts, though the surviving descriptions are insufficient to indicate much detail other than the fact that copper, marine shells, beads, and bracelets were present. Aerial photographs indicate that a small circular and two, possibly three, large rectangular enclosures were formerly present. The village site has been of particular interest because of its unusually large size and the abundance of surface debris present, particularly the presence of decorated pottery stamped with an engraved paddle which is rare to this area but common at the same time in southeastern states. Excavation has thus far produced no information regarding housing, but the material complement is becoming better documented. In addition to the use of readily available flints, bone, and shell, other raw materials include quartz crystal, Ohio flint, marine shell, jasper, mica, and obsidian. There is a well-developed flint industry, including the manufacture of great numbers of thin flake knives struck from prepared cores. The ceramics are commonly cord impressed, but a variety of stamped and incised wares and some painted sherds of clear middle-period provenience occur. Hunting appears to have been the major means of subsistence and there are quantities of bone debris which include most of the animals present in the region at the time. Also, fishing was of real consequence. The presence of earthwork enclosures at this Posey County site is unusual; the only other examples recorded from the immediate area are a large circle near Vincennes and a possible enclosure in Spencer County, though the latter is impossible to confirm at present.

In the Kankakee River valley in northwestern Indiana and eastward to at least Kosciusko County, there are numbers of mounds and camps which have affinities with the Middle Woodland cultures present in the Illinois River area.[15] Camps in northern Indiana tend to be small and were probably seasonally occupied, reflecting the cyclical availability of the food resources in the lake and moraine region. The mounds often occur in groups. Subfloor pits containing burials have been noted. Artifact inclusions were varied: pottery vessels which have stamped, incised, and punctate impressions grouped in zoned surface areas, cut animal jaws, corner-notched points (Snyders), plain platform pipes, effigy platform pipes (rarely), marine shell containers, a variety of ground-stone objects (celts, spheres, gorgets), shell and copper beads, mica, large drilled canines, and other copper artifacts.

There are in east-central Indiana a number of sites which, until quite recently, have been somewhat anomolous and, though their significance is not yet fully perceived, some greater understanding of them is becoming possible. The two best preserved of these are in Mounds State Park near Anderson and the New Castle State Hospital grounds.

The Mounds State Park group at one time comprised a dozen or more earthwork features. Road construction, cultivation, and a housing development have been responsible for some destruction, but much remains. The largest of these earthworks is circular in plan and has a diameter of 360 feet. It was constructed by first excavating a trench to a depth of nine feet below ground level and depositing the

15 George I. Quimby, Jr., *The Goodall Focus (Prehistory Research Series,* II, No. 2, Indiana Historical Society, 1941).

removed earth to the outside of the arc; the resultant embankment averages six feet in height. The central platform delimited by the trench is 140 feet in diameter. An unexcavated sector to the south and west permits ground level access through the embankment and onto the platform, near the center of which a small mound had been constructed. This same pattern of construction is exhibited by at least one large rectangular and two smaller circular enclosures.

There are three structures which are panduriform or "violin-shaped" in ground plan. There is a suggestion of a shallow defining trench and outside embankment in two cases and the largest, which measures approximately 180 by 120 feet, preserves a narrow entranceway into the interior. At least two other low earth mounds have been preserved.

Excavation of the platform of the large circular enclosure has disclosed that the small central mound consists of two parts. The lowest and earliest of these were three superimposed heavily burned clay floors raised in platform fashion above the old surface of the ground. A thick mantle of earth was then used to cover the burned area. Attributable to this last construction was a log tomb in which there was a disarticulated burial and portions of a cremation and two flexed burials in upper portions of the secondary earth mantle. On the platform surrounding the earth mound were numbers of small post molds suggesting that an irregular brush screen had guarded the activities occurring in the central region or that saplings had been bent over and tied to the heavy support posts located near the center to form a roofed shelter. Artifacts recovered, though few in number, included plain and distinctively incised pottery, bear effigy canines which were drilled and carved from bone, mica, and a plain platform pipe.

The New Castle State Hospital site is located about twenty straight-line miles east-southeast from Mounds State Park.[16]

[16] Summary reports of the seasonal work accomplished at the site are contained in Ball State University, *Archaeological Reports, Nos. 2 and 3.*

Of the dozen mounds comprising the group, at least six of them, possibly eight, were circular enclosures with ditches and external embankments. The largest of these was comparable in size with that described above and also apparently had a small mound located on the central platform. Unfortunately, this tumulus and four others were destroyed by a combination of hospital and road construction.

One of the more prominent features was a large mound about 215 feet in length and with a maximum width of 100 feet. A shallow ditch circumscribing the base was somewhat constricted near the center. This and two eminences provided good evidence that two major mound masses had originally been constructed adjacent to one another and overlapping. Excavation has produced a number of burials representing a variety of disposal practices, i.e., cremation, extended burials, reburials. Included among the artifacts are a broken platform pipe, effigy bear canines in copper, cut lynx jaws, mica, a marine shell container, and mortuary pottery vessels.

Both Mounds State Park and New Castle produce a distinctive ceramic complex characterized by tastefully incised decorations in the form of chevrons and diamonds. However, the typical and expected Middle Woodland design elements are conspicuous by their absence. The only exception is a single mortuary vessel from New Castle which has rocker-stamped elements arranged in zoned areas; its closest counterpart occurs in the Middle Woodland of the Kankakee drainage. The most obvious conclusion to be drawn from the ceramic information is that a highly localized cultural expression is represented at the two sites but one which is in contact with other Middle Woodland groups with whom there is some degree of shared ceremonialism. The earthwork features are allied with comparable ones in Ohio. To date no known camps or villages in the region can be assigned to the period of construction and use of these centers.

The definition of Late Woodland is based largely upon negative qualities; that is, those special features of culture which served to underscore our contemporary view of life during the Middle Woodland period become markedly attenuated or disappear. Earthwork complexes were no longer in use, though a few mounds continued to be constructed. However, these served as general cemeteries in many instances, rather than as repositories for the select few. The trade for exotic raw materials was substantially terminated and such items as mica, obsidian, copper, and marine shells occurred rarely, if at all. Craft specialization suggested by the work produced from these materials, as well as the effigy stone pipes, was no longer apparent. The material culture was often remarkably uniform and lacking in stylistic variation and evidence of experimentation. There was overall a sense of monotony, of sameness, and of local isolation.

A number of explanations have been proposed to account for what amounts to a significant change in the cultural orientation of the Woodland populations. However, most of these are unsatisfactory because they are not susceptible to testing. For example, one proposal is that the limited technological base was ultimately insufficiently productive to support the native institutions responsible for maintaining the inferred ceremonial practices. Another suggestion is that the system itself became so complex and highly developed that further elaboration of the pattern was not feasible. A third hypothesis and one which offers some opportunity for testing is that the Middle Woodland populations were displaced by intruders; the so-called hilltop forts, at least two examples of which are located in Dearborn and Clark counties, are cited as evidence for a struggle for control. This explanation is obviously allied with much earlier statements regarding the demise of the "mound builders," but it rests on the assumption that the intruders were American Indians, as were those intruded upon. A fourth suggestion, and one for which evidence can be marshaled, is ecological in nature. Plant cultivation is present during Middle Woodland, though it does not appear to have been intensively practiced, and it is possible that maize production provided the extra subsistence margin required for the indicated ceremonial development. Being near the northern limits of effective maize cultivation, slight climatic shifts could drastically alter the productivity of the then available seed. And a slight decrease in average temperatures is indicated beginning about A.D. 400, which accords reasonably well with the time when Middle Woodland begins to exhibit "decline." Interestingly, the cultural pattern maintains continuity farther to the south where the natural change would have had much less impact.

In southeastern Indiana the many small mounds constructed of limestone slabs and located on the high hills near the Whitewater, Ohio, and lesser streams are probably representative of Late Woodland.[17] These tumuli often contain well-defined central cists outlined with limestone slabs in which numbers of disarticulated burials had been deposited. Other human skeletal remains occur at various places within the mounds. The presence of artifacts is uncommon and seriously limits efforts to establish a cultural identification. Though reminiscent of the more highly developed Middle Woodland burial ceremonialism, it is much attenuated, and the ceramics consist of undifferentiated cord-marked vessels common to the later period recovered from nearby sites in Ohio.

There are a number of relatively small but intensively occupied sites in southwestern Indiana which reflect a comparable period of occupation. Named LaMotte, some of these seem to be comprised of a number of houses arranged in a circular pattern around an open "plaza." The ceramic remains associated with the villages have simple and check-stamped surface designs. The former consists of a series of broad parallel impressions; the latter resembles nothing more than the pattern made by a waffle iron. Both were made with a carved die. The specific technique and design patterns have a very long history in the southeastern states.

[17] Glenn A. Black, *Archaeological Survey of Dearborn and Ohio Counties* (*Indiana History Bulletin*, XI [1933-34]), 171-260.

Another Late Woodland expression in the lower Wabash and White River areas is referred to as Albee.[18] It was named for the Albee Mound in Sullivan County, which was in reality a natural elevation into which were intruded numbers of human burials. This same pattern of burial disposal is common throughout the lowland area of the state and a few to several dozen human skeletons often occur in the sand knolls of the region. Artifacts such as bone harpoons, shell beads, bone awls, rectangular slate gorgets, flint tools, and antler flakers occur, sometimes in association with thin well-made cord-marked pottery vessels. This same pottery is found in numbers of village sites in the same area.

Late Woodland is almost unknown in more northern portions of the state. However, the occurrence of pottery vessels with heavy corded design elements and well-defined collared rims indicate the presence of such populations.

Summarizing, the *Woodland Tradition* is a direct outgrowth of the *Archaic* initially recognized by the occurrence of pottery. While its most apparent trend relates to the development and ultimate decline of a specialized ceremonialism involving but not confined to funeral rites, there are several occurrences, some of which can only be inferred, of a more fundamental nature. Those of a basic technological nature include the introduction of pottery, the addition of cultivated plant foods to the subsistence base, and near the end, the initial use of the bow and arrow. These in varying degrees contributed to the possibility of a generally increased population size and, in some areas, larger local concentrations. Though such groups are difficult to perceive through the screen of archaeology, the large earthwork complexes are symptomatic of co-operative endeavor and the motivations for their long-term accretion and use must certainly rest in some form of institutionalized social control beyond that customarily present in the small kin group. The factors con-

18 J. Arthur MacLean, *Excavation of Albee Mound* (*Indiana History Bulletin*, VIII [1930-31]), 89-176.

tributing to the ultimate breakdown of the system cannot presently be precisely determined.

§   §   §   §

The *Mississippian Tradition* climaxes in what is the most complex of the several North American cultural developments. Unlike the Woodland apogee which is confined to a limited and somewhat esoteric segment of culture, that during Mississippian is reflected at many levels from the commonplace to the specialized. Also, elements of the development persisted into the period of early European settlement and limited insights were gained by direct observation, specifically in the southeastern states.

The basic tradition was dependent upon the intensive cultivation of maize, beans, and squash, as well as other lesser seed crops and tobacco, which in combination with resident plants and animals, provided an abundant and richly varied food supply. Settlements were permanently established and some evidence of intentional long-range planning is apparent in house distributions, the preservation of open areas within the towns, and the placement of community structures. Some of the larger towns extended over hundreds of acres and must have had populations of several thousand. The raw materials exploited differed little from those available and used for millenniums by the American Indian, but the artifacts produced from bone, stone, and shell and the ceramics were varied and occur in great numbers. The emergent picture is one in which marked social stratification is present and elements of social control are vested in institutions having a religious-political function. Undoubtedly, the town exercised a hegemony over nearby farmsteads.

At one time it seemed that Mississippian had appeared with relative suddenness at a very late time in the Mississippi River Valley. This, combined with the presence of a few startling characteristics having clear Middle American relationships, e.g., large community buildings erected upon the prepared surface of earth mounds, suggested that the genesis of the tradition might rest in an actual migration of populations from the South. The substantial distances involved and the absence of connecting material in the intervening area makes such an explanation improbable, but it has been only in recent years that the dimensions of the problem have been more clearly perceived, particularly the greater temporal insights made possible by the development of C14 dating.

The *Mississippian Tradition* becomes apparent in the central Mississippi Valley about A.D. 800. Some of the very earliest elements reflect practices and styles having a long history in the eastern United States, including the retention of some from Middle Woodland. Undoubtedly a significant stimulus was the development of more effective horticultural practices; this probably occurred in combination with or resulted from the appearance of a new variety of maize well suited to the natural conditions present in the region. There is also the inescapable fact that influences ultimately derived from Middle America played a part, though such elements usually give evidence of having been modified or reinterpreted to meet the local requirements. By approximately A.D. 1200 a distinctive culture type was present over much of the eastern United States, or had exerted influence upon surviving Woodland cultures in peripheral areas.

Though Indiana is not central to the major area of Mississippian development, there is evidence of societies living in the state prior to the presence of "climax" settlements and which share some of the emergent influences. The Yankeetown Phase in southwestern Indiana is one of these; another is the Oliver Phase in the central portion of the state.

The Yankeetown Phase dates to about A.D. 900 and is confined to a relatively small area in southwestern Indiana and the immediately adjacent sectors in Kentucky and Illinois near the Ohio River. There is at least the suggestion that maize was cultivated, though the association is not firmly established. Excavation has thus far failed to produce clear evidence for dwelling types. The ceramic complex is in some ways reminiscent of Woodland in vessel shape and in the presence of minor amounts of cord marking. However, in addition to a few wide-mouth bowls, its most distinctive attributes are systematically placed notched appliqued strips and fine-line incising in zoned areas. While the pottery, except possibly the bowl form, is not "mississippianized," other artifacts do reflect such a process: small stemless triangular projectile points, pottery disks, pottery trowels, stone discoidals, and stylistic characteristics exhibited by clay figurines. All of these occur in later *Mississippian Tradition* sites but are not generally a part of Woodland. The extreme localization of this Yankeetown Phase, the unique ceramics, and some of the artifact inventory are all suggestive of the cultural experimentation going on at the same time as cultural influences were diffused from and to many areas.

Further indication of this variability and the increased rate of interaction during this time is suggested by recent excavations in central Indiana. In the Indianapolis area there are or were a number of sites whose artifact complement was substantially similar in most details and which have been grouped into the Oliver Phase. C14 analysis suggests a period of occupation during the eleventh century.

One of the villages, the Bowen Site, was excavated almost in its entirety.[19] Somewhat more than an acre in size, the occupation was circular in plan and surrounded an open "plaza." No substantial evidence of structures was obtained. Within the midden deposit there were a number of human burials, commonly without artifact associations. The subsistence base included maize cultivation, as well as generous quantities of locally available game and wild plant foods. The artifact complex was not large and in addition to tools made from bone and antler, included the late small stemless

19 John T Dorwin, The Bowen Site: An Archaeological Study of Culture Process in the Late Prehistory of Central Indiana (in process of publication by the Indiana Historical Society in its *Prehistory Research Series*).

triangular flint projectile point, undoubtedly used with a bow-propelled dart. The pottery complex included a combination of modes from several sources. Cord marking, a common Woodland characteristic, was frequent. Shell tempering, a definitive Mississippian attribute, was present though not in abundance. The curvilinear guilloche, a series of interlocking scroll designs incised with a blunt pointed instrument in a still damp clay vessel, occurred; this is a characteristic motif of Fort Ancient ceramics in the middle and upper Ohio region. The most common decorative motifs, however, were several patterned variations produced with heavy cord impressions, commonly occurring on well-defined rims; this practice has a generally northern distribution. Similar pottery combinations occur from Orange County in the south to, perhaps, the Salamonie Valley in the north. The point of all this is that considerable cultural ferment was occurring during the early Mississippian period.

The outstanding "classic" Mississippian site in Indiana, Angel Mounds, is located a few miles east of Evansville in the flood plain of the Ohio.[20] A summary description of its physical remains serves to convey something of its importance.

The site extended over an area slightly in excess of a hundred acres and was shielded from the mainstream of the Ohio River by a narrow island. The residents undoubtedly were afforded some protection by this natural feature and, additionally, more than a mile of high bastioned stockade made of logs covered with clay daub covered the mainland approaches. A three-terraced flat-topped mound measuring 650 by 300 by 44 feet had been constructed near the approximate center of the settlement; a large structure reserved for a highly esteemed person or group undoubtedly occupied the broad platform. A number of smaller truncated pyramids were erected for yet other community structures. Just west of the large mound was an open plaza. Around this plaza and

[20] Glenn A. Black, *Angel Site: An Archaeological, Historical, and Ethnological Study* (2 volumes, Indiana Historical Society, Indianapolis, 1967).

throughout the village substantial houses were constructed. These were generally square to rectangular in plan and ranged from about sixteen feet to thirty feet on a side. Construction was accomplished by setting upright posts in a trench and then covering the frame with cane mats and these with daub. These houses followed consistent orientations in various segments of the community. While only a portion of the site has been excavated, projections from this suggest that about two hundred dwellings would have been present at any one time. The population estimate based on the number of houses produces a figure of at least one thousand residents. Food reliance was upon cultivated plants, game, fish and mussels, and wild plant products.

The Mississippian occupants of Angel Mounds were skilled craftsmen. They produced a good quality shell-tempered pottery having many vessel forms undoubtedly to serve specific functions. Though most of it is without surface decoration, some painted wares were manufactured. Using stone, bone, and shell, numerous tools necessary for daily life were manufactured in quantity as were other artifacts for personal adornment.

No other Mississippian village in Indiana duplicates the complexity of Angel Mounds, but there are many culturally related smaller sites in the Ohio and lower Wabash valleys. Some of these were undoubtedly supportive farmsteads for the Angel population and probably looked to that "town" for social, religious, and political leadership.

The culture described is commonly referred to as Middle Mississippian in recognition of the geographic area where it was thought to have been centered. The manifestations in Indiana are clearly intrusive. They appear without evidence of prior development about A.D. 1200 reflecting a clear migration of new peoples into the region. The distribution of such sites is also instructive on the same point. Angel Mounds is the most easterly of the major Mississippian centers in the Ohio Valley. There are a few related sites upstream as far as Clark County, but they are small and undifferentiated in surface features. There are one, possibly three, flat-topped mounds and several large villages downstream in Indiana. Mississippian is also distributed up the Wabash to about Vincennes; one site, a fortified ridge near Merom, though small, was intensively occupied.

Over-all, the distribution is largely confined to the Wabash Lowlands, a region characterized by natural features with a marked southern cast, i.e., cypress, bamboo, broad alluvial meander belts, etc. The Mississippian intruders must have felt "at home" in the area.

Because the period of residency in Indiana was short, removal taking place about A.D. 1500 for reasons presently unperceived, it should not be concluded that the picture is uniform and without change. To the contrary, there are differences between sites which seem to be a consequence of time rather than distance or function. The significance of these is yet to be studied.

The coeval culture in southeastern Indiana is somewhat loosely called Fort Ancient.[21] This occupation is confined to a very narrow strip in the Ohio Valley eastward from Madison. The subsistence pattern, house type, means of village protection, and much of the artifact complement is nearly identical with Middle Mississippi. The situation is one in which contact and diffusion of culture have been operative. However, the flat-topped foundation mounds are absent, as are other features of settlement pattern. Also, ceramics, while frequently shell-tempered and duplicating many Mississippian vessel forms, differ in the relatively high frequency of cord marking and the presence of the interlocking scroll design (curvilinear guilloche).

In northern Indiana a somewhat different adaptation was required. Though plant cultivation was certainly practiced, it was not as productive a technique here as in the south.

21 James B. Griffin, *The Fort Ancient Aspect* . . . (University of Michigan Press, 1943).

Therefore, some greater reliance was placed upon naturally
occurring foods and some greater degree of group mobility
was necessary to exploit these. Sites were smaller and they
often reflect the result of short-term occupancy where food
resources were seasonally available.[22] Even here, however,
such artifacts as pottery and projectile points reflect some
of the almost pan-eastern characteristics associated with the
Mississippian manifestations in the south.

§   §   §   §   §

Ideally, we should now be in a position, after summarizing
ten thousand years of Indiana prehistory, to relate all of this
to the Indian occupants of record. Actually, this is for the
moment at least, impossible. The explanation for this inability is simple. Various bands of the Miami and Potawatomi
occupied the greater portion of the state. Other residents
included the Delawares, Shawnee, and a few members of
other ethnic groups. These were without exception late
migrants into the region. For example, it is not until the
late seventeenth century that the Miami apparently moved
southeast from Wisconsin and Illinois. The Potawatomi
came at about the same time or a bit later. The Delawares
did not arrive until the middle of the following century. And
at least some of the Shawnee seemed to have wandered over
nearly all the eastern United States in the early historic
period before returning to what may have been their earlier
Ohio Valley homeland. The obvious fact is that the known
Indian occupants came into Indiana from the outside and
even though they might have lived here earlier, there is no
way to relate a fully prehistoric site or culture to a specific
ethnic group under these circumstances.

22 Charles H. Faulkner, The Late Prehistoric Occupation of Northwestern
Indiana: A Study of the Upper Mississippian Culture of the Kankakee (in
process of publication by the Indiana Historical Society in its *Prehistory Research Series*).

A necessary precondition for ethnic identification is that there be some distinguishing characteristics to permit separation. Since the archaeologist deals most directly with the substantive surviving materials, these characteristics must be discernible in the houses, pottery, tools, and the like. There are no such extant historic descriptions, however, which provide such a datum.

Another alternative is to excavate a village known to have been occupied by a particular group in order to determine the nature of the material remains. This has been done and the work at Ouiatanon, an eighteenth-century French trading post near Lafayette which served the Wea and others, was partially predicated on that basis.[23] Two seasons of excavation have produced five triangular projectile points and a handful of cord-marked potsherds. In contrast, there are hundreds of artifacts of European manufacture, duplicates of which were distributed by means of the Indian trade over half of North America. By 1700, the specifically Indian material culture had been replaced through a growing dependency on foreign glass, iron, and, ironically, flint for guns. The archaeologist-historian is faced with a problem of monumental proportions in the quest for ethnic identifications in Indiana.

§   §   §   §   §   §

Prior to 1950 there were no generally available methods for dating prehistoric archaeological sites, except in so far as they might be similar to or differ from one another. However, the development of the C14 dating technique, a technique based upon the regular rate of radioactive decay of a carbon isotope present in all organic material, changed all this. Though a precise calendrical date is not determined— only an average "date" and a plus and minus range of years around this average within which there are two chances in

[23] James H. Kellar, "In Search of Ouiatanon," *Indiana History Bulletin,* XLVII (1970), 123-133.

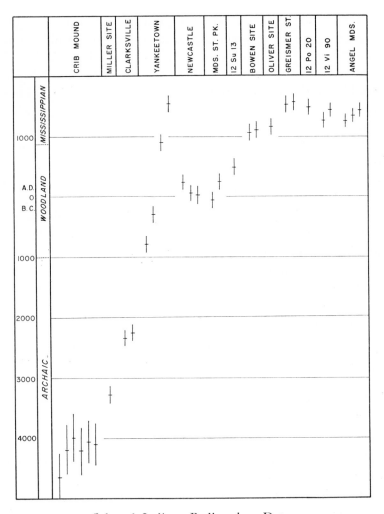

Selected Indiana Radiocarbon Dates

three that the correct calendrical date will occur—the results obtained permitted a degree of chronological control impossible at an earlier time.

A number of Indiana prehistoric sites and cultures have been dated through the medium of radiocarbon. The chart on

p. 54 is a summary of these results.[24] A few determinations from the state have not been included, either because the dates are so distorted as to suggest error or it is not known with reasonable precision to what prehistoric culture the date refers.

There has been a pronounced tendency to view the American Indian as an anachronistic element in the inexorable move towards the ultimate European domination of the New World. The native peoples, particularly those in the eastern United States, were thought to be so abjectly inferior and insensitive that even their earlier monumental earthworks were interpreted to represent the handiwork of a prior intellectually superior people, probably ultimately derived from an Old World heartland. Such interpretations, if they were ever warranted by evidence, grew out of the fact that Indian history was unwritten and by the time Europeans began to take a serious look at the cultures of the native peoples, they frequently had already been so thoroughly disrupted as to have reality only in the memory of the oldest generations.

[24] I am indebted to Robert Pace and E. V. McMichael, Indiana State University, and to Donald E. Janzen, Beloit College, for the use of their unpublished dates. Fresh water mussel shell was employed for the six Crib Mound dates. Experience has demonstrated that modern freshwater shell is routinely radiocarbon dated at about 1800 years old, hence, the Crib Mound chronology is probably too old by that much.

Site	Location (County)	Type
Crib Mound	Spencer	Shell midden
Miller Site	Harrison	Shell midden
Clarksville	Clark	Shell midden
Yankeetown	Warrick	Stratified occupation
New Castle	Henry	Mound group
Mounds State Park	Madison	Mound group
12 Su 13	Sullivan	Village
Bowen Site	Marion	Village
Oliver	Marion	Village
Greismer	Lake	Seasonal camp
12 Po 20	Posey	Village
12 Vi 90	Vigo	Village
Angel Mounds	Vanderburgh	"Town"

The prehistoric perspective which archaeology permits, while limited to only those aspects of culture likely to survive natural forces, results in quite a different picture than that suggested by the popular stereotype. Beginning at least 10,000 years ago, a widespread hunting base underwent a slow transition until human groups were ultimately able to utilize and become dependent upon a variety of natural resources. Some of this variety seems to occur coeval with alterations in the environment following the end of the Pleistocene. Mortuary ritualism, so conspicuous a part of the archaeological record from the first millennium before Christ to about A.D. 600, is an outgrowth of the more successful of these adaptations and with the addition of cultivated plant foods, reached a peak of development, particularly in Ohio. Following a short period of relative quiescence, developments in the Mississippi Valley involving a major reliance upon horticulture and undoubtedly influenced in some measure by the "high" cultures in Middle America, produced large settled town populations in some regions and contributed to the way of life in others. This pattern survived into the period of European settlement, though the area of Mississippian domination was much diminished during this later period and some regions seemed actually depopulated, e.g., the Ohio Valley. Indiana shares in these developments and preserves a host of archaeological sites reflecting upon them.

CHAPTER III

FRENCH EXPLORATION AND OCCUPATION

French dominion over the region that later became the state of Indiana is part of the larger story of French occupation of North America from the first attempts in the sixteenth century until their withdrawal in 1763. The first Frenchmen to visit the New World were fishermen who discovered early in the 1500s the bountiful fishing areas off the coasts of Newfoundland and New England and were making annual trips back and forth across the Atlantic to market their catch. The fishermen soon came in contact with the Indians on the mainland and learned they had still another product, the furs of wild animals, which they were willing to exchange for a few trifles of European goods. Soon the profits obtained from trading in furs dwarfed those obtained from fish.[1]

The fishermen were not interested in exploring the country they had discovered; this was left to the French explorers, the first of whom was Giovanni Verrazano (an Italian commissioned by France) who sailed along the Atlantic coast, probably from the present state of New Jersey northward in 1524 in search of a northern passage to Asia. The first Frenchman to venture inland was Jacques Cartier who explored the St. Lawrence River up as far as the Lachine rapids (above the present Montreal) during his three expeditions in 1534, 1535, and 1541, and took possession of the area in the name of the King of France. Though attempts were made during

---

[1] Louise Phelps Kellogg, *The French Régime in Wisconsin and the North-west* (Madison, Wis., 1925), pp. 8-9; George M. Wrong, *The Rise and Fall of New France* (2 volumes, New York, 1928), I, 46-76; John B. Brebner, *The Explorers of North America, 1492-1806* (New York, 1933), pp. 137-146; Paul C. Phillips and John W. Smurr, *The Fur Trade* (2 volumes, Norman, Okla., 1961), I, 15-22.

the sixteenth century to found a settlement, it was not until 1608 that the first permanent settlement was made at Quebec.[2]

In a very real sense New France was a monument to the persistence of a succession of Frenchmen who despite staggering hardships established a foothold for their country in North America. The first of these was Samuel de Champlain who not only founded Quebec but explored the country south to Lake Champlain, up the Ottawa River and its tributaries to Lake Huron, and across Lake Ontario into the land of the Iroquois Indians. He in turn sent out other young explorers such as Etienne Brulé and Jean Nicolet who explored the Great Lakes as far west as the present Green Bay.[3] Missionaries usually accompanied the explorers and it is from their writings that much information concerning the country and its inhabitants has come down to us.

The chief resource of New France was the fur trade, the center of which was at first about Tadoussac and Quebec but gradually moved westward, first to Three Rivers and then to Montreal. Though disappointed that French explorers had not found a short route to the Orient, or gold like the Spanish had found in Mexico and Peru, the King of France began to realize that perhaps in the fur trade lay the hopes of restoring French prosperity. Since there was no money in the French treasury for the promotion of colonization in North America, he adopted the practice of granting monopolies to certain commercial companies who in turn for the exclusive privilege of trade would establish settlements. Such a company was the Hundred Associates or the Company of New France which was organized in the 1620s. Its first attempts to send out settlers met with defeat at the hands of the English who were also interested in the fur trade and were contesting French claims to the St. Lawrence area and the islands off the coast. However, with the

[2] Brebner, *Explorers of North America*, pp. 113-136; Kellogg, *The French Régime*, pp. 9-50.

[3] Kellogg, *The French Régime*, pp. 44-83; Brebner, *Explorers of North America*, pp. 148-165.

settlement of differences between the French and the British in 1632 and the assumption of complete control of French interests in North America by the Company of New France, a new impetus was given to colonization and settlement.

Companies of immigrants were sent out composed of impoverished noblemen and peasants as well as Jesuit missionaries. Those of the upper class received large grants of land and became known as "seigneurs," while the peasants whom they settled on their land were known as *"habitans."* This plan of settlement was to serve as a model for the French posts later to be established in the west. The seigneurs and *habitans* were supposed to devote themselves to agriculture, but in this northern country agriculture did not prosper and both groups soon discovered in the Indian trade a more lucrative occupation. The Company of New France had a monopoly of the fur trade, buying the pelts from local merchants and exporting them. At first the Indians brought the furs east to the trading centers. It must have been a very colorful sight to see a flotilla of as many as one hundred canoes descend the St. Lawrence each spring loaded with the precious pelts. Later the traders accompanied the Indians into the interior and became known as *"coureurs de bois"* or "woods runners" because of their manner of living.[4]

The struggle for the expansion and control of the fur trade soon brought the French into conflict with the Iroquois Indians and their allies who lived south of the St. Lawrence; these tribes traded with the Dutch, who had come into New York, and later with the English, receiving in turn firearms as well as the usual trade goods. The French chose to ally themselves with the Hurons and related tribes of the Great Lakes region and this relationship was deepened by sending Jesuit missionaries among these Indians. The struggle between these two opposing forces was to continue for a century, with first one side and then the other gaining the advantage. During the cruel warfare of the 1640s and 1650s

[4] Kellogg, *The French Régime,* pp. 60-62, 101-103; Phillips and Smurr, *The Fur Trade,* I, 45-97, 204-219.

the Iroquois destroyed the Jesuit mission stations among the Hurons, interrupted the fur trade with the western Indians for which the Hurons acted as intermediaries, and drove their tribal victims westward.[5]

In 1663 Louis XIV took over the control of New France, or Canada as it was coming to be called, and made it a royal colony. The charter of the Hundred Associates was cancelled and a new form of government instituted consisting of a governor-general and intendant appointed by the King, who together shared the management of the colony. A superior council served in an advisory capacity and as a court of law. In addition, a portion of the Carignan-Salières regiment was sent to the colony for its protection and the pacification of the Iroquois. After making two expeditions into Iroquois country an armistice was signed with that tribe in 1667 which brought peace for a period of ten years. After the end of their term of service many of the soldiers remained in the colony as settlers.[6]

Three personalities dominated Canada during the second half of the seventeenth century. One was Intendant Jean Talon who was keenly interested in agriculture and manufac-

   [5] Kellogg, *The French Régime*, pp. 84-100; Phillips and Smurr, *The Fur Trade*, I, 97-102.

   [6] Wrong, *The Rise and Fall of New France*, I, 361-365, 374-380; Kellogg, *The French Régime*, pp. 118-119. The French colonies in America were governed through the Department of the Marine under the immediate control of the minister of that department who was in turn responsible to the King. The governor-general was usually a naval officer and was nominally in charge of the defense and general administration of the colony, while the intendant had jurisdiction over the police, finances, and the administration of justice. The council was composed of men drawn from the local citizenry and appointed by the King; the governor-general, intendant, and bishop were ex officio members.

   Royal troops were the chief arm of the governor-general for the defense of the colony; the number was never large—usually less than one thousand. Officers were appointed by the King upon recommendation of the governor-general. In addition, there was the colonial militia embracing all able-bodied men and officered by men commissioned by the governor-general. Norman W. Caldwell, *The French in the Mississippi Valley, 1740-1750* (*Illinois Studies in the Social Sciences*, XXVI, No. 3, Urbana, 1941), pp. 9-15.

turing as well as in exploration; the second was Bishop François de Laval, a bitter opponent of the liquor traffic with the Indians. It was through the encouragement of Bishop Laval and his immediate successors that some of the famous mission stations of the West were developed. Perhaps the most famous of all the leaders was the arrogant, quarrelsome "Iron Governor," Louis de Buade, Comte de Frontenac, who served from 1672 to 1682 and again from 1689 until his death in 1698. Under his administration New France reached new heights. It was in this period that heroic figures such as Louis Jolliet, Jacques Marquette, Nicolas Perrot, Robert Cavelier de La Salle, and Pierre Charles Le Sueur carried out important explorations in the West which extended the boundaries of the French colony to the Great Lakes and on to the Mississippi Valley.

Who was the first white man to reach the Indiana area? Possibly it was an obscure Frenchman whose adventures were never recorded—if he lived to tell the tale. Perhaps the first white visitor was the famous Jesuit, Jacques Marquette, who may have spent one or more of his last nights on Indiana soil. After Marquette and Jolliet returned from their exploration of the Mississippi in 1673, Marquette rested for a time at the St. François Xavier Mission at Green Bay before he received permission to found a mission among the Illinois Indians. Poor health forced him to spend the winter of 1674-75 near the site of Chicago and the following spring he tried unsuccessfully to get back to Michilimackinac before death overtook him. His homeward route followed the southern shore of the Lake of the Illinois, or Lake Michigan, a route which travelers often took because of currents which ran a northward course. It is quite possible that Marquette and his companions camped on Hoosier soil.[7]

[7] Reuben G. Thwaites, *Father Marquette* (New York, 1902), pp. 217-227. Claude A. Dablon's Journal of the trip around the lake is in Reuben G. Thwaites (ed.), *The Jesuit Relations and Allied Documents* (73 volumes, Cleveland, 1896-1901), LIX, 191-193.

The first white men who most certainly did touch Indiana were the Sieur de La Salle and his companions in 1679. The explorer's presence in Indiana was only a part of his experiences in the Illinois country, the scene of his main activities; his goal was the discovery of the mouth of the Mississippi.[8] Coming around the eastern shore of Lake Michigan in December, 1679, La Salle and his companions reached the mouth of the River of the Miami, known today as the St. Joseph of the Lake. While waiting for Henry de Tonti to join him, he built a fort, then proceeded up the St. Joseph, crossed the portage to the Kankakee near the site of South Bend, and continued down that stream to the Illinois River and the Illinois Indian villages. The following year, on his return journey to the St. Joseph, La Salle probably again crossed the northwest corner of Indiana.[9] Thus as the seventeenth century moved into the eighteenth, French influence had touched the Indiana area but as yet no permanent occupation had taken place.

French claims to the upper Great Lakes area and the Mississippi Valley, based on the explorations of La Salle and other explorers, did not go unchallenged. Though the English themselves were not prepared to enter into a direct struggle for the interior of North America, their allies, the Iroquois and other tribes of the Five Nations, were making raids on French posts and mission stations in the Illinois country by 1680. The Iroquois wished to act as intermediaries between the western tribes and the New York traders and did not want the French to establish trade relations with these Indians. To meet this opposition La Salle undertook

[8] Some historians contend that La Salle discovered and traveled down the Ohio River in 1669. For a discussion of the evidence concerning this discovery, see Frances Krauskopf, "The Documentary Basis for La Salle's Supposed Discovery of the Ohio River," *Indiana Magazine of History,* XLVII (1951), 143-153.

[9] Paul Chesnel, *History of Cavelier de La Salle, 1643-1687* . . . (New York and London, 1932), pp. 106-110, 116-117; Jean Delanglez, "A Calendar of La Salle's Travels, 1643-1683," *Mid-America,* XXII (1940), 278-305.

to form a similar confederacy of western tribes under direct French influence. In spite of repeated raids by Indians friendly to the English, the French continued to occupy the upper Great Lakes area and the Illinois country with strategically placed posts and missions. Then in 1696 Louis XIV issued a royal decree revoking all licenses for trading in furs or carrying goods into the Indian country in order to concentrate the trade at posts where troops were stationed. The reason for this reversal of policy was due to abuses in the license system as well as the decline in the market for furs and the temporary ascendancy for the moment of the anti-imperialist party in France which wished to restrict the colonists to the St. Lawrence Valley. Within two years the western posts were abandoned and all the *coureurs de bois* were called in, thus leaving the field to the English and their Indian allies. The year 1698 also marked the end of the war between France and England known as King William's War; parallel peace negotiations conducted at Montreal over a three-year period brought to an end, at least temporarily, the strife between the Iroquois and western tribes.[10]

The opening of the eighteenth century found the French seeking to recover their control in the west. Plans called for a policy of concentration with posts at three strategic points— at the site of Detroit, on Lake Peoria, and at the mouth of the Mississippi. They would try to gather the Indians close to these posts and make them trading centers for furs and

[10] Clarence W. Alvord, *The Illinois Country, 1673-1818* (Springfield, Ill., 1920), pp. 58, 72, 106-112; Kellogg, *The French Régime,* pp. 221-267. As early as 1680 the large number of *coureurs de bois* (estimated at eight hundred) and the difficulty of controlling them had become a concern of the King. He called upon Frontenac to encourage the inhabitants to engage in agriculture, fishing, and manufacturing rather than wandering in the woods; also, attempts were made to recall some and to allow only those operating under a *congé* or license to go into the Indian country. Lawrence H. Gipson, *The British Empire before the American Revolution* . . . (13 volumes, Caldwell, Idaho, 1936-1967), V, 43-45; Harold Innis, *The Fur Trade in Canada* . . . (Yale University Press, 1962), pp. 67-69. For the part played by the *coureurs de bois* in the fur trade, see Innis, *op. cit.,* pp. 59-62,

European goods as well as military posts. Antoine de La-
mothe Cadillac founded Fort Pontchartrain at the site of
Detroit in 1701; Henry de Tonti and François Daupin de la
Forest returned to their former post on Lake Peoria, and
the first settlement in the new colony of Louisiana was made
at Biloxi in 1699 under the guidance of two of the famous
Le Moyne brothers, Pierre le Moyne d'Iberville and Jean-
Baptiste le Moyne de Bienville. The former soon returned to
France, leaving Bienville, a youth of twenty, in charge.

Louisiana remained a royal colony until 1712, then finding
that instead of producing wealth it was proving to be a
serious drain on the treasury, the King granted Antoine
Crozat a monopoly of the trade with the colony for fifteen
years. When he did not find the rich mineral resources
he expected to discover and the trade with the Spanish
colonies did not materialize, Crozat surrendered the charter
at the end of five years. The colony was then taken over
by John Law's Company of the West, which soon merged
into the great Company of the Indies. In addition to a trade
monopoly this company received full authority to carry on
the local administration of affairs. Bienville continued as
governor of the colony until 1740 except for the years
between 1726 and 1734 when Louis de la Périer held the
office.[11] The government of Louisiana was much the same as

11 For a discussion of the establishment of Louisiana and its early development, see Alvord, *The Illinois Country,* pp. 127-167; Alcée Fortier, *A History
of Louisiana* (4 volumes, New York, 1904), I, 30-82, 98-140; *Historical
Collections of Louisiana,* compiled by B. F. French (3 volumes, New York,
1846-51), III, 10n-13n, 20n-22n; N. M. Miller Surrey, *The Commerce of
Louisiana during the French Régime, 1699-1763* (Columbia University *Studies
in History, Economics and Public Law,* LXXI, No. 1, 1916), Chap. XII.
La Salle had given the name Louisiana to the entire Mississippi Valley at
the time he laid claim to it for the French King in 1682. His own attempt
to found a colony there two years later ended in failure.

The implications of what the charter granted to Crozat might mean to
the English settlements on the eastern coast were expressed in a *Letter to a
Member of the P[arliamen]t,* published in London in 1713, a copy of which is
in the William Henry Smith Memorial Library of the Indiana Historical
Society.

that of Canada, with a governor and *ordonnateur* (intendant) appointed by the King; the two colonies were governed separately, but because Canada was older and more populous, Louisiana was somewhat dependent upon her.

In place of the fur trade which was the principal resource of the northern colony, Bienville promoted the development of agriculture since the climate was well adapted to the cultivation of sugar, cotton, tobacco, and rice. Since European colonists could not survive as agricultural laborers in the southern climate, Negroes were imported. Intercourse between Louisiana and the Illinois country was established almost immediately with furs from the north being transported down the Mississippi and explorers from the new post searching the Illinois country for mineral wealth. Bienville treated the Illinois country as belonging within his jurisdiction and made far-reaching plans for relocating the Indian tribes and establishing trading posts there, while at the same time Canada was also making plans for the area, expecting it to be continued under the jurisdiction of that government. Whereas the center of French activity had hitherto been on the Illinois River, after 1700 it became centered around Kaskaskia and Cahokia on the Mississippi where new missions were established. Also, the hostility of the Fox Indians led the French to develop the Maumee-Wabash route to connect Canada and Louisiana in place of the Kankakee-Illinois route.

§

In the eighteenth century both Indiana and Ohio became refuge areas for a large number of Indian tribes or segments of tribal groups. Some of them, such as the Mahican, Nanticoke, Delawares, Munsee, and Shawnee, were originally from the eastern seaboard and had been pushed westward by the press of white settlement. Others, such as the Kickapoo, Potawatomi, Miami, Piankashaw, Wea, and Hurons, were from the Great Lakes area.

Of the tribes which moved into Indiana, the Miami and two closely related groups, the Wea and the Piankashaw, occupy a foremost place. By 1680 the Miami had moved from their villages in the Wisconsin area to the region of Chicago and the St. Joseph River of the Lake. Twenty years later we find some of them in the neighborhood of Detroit. During the early part of the eighteenth century part of the tribe occupied the country north and northwest of the upper Wabash, whence they gradually moved eastward to the Fort Wayne area and into what is now northwestern Ohio. Kekionga (now Fort Wayne) at the junction of the St. Marys and St. Joseph rivers became their principal town.

Some of the Wea had shifted to the Wabash River in the area of the present Tippecanoe County, Indiana, by 1700; at that time another band was still at the site of Chicago but probably joined the rest of the tribe on the Wabash shortly thereafter. The Piankashaw had a village farther down the Wabash at the mouth of the Vermilion River; by 1750 a branch of the Kickapoo had also settled on the Vermilion and Wabash rivers.[12]

As in the previous century, wars between the various tribes continued. The Miami were first involved with the Ottawa, then with the Foxes, the Kickapoo, and the Illinois. Jean-Baptiste Bissot, Sieur de Vincennes, who was sent by the governor of New France to live with the Miami, became

---

[12] Erminie W. Voegelin, "Indians of Indiana," Indiana Academy of Science, *Proceedings,* L (1941), 27-32; Frederick W. Hodge (ed.), *Handbook of American Indians North of Mexico* (2 volumes, U. S. Bureau of American Ethnology, *Bulletin 30,* Washington, D. C., 1906, 1910), I, 684-685, 852-854; II, 240, 925. The Memoir of Pierre Deliette (also known as the De Gannes Memoir) describes these tribes as they were at the turn of the century before moving into the Indiana area. The Memoir is printed in *The French Foundations, 1680-1693,* edited by Theodore C. Pease and Raymond C. Werner (*Illinois Historical Collections,* XXIII, Springfield, 1934), pp. 302-395, and in Milo M. Quaife (ed.), *The Western Country in the Seventeenth Century . . .* (*Lakeside Classics,* Chicago, 1947). The spelling and pluralization of Indian names in the present volume are in conformity with Hodge.

a key figure in that tribe's relations with the French and with other Indian tribes.[13]

A description of conditions among the Indians in the Indiana area is given in a report made by Jacques-Charles de Sabrevois, former commandant at Detroit, in 1718. He described the lower Maumee region as a marshy area where game was very plentiful, especially in the spring and autumn. Thirty leagues [75 miles] from the mouth of the Maumee was La Glaise, where the buffalo ate clay and wallowed in it. At the source of the Maumee, sixty leagues [150 miles] from Lake Erie, the Miami nation numbered four hundred warriors. These Indians were described as being very industrious and fond of games and dances; the men were well tattooed and wore little clothing, but the women were adequately covered.

Down the Wabash, five villages of Wea and Piankashaw, with a population of a thousand or twelve hundred, were distinguished for their cleanliness. The people raised maize, melons, and pumpkins; buffalo grazed near by.[14]

Although the French had laid claim to the area west of the Appalachian Mountains, their ability to defend this claim

[13] Jean-Baptiste Bissot, Sieur de Vincennes, was born at Quebec in 1668. He was educated at the Seminary of Quebec and spent some time in France. In 1695 he signed himself as "ensign of the Navy." The following year he married at Montreal Marguerite Forestier. Seven children were born to this union, three boys and four girls; two of the boys died in infancy, the other, Francois-Marie Bissot, born in 1700, was destined to play an important role in Indiana history. It was apparently shortly after his marriage that Sieur de Vincennes, Sr., was sent to command at the garrison located at the Miami village on the St. Joseph River of the Lake. For his family and an account of his services, see Pierre-Georges Roy, *Sieur de Vincennes Identified* (Indiana Historical Society *Publications,* VII, No. 1, Indianapolis [1919]), pp. 31-75. Roy has also written *Le Sieur de Vincennes, Fondateur de L'Indiana et Sa Famille* (Quebec, 1919).

[14] "Memoir on the Savages of Canada . . . Describing Their Customs and Trade," *Wisconsin Historical Collections,* XVI, 375-376. The complete document is printed in *ibid.,* pp. 363-376. Estimates of Indian population vary; being almost continually on the move, it would have been impossible to get an accurate count.

depended on whether they could actually take possession of
the land and control the Indian tribes. The population of
the English colonies was increasing rapidly and explorers
and traders from Pennsylvania, Virginia, and the Carolinas
were pushing westward across the mountains. By 1700 a few
English traders had reached the lower Ohio and the Great
Lakes region, and the French feared they would in time secure
a portion of the fur trade. When the *congé* system of licensing French traders was temporarily discontinued in 1698, the
coureurs de bois did not all withdraw from the Indian country but instead scattered along the streams and traded whenever they could. Sometimes they sold their pelts to the English, sometimes they let the Indians be the middlemen and
take the furs east to the French trading centers. French efforts
to bring them under control only resulted in their wider
dispersal.[15]

The difference in the governments of the French and
English colonies contributed to the competition between the
respective groups of traders. Whereas the government of
New France was highly centralized and maintained a strict
control of the fur trade, the English colonies competed with
each other for the trade, and the mother country made no
attempt to control the price of furs or the price of goods
sold to the Indians. The only supervision was that which the
governors of such colonies as New York, Pennsylvania, Virginia, and the Carolinas exercised. The English were able to
provide cheaper goods to the Indians so the French had to
be on the alert continually to prevent their Indian allies from
going over to the English side.

Trade at the French posts was carried on at various times
under three different methods of exploitation: the plan of
farming out or leasing, the licensing plan, and the plan of
exploitation by the commandant of the post. In the first,

15 Alvord, *The Illinois Country*, pp. 101-102, 107-109, 123, 148; Pease and
Werner (eds.), *The French Foundations*, p. 7; Kellogg, *The French Régime*,
pp. 180, 202-203, 221, 230, 254-257; Alfred T. Goodman (ed.), *Journal of
Captain William Trent from Logstown to Pickawillany A.D. 1752* . . .
(Cincinnati, 1871), pp. 10-12.

the monopoly of the trade at a given post was sold, usually at public auction, to some individual or company, for a three-year period. The lessee agreed to exploit the post himself or send *engagés* to do it for him. He could send as many canoes with goods as he deemed necessary, but the content of his cargoes was strictly regulated, especially as to the amount of liquor they carried. The officer at the post was obligated to protect him in his trade monopoly and in turn the lessee would supply the officer with fuel, lodging, and the conveyance of his supplies.

Under the licensing system, private traders bought or were granted *congés* permitting them to trade at certain posts. Each *congé* designated the number of canoes the trader was allowed to send, the *voyageurs* who were to accompany him, as well as the route to be taken. Holders of *congés* were to carry in each canoe going to a post a certain amount of goods for the commandant. *Congés* were not sold at auction, but were issued upon application; sometimes they were given gratis. In the case of exploitation of the posts by the military commandant, this officer held a monopoly of the trade just as the "farmer" or lessee under the farming system.[16] The profit he derived therefrom apparently constituted part of his remuneration as commandant.

[16] Alvord, *The Illinois Country,* pp. 85-86; Caldwell, *The French in the Mississippi Valley,* pp. 51-53; Innis, *The Fur Trade in Canada,* pp. 61-62, 106-109. For a list of *congés* and permits registered at Montreal for trading at the various posts for the years 1720-30, 1739-52, and 1758, see *Rapport de L'Archiviste de la Province de Quebec,* 1921-22, pp. 189-223; 1922-23, pp. 192-265; 1932-33, pp. 245-304.

The term *coureurs de bois* gradually came to be applied to traders in the interior without official permission, although this was not the original meaning of the term. They received their supplies from licensed French traders or from the English in exchange for furs. Sometimes Indians served as agents between the *coureurs de bois* and their suppliers. Most of them took Indian women for their wives. The government continually tried to control them. They were especially numerous in Illinois which lay at the outskirts of both colonies, with the boundary between them indefinite. Phillips and Smurr, *The Fur Trade,* I, 197-203; Caldwell, *The French in the Mississippi Valley,* pp. 55-57; R. M. Saunders, "Coureur de Bois: A Definition," *Canadian Historical Review,* XXI (1940), 123-131.

The fur trade was carried on by means of an exchange involving raw furs and merchandise. The trading convoys usually left Montreal in May, reached Detroit in July, and from there fanned out to the different posts. After disposing of their goods to the savages and to French hunters and trappers, they returned home loaded with peltries. The return trip was scheduled to reach Montreal before bad weather began in November. From the more distant posts, the canoes did not return until the following spring, it being necessary to winter at the posts. In the colony of Louisiana it required four months for traders departing from New Orleans to reach Kaskaskia and from six weeks to two months for the return trip.

Articles suitable for the trade were those used by the savages and by the French woodsmen in their primitive life of hunting, trapping, and warfare. These might include hunting knives, guns, lead, balls, powder, steel for striking fire, gun flints, hatchets, kettles, beads, men's shirts, cloth (red and blue) for blankets and petticoats, vermilion and verdigris, tallow, blue and green ribbon, needles, thread, awls, blue, white, and red ratteen for making moccasins, woolen blankets, mirrors framed in wood, hats trimmed with variegated plumes, brandy, tobacco, razors, glass beads made after the fashion of wampum, and paints.

The furs chiefly in demand were skins of the beaver, bear, raccoon, otter, red fox, mink, fisher, wolf, and deer. Beaver was the most desirable. In Louisiana deerskins and buffalo hides were more plentiful.[17]

In 1715 the French government granted permission to re-establish the *congé* system which had been discontinued in 1696. One of the reasons given was that the officials hoped to conciliate the Ottawa, Miami, and Illinois who were all

17 Caldwell, *The French in the Mississippi Valley,* pp. 57-58. Frances Krauskopf (ed.), *Ouiatanon Documents* (Indiana Historical Society *Publications,* XVIII, No. 2, Indianapolis, 1955), pp. 195-204, lists trade goods brought to Ouiatanon in 1746.

middlemen in the fur trade with the more distant tribes. Along with this change in policy, the governor of New France was given authority to found and garrison as many posts in the interior as he thought necessary. Rumors which reported Englishmen among the Illinois and Miami Indians prompted this need for a military force to protect French claims.[18]

§ §

The first post to be established in the Indiana area was Ouiatanon near the present Lafayette. Plans called for a military force of a captain, one subordinate officer, a sergeant, and ten soldiers with instructions to break the supposed connection between the Wea and the English and to keep peace with the Illinois Indians. The post was not expected to be permanent, but only to continue until the Wea could be persuaded to return to the Chicago area or at least to the upper Kankakee where they would be less likely to trade with the English.[19]

[18] Claude de Ramezay and Michel Bégon, governor-general and intendant, to French minister, November 7, 1715; Proceedings of the Council of the Marine, January 6, 1717; and Phillipe de Rigaud de Vaudreuil, governor-general, to French minister, October 11, 1723, in *Wisconsin Historical Collections*, XVI, 332-333, 345-346, 437. Fort St. Joseph on the site of the present Niles, Michigan, which had originally been built under Frontenac's direction in 1691 and abandoned along with other posts in 1698, was reoccupied in 1715. F. Clever Bald, *Michigan in Four Centuries* (New York, 1954), pp. 43-44, 47, 57. A Jesuit mission was in existence here by 1690, and perhaps earlier. George Paré, "The St. Joseph Mission," *Mississippi Valley Historical Review*, XVII (1930-31), 24-36.

[19] Krauskopf (ed.), *Ouiatanon Documents,* pp. 140-141. Prior to the establishment of Post Ouiatanon a chain of events had taken place which well illustrates the difficulties of carrying out plans formulated in Quebec. In this instance, the governor-general, intendant, and commandants of western forts had made plans to end the war with the Renards (Foxes). Peace first had to be arranged between the Miami and Illinois, and then these two nations would be asked to unite with other tribes from the north to crush the Foxes. After receiving word from the Sieur de Vincennes of peace having been made between the Miami and Illinois, a rendezvous of French and Indian forces was arranged for Chicago in August of 1715. Emissaries dispatched to the Miami villages at the headwaters of the Maumee and

Ensign François-Marie Picoté, Sieur de Belestre, an army officer at Detroit, was chosen to carry out these plans in 1717; the commandant there supplied a blacksmith. Presents were sent to "cover" the deaths of several Wea chiefs and additional gifts were to be given to persuade the tribe to move. The site chosen for the post was on the north bank of the Wabash River approximately eighteen miles below the mouth of the Tippecanoe. Although no contemporary description has been preserved, it was apparently a palisaded fort sufficiently large to shelter twelve to twenty families, with an arsenal and storehouses. Instructions were sent to the Sieur de Vincennes, who by this time was living with the Miami at Kekionga, to use his influence with the Wea to get them to move back northward.[20]

Four trading licenses were issued by the governor-general of Canada for the new post in 1718. Pierre Comme dit Lajeunesse of Montreal and Claude Legris of Quebec set out in May, 1718, financed by the Montreal merchant Pierre de L'Estage. Joseph Larche of Quebec and Jacques Mon-

on the Wabash were accompanied by chiefs and members of that tribe; the latter had been exposed to measles while in Detroit and became ill on the journey; some died; those who survived carried the disease to others in the villages. The emissaries were not well received but finally extracted promises from the Miami and Wea that they would co-operate. Leaving the Wabash, one of the emissaries went on to the Illinois Indians to solicit their help. Upon arriving at the place of rendezvous at the appointed time, the Miami did not find any other Indians and returned home; likewise the Illinois Indians. It was found out later that the commandant at Michilimackinac and his Indians never started; the Detroit contingent arrived late. The Wea especially were disillusioned by the whole affair and to reassure them the hope was held out that the governor would send them an officer and a missionary. See the correspondence of French officials in *Wisconsin Historical Collections,* XVI, 303-307, 311-326.

20 Krauskopf (ed.), *Ouiatanon Documents,* pp. 141-142; Vaudreuil to the Council, October 28, 1719, and October 22, 1720; Proceedings of the Council, December 2, 1721, in *Wisconsin Historical Collections,* XVI, 380-383, 394-395, 399. An effort was made in 1968-69 to locate the exact site of Fort Ouiatanon by the use of archaeological methods. The explorations were conducted by Dr. James H. Kellar and students of the Anthropology Department, Indiana University; for a report of their findings, see *Indiana History Bulletin,* XLVII (1970), 123-133.

boeuf of Montreal also left in May; Etienne Roy of Montreal left in June.[21] The following year the home government
once more prohibited the issuing of licenses to traders and
requested that the Indians bring their pelts directly to Montreal. Phillipe de Rigaud de Vaudreuil, the governor-general,
warned French officials that the Indians could just as easily
take their furs to the English at Albany or Philadelphia.[22]

At the same time that the French were once again halting
trading licenses in the interior, eight or ten canoes of Miami
were observed going to Albany to trade. The English, for
their part, feared the growing French influence among the
Iroquois; they estimated that more than seven hundred of
that tribe had moved to French mission stations on the St.
Lawrence. Deputy-governor William Keith of Pennsylvania
was urging the English to reach out for the western Indian
trade by building four small forts, including one on Lake
Erie. Keith's report contains a fairly accurate description
of the Indiana area, although the estimates of distances are
faulty.[23]

During the winter of 1718-19, Sieur de Vincennes died in
the Miami village of Kekionga, and his son, a young man
of eighteen, continued the duties of his father as agent of
the French government. The death of the senior Vincennes
strengthened the resolve of the Miami to remain where they

21 Krauskopf (ed.), *Ouiatanon Documents*, pp. 162-164.

22 Phillips and Smurr, *The Fur Trade*, I, 453; French Archives Nationales,
Colonies, C11A40:54v (copies in Canadian Archives and in the Library of
Congress). Vaudreuil later got into trouble because he validated unused
congés issued before this prohibition. *Wisconsin Historical Collections*, XVI,
438-439. The home government explained that it had banned the trading
licenses because of representations made by missionaries who wished to prevent
the Indians from obtaining spirituous liquor. M. Edouard Richard, "Report
on Paris Archives," *Report on Canadian Archives*, 1904, Appendix K, 27.

23 Vaudreuil to the Council, October 28, 1719, in *Wisconsin Historical
Collections*, XVI, 383. Keith's report, which was in fact the work of James
Logan, is printed in part in Phillips and Smurr, *The Fur Trade*, I, 382-384.
A trading post was established at Oswego on Lake Ontario by the colony
of New York in 1722.

were, but Vaudreuil refused to give up plans for their removal. He proposed that Capt. Charles Renaud Du Buisson,
who had been designated to go to Ouiatanon, should go instead to the Miami village in the hope that he could persuade
that tribe to move to the St. Joseph area. If he failed, then
he should stay with them and establish a garrisoned post at
Kekionga to combat English influence.[24] But Du Buisson was
detained in Canada and in the interim Vaudreuil sent Ensign
Dumont and Simon Reaume, a former *voyageur* well known
to the Miami, to try and persuade the Indians to move. At
the Miami village Dumont's first duty was to expel all Frenchmen except the blacksmith so that they would not influence
the removal of the Indians. Dumont addressed an assembly of
Miami on February 11, 1721, after which they unanimously
declared they would not leave their present town where they
were safe from other Indians and the hunting was good. At
the St. Joseph of the Lake they would be in constant danger
from the Foxes and would have to travel a great distance to
reach their hunting grounds.[25]

When Du Buisson finally became free to go to the Miami
in August of 1721, he was instructed by Vaudreuil to proceed

[24] Vaudreuil to the Council, October 28, 1719, in Krauskopf (ed.), *Ouiatanon
Documents,* pp. 164-165, and in *Wisconsin Historical Collections,* XVI, 382-383.
Du Buisson, with thirty-three years of government service in America, was
considered the most capable officer available for the assignment. He and
the elder Vincennes had had an opportunity to become well acquainted back
in 1712 when Du Buisson was acting commandant at Detroit and had to
withstand an attack by hostile tribes in the neighborhood. On this occasion,
Vincennes and some of his faithful Miami from the St. Joseph River had
come to his rescue. Letter of Du Buisson to Vaudreuil, June 15, 1712, quoted
in Roy, *Sieur de Vincennes Identified,* pp. 45-68.

Commandants of French posts were officers detached from regular duty.
For important posts they usually held the rank of captain and received
gratifications up to three thousand livres annually; the amount was usually
taken out of the revenue received from the fur trade. Caldwell, *The French
in the Mississippi Valley,* pp. 14-15.

[25] Vaudreuil to Dumont, August 26, 1720, in Krauskopf (ed.), *Ouiatanon
Documents,* pp. 165-168; Vaudreuil to the Council, October 22, 1720, in *ibid.,*
pp. 168-169, and in *Wisconsin Historical Collections,* XVI, 394-395; Proceedings
of the Council, December 2, 1721, in *Wisconsin Historical Collections,* XVI, 399.

with the establishment of a garrisoned post at the Miami village where he was to live, at the same time exercising control over the Wea fort on the Wabash. By the following May he had completed a palisaded fort which he named Fort Saint Philippe des Miamis, or Fort Miamis, on the site of the present city of Fort Wayne. In reporting its construction to the Council, Vaudreuil described it as one of the finest forts in the upper country, strong enough to withstand an attack by the savages.[26]

For a time Du Buisson's charges gave him much trouble because they could not obtain all the brandy they desired, but his skill and prudence ultimately made them more docile than they had been. Meanwhile, the younger Vincennes had been transferred to Ouiatanon and placed in charge there under Du Buisson. The latter suggested to the Governor that Vincennes be given the rank of second ensign.[27] Bienville, the governor of Louisiana, had already recognized his ability and given him a commission of half-pay ensign under that government on May 20, 1722.[28]

The charter of 1718 under which the Company of the Indies received a monopoly of the trade in the colony of Louisiana also gave that company jurisdiction over the forts, depots, and garrisons of the province with the freedom of issuing orders regulating commerce and the relations with the Indians, and even extending to the appointment of all

[26] Letter of Vaudreuil, October 6, 1721, Archives Nationales, Colonies, C11A43:328v-329v; Vaudreuil to the Council, October 24, 1722, in Roy, *Sieur de Vincennes Identified*, pp. 82-83. The longer name was apparently used only briefly to designate the Miami fort. A village of St. Philippe was established north of Fort de Chartres in the Illinois country about 1725. Alvord, *The Illinois Country*, p. 204.

[27] Vaudreuil to the Council, October 24, 1722, in Roy, *Sieur de Vincennes Identified*, pp. 83-84. In all except one of the years between 1721 and 1726 the mother of Sieur de Vincennes sent canoes loaded with goods from Montreal to her son at Ouiatanon. Canoes were also sent to Du Buisson during these same years. *Rapport de L'Archiviste de la Province de Quebec*, 1921-22, pp. 196-314 *passim*.

[28] Roy, *op. cit.*, p. 82.

officials.[29] It was at this time that the Illinois country was formally incorporated into the Louisiana colony and it marked the beginning of a period of more active colonization and exploitation as well as rivalry between that colony and Canada.

Pierre Dugué, Sieur de Boisbriant, age forty-three, was appointed commandant of the Illinois district in 1718 and arrived at Kaskaskia accompanied by a hundred officers and troops, plus employees of the Company of the Indies, engineers, workmen, and others. The new commandant began the erection of Fort de Chartres about fifteen miles north of Kaskaskia, which became the seat of government for the district, while Kaskaskia remained the center of the religious and social life. Boisbriant and those who came with him introduced a period of gaiety and romance into the social life of the community to which it was but natural that the young Sieur de Vincennes at his lonely outpost on the Wabash would have been drawn.[30] The Illinois commandant soon recognized that Vincennes could be useful to the Louisiana colony and no doubt recommended that he receive a commission.

The need for one or more additional posts on the lower Wabash and Ohio rivers was recognized by both the government of Louisiana and the Company of the Indies; if and when a post was established, they wanted Vincennes to take charge of it and invite some of the Wabash Indians to locate there.[31] As early as 1720 the governor-general of Canada

[29] Alvord, *The Illinois Country*, pp. 150-151.

[30] *Ibid.*, pp. 152-153; Natalie Belting, *Kaskaskia under the French Regime (Illinois Studies in the Social Sciences,* XXIX, No. 3, Urbana, 1948), pp. 10-18; Joseph J. Thompson, "Catholic Statesmen of Illinois," *Illinois Catholic Historical Review,* III (1920-21), 202; Edward G. Mason, "Kaskaskia and Its Parish Records . . . ," *Fergus Historical Series,* No. 12 (Chicago, 1881), p. 15. The parish records show that Vincennes attended a wedding at Kaskaskia in 1727; he himself courted and later married a Kaskaskia girl.

[31] Paul C. Phillips, "Vincennes in its Relation to French Colonial Policy," *Indiana Magazine of History,* XVII (1921), 311-318. Phillips used the correspondence between French officials in Paris and those in Canada and Louisiana in his account of Sieur de Vincennes and the founding of Post Vincennes.

represented to the French Council that Boisbriant was influencing the Piankashaw (located below Ouiatanon) to remain where they were by promising to send an officer and a garrison to their village, while the Canadian government wanted them to move farther north. To the Illinois commandant as well as to the Council, the Canadian governor-general also pointed out how important it was that the Sieur de Vincennes should remain at Ouiatanon "on account of the esteem in which he is held by the savage nations at that post." If it had not been for him, the Ouiatanons would have waged war against the Illinois Indians.[32] On April 23, 1726, Vincennes received his promotion as second ensign in the detachment of marines serving in New France, for which he had been recommended four years earlier.[33] Being in a strategic location to watch the movements of the English, his correspondence shows that he made reports to both the governments of Louisiana and Canada.

The Wea had been promised a missionary as early as 1715, but it was not until ten years later that this promise was fulfilled. In May, 1725, Vaudreuil issued a permit to R. P. Guimoneau, a Jesuit, to leave for the Miami and Ouiatanon posts; he was still there the following year but his labors apparently had no permanent results.[34]

In August, 1726, Charles de la Boische, Marquis de Beauharnois, succeeded Vaudreuil as governor of Canada. He was about fifty-five years of age, had been trained for the French Navy, and heretofore had had only a brief period of service in America in the early 1700s. The instructions of

---

[32] Vaudreuil letters of October 22, 1720, October 11, 1723, and August 17, 1724, in *Wisconsin Historical Collections*, XVI, 392-395, 436, 442-443. The 1720 letter is printed in part in Krauskopf (ed.), *Ouiatanon Documents*, pp. 168-169, and the 1724 letter in Roy, *Sieur de Vincennes Identified*, pp. 84-85.

[33] Roy, *Sieur de Vincennes Identified*, p. 86.

[34] Krauskopf (ed.), *Ouiatanon Documents*, pp. 143, 176-177. Missionaries among the Indians were allowed 600 livres annually by the King. They rendered an important service in keeping tribesmen loyal to the French. Caldwell, *The French in the Mississippi Valley*, pp. 19, 22. Guimoneau had been a missionary priest in the Illinois country prior to 1725.

Louis XV to the new governor included the following ad-
monitions:

The Indian Nations inhabiting . . . [New France] exact continual
foresight and attention to make them live in peace, and to prevent the
Europeans, who occupy the same Continent, penetrating and carrying
on a trade among them. . . . He will require firmness to maintain the
possessions of France against those neighbors who, for a long time, have
been endeavoring to encroach thereon.

It is necessary to blend mildness, justice and disinterestedness with
this firmness, in the government of the French inhabiting the Colony,
who are more inclined to run loose in the woods, and to live like
Indians, than to cultivate and remain on their farms.[35]

That same year, as a countermeasure to British encroach-
ments, the French government re-established the *congé* system of regulating trade in the northern colony.[36]

Louisiana also received a new governor in 1726, Bienville
being succeeded by Louis de la Périer. The Company of the
Indies immediately took up with him the need of establishing
a post on the Wabash or lower Ohio to prevent English
expansion in that area. Correspondence between the company
and the governor of Louisiana, the commandant of the
Illinois country, the governor-general of Canada, and Count
Maurepas, minister for the colonies, reveals a deep concern
and the need for co-operation between the officials of the two
American colonies. Vincennes' influence with the Miami and
the government's need of the help of that tribe was definitely
recognized, also the importance of satisfying the needs of
the Indians so far as trade goods were concerned in order that
they need not go to the English.[37] Although the Company

[35] *Documents Relative to the Colonial History of the State of New York* . . . ,
edited by Edmund B. O'Callahan and B. Fernow (15 volumes, Albany, 1853-
87), IX, 956, cited hereafter as *New York Colonial Documents*.

[36] Phillips and Smurr, *The Fur Trade*, I, 453.

[37] See correspondence in Phillips, "Vincennes in its Relation to French
Colonial Policy," *Indiana Magazine of History*, XVII, 318-322; in Roy, *Sieur
de Vincennes Identified*, pp. 85-91; and in *Mississippi Provincial Archives*,
compiled and edited by Dunbar Rowland and Albert G. Sanders (3 volumes,
Jackson, 1927-32), II, 253-260, 580-581.

of the Indies allocated money in 1727 for Vincennes' salary and for construction of a fort and garrisoning it, nothing was done at that time, perhaps because of reverses suffered by the Company which made it necessary that they cut expenses. For a time it appeared that even the Illinois fort would be abandoned.

The influence of the English was not confined to the northern tribes. South of the Ohio the English had acquired considerable influence among the Chickasaw, Natchez, and Cherokee; sometimes English goods tempted even the Choctaw, who could usually be counted on as an ally of the French. The economizing policies and weaknesses of the Company of the Indies prevented any effective countermeasures; the expenses of a punitive expedition against the English in 1730 helped to persuade the Company to ask the French King to resume once more the responsibility of governing Louisiana.[38] When Canadian officials learned of these plans, they asked that jurisdiction over the southern half of the Illinois and Wabash country be returned to the northern colony,[39] but this appeal was of no avail.

In 1730 Vincennes, who had been confirmed half-pay lieutenant by the Louisiana government, took some Indians from the Ouiatanon area into the jurisdiction of the southern colony. As the result the chagrined Beauharnois considered barring *voyageurs* from going to the new location as a means of forcing the Indians to return to Ouiatanon for supplies. However, he relented and allowed Frenchmen sent to escort missionaries to the Illinois country to take along goods which

38 Fortier, *History of Louisiana,* I, 110-118; Alvord, *The Illinois Country,* pp. 158-160, 166-167.

39 *Wisconsin Historical Collections,* XVII, 145-147n. The boundary between Louisiana and Canada was never definitely defined but lay somewhere between Ouiatanon and Post Vincennes. An undated itinerary made by a British official traveling between Detroit and the Illinois country located it on the Wabash River at "The Highlands," the English name for Terre Haute. Jacob P. Dunn (ed.), *Documents Relating to the French Settlements on the Wabash* (Indiana Historical Society *Publications,* II, No. 11, Indianapolis, 1894).

they sold to the Indians as usual.[40] The Louisiana government was happy with Vincennes' decision to move the Wea down the Wabash, but they insisted it was absolutely necessary to fortify the place where they were to be located.[41]

The Louisiana budget for 1732 included 800 livres salary and "perquisites" for M. de Vincennes, commandant at the Wabash. It was probably that year that he began the erection of a fort on the site of the present city of Vincennes. The following March he described its location as eighty miles above the junction of the Wabash and the Ohio. He stated that the place was suitable for a large establishment and that he would have made one if he had had the necessary force. He complained that he had no goods with which to trade and the English were carrying away all the furs collected in that area. If this trade could be diverted to the French, he estimated that every year thirty thousand skins could be obtained. He suggested that a garrison of thirty men and one officer was needed to man the fort, and that a guard house and barracks should be erected.

Regarding the Indians of the Wabash area, Sieur de Vincennes wrote: they are

composed of five nations who compose four villages of which the least has sixty men carrying arms, and all of them could furnish from six to seven hundred men if it were necessary to assemble them for the welfare of the service and for their own welfare. On account of the nearness of the English, it has been impossible for me to bring together all these nations because there has always been a lack of merchandise in this place. . . . I have never had a greater need of troops . . . than at the present time. The savages, the Illinois, as well as the Miamis and others are more insolent than they have ever been.[42]

The builder of Indiana's newest fort still lacked a few months of being thirty-three years of age. He had indeed done well in the fourteen years since his father's death.

[40] Roy, *Sieur de Vincennes Identified*, pp. 89, 90-91; *Wisconsin Historical Collections*, XVII, 133.

[41] Archives Nationales, Colonies, C13A12:344-347.

[42] Letter of March 7, 1733, to the Department of the Marine in France, in Roy, *Sieur de Vincennes Identified*, pp. 91-93.

About this time Vincennes received word from the governor-general of Canada about plans to unite all the northern tribes for an attack on the Chickasaw in the spring. This tribe, brave, independent, and warlike, were among the most haughty, cruel, and insolent of the southern Indians. They numbered above five hundred warriors and had forty villages in what is now northern Mississippi. The Chickasaw war had its origin in the massacre of the French garrison at Fort Rosalie (Natchez) by the Natchez Indians in 1729. For this deed, the Louisiana governor determined to wipe out that nation and nearly succeeded except for a remnant which took refuge with the Chickasaw. When the latter refused to obey the Governor's order to give up the refugees, the French turned their wrath on that tribe and sought the aid of the Canadian governor and the northern Indians in destroying them.[43]

Concerning the Chickasaw war, Vincennes wrote in 1733 that "all the nations of Canada and the lakes start this spring to go there. Both nations here have gone, even their chiefs. Not a single man remained in all these villages." He went on to say:

In this post we lack everything. I am obliged to borrow from travellers and to give the little that I have myself to take care of all the affairs which come up daily. . . . When these nations return and when all the prisoners, which they have taken are given to us, it will be necessary to pay for this sort of thing as well as to look for the dead if we lose any one.

The governor-general of Canada, he wrote, had given him permission to go to Canada to attend to some family matters, but he promised not to leave "unless I see everything in good shape in this continent." If he should go, he would ask Sieur

---

[43] *Ibid.,* pp. 93-94; Hodge (ed.), *Handbook of American Indians,* I, 260-261; II, 35-36; *Dictionary of American History,* edited by James Truslow Adams (5 volumes and Index, New York, 1940), I, 360; IV, 56-57.

de St. Ange, Senior, commandant at Fort de Chartres, to send his son to Post Vincennes during his absence.[44]

The "family matters" to which the young commandant referred apparently would have included his marriage to Marie, the daughter of Étienne Philippe Dulongpré, a prominent citizen of Kaskaskia, which took place sometime in 1733, and probably at Kaskaskia.[45] It would have been the natural thing for Vincennes to want to take his bride to Montreal to meet the members of his family.

The journey to Canada was not entirely of a personal nature. The Chickasaw had expressed a desire to remain at peace with the northern tribes and sent a calumet as a token of their bid for peace; Sieur de Vincennes carried this token with him to the Canadian governor-general. Regardless of this gesture, Beauharnois wrote that he would continue to make war on the Chickasaw until he received further word from the governor of Louisiana.[46]

Meanwhile, on the upper Wabash, Du Buisson, the builder of Fort Saint Philippe, continued at this Miami post until 1727. The next commandant of whom we have any record was Nicolas-Joseph de Noyelle who was there in 1730. In the expedition against the Foxes that year he appeared with ten Frenchmen and two hundred Indians but only half of these were warriors.[47]

44 Sieur de Vincennes to the Department of the Marine in France, March 21, 1733, in Roy, *Sieur de Vincennes Identified*, pp. 93-94.

45 Roy, *op. cit.*, p. 18. Unfortunately the records of the Catholic Church at Kaskaskia are not available for this period. The dowry which Dulongpré paid to Sieur de Vincennes included land, provisions, cattle, and a Negress, and is believed to have been one of the largest ever paid in the Illinois country. Belting, *Kaskaskia under the French Regime*, p. 77n.

46 Phillips, "Vincennes in its Relation to French Colonial Policy," *Indiana Magazine of History*, XVII, 325-328; letter of Beauharnois, July 31, 1733, in *Michigan Historical Collections*, XXXIV, 109-110.

47 *Michigan Historical Collections*, XXXIV, 307-308, 323; *Wisconsin Historical Collections*, XVII, 112, 114, 116, 130. The last permit issued to Madame Du Buisson to send provisions to her husband, commandant at Fort Miamis and Ouiatanon, was on August 20, 1726. *Rapport de L'Archiviste de la Province*

In 1732 before turning the Miami post over to Nicolas-Marie Renaud (D'Arnaud), Sieur de Desmeloises, Noyelle put in claims for about one thousand livres which he had provided in merchandise at the post, while Simon Reaume asked to be reimbursed for 223 livres which he had expended at Ouiatanon. During 1732-33 Reaume served as commandant at the Wea post, where he furnished supplies to war parties going to and returning from attacks on the Chickasaw. He also gave the Piankashaw chiefs of the Vermilion River powder and bullets to persuade them to move to the Ouiatanon area.[48]

In 1732 Pierre and Charles Papin of Canada formed a trading partnership just before they left for the Wea post, where they planned to spend the next three years. At the end of that period they agreed to bring back all of the furs they had collected so that they could pay the merchants who had supplied the necessary equipment.[49]

At Fort Saint Philippe (or Fort Miamis) during this same period we have an example of the commandant having a monopoly of the trade. Needing help in the enterprise D'Arnaud formed a partnership with Pierre Roy in which they agreed to share all expenses and profits for a three-year period unless D'Arnaud should be relieved of his command. Since Roy could neither read nor write, he pledged himself to show his accounts and ledgers to his partner twice a year or oftener. The sum due the King for the monopoly of the trade was to be paid out of the partnership funds. D'Arnaud was to put into their common magazine the presents he was obliged to give the Indians, and whatever gifts of pelts he might receive from them. Roy was to act as

---

de Quebec, 1921-22, p. 214. Noyelle was born in France in 1694, was an ensign in the colonial troops at the age of sixteen, a lieutenant by 1721, and captain in 1732. He later commanded at Detroit and Michilimackinac. *Wisconsin Historical Collections*, XVII, 112n.

[48] Archives Nationales, Colonies, C11A57:340; C11A62:65v; C11A63:134-136; Krauskopf (ed.), *Ouiatanon Documents*, pp. 145-146.

[49] Krauskopf (ed.), *op. cit.*, pp. 179-181.

interpreter whenever the need should arise, for which he would receive fifty écus annually. D'Arnaud was to receive the income from the forge. At the conclusion of the three-year period, the partners would divide the merchandise and assets at the post while they would share the furs and other funds at Montreal. One stipulation specified that the *engagés* who were to come from Montreal the following autumn would have to agree to work on the construction of a new fort during the winter.[50]

Very early in D'Arnaud's tour of duty an epidemic attacked the Indians of the Miami post, causing the death of at least one hundred and fifty. Although the commandant blamed the casualties on a subtle poison which the English had added to four hundred kegs of brandy the Indians had brought from the English post of Oswego, it is much more probable that they died from smallpox. The Miami were not the only victims of the epidemic. Large numbers of Wea and Piankashaw came to get a share of the brandy and carried the malady back to their villages, thus causing many deaths among their people also. To avoid the plague many of the Miami fled from their village. After the epidemic subsided, Beauharnois dispatched Noyelle to bring all the Miami back again to the village of Kekionga, and to offer inducements to the Shawnee to join them. Noyelle coaxed the scattered Miami back with the assistance of D'Arnaud, the commandant.[51]

After Sieur de Vincennes returned to the Wabash in the early spring of 1734, he again described the state of his post. The garrison consisted of ten men but he expected it to be increased to thirty. The fort was very small, he reported, and needed to have a double wall of stone built around it. Within

[50] The original document, one of the few in which the official name of the post appears, is in the Chicago Historical Society Library. For a biographical note on D'Arnaud, see *Wisconsin Historical Collections*, XVII, 211n.

[51] D'Arnaud to Beauharnois, October 25, 1732, in Krauskopf (ed.), *Ouiatanon Documents*, pp. 146, 181-182n; *Wisconsin Historical Collections*, XVII, 185-186.

the fort he had built a house at his own expense and the soldiers had built their own barracks. The Piankashaw, he wrote, were thinking of moving one of their villages down to Post Vincennes, and the commandant liked the idea because it would help secure his establishment and remove a temptation for the Indians there to trade with the English.[52] Bienville had given orders to the commandant at Fort de Chartres to send thirty additional men and two officers to the post, but there is no record of his compliance.[53]

In 1734 a large number of Miami went south to attack the Chickasaw. The Wea did not go because they were uncertain about what action the French were planning against the Foxes and wanted to be ready to defend their village. That same year, the Wea post, now under the command of François de l'Espervanche, was the scene of tumult and apprehension resulting from a brawl between a Frenchman and an Indian in which the white man gained the advantage. The disgruntled Indian aroused his friends who pillaged the post. At the time the commandant was absent but on his return he appealed to Detroit for help. A force of one hundred twenty Frenchmen and some two hundred Indians were assembled under the leadership of D'Arnaud, commandant at the Miami post, who happened to be at Detroit. When the expedition reached Fort Miamis, word came from Ouiatanon that the difficulty had been settled and all was quiet, whereupon the expedition was dismantled. The prompt action of the French officials impressed the natives and served to instill a greater respect and fear of the French; Beauharnois used the episode to point out to the home government the need for strengthening the garrisons at the posts.[54]

---

[52] Bienville and Salmon (the *ordonnateur*) to the French minister, April 8, 1734, and Bienville to same, July 27, 1734, in Roy, *Sieur de Vincennes Identified*, pp. 95-97.

[53] Bienville to the French minister, July 27, 1734, in *ibid.*, p. 97.

[54] Krauskopf (ed.), *Ouiatanon Documents*, pp. 146-147, 183-184; *Wisconsin Historical Collections*, XVII, 211-212.

Parties of Miami, Wea, and Piankashaw continued to join other northern tribes in raids against the Chickasaw in 1735, but their efforts accomplished little because they were not united.[55] That year there was again a new commandant at the Wea post, Louis Godefroy, Sieur de Normanville. On June 6 he subleased the right to trade at his post to François Augé and René Bissonet La Faverez for 2,500 livres a year, they agreeing to furnish flour, three barrels of brandy, four of wine, one of powder, and fifty pounds of tobacco to the garrison each year.[56]

During the summer of 1735 Sieur de Vincennes again warned of English aggression on the Ohio. According to his information the Miami of Kekionga and the Wea were planning to move closer to the English in the autumn, but the Indians of his post had refused the English belts.[57]

Meanwhile, Bienville, the governor of Louisiana, was planning a new concerted effort against the Chickasaw; he hoped to raise five hundred French and Indians in the southern province and three hundred in the Illinois country. Pierre d'Artaguiette, now commandant in the Illinois country, was to command the northern forces; Sieur de Vincennes was to join him with all the French and Indians he could get together. The rendezvous of all the forces was set for the end of March, 1736, at Prud'homme Bluffs, near the present Memphis. Early in February the Governor realized he was not going to be able to meet the northern forces at the ap-

[55] Beauharnois to the French minister, October 9, 1735, in *Wisconsin Historical Collections,* XVII, 220; Archives Nationales, Colonies, C11A65:49v-51v, 116v-117v, 119v. The number of northern Indians who joined the southern expeditions in 1735 was somewhat lessened by Noyelle's unsuccessful expedition against the Fox Indians in the winter of 1734-35; those who participated in the latter wished to return home and provide for their families at the end of that campaign. *Wisconsin Historical Collections,* XVII, 228.

[56] Krauskopf (ed.), *Ouiatanon Documents,* pp. 184-185.

[57] Bienville to the French minister, August 20, 1735, in *Mississippi Provincial Archives,* I, 264-269; the French minister to Bienville, December 27, 1735, photostat in Indiana Historical Society Library.

pointed time because of failure to receive expected supplies and sent a courier to d'Artaguiette telling him to delay his departure from the Illinois country until the end of April. The latter failed to receive the message and left Kaskaskia on February 20 with the forces he had been able to recruit.[58]

Arriving at the agreed meeting place on March 4, d'Artaguiette dispatched a courier to Bienville, whom he presumed to be approaching from the south, stating that he had in his company thirty soldiers, one hundred *voyageurs* and colonists, and almost all the Indians of the village of Kaskaskia; he was expecting the arrival of others from Cahokia and the Arkansas post and Sieur de Vincennes with the Indians of the Wabash plus forty Iroquois. He had brought food and was prepared to wait for Bienville's forces. After the arrival of Vincennes, their combined forces started advancing slowly toward the Chickasaw villages in order to give time for the others from the north to join them. It was at this time that a courier from Bienville's army met them with the news of the delay in their departure from Mobile and that they would not be able to join the northern forces until the end of April.

Upon calling a council of officers and Indian chiefs to determine what to do, the chiefs pointed out to d'Artaguiette the lack of provisions for such a long sojourn in enemy territory and the necessity they would be under of abandoning the expedition in the event the French decided to wait. Scouts reported there was a Chickasaw village separate from the others that would be easy to take and would supply needed provisions. The decision to attack was made, but the Chickasaw had been alerted to the movements of d'Artaguiette's forces and were ready. Some four or five hundred Indians fell upon the attackers with such force that they were forced

---

[58] Bienville to the French minister, February 10 and June 28, 1736, in *Mississippi Provincial Archives*, I, 293, 297-310. At the time of the writing of the first letter, Bienville was doubtful of the co-operation of the northern Indians.

to retreat, with the Indians in full pursuit. Two days' march from the Chickasaw villages, the remnant of the troops met the reinforcements from Cahokia and with them returned to Illinois with the wounded. Among those taken prisoner were d'Artaguiette, Vincennes, and Father Antoine Senat, Jesuit priest. After suffering the cruelest of Indian torture they were burned at the stake. From letters found on the prisoners the Indians learned of Bienville's plans and were also ready for him when his forces attacked on May 26. They too suffered defeat and began a retreat to Mobile. Not until his arrival there did Bienville receive definite confirmation of the disaster that had overtaken the northern army.[59] Thus the plans to humble the perennial enemy ended in failure and chagrin. It was a defeat that France could ill afford.

As word of the disaster filtered through to the French and Indian villages on the upper Mississippi and Wabash, those who had not joined the expedition were stunned—none more so than those at Post Vincennes which had lost its commandant, most of its garrison, and the adult males of some of the French families that Vincennes had persuaded to settle around the post. As the word reached the officials in Canada, plans were laid for a new expedition against the Chickasaw

[59] The accounts of the expedition and battle do not agree on all points. The one given here is from Bienville's reports to the French minister, June 28, 1736, in *Mississippi Provincial Archives,* I, 297-310, 311-316. Various accounts, including that of Drouet de Richardville, a member of the expedition who was taken prisoner, escaped, and reached Montreal, are in *Indiana's First War,* translated by Caroline and Eleanor Dunn (Indiana Historical Society *Publications,* VIII, No. 2, Indianapolis, 1924). See also Roy, *Sieur de Vincennes Identified,* pp. 98-103; *Historical Collections of Louisiana,* II, 82-83 (refers to an account by Edmund J. Forstall); Richard, "Report on Paris Archives," *Report on Canadian Archives,* 1905, Vol. I, Pt. 6, p. 458. The historical marker erected to commemorate the battle mistakenly gives the date as May 20. See illustration, p. 176. The marker is located southwest of Tupelo, on Mississippi State Road 41, 3.9 miles from its junction with State Road 15.

Bienville reported that d'Artaguiette's forces made their attack on March 25; another account says the prisoners were burned at the stake on that day. Under the Gregorian calendar which was adopted in 1752 the date would be eleven days later or April 5.

to avenge the recent defeat. Vincennes' wife and two little girls were left to mourn his death.[60]

Realizing the seriousness of the situation in the Illinois country, Bienville dispatched a convoy up the Mississippi with forty-three picked soldiers to replace those from the Illinois and Indiana garrisons that had been killed. Two hundred French, Indians, and Negroes accompanied the convoy to ward off any possible attack. Alphonse de La Buissonnière, who had been acting commandant in d'Artaguiette's absence, was appointed to succeed him and continued to serve for four years. Louis Bellerive, Sieur de St. Ange, one of the sons of the elder St. Ange, commandant at Fort de Chartres, was called from a fort on the Missouri to succeed Sieur de Vincennes at the Wabash post. Most of the Piankashaw living around the fort now decided to return to their former village on the Vermilion River. St. Ange reported in 1737 that only about twenty-five men remained and if they should decide to leave it would be necessary to add to the strength of the garrison. In reporting the situation to the French minister, the Louisiana *ordonnateur* expressed the view that the cost of keeping up the fort was more than it was worth; however, he believed it was necessary to maintain it to keep the English from settling there.[61]

Although St. Ange was to remain at Post Vincennes for over a quarter of a century, with the death of its founder a curtain seemed to fall over its activities and only occasionally does one get a glimpse of what was happening. Not until the advent of the English and the Americans does it again come to life and assume the importance that its founder ex-

[60] Charles Dulude, a gunsmith of Kaskaskia who had married the widow of Étienne Philippe Dulongpré, the grandmother of Vincennes' children, was appointed guardian of one of the daughters; Antoine Girard, a militia officer at Kaskaskia, was guardian of daughter Marie in 1744. Belting, *Kaskaskia under the French Regime,* pp. 91-92, 96.

[61] Alvord, *The Illinois Country,* pp. 179-180; Bienville to Maurepas, June 21, 1737, and Salmon to Maurepas, June 22, 1737, in Roy, *Sieur de Vincennes Identified,* pp. 104-105.

pected it to have. Part of this is due to the fact that the scene of rivalry between the English and French now shifted to the upper Ohio.

A census of the Canadian tribes taken in 1736 listed the Miami as divided into two groups with a total of two hundred warriors. The Wea, Piankashaw, and Petikokias (or Pepikokia) were listed as having three hundred and fifty warriors.[62]

The movement of war parties down the Wabash continued in spite of the 1736 defeat. The commandant at Ouiatanon wrote in February, 1738, that the savages of his post were going south "to avenge their father for the insult which had been done him and at the same time to [avenge] the blood of their brothers which had been shed." The commandant of the Miami post reported in June of the same year that the young men of his post were leaving every day to go to war on the Chickasaw. War parties from other tribes also passed down the Wabash; for example, on July 25 the commandant at Ouiatanon wrote that a party of eighteen Ottawa had just passed by as well as twenty-eight Miami. Letters also tell of the return of the war parties with prisoners, some of whom were burned.[63]

Late in 1738 or early the following year Charles François Tarieu de La Pérade *fils* succeeded d'Amours de la Morandière as commandant at the Miami post. Ouiatanon also received a new commandant in the fall of 1739, but he died soon after his arrival. The following summer Henri Albert

---

[62] *New York Colonial Documents*, IX, 1057. The last group mentioned had previously lived in Wisconsin; they disappear from history by 1750 and may have been absorbed by the Piankashaw. Hodge, *Handbook of American Indians*, II, 228-229.

[63] Extracts of letters of René Godefroy, Sieur de Linctot, and Philippe d'Amours, Sieur de la Morandière, to Beauharnois, July 25, 1738, C11A69:107, and Krauskopf (ed.), *Ouiatanon Documents*, pp. 186-187. René Godefroy apparently became commandant at Ouiatanon in 1736 or 1737. He may have been a brother of Louis Godefroy, who was appointed in 1735. Bienville, writing on June 21, 1737, refers to René as commandant at Miamis and Ouiatanon. *Ibid.*, pp. 185-186. D'Amours may have gone to Miamis the latter part of 1737 or early in 1738.

de St. Vincent *fils* became the commandant at that post. Soon after his arrival he and La Pérade had to settle the affair of La Peau Blanche, a Wea who had killed a Miami when the latter was returning from visiting the English. The Miami wanted to fall upon the Wea tribe to avenge the insult but the commandant at Miamis succeeded in stopping them on the promise that the murderer would be turned over to them for any punishment they wished to inflict. La Pérade set out for the Wea post with five Frenchmen to bring back La Peau Blanche. His expense account for the journey has been preserved and shows that in addition to paying each of the men fifty livres, they received brandy, corn, tobacco, powder, and lead. The Indians furnished them meat along the way, receiving vermilion as their compensation. The punishment meted out to the Wea murderer is not recorded.[64]

Bienville, the governor of Louisiana, sought to wipe out the criticism that fell upon him for the 1736 defeats by the Chickasaw by organizing a new army to march against them in 1739-40; he was aided by an expedition recruited in Canada but there was no organized participation by the Indians of Indiana.[65] This time the Chickasaw sued for peace and Bienville entered into a treaty with them. Following this the Louisiana governor returned to France but remained under a cloud of censure the rest of his life. He had served for more than forty years, most of the time in Louisiana. His successor was Pierre Rigaud de Vaudreuil, son of the former governor-general of Canada. The treaty brought only a brief interlude of peace and within a few months the Chickasaw were again fighting with their neighbors and with tribes north of the Ohio.[66]

[64] *Ibid.,* pp. 149, 189-190.

[65] *Historical Collections of Louisiana,* III, 20n-22n. For an account left by a participant in the expedition from Canada, see *Expedition of Baron de Longueuil (Historic Pennsylvania Leaflet No. 16,* Pennsylvania Historical Commission, 1953).

[66] In the fall of 1740 members of this tribe killed nineteen men, a woman and her daughter, and a small boy, all of Post Vincennes, as they were returning home from the Illinois country. *Wisconsin Historical Collections,* XVII, 336.

In 1741 wars among the northern tribes caused a decrease
in the attacks upon the Chickasaw. That fall Jacques Le
Gardeur, Sieur de St. Pierre succeeded La Pérade at the
Miami post. As usual, the commandants of all three Indiana
posts were kept busy with tribal movements and war parties,
but when accounts of high expenses and meager results
reached the French court, the official reaction was that these
excursions had not been as successful as might have been expected.[67] In April, 1741, eight "cabins" of Mascoutens from
Wisconsin came to join a chief already at Ouiatanon, giving
as their reason their fear of the Fox tribe.[68]

In the summer of 1742 an unusually large number of
Indians went to Montreal to pay their respects to the Governor-General, but the Miami did not go. In response to the
Governor's request that the tribesmen make known their
grievances, the Wea, Kickapoo, Petikokia, and Mascoutens
addressed him on July 8. The Wea said they had not ceased
to weep for Sieur de Vincennes and were continually on the
warpath against the Chickasaw to avenge his death. They
asked that Noyelle be sent to command at their post and that
it be put under the license system so that everyone who wished
could trade there. The Petikokia speech was much the same
as that of the Wea. The Kickapoo asked for permission to
leave Post Ouiatanon and settle on the prairie of the Mascoutens; they also asked for a "chief" (probably meaning
a commandant), a blacksmith, and Frenchmen to bring what
they needed. The two bands of Mascoutens wanted only to
go home before the inclement season began.

In his reply to the Wea, the Governor said, "You do
rightly in weeping for the death of Monsieur de Vincennes.
I had given him to you because I knew he loved you and you
loved him greatly. . . . I ask you to continue to avenge his

[67] St. Ange recorded that between March and August of 1741, some
six hundred warriors brought back only nineteen prisoners and sixteen
scalps. *Wisconsin Historical Collections,* XVII, 419.

[68] *Ibid.,* XVII, 336.

death." He promised to take their other requests under consideration. "There will be several traders, and you will be Masters to seek a cheap market," he told them. He granted the request of the Kickapoo to move and promised to send them a "chief" and blacksmith after "your fire is well lighted."[69]

Before the year was over the King ordered that the trade with the Indians at the posts of the River St. Joseph, Miamis, and Ouiatanon should be auctioned to the merchants of the colony the following year, and that the pay of the commandants should be prorated according to the amount of trade at each post. The governor protested. The Indians, he said, were already complaining of the high prices and they would be still higher if the posts were auctioned. "It is to be feared ... they will all go over to the English."[70]

When the posts were auctioned the following year, Ouiatanon brought 3,000 livres and Miamis, 6,850. The governor ordered the lessees of the posts to set up several places where merchandise could be sold, in the hope that the Indians could find in one of the stores the bargains they could not find in a single store.[71]

---

[69] *Wisconsin Historical Collections,* XVII, 377-409, especially pp. 380-386.

[70] *Ibid.,* XVII, 409-412; Innis, *The Fur Trade in Canada,* pp. 107-108.

[71] *Wisconsin Historical Collections,* XVII, 444; Krauskopf (ed.), *Ouiatanon Documents,* pp. 151, 193-194.

CHAPTER IV

FRENCH AND BRITISH RIVALRY

The year 1744 marked the end of a thirty-year truce between France and Great Britain and the beginning of a new series of wars that would affect their colonies in America. By this time English penetration into the Ohio Valley was such that unless there was some drastic change in the tide of events the English were well on the way to colonial supremacy in North America. The fight for the fur trade of the Ohio and Wabash valleys was to be especially bitter.[1]

By this time the trade at Vincennes was decreasing and some of the *habitans* were taking up farming, but at the Wea and Miami posts the trade continued to be of some consequence.[2] And the Wabash Valley was still vitally important to the French as offering the best line of communication between Canada and Louisiana.

As France fought to maintain her colonial empire in America, she was to be greatly hampered by the lack of trade goods and presents available for the western tribes. This shortage had become apparent during the wars with the Chickasaw and was to become greater as English warships interfered with French shipping and the demand for goods for war purposes increased. The effect this would have on the Indians was a matter of concern to Beauharnois, the governor-general, who wrote to the French minister on October 28, 1745, "whatever attachment they [the Indians]

[1] Phillips and Smurr, *The Fur Trade,* I, 377-378, 500-501. One clause in the Treaty of Utrecht (1713) which closed the War of the Spanish Succession (known as Queen Anne's War in America) had granted both Great Britain and France unrestricted trade with their respective Indian allies, while another clause gave the Indians liberty to trade with either the English or French.

[2] *Ibid.,* I, 502-503.

may entertain towards the French . . . 'tis impossible for me to flatter myself with continuing them in it when the posts will be stript of every necessary, as I expect they will be entirely next year."[3]

A new enclosure had been built around Fort Miamis during the winter of 1743-44, requiring 900 oak stakes 14 feet long. A sentry box was also constructed.[4] Despite the scarcity of goods, the French were able to send a large quantity to Ouiatanon for distribution by the commandant to the Wabash Indians in 1746-47, in order to maintain the friendship and loyalty of those tribes.

Also, the incumbent lessees at Ouiatanon and the River St. Joseph were allowed to retain their trading privileges free of charge "in order to maintain the savages . . . until times change."[5]

Though the English trader was often able to undersell his French counterpart, prices alone were not always sufficient to hold the affections of the Indians. The French understood the Indian way of life; through their many years of association with them they had come to know them intimately. The English had no officer to compare with the French commandant, a gentleman and soldier who commanded the respect of the tribesmen. The loyalty of the Miami to the person of the Sieur de Vincennes and later to his memory is an example of the hold the French had on the affections of the Indians.

In 1746 the Louisiana colonial government took a census of the adult males at its various posts. At the Petit Ouyas (Vincennes) were forty *habitans* and five Negroes engaged principally in hunting and the raising of wheat and tobacco. The warrior strength of the Piankashaw was estimated at

---

3 *New York Colonial Documents,* X, 21; Caldwell, *The French in the Mississippi Valley,* p. 86; Innis, *The Fur Trade in Canada,* pp. 114-118.

4 C11A84:275.

5 C11A85:19; C11A118:9-14v, printed in Krauskopf (ed.), *Ouiatanon Documents,* pp. 195-205.

one hundred fifty, of the Shawnee two hundred, and the Illinois four hundred. At the Grand Ouyas (Ouiatanon) only twenty *habitans* were listed and the warrior strength was six hundred. At Fort Miamis there were about three hundred warriors.[6]

Canada received a new governor-general in the summer of 1747 in the person of Roland-Michel Barrin, Comte de la Galissonière. He had no more than arrived at Quebec when he was faced with a revolt among the Miami. Some disaffected Hurons of Nicolas' band at Sandusky had won over a party of Miami and as a result the latter seized eight whites in the fort at the Miami post, looted the property, and burned part of the buildings. Rumors spread among the Indians of the Indiana area warning them to abandon the French or they would be killed. French officials tried to counteract these reports and show that they were prompted by misinformation. The Governor placed the blame for the unrest on "the presents of the English, and the rumors which they have spread abroad" and "above all the lack of goods in the posts."[7]

Following the burning of the fort one band of the Miami under the leadership of La Demoiselle (also known as Old Briton) left the main body of the tribe at Fort Miamis and established a village of their own called Pickawillany, northwest of the present Piqua, Ohio. It soon became a thriving center of English trade.

By this time the supremacy in the English fur trade had passed from the Iroquois and the New York traders to

---

[6] Memoir of the State of the Colony of Louisiana, C13A30:252, 256, 258, 268-269, published in part in Krauskopf (ed.), *Ouiatanon Documents,* p. 194.

[7] Theodore C. Pease and Ernestine Jenison (eds.), *Illinois on the Eve of the Seven Years' War, 1747-1755* (*Illinois Historical Collections,* XXIX, Springfield, 1940), pp. 32-33, 38-39, 42-47, 54; *New York Colonial Documents,* X, 142-143, 220; Goodman (ed.), *Journal of Captain William Trent,* pp. 15-22n; Catherine E. Gregory, The Miami Revolt, 1748-1752 (Unpublished M.A. thesis in history, University of Illinois, 1936). An excellent discussion of events in the Ohio Valley for the next few years can be found in Gipson, *British Empire before the American Revolution,* IV, 186-224.

Pennsylvania and white traders from that state who took their furs to Philadelphia. Friendship with the Miami Indians gave them an opening through which they could extend their trade to the Wabash River and the Illinois country. Before 1748 the Virginia traders ordinarily avoided the region north of the Ohio although her colonial charter gave her a claim to the region. In order to compete with Pennsylvania in the trade of that region, the Ohio Company of Virginia was organized in 1747 for the purpose of land speculation and trade with the Indians; they asked for and received a grant of some two hundred thousand acres under the condition that they would build a fort as well as settle the land. Christopher Gist who was sent to explore and survey for the company traveled as far as Pickawillany in 1750 looking for a likely site and at the same time making friends with the Indians and trying to woo them away from the French.[8]

When early in the winter of 1747-48 the loyal Miami begged the Detroit commandant not to deprive them of French aid the latter sent Ensign Louis-Jacques-Charles Renaud Du Buisson with thirty Frenchmen to spend the winter in a small establishment near the Miami village. Throughout the winter the men suffered many hardships from unfriendly Indians. They had brought few supplies because goods were scarce at Detroit, but managed to exist until spring while Du Buisson kept up negotiations with the chief of the hostile Miami faction. In the spring of 1748 Du Buisson returned to Detroit with that part of the plundered property which had been given up.[9] His negotiations apparently availed nothing for that same year at Logstown, a village on the upper Ohio, the Pennsylvania traders met agents of the rebel Miami who asked for an alliance with the English.

[8] Surrey, *The Commerce of Louisiana during the French Régime,* pp. 326-332; Phillips and Smurr, *The Fur Trade,* I, 507-510.

[9] La Galissonière to the French minister, October 27, 1748, in *New York Colonial Documents,* X, 181; Krauskopf (ed.), *Ouiatanon Documents,* p. 207.

The deputies were taken to Lancaster, Pennsylvania, where a treaty was signed which admitted the Miami to English friendship; the famous Indian traders Croghan and Conrad Weiser witnessed this event which opened the Miami hunting grounds to the English.[10]

The French sent Du Buisson back to the Miami in the fall of 1748 together with a large detachment under La Pérade, who had orders to re-establish the Miami post and maintain the loyalty of the Indians in that area. Disaffection among the Wabash tribes was also reported to be growing because of the English influence. The Wea had remained calm during this period of unrest but the French naturally were on the alert for signs of trouble. Apparently both the Wea and Miami posts still had their own commandants, but the military force under La Pérade operated on both the lower and upper Wabash. Du Buisson signed as commandant at the Miami post in 1747 and 1748, his last voucher being dated July 24. After that date La Pérade was apparently the commandant. Claude Drouet de Richardville, Sieur de Carqueville, became commandant at Ouiatanon in May, 1748.[11]

That same year the manner of paying Canadian commandants was changed. Up to that time each had received three thousand livres without distinction as to military rank or expenses involved in the various posts. Now La Galissonière promised Carqueville only two thousand livres when he went to Ouiatanon because his rank was inferior and because one could live more cheaply at this post than at several others. The Miami commandant continued to receive three thousand livres.[12]

---

[10] *Minutes of the Provincial Council of Pennsylvania* (10 volumes, Harrisburg, 1851-1853), V, 299-300, 307-319; Nicholas B. Wainwright, *George Croghan. Wilderness Diplomat* (Chapel Hill, N.C., 1959), pp. 18-20.

[11] La Galissonière to the French minister, October 23, 1748, in *New York Colonial Documents*, X, 181-182; sketch of Carqueville in Pease and Jenison (eds.), *Illinois on the Eve of the Seven Years' War*, p. 123n.

[12] Archives Nationales, Colonies, C11A116:156, 158v, 159; C11A117:32; C11A118:97-102v, 149v-150, 205-211v, 217, 227, 283, 410, 411, 418, 419, 424,

The Treaty of Aix-la-Chapelle in 1748 brought a nominal peace between England and France which was to last for eight years. Everywhere except in North America the war had been a triumph for France; only there had she met reverses. The English advance into the area south of the Great Lakes had now reached the point where the French fur trade was jeopardized and communications between Canada and Louisiana were threatened. The French ministry decided it was time to take stock and find out what was wrong in the administration of the two North American colonies, and especially why they were a drain on the finances of the mother country instead of bringing in an income. There was some feeling that unless costs could be reduced, it would be better to abandon them.

Inasmuch as the costs of the Louisiana government were especially high, the French minister, Count Maurepas, suggested detaching the Illinois country from the jurisdiction of that colony and placing it under the supervision of the governor-general of Canada, and requested the opinion of the respective governors. Louisiana had failed to attract resourceful and enterprising immigrants who would have utilized and developed its soil and mineral resources; also, corruption was widespread among its officials.

La Galissonière, the recently appointed governor-general of Canada, was the first to reply. The value of the Illinois country had been overestimated in the beginning, he felt, but now opinion was swinging too much in the opposite direction because of the lack of profit realized from the mining and the fur trade. Its real wealth, he pointed out, lay in the extreme productiveness of its soil and its capability of supporting an extensive population. Canada was in a

431, 434; C11A119:64, 67, 76, 77, 87, 95, 98, 101, 118, 127, 130, 134-136. La Pérade repaired the Miami fort and built a powder magazine. Four oxen were taken from the Wea post to Miamis to haul wood for the barracks as well as firewood for the garrison of thirty. Krauskopf (ed.), *Ouiatanon Documents*, pp. 207-208, 213.

better position to colonize the country than Louisiana and in so doing an effective barrier would be built up against English aggression. He warned that it would be a long time before the King would realize any revenue from that source but in the end he believed it would be worth the sacrifice. Vaudreuil, the Louisiana governor, was not willing to see the Illinois province detached from his administration, and pointed out its great value to that colony. Which letter would have had the greatest influence on Maurepas is not known, for at this juncture he was replaced by a new minister, Antoine-Louis Rouillé, Comte de Jouy, who apparently favored leaving the Illinois country under the jurisdiction of Louisiana.[13]

Both the French and English determined to use the interim of peace following the treaty of 1748 to strengthen their position in North America. La Galissonière believed that France should adopt a firm policy of aggression in asserting her rights to the region south of the Great Lakes and proceeded to act along this line by establishing a new trading post at Toronto to divert trade from the English post of Oswego; by strengthening the post at Detroit and giving the commandant there supervision over the posts at Miamis, Ouiatanon, and Sandusky; and most important of all by sending a large detachment of French and Indians into the Ohio

[13] Maurepas to Vaudreuil and La Galissonière, April 25, 1748, in Pease and Jenison (eds.), *Illinois on the Eve of the Seven Years' War*, pp. 61-67; La Galissonière's reply, dated September 1, 1748, is in *New York Colonial Documents*, X, 134-136. See also Gipson, *British Empire before the American Revolution*, IV, 116-122, 128-135.

At the time Canada was surrendered to the English in 1760, Vaudreuil (who was then governor-general of Canada) is supposed to have said that the Wabash River was the eastern boundary of the Illinois district; this would have placed Post Vincennes under the jurisdiction of Canada, yet the British made no move to occupy it until after the Treaty of Paris in 1763. See the discussion in Theodore C. Pease (ed.), *Anglo-French Boundary Disputes in the West, 1749-1763* (*Illinois Historical Collections*, XXVII, Springfield, 1936), pp. 398-408, and map following p. 568.

country to take possession of it in the name of the King of France. He determined to secure the Allegheny and upper Ohio rivers as the eastern boundary of French possessions; this must be her first line of defense.

In pursuance of this last objective, Pierre-Joseph Céloron de Blainville was selected by the Governor-General in 1749 to lead an expedition of some two hundred Frenchmen and thirty Indians into the area to win back the recreant Indians and remove the English traders who proposed to build a post on the Ohio River. Céloron had been appointed commandant at Detroit; in his absence Sabrevois, a former commandant, was in charge there.

In May of 1749 Charles de Raymond succeeded La Pérade at Fort Miamis. The new commandant kept a journal of happenings at the post, thus we have more information than usual during his period of service. Raymond reported that the English were still courting the savages, who were more inclined toward evil than ever. In the seventy or eighty Indian villages of the Ohio country, the English had distributed forty pack loads of powder, swords, and bullets. Three hundred British subjects were supposed to be scattered through the villages. They had built three forts equipped with swivel guns and grenade mortars.

Le Pied Froid, chief of the loyal Miami, informed Raymond that it would be impossible to detach the rebel Miami from the English who gave them cheap goods. Later this chief revealed the existence of a general conspiracy to attack the Miami post and destroy all the French stationed there. Although the loyal Indians promised to reject overtures of the enemy, Raymond determined to be on guard and to fortify the fort—which was almost impossible without building a new structure.[14]

---

[14] Raymond to the governor-general, September 4 and 5, 1749, in Pease and Jenison (eds.), *Illinois on the Eve of the Seven Years' War*, pp. xxvn, 105-111.

News of Céloron's expedition filtered through to Fort Miamis.[15] It had followed the usual French route across Lake Ontario to Fort Niagara, down the Allegheny to its confluence with the Monongahela to form the Ohio, and down the latter stream to the mouth of the Miami River. From thence some of the members traveled overland and some by water to Pickawillany. Both Céloron and the Jesuit Father Joseph Pierre de Bonnécamps, who accompanied the expedition, kept a record of what transpired. At the mouth of each important stream, Céloron buried a lead plate with an inscription that asserted possession of the surrounding region in the name of the King of France. On a near-by tree he would nail a tin plate bearing the royal arms and a statement calling attention to the buried plate. These proceedings, repeated over and over, naturally aroused the suspicions of the Indians. Chabert de Joncaire, the half-breed son of a Frenchman, was sent ahead of the main body to assure the Indians of the peaceful intentions of the troops. At every Indian village where they found English traders, or met them along the way, they warned the traders to leave the territory. In some instances protests were sent with the traders back to the governors of the states whence they were operating.

At the Lower Shawnee town, at the mouth of the Scioto, the French were warned of a possible ambush by the Indians, but Céloron put on a bold front and the attack did not occur. Arriving at Pickawillany in September they found that most of the traders had already departed from this important center. The Miami were urged to return to their former home at Kekionga, but gave only vague promises. On September 20 the expedition started overland for Fort Miamis after burning the canoes they could no longer use. They

15 Beverley W. Bond, *The Foundations of Ohio (The History of the State of Ohio,* Vol. I, Columbus, 1941), pp. 115-120, gives a good general account of the expedition. Céloron's Journal, edited by A. A. Lambing, is printed in Ohio Archaeological and Historical Society *Quarterly,* XXIX, 335-396; that of Father Bonnécamps in *ibid.,* pp. 397-423.

found the fort in a miserable condition with most of the stakes enclosing it rotten and dilapidated. Within the enclosure were eight houses or miserable huts; the commandant and the twenty-two Frenchmen were all ill with fever. Since Raymond disliked the location of the fort and wanted to move it to the St. Joseph River, plans for a new fort were drawn.

Céloron left the Miami post on September 27 and arrived at Detroit on October 6. From there he went on to Montreal where he reported to La Galissonière's successor, Pierre-Jacques de Taffanel de La Jonquière, that the Indians were for the most part friendly to the English and ill-disposed toward the French. If violence were to be employed to try to win them back, he feared they would seek refuge with the western tribes. He also observed that it would be impossible for the French traders to compete with the English in prices offered for furs or in prices charged for goods. He made no specific recommendations. The new governor-general seemed pleased with the work accomplished by the expedition and favored taking a strong hand against the English.

Early in October, 1749, Le Gris, the young chief of the Tippecanoe Miami, came fifteen or twenty leagues to the Miami post to deny that he had accepted a belt to strike the French. He said La Demoiselle's belt had been passed from village to village including his own. In order to keep this band faithful, Raymond wanted to move them nearer to Kekionga. Most of Le Pied Froid's band there was ill-disposed, but the Chief himself still favored the French.[16]

16 Raymond to the governor-general, October, 1749, in Pease and Jenison (eds.), *Illinois on the Eve of the Seven Years' War,* pp. 119-123. In the midst of these unsettled times, at least one peaceful event occurred: the establishment of the parish of St. Francis Xavier at Vincennes by the Jesuit priest Father Sebastian Louis Meurin. Its records date from April 21, 1749. Father Meurin began his missionary career in the Illinois country in 1742. He was followed at Vincennes by Fathers Du Jaunay (1752), Louis Vivier (1753-56), and Julian Duvernay (1756-63). Gilbert J. Garraghan, *Vincennes: A Chapter in the Ecclesiastical History of the West,* pp. 9-10 (reprinted from *Mid-America,* II, No. 4 [April, 1931]); Mary Salesia Godecker, *Simon Bruté de*

During 1750 the French heard rumors of La Demoiselle's conspiracies among tribes as far away as the Mississippi. The Miami, Wea, and Piankashaw were invited to send representatives to Rivière à la Roche (the Miami) to plan a general revolt. These uncertainties discouraged traders and residents at the Miami post and many decided to withdraw to Detroit. Rumor had it that the Indians were boasting that within a year the British would be at the forks of the Wabash, along the only route to the Wea, thus cutting communications between them and Raymond's post.

About this time Raymond was recalled from the Miami post, partly because he was considered to be an alarmist. Soon after his departure Le Pied Froid's band joined the rebels, leaving only the Chief and his family loyal to the French.[17] The new commandant was Lieut. Louis Coulon de Villiers, a friend of La Demoiselle who was expected to use his influence to bring him and the rebellious tribe back to the French. If it proved necessary he was to go to La Demoiselle's village and take along the son of Le Gris, who had much influence over the rebel chief. In any meeting he was to promise forgiveness and amnesty.[18]

De Villiers found that construction of the new fort at Post Miamis had not yet been started. Since the old one had served as an asylum for *voyageurs* and *engagés,* colonial officials decreed that they should help with the construction work on the new one. De Villiers was given authority to commandeer some of them to work at the most pressing tasks, such as cutting stakes.[19]

Rémur, First Bishop of Vincennes (St. Meinrad, Ind., 1931), pp. 155-156. Photostats of the original church records are in the Genealogy Division, Indiana State Library. They are printed in *American Catholic Historical Society Records* (Philadelphia, 1884-   ), XII, 41-60, 193-211, 322-336.

[17] Letters of Raymond in 1750 enclosing reports, in Pease and Jenison (eds.), *Illinois on the Eve of the Seven Years' War,* pp. 149-156, 166-178, 188-193, 194-216, 394-397; letter of October 1, 1751, written in his defense, in *ibid.,* pp. 394-397.

[18] Instructions for De Villiers, July 10, 1750, in *ibid.,* pp. 217-223.

[19] *Ibid.,* pp. 221-222. Bert J. Griswold in his *Pictorial History of Fort Wayne* (2 volumes, Chicago, 1917), I, 47, states that Captain Raymond

George Croghan, English trader, visited the Miami at Pickawillany in November, 1750, with a small present to renew their friendship. Several Wea and Piankashaw appeared and asked to be admitted into the chain of friendship between the English and the Iroquois and their allies. Croghan granted their request, had a treaty of friendship drawn up and signed, and gave them presents. After he had returned to his home in Pennsylvania, the legislature of that state rejected the agreement and reprimanded him for exceeding his authority and laying additional expense on the government. Further rejections of Croghan's aggressive policies during the next few years by an economy-minded Pennsylvania Assembly caused that state to forfeit to Virginia the leadership it had heretofore exercised in the struggle for the Indian trade and western lands. As the same time Croghan's financial reverses caused by an over-expansion of trading interests and a decrease in the price of furs brought a temporary eclipse in his influence with the Indians.[20]

erected the fort and that it was finished by the spring of 1750. However, John Pattin, a trader from Pennsylvania who was captured by De Villiers at the fort in November or December, 1750, left this account: ". . . the River at the Fort is about three Rods wide, on the other side of which about a mile & half from the Fort is the French Miamis Town, where there are about 150 Indians the remainder of those who came over [did not go] to the English . . . the Fort is small, stuck round with Pallisadoes and had . . . a Capt. Lieut. & 50 Men, but that most of these men were traders, who were continually passing to & fro, & by what he could hear there were but about 9 or 10 who constantly resided there; that the French talk of destroying this Fort, & building one three Miles below on the other side of the River, in a Fork between the Miamis [Maumee] River & a River which leads to a Portage near the head of Wabach [Wabash]." Howard N. Eavenson, *Map Maker & Indian Traders* . . . (University of Pittsburgh Press, 1949), pp. 118-119. Before he departed, Captain Raymond apparently built a barn to house cattle and hay. Vouchers were issued to cover various phases of its construction. Archives Nationales, Colonies, C11A119:111, 113, 120, 123, 154, 157, 159, 164, 306.

[20] Albert T. Volwiler, *George Croghan and the Western Movement, 1741-1782* (Cleveland, 1926), pp. 72-73; Wainwright, *George Croghan*, pp. 37-40, 43-46.

The relocation of the Mascoutens was a topic of discussion in 1750-51 between the governors of Louisiana and Canada. The former had heard that these Indians were planning to leave the neighborhood of the Wea post and feared they might join their allies, the Foxes; he wanted the assistance of the Canadian governor in persuading the Mascoutens to settle farther down the Wabash near the Piankashaw. The Canadian governor did not think this would be a wise move and explained that it was very important to keep the Kickapoo and Mascoutens near the Wea because of unsettled conditions in the area.[21]

The beginning of 1751 found the French continuing to coax the Miami rebels to return to Kekionga. Four of the headmen promised De Villiers they would settle near his post and deal no more with the English, but this turned out to be a false hope. When they had not returned by the end of March, De Villiers went to their village on the Great Miami, only to be insulted and ordered to leave. When Céloron, who had returned to Detroit as commandant, heard of this he recommended to the Governor-General that an attack be made on the Indian villages on both the Miami and Ohio rivers. While the water was high in the Maumee he could transport provisions to Fort Miamis which could serve as a base of supplies for any expedition that might be undertaken.[22]

La Jonquière agreed that an attack should be made and instructed the Detroit commandant to go ahead. If he could not leave his post he was to turn over the command of the expedition to François-Marie le Marchand de Ligneris who had been assigned to the Wea post in June, 1751. The Governor thought the Indians around Detroit would be

[21] La Jonquière to the French minister, September 27, 1751, in Pease and Jenison (eds.), *Illinois on the Eve of the Seven Years' War,* pp. 376-377.

[22] Céloron to Vaudreuil, April 23 and August 4, 1751; Raymond to the French minister, October 1, 1751; Vaudreuil to the French minister, October 10, 1751, in Pease and Jenison (eds.), *Illinois on the Eve of the Seven Years' War,* pp. 247-250, 283-289, 397, 403-404.

more likely to participate if De Ligneris could persuade the Wea and the tribes of the River St. Joseph to do so. In spite of these instructions, Céloron decided against the undertaking, giving as his reasons that the Governor had failed to send sufficient troops to augment those he could muster at Detroit, and, secondly, some of the western Indians that he had counted on had refused to go against other Indians with whom they had a blood relationship. When the news reached La Jonquière that the expedition had not materialized, he was much perturbed and criticized Céloron for not going ahead with the forces at his command. He still hoped that something could be done that fall, but with the departure of the Indians to their winter hunting grounds, any action had to be postponed until spring.

De Ligneris was disappointed in the postponement and predicted that if the French delayed much longer most of the Wea and Piankashaw would join the English. A small group of Nipissing Indians who had come to Detroit to participate in the expedition were also disappointed and decided to go ahead on their own. Their force was too small to attack La Demoiselle's fort so they contented themselves with capturing a couple of the inhabitants outside the walls and scalping them. This only served to anger the rebel Miami and stir them to revenge.[23]

Meanwhile, during the spring and summer of 1751 some of the Miami took part in the council held at Logstown with Croghan and the Pennsylvania traders. In addition, three canoe loads of Miami appeared at Oswego, where they

---

[23] La Jonquière to Céloron, October 1, 1751, in Pease and Jenison (eds.), *Illinois on the Eve of the Seven Years' War*, pp. 381-392. The correspondence between the two officials during the preceding summer is not available but can be surmised from the content of the above letter as well as those of De Ligneris to Vaudeuil, October 25, 1751 (*ibid.*, pp. 414-417), and Charles le Moyne, second Baron de Longueuil, to the French minister, April 21, 1752, in *Wisconsin Historical Collections*, XVIII, 104-108. Upon the death of La Jonquière on March 17, 1752, Longueuil served as governor until the new appointee could arrive from France.

reported that most of their nation favored the English, and that 125 canoes had gone to trade with the Philadelphians. As a mark of sentiment, the English at Oswego gave them a flag, rum, pipes, and tobacco.[24]

It was at this critical juncture that a new commandant, M. de Macarty Mactigue, took over the administration of the Illinois country. Macarty had been appointed in the summer of 1750 but did not leave New Orleans for his new assignment until a year later. Detailed instructions formulated for his guidance included the stipulation that he was to exercise supervision over St. Ange, commandant at Post Vincennes, and supply that officer with the presents needed to keep the Indians of his post attached to the French, as well as the goods needed to supply war parties on their way south to fight the Chickasaw. Also, Macarty was to keep in close touch with the commandants at Ouiatanon, Fort Miamis, and Detroit, and keep informed of the designs and movements of the Indian tribes and report the same to his superior in New Orleans.[25]

Upon his arrival in the Illinois country in December, 1751, Macarty found the Wabash and Illinois tribes in a state of ferment due to the efforts of the English to extend their

[24] George Croghan's Journals, in Reuben G. Thwaites (ed.), *Early Western Travels, 1748-1846* (32 volumes, Cleveland, 1904-1907), I, 58-69; Report of John Lindesay, June 25, 1751, in *The Papers of Sir William Johnson*, prepared by New York Division of Archives and History (13 volumes, Albany, 1921-62), IX, 82, hereafter cited as *Johnson Papers*.

[25] Order of command for Macarty, August 8, 1751, in Pease and Jenison (eds.), *Illinois on the Eve of the Seven Years' War*, pp. 293-319, especially pp. 309-310, 316. Macarty was born in 1708 in France, the son of Irish refugees, and had served previously under both the Louisiana and Canadian governments. At Fort de Chartres he succeeded M. le Chevalier de Bertet who died on January 7 (or 9), 1749. William P. McCarthy, "The Chevalier Macarty Mactigue," *Journal* of the Illinois State Historical Society, LXI (1968), 41-57; Pease and Jenison (eds.), *op. cit.*, pp. xxxviii, 99. Macarty found plenty to report on the movements of the Indians; his first report, dated six weeks after his arrival, runs to twenty-five printed pages. *Ibid.*, pp. 432-469 (French and English text). In a letter of March 27, 1752, Macarty said he had used more writing paper in three months than he would have used in ten years at any other place. *Ibid.*, p. 557.

influence over them. Instead of a direct approach, the rebel
Miami were being used to stir the Indians to revolt against
the French. The Vermilion Piankashaw were apparently
the first to turn against the French and they in turn persuaded
other members of that tribe as well as the Wea to revolt.

On December 7 a party of twenty-three Piankashaw appeared in the neighborhood of Kaskaskia, supposedly plotting an attack. After scalping a soldier and wounding a
civilian, they were discovered and a retaliatory French scouting party killed five of the Indians and took four prisoner,
including Le Loup, a chief. Later in the month a party of
Piankashaw who came to the house of Toussaint la Framboise
on the lower Wabash to trade warned him that some of their
tribe plus ten Miami planned to attack Post Vincennes. That
same night four young Piankashaw killed two *voyageurs*
below the post after they had eaten with them, and just
before Christmas these Indians also killed two slaves who
were working on the fort. At the end of December the
Vermilion Piankashaw killed five Frenchmen who were bringing them needed goods. The rebels next approached the
Illinois Indians, warning them that the word of the English
chief was to strike the French with the combined forces of
eleven tribes, including some from the South; "we are a
thousand men," they boasted. The faithful Illinois reported
the threat to Macarty who sent warnings to the other
commandants.[26]

The defection of the Piankashaw threatened to leave Post
Vincennes without any Indians and since the fur trade depended upon them, the *habitans* were threatening to leave
also. Macarty urged the latter to turn to agriculture for
their livelihood, even promising to help them erect a mill

[26] Macarty to Vaudreuil, January 20 and March 18, 1752, in Pease and
Jenison (eds.), *Illinois on the Eve of the Seven Years' War*, pp. 432-435, 507-
509; Gipson, *The British Empire before the American Revolution*, IV, 146-
152.

to grind their grain. St. Ange prepared to defend his post
and wrote to De Ligneris to prepare for the worst.[27]

At the same time that Macarty was trying to hold the
Illinois tribes for the French, he was also trying to collect
flour and corn to send to Detroit to feed the troops there;
this was in addition to the flour, pork, lead, and tobacco
he was already sending to Posts Vincennes, Ouiatanon, and
Miamis. Early in 1752 Macarty heard rumors that the
English were at Ouiatanon and that the Miami were trying
to persuade the Kickapoo to help them besiege the French
at that post. He also complained that the failure of crops
in the Illinois country and the lack of men and boats were
intensifying the difficulties of shipping provisions to the other
posts. He asked Canadian officials to send men and boats
to get the provisions that his colony could spare.[28] De
Ligneris asked the Kickapoo to move closer to his fort as a
protection against treachery.[29]

Meanwhile, from Canada came reports that a smallpox
epidemic was taking the lives of some of the principal Miami,
both among the rebels as well as among those friendly to
the French. It soon spread to other tribes and to the French
posts. Famine was also present in Canada because of crop
failures. In spite of these circumstances Longueuil, the acting
governor, expected to send four hundred soldiers to Detroit
during the summer of 1752 whence they would go into the

27 Pease and Jenison (eds.), *Illinois on the Eve of the Seven Years' War,*
pp. xliii-xliv; St. Ange to Vaudreuil, February 28, 1752, and Macarty to
Vaudreuil, March 18, 1752, in *ibid.,* pp. 483-487, 507-509, 533-535; *Wisconsin
Historical Collections,* XVIII, 109-110. St. Ange enlarged the fort to include
the church and shelters for the *habitans,* but only small pickets were used
for the enclosure. The buildings were described as in a state of decay and
needed to be rebuilt.

28 Macarty to Vaudreuil, March 18, 27, 29, 1752, and Vaudreuil to Céloron,
April 25, 1752, in Pease and Jenison (eds.), *Illinois on the Eve of the Seven
Year's War,* pp. 506-507, 509-510, 519-520, 563, 569, 610; Surrey, *The Commerce
of Louisiana during the French Régime,* pp. 297-299.

29 De Ligneris to Vaudreuil, October 3, 1752, in Pease and Jenison (eds.),
op. cit., pp. 731-732.

Indian country and spend the winter at the camps nearest the English; the following spring they would be joined by another contingent of troops. With this show of force, it was hoped the Indians would return to the French and the English would leave the Ohio country.[30]

By this time the new Fort Miamis on the St. Joseph of the Maumee was finished, at no cost to the King because the *voyageurs* and *engagés* had borne the expense of the work. De Villiers was supposed to add a powder magazine. While the old fort was on low ground, the new one occupied a commanding position on the east bank of the St. Joseph River. Among the vouchers for 1752 were requests for payment of the *voyageurs* who had taken Father Du Jaunay, a Jesuit, to Post Vincennes.[31]

Meanwhile, Michel-Ange de Menneville, the Marquis de Duquesne, had been appointed to succeed La Jonquière as governor of Canada. The usual lengthy briefing on conditions plus the instructions drawn up for his guidance reveal the thinking of French officialdom on affairs in North America at this critical time. In their opinion the Ohio and its tributaries belonged indisputably to France because of La Salle's discoveries and subsequent French possession. Although by the Treaty of Utrecht the English were permitted to trade with the Indians west of the mountains, it did not mean that they could trade in French territory. English pretensions were based on Iroquois mastery of the region, but the French denied that this tribe had any valid claim to the land and the pretended sovereignty of the English over the Iroquois was foolish fancy. They apparently ignored

[30] Longueuil to the French minister, April 21, 1752, in *Wisconsin Historical Collections*, XVIII, 108, 115-117.

[31] C11A98:458; C11A119:306v, 307v, 308. The French government said the post had been established for the benefit of the *voyageurs*. Father Du Jaunay performed a baptismal service at Ouiatanon for Charles, son of Charles Boneau and Genevieve Dudevoir, on May 21, 1752. *Combination Atlas Map of Tippecanoe County Indiana* (Kingman Bros., Chicago, 1878), p. 13.

the charters granted some of the colonies which included in their boundaries the lands west of the mountains.

Regardless of the conditions Duquesne might find when he reached Canada, he was instructed to avoid an Indian war if at all possible because such wars were very expensive and did not bring any real returns. Instead, he should try to drive out the English by seizing their goods and destroying their trading posts. At the same time he should convince the Indians that the French had no designs on them; they could go to trade with the English as much as they desired, but they could not receive them on French territory. If Duquesne could accomplish these two objects and keep the French posts well supplied with trade goods, it was believed he could soon regain superiority over the English traders. He was ordered to guard against the French traders imposing on the Indians, an acknowledgment that graft and corruption were present. These instructions were a reversal of the earlier policy to the extent that instead of using Indians to attack other Indians, the Canadians should attack the English; once they were dispersed the Indians were expected to fall into line.[32]

However, before the Governor had an opportunity to put this new policy into effect an event occurred which put new life and new hope in the French and their Indian allies. The hero of this event was young Charles-Michel Mouet, Sieur de Langlade, of Michilimackinac, who though unskilled in military methods was thoroughly familiar with Indian ways having lived with them all his life. Burning with a desire to retrieve French honor and turn the tide of French defeat in the West, he enlisted a force of two hundred and forty Chippewa and Ottawa Indians and offered his services to the Detroit commandant who gave him authority to attack the rebel Miami town of Pickawillany.

The fort which the English had erected there was exceptionally strong, and surrounding the main structure was a

---

[32] The French minister to Duquesne, May 15, 1752, in *Wisconsin Historical Collections*, XVIII, 118-122.

high log stockade with three gateways. The traders' houses were within the stockade. Keeping their movements a complete secret, Langlade and his Indian followers swept down on the fort the morning of June 21, 1752. Many of the warriors were away hunting and a few of the women who were outside the enclosure escaped. Within the fort were twenty men and boys including three of the English traders. After firing on the fort for several hours, the attackers let it be known that they would cease if the white men were delivered to them. Being decidedly outnumbered, the Indians acquiesced. One of the traders who had been wounded in the firing was killed and the other two were taken prisoner along with three who had hidden in one of the houses outside the fort. Of the Indian inhabitants of the town only five were killed but one of these was La Demoiselle, the leader of the rebel Miami, whose body was supposedly boiled and eaten. After burning the cabins of the traders and raising two French flags over the fort, the raiders hurriedly departed with their English prisoners and goods estimated as worth three thousand pounds sterling. According to some of the accounts they were accompanied by a few of the inhabitants who now decided to return to Kekionga.[33]

---

[33] Gipson, *The British Empire before the American Revolution*, IV, 221-224; Kellogg, *The French Régime*, pp. 420-422; Bond, *Foundations of Ohio*, pp. 127-128; Duquesne to the French minister, October 25, 1752, in *Wisconsin Historical Collections*, XVIII, 128-131. Duquesne was pleased with Langlade's feat and asked the French minister to grant him a pension of one hundred fifty livres; when this was not forthcoming, the Governor asked that he be given a commission as ensign *en second,* with half pay. Duquesne to the French minister, October 12, 1754, in Pease and Jenison (eds.), *Illinois on the Eve of the Seven Years' War,* pp. 904-905. Langlade was given a commission as ensign on March 15, 1755. *Wisconsin Historical Collections,* XVIII, 149. William Trent, a Pennsylvania trader, learned of the attack while at a Shawnee town on the Ohio River, and set out with a few companions to visit the scene, arriving on July 20. They found the once thriving town deserted; the French flags were still flying but were quickly taken down and replaced by the English colors. The following day the party gathered up the furs that were still there and returned to the Shawnee town. Goodman (ed.), *Journal of Captain William Trent,* pp. 86-91.

Though the fall of Pickawillany marked a turning point in French colonial affairs, it received scant attention from the commandants of the western posts. De Ligneris wrote that Langlade's feat was "not of great account as they only killed five or six men. But what was better was their killing three English and taking six prisoners." He acknowledged, however, that as soon as the English traders who were with the Piankashaw learned of it, they left because they no longer considered it safe to trade with the Miami.[34] These same officials were, however, much interested in Longueuil's proposal to send a Canadian force against the English and their Indian allies. Macarty thought that the four hundred who were to winter in the area and the six hundred who would descend the Ohio the next spring should be able to take care of both the English and Indians, the fighting strength of the latter being estimated at only two hundred. The Illinois commandant was ready to do his part in furnishing men and supplies. Before the year 1752 came to an end, however, Macarty received word that there would be no movement of troops before spring. "If Longueuil's detachments do not come," he predicted, "everything will begin again worse than ever."[35]

With the arrival of the new Canadian governor the latter part of 1752 with instructions to occupy the line of the Ohio and drive out the English traders but to avoid any conflict with the Indians, Longueuil's plans were tossed aside. The best way to enforce French claims to the Ohio Valley, in Duquesne's estimation, was to build a string of forts beginning on Lake Erie and then on the Allegheny and the Ohio. Pierre Paul Marin was placed in command of an expedition to carry out this plan with Michel Péan second in command. Food was still very scarce because of another crop failure

34 De Ligneris to Vaudreuil, October 3, 1752, in Pease and Jenison (eds.), *Illinois on the Eve of the Seven Years' War*, pp. 733-734.

35 Macarty to Vaudreuil, September 2 and December 7, 1752, in *ibid.*, pp. 688, 748, 751, 761.

but the Governor used extreme measures to obtain a supply from the *habitans* for the troops. The two leaders with approximately a thousand men landed at the site of the present Erie, Pennsylvania, in the summer of 1753 and erected Fort Presque Isle there, then cut a road through to the Rivière aux Boeufs on French Creek where they erected another fortification. The plans called for the erection of a third fort at the outlet of French Creek into the Allegheny River, but low water prevented the carrying out of this plan. Instead, a few men were sent by pack horses and erected a small fortification called Venango at this location. Three hundred men were left to guard the three forts and the remainder of the troops were sent back to Montreal for the winter. In the meantime, Marin had died on October 29, 1753, and Jacques Le Gardeur, Sieur de St. Pierre, was sent to take charge of the new forts, with headquarters at Fort Le Boeuf.[36]

In addition to implementing a new Indian policy, Duquesne adopted a stern policy of discipline among the soldiers as well as among those in command at the various posts. He was horrified by the lack of discipline that had crept in as well as by the methods being used by officials to get rich at the expense of the King. "It is necessary that I have my sword always lifted to maintain subordination and good order," he wrote on October 26.[37]

Duquesne also undertook to change the method of carrying on trade at the western posts. At Post Vincennes (which had never been under the jurisdiction of the Canadian govern-

---

[36] Gipson, *The British Empire before the American Revolution,* IV, 270-275; Bond, *Foundations of Ohio,* pp. 129-130.

[37] Letter to French minister, in Pease and Jenison (eds.), *Illinois on the Eve of the Seven Years' War,* pp. 832-838. He was especially critical of Macarty whom he wrote was following "an infamous line of conduct at Fort de Chartres"; he was accused of limiting his trade to brandy, which he not only drank to excess himself, but dispensed to the Indians and the French. The latter "have become as drunken as the Indians and . . . neglect their farms." *Ibid.,* pp. 845-847.

ment) he granted a monopoly of the trade to a Sieur Monière [probably Alexis Lemoine Monière]. Under an agreement dated May, 1754, Monière's agent was to leave from Montreal with one canoe manned by seven men and carrying provisions for them. At Detroit they apparently expected to get other canoes and trade goods. The *habitans* at Vincennes who were accustomed to engaging in the trade of the post objected strenuously to this new arrangement and threatened to leave. They appealed to the governor of Louisiana, who in turn wrote to the French minister in their behalf. Since Duquesne was replaced on January 1, 1755, by Vaudreuil, the former governor of Louisiana, it may be presumed that the people of Vincennes were able to continue trading as in former years.[38]

The appearance on Lake Erie during the spring of 1753 of the large number of batteaux and canoes filled with troops frightened the Indians of that area. The Iroquois appealed to Virginia for aid and William Trent was sent with some of the supplies requested, but could promise no military help. He wrote on April 10 that he expected many of the Indians would return to the French. Already in December, 1752, De Villiers had sent the Canadian governor two English scalps which the rebel Miami had brought to Fort Miamis in penitence; their sincerity was doubted, however, when they continued to trade during the winter with the English, but in July, 1753, they journeyed to Montreal along with other tribes to ask forgiveness and acceptance once more into the good graces of the French. Duquesne reported that unless one witnessed the penitent attitude of the tribesmen, it would be hard to believe the prodigious effect the troop movement had had on all the Indians in general. The Miami chose as their

[38] The trade agreement is in Pease and Jenison (eds.), *Illinois on the Eve of the Seven Years' War*, pp. 854-857; Kerlérec to the French minister, December 17, 1754, in *ibid.*, pp. 920-924. Louis Billouart, Sieur de Kerlérec, had become governor of Louisiana in 1753 when Vaudreuil departed for France where he remained until his appointment as governor-general of Canada. He had expressed his disapproval of Duquesne's trade arrangements.

spokesman for the occasion one of the most rebellious of their number. Duquesne accepted their submission with tongue in cheek for he realized it had been prompted by fear, but later in the year he was able to report that the revolting Miami had turned over to him the murderers of the French as proof of their good intentions. The Governor informed the Indians that he wished only to procure for them "peace and tranquility" and would exterminate only those bold enough to oppose his will.

At Ouiatanon, the Piankashaw who had defected to the English, also came to ask pardon and to be restored to favor, but De Ligneris informed them that they could be accepted only on orders of the Governor-General. The latter asked that they meet Sieur Péan who was to visit that post on his way to Vincennes, and who had instructions to pardon them if they acknowledged their fault and surrendered those who had committed murders on the French. When Péan's plans were changed and he did not make the trip, Duquesne ordered De Ligneris to pardon the Piankashaw on the condition that they would deliver the murderers to the Governor-General the following year.[39]

The Canadian governor apparently had planned for the expedition of Marin and Péan to be well on its way down the Ohio River by the fall of 1753 for he had asked Macarty to send provisions and a detachment from the Illinois country to meet the expedition there. One hundred men left Fort de Chartres the first of September and traveled up the Ohio River as far as the Falls of the Ohio, whence one of the officers and a few soldiers went on by land to meet the Canadians. After several days they reached a Shawnee village where they learned that the troops they were to meet had

[39] Randolph C. Downes, *Council Fires on the Upper Ohio* . . . (University of Pittsburgh Press, 1940), pp. 62-63; Duquesne to the French minister, October 27 and 31, 1753, in Pease and Jenison (eds.), *Illinois on the Eve of the Seven Years' War*, pp. 838-843, 843-844, 847-849; Duquesne to the French minister, October 13, 1754, in *New York Colonial Documents*, X, 263.

returned to Canada after erecting the three forts mentioned above. Meanwhile, when the scouting party did not return to the Falls at the expected time, the main Illinois detachment made a shelter to store the provisions, and returned home. The scouting party reached Fort de Chartres a few days later. Once again, the difficulty of communications in the wilderness had been demonstrated.[40]

The Marin expedition had met no opposition from English forces as they erected the French posts of Presque Isle, Le Boeuf, and Venango, but when Lieutenant Governor Dinwiddie of Virginia received word of what the French were doing he dispatched a messenger to warn the French commander that he was on British territory and should get out. This first messenger ventured only as far as Logstown. Dinwiddie decided to try again and this time chose as his emissary young George Washington, then only twenty-two but already an adjutant general in the Virginia militia. He was to proceed to the French headquarters, give the commander a letter from the Virginia governor, and await a reply. On the journey to and from his destination he was to gather all possible information on French forts and military forces.

From Logstown Washington was accompanied by Half King, the Seneca chief, and two other Indians. His first contact with the French was at Venango where he observed that the French officers were doing everything possible to influence the Indians in his party against the English. Arriving at Fort Le Boeuf on December 11, 1753, he presented his credentials and the letter in which the Governor courteously asked for an explanation of the presence of French troops in territory that belonged to Great Britain. St. Pierre's official answer was evasive but he promised to send the communication on to the Governor-General. In personal conversation with Washington, the French officer affirmed French ownership of the region and asserted that the English had

---

[40] Kerlérec to the French minister, August 20, 1753 and June 23, 1754, in Pease and Jenison (eds.), *op. cit.*, pp. 824-825, 861-867.

no right to trade there. The French paid little or no heed to Governor Dinwiddie's letter, but the trip did point up the need for co-operation between the colonies if the French were to be driven out. Representatives of most of the colonies met at Albany on June 19, 1754, but this attempt at unity came to naught.

Although desirous of joint action, the Virginia governor continued his efforts to do what he could to thwart the French. Before Washington had returned home, Trent was sent to establish a fort at the forks of the Ohio. Before it was completed, in April, 1754, a French force from Fort Le Boeuf, augmented by fresh recruits from Canada, captured the fort and upon its completion named it Fort Duquesne. Another French contingent from Le Boeuf drove the English traders from Logstown and erected a French fort there. With the forks of the Ohio and Logstown in their control, in addition to Presque Isle, Le Boeuf, and Venango, the French were now seemingly masters of the upper Ohio Valley.[41]

Before the news of the recent French success had reached Williamsburg, the Virginia Assembly had dispatched Washington with a force of one hundred men to aid Trent. En route he heard of the surrender of the fort. While awaiting further orders, he encamped at the Great Meadows, ten miles east of the present Uniontown, and with the aid of some friendly Indians attacked a French party in the neighborhood, killing several including the commander and capturing some. Realizing that the French would be quick to seek revenge for this defeat, he erected Fort Necessity, which constituted

[41] Gipson, *The British Empire before the American Revolution,* VI, Chaps. II-IV, VI-VII; Vol. VII, Chaps. II-IV, VII-IX, XI-XIV; Bond, *Foundations of Ohio,* Chaps. V-VI; and Downes, *Council Fires on the Upper Ohio,* Chaps. III-V, are among the excellent secondary sources for the final events that led up to the French surrender of her North American colonies. Inasmuch as the present volume deals particularly with those events which touched the Indiana area, the final struggle between France and England in North America is presented only in summary form.

the last important stand of the English on the west side of the mountains. The expected attack came early in July of 1754 when in the face of overwhelming odds Washington was forced to surrender. De Villiers, former commandant at Fort Miamis, was at the head of the force of six hundred French and one hundred Indians that defeated Washington.[42] A few Miami had taken part in the French expedition of 1753, and some of the Indians with De Villiers were probably from that tribe. It was not, however, until 1755 that large detachments of Indian auxiliaries were recruited to aid the French troops. De Ligneris, who had been transferred from Ouiatanon to Fort Duquesne in the fall of 1754, had Miami, Mascouten, Kickapoo, and Wea tribesmen among his forces the following year while the northern tribes were under Langlade of Pickawillany fame.[43]

The French success in erecting their forts on Lake Erie and the Allegheny River and in taking over Forts Duquesne and Necessity brought to a standstill British trade with the Indians. After several disastrous occurrences in 1753 the traders did not venture into the Ohio country and the Indians no longer brought any furs and pelts into the trading posts. The tribes of western New York and Pennsylvania were bewildered by the turn of events; they could not understand the failure of the colonists to unite and defend their frontiers against the French advance, nor could they understand why their own needs were being ignored. Though desiring to remain loyal to the English, the defeat of the Virginia troops led some of the eastern tribes also to turn to the French.

Meanwhile, the burden of restoring English power and prestige in the Ohio Valley had shifted to the home government which dispatched Gen. Edward Braddock with instruc-

---

[42] Gipson, *The British Empire before the American Revolution,* VI, 36-43. One account of the battle gives the number of French as nine hundred and two hundred Indians. An extract of De Villiers' journal of the expedition is printed in *New York Colonial Documents,* X, 261-262.

[43] Kellogg, *The French Régime,* pp. 425-426.

tions to drive out the French and to build a fort for the
protection of the Indians. April of 1755 found Braddock with
a force of one thousand continental troops and an equal
number of militia facing in western Pennsylvania a French
force of comparative size. The details of Braddock's defeat
are well known and need not be repeated here. At the same
time that the two governments were attempting to decide the
fate of the western country on the battlefield, French and
English diplomats were arguing the merits of the claims of
their respective countries. They were not able to come to
any agreement, and the difficulties in the Ohio Valley became
merged in other differences which prompted England's declaration of war against France on May 18, 1756.

In addition to traders, English settlers had also crossed
the mountains to found homes in the Ohio Valley. The Indians viewed with alarm this encroachment on their hunting
grounds and it required little urging from the French for
them to begin raiding the settlements on the frontiers of
Pennsylvania and Virginia. This marked the beginning of the
settlers' hatred for the Indians and their spirit of vengeance
toward members of the race.

An insight into French warfare is given in the journal of
Maj. John Smith of the Virginia Rangers who was captured
along with ten of his men in a blockhouse near the head of
the James River in June of 1756. His captor was none other
than Marie-François Picoté, Sieur de Belestre (who had
replaced De Villiers as commandant at Fort Miamis) who
had come all the way from the Wabash Valley at the head
of a party of 25 French Canadians and 205 Miami and Wea
Indians. They killed or captured in all about three hundred
persons. All the cattle were driven together and killed, while
the raiders used 120 horses to carry away the booty. Belestre
was wounded. During the eleven months that Smith was held
prisoner he was taken across the Appalachians to the Ohio
country, then to Fort Miamis and Detroit, and finally through
the Great Lakes to Niagara and Fort Frontenac. On the way

he noted many evidences of French aid to the tribes of the
Miami confederacy and to other western tribes. According
to Smith's account, the Miami post had only 16 regulars and
no guns. He thought the English could win back 1,400 Miami
and 2,000 Potawatomi, and after his return home proposed
that a party be sent into the interior to capture the forts at
Miamis, St. Joseph, and Detroit.[44]

A famous memoir of 1757 alleged that Belestre had the
lease of the trade at Fort Miamis for three years at 1,200
livres a year, with exclusive trading privileges and all expenses, including the wages of the interpreter. He received
no pay, while the garrison was paid in powder and lead.[45]
According to the memoir, the Miami and Tippecanoe branch
of that tribe, who traded at this post, could raise 150 warriors. Its trade averaged 250 to 300 packages of pelts. At
Ouiatanon, Ensign Camet Bayeul had the post on the same
footing. The Wea, Kickapoo, Mascoutens, and Piankashaw
who traded there could supply 300 warriors, and the post
produced 300 to 400 packages of pelts a year. Vincennes
was reported to be a pretty little village with three horse
mills and about 75 inhabitants who worked the land and
gathered wheat. The Piankashaw traded there and the post
produced about 80 packages of pelts.[46]

[44] Charles F. Mullett, "Military Intelligence on Forts and Indians in the
Ohio Valley, 1756-1757," *William and Mary Quarterly* (3d series, Williamsburg, Va., 1944-   ), III, 407-410; Bond, *Foundations of Ohio,* pp. 153-154.

[45] Belestre acquired considerable property at Fort Miamis in connection
with his trading activities. An inventory of the same made in 1761 listed two
houses valued at a thousand crowns (probably around $1,250), three houses
valued at £1,200, and two sheds worth £800. *The Papers of Col. Henry
Bouquet,* edited by Sylvester K. Stevens and Donald H. Kent (17 volumes,
Pennsylvania Historical Commission, 1940-1943), Series 21645, p. 267. Belestre
became commandant at Detroit in 1758. *Wisconsin Historical Collections,* XVII,
459n.

[46] "Last Official French Report on the Western Posts," *Journal* of the Illinois State Historical Society, XXIV (1931-32), 578-584. The author of the
memoir is not known. It had previously been published in French in *Rapport
de l'Archiviste de la Province de Québec,* 1923-24, pp. 42-70, and was translated for the *Journal* by William R. Riddell. It is printed in *Wisconsin His-*

In addition to taking over the military defense of their North American domain, the British government also took over the management of Indian affairs. Two separate departments were created with a superintendent for each. In April, 1755, Sir William Johnson of New York received a royal commission as superintendent for the northern department. He had been active in handling Indian affairs in his home colony and now proposed to use his friendship with the Iroquois to counteract French intrigues among the Pennsylvania and Ohio Indians and win back their friendship. Profiting by their earlier experience of neglecting the tribesmen, they now promised them an abundant supply of goods at cheap prices. George Croghan, the Pennsylvania trader, now restored to favor, was chosen as Johnson's deputy. Their efforts brought a lessening if not a discontinuance of the raids on settlements.

The French were having difficulty supplying their new posts in the Ohio country because of their distance from the home base and their lack of man power. The settlements in the Illinois country were able to give valuable assistance, sending supplies both by way of the Ohio River and by way of the Wabash. The need for a French fort at the Falls of the Ohio was urged upon French officials but none was ever built. Fort Massac was constructed on the lower Ohio in 1757, and Fort Duquesne was strengthened in anticipation of a new English offensive.

Indians sent to reinforce Gen. Louis Montcalm, who was preparing to attack the English stronghold of Oswego on

torical Collections, XVIII, 167-195, as the memoir of Louis Antoine Bougainville.

When Kerlérec, governor of Louisiana, reported on conditions in that colony in 1758, he listed a garrison of fifty at hastily built Fort Massac on the lower Ohio. At Vincennes, he said the fort was protected by only a simple fencing of very old stakes. St. Ange had forty in the garrison with about eighteen or twenty inhabitants who raised wheat, tobacco, and corn. In the vicinity were eighty Piankashaw warriors. Archives Nationales, Colonies, C13A40:136-156.

Lake Erie, were able to intercept English reinforcements and pave the way for Montcalm's victory on August 14, 1756. The capture of this English fort made a deep impression on the western Indians for this was the place to which they had carried their furs when seeking the advantages of English prices and an English alliance. It had been under the protection of the Iroquois and its fall seemed to foreshadow complete victory for New France. The following year Montcalm moved to the Lake Champlain frontier which the English had strongly fortified and captured Fort William Henry. Here the Indians were responsible for the massacre of unarmed English soldiers and their families after the surrender. The smallpox had been prevalent among the English troops and was transmitted to the Indians as if in revenge for their cruelty. From this time on French fortunes began to wane.

With the coming to power of William Pitt in England in 1757, there was a stepping-up of preparations for driving the French out of the Ohio Valley. Gen. John Forbes was chosen to head a new expedition aimed at the capture of Fort Duquesne. His force of over seven thousand included about fifteen hundred continental troops and the remainder from the colonies. Simultaneous with the military preparations there was a concentrated effort to conciliate the Indians and win them over to the English side. In addition to Johnson and Croghan, Christian Frederick Post, a Moravian missionary, performed a valuable service in this connection at the risk of his own life. To overcome their suspicion that English success over the French would lead to the former then taking over the Indian lands, the Pennsylvania governor and council in the Treaty of Easton (1758) relinquished all claim to land west of the mountains.

When news of the Forbes expedition reached Detroit in May, 1758, the commandant immediately set out to rally the tribes in that area for the defense of Fort Duquesne. Forbes was in no hurry, figuring that the longer he delayed the attack the more impatient the Indians would become and the more pressing the need for them to return home to hunt. This proved to be the case, for after defeating a detachment from the main body of Forbes's troops, the Indians were content to withdraw, leaving it up to the French to hold the fort. Deprived of Indian support, Captain De Ligneris decided to withdraw up the Allegheny to Venango, after first setting fire to the buildings. The English took possession that same evening, November 24, 1758, and renamed the fort for William Pitt. A convoy from the Illinois country had reached the fort before it was abandoned by the French, although it had taken twenty days to pass the Falls of the Ohio.

The Indians were told that the French retreat was only temporary and that plans were being made to take the offensive in the summer of 1759 and retake the fort. However, on July 12 De Ligneris was called on to rush reinforcements to Fort Niagara to which the English had laid siege. Before these troops and other reinforcements were able to join the main body of the French, they were surprised by the English and many lost their lives. The fort was surrendered. These reverses created grave doubts in the minds of the Indians about the ability of the French to withstand the English. Not wanting to be on the losing side, more and more of them began to look toward the English. George Croghan was ever ready to encourage their defection.

Expecting Detroit to be the next objective of the English, the fort there was enlarged and strengthened but the expected attack never materialized. Instead the war centered in the East with the result that Frontenac, Louisburg, Ticonderoga, and Quebec were in English hands by the end of 1759. In a final effort to hold the colony, the Governor-General called for the use of all available Indians from the West. About 1,500 went to Montreal during the summer, including one hundred under the Wea commandant and perhaps six or seven hundred under the Miami commandant.

Meanwhile, Croghan was busy preparing the Indians for the British victory he was certain would come. He gave

presents to those who visited Fort Pitt and assured them of
an abundance of trade goods and rum. In July he accompanied Col. Henry Bouquet and a detachment of soldiers
to Venango and Presque Isle where British garrisons replaced
the French. All of the Indians as far west as the Wabash
were invited to a conference at Fort Pitt the following month.
From August 12 to 20, 1760, a goodwill assembly was held
at the fort which was attended by one thousand Indians from
the West representing many different tribes, including the
Miami, Potawatomi, and Kickapoo. The English promised
a restoration of the disrupted trade and said they had no
designs on the land. Representatives of various tribes pointed
out the need of having their guns repaired and of having a
sufficiency of powder and lead; without these necessities they
were scarcely able to sustain their families. The English em-
phasized that the Indians must return the English captives
they were holding, a requirement with which they were slow
to comply.

The capitulation of Canada came at Montreal on September 8, 1760, with all of the province included in the surrender. The inhabitants of the western posts were to be left
in possession of their property and were free to exercise their
own religion; they were free to migrate to French territory
if they wished or they might remain as subjects of the English King. At Detroit, Belestre made ready to receive the
English. A detachment of the famous Rogers Rangers received its capitulation on November 29, 1760. From there
a party of Rangers was sent to Miamis and Ouiatanon.[47]

Vincennes, being still under the jurisdiction of Louisiana,
was not affected as yet, but by the terms of the Treaty of

[47] *Journal of Major Robert Rogers* . . . (London, 1765), pp. 197-230;
Griswold, *Pictorial History of Fort Wayne,* I, 55-56; Capt. Donald Campbell to
Col. Henry Bouquet, December 11, 1760, in *Michigan Historical Collections,*
XIX, 47. The Rangers apparently did not go beyond Fort Miamis and it was
not until a year later that the British took over Ouiatanon. Lieut. Edward
Jenkins to Bouquet, November 4, 1761, and Campbell to Bouquet, November
8, 1761, in *Michigan Historical Collections,* XIX, 118, 120.

Paris, signed in 1763, France ceded to England not only all of Canada but all of Louisiana east of the Mississippi River except for New Orleans. The remainder of Louisiana was given to Spain in return for Florida. St. Ange, who was still at Vincennes, was ordered to proceed to Fort de Chartres where he formally surrendered that post to the English on October 10, 1765. Before taking leave of the people of Vincennes with whom he had lived for almost a quarter of a century, St. Ange issued his final instructions:

By virtue of the order of M. de Neyon, Major Commandant of the Illinois country, to name a person to attend to the police, and to maintain good order among the citizens of this post, as also of the voyageurs and the Indians—I . . . have named M. Deroite de Richardville, performing the functions of captain of militia, jointly with Sr. le Caindre, soldier of the troops. Their first care should be to maintain good feeling among the Indians to prevent disorder so long as they are in charge. Whenever complaint shall be made to them against any one they will proceed to call an assembly of the more notable of the citizens of the place, where the matter shall be decided by a plurality of votes.

Messieurs Deroite de Richardville and de Caindre can not watch too carefully that the citizens keep up their fences, it being to the public interest that the cattle should not pass from the commons to the grain fields. They will check as far as they are able the disorders which occur too frequently, occasioned by drinking. Whenever any news shall come to them . . . of importance to the good of the service they will take care to apprise me of it. . . . in all cases which I have not been able to foresee, I depend on their good management and their devotion to the public welfare.

Given at Post Vincennes the 18th of May, 1764.[48]

And so ended French control of the great interior valley systems. In the Indiana region, the three tiny posts never reached first-rank importance even though many French officials thought control of the Wabash-Ohio valleys was the key to French security. While the immediate cause for the estab-

---

[48]Dunn (ed.), *Documents Relating to the French Settlements on the Wabash*, p. 408.

lishment of the posts was a mixture of political and imperial motives, these factors were based on the need to protect the entire colony from Indian warfare and from English encroachment in the valley. The chief factor in keeping the savages peaceful and contented was a continuous and liberal supply of the necessities, trinkets, and liquor which they needed or desired.

Although the immediate cause of the capitulation of Canada was the superiority of the English forces, there were deeper causes underlying French defeat in North America, namely, the type of government, the monopoly of the trade which stifled free enterprise, the political and religious orthodoxy of the colony, the over expansion of settlements, and the corruption of its officials. New France was a world of officials (some of whom had little knowledge of local conditions), of decrees and ordinances issued by a government far removed from the colony, and of the King's soldiers, from all of which the inhabitants sometimes sought to escape by living in the wilderness. Placing the governor-general and intendant on an equal basis made for rivalry between the two officials as well as a divided responsibility.

With the government having a monopoly of the trade, free enterprise was discouraged. The French fur trader received a low price for his furs and pelts but paid a high price for the goods received in return and thus was unable to compete with his English counterpart who had an unlimited supply of goods of a superior quality which he could trade with the Indians for a lower price. As a result the greatest single source of the country's wealth was diverted to their rival to such an extent that New France became a liability rather than an asset to the home government.

Expansion was overdone. A population equal to only one twentieth of that of the English colonies was scattered from the islands off the coast of Canada to the mouth of the Mississippi; only on the lower St. Lawrence and the lower Mississippi was there any concentration of settlement. The failure of communications over this vast area was demonstrated over and over. In contrast with the English colonies, there was no emigration of political or religious refugees from Europe to Canada. Apparently no effort was made to attract such settlers, and all but Catholics were excluded. Not the least of the causes for defeat was the corruption which permeated officialdom from those of high position to the lowest, each seeking his own private gain at the expense of the King.

Yet in reading the history of New France one cannot forget the zeal, the bravery, and sacrifices of individual Frenchmen that made possible the planting of the two colonies of Canada and Louisiana and their continuation for a century and a half. Of those that touched Indiana there was first La Salle, who feared neither man nor beast as he spent that first night on Indiana soil in 1679; the senior Sieur de Vincennes who so endeared himself to the Miami that they refused to leave Kekionga where he was buried; the junior Sieur de Vincennes who founded the town that bears his name and died at the stake in defense of French claims to Louisiana; his name, too, was so revered by the Wea that they continued to revenge his death for many years. Bancroft, the historian, wrote in the 1850s, the name of Vincennes "will be perpetuated as long as the Wabash shall flow by the dwellings of civilized man," yet how many Hoosiers today, outside of the city of Vincennes, know of him or his father. Lastly, Sieur de St. Ange who succeeded Vincennes on the lower Wabash, continued as commandant there for a quarter of a century, preserving peace among the traders and the Indians who lived near by as well as among those that frequented the place from time to time.

French civilization did not leave an abiding influence in the Indiana area except in the names given to streams and places: for example, Aboite, Brouillet, Busseron, Deshee, L'Anguille, and La Belle Rivière to mention some of the streams; and Fontanet, French Lick, La Crosse, La Grange,

La Porte, Lagro (Le Gros), Terre Coupee, Terre Haute, and Vincennes, French place names. The main contribution of the French lay in exploring and mapping the region; knowledge of French discoveries filtered through to the English settlers and to the home government via the Indians and the *coureurs de bois* who trafficked with the English. The French brought useful items to the Indians, but also the diseases and liquor which annihilated large numbers and left others debilitated.

In the early years of contact with whites, the Indians noticed little difference between the two European nations: both could supply what they wanted, and their unstable affections— but certainly not unswerving loyalty—quite naturally went to the one which furnished the best goods at the lowest cost. Life at the posts must have been a dreary round of encounters with childlike savages who for the most part could never be trusted completely, either at hand or out of sight. Occasionally news of the outside world filtered through, but rumors, sometimes true, mostly false, were so rampant that one could never have been quite sure what to believe. When one considers the motives which could have induced a civilized man to remain in such surroundings, one is impressed with Bonnécamps' comment that only the hope of profit could make such an existence endurable.

When France transferred the Wabash Valley to the British, the wilderness was almost physically untouched. But the French had planted the blight which continued to sap the strength of the tribesmen, so that they inadvertently lightened the task of conquest facing the British and Americans. Nevertheless, the westward movement experienced bitter warfare and heartbreak before Indian resistance was finally crushed.

CHAPTER V

THE BRITISH INTERLUDE

The struggle between Great Britain and France for control of North America came to an end with the surrender of Montreal and Quebec by the French in the fall of 1760 and the signing of the Treaty of Paris three years later. The first of these events opened the way for the British to take possession of the province of Canada; the second gave them in addition that portion of Louisiana which lay east of the Mississippi River. That part of the French cession about which we are most concerned, the Old Northwest as it came to be called, was a vast fertile region stretching from the Mississippi River to the Appalachian Mountains and lying between the Great Lakes and the Ohio River. This area seemed to hold amazing prospects for not only the English-speaking people, but for others who might join them in clearing and cultivating the land and building homes. The French had done little to colonize or develop its resources, but settlers on the frontiers of the English colonies had long anticipated the day when it would be open to them. Before this could happen something had to be done about the Indians, some ten thousand of whom inhabited the region[1] and exchanged skins for a quantity of goods valued at 1,500,000 livres at Montreal, of which 140,000 livres was with the Miami and Wea in the Indiana area.[2]

[1] The figure represents the number of adult males or hunters. *Johnson Papers*, IV, 243-246; X, 544-545; *Historical Account of Bouquet's Expedition against the Ohio Indians, in 1764* (Cincinnati, 1868), pp. 154-155; Croghan's Journals in Thwaites (ed.), *Early Western Travels*, I, 141-150, 168.

[2] *Michigan Historical Collections*, XIX, 14 (copy of letter to Governor James Murray, August 10, 1761). The value of goods at Montreal represented an advance of 30 per cent to cover freight and other charges. A survey made in 1764, which included the Great Lakes region and the Ohio country, showed

To win the support of the Ohio Indians during the French and Indian War the Pennsylvania government in the Treaty of Easton in 1758 had promised that white men would be restrained from settling on the lands west of the mountains, and the British government had recognized the treaty as binding on them. Now that victory had been achieved this commitment was in part responsible for the provision in the Proclamation of 1763 forbidding settlement in this area, but the desire to indulge in the fur trade of the region without any competition was the prime consideration.

After Sir Jeffrey Amherst, the commander in chief of the British forces in America, received the capitulation of Canada on September 8, 1760, he appointed military governors for each of the Canadian districts: Brig. Gen. James Murray for the district of Quebec, Brig. Gen. Thomas Gage for Montreal, and Lieut. Col. Ralph Burton for Three Rivers. Military control of Canada continued until August 10, 1764, when a civil government took the place of military occupation. The military government was not one of coercion, but one in which French laws and customs were followed as a general rule. British troops were dispatched to take over the western forts with instructions to grant the garrisons at these posts the same honors of war that were granted to those at the eastern posts.

Maj. Robert Rogers and his Rangers received the surrender of Detroit on November 29, 1760, and sent Lieut. John Butler with a party of Rangers to occupy the French posts of Miamis and Ouiatanon, while he himself set out for Michilimackinac but was turned back by the ice.[3] Capt.

that the fur trade employed fully ten thousand Indian hunters and that goods of an annual value of £179,594 were being exchanged for furs. *New York Colonial Documents*, VII, 637-641.

[3] *Journal of Major Robert Rogers*, pp. 197-230; Downes, *Council Fires on the Upper Ohio*, pp. 103-104; Howard Peckham, *Pontiac and the Indian Uprising* (Princeton University Press, 1947), pp. 63-67. It was September of the following year before another party, headed by Capt. Henry Balfour, took possession of Michilimackinac. Peckham, *op. cit.*, p. 89.

Donald Campbell and a company of Royal Americans (60th Regiment), who had accompanied Rogers to Detroit, were left in command there. Campbell considered Fort Miamis to be "of great importance" to Detroit and Butler, who could speak French, was ordered to maintain it if possible with a few men during the winter. "From there is a great carrying place of nine miles into the waters of Ouabache and it would prevent a surprize in the Spring. We have given Mr. Butler a good quantity of Ammunition and some Indian goods."[4]

In the change-over at Detroit, the Indians were not forgotten. George Croghan, assistant to Sir William Johnson, superintendent of the northern department of Indian affairs, had also accompanied the Rogers' expedition and met representatives of the Ottawa, Potawatomi, and Wyandots (formerly called Hurons) in council on December 4. These tribes had heretofore known only French rule and the importance of this first meeting with them was well understood by Croghan as he presented to them the main outlines of English plans that previously had been given to the more eastern tribes, including the promise of an early restoration of the fur trade. They were told that the delivery of their white captives would be proof of their sincerity and intention of living in peace and friendship with the English. In their replies the Indian spokesmen stressed the dire necessity for an early resumption of trade and for low prices of the goods they needed. So far as the captives were concerned they were willing to give up only those who wished to return; some had taken up the Indian way of life and been adopted into the tribes.[5]

On returning to Fort Pitt, Croghan wrote enthusiastically to Johnson about the countryside around Detroit and about

4 Campbell to Col. Henry Bouquet, Fort Pitt, December 11, 1760, in *Michigan Historical Collections,* XIX, 47. It is not clear whether Campbell expected "a surprize" from the French or the Indians. Butler apparently did not go on to Ouiatanon.

5 Downes, *Council Fires on the Upper Ohio,* pp. 104-105; Peckham, *Pontiac and the Indian Uprising,* pp. 66-67.

the fort and its inhabitants, which he considered was far from being an uncivilized outpost in the wilderness. He was greatly pleased at the prospects of a good trade with the Indians, but warned that unless it was well regulated the interest of the Indians would suffer.[6] Johnson passed these recommendations on to General Amherst, with the comment that since the key man in relations with the Indians was the post commander, that officer should have it in his power to supply the savages with arms and ammunition with which to hunt, a smith to repair their guns, and clothing if needed. They were accustomed to receiving these items from the French and their continuance would smooth the transition to English rule.[7] In his reply, Amherst gave a hint of the new policy of economy which was to pervade British-Indian relations. Instead of the government furnishing the items mentioned, he thought the Indians should obtain them from the traders in exchange for the furs they brought in. As to the giving of presents, he considered this a form of bribery which should not be tolerated.[8]

Meanwhile, Captain Campbell was trying to be a friend to both the French and the Indians in the vicinity of Detroit. The demands of the latter worried him as he was unable to give them the presents and ammunition which they had been accustomed to receiving. English traders began to arrive in the spring of 1761. William Trent and Alexander Towery who went out from Fort Pitt were instructed "to cultivate a good understanding with the Indians . . . by doing them strict Justice in the course of your Trade with them." They were given a list of prices to charge in their barter for furs.[9] Some English and Scottish merchants moved from New

[6] Croghan to Johnson, January 13, 1761, in *Johnson Papers,* III, 301-303.

[7] Johnson to Amherst, February 12, 1761, in *ibid.,* III, 331-334.

[8] Amherst to Johnson, February 22, 1761, in *ibid.,* III, 345. See also Johnson's letter of August 9, 1761, in *ibid.,* III, 514-516.

[9] Campbell to Bouquet, December 11, 1760, in *Michigan Historical Collections,* XIX, 46-49; Croghan to Trent and Towery, February 5, 1761, in *ibid.,* XIX, 58-59.

York to the St. Lawrence and secured the services of the now idle *coureurs de bois* and *voyageurs* to carry on a trade for them, thus capitalizing on their long experience.[10] The hopes and expectations of the British merchants for a prosperous trade, however, were soon to be cut short by trouble with the Indians.

Unrest among the Indians and the discovery by Campbell of a plot against the English prompted Sir William Johnson and Croghan to go to Detroit in the summer of 1761 to hold a grand council with the tribes. With them Amherst sent a detachment of 360 soldiers under the command of Maj. Henry Gladwin who were to complete the occupation of the western posts and relieve the Rangers at Miamis. The trip by way of the lakes proved very rough and a part of the provisions and ammunition were lost as well as some of the soldiers. But once arrived, both Johnson and Gladwin were feted and dined by Campbell's soldiers and the French inhabitants and greeted by the Indians.[11]

Johnson immediately called a council of the tribal leaders, but found himself greatly handicapped by the want of provisions, a necessity in any negotiation with savage tribes. Some that he had brought with him were lost on the way and those ordered from Fort Pitt had failed to arrive. To feed the Indians, he was obliged to purchase cattle from the inhabitants of the post at great expense. Also, some of the goods intended as presents for the Indians (to be presented

---

10 The French practice of exploiting the trading posts was abolished when the British took over the country and the traders were allowed to choose where they wished to go. General Gage thought trade should be carried on only at a limited number of posts where troops were stationed. Ouiatanon was among the five posts Gage recommended as trading centers. Gage to Amherst, March 20, 1762, in *Michigan Historical Collections*, XIX, 16-18; Wayne E. Stevens, *The Northwest Fur Trade, 1763-1800* (University of Illinois, Urbana, 1928), p. 21.

11 Edward Jenkins, Fort Niagara, to Amherst, August 21, 1761, in *Michigan Historical Collections*, XIX, 105; Johnson's Detroit Journal, September 4-6, 1761, and letter to Amherst, September 10, 1761, in *Johnson Papers*, XIII, 250-251; III, 524; Peckham, *Pontiac and the Indian Uprising*, pp. 76-79.

at the close of the council) had been damaged by water during the journey. Much of the speechmaking had to do with the Indians' disavowal of any guilt in the plot against the English. Again they pointed out their great need of powder and lead if they were to be able to hunt. A request that the English give them guns and ammunition on credit, as the French had done, was refused. Johnson did not tell the Indians that General Amherst had ordered the discontinuance of the giving of any presents.[12]

Before leaving Detroit, Johnson mapped plans with Gladwin for garrisoning the interior posts. Here again they were greatly hampered by the scarcity of provisions and ammunition. Ordinarily such troops would be expected to take with them enough supplies for eight or ten months, but under the circumstances it was necessary to try to divide on an equitable basis what was available. The posts of St. Joseph, Ouiatanon, and Miamis were each allotted an officer and fifteen men.[13]

The officers were instructed to keep up a good understanding with all the Indians who lived near their posts as well as with those who might resort there for business; to see that no injustice was done them in trade or otherwise; and to prevent the garrison from having intercourse with the Indians. They should choose from among the French inhabitants the most honest and best qualified persons for interpreters, and if applied to for the repair of arms they should have the work done by an inhabitant of the post on the most reasonable terms possible. In order to prevent abuses in the fur trade, only those persons who had a "passport" from Johnson or his deputy were to be allowed to trade and they could only do so at a garrisoned post. No one was to enter the Indian country for purposes of trade.[14]

---

[12] Johnson's Detroit Journal, September 4-18, 1761, in *Johnson Papers*, XIII, 250-259; Downes, *Council Fires on the Upper Ohio*, pp. 108-109; Peckham, *Pontiac and the Indian Uprising*, pp. 79-81.

[13] Johnson's Detroit Journal, September 4, 1761, in *Johnson Papers*, XIII, 250.

[14] Johnson to officers at western posts, Detroit, September 16, 1761, in *ibid.*, III, 527-528.

Each officer was also given a list of the prices to be charged for various trade goods. Those for the Miami post included the following: a stroud (coarse cloth) two yards long was to be sold for three beavers or four buckskins; a plain shirt for one beaver, or one buck and one doe; ruffled shirt for two beavers or three buckskins; vermilion, per pound, three beavers or four buckskins; a silver "broach" required one raccoon; ear bobbs, one doe or small beaver.[15] In January, 1762, Amherst sent orders to the commanding officers of the various posts to forbid the traders bringing spirituous liquors to the posts. However, Johnson reminded him that it would be impossible for the garrisons to prevent the inhabitants of the posts from bringing it in.[16]

Ensign Robert Holmes was selected to go to the Miami post to relieve Lieutenant Butler, but illness prevented him from leaving Detroit immediately.[17] In the meantime another officer was sent to hold a council with the Indians at that post. He arrived on September 25, 1761, and was greeted by the tribesmen who had gathered to receive the "expected" presents. A council was immediately called and continued for several days. The officer tried to dodge the issue of "presents" by telling the chiefs they should have gone to Detroit to receive their share from Sir William Johnson. But during the next few days he doled out powder and lead, strouds, needles and thread, shirts, blankets, vermilion, and rum, and assured the Indians that the British wished to be their friends. The Indians complained of the high prices they were forced to pay for goods, while at the same time

15 Indian trade regulations at Miamis, September 18, 1761, in *ibid.*, III, 533-535. Apparently no English traders had yet reached the post and a French trader was permitted to carry on the trade there. When he went to Fort Pitt for goods, Colonel Bouquet, the British officer at the fort, persuaded some of the English traders to give him some on credit. Bouquet to Gen. Robert Monckton, February 24, 1761, in *Michigan Historical Collections*, XIX, 61-62.

16 *Johnson Papers*, X, 354, 496.

17 Johnson to William Walters, commandant at Niagara, September 10, 1761, in *ibid.*, III, 525; Peckham, *Pontiac and the Indian Uprising*, pp. 90-91; James McDonald to Bouquet, September 18, 1761, in *Michigan Historical Collections*, XIX, 110.

receiving low prices for their furs; they also needed someone
to repair their guns. Lieutenant Butler commended the Indians for their good behavior during the past year and told
the new officer that they had faithfully supplied the garrison
with venison. When asked to give up their British prisoners,
the chiefs sidetracked the question, saying the prisoners were
being held in place of Indians who had been killed. However,
they finally agreed to do what they could to persuade those
tribesmen holding prisoners to give them up.

Any good feeling that might have been generated by the
council was dispelled the last day when one of the soldiers
threw a bayonet at a horse belonging to an Indian and killed
the animal. The Indians immediately threatened to kill every
horse and cow belonging to the garrison if the owner of the
dead animal was not given another horse immediately. By
giving him a gallon of rum, two English blankets, and two
pounds each of powder and lead, in addition to promising to
replace the horse as soon as possible, the officer was able to
pacify the angry tribesmen. The soldier was given one hundred lashes for disobedience of orders.[18]

The Indians were learning that life under British rule was
going to be different than that to which they were accustomed.
Though the French commandant had wielded a strict control
over the Indians at his post, yet he was always courteous and
avoided wounding their self-respect. The English officer felt
his superiority over the savages and was apt to show it at
every opportunity. The presents which they were accustomed
to receive were now either discontinued entirely or measured
out grudgingly. Also, the French trader was a friend of the
Indian, and when the latter brought in his peltry it was an
occasion for festivity; the British trader was apt to be greedy,
eager to make the best trade possible, and there was no rum
with which to celebrate.

---

[18] Report of Indian council, September 25-October 3, 1761, in *Johnson
Papers*, X, 325-329. The report is not signed. The wording is very similar
to the report made by James Gorrell of an Indian conference held at Green
Bay a few weeks later.

Holmes evidently took up his duties at Fort Miamis sometime in the fall of 1761. The following March he wrote to
Colonel Bouquet at Fort Pitt that the garrison had ten
pounds of powder, two barrels of flour, one and one half
barrels of pork, and seven or eight bushels of Indian corn
which had to last them until late in the summer. For meat
brought in by the Indians, he had to pay an extravagant
price. "They are continuly tormenting me for presents," he
reported, and he had had to put them off with trifles.[19]
Though he had written to Croghan the previous fall about
gifts, he had not yet received a reply. Likewise, he apparently
had not heard about Amherst's order prohibiting liquor at
the posts, for he had given a Mr. Crafford liberty to bring
in a quantity.

In January, 1762, George Croghan was instructed by Sir
William Johnson again to visit Detroit and the Indian posts
or to send an assistant to examine into the condition and
behavior of the Indians and to regulate or transact any necessary business with them. He did not neglect to add that "As
maters are Now happily Established between us you will for
ye futer Retrench all Indian Expences and Make use of all the
Oconemy which ye good of ye Service will in any wise ad-
mitt...."[20]

Thomas Hutchins was dispatched the following April to
make the required tour. He found 230 Twightwees (Miami)
at their village of Kekionga, while in the neighborhood of
Post Ouiatanon there were 200 Wea, 180 Kickapoo, 90 Mascoutens, and 100 Piankashaw.

The Settlement of Ouiatanon Consists of about fifteen french families
Situate in a pleasant firtile Country which would produce all kinds
of Grain Natural to the Climate were the Inhabitants to turn their
minds to Cultivate the Lands which they seem Intirely to neglect,
except some small Gardens and raising Indian Corn which they chiefly
make their Bread of: Their whole Genius seems to be turned to the
Indian Trade which they carry on very largely with the Natives: This

---

[19] Ensign Robert Holmes to Bouquet, March 17, 1762, in *The Papers of Col.
Henry Bouquet,* Series 21648, part 1, pp. 52-53.

[20] *Johnson Papers,* III, 604-605.

Country abounds with very Extensive Natural Meadows which makes it very fitt for raising Stock.[21]

In the fall of 1762 Alexander McKee was sent on a similar mission to verify reports that the French in the Illinois county were endeavoring to poison the minds of the Indians and stir them up to murder the British officers and soldiers stationed at the various posts.[22]

Lieut. Edward Jenkins who had come to Detroit with Major Gladwin left there on November 6, 1761, to take charge of the Wea post (Ouiatanon). He found it necessary to give presents to the Indians there before he could go about establishing his small garrison of fifteen men. Ensign Francis Schlosser took command of Fort St. Joseph with the same number of men on November 9.[23]

The following June a Wea chief from Ouiatanon and a Piankashaw from Fort Miamis appeared at Fort Pitt with a few of their tribesmen and some from farther west and requested an audience with Colonel Bouquet. When informed that neither the Colonel nor Croghan were at the fort, they delivered their message to Maj. Edward Ward. After affirming their friendship with the British, they presented a large pipe and a beaver blanket to confirm the truth of what they had said, after which they requested ammunition and cloth-

[21] *Ibid.,* III, 732; X, 521-529, 544-545; Explanations and Table from Hutchins' Map, 1762, in Beverley W. Bond, Jr. (ed.), *The Courses of the Ohio River Taken by Lt. T. Hutchins* . . . (Cincinnati, 1942), 82-83. At Ouiatanon Hutchins met with the various tribes and learned that their principal grievance against the British was the failure to send them a gunsmith and give them presents. None of their people had as yet gone to visit the French at the Illinois fort though they were certain the French would at least give them some ammunition. The Miami at Fort Miamis likewise complained of the lack of presents and the fact that they did not have a gunsmith. At both places Hutchins found many of the Indians ill.

[22] Croghan to McKee, October 5, 1762, and McKee's Journal, October 12-November 27, 1762, in *Johnson Papers,* X, 547, 576-580.

[23] Jenkins to Bouquet, November 4, 1761; Campbell to Bouquet, October 12 and November 8, 1761, August 26, 1762, in *Michigan Historical Collections,* XIX, 116-117, 118, 120, 161-162; Peckham, *Pontiac and the Indian Uprising,* pp. 90-91. Constant Vien was selected as interpreter at Ouiatanon. Clarence W. Alvord and Clarence E. Carter (eds.), *The Critical Period, 1763-1765* (*Illinois Historical Collections,* X, Springfield, 1915), p. 19.

ing for their nations. Upon being refused they decided to wait for Croghan's return. They complained that the traders at Ouiatanon were taking advantage of them in their exchange of furs for goods, charging ten buckskins for one stroud.[24]

Failure of the British to reciprocate with gifts for the chiefs could not be understood, therefore it is not surprising to find Jenkins writing in the following month that the Indians were anxious for the French to come back and take over their former posts. He surmised that the French-Canadians were encouraging them to believe this would take place, also that the British planned to attack the Indians—otherwise, why were they restricting the giving of powder and lead with which to hunt and to carry on the war against the southern Indians, their natural enemies. As soon as they should give up the remainder of the British prisoners they were holding, the Ouiatanon tribes believed the British would attack.[25] Upon receiving word of this apprehensive feeling among the Indians, Croghan observed: "Itt is very luckey for us that those Indians [to the west] & them over ye Lackes are Nott upon a good understanding with Each other. If they were united I am of opinion we should Soon have an Indian warr."[26]

This lack of unity was soon to be changed by the appearance on the scene of a new Indian leader named Pontiac. Little is known about Pontiac except that he belonged to the Ottawa nation by birth, and grew up among that tribe, and was loyal to the French during the Seven Years' War; he was one of several war chiefs of that tribe, but not one of the head chiefs. About fifty years of age in 1763, he had a commanding appearance and was gifted as an orator.[27]

---

24 Edward Ward to Bouquet, June 15, 1762, in *The Papers of Col. Henry Bouquet,* Series 21648, part 1, pp. 155-156.

25 Jenkins to Gladwin, July 29, 1762, and Croghan to Bouquet, December 10, 1762, in *Johnson Papers,* X, 476, 596-597; Croghan to Johnson, December 10, 1762, in *ibid.,* III, 964-966.

26 Croghan to Johnson, December 10, 1762, in *ibid.,* III, 964-965.

27 Peckham, *Pontiac and the Indian Uprising,* Chaps. II-III; Gipson, *The British Empire before the American Revolution,* IX, 96-97.

As early as the summer of 1761 two Seneca had appeared at an Indian council of Ottawa, Wyandot, Chippewa, and Potawatomi chiefs near Detroit and urged the Great Lakes Indians to cut off the English at Detroit, while they in turn would seek to do the same at the posts east of there; their resentment seemed to be a personal one against General Amherst. At that time the western Indians were not prepared to act.[28] A year later Croghan learned of another Indian council held at an Ottawa town near Detroit. This highly secretive gathering was apparently called by two Frenchmen and at its conclusion runners hurried off with a message for the Wabash tribes. Early the following year (1763) war belts were again sent by the Seneca to the Great Lakes and Ohio Indians urging immediate action against the British.[29] With the growing resentment of the Wabash and Great Lakes tribes thus being fanned from both the west and the east, the time was ripe for action. Pontiac became the leader in a widespread plot to strike simultaneously all of the English forts west of the Appalachians.

Execution of the plot began logically at Detroit on May 7 with plans to attack the fort and murder the British officers, but word of the plot had leaked out and Major Gladwin and the troops were prepared. After attempting on three successive days to enter the fort the attack was called off by Pontiac; the Indians, about five hundred in number, then laid

[28] Gipson, *The British Empire before the American Revolution,* IX, 92-93; Campbell to Bouquet, June 16, 1761, in *Michigan Historical Collections,* XIX, 76-77. It was the discovery of this plot that prompted Johnson to go to Detroit in the fall of 1761. See above, pp. 135-136.

[29] Gipson, *The British Empire before the American Revolution,* IX, 93-94. Ensign Robert Holmes discovered a belt of wampum at Fort Miamis and requested that it be given to him. The Indians told him they had received it from the Shawnee at a council held in Pennsylvania. They had received it from the Delawares, and they in turn from the Seneca "who are much enraged against the English." The Miami were apparently supposed to pass it on to the Wea. Speech of Miami Chiefs, March 30, 1763, in *The Papers of Col. Henry Bouquet,* Series 21634, pp. 148-149, and in *Michigan Historical Collections,* XIX, 181-182.

siege to the place, waiting for an opportunity to capture or destroy it, but without success. Pontiac was supported not only by warriors of his own tribe but by Potawatomi, Wyandots, and Chippewa.[30] At the other British posts, the Indians were more successful, and by June 21 all the garrisons west of Fort Niagara—Michilimackinac, Sandusky, Le Boeuf, Presque Isle, Venango, St. Joseph, Miamis, and Ouiatanon— had abandoned their posts or surrendered. At Fort St. Joseph Ensign Francis Schlosser and three of his garrison were taken prisoner and the remainder killed. At Fort Miamis, Ensign Holmes was lured from the fort by a Miami girl and shot, after which the garrison surrendered. At Ouiatanon, the Potawatomi persuaded the Wea, Kickapoo, and Mascoutens to join in the attack. After Lieutenant Jenkins and two or three of the garrison were seized, the rest surrendered; all were taken as prisoners to Fort de Chartres.[31] Jenkins was permitted to send word of his capture to his superior officer at Detroit. If it had not been for Alexander Maisonville and another Frenchman at Fort Ouiatanon, he reported that he and all his men would probably have been killed. As it was they were being well treated in their confinement.[32]

Word of the Indian uprising did not reach General Amherst until the end of June. It must have come as a rude awakening for as late as May 29 the General had written to Johnson that he did not believe the Indians had it in their power to execute anything serious against the British. He betrayed his feeling of superiority when he referred to the *Contemptible Figure* the savages presented. By June 19 he was ready to admit that the "Motions of the Savages

30 For an account of the proposed attack and siege, see Peckham, *Pontiac and the Indian Uprising*, pp. 130-155, 180-242.

31 *Ibid.*, pp. 159-161; Gipson, *The British Empire before the American Revolution*, IX, 99-102; affidavit of James Burns, soldier in the 60th Regiment at Fort Miamis, July 6, 1763, in *Johnson Papers*, X, 731-732; Griswold, *Pictorial History of Fort Wayne*, I, 57-62.

32 Jenkins to Gladwin, June 1, 1763, in *Johnson Papers*, X, 690-691, and in Alvord and Carter (eds.), *The Critical Period*, pp. 12-13.

seem to be more General" than he at first imagined. But he seemed to be ignorant of the causes of the unrest "unless it has been owing to a War Belt, which was Sent some time ago from the Southward, and is Supposed to have been Laying with the Miamis Ever Since."[33]

General Amherst was short of Royal troops with which to meet the Indian onslaught and when he called on the colonies for help they were slow to respond. Capt. James Dalyell with two hundred and sixty Royal troops sailed from Niagara in July to the relief of Detroit, but after a successful voyage the over-confident leader and several of his men were killed while trying to make a surprise attack on the Indians.[34]

After capturing all the forts west of Niagara except Detroit, the Indians had swept on east to the Pennsylvania frontier. Colonel Bouquet, the commander at Fort Pitt, was absent from his post but when word reached him in Philadelphia of the Indian uprising he hastily assembled a force of some four hundred Royal troops and Rangers and marched to the relief of Fort Pitt. The first week in August they won a decisive victory over the Indians at Bushy Run twenty-five miles east of the fort. Because of the lateness of the season, Bouquet decided against following up his victory with any large-scale operation until the following spring. By then General Amherst had returned to England leaving his successor, Gen. Thomas Gage, the task of subduing the Indians and retaking the forts.[35]

After an unsuccessful siege of Detroit of over four months, some of Pontiac's followers began to disperse; then at the

[33] *Johnson Papers*, X, 689; Amherst to Governor James Hamilton of Pennsylvania, June 19, 1763, in *The Papers of Col. Henry Bouquet*, Series 21634, p. 194.

[34] Peckham, *Pontiac and the Indian Uprising*, pp. 201-209.

[35] *Ibid.*, pp. 171-174, 176-179, 210-213; Gipson, *The British Empire before the American Revolution*, IX, 106-113. Amherst was so outraged by the revolt of the Indians that he suggested the possibility of getting rid of them by spreading smallpox among them; he also approved Bouquet's suggestion of using dogs against them, but thought it would be difficult to procure the animals. Gipson, *op. cit.*, IX, 108-109.

end of October, 1763, a messenger arrived from Fort de Chartres with the information that peace had been made between England and France and that fighting should cease. Pontiac, who had secretly hoped that a French expedition might be sent from Louisiana to aid the Indians, now sent word to Gladwin that he and his followers were ready to bury the hatchet. Gladwin replied that since he had not started the war, he could not make peace; he would refer the matter to the British commander in chief. With the approach of winter, the Indians scattered to their hunting grounds and Pontiac with a few Ottawa and some renegade Frenchmen settled down for the winter at an encampment on the Maumee.[36]

§

Word of the signing of the definitive treaty of peace at Paris on February 10, 1763, by which the province of Louisiana was ceded to Great Britain in addition to the province of Canada, had reached the Illinois country on September 28. Pierre Joseph Neyon de Villiers, commandant at Fort de Chartres, not only sent the message to the Indians besieging Detroit but also to those on the Wabash as well, urging them to cease hostilities against the English. The Piankashaw, Kickapoo, Mascoutens, and Wea tribes accepted the "talk" and promised to remain at peace.[37]

Spain had been drawn into the war on the side of France in 1762, with the guarantee that she would be indemnified for any losses she might sustain. By the terms of the definitive treaty Spain ceded Florida to Great Britain to offset the

[36] Peckham, *Pontiac and the Indian Uprising*, pp. 236-240, 243; Gipson, *The British Empire before the American Revolution*, IX, 103-104.

[37] De Villiers to Dabbadie, December 1, 1763, in Alvord and Carter (eds.), *The Critical Period*, pp. 50-51. Dabbadie had replaced Chevalier de Kerlérec as acting governor of Louisiana and was to take charge of the cession of that province to the British. *Ibid.*, 57n. The text of the treaty is printed in Adam S. Shortt and Arthur G. Doughty (eds.), *Documents Relating to the Constitutional History of Canada, 1759-1791* (2 volumes, Ottawa, 1918), I, 113-122.

return of Cuba which the British had conquered. As a compensation for her loss of Florida, Spain received from France, by the secret Treaty of Fontainebleau (November 3, 1762), that part of Louisiana which lay west of the Mississippi plus the city of New Orleans.[38] The news of this last cession did not reach North America until the fall of 1764.

How to take possession of the Illinois country was to become one of the main problems of General Gage. Whether the British approached from the south by way of the Mississippi or from the east by way of the Ohio or Wabash rivers, hostile Indians stood in the way.

De Villiers was anxious to leave Fort de Chartres, but the French could not pull out and leave the fort unattended. St. Ange, who had been commandant at Vincennes since 1737, was ordered to leave there and occupy the Illinois post until the British arrived. Presumably the small garrison at Vincennes accompanied their commander.[39] Upon their arrival at the Illinois post in April of 1764, De Villiers and most of the troops there departed for New Orleans.[40] St. Ange's new position was anything but enviable. He was governing in the name of the King of France a country that had been surrendered to another king; in addition, he was surrounded by crowds of begging, thieving savages who constantly were importuning him to join their side against the British.

The first attempt made by the British in the spring of 1764 to send an expedition to the Illinois country by way of the Mississippi proved unsuccessful. The troops were attacked by

[38] *Dictionary of American History,* II, 294; IV, 216.

[39] Amherst estimated that there were between twenty and thirty soldiers at Post Vincennes. Letter to Bouquet, August 7, 1763, in *The Papers of Col. Henry Bouquet,* Series 21634, p. 237.

[40] Journal of Dabbadie, July, 1764, and De Villiers to Dabbadie, April 20, 1764, in Alvord and Carter (eds.), *The Critical Period,* pp. 189-190, 243. St. Ange was a brother-in-law of De Villiers. He was about sixty years old at this time. J. Thomas Scharf, *History of St. Louis City and County* (2 volumes, Philadelphia, 1883), I, 71. For St. Ange's farewell letter to the inhabitants of Post Vincennes, see above, p. 127.

unfriendly Indians and forced to turn back.[41] General Gage immediately gave orders to prepare another expedition; only this time he advised that efforts be made to obtain permission from the chiefs of the hostile tribes before setting out. However, the way had not yet been cleared by the summer of 1764.[42]

§ §

The success of Pontiac's conspiracy in the summer of 1763 had hastened the need for an immediate declaration of policy by the British government for governing her new possessions in North America. In the absence of any instructions from London, General Amherst and Sir William Johnson had devised their own plans for dealing with the Indians, regulating trade, and trying to keep the settlers off the Indian lands. The latter had deprecated the economy measures which Amherst had instituted in dealing with the Indians and warned him of the possible consequences, while George Croghan at Fort Pitt often used his own private funds to buy presents for the Indians with whom he was dealing.

The development of a definite colonial policy had been delayed because of the changes in the British government brought about by the death of George II in October, 1760, and the succession to the throne of the young George III. The next few years saw the rise and fall of a half dozen different ministries and a consequent change of personnel in the departments dealing with colonial affairs. In the various attempts to institute a colonial policy, four crucial issues were debated: (1) establishment of governments for newly acquired territories; (2) defense and security of the colonies, with the alternatives of concentrating the forces or scattering them; (3) relations with the Indians, whether there should be a strong centralized Indian department subordinate to military authority or whether Indian affairs should be left in the hands of the colonies; (4) where should the boundary

41 Alvord and Carter (eds.), *The Critical Period,* pp. xli-xlii.
42 *Ibid.,* pp. xliv-xlv.

line be drawn between the Indian country and the land opened
for settlement, and should it be a permanent or temporary
line. The proper means of financing the cost of protection
and administration of the colonies, while not an issue in itself,
was a determining factor in any decision regarding the colonies. An attempt was made to resolve the above questions
in the Proclamation issued on October 7, 1763.[43]

By the provisions of the Proclamation the former French
possessions were divided into four colonies: Quebec, East
Florida, West Florida, and Grenada; civil government was
to be inaugurated in Quebec the following year with a
guarantee of a legislative assembly.

To conciliate the Indians the Appalachian divide was established as the temporary boundary between the colonies and
the Indian country. The region between this line and the Mississippi was not included in the boundaries of any of the
colonies, but was reserved for the Indians, and persons who
had already settled there were to leave. No provision was
made for the French settlements such as Vincennes and
Kaskaskia; the only government in the area was to be that
of the military authorities. This omission may have been
caused in part through ignorance of the extent of these
settlements or a belief that the French inhabitants would
leave.

The setting apart of the interior of the country as Indian
land came as a great disappointment to prospective settlers

---

[43] For the background of the Proclamation of 1763, see Gipson, *The British
Empire before the American Revolution*, IX, Chap. 3, and Jack M. Sosin,
*Whitehall and the Wilderness. The Middle West in British Colonial Policy,
1760-1775* (University of Nebraska Press, Lincoln, 1961), Chaps. II and III;
Clarence W. Alvord, *The Mississippi Valley in British Politics. A Study of
the Trade, Land Speculation, and Experiments in Imperialism Culminating in
the American Revolution* (2 volumes, New York, 1959), I, Chaps. VI-VII.

The Proclamation is printed in Alvord and Carter (eds.), *The Critical
Period*, pp. 39-45, and in Shortt and Doughty (eds.), *Documents Relating to
the Constitutional History of Canada*, I, 163-168. Sosin points out that it did
not institute a new policy, but rather gave legal sanction to the *ad hoc* measures
of the war years.

who had hoped that with the war at an end and the signing
of the treaty of peace they would be free to enter. Instead,
the policy which the military had been trying to enforce ever
since the treaty with the Indians in 1758 was now to be continued. The settlers were not the only ones that were disappointed; both in the colonies and in England vast colonization
schemes were being developed. These were halted temporarily
but not given up entirely.

The desire to increase and protect the fur trade accounted
in large measure for the above provision. Imperial control
of the trade which had been instituted to some extent during
the war was to be continued instead of permitting it to revert
to the colonies. The Proclamation decreed that the trade
should be open to all English subjects upon their obtaining a
license from their respective governors and giving adequate
security that they would obey such rules regulating the trade
as should be made in the future. This was supplemented the
following year by a detailed plan of administration and control which continued the offices of the two superintendencies,
instituted in 1755, but made them independent of the military
and of the provincial governments. The northern department
was to be divided into three subdivisions in each of which
the superintendent was to be represented by a deputy. Trade
was to be confined to the garrisoned posts, and schedules of
prices were to be established by officers known as commissaries acting in concert with the Indians and merchants.

Upon obtaining a license a trader should designate the post
where he intended to trade; upon entering the Indian country
he would be under the supervision of the commissaries who
would establish the prices of goods to be sold, prevent the
sale of rum, and establish the limits beyond which the trader
could not go.

The inability of Parliament to raise the necessary money
to finance the program prevented it from being carried out
in its entirety, but after some delay Sir William Johnson, who
was continued as superintendent of the northern department,

undertook to carry out the plan to some extent. He designated Fort Pitt, Detroit, Niagara, Oswego, Michilimackinac, and Fort de Chartres as trading posts or centers and appointed a deputy for each of three subdistricts in 1766: George Croghan for Ohio and the West, Daniel Claus for Canada, and Guy Johnson for the middle district. He also appointed commissaries for each trading center, with Edward Cole being appointed for Fort de Chartres.[44] By this time, however, it was recognized that instead of being independent of the military, the superintendent should take orders from the commander in chief "on all material occasions."

Since none of the designated trading posts were in the Indiana area, the furs and skins collected there would have to be taken to Detroit or Fort de Chartres.

§   §   §

During the winter of 1763-64, while the Indians were scattered in their various hunting camps, there had been no further hostilities, but with the return of spring General Gage and Johnson took up the task of making peace with those tribes which had participated in Pontiac's conspiracy. The signing of the treaty of peace between France and Great Britain and the issuance of the Proclamation of 1763 should have made their work easier, but there was still considerable unrest among the Indians. Also, as long as Pontiac remained alive his influence upon the tribesmen could not be discounted. In the hopes of bringing about a general amnesty between the British and all the tribes east of the Wabash, Sir William Johnson arranged for a council to be held at Fort Niagara in the summer of 1764. Representatives of nineteen tribes attended—more than two thousand in all, but the Potawatomi, Miami, Delawares, and Shawnee were not represented

44 Alvord, *The Mississippi Valley in British Politics,* I, Chap. 8; Gipson, *The British Empire before the American Revolution,* IX, Chap. 3, X, Chaps. 1, 10-12; Sosin, *Whitehall and the Wilderness,* pp. 73-78; Phillips and Smurr, *The Fur Trade,* I, 545-585; Stevens, *The Northwest Fur Trade,* pp. 23-24, 26-27. The detailed plan for Indian trade as worked out by the British government is printed in *New York Colonial Documents,* VII, 637-641.

and Pontiac did not attend. Johnson negotiated separately with each tribe, but in each instance the talks were much the same and included requests for the immediate delivery of all prisoners, compensation of traders for their losses suffered at the hands of the Indians, and freedom of movement for traders by land and water. In the future, any grievances the Indians might have were to be submitted either to the superintendent of the northern department or to the commandant at Detroit. Johnson's conciliatory attitude and a liberal distribution of presents helped to smooth troubled waters.[45]

Col. John Bradstreet, who had been ordered to Detroit with reinforcements, was present at the negotiations and left at the close of the council supported by some 250 Indians. His instructions were to avenge the insults and injuries suffered by the British at the hands of those savages who had not asked for forgiveness nor were ready to give any surety for their future behavior.[46] Before reaching Detroit, Bradstreet dispatched Capt. Thomas Morris and a small party of friendly Indians plus two Frenchmen by way of the Maumee and Wabash rivers to the Illinois country to take possession of that territory for the British. Almost immediately the party ran into Pontiac and some of the Indians he had gathered around him on the Maumee. Only through the intervention of one of the Frenchmen was Morris' life saved. Proceeding on to Fort Miamis he was again threatened with death by the Indians there, but was saved by the intervention of Pacan, a Miami chief. Warned not to go on to Ouiatanon, he then retraced his steps and joined Bradstreet at Detroit.[47]

45 Gipson, *The British Empire before the American Revolution*, IX, 118-119; Peckham, *Pontiac and the Indian Uprising*, p. 253; *Johnson Papers*, IV, 466-501, 511-514; XI, 245-247, 250-254.

46 Gipson, *op. cit.*, IX, 119-121.

47 *Ibid.*, IX, 121-122; Journal of Thomas Morris in Thwaites (ed.), *Early Western Travels*, I, 301-328, reprinted in *Old Fort News*, published by Allen County—Fort Wayne Historical Society, VI, No. 1 (February, 1941), and in part in *Travel Accounts of Indiana, 1679-1961* (Indiana Historical Collections, XLVII, Indianapolis, 1970), pp. 12-17. See also the testimony of Thomas King re the party's treatment, in *Johnson Papers*, XI, 369-372.

Foiled in the attempts to reach the Illinois country by way of the Wabash as well as from the south, the Ohio route now remained as a third alternative. While Johnson and Bradstreet were negotiating with the Indians around Lake Erie, Colonel Bouquet went down the Ohio from Fort Pitt to meet the Shawnee and Delawares in an effort to bring them to terms. He was seemingly successful though it was necessary to continue negotiations with some bands before a general peace was established.[48] Having thus made some headway with the northern tribes and those along the Ohio, it still remained for the British to treat with those on the Wabash and in the Illinois country.

In the meantime, Pontiac had left the Maumee in the spring of 1764 and gone to Fort de Chartres, stopping on the way at Fort Miamis, Ouiatanon, and Vincennes. The expeditions of Bouquet and Bradstreet had reduced his potential strength, but there had been no military defeat nor punishment of his followers. Pontiac had not yet been brought into a treaty council and instead of submitting to the British he was again plotting against them. On the Wabash and in the Illinois country his name was still magic and in no time he had undone the work of De Villiers in preparing for the peaceful transfer of the territory to the British. On his arrival at Fort de Chartres, he implored the commandant to ask the French King not to abandon the Indians. "They would rather die with their tomahawks in their hands than live in slavery with which the English menace them." In his reply, De Villiers accused Pontiac of continuing a war that would benefit neither the Indians nor the French, and advised him to return to his village and keep quiet.[49]

To negotiate with the Wabash and Illinois tribes, General Gage picked George Croghan, veteran in the field of Indian diplomacy, who was to proceed down the Ohio and assure

48 Gipson, *The British Empire before the American Revolution*, IX, 123-126; Alvord and Carter (eds.), *The Critical Period*, pp. xlv, xlvii, li-lii.

49 Peckham, *Pontiac and the Indian Uprising*, pp. 243-251.

the tribes of the peaceful intent of the British, backing up his words with presents. Lieut. Alexander Fraser was to accompany him and go on to Fort de Chartres with letters to the commandant and a proclamation to the inhabitants. Croghan's departure was delayed and Fraser finally went on without him and reached the Illinois post the last of April, 1765.[50]

In the meantime, another expedition directed toward Fort de Chartres had set out from Mobile in December, 1764, under the command of Lieut. John Ross. Avoiding the Mississippi, they worked their way north through the Indian country to the mouth of the Tennessee, then down the Ohio to its confluence with the Mississippi, and up that stream to the fort, reaching there in February, 1765, two months before Fraser arrived from the East. Ross's efforts to negotiate with the Illinois Indians and representatives of tribes west of the Mississippi proved unsuccessful and he and his companions were forced to flee for their safety.[51]

Ross and his party had scarcely departed when Fraser arrived at Fort de Chartres from Fort Pitt. He reported that some of the Indians were in a state of destitution and inclined toward peace, but as a whole they were hostile and unwilling to listen to any overtures from the British. He was thrown into prison and his life threatened; only through the intervention of Pontiac was his life spared. Before departing by way of the Mississippi for New Orleans he received from Pontiac the assurance that if the Indians on the Ohio made a permanent peace he would do likewise, thus opening the way for Croghan to negotiate with the Illinois and Wabash tribes.[52]

---

[50] Alvord and Carter (eds.), *The Critical Period*, pp. li-liii.

[51] *Ibid.*, pp. xlvii-l; Peckham, *Pontiac and the Indian Uprising*, p. 269.

[52] Alvord and Carter (eds.), *The Critical Period*, pp. lii-liii. Word of the secret treaty of 1762 by which France had transferred to Spain the city of New Orleans and all of her possessions west of the Mississippi River had no doubt reached Kaskaskia by this time. Pontiac's hope of receiving any help from France must have dropped considerably when he learned this news.

Croghan had finally set out by boat from Fort Pitt on May 15, 1765, accompanied by several white companions and a party of Shawnee. All went well until near the mouth of the Wabash they were attacked by a party of Mascoutens and Kickapoo, who apparently mistook them for a band of hostile Cherokee. Two of the whites and several Indians were killed and the rest were taken as prisoners to Vincennes, whence Croghan was taken on to Ouiatanon. His capture turned out to be a blessing in disguise, for at the latter place he was released and met deputations from various tribes assuring him of their desire for peace and offering to escort him to Fort de Chartres to meet Pontiac. They had gone only a short distance when they encountered that chief and a number of his followers, whereupon they all returned to the Wabash post for a council during which Pontiac promised to make no further resistance to the coming of the British. Since it was no longer necessary that he go to Fort de Chartres, Croghan proceeded to Detroit where another Indian council was held in which a general peace was made with all western Indians.[53] This in turn was followed by a council at Oswego the next summer conducted by Sir William Johnson, aimed at consolidating the gains thus far made. Pontiac participated in these councils but held to his thesis that the French had only occupied the land as tenants of the Indians and had no right to cede it to the British; in other words, the land still belonged to the Indians.[54]

[53] *Ibid.*, pp. liii-lv; the Indiana portion of Croghan's Journal is reprinted in *Readings in Indiana History* (*Indiana Historical Collections,* XXXVI, Indianapolis, 1956), pp. 17-25, from Clarence W. Alvord and Clarence E. Carter (eds.), *The New Régime, 1765-1767* (*Illinois Historical Collections,* XI, Springfield, 1916), pp. 29-36.

[54] In the midst of any seeming success that the British might feel they were making in establishing peaceful relations with the Indians, they were almost certain to have received reports of continued disaffection on the part of some. For example, in between the two councils mentioned above, Johnson wrote to Gage concerning the Potawatomi of the St. Joseph and the Chippewa who were believed to have formed a conspiracy against the British; they were spreading the word that the French would come and attack Detroit in the

After word was received at Fort Pitt of the success of Croghan's mission, Capt. Thomas Stirling and a detachment of about one hundred men of the 42d Regiment set off down the Ohio for Fort de Chartres on August 24, 1765. Due to difficulties of navigation at that time of year the journey required forty-seven days. The day after their arrival, on October 10, 1765, St. Ange and the French garrison turned the post over to the British and moved across the river to St. Louis.[55] Stirling remained in command at Fort de Chartres until December 2 when Maj. Robert Farmar arrived from Mobile. The British at last had achieved their goal of taking possession of the Illinois country; the still greater problem of governing the area remained.

§ § § §

Before leaving Vincennes in May, 1764, St. Ange had appointed Drouet de Richardville, captain of militia, with Sieur le Caindre, "soldier of the troops," to maintain good order among the citizens, *voyageurs,* and Indians. "Their first care should be to maintain good feeling among the Indians to prevent disorder." Whenever any complaint should be made to them against any one they were "to call an assembly of the more notable of the citizens . . . , where the matter shall be decided by a plurality of votes." From his long acquaintance with the place, St. Ange cautioned Richard-

spring and that the French traders would see that the Indians wanted for nothing. Johnson to Gage, December 21, 1765, in *Johnson Papers,* XI, 982-983. War belts and false rumors continued to be circulated after the Oswego council but Pontiac refused to have anything to do with them. In April, 1769, he was assassinated by a Peoria brave while at Cahokia. Peckham, *Pontiac and the Indian Uprising,* pp. 311-316.

55 St. Louis was founded in 1764 as a trading post of the firm of Maxent, Laclede & Company of New Orleans, which had been granted exclusive control of the fur trade of the upper Mississippi by the governor of Louisiana. St. Ange continued to live at St. Louis until his death on December 27, 1774. He was held in such high esteem by the French that they asked him to administer their civil government and after the arrival of the Spanish he was given the rank of captain of infantry in the Spanish service. Scharf, *History of Saint Louis City and County,* I, 62 ff, 203 ff.

ville and Le Caindre to see that the fences were kept up
so the cattle could not pass from the commons to the grain
fields, and to check the disorders that frequently arose from
drinking. They were to apprise St. Ange of any news of
importance.[56]

Col. James Robertson, a British officer who visited Vincennes soon after St. Ange's departure, deemed the place too
distant from Fort de Chartres to be occupied by the British,
but he recognized it as a useful link between Louisiana and
Canada. He wrote that it formerly had been occupied by
about twenty soldiers; the nearby Piankashaw village had
about sixty warriors. "The ground is extremely fertile &
produces Corn & Tobacco."[57]

Croghan, who was taken there as a captive in 1765, estimated the population at eighty or ninety French families;
the inhabitants were pictured as "an idle lazy people a parcel
of Renegadoes from Canada" who were much worse than
the Indians. He, too, recognized its importance as "a place
of great consequence for Trade being a fine hunting country
all along the Cuabache and too far for the Indians which
reside hereabouts to go either to the Iillionois or elsewhere
to fetch their Necessaries."[58]

The following year, Lieutenant Fraser wrote that there
were about sixty farmers at Vincennes "who raise a considerable quantity of Wheat and Tobacco and have a good stock
of cattle."[59]

Ouiatanon, it will be recalled, had fallen to the Indians in
1763, and the English commandant, Lieutenant Jenkins, and

[56] Dunn, *Documents Relating to the French Settlements on the Wabash,* p.
408.

[57] Report of Robertson, March 8, 1764, in Alvord and Carter (eds.), *The
Critical Period,* p. 218.

[58] *Readings in Indiana History,* pp. 20-21.

[59] Dunn, *Documents Relating to the French Settlements on the Wabash,* p.
410.

the small garrison there were taken to Fort de Chartres.[60] In the months that followed the British made no attempt to reoccupy the fort. Reinforcements were sent to Detroit, but General Gage wrote that he did not think it worthwhile to try to reoccupy any of the smaller posts.[61]

Being on the route between the Illinois fort and Detroit, Ouiatanon continued to be a place of some importance. Croghan wrote of it in 1765:

About 14 French Families are living in the Fort which Stands on the North Side of the River: The Kicapoos & Musquatimes . . . live nigh the Fort on the Same Side of the River where they have two Villages and the Cauatanons have a Village on the South Side of the River. . . . The Country hereabouts is exceedingly Pleasant being open and clear for many Miles the Soil very rich and well watered. . . . This Post has always been a very conciderable Trading place the Great Plinto [plenty of furs] taken in this Country induced the French to establish this Post which was the First on the Cuabache and by a very advantageous Trade they have been richly recompensed for their Labour.[62]

Likewise, Sir William Johnson recommended in 1764 that Fort Miamis be abandoned. "It will create a Saveing, & I apprehend the Twighties [Miami] can be conveniently supplied at Detroit." The following year he described the French inhabitants as of "the worst sort." Although they

---

[60] De Villiers mentioned Jenkins being at the fort in a letter to the governor of Louisiana, December 1, 1763. Alvord and Carter (eds.), *The Critical Period*, p. 53.

[61] Peckham, *Pontiac and the Indian Uprising*, p. 255. A similar opinion was expressed in letters of Col. William Eyre, chief military engineer in America, to Sir William Johnson early in 1764: "For a Party to go between Miamis and St. Josephs or Ouatanau [Ouiatanon] would require an Army . . . and tho' it was possible to maintain one there, and repulse the Indians at every Attack they would make, we should even in these Victories lose ten Men for one, nay twenty if we consider Sickness and Accidents. In short to pretend to keep Posts in these distant Places without the consent of the Indians, or without having them by their own Desire and under their Protection, I consider as vain and delusive. . . ." *Johnson Papers*, XI, 6, 20-24.

[62] *Readings in Indiana History*, pp. 22-23.

frequently deceive the Indians, still the latter have a blind partiality for them.[63]

Stopping there on his way to Detroit in 1765, Croghan wrote: "The Twightwee Village is situated on both Sides of a River called St. Josephs." It "Consists of about 40 or 50 Cabins besides nine or ten French Houses a Runaway Colony from De Troit during the Late Indian War, they were concerned in it and Being affraid of Punishment came to this Post where ever since they have Spirited up the Indians against the English." As at Vincennes, Croghan considered the French at Miamis as lazy and indolent.[64]

One disadvantage that Johnson feared might result from the abandonment of these outposts in Indiana was that in the absence of garrisons commercial companies would attempt to acquire property and make settlements there. Being without restraint they would do as they pleased. Also, he foresaw that the French inhabitants might present the English traders in a bad light to the Indians, and if traders and goods fell into Indian hands the British might be drawn into war.[65]

Representatives of some of the large trading companies of the East prepared to take advantage of the opening of the Ohio and Mississippi valleys to trade. Fort Pitt became the great rendezvous for traders. The Philadelphia firms of Baynton, Wharton and Morgan and of David Franks and Company were two of the principal eastern companies that sent their agents into the Indian territory. But the British expectations of the trade were to be disappointing, for the French traders continued to operate from bases west of the Mississippi. Their friendship with the Indians worked in their favor and the furs and skins that should have gone to Fort de Chartres went to St. Louis, instead; and when

---

[63] Johnson to Lords of Trade, October 8, 1764, and May 24, 1765, in Alvord and Carter (eds.), *The Critical Period*, pp. 324, 508-509.

[64] *Readings in Indiana History*, pp. 23-24.

[65] Johnson to Gage, January 7, 1766, in *Johnson Papers*, V, 1-5.

shipped from New Orleans they brought a higher price than in the East. Even some of the British traders were tempted to use that market.[66] The net result was that the British government found the expenses of administering her new possessions mounting while the profits from the trade were decreasing. Passage of the Stamp Act by Parliament in 1764 to help defray the cost of defense and administration of new territories met such a storm of protest in the colonies that it was repealed the following year. This meant the budget for America would be still further cut unless another source of revenue could be discovered.

Edward Cole had been appointed commissary of Indian affairs for Fort de Chartres in 1766 and arrived there at the end of August from Detroit. En route he stopped at Miamis, Ouiatanon, and Post Vincennes (called Post Vincent by the English). From the first of these he wrote:

> Upon my arrival here The Chiefs Sent for me, to take me by the hand, and well come me to their Village, and made a speach in which they Declared their firm Resolution to adhear Strictly to the peace they had made. Then I acquainted them, where I was goeing, and my business, and gave them a little milk   they Seem'd much pleased with the new regulations and hoped everything would go wright.

Cole purchased some sundries for the remainder of his journey at Miamis for which he paid F. Hambach 147 livres. At Ouiatanon he purchased other items from Joseph Pallier for

---

[66] Charles M. Thomas, "Successful and Unsuccessful Merchants in the Illinois Country," *Journal* of the Illinois State Historical Society, XXX (1937-38), 429-440; Stevens, *The Northwest Fur Trade*, pp. 25-26. For the activities of Baynton, Wharton and Morgan in the Illinois country, see Max Savelle, *George Morgan. Colony Builder* (Columbia University Press, 1932), Chaps. II and III.

In a letter to Sir William Johnson on December 1, 1766, General Gage wrote: "I find the trade to the Ilinois from . . . [Fort Pitt] has turned out as I Expected it would. The Traders bring back no Furrs or Skins. They carry them down the Mississippi & will tell us that they carry them to West Florida; But You may depend upon it, they all go to New Orleans, where they get a better Price, than at any of our Markets: And I wish they may not go up the Mississippi again with French Goods. . . ." *Johnson Papers*, XII, 226.

230 livres. At Post Vincent J. B. Vodrie (Vaudry) and Anthony La Framboist (Framboise) acted as interpreters and from Vaudry and Maisonville he hired horses for the trip overland to Fort de Chartres. Provisions for their stay at that place and for the remainder of their journey were purchased of Mr. Nicholas for 469 livres.[67]

Upon his arrival at Fort de Chartres, Cole found Croghan there and reported his observations to him. The latter's recommendation to Johnson that a trading post be erected on the Wabash "from whence the five nations who are settled on that river may be supplied with British goods," no doubt stemmed in part from Cole's observations. All the French, except those who become English subjects, should be barred from trading there, Croghan advised.[68]

Croghan did not indicate where he thought the trading post should be located, but the Miami Indians were complaining that they must go to Detroit for everything, even to shirts and leggings; and since they had no blacksmith to repair their guns and tomahawks, how could they support their families; they also complained of the traders bringing brandy to their village, and begged that this not be permitted.[69]

[67] Cole to Johnson, July 15, 1766, in *Johnson Papers,* XII, 143-144. Cole's expense account for his journey is printed in Alvord and Carter (eds.), *The New Régime,* pp. 388-389. Though Cole found the Miami Indians inclined to keep the peace, Johnson was receiving reports from Fort St. Joseph, Detroit, and Michilimackinac to the contrary. See Johnson to Gage, August 23 and December 12, 1766, in *Johnson Papers,* XII, 159-160, 227-228.

[68] Report of Croghan, Detroit, January 18, 1767, in *Johnson Papers,* XIII, 412. Croghan had held a conference with the tribes in the vicinity of Fort de Chartres on August 25-26 and reported a "General Peace & Reconciliation" had been reached with all the western nations except those which the French had influenced not to attend. He had found Col. John Reed and all the garrison at the fort ill and Croghan himself later became ill. Croghan to Johnson, September 10, 1766, and Baynton, Wharton and Morgan to Johnson, December 28, 1766, in *Johnson Papers,* XII, 176-177, 235-236.

[69] Miami Indians to traders, May 7, 1767, and to commander at Detroit, May, 1767, in *Johnson Papers,* V, 546-547, 557-558.

Alexander Maisonville, a Frenchman who lived on the Wabash (sometimes at Ouiatanon and sometimes at Vincennes), reported to Croghan that the tribes there were much dissatisfied that they did not have a trading post in their country. For lack of one they sold their furs to French traders who followed them to their hunting grounds and in their contacts did not hesitate to poison the minds of the Indians against the English.[70]

Andrew the Huron, who had been sent to the Wabash and Illinois country to gain intelligence on the state of Indian affairs, gave a similar report. He found the chiefs and principal warriors well pleased with the English traders but incensed because the English had not established a trading place for them on the Wabash. It had been promised to them and if this promise was not fulfilled the Indians would not keep their promises to the English. He cited an instance of the Indians near Vincennes plundering a hunting boat from Fort de Chartres and killing two of the Englishmen aboard and thought it likely that the Indians would rob and plunder all the traders unless they were allowed a post with free trade as at Detroit and Fort de Chartres.[71]

Jehu Hay, commissary at Detroit, also voiced his opinion that the distance between Detroit and the Illinois was so great "that it would be Better if there was a place of trade

---

[70] Croghan to Gage, October 18, 1767, in *Johnson Papers*, XII, 372-373. Maisonville was carrying on trade with the Indians with goods belonging to English merchants. See his letter of November 20, 1767, in *Johnson Papers*, V, 803. Croghan met Maisonville near Fort Pitt while he was on his way to Detroit to hold a council with the western tribes. In his Journal of the trip, Croghan gives a somewhat different version of what Maisonville said regarding the Wabash Indians: after complaining to the British both at Fort de Chartres and Fort Pitt about their failure to establish a trading post on the Wabash, the Wabash chiefs decided it was because the British despised them, and if they did not get the post they would plunder both the English and the French as they must live. *George Croghan's Journal of His Trip to Detroit in 1767 . . .* , edited by Howard H. Peckham (Ann Arbor, Mich., 1939), pp. 32-33.

[71] Peckham (ed.), *George Croghan's Journal*, pp. 37-38.

between this and that, as to Complaints or requests from
the Indians with regard to the traders being Confin'd to
the posts, I have never heard any But from the Miamies and
the people on the Wabache," and he believed these complaints were instigated by the French living among them.[72]

In a memorial of English traders at Detroit, perhaps in
answer to Hay, they voiced their objection to the regulation
that they could not go to the Indian villages to trade, and
pointed out that the French and Spanish were carrying on
an illicit trade at these same villages. And because the Indians could not get the necessary powder and ball needed
for hunting close at hand they were often obliged to cease
hunting and go two or three hundred miles to replenish their
supplies. Also, these traders complained that one third of the
British Indian trade at Detroit was carried on by people without character or property who furnished the Indians with
rum, thus keeping them drunk and idle.[73]

General Gage protested to Don Ulloa, Spanish commandant
at St. Louis, about the French and Spanish traders crossing
the Mississippi to trade and asked that they be prohibited
from doing so; at the same time he ordered the commander
at Fort de Chartres to scour the Illinois, Ohio, and Wabash
rivers with armed boats, and take prisoner anyone found
acting contrary to British orders.[74]

Johnson opposed granting the requests of the merchants
and traders that they be allowed to go into the Indian country,
and thought the French traders were responsible for the

[72] Jehu Hay to traders of Detroit, September 4, 1767, in *Johnson Papers,*
V, 657-658.

[73] Memorial enclosed in Henry Van Schaak to Johnson, November 26, 1767,
in *ibid.,* V, 826-830.

[74] Gage to Lord Shelburne, April 24, 1768, in Clarence W. Alvord and
Clarence E. Carter (eds.), *Trade and Politics, 1767-1769 (Illinois Historical
Collections,* XVI, Springfield, 1921), pp. 267-268. In accordance with Gage's
orders, Col. John Wilkins, commander, purchased a boat from Baynton, Wharton
and Morgan and was fitting it up to patrol the Ohio on which so many depredations had been taking place. He expected to use it to convey a detachment of his
regiment to Vincennes if orders came through to that effect. George Morgan to
Baynton and Wharton, October 30, 1768, in *ibid.,* p. 440.

Indians' resentment against the British for not permitting it. He did, however, come around to the point of advocating the establishment of additional trading posts, including Miamis and Ouiatanon. Since the Indians wanted the posts, he thought it would be safe to place small garrisons there, and to save expenses the soldiers should raise some of their own food supplies.[75] But any decision regarding their establishment must await approval of the home government.

Complaints were also voiced about the lack of a trading post on the lower Wabash. George Morgan of the trading firm of Baynton, Wharton and Morgan reported to his company on December 10, 1767:

An English Trader cannot at present with the least Security of his Life venture even to Post Vincent for want of a garrison there—to ascend the Mississippi or the Illinois Rivers with Goods would be certain Death, so great is the Influence of the French in that Part. . . . The Peltries which would be taken at those Places alone Were proper Measures fallen on, would pay a sufficient Duty to support the Garrisons—by Which the Nation would reap a double Advantage, as our Natural Enemies would be deprived of the Benefit of that Trade & thereby considerable Numbers of English Subjects would find profitable Employment.

In short, unless very diff[eren]t Measures . . . are taken, the Country had much better be abandon'd, as it is very evident that not a single Advantage can arrise from it as yet, otherways than by a proper Regulation & Encouragement of the Peltry Trade, which . . . would be more than 3000 Packs P Annum were suitable Posts established at the Illinois River and Post Vincent.[76]

Edward Cole, commissary at Fort de Chartres, wrote in a similar fashion to Croghan on December 19, 1767:

You wish Some Stop could be put to French traders going out into the Indian Country, So do I with all my hart but unless the Posts are

---

[75] Johnson to Gage, January 15, 1767, in Alvord and Carter (eds.), *The New Régime,* pp. 482-484; Johnson to Lords of Trade, January 15, 1767, in *New York Colonial Documents,* VII, 894-895; Johnson's Review of Trade and Affairs of the Northern District, September 22, 1767, in Alvord and Carter (eds.), *Trade and Politics,* pp. 60-61.

[76] Alvord and Carter (eds.), *Trade and Politics,* p. 131.

Established . . . [at the mouth of Illinois River, the Cherokee fort, and Post Vincent] it never can be prevented, that being done and all peltrys obliged to be bonded for an English post, and a duty or prohibition Laid on all French goods, landed on this Side would in a great measure through [throw] the Trade into our hands, make our Influence much greater with the Indians, and the moneys arising from the dutys of the peltry, and French goods, would go far towards paying the Expence of the Country. . . .[77]

§ § § § §

It may have been in connection with the desire to see a garrison and trading post established at Vincennes that a census was taken in 1767, entitled "State of the Settlement at St. Vincents on the Ouabache."[78]

Inhabitants, Men, Women & Children.................232
Strangers 168

Negro Slaves 10	Hoggs	295
Savage Do 17	Mills	3
Oxen 352	Bushels Corn to be reaped	5,450
Cows 588	Bushels Indian Corn to be reaped	5,420
Horses 260	Tobacco growing n^t Pounds	36,360

A list of the inhabitants at the three Indiana posts was apparently taken two years later.[79]

List of the Inhabitants at Fort St. Vincents on the Ouabache as they were in 1769, since which they have increased rather than diminished.

Mr. Nicholas	Pierre Cornville
De Lorier	François Godere
Mrs. Mallé	François Barois
Antoine Marie	Jean Jazon
Dubois	Bordelot
Nouveau	Peleteree
St. Aubin	Provencalle
Mrs. Richarville	Joseph Sabotte
Antoine La Framboise	Langlois
Jaque Suinaitte	De Comte
Pierre Lefevre	Valcour
Charle Harbonnaux	Denoiyon
	Mallé fils

[77] Alvord and Carter (eds.), *Trade and Politics*, pp. 147-148.

[78] Alvord and Carter (eds.), *The New Régime*, pp. 469-470.

[79] The Indiana Historical Society Library has a transcript of the census from the Haldimand Papers.

Antoine Peradort
Orlans
St. Marie
Lagaissie
Brunett
Desnott
Panat
Arpain
Bourcier
Jean Millehomme
Michelle Depè
Legar
Dutremble
Millet Cardinal
Cardinal
Joseph Deroin
Pierre Quiret
Duchesne
Bailoup
Languedoc
Chapeaux
Vaudrille

Pierre Peron
Lagarouche Godere
Mallèt
Josephe Chapot
Josephe Metaige
Sanschagrin
St. Louis dit-pluechon
La fulliade
Clairman
De Ligne
Grimar
Alexis Delaronte
Magnifique Desne
Jean Lagarde
Sanspeur
Baullon
Charle Lachisne
St. Martin
Rapicaut

N. B. Nicholas is the most substantial Inhabitant and has been employed as Justice of the Peace there, by some authority from the commanding officer at the Illinois.

When this list was taken there were fifty women and One Hundred and Fifty Children belonging to the Inhabitants, and Fifty Men able to bear arms including Servants.

Names of Inhabitants at Fort Ouiattanon.

Maisonville
Maignian
Paillé
Lamorceau
J. Cardinal
Lefevre
Vernette
La Riviere
Clement
Pierre Bertin
Crepo
Aijot

Names of the Inhabitants at Fort Miamie.

Capucin
Baptiste Campau
Nicolas Perot
Pierre Barthè
Bergeron
Berthelemy
Dorien
François Maisonville
Laurain

Six more slaves were ordered by Monsieur Nicholas in 1768 at $360 each, but the order was later cancelled when he could not raise sufficient funds for their purchase.[80]

Commissary Cole continued his efforts to get a trading post at Post Vincent. On April 18, 1768, he wrote to Johnson: "I think there is an absolute Necessity of Establishing a Post at Post Vincennt . . . it being the great path throu which all the Northward Indians pass, and a great place of Trade." James Rumsey, formerly of the 42d Regiment, was anxious to go to Vincennes and Cole recommended him for any employment Johnson might feel inclined to give him.[81]

In the meantime, in the northern part of Indiana two traders, presumably Frederick Hambach and ———— Rogers, had been killed by Indians of Fort St. Joseph at the instigation of the French.[82]

In fulfillment of a request from the principal inhabitants of Post St. Vincent to send them a supply of merchandise for their own use, Baynton, Wharton and Morgan sent the goods

[80] George Morgan to Baynton and Wharton, February and April 5, 1768, in Alvord and Carter (eds.), *Trade and Politics*, pp. 161-162, 228, 233. Other letters of Morgan indicate he was trying to exchange slaves for cattle or peltry. *Ibid.*, pp. 259-260; Morgan to Nicholas Chapau, January 19, 1768, in Baynton, Wharton and Morgan Papers, Pennsylvania Historical and Museum Commission, Harrisburg. If Chapau took four Negroes the price was to be twelve cattle for each one or 200 otter, or 450 beaver, or 1,700 raccoon. If he purchased a larger number of Negroes the cost in cattle and peltry would be reduced proportionately.

[81] *Johnson Papers*, VI, 197; Alvord and Carter (eds.), *Trade and Politics*, pp. 255, 640. After Rumsey failed to get an appointment in the Indian Department, he sought a commission in the British army. No record of an appointment has been found, but in 1777 Lieutenant Governor Edward Abbott referred to him as having been at Post Vincennes and granted land to the inhabitants there. Abbott to Sir Guy Carleton, May 26, 1777, in Colonial Office Records, Q Series, XIV, 61-63, microfilm in Indiana State Library from transcripts in Canadian Archives; the letter is printed in the *Illinois Historical Collections*, Vol. I, edited by H. W. Beckwith, pp. 313-316, with the editorial note that Rumsey was appointed judge advocate of the province of Illinois in November, 1768, with power to examine land titles and administer the oath of allegiance to the French inhabitants.

[82] Gage to Johnson, May 2, 1768, in *Johnson Papers*, XII, 486-487. See also *ibid.*, VI, 121-122.

by boat in the summer of 1768, and an agent, Alexander Williamson, by land. He was instructed to apply for advice and assistance to "Mr. Neauveau, Mr. Flamboice, or Mr. Vadrie." "If you shou'd not find a House belonging to the King which you can make tennantable & convenient, You must rent One at as low a Rate as possible with a good Cellar to keep your Peltry in as to the disposal of your Merchandize the Prices &c I cannot give you any Directions except that you are not to credit any Pson whatsoever without good Security. . . ." The goods were "expressly assorted for the Trade there both for the French Inhabitants & the Indians, I flatter myself you will make a very handsome Remittance to me in the Spring in Peltry & Cattle . . ."[83]

The available correspondence does not reveal exactly what happened to the boatload of goods and to Williamson, but apparently the boat was attacked and perhaps some of the goods lost. The following year the store in Vincennes was plundered by Indians. No further mention has been found of Williamson until 1771 at which time he was living at Cahokia.[84]

Hopes for the establishment of a trading post and garrison on the Wabash were greatly lessened in 1768 when the British government abandoned the plan of 1764 as impracticable because of the expense involved and turned the regulation of the fur trade back to the individual colonies. The

[83] Morgan to Baynton and Wharton, June 20, and Morgan to Williamson, July 8, 1768, in Alvord and Carter (eds.), *Trade and Politics,* pp. 329, 344-347. The last letter contained detailed instructions regarding the sale of merchandise assigned to Williamson and goods he was to take in exchange. Morgan expected that a garrison would be established there and wanted to be ready to supply its needs. See also Savelle, *George Morgan,* p. 61.

[84] Morgan to Baynton and Wharton, July 20, 1768, in Alvord and Carter (eds.), *Trade and Politics,* pp. 362-363; George Croghan to Sir William Johnson, August 8, 1769, in *Johnson Papers,* VII, 78-79; John Finley to Windsor Brown, November 1, 1769, and James Rumsey to Windsor Brown, November 3, 1769, in Baynton, Wharton and Morgan Papers. Williamson is supposed to have written at least one letter from Vincennes, but it is not in the papers of the firm.

general organization of the Indian Department was retained, including the superintendents of the northern and southern departments, but the commissaries were to be recalled. The troops were withdrawn from all but a few of the posts, and the garrisons at these were reduced. Cole was recalled the following year and left Fort de Chartres on April 25, 1769. The garrison at the fort was continued with fifty soldiers and now took on the additional task of managing Indian affairs.[85]

General Gage was not surprised at this change in policy since "the Noise and Complaints of Indian Expences" had been so great. Earlier, Gage had protested the sum of £ 10,742 which Cole had expended in one year, saying it was more than had been spent at Detroit and Michilimackinac combined.[86]

Lieut. Col. John H. Wilkins, who had taken command at Fort de Chartres in 1768, was extremely unpopular and was dismissed in 1772 after his own men filed charges against him. Maj. Isaac Hamilton succeeded him temporarily and it was during this interim that the old fort was destroyed because the ravages of the Mississippi River threatened its security, and a new one was erected at Kaskaskia which was christened Fort Gage. The administration of Capt. Hugh Lord, who replaced Hamilton, was characterized by a policy of conciliation which won for himself the confidence and respect of the French and English inhabitants.[87]

§   §   §   §   §   §

At the same time that the British government abandoned its regulation of the trade with the Indians, it was also endeavoring to establish a more permanent line between

[85] Clarence E. Carter, *Great Britain and the Illinois Country, 1763-1774* (American Historical Association, 1910), pp. 73-74; *New York Colonial Documents,* VIII, 57-58, 105-106, 151; Stevens, *The Northwest Fur Trade,* p. 31.

[86] Gage to Johnson, April 4 and August 7, 1768, in *Johnson Papers,* VI, 176-177, 221, 313.

[87] Carter, *Great Britain and the Illinois Country,* pp. 155-157.

the eastern colonies and the Indian territory. By the treaty of Fort Stanwix, signed in November, 1768, with the Iroquois and their allies, the boundary was designated as running from the eastern end of Lake Ontario southerly to the Delaware River, then west to Kittanning where it turned down the Allegheny, then down the Ohio to the mouth of the Tennessee. The Indians ceded the lands east and south of this line for "a valuable consideration." The line was continued southward by treaties made with the Cherokee who ceded their claims to lands in the present state of West Virginia.[88] With the western parts of Pennsylvania and Virginia thus opened to settlement, settlers began pouring into the area. Deprived of their hunting grounds, the Indians denied the validity of the cessions and the hostility engendered between settlers and Indians broke out into declared war in 1774.

§   §   §   §   §   §   §

In January, 1769, General Gage presented to his superiors an additional recommendation for the establishment of a garrison at Vincennes. "This . . . Settlement has increased within a very Short time, in a Manner that is Surprizing. I find that Strollers and Vagabonds from Canada, Detroit, Ilinois, and other Places, have assembled there, to live a lazy kind of Indian life, or take shelter there from Justice.[89] Again in March he wrote to Colonel Wilkins: "St. Vincent should certainly have a detachment, was it only to keep the Inhabitants within bounds. . . . those Interior Settlements must not be Suffered to increase with the fugitive French and Canadians, who go thither to get Shelter from Creditors, or escape from Justice, for their Crimes." He was evidently still hopeful of receiving orders from London to go ahead and establish a fort at Vincennes, for he included in his

88 *Dictionary of American History,* V, 159; Alvord, *Mississippi Valley in British Politics,* II, 68-72; Gipson, *The British Empire before the American Revolution,* XI, 446-448.

89 Gage to Lord Hillsborough, January 6, 1769, in Alvord and Carter (eds.), *Trade and Politics,* p. 485.

letter to Wilkins the statement, "I must wait for Resolutions from home respecting the future destiny of the Ilinois. I am told it will be determined soon. . . ."[90]

The inhabitants themselves recognized matters were getting out of hand and asked Bishop Briand of Quebec to send them a priest.[91] This request was supplemented by one from Father Meurin, vicar general in Illinois, who wrote on June 14: "The inhabitants of Post Vincennes are in great need of a missionary; they have not seen one since October, 1763, when Father Duvernay was taken from them. The place is large, and disorders are beginning to have full sway over them."[92]

Father Pierre Gibault, who had come to the Illinois country from Canada as a missionary priest in 1768, had been prevented from going to Vincennes by illness and the dangers of the overland trip. He finally reached there in October, 1769, where he found "religion nearly extinct."

Everything is lax, and free thinking and irreverence have come in. . . . I am having the church of this post rebuilt of wood, but it is well put up and very neat; there is a rather large parsonage-house, a beautiful orchard, a garden, and good ground for the benefit of the curé, who could live there comfortably. There are only eighty men who sow, but there are many people of all trades, and many young people who are taking up residence every day. There are in all from seven to eight hundred persons who desire to have a priest. This post would become very quickly populated if it had a missionary.[93]

Unrest among the western tribes continued. Every communication which Johnson or Gage received from the West spoke of depredations committed by the Indians, while on their part the Indians complained of the treatment they received at the hands of the British. *"Since you entered this*

[90] Gage to Wilkins, March 24, 1769, in *Trade and Politics*, pp. 509-510.

[91] Ste. Marie (Jean Baptiste Racine), commandant at Vincennes, to Bishop Briand in Canada, April 22, 1769, in *ibid.*, pp. 520-523. The letter was written in behalf "of all the inhabitants."

[92] Meurin to Briand, June 14, 1769, in *ibid.*, p. 552.

[93] Gibault to Briand [October, 1769], in *ibid.*, pp. 609-611. Garraghan uses a different source for this letter and thinks it was not written until 1770. *Vincennes: A Chapter in the Ecclesiastical History of the West*, pp. 11-12.

*country you alone have caused the misfortunes which have
come upon us,"* Chief Maringouin of the Wabash Indians
charged. "The road of the Illinois is covered with the bones
of my brothers."[94] There was evidence that the Indians were
trying to form a confederacy and unite for a blow at the
British, and this Johnson wished to prevent.[95] Alexander
McKee was sent to the Ohio country in 1769 to watch the
movements of the Indians there, while the following summer
Johnson called a council of the tribes in New York. Nearly
2,400 Indians attended and the superintendent of Indian
affairs was optimistic that the threat of war was at least
postponed for a time.[96] However, by the following spring
rumors were again afloat that the Indians (including those
on the Wabash) were preparing to strike the English forts.
In September of 1770 General Gage reported to Johnson
that the "Ouabache Indians Instead of becoming More
Peaceable . . . are grown worse; and the Navigation of the
Ohio will be more precarious daily, unless Some Measures
are taken to bring them to Reason."[97]

The following year Gage reported to the British colonial
secretary that neither the Potawatomi nor the tribes on the
Wabash would suffer an English trader to come amongst
them. For this hostility he blamed the French who were
"thick" on that stream. He believed they were migrating
to Vincennes from St. Louis because of their dislike of
Spanish rule.[98]

[94] Excerpt from speech of Indians to Colonel Wilkins, enclosed in letter of
Johnson to Lord Hillsborough, August 26, 1769, in *Johnson Papers,* VII, 136-139.

[95] See, for example, Croghan to Johnson, August 8, 1769, and Johnson to
Thomas Penn, September 15, 1769, in *ibid.,* VII, 77-78, 177.

[96] Croghan to Johnson, September 18, 1769, and Johnson to Gage, July 31,
1770, in *ibid.,* VII, 182, 817. McKee kept a journal of his observations which is
printed in *ibid.,* VII, 184-185.

[97] Information concerning an Indian conspiracy related by two Stockbridge
Indians, March 7, 1771, and Gage to Johnson, September 10, 1771, in *ibid.,* VIII,
6-8, 252.

[98] Gage to Lord Hillsborough, October 1, 1771, in Clarence E. Carter (ed.),
*The Correspondence of General Thomas Gage with the Secretaries of State
. . . 1763-1775* (2 volumes, Yale University Press, 1931, 1933), I, 310.

Alexander Maisonville, a Frenchman who had proved himself useful to the British on a number of occasions, was instructed by Johnson in the fall of 1771 to act as his agent or representative on the Wabash.[99] From Fort Stanwix, where he conversed with Johnson, he traveled the northern route by way of the lakes to Detroit and then by way of the Maumee and Wabash rivers to Miamis and Ouiatanon. At Miamis he estimated the number of Indians to be one hundred; at Ouiatanon, about six hundred men who could bear arms (Ouiatanons and Kickapoo) living in two villages opposite each other. He reported that a fort had been built at Vincennes that year on account of an alarm that the Indians intended to cut off the inhabitants. If true, it must have been built by the people of the village since no record has been found of the British erecting one at that time. Maisonville continued to report on happenings taking place on the Wabash for a couple of years.

In response to complaints against settlers at Vincennes, the British secretary informed Gage that it was the King's pleasure that they be removed.[100] After receiving the order, Gage moved slowly in carrying it out, not wishing to give offense to the Indians.[101] The proclamation which he finally prepared was dated April 4, 1772, and with it went a letter of explanation to the neighboring tribes. Both documents were apparently conveyed to Vincennes through Capt. Hugh Lord, then commanding at Kaskaskia.[102] The order to vacate

[99] Instructions to Maisonville, October 8, 1771, and Maisonville's Account of Indian Nations, in *Johnson Papers*, XII, 930-932; Johnson to Gage, November 16, 1771, in *ibid.*, VIII, 319. Maisonville received £50 for his services during one six-month period in 1772. *Ibid.*, VIII, 600.

[100] Lord Hillsborough to Gage, December 4, 1771 and July 1, 1772, in Carter (ed.), *Correspondence of General Gage*, II, 137-138, 145.

[101] Gage to Lord Hillsborough, March 4, 1772, in *ibid.*, I, 319-320; Gage to Johnson, March 9, 1772, in *Johnson Papers*, VIII, 417; Johnson to Gage, March 20, 1772, in *ibid.*, XII, 942.

[102] The proclamation is printed in John B. Dillon, *A History of Indiana* . . . (Indianapolis, 1859), pp. 86-87. The letter to the Indians was composed from Johnson's letter of March 20, cited above. Gage to Johnson, April 7, 1772, in *Johnson Papers*, VIII, 441.

the town was received with consternation by the inhabitants and a memorial was duly prepared giving the history of the village and pleading that they were not vagabonds but "peaceful settlers, cultivating the land which His Most Christian Majesty granted us, or which we have purchased, and often watered with our blood." They then went on to answer the various misdeeds with which they were charged. Although the memorial was dated September 18, 1772, it did not reach Gage until the following March.[103] By that time Lord Hillsborough had fallen from power and was succeeded by Lord Dartmouth. The latter was much more sympathetic with the French inhabitants than his predecessor and notified Gage that he considered that they had a right to their possessions, and instead of being lawless vagabonds they were English subjects claiming the protection of the King.[104]

In the meantime Gage had instructed the inhabitants to transmit additional information regarding their titles to their lands and where the same were registered, whether at Quebec or Louisiana.[105] At this point Gage returned to England on leave and Frederick Haldimand assumed command in his absence. The latter was opposed to the plan of removing the inhabitants and encouraged the settlers to furnish all possible proof of their grants.[106] In due time a document was received listing the names of eighty-eight citizens, the name of the commandant who granted each of them his land, and the date of the grant together with a letter from Ste. Marie, commandant of the local militia, and one from St. Ange, their former commandant, under whom most of the grants had been made. In a number of cases the titles had

---

103 It is printed in "Some Vincennes Documents of 1772," translated and edited by Florence G. Watts, *Indiana Magazine of History,* XXXIV (1938), 206-212.

104 Lord Dartmouth to Gage, March 3, 1773, in Carter (ed.), *Correspondence of General Gage,* II, 156-157.

105 Gage to Lord Dartmouth, April 7, 1773, in *ibid.,* I, 347-348; Dillon, *History of Indiana,* pp. 87-88.

106 Phillips, "Vincennes in its Relation to French Colonial Policy," *Indiana Magazine of History,* XVII, 337.

been lost, either by accident or by the bad conduct of a notary named Baumer.[107] Although the proof was not such as would have been accepted in a court of law, Dartmouth recommended that the citizens be allowed to remain on their lands, but that someone should be sent to govern them.[108] This last problem was taken care of by the passage of the Quebec Act on June 2, 1774, which added the territory north of the Ohio and east of the Mississippi to the province of Quebec. The act also secured to the inhabitants the free exercise of their religion and restored to them French laws and customs in civil cases.[109]

In his letter of January 5, 1774, Haldimand also reported the recent purchase of Indian lands on the Mississippi by a private company. The British government had steadfastly rejected all propositions of the various land companies that had been organized to purchase lands in Indian territory and establish colonies. But on July 5, 1773, an association of English traders called the Illinois Land Company had obtained from ten chiefs of the Kaskaskia, Cahokia, and Peoria tribes a deed for two large tracts of land on the east side of the Mississippi, giving in return two hundred fifty blankets and other Indian goods. The transaction was handled by William Murray, a trader and member of the company. Two years later Louis Viviat, acting as agent for the Wabash Land Company, purchased two tracts on the Wabash River, comprising some 37,497,600 acres, from eleven Piankashaw

107 Printed in Dunn (ed.), *Documents Relating to French Settlements on the Wabash*, pp. 421-431.

108 Haldimand to Gage, January 5, 1774, in *ibid.*, pp. 431-434; Louise Phelps Kellogg, "A Footnote to the Quebec Act," *Canadian Historical Review*, XIII (1932), 147-156.

109 Dillon, *History of Indiana*, p. 89; *Dictionary of American History*, IV, 389. The text of the Quebec Act is printed in Shortt and Doughty (eds.), *Documents Relating to the Constitutional History of Canada*, I, 570-576.

chiefs. These purchases were never recognized by the British government nor by the new American government.[110]

The remaining detachment of British troops under Captain Lord was withdrawn from Fort Gage in 1776. That officer was instructed to entrust the administration of affairs to such persons as he deemed proper. Instead of choosing an Englishman as might have been expected, Lord chose Philippe François de Rastel, Chevalier de Rocheblave, a Frenchman who had come to Canada in 1748, fought in the French and Indian War, and located at Kaskaskia as a trader in 1763. When the British arrived two years later, he moved to the west side of the Mississippi, but sometime after 1770 returned to Kaskaskia. Despite his French heritage, Rocheblave seems to have been faithful to the British government and did all he could to warn them of the schemes of the Spaniards and the colonists. He asked for troops but none were ever sent.[111]

Instructions were sent to Sir Guy Carleton, governor of the Province of Quebec, regarding the government of the new territory over which he had been given jurisdiction.[112] Courts of criminal and civil jurisdiction were to be established for the districts of Illinois and Vincennes as well as for Detroit, Michilimackinac, and Gaspé, and lieutenant governors or superintendents appointed for each district. No one was ever

110 Dillon, *History of Indiana*, pp. 104-109n; Gipson, *The British Empire before the American Revolution*, XI, Chap. 13, discusses these and other land companies formed for speculative purposes.

111 Edward G. Mason (ed.), *Early Chicago and Illinois (Chicago Historical Society's Collection*, IV, Chicago, 1890), pp. 360-381; Introduction to *Illinois Historical Collections*, II, xxvi-xxvii. As proof of his confidence in Rocheblave, Captain Lord left his own family in his charge and after the latter was imprisoned by Virginians, they lived with Madame Rocheblave.

112 The instructions are dated January 3, 1775, and are printed in Shortt and Doughty (eds.), *Documents Relating to the Constitutional History of Canada*, II, 594-614. A plan for the future management of Indian affairs was also sent to Carleton, and appears in *ibid.*, pp. 614-620.

sent to Illinois; Edward Abbott was sent to Vincennes, Henry Hamilton to Detroit, and Arent S. de Peyster to Michilimackinac. The government which the British had at last provided for the Old Northwest was doomed to short duration for the revolt of the colonies in the East would in due time spread to the West.

The French capitulation at Montreal in 1760 and the subsequent Treaty of Paris which ended the Seven Years' War left Great Britain in sole possession of Canada and the region between the seaboard colonies and the Mississippi River. Within the area were some 80,000 French Canadians for whom a government must be provided and numerous Indian tribes for whom some provisions should be made in order that the trade in furs might be resumed. The prospect appeared bright for the development of a prosperous trade but the accession of George III to the throne in the fall of 1760 and the subsequent fall of the ministry of William Pitt brought a reversal of colonial policy.

The huge war debt with which Great Britain was saddled brought demands for economy in colonial administration at the very time when more money was needed in America to provide adequate troops and supplies for frontier garrisons and to meet the needs of the Indians and win their friendship. Sir Jeffrey Amherst and his successor Gen. Thomas Gage together with Sir William Johnson and John Stuart, superintendents of Indian affairs, who were charged with the administration of various colonial measures dictated by a succession of British ministries, had to turn a deaf ear to pleas of officers and agents at western posts for the help they desperately needed to prevent an Indian uprising. After two years of conflict with the Indians, during which the trade was again disrupted, an unstable peace was concluded and British officialdom once more endeavored to produce a workable policy of dealing with the Indians, with trade, and

Marker near Site of French Defeat by the Chickasaw

Silver Cross and Lead Baling Seal found at
Site of Fort Ouiatanon, 1969

Letter of George Croghan written from Ouiatanon, July 12, 1765

with government only to see their plans defeated by the unwillingness of the seaboard colonies to help bear the cost. By the time the Quebec Act was passed in 1774 providing a government for the area between the Great Lakes and the Ohio River, it was too late for the storm clouds that were gathering in the East would spread westward and engulf the area in a new war.

CHAPTER VI

THE AMERICAN REVOLUTION
IN THE OHIO VALLEY

With "five & thirty Canadians, Seven Ottawa, two Chippe-was, & three Peankishaw Chiefs," but without troops to form a garrison, Lieutenant Governor Edward Abbott left Detroit, April 15, 1777, for his new post, Vincennes, on the lower Wabash River. To escort Abbott to his post of duty, the Piankashaw who lived along the lower Wabash had come to Detroit.

Though Governor Guy Carleton's instructions to Abbott have not been found, the latter perhaps paraphrased them when he expressed the hope before leaving Detroit that he would be able to "prevent the machinations of His Majesty's Enemies, and if possible hinder any Succour they might receive by the river Mississippi.—It is true I am without troops, but I make not the least doubt I shall be able to perswade the Indians to keep in our interest, who are now wavering, & engage them to act offencively if your Excellency thinks proper." And then in a less optimistic vein he added, "Your Excellency will not I hope forget to send me a garrison as soon as convenient, for without troops, I may be looked upon as a Cypher. . . ."[1]

When Abbott arrived at Miamis Town at the head of the Maumee, he was met by a picturesque reception committee, of whom Jean Marie Phillipe Le Gras, a native of Montreal, and one of the principal residents of Vincennes, was the leading member. With him had come twenty-four other residents

[1] Abbott to Sir Guy Carleton, April 15, 1777, in Colonial Office Records, Q Series, XIV, 46-47, transcripts in the Canadian Archives, Ottawa, Canada. The Indiana State Library has microfilm copies of most of the Abbott transcripts.

of Vincennes, and thirty-six Indians—Piankashaw, Wea, Mascoutens, Kickapoo, Shawnee, and Delawares. Abbott estimated that altogether there were some five hundred Indians
assembled at the Miami village.[2] Abbott's colorful caravan
moved across the portage to the Little River and down
it to the Wabash. "The Wabache is perhaps one of the
finest rivers in the world," he wrote, "on its banks are several
Indian Towns, the most considerable is the Ouija [Wea or
Ouiatanon], where it is said there are 1000 men capable
to bear arms."[3]

According to a long-established custom, the Indians along
the route expected gifts from the new official, and Abbott
found that he could not ignore them.

I found them so numerous, and needy, I could not pass without great
expense; the presents though very large, were in a manner dispised.
. . . [They said] their antient Father (the french) never spoke
to them without a barnfull of goods; having no Troops and only a
handfull of french obliged me to esquiese in part of their exorbitant
demands . . . but I believe it not thrown away, as I left them
seemingly well disposed for his Majesty's Service.[4]

The journey cost the British a considerable sum of money,
some of which might have been avoided if the Lieutenant
Governor had been accompanied by a body of soldiers. On
Abbott's arrival at Vincennes, May 19, 1777, he found things
in a state of confusion.

[2] Abbott to Carleton, written from Miamis, May 4, 1777, in *ibid.*, XIII,
310-311. The British term for the French Fort Miamis was Miamis Town or
simply Miamis.

[3] Abbott to Carleton, from "St. Vincennes," May 26, 1777, in *ibid.*, XIV,
48-50. Abbott probably overestimated the number of warriors. George Morgan,
Indian agent for the colonies at Pittsburgh, estimated that the Kickapoo, Wea,
and other small tribes of the Wabash numbered only eight hundred. James A.
James, *The Life of George Rogers Clark* (University of Chicago Press, 1928),
pp. 31n, 44.

[4] Abbott to Carleton, May 26, 1777. In this same letter Abbott informed
Carleton that he had drawn on Mr. Dunn for £7,532 New York currency and
trusted he would order payment.

In the fourteen years since the settlement had passed into British hands, no British official had been sent to assume control over the village that had grown steadily until it now numbered some eighty or ninety French families. The original inhabitants had come from Canada but these had been augmented from time to time by the arrival of others from the French villages on the Mississippi. Civil and military affairs were in the hands of local officials. British traders passed to and fro operating under licenses issued by the governors of their respective colonies, while unlicensed French traders from west of the Mississippi journeyed as far east as the Wabash to trade with the Indians and no doubt stopped at Vincennes. When complaints had reached Great Britain concerning the lawlessness of the place, British officials had ordered it evacuated. Against this severe measure the French inhabitants united and were able to prove that they were not mere squatters but had a right to their lands and homes. With the danger of eviction seemingly past and the promise of better days ahead under the provisions of the Quebec Act of 1774, it is not surprising that they dispatched a delegation up the Wabash to meet their first British commandant. On Abbott's arrival, most of the inhabitants presumably took the oath of fidelity to the government of Great Britain.[5]

§

Meanwhile, events were transpiring in the East which were destined to change the course of history in the West. That part of the Quebec Act which added the area north of the Ohio to the Province of Quebec also provided for a government upon French monarchial principles and secured to the inhabitants the free exercise of the Roman Catholic religion. The interior of the country was thus to remain closed to the extension of the liberal traditions of the English colonies on the seaboard and the hopes of land speculators would continue to be thwarted. This along with such other British

5 The oath is printed in Dillon, *History of Indiana*, p. 110.

measures as the sugar and currency acts of 1764, the stamp act and one regarding the quartering of royal troops in 1765, plus the act levying duties on tea, paper, and other products in 1767 were deemed oppressive and had brought the colonists to the brink of revolution. At first they wished only a retraction of the oppressive acts, but after two years this was changed to a declaration of independence from the mother country.

With British troops withdrawn from Fort Pitt as well as from Kaskaskia in 1772, Detroit became the main base of British operations in the West. Col. Henry Hamilton was sent there as lieutenant governor in 1775, charged with holding the vast area for the British. He was supported by a garrison of one hundred and twenty soldiers under the command of Capt. Richard D. Lernoult plus a small navy. Hamilton kept in touch with Rocheblave, the British agent at Kaskaskia at the western edge of British territory, and with Alexander McKee and other British agents on the eastern extremity. Jean Baptiste Céleron was sent to Ouiatanon to watch movements there and Charles Beaubien acted as interpreter and agent at Miamis Town. Louis Chevalier was with the Potawatomi at Fort St. Joseph, while Maj. Arent S. de Peyster was lieutenant governor at Michilimackinac with a small garrison.[6] Vincennes was considered important enough to have a lieutenant governor, but his appointment was delayed for two years (until after the Declaration of Independence by the colonies) and then for the sake of economy he was left without a garrison.

From the opening of the Revolution, American leaders including General Washington desired to send an expedition against Detroit, feeling that it was the key to the control

[6] John D. Barnhart, *Henry Hamilton and George Rogers Clark in the American Revolution with the Unpublished Journal of Lieut. Gov. Henry Hamilton* (Crawfordsville, Ind., 1951), pp. 15, 38, 43-44. The list of officers attached to the Indian Department at Detroit, September 5, 1778, are printed in "The Haldimand Papers," *Michigan Historical Collections,* IX, 470, hereafter cited only to the *Collections.*

of the Indian tribes northwest of the Ohio who were estimated to number some eight thousand warriors. Plans for
such an expedition, however, were temporarily shelved in 1776
due to several reasons, one of which was the refusal of the
Six Nations to permit passage of an army through territory
which they claimed.[7]

Both the Americans and the British sought to win the
allegiance of the Indians. The tribesmen listened to the promises held out by both sides and at first seemed to favor the
former, but after viewing the poverty of the Americans they
were inclined to believe the British could offer them more in
the way of presents. Then, too, the Indians were angered
because of American encroachment upon their lands and
feared this would continue until they were dispossessed.
While American tactics were aimed more at keeping the
Indians neutral, the British tried to stir them to "take up
the hatchet."[8] Apparently wishing to have the backing of
the British Colonial Office for the course he was pursuing,
Hamilton wrote to Lord Dartmouth, British secretary for

[7] Worthington C. Ford *et al.* (eds.), *Journals of the Continental Congress,
1774-1789* (Library of Congress edition, 34 volumes, Washington, D. C., 1904-
1937), IV, 301, 318, 373; John C. Fitzpatrick (ed.), *The Writings of George
Washington . . . 1745-1799* (39 volumes, Washington, D. C., 1931-1944), IV,
493-494; Reuben G. Thwaites and Louise P. Kellogg (eds.), *The Revolution on
the Upper Ohio, 1775-1777* (Madison, Wis., 1908), pp. 145, 147-151, 172, 189.

[8] James A. James (ed.), *George Rogers Clark Papers, 1771-1781 (Illinois
Historical Collections,* VIII, Springfield, 1912), Introduction, pp. xiv-xxxv;
Savelle, *George Morgan,* pp. 132-141. Recognizing the importance of cultivating
and strengthening friendly relationships with the Indians, the Continental
Congress had organized on July 12, 1775, an Indian department to deal specifically with problems relating to the tribes. The frontier was divided into
three districts and commissioners appointed for each district to work under the
direction of a Congressional committee. The commissioners in turn were to
appoint agents to reside among or near the Indians. Benjamin Franklin,
Patrick Henry, and James Wilson were appointed commissioners for the
middle district centering around Fort Pitt, which had been reoccupied and
repaired by the colonists. Richard Butler was first appointed the agent for
that district, but early in 1776 George Morgan, formerly a partner in the
trading firm of Baynton, Wharton and Morgan, became agent. *Journals of the
Continental Congress,* II, 174-176, 183; Savelle, *George Morgan,* pp. 133, 136.

the colonies, in the fall of 1776 that he was having a difficult time restraining the Indians and suggested using them to attack the American settlements on the frontiers of Pennsylvania and Virginia, thus creating a diversion which would work against the American cause in the East. Lord George Germain, who replaced the Earl of Dartmouth during the winter of 1776-77, replied through Governor Carleton that it was the King's command that Hamilton assemble groups of Indians and after placing proper persons at their head, send them out on raiding parties against the American frontier. They were to be restrained from committing violence "on the well affected and inoffensive Inhabitants."

In hopes of winning some of the American frontiersmen to the British side, Hamilton was directed in the same letter to invite all loyal subjects to join the British forces, assuring them of the same pay as that given to members of the King's army in America plus a land bounty of two hundred acres if they served until the rebellion was suppressed.[9] Governor Carleton considered this letter as taking the responsibility for the conduct of the war in the West out of his hands and refused to give Hamilton any further advice or direction.[10] His successor, Frederick Haldimand, apparently did not share this view, but considering the time and difficulty it took to transmit a letter from Quebec to Detroit and then receive a reply, the Governor could exercise little effective control and Hamilton was left to use his own judgment.

Up to this time various desultory expeditions by the Indians had kept the frontiers in a state of alarm, but the execution of the King's order intensified warfare between the "savages," as Hamilton called them, and the frontiersmen. Re-

[9] Lord Germain to Guy Carleton, March 26, 1777, enclosed in Carleton to Hamilton, May 21, 1777, in *Michigan Historical Collections*, IX, 346-348; also printed in *Wisconsin Historical Collections*, XI, 175-177.

[10] Carleton to Hamilton, September 26, 1777, and March 14, 1778, in *Michigan Historical Collections*, IX, 351-352.

gardless of whether the Detroit lieutenant governor was sincere in his efforts to prevent the worst features of Indian warfare, after a few weeks barbarism soon became all too common and Hamilton became known as the "Hair-Buyer." The year 1777 was to be long remembered as the "bloody year" in the history of border warfare. In addition to Detroit, other points of origin for Indian raiding parties included Niagara, Michilimackinac, and Green Bay, so that Hamilton was not the only officer involved in sending out the Indians.[11]

Another problem confronting British officials in the West was how to stop the aid which the rebels were receiving from the Spanish at New Orleans. In July, 1776, Capt. George Gibson and Lieut. William Linn had left Fort Pitt for the Spanish capital, where they obtained supplies through the aid of Oliver Pollock, an unofficial agent in New Orleans for Virginia. Gibson was arrested to check English suspicion, but Linn was permitted to take some nine thousand pounds of powder up the Mississippi and Ohio, arriving at Pittsburgh, May 2, 1777. At New Orleans Gibson was soon released and with the remainder of the powder sailed for Philadelphia. The trans-Appalachian settlements were in dire need of powder and Linn's shipment was vital to their existence.[12]

Gibson's successful journey to obtain supplies and powder from the Spanish made a strong impression on Rocheblave at Kaskaskia, as well as on Abbott at Vincennes. The former not only wanted to stop such aid from reaching the Americans, but he also feared that another expedition might attack the French villages in the Illinois country. He wrote a long letter on May 7, 1777, telling Lieutenant Governor Hamilton

[11] The extent to which Hamilton was guilty of inciting the savages to barbarism is dealt with more fully in Barnhart, *Hamilton and Clark*, pp. 21-36.

[12] John W. Caughey, *Bernardo de Gálvez in Louisiana, 1776-1783* (Berkeley, Calif., 1934), pp. 56, 86-87; Thwaites and Kellogg (eds.), *The Revolution on the Upper Ohio*, pp. 144n-145n, 226n, 252n-253n; James A. James, *Oliver Pollock. The Life and Times of an Unknown Patriot* (New York and London, 1937), pp. 61-73.

how he had tried to organize an attack on Linn's boats as they made their way back to Pittsburgh, but the French and Indians would not support him nor was there any aid from the Spanish across the Mississippi. On the contrary, Thomas Bentley, a trader at Kaskaskia, had furnished Linn with supplies at the mouth of the Ohio. The following day Rocheblave urged the transfer of Abbott to Kaskaskia where he could "give orders for the common safety" of the two villages, and offered either to assist him or leave if the transfer was made.[13]

While Abbott was at Vincennes, James Willing passed down the Ohio to repeat the accomplishment of Gibson and Linn and to bring back powder and goods which Spain had sent to New Orleans. He left Pittsburgh on January 10, 1778, with some thirty men. At the mouth of the Ohio he took prisoner the Becquet brothers and a Mr. LaChance, traders. At Natchez, Willing seems to have yielded to the temptation of a career of "confiscation and cruelty." After wearing out his welcome in New Orleans he returned to New York by sea, but gave Robert George orders to proceed up the river with the men and cargo[14]

In addition to aiding the colonists with supplies, Abbott informed Governor Carleton that the Spanish were sending belts among the Indians on the Wabash inviting them to

[13] Rocheblave to Hamilton, May 7 and 8, 1777, in Colonial Office Records, Q Series, XIV, 56-62, transcripts in Canadian Archives. The letter of May 8 is printed in Mason, *Early Chicago and Illinois,* pp. 391-392. See also Rocheblave to Abbott, June 1 and July 1, 1777, in Mason, *op. cit.,* pp. 392-394. The suggestion that Abbott be transferred to Kaskaskia was disregarded. Bentley was arrested by the British shortly afterwards and imprisoned in Canada. See Clarence W. Alvord (ed.), *Kaskaskia Records, 1778-1790 (Illinois Historical Collections,* V, Springfield, 1909), pp. xvii-xxv, and documents pertaining to his case printed in the same volume.

[14] Caughey, *Bernardo de Gálvez in Louisiana,* pp. 102-134 *passim.* For a more detailed account of Willing's expedition, see Caughey's article in the *Louisiana Historical Quarterly,* XV (1932), 5-36. See also Willing to George Rogers Clark, August 22 and September 1, 1778, in James (ed.), *Clark Papers, 1771-1781,* pp. 66, 67-68. George served under Clark during the remainder of the war. *Ibid.,* p. 311n.

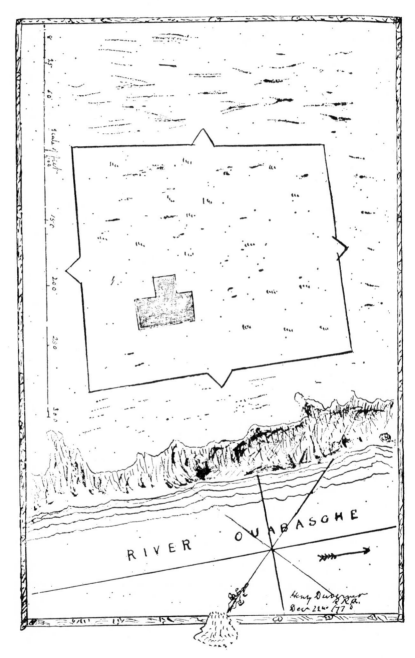

Plan of Fort Sackville
AT VINCENNES.

trade with them. This had the effect, he reported, of the savages carrying all their peltry to the Spanish settlements where they not only received a better price but also rum to drink. Unless some measures were taken to prevent this trade, he feared the British traders would be ruined.[15]

§   §

Upon his arrival at Vincennes, Abbott organized the citizenry into three militia companies of fifty men each, but he realized they would not be adequate for the defense of the village. The Indians frequented the place in such large numbers (sometimes three hundred at a time) that he apparently feared for his own life. "It's true," he wrote during the summer, "I have a guard from the militia . . . but having no fort and the village so extensive makes me continually subject to their importunities." He believed the Indians were striving "to sett the French against the English government & has told many of them I should not live long." To secure himself, Abbott reported that he was stockading the cabin in which he was living and asked Monsieur Rocheblave to send him four pieces of cannon from Kaskaskia. There is no further mention of the erection of a stockade or fort in Abbott's correspondence so this may be part of the fort which Abbott named Fort Sackville in honor of Lord George Sackville (later known as Lord George Germain). A drawing of it made in December, 1778, indicates it was about two hundred feet square with an angle on each side, and a building in the southwest sector. Not having a garrison, there would have been no necessity for erecting barracks.[16]

[15] Abbott to Sir Guy Carleton, November 16, 1777, in Colonial Office Records, Q Series, XV, 99.

[16] Abbott to Carleton, July [June?], 9, 1777, in *ibid.*, XIV, 61-63. The drawing was made by Lieut. Henry Duvernet who accompanied Lieutenant Governor Hamilton to Vincennes in the fall of 1778. It is reproduced on p. 186, from the *Transactions* of the Illinois State Historical Society, 1907, facing p. 62. It also appears in the *Illinois Historical Collections,* I, 230. One of the walls of the stockade was located during an archaeological exploration of the site in the fall of 1970.

Because of his expenditures, particularly for presents to the Indians, Abbott was criticized quite severely by Governor Carleton, to whom he replied:

I am extremely sorry to have done anything to occassion your displeasure. I have done to the best of my judgment to keep the Indians of the Wabache (who are numerous) and the Delawares, in his Majesty's interest. this I have accomplished, and at this time can have a thousand at my command to act wherever Your Excellency may think proper.[17]

The Governor's rebuke apparently had the effect of discouraging Abbott from continuing his efforts to keep the Indians friendly; henceforth his letters to the Governor become very brief. On September 26 he wrote that he had stopped all expenses, except the pay of the interpreters. "I lately received advice from Indians of different Nations, [that] the Rebels intend an attack on this place, should they succeed it will render them masters of the Wabache and of course procure them the interests of the Indians on this River." The Wabash Indians, he reported, had refused "the Hatchet" which Lieutenant Governor Hamilton had tried to present to them.[18]

Finally, on February 3, 1778, after instructing the commandant of the local militia to take charge of affairs, Abbott left Vincennes and after a painful journey of thirty-three days reached Detroit where he resigned his lieutenant governorship. From that place he addressed Governor Carleton on April 25 :[19]

[17] Abbott to Carleton, August 3, 1777, in Colonial Office Records, Q Series, XV, 96-97.

[18] Abbott to Carleton, September 26, 1777, in *ibid.*, XV, 98.

[19] Abbott to Carleton, April 25, 1778, in *Michigan Historical Collections,* IX, 488. Rocheblave traveled from Kaskaskia to Vincennes the last of January and tried unsuccessfully to dissuade Abbott from leaving that place or at least to withdraw to Kaskaskia and take charge there. Frederick Haldimand Papers, B 122, p. 12, copy in Canadian Archives. Abbott drew his salary as lieutenant governor from April 1, 1777 to July 20, 1778, at the rate of £200 sterling annually. *Illinois Historical Collections,* I, 311. He had had no previous experience in dealing with Indian tribes; he was later sent to the West Indies. *Ibid.,* I, 311-312.

I once flattered myself . . . of being able to remain without incurring any great expence, experience has convinced me to the contrary, which determined me to leave the place before the Indians returned from their winter Hunt, knowing they would be much exasperated [by] my not making large presents.

I hope your Excellency will approve my conduct, it was the only alternative left, under the restrictions you was pleased to lay on me; it was not possible for me to meet thousands of savages, without presents of ammunition, Liquor, & Merchandize, notwithstanding every precaution in my power, I have been obliged to incurr a great expence to keep the Indians in the crown's interest.

Abbott also wrote to Lord Germain that he was obliged to leave Vincennes because of Carleton's order not to incur any expense. He then continued:

I cannot help mentioning to your Lordship my regret for a poor people so entirely attached to the Crown, who now think themselves cast off from His Majesty's protection, but firm in their allegiance to defend Fort Sackville against all enemies of Great Britain. . . . I must not omit mentioning . . . a number of people at & near Fort Pitt on hearing of my arrival at Vincennes was determined to take the benefit of my placart and retire from the oppression of the Rebels, some hundreds wou'd have been there this Spring had I not been obliged to quit the place.[20]

Abbott enclosed with his letter to Lord Germain a complimentary address presented to him by the citizens of Vincennes at the time of his departure.

In a later letter Abbott criticized severely the British government's policy of employing Indians to attack the frontier settlements, saying it had been of

great hurt to the cause, for many hundreds [of the settlers] would have put themselves under His Majesty's protection was there a possibility: that not being the case, these poor unhappy people are forced to take up arms against their Sovereign, or be pillaged & left to starve; cruel alternative. . . . Your Excellency's known humanity will certainly put a stop if possible to such proceedings, as it is not people in arms that Indians will ever daringly attack; but the

[20] Abbott to Lord Germain, April 3, 1778, in Colonial Office Records, Q Series, XV, 209-210.

poor inoffensive families who fly to the deserts to be out of trouble, and who are inhumanely butchered sparing neither women or children. It may be said it is necessary to employ Indians to prevent their serving our enemies, I will be bold to say, their keeping a neutrality, will be equally (if not more) serviceable to us. . . .[21]

Hamilton's own figures reveal clearly the inhumanity of Indian warfare. He reported that seven parties of Indians with white leaders had been dispatched by July 18, 1777, which totaled 178 warriors and 22 white officers, an average of 25 Indians and 3 officers to each party. During the next nine days, eight groups, totaling 111 warriors, were sent to the frontiers. These groups were somewhat smaller and each had only one white officer. By September 5, 1777, Hamilton wrote that he had dispatched seven hundred warriors and that an additional 450 had been sent out by other officers.[22] During the winter of 1777-78 the attacks decreased somewhat, but on January 15, 1778, Hamilton summarized another facet of this type of warfare: the Indian raiders had taken seventy-three prisoners but only twenty of them had been turned over to the British officer. The fate of the others was not known. At the same time he mentioned the loss of one of his best interpreters, and one of his most spirited officers, and added: "The Indians have [also] lost men enough to sharpen their resentment."[23]

As the early spring days of 1778 arrived, the Indians renewed their attacks on the frontier settlements. Charles Beaubien, British agent among the Miami, failed to induce that tribe to take up the hatchet, but with the aid of Peter Lorimer and eighty Shawnee he was able to capture the renowned Daniel Boone with some twenty of his men at the salt licks on Licking River in Kentucky. The Indians were so pleased with this achievement that they refused to surrender their

21 Abbott to Carleton, June 8, 1778, in *Michigan Historical Collections*, IX, 488-489.

22 Hamilton to Lord Germain, July 27 and September 5, 1777, in Colonial Office Records, Q Series, XIV, 72-73, 225-228.

23 Hamilton to Carleton, in *Michigan Historical Collections*, IX, 430-433.

prisoner, but in time he managed to escape. Pressure was put on the Delawares in a council at Detroit, June 14-17, 1778, and in time this tribe joined the other Indians in raiding the settlements.[24]

§   §   §

As Indian warfare became more intense, a young Virginian by the name of George Rogers Clark assumed the leadership in military matters in the Kentucky settlements. As early as June, 1772, Clark had begun to seek land on the east bank of the Ohio River between Pittsburgh and the mouth of the Kanawha River. During the next two years he was on the Ohio and became involved in Dunmore's War. Surveying lands for the Ohio Company took him to Kentucky after the war, where he had the opportunity to locate land for himself. So pleased was he with the region that he determined to make it his home. Virginians had already made settlements at Leestown and Harrodsburg while Richard Henderson and the Transylvania Company, largely made up of North Carolinians, had founded Boonesboro and other stations. The latter based their claim to the land on a grant from the Cherokee Indians and planned to establish a proprietary government, while the Virginians claimed the land under the laws of Virginia and expected to have a voice in their government. In the contest that followed between the two groups, Clark naturally took sides with the Virginians.

In 1776 Clark was chosen one of the two delegates to represent the people of Kentucky in the Virginia House of Burgesses and to present a petition requesting the organization of a county government in Kentucky as a part of Virginia and for aid in protecting the people from the Indians. The quest was successful—the formation of Kentucky County was authorized and five hundred pounds of powder was

[24] Hamilton to Carleton, April 25, 1778, in *ibid.,* IX, 435; Proceedings of Council, *ibid.,* IX, 442-452. On June 29 to July 1 Hamilton held a council with the Wea, Kickapoo, and Mascoutens of the Wabash and presented the war axe to them. *Ibid.,* IX, 452-458.

granted for the protection of the people. The journey to
Williamsburg, the Virginia capital, was important for Clark
and for the future of the western country he represented.
Henderson's plans for a proprietary colony were defeated by
the Virginia Assembly and Kentucky's future was assured as
a county of Virginia and not as an independent state as Clark
had threatened if Virginia did not extend aid and protection.
Also, Clark had the opportunity to become acquainted with
Governor Patrick Henry and to tell him something of his
hopes and dreams for the new county.[25]

Upon returning to Kentucky from Williamsburg, Clark
received a commission as major and was entrusted with the
organization of the local militia. Secretly, on April 20, 1777,
he sent Benjamin Linn and Samuel Moore as spies to the
Illinois country. They returned in two months, well informed
of British defenses—or lack of them. According to a previous
promise, Clark wrote Governor Henry a brief summary of
their findings.[26]

Then on October 1, 1777, he set out again for Williamsburg in order to submit his plan for the defense of Kentucky
to Governor Henry. Clark's objective was to attack and take
the old French villages on the Mississippi and Wabash rivers.
If successful in taking these, he hoped to be able to move on
Detroit, but he did not mention the latter even to the Governor. After listening to Clark, the Governor sought the
advice of Thomas Jefferson, George Mason, and George
Wythe, members of the Virginia Council. Finally, the proposal was laid before the privy council which advised the
Governor to "set on foot the expedition against Kaskasky
with as little delay & as much secrecy as possible" and
advanced Clark £1,200. The Governor was further advised

[25] Temple Bodley, *George Rogers Clark. His Life and Public Services*
(Boston and New York, 1926), pp. 8-36; James, *Clark,* pp. 9-27.

[26] Bodley, *Clark,* pp. 37-43; James, *Clark,* pp. 56, 69, 112. The letter published in James (ed.), *Clark Papers, 1771-1781,* pp. 30-32, is believed to be the
one written to Governor Henry.

to draw up the proper instructions. The consent of the Virginia Assembly was obtained through the plea that the expedition was designed as a defense of Kentucky. Governor Henry drew up two sets of instructions: the public one authorized Clark to enlist three hundred and fifty men, ostensibly to defend Kentucky, while a secret one directed him to attack the British post at Kaskaskia. Clark was now promoted to the rank of lieutenant colonel.[27]

Elated over the success of his plans thus far, Clark hastened to Redstone Fort (now Brownsville), Pennsylvania, the place set for the rendezvous of his troops. But he found recruiting difficult and slow because of the Indian warfare which threatened to destroy the settlements in western Pennsylvania and Virginia. After three and a half months only one hundred and fifty men had signed up to accompany him, but these were picked men under two trusted leaders, Capts. Joseph Bowman and Leonard Helm. Two hundred additional men promised from the Holston River area and from Kentucky were expected to join Clark when he reached the Falls of the Ohio.[28]

From the mouth of Redstone Creek the small army of one hundred and fifty men set out on May 12, 1778, following the Monongahela to its junction with the Ohio and then down that stream to the Falls where a blockhouse was built on Corn Island. The twenty families who had accompanied the expedition for the protection the troops afforded were given land to cultivate here. Only a small number of the additional men that had been promised showed up and some of these tried to escape when Clark divulged that the real object of the expedition was the capture of the British posts north of the Ohio. But Clark did not waver from his purpose. One good

[27] Bodley, *Clark,* pp. 43-48; James, *Clark,* pp. 112-115. The order of the council and Henry's letters of instruction are printed in James (ed.), *Clark Papers, 1771-1781,* pp. 33-36. The original letter containing the secret instructions is in the Indiana Historical Society Library.

[28] Bodley, *Clark,* pp. 48-49. The area in which Clark was recruiting was claimed by both Pennsylvania and Virginia at this time.

bit of news that reached him before he and his men departed was word of the French alliance with the colonies.[29]

On June 26, 1778, with one hundred and seventy-five men (all that stayed with him) Clark rowed about a mile up the Ohio to reach the main channel and "shot the Fall" at the very moment of an eclipse of the sun. We "double Man'd our Oars and proceeded day and Night until we run into the mouth of the Tenesse River the fourth day," Clark later wrote. Near the site of old Fort Massac the army secreted their boats and struck across Illinois to Kaskaskia, carrying only what equipment was absolutely necessary. On the third day the hunter, John Sanders, who was serving as guide, lost his way and was suspected of treachery but after a few hours he got his bearings and the march was resumed. On the following day the supply of food ran out but the men pushed on, determined to take Kaskaskia "or die in the attempt." In the evening of the sixth day (July 4), they reached the eastern bank of the Kaskaskia River. Boats were found and a crossing was quickly made. One half of the soldiers surrounded the village while the others took possession of the fort and then spread through the streets. Rocheblave was taken captive and the inhabitants were ordered to go to their homes and remain indoors. The following morning Clark addressed the principal men, told them of the alliance between France and the United States, and assured them that he had come to free them and not to enslave them. On inquiry by the priest Clark informed them they would be free to worship as they pleased. No sooner had they heard these statements than some "fell into Transports of Joy" and assumed a carefree and friendly attitude toward Clark.[30]

[29] Bodley, *Clark,* pp. 49-52; James, *Clark,* pp. 115-117.

[30] Clark to George Mason, November 19, 1779, in James (ed.), *Clark Papers, 1771-1781,* pp. 118-122; Clark's Memoir, in *ibid.,* pp. 223-232. The eclipse took place June 24 instead of the 26th, the day Clark said they left. The letter to Mason and Clark's Memoir are the two principal sources for the expedition. The latter was written by Clark between 1789 and 1791 and without having the former at his disposal. Sometimes one best narrates an

Capt. Joseph Bowman led a body of Clark's soldiers to Cahokia about sixty miles to the north and received the submission of the people there without resistance. To Vincennes, Clark sent the priest, Father Pierre Gibault, a doctor, Jean B. Laffont, and a small group of persons who were acquainted with the residents of that place. They were greeted cordially and the inhabitants joined the residents of the Illinois villages in taking the oath of allegiance to Virginia. Capt. Leonard Helm was sent to take command there and to act as agent for Indian affairs.

To win the Indians around the French villages Clark resorted to artifice. Lacking presents to buy their support and the men necessary to control them, he put up a bold front, and by audacious acting gave them an exaggerated idea of his power. In this manner he was able to win the friendship of most of the tribes with whom he came in contact.[31]

§   §   §   §

In Detroit, on August 8, 1778, news from the Illinois interrupted the dispatching of raiding parties against the frontiers. On that day Hamilton informed Governor Carleton:

. . . an Express is arrived from the Illinois, with an account of the arrival of a party of Rebels in number about three hundred who have taken Mr. de Rocheblave prisoner have laid him in Irons, and exact an oath from the Inhabitants binding them to obedience to the

event or supplies an omission in the other. See *ibid.*, pp. 619-629; Bodley, *Clark*, pp. 35-36, 49, 60. Clark did not mention running out of food before reaching Kaskaskia, but Joseph Bowman supplied this bit of information in a letter to John Hite, July 30, 1778, in James (ed.), *Clark Papers, 1771-1781*, p. 613.

[31] Clark to Mason, November 19, 1779, in James (ed.), *Clark Papers, 1771-1781*, pp. 122-129; Clark's Memoir, in *ibid.*, pp. 232-258; Alvord (ed.), *Kaskaskia Records*, pp. xxv-xxxii, 541-542. Clark's proclamation to the inhabitants of Vincennes and the names of those who signed the oath of allegiance are printed in *Transactions* of the Illinois State Historical Society, 1907, pp. 265-276.

Congress &c. There is an officer with 30 men detached by the Rebels to Cahokia to receive the allegiance of the people at that Post. . . .[32]

The messenger, Francis Maisonville, thought that by this time the people of Vincennes also would have capitulated as the French priest had his horse saddled ready to go there. Somewhat exaggerated but otherwise fairly accurate, the news had covered the distance between Cahokia and Detroit in five weeks.[33] Additional reports arrived from time to time and Hamilton in turn informed Lord Germain in England and Governor Carleton in Quebec of developments. Hamilton was somewhat skeptical of the reports, but he sent Céloron with belts and speeches to the Miami and Wabash Indians promising them British support if they would move against the rebels. Céloron was ordered to have the four cannon at Vincennes "spiked and Trunnions knocked off." Further than that he awaited instructions from his superiors.[34]

Before Hamilton's letters reached Quebec, Governor Carleton had been succeeded by Gen. Frederick Haldimand. Although an able officer, he was new to the situation and was

[32] Hamilton to Carleton, in *Michigan Historical Collections,* IX, 459-460; this same letter and an undated one probably of the same day are also in *Illinois Historical Collections,* I, 330-332.

[33] Journal of Henry Hamilton, in Barnhart, *Hamilton and Clark,* pp. 102-103; Hamilton to Carleton, August 8, 1778, in *Michigan Historical Collections,* IX, 459.

[34] Hamilton to Carleton, August 11, 1778; to Hector T. Cramahé, lieutenant governor of Quebec, August 12, 1778; to Frederick Haldimand, September [5], 16-17, September 22-October 3 [8], 1778, in *Michigan Historical Collections,* IX, 460-461, 462, 464-469, 475-477, 477-482, 486-487. Upon learning of Céleron's arrival at Ouiatanon with a considerable quantity of goods with which to gain the "affections" of the Indians in that quarter, Helm requested permission to lead an expedition against that place. Clark not only acquiesced but sent reinforcements from Kaskaskia. Helm's force completely surprised some forty Chippewa Indians who were assembled in the fort for a council, but they discovered that the British agent had deserted the place a few days earlier. After making a treaty of friendship with the Wabash chiefs, Helm returned to Vincennes. However, upon Lieutenant Governor Hamilton's arrival at Ouiatanon a few weeks later, both the Wea and Kickapoo chiefs were willing to renounce their friendship with the Americans. James (ed.), *Clark Papers, 1771-1781,* pp. 130, 259-260; Barnhart, *Hamilton and Clark,* pp. 134-139.

hardly prepared to advise the Lieutenant Governor. In some haste he wrote Hamilton on August 26,

the expediency of supporting the Ouabash Indians is very evident & I cannot therefore but approve of such steps as you shall find necessary to take for this purpose. . . . it might be expected that some of . . . [the Indians] might easily be induced to undertake expeditiously to clear all the Illinois of these Invaders. . . .[35]

This was followed by a secret and confidential message the following day:

. . . As you must now be so well acquainted with the degree of confidence which is to be placed in the Savages, and what numbers of them you could collect to serve upon emergency; with the number also and disposition of the Militia of your District . . . with a competent knowledge of all the different modes and Routes by which Forces of every nature can pass thro' the adjacent Countries; of the difficulties they have to encounter . . .; in short with all the resources to be made use of and all the obstacles to be met with. I must therefore desire that you will immediately . . . acquaint me with your Idea of the practability of recovering the possession of the Illinois and of the means which . . . you should advise to be employed for that purpose with a probability of success.[36]

By the time Hamilton received the Governor's dispatches, he had made up his mind to lead an expedition to retake Vincennes and Kaskaskia. Believing from the reports received from the Indian country that the Wabash and other Indians were hostile to the idea of the Virginians settling in the Illinois country, he concluded "no time was to be lost in supporting & encouraging them." "Your Excellency is no doubt aware that in an undertaking depending so much on Indians, and in a settlement where I am but too sensible there are many disaffected persons, secrecy is impracticable, I hope notwithstanding to second your Excellency's views by preventing the Rebels from confirming themselves at Ilinois."[37]

35 *Michigan Historical Collections,* IX, 402.

36 Haldimand to Hamilton, August 27, 1778, in *ibid.,* IX, 404.

37 Hamilton to Haldimand, September 16-17, 1778, in *ibid.,* IX, 476.

Detroit took on a new air of activity as preparations went forward for the departure of the expedition which at first was set for the first of October and then postponed a week. Hamilton himself seemed a changed man as he planned and watched over all the details of preparation. Biscuits were baked, provisions packed in small barrels and bags, boats repaired, and artillery stores prepared. Provisions and stores were sent ahead by boat, and oxen and horses were dispatched to transport supplies over the portage between the Maumee and Little Wabash. The Indians around Detroit were assembled and Hamilton joined them in singing their war song. De Peyster at Michilimackinac was asked to encourage the Indians near his post and around Fort St. Joseph to cooperate by way of the Illinois River. Inhabitants of Detroit, most of whom were French, were urged to join the militia and their officers might be seen daily holding drill practice.[38]

Rumors reached Detroit that the rebels were advancing on that place, but Hamilton did not let this alter his plans. His optimism is revealed in a statement made in one of his letters to Haldimand:

The Spaniards are feeble and hated by the French, the French are fickle and have no man of capacity to advise or lead them, the Rebels are enterprizing & brave, but want resources, and the Indians can have their resources but from the English if we act without loss [of] time in the favourable conjuncture. This may appear [to be] a picture with strong lights & little or no shade, but as the effects of pushing a force supported by the zeal of the Indians (who have hitherto acted with perfect compliance) have not yet been tryed, I hope to be excused if perhaps too sanguine.[39]

Reinforcements for the Detroit garrison arrived just as the expedition was leaving and a part of these made a welcome addition to Hamilton's forces which now consisted of 33 men and officers of the King's Regiment, two companies

---

[38] Hamilton to Haldimand, September 16-17, September 22-October 3, 1778, in *Michigan Historical Collections*, IX, 475-476, 477-482.

[39] *Ibid.*, IX, 478.

of militia (125 men and officers), ten officers of the Indian Department, and three artillery men to take care of the six-pound cannon which was being transported, a total of 171. At the time of leaving Detroit there were 70 Indians in the entourage but as the expedition progressed up the Maumee and down the Wabash rivers other Indians joined until there were approximately 350 in all. Hamilton had not neglected to take along presents for the tribesmen who accompanied the army.[40]

The troops arrived at the rapids of the Maumee on October 11 and found it quite difficult to get the boats and supplies over the obstruction. Boats were then repaired and equipment and supplies dried. Feasts for the Indians were held at which time they again sang their war song. Proceeding up the Maumee, the expedition reached Miamis Town on the 24th, where again there were feasts and war songs to keep the spirits high. Miamis was described by Lieutenant Duvernet as being on a high point along the St. Joseph River and consisting of a few dirty huts inhabited by "a worthless set, deserters from Canada or Detroit." There was no mention of a fort except that the location was a most advantageous spot for one. The Indian village was described as opposite the French town and consisting of "150 or 160 Cabbins the Inside much preferable & Cleaner than the French." From Mr. Beaubien they learned that the floods which occurred each spring "drowned" the Indian cabins and reached even the French town.

The crossing of the portage proved very difficult and required two weeks even with the aid of the axles and wheels which Hamilton had sent ahead from Detroit. This accomplished, the flotilla of forty boats set off down the Wabash on November 14. But progress was slow what with the rapids a mile above the mouth of the Eel (where the boats had to

---

40 The number of troops varies in the different accounts. See *ibid.*, IX, 477, 484-485, 487; Barnhart, *Hamilton and Clark*, p. 41; "Lieutenant Governor Henry Hamilton's Apologia," *Indiana Magazine of History*, LII (1956), 388, 389.

be unloaded and supplies carried around them), the freezing weather, and low water.[41]

Hamilton took time to record in his Journal many of the geographical features noted along the way such as the Sugar Loaf (about two miles below the present Lagro), the "Ship" on an island at the present Logansport, and several small rivers that flowed into the Wabash. Ouiatanon was described as a small village inadequately protected by a palisade ten feet high; within the stockade were twelve cabins inhabited by Frenchmen and their families. About the village were some ninety Indian cabins which were estimated to house some nine hundred Indians. Here Hamilton burned a copy of the Wabash land purchase and blamed the Virginians and other Americans for having bought the Indians' land. He assured the tribesmen that the King would not approve the purchase and that their welfare would be in better hands if they remained loyal to the King.[42]

A few miles south of Ouiatanon was the Kickapoo village of ninety-six cabins. From this place the depth of the Wabash ceased to be a major problem but the temperature dropped below freezing and ice on the river made the work of the canoemen very unpleasant. Four men who had been sent from

[41] The progress of the expedition can be followed in Hamilton's Journal, printed in Barnhart, *Hamilton and Clark,* pp. 106-149, and in Hamilton's letters to Governor Haldimand written from Rocher du Bout, Miamis Town, Camp at Petite Rivière, and Ouiatanon on October 14 and 28, November 1, and December 4, 1778, in transcripts of Frederick Haldimand Papers in Canadian Archives. The Indiana State Library has microfilm copies of these as well as of other Hamilton letters written from Vincennes. Some of the letters are printed in the *Illinois Historical Collections,* Vol. I, some in *Michigan Historical Collections,* Vol. IX, and in *Wisconsin Historical Collections,* Vol. XI. A photostatic copy of Lieut. Henry Duvernet's sketch of the Maumee River and his description of the route to Miamis is in the Indiana Historical Society Library.

[42] Barnhart, *Hamilton and Clark,* pp. 124, 126, 133-134. In his Journal Hamilton estimated the number of Indians in each cabin or family as ten, while in his letter of December 4 from Ouiatanon, he estimated five men to a cabin. Of the French settlers, he wrote that they were "few & as inconsiderable as debauchery and idleness" could make them.

Vincennes by Captain Helm to reconnoiter were captured, and from them Hamilton was able to extract information that aided in planning the attack on that place. On December 16 the Commander sent Maj. Jehu Hay with one company of the militia and a few of the Regulars to reconnoiter Vincennes, to take possession of it if conditions were favorable, and to place small groups of men on the roads leading to Kaskaskia and the Falls of the Ohio in order to prevent knowledge of the British expedition reaching Clark and the Kentuckians.

Hamilton and the rest of the troops followed a day later and upon seeing the rebel flag still flying over the fort,[43] Hamilton came to the conclusion that the Virginians had been reinforced and that Hay was having trouble. The Lieutenant Governor ordered his men ashore, drew up in battle formation, and marched through snow to the gate of the fort. Instead of being reinforced, the French militia guarding the fort had almost all deserted at the first sight of the British, leaving Helm with three militiamen, one Virginian, and a civilian to face Hamilton's troops. Though resistance was impossible, Helm put up a good front and demanded the honors of war before surrendering the fort and being taken a prisoner.

At this juncture Hamilton tried unsuccessfully to prevent the Indians who were with him from entering the fort, but "the torrent was too strong" for the sentries he had posted

[43] This was probably not the Stars and Stripes described as the United States flag in the act of the Continental Congress of June 14, 1777, but a pennant or company banner that Helm had ordered made from material available in Vincennes. The account book of Francis Bosseron reveals that Helm purchased in November, 1778, five ells of red and three and three fourths ells of green serge and paid Madame Goderre 25 livres for making a flag. The French word "pavillon" is used instead of "drapeau," meaning a national flag. Janet Shaw (ed.), "Account Book of Francis Bosseron," *Indiana Magazine of History*, XXV (1929), 236-237. R. C. Ballard Thruston describes the various flags or banners that Clark is believed to have used in "Colors of the Illinois Campaign under George Rogers Clark," *Indiana History Bulletin*, IX (1931-32), 230-239.

at the gate and at the door of the commandant's house. The Indians went through the gun ports of the stockade and through the windows of the house while the troops looked on helplessly. They were allowed to keep the thirty-two horses they found inside the stockade, but Hamilton persuaded them to restore to Helm his personal property. The British permitted Helm to take down "the continental flag" before they hoisted their own. Thus Vincennes once more was in British hands without a single shot having been fired; if there had been a single shot, Hamilton wrote, "probably the settlement would have been destroyed in an hour's time."[44] The Vincennes militia along with the other inhabitants of the town were then called together by the ringing of the church bell, whereupon Hamilton reminded them of the oath they had taken before Lieutenant Governor Abbott and the grateful address they had given him when he departed. Their oath of allegiance to the British was then reaffirmed.[45]

Hamilton described the fort which he had taken as a "miserable picketted work" in which "was found scarce anything for defense, the want of a well was sufficient to evince its being untenable—two Iron three pounders mounted on truck carriages and two Swivels not mounted constituted its whole defence, for there were not even platforms for small arms, nor men to use them."[46]

Hamilton set his men at strengthening the fortifications. By December 28 they had constructed a barracks for fifty men and a guard house near the gate while others were at work

[44] Barnhart, *Hamilton and Clark*, pp. 146-149; Bessie T. Conkwright, "Captain Leonard Helm," *Indiana History Bulletin*, X (1932-33), 417-421; Hamilton to Haldimand, December 18, 1778, in Haldimand Papers.

[45] Barnhart, *Hamilton and Clark*, pp. 149-151. Hamilton reported the number of inhabitants at Vincennes as 621, of whom 217 were fit to bear arms. A number of the men were absent buffalo hunting. James (ed.), *Clark Papers, 1771-1781*, p. 182. The text of the oath is printed in *ibid.*, p. 183.

[46] Barnhart, *Hamilton and Clark*, p. 149. In the village Hamilton confiscated all the spirituous liquors and destroyed two billiard tables, "the source of immorality & dissipation." Hamilton to Haldimand, December 30, 1778, in Haldimand Papers.

digging a well. By early January, work was progressing on a second barracks, 40 x 18 feet in dimension. Local inhabitants were called in to square logs for two blockhouses; the east one was raised on January 28 and in two days a three-pounder was mounted in it. The second blockhouse was completed in February and a magazine for powder was also constructed.[47]

Hamilton at first planned to strengthen the fort by changing its form to a triangle with a blockhouse in each angle, but upon reconsideration decided not to change the form but to erect a blockhouse at the northwest angle and another at the southeast angle, "each scouring two faces of the square." The existing small "saillant" angles in each face of the square were to be removed. The blockhouses were to be musket proof and each was to have five portholes. The cannon which Rocheblave had sent to Abbott were to be mounted in the blockhouses. The two other angles of the fort were to be "loop holed & lined," with platforms for musketry.[48] Hamilton failed to have palings placed between the logs of the stockade which he was soon to learn was a serious error.

During the time that the physical properties of the fort were being strengthened, Hamilton's army was dwindling away. On December 23 he reported, "Several of the Indians came this day for provision and powder being on their return to their respective Villages." Five days later, "others came desiring leave to return to their own homes. . . ." Officers of the Indian Department were also involved. Three Lieuts. De Quindre, brothers, asked for leave to return to Detroit. The Detroit militia, which had been engaged only for the campaign, in a few days asked for leave and on January 3, 1779, set off for home. By the end of January militia returns indicated that seventy-five had left. A corporal and six men of Captain La Mothe's Volunteers deserted a week later. During January the Miami Pacan and two of his warriors, Wabangi and Old Reaume,

47 Barnhart, *Hamilton and Clark,* pp. 158, 162, 171, 172, 175, 177.
48 Hamilton to Haldimand, January 24, 1779, in Haldimand Papers.

requested leave to return to their villages. Lieut. Henry
Duvernet of the King's Regiment complained of being subordinate to some of the officers and asked permission to return
to Detroit. A Chippewa chief left after promising to bring
his people back in the spring. A captain, a lieutenant, and
Charles Beaubien, agent at Miamis, returned north on January 27. In view of later developments, one wonders why
Hamilton remained in Vincennes and allowed his army to
dwindle away. First and foremost, it was no doubt a matter
of economy. Having decided to wait until spring before
marching on Kaskaskia, he could save on provisions during
the winter months and hope for reinforcements in the way of
troops and supplies in the spring as well as the return of
some of the northern Indians plus others from the south.
From various reports brought in by the tribesmen, he learned
that the southern Indians were planning attacks against the
Virginians at Kaskaskia and Vincennes in the spring. A "long
white belt" sent by a Creek chief was presented at an Indian
council held at Vincennes on January 26 as witness of their
desire to open a road for friendship with northern tribes and
their enmity toward the rebels. Also, from various scouting
parties Hamilton had learned that Clark had received no
reinforcements and had only about one hundred and ten men.
By sending out small parties to harass the settlers in Kentucky
and cut off any reinforcements and supplies intended for
Clark, the British leader thought he was safe from attack.[49]

The scouting parties covered the roads to Kaskaskia and
the Falls of the Ohio so effectively that word of the presence
of Hamilton in Vincennes was not known to Clark until the
latter part of January, 1779. Near the end of the month,
Francis Vigo, a trader who had been captured and released
by Hamilton, was able to give Clark accurate information of

[49] Hamilton to Haldimand, January 24 and 30, 1779, in Haldimand
Papers; Barnhart, *Hamilton and Clark*, pp. 155-177 *passim;* Hamilton's Report
in James (ed.), *Clark Papers, 1771-1781*, p. 182.

what had taken place.⁵⁰ Up until the first of January, Clark and his men were in daily expectation of receiving word that an expedition being sent out from Fort Pitt under Gen. Lachlan McIntosh would have succeeded in capturing Detroit and taken Governor Hamilton prisoner. But on intercepting a letter being sent from Cahokia it was learned that the expedition had been abandoned and instead Hamilton was planning to retake the Illinois country. Supposing that his first objective would be Kaskaskia, Clark had sent out spies to watch for him but they were captured by one of Hamilton's scouting parties. Indeed, Clark and some of his officers narrowly escaped capture by an Ottawa chief acting as a spy for Hamilton. Thus, it was not until the arrival of Vigo that Clark learned that the British had taken the easier route by way of the Wabash and were in possession of Vincennes.

No time was to be lost; Clark determined to take the initiative and march on Vincennes while Hamilton waited for more favorable weather and reinforcements to retake Kaskaskia.⁵¹ The "Willing," an armed galley, was stocked with supplies, and with a crew of 40 set out February 5 for Vincennes by way of the Mississippi, the Ohio, and the Wabash. With 170 men, about half of whom were French volunteers, Clark left Kaskaskia the next day to proceed overland some

---

⁵⁰ James (ed.), *Clark Papers, 1771-1781*, pp. lxxv, 138, 170; Dorothy Riker, "Francis Vigo," *Indiana Magazine of History*, XXVI (1930), 14-15. Vigo, a Sardinian by birth, had served in the Spanish army at New Orleans before becoming a trader. Clark had become acquainted with him earlier and had borrowed money from him to purchase supplies for his troops. See the memorial of Vigo, dated 1834, in U. S. *House Reports*, 30 Congress, 1 session, No. 216, pp. 41-44, and Papers filed in U. S. Court of Claims by Vigo's heirs, October 31, 1873, No. 7912, in Indiana State Library.

⁵¹ James (ed.), *Clark Papers, 1771-1781*, pp. lxxiii-lxxv, 138, 169-170, 261-268; Bodley, *Clark*, pp. 101-107. Clark wrote to Governor Henry on February 3 that "the Case is Desperate but Sr we must Either Quit the Cuntrey or attact Mr. Hamilton no time is to be lost . . . who knows what fortune will do for us Great things have been affected by a few Men well Conducted perhaps we may be fortunate we have this Consolation that our Cause is Just and that our Cuntrey will be greatful." James (ed.), *Clark Papers*, p. 99.

180 miles to the same village. Clark and his men met unexpected hardships on the march, for a period of warm weather melted the snow and ice and flooded the river bottoms between the Mississippi and the Wabash rivers. The soldiers only occasionally found dry ground on which to camp and they often waded in cold water up to their waists. Animals had generally fled northward to escape the flood thus depriving the men of the opportunity of replenishing their food supplies. The wet lands of southern Illinois were bad but they did not compare with the flooded valleys of the Little Wabash, the Embarrass, and the Wabash. The two branches of the Little Wabash had overflowed until they formed a single body of water five miles wide. Crossing the Embarrass was not attempted. Clark's army made its way along its banks until they reached the Wabash River; then obtaining two small canoes, the men crossed over and landed on a small hill on February 21, from which they were able to reach another hill called the Sugar Camp. Another march brought them to a third piece of dry land. The canoes ferried the weakest, and the stronger helped the most exhausted. Meat was taken from some Indian squaws and broth made to overcome the men's hunger. Soon the army reached Warriors Island which was in sight of Vincennes. The fires built by Clark's men were discovered by a British scout and reported to Hamilton, although it was not known at that time who had built them. Captain La Mothe with two other officers and twenty men were sent to reconnoiter and the fort was made ready for defensive operations.

The Virginians moved closer to the village on February 22 and Clark sent a message to the inhabitants asking them to stay in their homes and by so doing they would be recognized as friends of the Americans. If they were friends of the British they were advised to join Hamilton in the fort. Before the army marched into town, the men paraded over a small rising piece of land in such a manner that the people of Vincennes could see the flags and not the men; by this ruse

Clark's forces were estimated at about a thousand men instead of less than two hundred.[52]

A portion of the Virginians under John Bailey (Baley, Bayley) were sent to attack Fort Sackville while Clark led the remainder in taking possession of the town. Kickapoo and Piankashaw Indians, about one hundred in number, came to Clark and volunteered to aid in taking the fort, but Clark rejected their services. Firing was kept up during the night between the British in the fort and the Americans; the former discovered that their failure to put palings between the logs left them greatly exposed to the rifle fire of the enemy. At eleven o'clock on the morning of the twenty-third one of the Vincennes militiamen advanced towards the fort gate with a flag of truce and on being admitted delivered a letter from Clark demanding that Hamilton surrender the fort, and warning him not to destroy any supplies, letters, or papers, to which Hamilton replied that neither he nor his garrison were disposed to be awed into any action unbecoming the character of British subjects. The attack on the fort was then renewed and continued for a few hours when Hamilton asked for a three-day truce which was refused.

Upon consulting his men about fighting it out, Hamilton found that the Regulars were willing to stand to the last, but the French were unwilling to fight against their friends and relations in the town. Hamilton believed that half of his garrison was disloyal to him. "I determined from that moment to accept honorable terms if I could procure them. . . ." Clark threatened that if Hamilton did not surrender, "not a single man should be spared." At a later negotiation terms were arranged.

52 James (ed.), *Clark Papers, 1771-1781,* pp. lxxvi-lxxxii, 139-141, 268-277. In addition to Clark's two accounts of the expedition contained in his letter to Mason and in his Memoir, Joseph Bowman kept a Journal which is printed in *ibid.,* pp. 155-160. For the route followed by Clark and his men, see the article by F. M. Woolard in *Transactions* of the Illinois State Historical Society, 1907, pp. 48-63.

The fort was surrendered to the Virginians on the morning of February 25, and Hamilton's soldiers were ordered "to deliver themselves up prisoners of war, and to march out with their arms accoutrements and Knapsacks."[53]

Clark wanted to punish Hamilton and his men severely because of their part in sending the Indians against the white people. The first demand made by Clark to Hamilton contained the threat of treating him as a murderer. Between the time of the first demand and the meeting of the two leaders occurred the scalping (but not killing) by Clark's men of Francis Maisonville of the British Indian Department and the killing of several Indians who had been on a raid into Kentucky. The treatment given these men indicates that the Indians were not the only ones who used barbaric methods. Clark's responsibility in these incidents depends in part upon whether one accepts the American or British reports. Capt. Joseph Bowman stated in his Journal that Clark was talking to Hamilton about the terms of surrender when the Indians were killed. Clark defended the action of his soldiers, saying that it gave them the opportunity to impress on the Indians the fact that Hamilton could not give them the protection that he had promised.[54]

Learning that Hamilton had dispatched men and boats to bring down the river provisions left at Miamis Town, Clark lost no time in sending three boats and fifty men under the

[53] For Clark's and Bowman's accounts of the attack and surrender, see James (ed.), *Clark Papers, 1771-1781*, pp. lxxxii-lxxxiv, 141-145, 160-161, 277-289; for Hamilton's Report, *ibid.*, pp. 185-195; for Hamilton's account in his Journal, see Barnhart, *Hamilton and Clark*, pp. 74-76, 177-186. Hamilton gives the date of surrender as February 24 in his Journal. Other known accounts of the attack and surrender are those of Jacob Schieffelin, Hamilton's secretary, which was printed in the New York *Royal Gazette*, July 17, 1780 (after his escape from the Williamsburg prison), and of Isadore Chene (Chesne), a French-Canadian who returned to Detroit. Copies of both of these accounts are in the Indiana State Library.

[54] James (ed.), *Clark Papers, 1771-1781*, pp. 144-145, 161-162, 288-289; Hamilton's Report, in *ibid.*, pp. 188-190; Hamilton's Journal, in *Hamilton and Clark*, pp. 182-183.

The Fall of Fort Sackville

Painted by Frederic C. Yohn for the *Youth's Companion* and presented
jointly by the artist and publisher to the State of Indiana

Clark Statue in George Rogers Clark Memorial, Vincennes
Executed by Hermon A. MacNeil, New York City

command of Captain Helm to intercept them. Near Ouiatanon they surprised and captured seven British boats loaded
with goods and provisions and manned by forty men. Some
of the Vincennes militia were members of the expedition and
their triumphant return to Vincennes was greeted with the
wildest excitement. In the meantime, the "Willing" which
Clark had dispatched from Kaskaskia on February 5 arrived
at Vincennes two days after Hamilton's surrender bringing
the first news from Virginia that the officers and men had
received in a year. Flushed with victory, Clark's men were
eager to proceed at once against Detroit, but many were ill
from the effects of their recent exposure and in no condition
to undertake another long and hazardous march. This and
other circumstances led Clark to decide to wait until summer
for reinforcements expected from Virginia and Kentucky.
What the outcome would have been had Clark proceeded
against Detroit at this time has often been the subject of
conjecture. Viewed from the vantage point of later events,
it would seem to have been the most opportune moment.
"Never was a person more mortified than I was at this time,"
Clark wrote, "to see [slip] so fair an opportunity to push a
victory,—Detroit lost for want of a few men."[55]

One of the reasons for Clark's hesitancy in undertaking a
second expedition at this time may well have been the large
number of prisoners he was holding in proportion to his small
force. Arrangements had to be made for sending Governor
Hamilton and the other British officers under guard to Williamsburg, Virginia. For this purpose the large oak boat
which Hamilton had used in transporting the six pounder
from Detroit was outfitted and on March 7 (or 8) took off
with twenty-five or twenty-six prisoners and an equal number

[55] Bodley, *Clark*, pp. 134-137; James, *Clark*, pp. 147-151; William H.
English, *Conquest of the Country Northwest of the River Ohio, 1778-1783
and Life of Gen. George Rogers Clark* (2 volumes, Indianapolis, 1897), I, 358-
364; James (ed.), *Clark Papers, 1771-1781*, pp. cvii, 145-146, 290-294. Many
of the documents regarding Clark's campaign that have been cited to the *Clark
Papers*, edited by James A. James, also appear in the volumes by English.

of soldiers. The Ohio Valley had received heavy rains and the river was out of its banks. Progress was slow and the journey to the Falls of the Ohio took three weeks. From that point the prisoners were taken overland under a guard of Kentucky militiamen. On June 16 they reached the capital of Virginia where Hamilton was imprisoned until October 10, 1780, when he was paroled and permitted to join the British in New York. The following March he was exchanged and reached England on June 21, 1781, more than two years after his surrender.[56]

Following Hamilton's surrender Clark permitted the French-Canadian militiamen who had been captured to return to Detroit after first taking an oath of neutrality. By this gesture, Clark hoped to win the friendship and good will of their friends and relatives in Canada.[57]

Once more, as after the capture of the Illinois towns, Clark was faced with the important problem of how to deal with the Indians, only this time it was the Wabash tribes. Since they far outnumbered his forces, he had to win the friendship of all that he could and let the remainder know he was master of the situation. Those who had withstood the advances of the British he extolled for their "Manly behaviour and

56 James (ed.), *Clark Papers*, pp. 146, 290-294; Barnhart, *Hamilton and Clark*, pp. 79-92, 191-205; English, *Conquest of the Country Northwest of the River Ohio*, II, 605-661. Hamilton returned to Canada as lieutenant governor of Quebec in November, 1784, and served a year; he later held the same office in other British colonies. Rocheblave, commandant at Kaskaskia, who was also imprisoned at Williamsburg, made his escape in April, 1780, and safely reached New York. English, *op. cit.,* II, 651. Hamilton was apparently treated at first as any other prisoner without any consideration for his military rank, to which he strenuously objected. Thomas Jefferson, who had succeeded Patrick Henry as governor of Virginia in June, 1779, consulted General Washington, who at first agreed with the Virginia authorities but later changed his views and thought he should receive special consideration. For correspondence regarding Hamilton's imprisonment, see Julian P. Boyd (ed.), *The Papers of Thomas Jefferson* . . . (Vols. 1- , Princeton University Press, 1950-   ), Vols. II and III, Index.

57 James (ed.), *Clark Papers*, pp. lxxxviii, 291-292; English, *Conquest of the Country Northwest of the River Ohio*, I, 364-365.

fedility," while those that had accompanied Hamilton were threatened with extermination if they did not lay down their arms at once. He assured the Indians that he had no design on their lands, that it was only necessary that he should be in their country during the war and keep a garrison there to drive off the English.[58]

Having met the Indians and dispatched most of the prisoners, Clark had one last item of business to take care of before returning to Kaskaskia—providing a civil government and military protection for Vincennes. Captain Helm was appointed to take care of civil matters and to act as superintendent of Indian affairs; Moses Henry was made Indian agent. A garrison of forty men was left at Fort Patrick Henry (the new name given Fort Sackville) under the command of Lieut. Richard Brashers, assisted by Lieuts. John Bailey and Abraham Chapline.[59] This accomplished, Clark set out for Kaskaskia on March 20 with eighty of his men and the remaining prisoners of war. The last two months had indeed been momentous, and demonstrated Clark's own statement that "Great things have been affected by a few Men well Conducted."

§ § § § §

Word of Hamilton's surrender reached Detroit by March 21, 1779, but it was probably six weeks later before the news reached Quebec. The Governor had sent Capt. D. Brehm, his aide-de-camp, to Detroit the first of April to learn the exact state of things in the upper country; he was to

[58] James (ed.), *Clark Papers, 1771-1781,* pp. xcii-xciv, 146-149, 295-297.

[59] *Ibid.,* p. xciv. A new assignment of troops was made the following August. By Clark's general orders of August 5, 1779, Capt. James Shelby was placed in charge of the garrison at Fort Patrick Henry together with the companies of Capts. Abraham Kellar and Isaac Taylor. *Ibid.,* p. 354. Shelby wrote to Clark on October 10 that the garrison was much in need of provisions; the lack of salt had made it useless to hunt. He and thirty of his men had gone to the relief of Capt. Godefroy Linctot at Ouiatanon in August, he reported, but lack of shoes had prevented them from going on an expedition against Fort St. Joseph. *Ibid.,* pp. 362-363, 366, 370; note 62, below.

consult with Captain Lernoult "in regard to what may be done respecting the post of Vincennes, and the further steps advisable for Lieut. Govr. Hamilton to take." He had written to Hamilton on April 8, after receiving word of the taking of Vincennes, that he would know what further could be done in those parts for the King's service. "Before you undertake anything considerable, I must recommend you weighing well the difficulty and expence, that must attend the Transport of every article you are to be furnished with from hence, and whether they are likely to be compensated by the advantages expected to accrue from such an undertaking." But after learning of Hamilton's defeat, the Governor wrote to Lord Germain, "it is to me astonishing and unaccountable how any Officer of his Good Character could remain at Vincennes when he knew the impracticability of my supplying him with Provisions, or assistance, and after he must have received notice of the Rebels approaching towards Detroit." He expected disagreeable circumstances to arise from the defeat inasmuch as the Indians would think Great Britain had become the weaker side. In another letter written on June 17, Haldimand referred to Hamilton's "unhappy expedition" which had been "undertaken without my orders and which, however, might have been useful, had he had the prudence to retire in time."[60]

Officials at Detroit were not long in feeling the effects of the defeat. The Indians that Colonel De Peyster, commander at Michilimackinac, had been collecting to assist Hamilton in driving the Americans out of the Illinois villages quickly dispersed upon learning of the latter's surrender. Those to whom Hamilton had made promises of protection against the Americans now appeared and expected food and clothing, neither of which could be supplied them. Rumors were rife

[60] Haldimand to Hamilton and to Captain Lernoult, April 8, 1779, in *Michigan Historical Collections,* IX, 406-408; Haldimand to Lord Germain, June 7, 1779, and Haldimand to General De Bude, June 17, 1779, in *Illinois Historical Collections,* I, 445-446, 450.

at Detroit that the rebels were advancing on that post both from the direction of Fort Pitt and from Vincennes and the Illinois country.[61] Captain Lernoult made strenuous efforts to place his fortifications in a state of defense and to gather about him the Indians that could be trusted. The Wabash tribes, he learned, were either neutral or actively engaged with the Americans; the Wyandots were favorably considering an invitation to visit the Americans at Fort Pitt, and the Ottawa, Chippewa, and Potawatomi were ready to follow their example. Of the Ohio tribes, only the Shawnee continued to resist American overtures and to raid the Kentucky settlements.[62]

§   §   §   §   §   §

Meanwhile, the state of Virginia had established the County of Illinois on December 9, 1778, to include all the area north and west of the Ohio River. Following the pattern established in Kentucky, the chief officer was to be a county lieutenant, who was authorized to appoint deputies, militia

[61] Typical of the rumors circulating was one that 1,400 Bostonians and 600 Frenchmen had joined Clark and were marching towards Miamis Town with seven pieces of heavy cannon and four mortars, two weighing fifty pounds and two smaller ones. Michael Lorraine, Miamis Town, to Captain Lernoult, July 18, 1779, in *Michigan Historical Collections,* X, 342.

[62] Capt. D. Brehm to Haldimand, May 28, 1779, in *Michigan Historical Collections,* IX, 410-411; De Peyster to Haldimand, May, 1779, in *Wisconsin Historical Collections,* XI, 126, 128, 132, 134; Kellogg (ed.), *Frontier Advance on the Upper Ohio,* pp. 29-41.

Godefroy Linctot, a French trader at Cahokia who had espoused the American cause and been elected captain of the local militia and appointed Indian agent in the Illinois country, was sent by Clark to the small fort on the Illinois River, to Ouiatanon, and the Indian country in between to enlist as many French and Indians as possible and hold them in readiness for any new expedition that might be undertaken against the British. In June he wrote to Clark from Ouiatanon that he needed guns and provisions if he was to keep the Indians friendly to the American cause. On receiving word that no expedition would be undertaken that summer, the tribesmen dispersed. Linctot's movements and his influence over the Indians caused the British much uneasiness. James (ed.), *Clark Papers, 1771-1781,* pp. 341-342, 359-360, 362-363; George A. Brennan, "De Linctot, Guardian of the Frontier," *Journal* of the Illinois State Historical Society, X (1917-18), 323-366.

officers, and commissaries. The civil officers were to be elected by the citizens of the respective districts. The governor was authorized to enlist five hundred men to garrison the forts already established in the Illinois County and any others that might be necessary. George Rogers Clark was to continue in command of the Virginia and Pennsylvania troops. Governor Patrick Henry appointed John Todd county lieutenant and advised him to consult with the most intelligent and upright persons in the territory regarding the government and to inculcate in the people the value of liberty. Upon arriving at Kaskaskia in early May of 1779, Todd assured the people that Virginia "was not moved by the love of conquest" but had come to invite them to participate "in the blessings of a free and equal independence and to be governed and judged by officers who shall be placed in power by the people."[63] Todd was warmly welcomed by Clark, whom he had known in Kentucky; his arrival left Clark free to devote his full time to military affairs.

Vincennes and the surrounding area constituted one of three districts set up by Todd in the new county. Nine judges (also called justices of the peace) were elected, among whom J. M. P. Le Gras and Francis Bosseron were the best known. They also headed the list of militia officers. The court proved to be unpopular with the people; the judges were criticized for charging high fees and for granting themselves large tracts of land. Their records seem not to have been preserved.[64]

[63] William Waller Hening (ed.), The Statutes of Virginia (13 volumes, Richmond, New York and Philadelphia, 1819-23), IX, 552-555; Official Letters of the Governors of the State of Virginia, edited by H. R. McIlwaine (3 volumes, Richmond, 1926-29), I, 338-344; Clarence W. Alvord (ed.), Cahokia Records, 1778-1790 (Illinois Historical Collections, II, Springfield, 1907), pp. lii-lxiii. John Todd's Record Book and Papers are printed in Mason (ed.), Early Chicago and Illinois, pp. 289-359.

The act creating Illinois County was to be in force only for a year or until the end of the next general assembly. It was continued at that time (May, 1780) for another year or to the end of the next assembly. Hening (ed.), Statutes of Virginia, X, 303-304.

[64] Mason (ed.), Early Chicago and Illinois, pp. 295-296; Alvord (ed.), Cahokia Records, pp. lvii-lviii, lxiii; John Law, The Colonial History of

After three months of wrestling with the various problems that arose in extending American government to the new area, Todd wrote that he would stay on during the winter but wished to be relieved of the office in the spring. In addition to the ordinary administrative and judicial problems that might be expected to arise, there were those of a depreciated currency, unauthorized land grants, and undisciplined militia. The elected officials apparently expected to be paid, yet there was no provision in the law for their payment. Jefferson advised limiting the number of officials as much as possible and requiring litigants or the people at large to contribute toward their salaries. "As to the rules of decision and modes of proceeding I suppose ours can be only gradually introduced," the Governor wrote.[65]

Clark returned to Vincennes on July 1, 1779, to meet the reinforcements expected for the expedition against Detroit. Instead of the five hundred men promised by Virginia only one hundred and fifty were on hand. He still had hopes of the three hundred Col. John Bowman was to bring from Kentucky, but here again he was disappointed. Before joining Clark, Bowman had led his troops against the Shawnee towns in Ohio, and although they succeeded in burning part of their principal town and taking a quantity of plunder, they had been repulsed by the enemy and forced to retreat. As a result the

---

Vincennes . . . (Vincennes, 1858), pp. 109-120. Jean Marie Philippe Le Gras was born about 1734 in Montreal and died at Vincennes on February 8, 1788. The esteem in which he was held is attested to by the fact that all of the village attended his funeral. Records of St. Francis Xavier Church, Vincennes. Bosseron, a merchant, was fourteen years younger than Le Gras, and had lived at Kaskaskia prior to locating at Vincennes. See sketch by Janet Shaw in *Indiana Magazine of History*, XXV (1929), 204-211, and his account book for the period 1778-1779, in *ibid.*, pp. 212-241.

65 Todd to Jefferson, August 18, 1779, and Jefferson to Todd, January 28 and March 19, 1780, in Boyd (ed.), *Papers of Thomas Jefferson*, III, 70-72, 271-272, 319-321. Jefferson's second letter acknowledged one from Todd written from the Falls of the Ohio on December 22, indicating that he had decided not to stay in the Illinois country even through the winter. The following spring he was elected to represent the county of Kentucky in the Virginia legislature.

men were not willing to join another expedition immediately and Bowman was able to bring only thirty men to Vincennes. The new recruits plus the men already with Clark numbered only three hundred and fifty; many of the latter were barefoot. The supplies and clothing that Clark expected to find at Vincennes were likewise deficient. As a result the Detroit expedition had to be abandoned, at least temporarily, while Clark returned to his former tactics of maneuvering "to Keep the enemy in hot water and in suspence," in hopes they would not engage in offensive operations.[66]

Since his arrival in the Illinois country Clark had been issuing bills of credit or drafts on Virginia in exchange for supplies; these were to be paid in silver by Oliver Pollock, Virginia's agent at New Orleans, on whom the bills were drawn. However, the war in the East had prevented Virginia and the United States from providing Pollock with funds and by July, 1779, he had exhausted his credit and could not honor any more drafts presented to him for payment. The paper currency issued by the Continental Congress passed at par value in the West for a time even after it began to depreciate in the East, but after traders began bringing it in in quantities it depreciated rapidly; also, there was considerable counterfeiting of this currency including some by the British. By May of 1779 the price of provisions in the West had tripled from what they were two months earlier. Clark was thus finding it increasingly difficult to obtain the necessary supplies and provisions for his men. At this point he took the imprudent step of directing his commissary, Capt. William Shannon, to purchase the necessary stores by giving notes on himself; these Clark accepted and personally endorsed, thus making himself liable for payments for some of which he was never reimbursed. Some of the other officers likewise pledged their personal resources to obtain food and supplies.

[66] James, *Clark,* pp. 169-172; Bodley, *Clark,* pp. 140-142; James (ed.), *Clark Papers, 1771-1781,* pp. 299-300.

The other alternative, which was resorted to by some of the officers, was to order impressments of food and clothing from local residents. Sometimes the cold and hungry soldiers did not wait for impressments but helped themselves to fuel, food, and clothing wherever it could be found. Thus the soldiers and the inhabitants were brought to the point of war. Jefferson and the Virginia Assembly were not unmindful of the pleas for help from Pollock, from the western troops, and from the French inhabitants, but the state treasury was empty. Taxes and debts could only be paid with tobacco. The conduct of the war in the East had exhausted her finances as well as her fighting strength. With neither money nor credit, the government and people alike suffered at the hands of the unscrupulous who often took advantage of the situation to seek personal profit at the public expense.[67]

Before leaving Vincennes in August, 1779, to take up his headquarters at the Falls of the Ohio, Clark assigned small contingents of his veteran troops and the new recruits to the Illinois posts and Vincennes. They were ordered to begin collecting supplies for an expedition against Detroit the following year.[68]

[67] James, *Clark*, pp. 123-127, 155-157, 166-168; Bodley, *Clark*, pp. 139-140, 148-153; James, *Oliver Pollock*, pp. 138-178. Boyd (ed.), *Papers of Thomas Jefferson*, III, contain many references to the efforts of the Virginia government to meet the demands created by the war in the West. Colonel Le Gras went to Williamsburg to present his own claims and those of other Vincennes residents who had aided Clark at the time of his capture of the fort and suffered subsequently from the depredations of his troops.

For an article on the methods used by Clark in supplying his troops, see James G. Randall, "George Rogers Clark's Service of Supply," *Mississippi Valley Historical Review*, VIII (1921-22), 250-263.

[68] James (ed.), *Clark Papers, 1771-1781*, pp. cx-cxi, 354-355. After the capture of Kaskaskia Clark had ordered Capt. William Linn to return to the Falls and establish a fort on the Kentucky side of the river. With its completion, the settlers that had been left on Corn Island removed to the mainland. It was at this location, at the foot of Twelfth Street in the present Louisville, that Clark set up his headquarters in the fall of 1779 and from there he continued to carry on operations during the war. Reuben T. Durrett, *The Centenary of Louisville* . . . (Louisville, 1893), pp. 30-32n.

The failure of either Clark or the commander at Fort Pitt to march on Detroit in the summer of 1779 gave the British time to recoup their forces and place themselves in a position to take the offensive the following year, while the Americans would be forced to assume a defensive role. Then in October of 1779 an episode occurred which greatly encouraged the British and affected the decision of hundreds of tribesmen who were wavering between supporting the Americans or the British. A party of warriors intent on making another raid into Kentucky arrived at the site of Cincinnati and were preparing to cross the river when they discovered a flotilla of boats ascending the Ohio, laden with a rich store of supplies and ammunition. This was the expedition of Col. David Rogers returning from New Orleans with a large store of goods and specie which he had obtained from the Spanish. Clark had furnished a guard for the boats but they were not able to fight off the savages. In addition to the loss of men and supplies, letters written by Clark and Todd to officials in the East were captured; these revealed the true state of affairs regarding finances and the military in the West, information that was invaluable to the British in helping them win back the Indians to their side and in planning an offensive campaign.[69]

Colonel De Peyster was transferred from Michilimackinac to the command of Detroit in October, 1779, and resumed Hamilton's policy of arousing the Indians to attack the Americans, supplying them with arms and provisions and sending them out on raiding parties, often under the direction of white officers.[70]

[69] James, *Clark,* pp. 183-184; Louise Phelps Kellogg (ed.), *Frontier Retreat on the Upper Ohio, 1779-1781 (Wisconsin Historical Collections,* XXIV, Madison, 1917), pp. 16-18.

[70] See De Peyster's correspondence in J. Watts de Peyster (ed.), *Miscellanies by an Officer. Colonel Arent Schuyler de Peyster . . .* (2 parts, New York, 1888), Part II, and in *Michigan Historical Collections,* Vols. X and XI. In justice to De Peyster it should be noted that he encouraged the Indians to bring in prisoners instead of scalps and apparently treated the prisoners well. Agnes (Mahan) Wilson who was taken in one of the raids into Ken-

§ § § § § § §

The establishment of a strong fortification at the mouth of the Ohio River had been contemplated as early as 1777 by Governor Henry, and his successor, Governor Jefferson, also favored the project as did Colonel Clark. It was envisioned as becoming an important place of trade and a protection against the British capture of American supplies being brought up the Mississippi from New Orleans; also it would stop the escape of Tories and American deserters down the river. To encourage a settlement growing up around the post, grants of land would be made to prospective settlers. The choice of a site and plans for construction took definite form during the summer of 1779, but the fall and winter passed without anything being done. In the meantime, Spain had declared war against Great Britain and the British posts of Baton Rouge, Manchac, and Natchez were all in Spanish hands. Though Spain had rendered valuable assistance to the colonies in the way of supplies, it is likely that Jefferson now also was aware that the erection of the fort would serve to forestall any future claim Spain might make on the country to the east and north of the fort. Also, British preparations to take the offensive in the spring of 1780 made construction of the fort imperative.

On April 14, 1780, Clark set out from the Falls of the Ohio with a small force which proceeded to erect several blockhouses and a stockade at the chosen site on the Missis-

tucky testified that the prisoners were well treated after they reached Canada. Major De Peyster "was a great friend to the prisoners. We had no want of food." "We had a very good house to stay in." Kentucky Historical Society *Register,* LIV (1956), 313-314. Delilah (Mrs. Charles) Polke and her four children, taken from Kentucky in August of 1782, were housed at the fort in Detroit where a fifth child was born shortly after their arrival. De Peyster wrote in June, 1783, that every attention was being shown them, and when Mr. Polke came to claim his family at the close of hostilities, he was given "every assistance for their safe return" with a guide to pilot them through the wilderness. *Michigan Historical Collections,* XI, 366-367; "Polke Memoirs," *Indiana Magazine of History,* X (1914), 89.

sippi, approximately five miles below the mouth of the Ohio. When completed the troops stationed at Vincennes were withdrawn to the new post which was named Fort Jefferson. They and the rest of the new garrison ran into immediate trouble for the Chickasaw Indians contested Virginia's right to build the fort which they claimed was on their land. Some one thousand of them laid siege to it in July and were not dispersed until Clark sent reinforcements.[71]

§ § § § § § § §

By early spring of 1780 the British at Detroit had recovered sufficiently from the effects of Hamilton's defeat to be ready to take part in a comprehensive plan of conquest. From East Florida attacks were to be made on the Spanish post of New Orleans and other points on the Mississippi; from Michilimackinac an expedition would pass down the Mississippi River to St. Louis and the Illinois towns and then unite with the above expedition coming up the river; at the same time two parties would move from the southern end of Lake Michigan, one down the Illinois while a second watched the plains between the Mississippi and the Wabash; and a fourth group would move simultaneously from Detroit through northern Ohio and down the Miami River to Kentucky. Indians were to make up the greater part of the northern expeditions.[72]

The first stroke was from the north against Cahokia and then across the river to St. Louis. Clark reached the former place with reinforcements in time to help repulse the enemy

[71] James (ed.), *Clark Papers, 1771-1781*, pp. cxxi-cxxvi, 364-365, 386-387; Bodley, *Clark*, p. 143; English, *Conquest of the Country Northwest of the River Ohio*, II, 666-675. The continued threat of attack by Indians prevented a settlement growing up around the fort to provide the garrison with food; as a result some soldiers deserted for want of provisions while others subsisted on a starvation diet. The fort was evacuated on June 8, 1781. James (ed.), *Clark Papers*, p. 585.

[72] James (ed.), *Clark Papers, 1771-1781*, pp. cxxv-cxxix; James, *Clark*, p. 198; Bodley, *Clark*, pp. 160-161; English, *Conquest of the Country Northwest of the River Ohio*, II, 677-679.

there; the attack on the Spanish forces at St. Louis was more successful and several were killed and others taken prisoner before the British and the Indians retreated. Clark sent a force of three hundred and fifty French and Spanish volunteers in pursuit of the tribesmen that had participated in these attacks. They burned a number of villages but failed to meet any Indians.[73]

The British attack from the south was foiled by the Spanish governor Galvez,[74] but the expedition from Detroit proceeded on schedule with Capt. Henry Bird, a British officer, with a force of 150 whites and several hundred Indians setting out early in May. When the expedition reached the Ohio, the plan to attack the Americans at the Falls was changed (evidently because of the Indians' fear of Clark) and instead a stroke was made at Martin's and Ruddle's forts on the Licking River in eastern Kentucky, killing a number of their defenders and taking prisoner between three and four hundred including women and children. On learning of this cruel attack, Clark rushed across country from the Mississippi to launch a retaliatory raid against the Indian towns in Ohio. Upon reaching the Shawnee town of Chillicothe, the troops found it deserted but burned the cabins and destroyed the growing crops. At Piqua a few miles farther north the Indians put up a fight but could not hold the town and it too was burned and the crops in the surrounding area destroyed, after which the Americans returned to Kentucky. This expedition had the effect of relieving that county from any new raids for a year.[75]

[73] Bodley, *Clark*, pp. 161-163; James (ed.), *Clark Papers, 1771-1781*, pp. cxxix-cxxxv; James, *Clark*, pp. 202-209; Abraham P. Nasatir, "The Anglo-Spanish Frontier in the Illinois Country," *Journal* of the Illinois State Historical Society, XXI, 310-322.

[74] James, *Clark*, pp. 201-202. Galvez did not wait for the British to move against New Orleans, but instead launched an expedition against Mobile and received its surrender in February, 1780. A year later the Spanish also captured Pensacola.

[75] James, *Clark*, pp. 209-213; Bodley, *Clark*, pp. 163-167; account of the expedition into Ohio by Henry Wilson, in James (ed.), *Clark Papers, 1771-*

The expeditions that were to proceed from Lake Michigan toward Kaskaskia and Vincennes apparently were composed only of Indians and accomplished nothing. The Potawatomi refused to proceed when they heard a rumor that there were four thousand Frenchmen at Vincennes with all the artillery Admiral d'Estaing of the French Navy had taken at Jamaica. By the time it was learned that there were only twenty-three Virginians at that place the Indians had dispersed. This episode caused De Peyster to remark that no dependence could be placed on Indians without British troops to lead them, and that the Canadians at Vincennes (who apparently spread the rumor) were the worst enemies the British had.[76]

Clark had been too busy defending his earlier conquests to make any further move against Detroit, but an expedition of a different sort was being organized against that place. During the summer of 1780 Augustin de la Balme, a Frenchman who had come to America with the Marquis de La Fayette and joined the American cause, appeared in the Illinois country with the idea of enlisting the French and French-Canadians and their Indian allies for an expedition against Detroit, where it was hoped they would be joined by other French and Canadians in taking the town. Having become disillusioned by their treatment at the hands of the American soldiers, the French residents of Vincennes rallied to his cause. Seventeen of them, including Le Gras, signed a memorial to Chevalier de la Luzerne, the French minister to the United States, asking his country's help for the proposed expedition. According to one observer La Balme was received at Kaskaskia in the same manner that the Jewish people would receive the Messiah.

1781, pp. 476-484; English, *Conquest of the Country Northwest of the River Ohio*, II, 676-677, 680-687; Maude W. Lafferty, "Destruction of Ruddle's and Martin's Forts," Kentucky Historical Society *Register*, LIV (1956), 293-338; Charles G. Talbert, "Kentucky Invades Ohio—1780," Kentucky Historical Society *Register*, LII (1954), 291-300.

[76] Correspondence of De Peyster in *Michigan Historical Collections*, X, 391-392, 395-396, 398-399, 406-407.

In spite of the warm welcome accorded him in Vincennes and the Illinois villages, La Balme was able to recruit less than a hundred Frenchmen. In October they moved up the Wabash to Miamis Town where they made the mistake of raiding the stores of one or more of the British trading houses, thus incurring the anger of Indians in the vicinity. While La Balme and his little army were encamped near the town that night the Indians attacked and killed him and most of his men. The expedition did not have the backing of Virginia nor the Continental Congress, but La Balme was apparently acting under authority of the French minister to the United States. There is some evidence that General Washington had at one time spoken of the possibility of using the French in such a movement against Detroit. La Balme's defeat had the effect of destroying French influence with the Indians and further restoring some of the British prestige with the tribes that they had lost by Hamilton's defeat.[77]

[77] Alvord (ed.), *Cahokia Records, 1778-1790*, Introduction, pp. lxxxix-xciv; James (ed.), *Clark Papers, 1771-1781*, pp. 438-450; James, *Clark*, pp. 213-215; Griswold, *The Pictorial History of Fort Wayne*, I, 76-80.

Le Gras wrote Clark from Vincennes that La Balme wished to capture Beaubien (probably Charles the British agent at Miamis) and when they did not find him they plundered his store. James (ed.), *Clark Papers*, pp. 469-470. According to the report De Peyster received from one of La Balme's men who was taken prisoner, the French were at Miamis for twelve days waiting for reinforcements before plundering the trader's store. De Peyster was chagrined that the expedition was able to reach Miamis and remain there for several days without his knowing of it, and reported that if they had reached Detroit and been joined by the French there they could have given the British a "deal of trouble." The British commandant believed it was only the loss of their goods that caused the Indians to attack La Balme's party. De Peyster to Haldimand, November 16, 1780, and May 27, 1781, in *Michigan Historical Collections*, X, 448-449, 481-482.

La Balme sent a small detachment of sixteen men from Cahokia, under the command of Jean Baptiste Hamelin to raid the trading post at Fort St. Joseph. They arrived around the first of December and finding most of the Indians absent were able to capture a quantity of goods. One of the Lieuts. De Quindre hastily assembled the Indians and overtook the raiders at a place called the Petite Fort, near the present Tremont in Porter County, where they killed four, wounded two, and took seven prisoners; the other three escaped. Report of De Peyster, January 8, 1781, in *Michigan Historical Collections*, XIX, 591-592; Alvord (ed.), *Cahokia Records*, p. xcii.

The following year an expedition under Spanish leadership was more successful. Early in 1781, Spanish Capt. Don Eugenio Pourée left St. Louis with a detachment of sixty-five men to attack the small British outpost of St. Joseph on the river of that name. They were joined by an equal number of Indians and met no opposition in their march across Illinois and around the southern end of Lake Michigan. After capturing the few British traders they found at the post and confiscating their goods, they took possession of the post and the country they had traversed in the name of the King of Spain. The Spanish commandant at St. Louis sent an exaggerated account of the expedition to the home government which was used in the treaty negotiations with Great Britain as a basis for Spain's claim to the land east of the Mississippi River.[78]

§ § § § § § § § §

In the East the British were successful in 1780 in reconquering Georgia, South Carolina, and part of North Caro-

[78] Dillon, *History of Indiana,* p. 173; De Peyster to Haldimand, January 8 and May 27, 1781, in *Michigan Historical Collections,* X, 450-451, 481-482; Nasatir, "The Anglo-Spanish Frontier in the Illinois Country," *Journal* of the Illinois State Historical Society, XXI, 330-351; Lawrence Kinnaird, "The Spanish Expedition against Fort St. Joseph in 1781. A New Interpretation," *Mississippi Valley Historical Review,* XIX (1932-33), 173-191. The motive for the expedition has been subject to various interpretations by historians depending upon the sources available to them. Based on the account in the Spanish paper and the writings of American peace commissioners, it could only be explained as a diplomatic move on the part of the Spanish government to establish a claim to the territory east of the Mississippi. With the publication of additional source material, it was interpreted (1) merely as a frontier foray undertaken by the French of Cahokia and Spanish of St. Louis for plunder and revenge for La Balme's defeat; and (2) as a defensive measure on the part of Spaniards to prevent a threatened British attack upon St. Louis. With the finding of a letter written by the Spanish commandant at St. Louis shortly after the start of the expedition, Kinnaird believes the last two conflicting opinions can in a measure be reconciled: two Milwaukee chiefs desired to undertake the expedition for the sake of plunder and the St. Louis commandant consented, believing that it would aid in keeping the Indians attached to the Spanish cause, and also it would make more difficult the outfitting of any future British expedition.

lina; the only American victory occurred when the militia of the back country defeated the British at the battle of King's Mountain on October 9. As the year came to a close the American cause seemed well-nigh hopeless. France was appealed to for additional aid and responded with a substantial monetary loan as well as military assistance.

Jefferson had considered the possibility of an expedition against Detroit by Clark early in 1780 and had written General Washington to that effect, but in the face of British offensives both in the West and East, had reluctantly given up the idea. "That nest is too troublesome not to render the relinquishment of the attempt to destroy it very mortifying to us," he had written Washington on March 19.

The subject was again taken up when Clark visited Richmond in December, and on Christmas Day the Governor authorized Clark to go ahead with plans for an expedition against the British post in spite of the demands of the eastern war, hoping it would "throw the enemy under the embarrassments of a defensive war" in the West. The best time for the movement northward was believed to be in the spring between the breaking up of the ice in the Wabash (to allow transportation of men and baggage by that route) and before the ice left Lake Erie (when the British armed vessels would be free). Militia detachments from the counties of western Virginia as well as the forces already under Clark's command were to participate, making in all about two thousand men.[79]

Clark had asked for an advancement in military rank, asserting that he did not "wish to be disturbed in the execution of orders by any 'Continental Colonel'" that might be in the same area with him. There was apparently some opposition to this but on January 22, 1781, he was commissioned by the Governor "Brigadier General of the forces

---

[79] Boyd (ed.), *Papers of Thomas Jefferson,* III, 291-292, 312, 321; IV, 233-234. Jefferson's letter of December 25, 1780, is also in James (ed.), *Clark Papers, 1771-1781,* pp. 485-490.

to be embodied on an expedition westward of the Ohio."[80]

Recruiting of men and supplies proved even more difficult in 1781 than it had been three years earlier when Clark was planning his first expedition. The British invasion of Virginia prevented the militia of the western counties from joining. In some places there were men but no arms. A supply of powder was located in Philadelphia but the scarcity of wagons prevented it being sent west for several weeks. When cloth was found for clothing for the men there was no money to buy it. One hundred thousand pounds of beef collected in Kentucky for use of the troops was found to be spoiled. Although Jefferson sent an urgent request to Col. Daniel Brodhead at Fort Pitt to allow Col. John Gibson's regiment to join Clark, Brodhead refused and instead led a small force against the Delaware towns in Ohio. Brodhead also opposed allowing provisions intended for the troops at Fort Pitt to be sent down the Ohio. In spite of these and many other discouraging circumstances, Clark hoped to be able to set out by June 15, although his optimism had waned to the point that he wrote, "I doubt Sr we shall as utial be obligd to play a desperate gaim this campaign." His spirits must have sunk still lower as he delayed his departure six weeks longer and then left the upper Ohio with only about four hundred men. He still hoped to "make some stroke among the Indians," and predicted "dreadful consequences" if nothing were done.[81]

80 Boyd (ed.), *Papers of Thomas Jefferson*, IV, 424; James (ed.), *Clark Papers*, pp. 500-501. Boyd states that Clark had desired a continental commission, but established rules did not permit the granting of such a commission to officers of state regiments.

81 See the correspondence of Clark and others during this period in Boyd (ed.), *Papers of Thomas Jefferson*, especially IV, 597-598, 598-599, 653; VI, 11-12, 40, 69; James (ed.), *Clark Papers, 1771-1781*, pp. 494-580 *passim*. Jefferson had resigned the governorship on June 3, 1781, due to criticism of his conduct of the war then being fought on Virginia soil. In place of Jefferson's support, Clark now had to contend with a resolution of the Virginia Assembly authorizing the new governor, Thomas Nelson, "to put a stop to the Expedition lately ordered against Detroit." Bodley, *Clark*, p. 174. Rumors of a possible

Col. Archibald Lochry with 107 men recruited largely in Westmoreland County, Pennsylvania, set out late in July to join Clark. The latter had waited for him at Wheeling for several days, then moved on down the Ohio. Lochry sent a captain and seven men on ahead to catch up with Clark, but they were captured by the Indians along with a letter revealing the whereabouts of the main party. The Indians waited for them a few miles below the mouth of the Great Miami, where on August 24 they attacked and killed nearly half of the men including their leader and took the others captive.[82] The loss of Lochry's reinforcements proved to be the finishing blow to Clark's hope of a successful campaign against Detroit as well as any hope of an immediate campaign against the Indians.

While disaster was striking in the West, the war in the East was taking a turn for the better. After invading western Virginia in May, Cornwallis had gradually moved toward the coast and by August had settled down with his army at Yorktown. Admiral De Grasse arrived in Chesapeake Bay on August 31 with a powerful squadron of the French fleet from which additional troops were disembarked to join Lafayette's forces in blocking Cornwallis' escape. General Washington quickly moved his forces south to join those of Lafayette and together they bombarded the British. With the French fleet preventing any help from the British Navy,

invasion of the Ohio country by Brodhead and Clark made the Indians in that quarter very uneasy during the summer of 1781, but Haldimand reassured the Detroit commandant that such a movement was not likely. *Michigan Historical Collections,* X, 478-479, 490-491.

[82] Charles Martindale, *Loughery's Defeat and Pigeon Roost Massacre* (Indiana Historical Society *Publications,* II, No. 4, Indianapolis, 1888), pp. 106-127; James (ed.), *Clark Papers, 1771-1781,* pp. 583-584, 588-589; Bodley, *Clark,* pp. 175-176. The Indians were under the leadership of the noted Mohawk chief, Joseph Brant, who had received intelligence of the expedition and was laying in wait. Though the British were jubilant at the news of Brant's success, they were disappointed that another party of Indians under Alexander McKee, that were on the Ohio at the same time, had not taken advantage of Clark's weakness and attacked him, thus ending any future threat from that quarter. *Michigan Historical Collections,* X, 510-548 *passim.*

Cornwallis was forced to surrender on October 19, thus bringing to an end the fighting in that sector. But during the remainder of 1781 and most of the next year the control of the West hung in the balance. From his headquarters at the Falls Clark would continue to exercise a minimal control over the Illinois posts and try to defend the Kentucky settlements, while the British at Detroit would strive to hold the friendship of the Indians and regain control of the Illinois country.

During 1780 and 1781 conditions had gone from bad to worse in the area north of the Ohio over which Virginia had extended her jurisdiction. Colonel Todd, the county lieutenant, had returned to Kentucky leaving affairs in the hands of his deputy, Richard Winston, with instructions to avoid coming into conflict with the military establishment. But under the circumstances, disagreements were unavoidable. Although the act creating the county of Illinois expired in 1781, Winston apparently continued to carry out the duties of the office of county lieutenant and during his absence in 1783 appointed Timothé de Monbreun to act in his place.[83]

Morale among Clark's troops reached a very low ebb: desertions were frequent; those whose terms of enlistment expired were unwilling to re-enlist; officers were accused, often by fellow officers, of misuse of funds and supplies as well as of their authority. After receiving complaints from various correspondents, Clark must have wondered whom he could trust. He determined to learn the truth about the charges and see that those who were guilty were punished. "I have long Since determined to Conduct myself with a particular Regour towards every person under me, they Shall feel the Stings of Remorce (if Capable) or the Sweats of publick applause either as they demean themselves," he wrote Governor Jefferson on March 27, 1781.[84]

---

[83] For Winston's difficulties, see the Index in Alvord (ed.), *Kaskaskia Records*, under his name and that of Todd. The commission he gave De Monbreun is printed in *ibid.*, pp. 320-322.

[84] James (ed.), *Clark Papers, 1771-1781*, pp. 516-517.

When later that year the Virginia Assembly appointed four commissioners to investigate the conduct of all officers, agents, contractors, and other persons who had disbursed public money in the West, Clark interpreted the act as a reflection upon himself and his conduct of public affairs and sent in his resignation but it was not accepted.[85]

§ § § § § § § § § §

Clark had tried to give Vincennes some measure of military protection after its capture from the British. When the Virginia troops were withdrawn in the spring of 1780 and sent to Fort Jefferson, Francis Bosseron was placed in charge of Fort Patrick Henry with authority to raise a militia company which was to be paid and supplied rations by Virginia.[86]

By February, 1781, Capt. John Bailey and twenty-five of Clark's troops had returned to the Wabash fort but conditions were such that on August 6 Bailey wrote Clark that he could not keep his garrison much longer without some speedy relief, his men having been on half rations for two weeks. Help was not forthcoming and the troops were

[85] The Journal of the commissioners is in James A. James (ed.), *George Rogers Clark Papers, 1781-1784* (*Illinois Historical Collections*, XIX, Springfield, 1926), pp. 290 ff. Clark's accounts with Virginia are in *ibid.*, pp. 254-289. These accounts reveal the meticulous fashion in which Clark tried to keep a record of every purchase and every service rendered for him in his years of command. In view of the fact that he was operating in a wilderness much of the time, paper was difficult to find for the keeping of records and for correspondence, and no system of accounting had been set up for him to follow, the records show Clark's deep sense of responsibility for the administration of public funds.

[86] John Todd to Jefferson, June 2, 1780, in James (ed.), *Clark Papers, 1771-1781*, p. 422. To prevent the troops being evacuated at an earlier date because of a lack of supplies and provisions, Clark sent Bosseron an order on Col. John Montgomery for fifteen hundred livres of peltry to defray expenses for a few weeks. Clark to Bosseron, February 28, 1780, printed in *Indiana Magazine of History*, XXV (1929), 207-208, from the original letter in Indiana State Library.

shortly withdrawn.[87] The militia probably took over complete control again to guard against any surprise attack by the British or by Indians friendly to them. Clark kept in constant touch with happenings at the village through J. M. P. Le Gras who signed his communications as "Lieutenant Colonel in Command." Clark also corresponded with Lieut. Valentine Thomas Dalton who had been in charge of artillery at the fort in 1779; he was taken prisoner in 1782 and sent to Quebec.[88]

In the meantime, the French inhabitants of Vincennes set forth their grievances against the military establishment in a memorial to the governor of Virginia on June 30, 1781. They told how they had been forced to take depreciated currency in payment for the provisions and goods furnished Clark's men, and how in recent months their property had been taken without compensation. Their cows and hogs had been killed in the fields, flour taken from their mills, and corn from their granaries; their very lives had been threatened if they tried to resist such seizures. In addition, they complained that the soldiers had carried off all their artillery and ammunition, leaving them with nothing to defend themselves. The memorial was signed by the principal

[87] Robert George to George Slaughter, February 15, 1781, and Bailey to Slaughter, August 6, 1781, in James (ed.), *Clark Papers, 1771-1781*, pp. 506, 581. Clark informed the county lieutenants of Kentucky on September 5, 1781, that the evacuation of the troops would shortly take place. *Ibid.*, p. 597. Le Gras wrote Clark on December 31, 1782, that he had sold the barracks of the fort "which the Americans, French and Indians have reduced to ruins." James (ed.), *Clark Papers, 1781-1784*, p. 176.

[88] See *Clark Papers, 1781-1784*, pp. 37-38, 83-85, 100-101, 145-147, 175-176, for Clark's correspondence with residents of Vincennes. In a letter from Quebec (*ibid.*, pp. 145-147) Dalton gave information on Ouiatanon and Miamis Town at the time he passed through those places in July, 1782. At the former John Baptiste had charge of the British store, while at the latter a Mr. Bawbee was in charge of the store and a Mr. Truchey, formerly employed by Mr. Le Gras, was working for him. He wrote of the "compact Picket Fort on the Bank of the River." According to a letter of De Peyster, Dalton was commandant at Vincennes. *Michigan Historical Collections*, XX, 54-55.

citizens, including Francis Bosseron, Pierre Gamelin, and J. M. P. Le Gras.[89]

Kentucky had been receiving a flood of new immigrants during 1780 and 1781 in spite of the almost constant state of alarm under which the settlements labored. The population had increased to such an extent that the county of Kentucky was divided in November, 1780, into the three counties of Fayette, Jefferson, and Lincoln. Being principally interested in locating and gaining a title to the best land possible, the new settlers sometimes failed to see the necessity of uniting their efforts for defense against their common enemy, the Indians; instead, those in each county wanted the best possible protection for their own area. Only a few leaders like Clark could see the need of a defense system that was calculated to be the best for all the settlements.

Following the capture and massacre of most of Lochry's company, Clark called together the county lieutenants of the three Kentucky counties and the principal field officers to consult on the best measures of future defense. The council advised against undertaking any offensive operation and suggested instead the establishment of more garrisons on the south side of the Ohio River. The members favored a strong fort at the mouth of the Kentucky River, but General Clark thought the Falls of the Ohio a better location. His preference prevailed and Fort Nelson was built in 1782 within the bounds of the present city of Louisville. Clark also suggested the construction and arming of boats to patrol the Ohio; with a reasonable number of these he thought any

[89] The memorial is printed in James (ed.), *Clark Papers, 1771-1781*, pp. 430-433. The commissioners appointed to settle western accounts denied reports that were circulating at Vincennes that the citizens were to be ignored and their claims not considered. However, they did balk at the high prices charged at that place. Clark explained that the merchants had been cut off in all directions from obtaining fresh supplies, and that only about one fourth of the population engaged in farming, producing only a sufficiency to supply the inhabitants. *Clark Papers, 1781-1784*, pp. 243-244, 376-377.

future invasion from the north could be halted. Not receiving any aid from Virginia, he proceeded to go ahead with the construction of four armed galleys; at least one of these was completed by July, 1782, but not in time to prevent an attack on Estill's Station near the present Richmond by a small party of Indians in May of that year. Three months later several hundred Indians under the leadership of Simon Girty crossed the Ohio and attacked Bryan's Station near Lexington but withdrew toward the north after losing several of their number. A force of approximately two hundred militia under the leadership of some of Kentucky's most prominent citizens pursued them only to be defeated in a disastrous battle at the Blue Licks which cost the lives of over one third of their number, including Col. John Todd.[90] This disaster aroused the citizens to action and General Clark assumed command of a force of one thousand which marched north in November, 1782, against the Indian towns on the Miami River where they destroyed several villages and captured considerable plunder but failed to meet the enemy.[91] With this expedition the western phase of the Revolution came to an end. A provisional treaty of peace with Great Britain was signed on November 30, 1782, and a cessation of hostilities was to take place upon ratification of the preliminary articles by the two countries.

Peace negotiations were complicated because France and Spain with their interests were involved in addition to the United States and Great Britain. The American peace commissioners were instructed by Congress not to negotiate a

---

[90] Bodley, *Clark,* pp. 177-187, 199-209.

[91] Correspondence between Clark and Governor Benjamin Harrison, in James (ed.), *Clark Papers, 1781-1784,* pp. 157-158, 170-172, 181-182; Charles G. Talbert, "Kentucky Invades Ohio—1782," Kentucky Historical Society *Register,* LIII (1955), 288-297. Governor Harrison was at first critical of the invasion, which was undertaken without consulting him, but after learning of its success he congratulated Clark and commented that it would "teach the Indians to dread us, and convince them that we will not tamely submit to their depredations."

peace with Great Britain without the knowledge or concur-
rence of their ally, France, but it proved to be to the best
interests of the United States to disregard this mandate. In
the end the different countries signed separate definitive
treaties at Versailles and Paris on September 3, 1783. The
principal terms of the Anglo-American treaty were: recognition of American independence; evacuation of British troops
from United States soil; and a guarantee against legal obstacles in collecting pre-war debts due British creditors. The
boundaries of the United States were to be the Mississippi
River on the west, the St. Lawrence River and the Great
Lakes on the north, and East and West Florida on the south.
In the treaty between Spain and Great Britain, all of Florida
was given to Spain.

Whether Clark's conquest of the British posts north of the
Ohio had any bearing on the fact that the Old Northwest
(the area between the Mississippi and the Alleghenies, the
Great Lakes and the Ohio) became a part of the United
States by the terms of the treaty of 1783 is still a moot
question among historians. Of those writing in the nineteenth
century who gave Clark and his men credit for the extension
of American boundaries to the Mississippi were John Fiske,
Lyman C. Draper, John Law, John B. Dillon, John Reynolds,
Jacob P. Dunn, and William H. English. Reuben G. Thwaites
thought England's jealousy of Spain and the shrewd diplomacy of the American peace commissioners were equally if not
more important in the peace negotiations, while Henry Pirtle
of Kentucky was also somewhat restrained on the importance
of Clark's expedition.[92]

With the coming of the twentieth century, historians have
been more divided on the subject. Consul W. Butterfield,

---

[92] English, *Conquest of the Country Northwest of the River Ohio,* II, 909-
922; Consul W. Butterfield, *History of George Rogers Clark's Conquest of the
Illinois and the Wabash Towns 1778-1779* (Columbus, Ohio, 1904), 790-797;
James A. James, "The Old Northwest: Conquest or Gift?" *Indiana Magazine
of History,* XXX (1934), 10-15.

writing in 1904, expressed the view that while it was "most fortunate that the Virginia troops were in possession of the Illinois and the Wabash at the close of the war, . . . there is no reason to think that the Clark conquest, separate and apart from the colonial titles, ever would have given the United States the Great West. . . . It is highly probable that the British ministry, seeing that the West would go to Spain if not to the United States, preferred to give it the latter direction." The following year Claude H. Van Tyne expressed the view that the capture of the British posts was sufficient to insure an American hold upon the region until Clark's military prowess could be "followed up by the diplomatic triumph of Jay."[93]

Clarence W. Alvord, writing in 1916, took the position that while the American peace commissioners may have felt that their position in claiming the West was somewhat strengthened by the knowledge of Clark's success, yet it was unbelievable that they would have demanded less, even had he failed. In Alvord's opinion the basis for the success of American diplomacy lay in the liberal principles held by Lord Shelburne, the British minister in charge of the negotiations.[94]

Clark's principal biographers—Temple Bodley, James A. James, and Frederick Palmer—writing in the 1920s took the position that American possession of the area at the close of the war was the determining factor in the decision to give the territory to the United States. In Bodley's opinion all the diplomatic talk that went on during the peace negotiations regarding legal and moral rights, charter grants and repeals, royal proclamations, and other argumentative "make weights" was merely superficial and that the real question was whether Shelburne would continue the war to reconquer the western country or whether American negotiators would give it up

[93] Butterfield, *History of George Rogers Clark's Conquest,* pp. 795-796; Van Tyne, *The American Revolution, 1776-1783 (The American Nation: A History,* IX, New York and London, 1905), p. 284.

[94] Clarence W. Alvord, "Virginia and the West: An Interpretation," *Mississippi Valley Historical Review,* III (1916-17), 34-38.

to get peace. Since Great Britain was financially exhausted and unable to continue the war, Shelburne conceded to American demands.[95]

James A. James also believed that Clark unquestionably was in military control of the greater part of the Northwest when negotiations for peace were begun, and that this was the foundation for the demand that the Great Lakes and the Mississippi were to constitute the boundaries. That indisputable right to this territory had been asserted as an offset to Spanish claims after their so-called conquest in 1780, is borne out in a letter prepared by a committee of Congress for American ministers in France and Spain.[96]

Samuel F. Bemis, diplomatic historian, took the opposite view and wrote in 1935 that any effect Clark's victories of 1778-79 might have had was wiped out by the fact that by 1782 the greater part of the territory north of the Ohio was more subject to the influence of British garrisons at Detroit and Michilimackinac than to Clark at Fort Nelson.[97]

Likewise, A. L. Burt in his monograph on British-American relations from the Revolution to the War of 1812, gave little credit to Clark. Although Great Britain had an excellent title to the country north of the Ohio, he maintained that she gave in to American demands because the people were sick of the war and in no mood to continue it. The cost of keeping military posts and garrisons in the West were fresh in their minds; also by ceding the land she would draw the United States away from her enemy France and lay a foundation for a lasting peace with the new republic. Though the Montreal merchants were in a panic over the thought of losing the fur trade, the British leaders reasoned

95 Bodley, *Clark,* pp. 240-253.

96 James, "The Old Northwest: Gift or Conquest?" *loc. cit.,* XXX, 10-15; James, *Oliver Pollock,* pp. 242-249. Regarding the Spanish claim, see also "The Rayneval Memorandum of 1782," edited by Florence G. Watts, *Indiana Magazine of History,* XXXVIII (1942), 167-207.

97 Samuel F. Bemis, *The Diplomacy of the American Revolution* (New York and London, 1935), p. 219n.

that regardless of boundaries the furs would still find their way to London and, in the absence of competing American industries, England would still have the opportunity of supplying the natives with manufactured goods.[98]

Dexter Perkins and Glyndon G. Van Deusen in their recent history of the United States return to the earlier view that Clark's expedition "strengthened the American claim to what was to become known as the Old Northwest."[99]

Though historians may disagree on the significance of Clark's expedition in the treaty negotiations, all have praise for the sagacity, valor, perseverance, and patriotism displayed by the Virginia leader and his men.

The Indians were not a party to the Anglo-American treaty and for them it would mark only a lull in hostilities while they waited to learn what the new turn of events would bring.

[98] Alfred L. Burt, *The United States, Great Britain, and British North America from the Revolution to . . . 1812* (Yale University Press, 1940), pp. 32-37.

[99] Perkins and Van Deusen, *The United States of America: A History* (2 volumes, New York, 1962), I, 163.

CHAPTER VII

AMERICAN BEGINNINGS AFTER THE REVOLUTION

It was over a year after the surrender of Cornwallis that the provisional treaty of peace between Great Britain and the United States was signed on November 30, 1782. The treaty recognized the independence of the United States and defined its boundaries as the Mississippi River on the west, East and West Florida on the south, and roughly the northern boundaries of Maine and New York and a line through the middle of lakes Ontario, Erie, Huron, and Superior on the north. Great Britain was to withdraw her armies and garrisons from United States territory; no impediments were to be placed in the way of collecting debts due in America to British subjects; and Congress would recommend to the states that they deal leniently with the Tories in the restoration of their confiscated estates.[1] No mention was made of the Indians even though they were in possession of the land between the Appalachians and the Mississippi and considered it as their own. The above provisions became a part of the definitive treaty concluded between Great Britain and the United States at Paris on September 3, 1783, and

[1] For the terms of the treaty, see William M. Malloy (comp.), *Treaties, Conventions, International Acts, Protocols and Agreements between the United States of America and Other Powers, 1776-1909* (2 volumes, Washington, D. C., 1910), I, 580-583. Great Britain signed separate provisional treaties with France and Spain, with whom she was also at war, in January, 1783. Spain regained East and West Florida, which she had held prior to 1763. All of the country west of the Mississippi to the Pacific coast was already Spanish territory by the treaty of 1763. With the lower Mississippi thus in Spanish hands, that provision of the Anglo-American treaty which stated that the navigation of the Mississippi was to remain open to subjects of both Great Britain and citizens of the United States was nullified.

was ratified by the Congress of the Confederation on January 14, 1784.[2]

Though historians are not agreed as to the importance of George Rogers Clark's victories at Kaskaskia and Vincennes in 1778-79 in determining the boundaries of the United States at the end of the war, these victories did give the Americans a foothold in the Illinois country.[3] Virginia had tried to extend a modicum of control over the area in 1779 by setting up the county of Illinois with John Todd as county lieutenant. He in turn had set up courts in the French villages. When Todd returned to Kentucky, his deputy, Richard Winston, was left in charge, and he in turn appointed Timothé de Monbreun in January, 1783.[4] A year later Virginia ceded her western lands to the United States, thus ending her responsibility for civil and military government in the Illinois country.

When British officials in Quebec received a copy of the provisional treaty of peace in late April, 1783, and learned that the land south of the Great Lakes had been ceded to the United States, they were shocked and felt considerable concern over the effect this news would have on the Indians. Governor Frederick Haldimand immediately sent word of the treaty to Brig. Gen. Allan Maclean at Niagara who forwarded the news on to Colonel De Peyster at Detroit where it was received on May 6. For the past several months De Peyster had been trying to restrain the Indians from committing any further depredations on the American settlers that might affect the pending negotiations. He now dispatched Charles Beaubien to the Miami and Wabash tribes with the news that the war was over.[5]

---

[2] *Ibid.,* I, 586-590.

[3] See above, pp. 233-236.

[4] Alvord (ed.), *Cahokia Records, 1778-1790,* pp. lii-lviiin, lxxix, lxxxvi. The provisions of the act creating the county of Illinois were to expire at the end of 1782, so there was no legal basis for De Monbreun's appointment.

[5] Burt, *The United States, Great Britain, and British North America,* p. 87; *Michigan Historical Collections,* XI, 336, 342, 359-360, 361, 362-364. Haldimand's letter to Maclean stated only that he had received His Majesty's Proc-

The Americans also took steps to inform the Indians of the peace treaty. The Congress of the Confederation officially proclaimed an end to hostilities on April 11, 1783, and the following month Ephraim Douglass and John Bull were sent to carry the news to the Indians. The message that they carried told only of the boundary drawn between the United States and Canada, and that the Indians living south of that line should cease hostilities and look to the United States as their "father." The forts within the United States would be evacuated by the British, and treaties of peace and friendship would be entered into with the tribes. Douglass reached Detroit early in July but was prevented by De Peyster from calling the Indians together to deliver his message although he was treated with the utmost courtesy. Bull met with similar treatment in his efforts at Oswego and Niagara.[6] Later in the summer a representative sent to confer with the governor of Canada on a plan for the transfer of the British posts was informed that as yet no instructions had been received from London regarding the transfer.[7] These posts in-

lamation for a cessation of arms in consequence of the preliminary articles of peace having been signed. However, the text of the treaty was printed in the Philadelphia *Pennsylvania Gazette* on April 16 and no doubt in other newspapers about that time; it seems likely that the Canadian governor would have received a copy by the end of the month. De Peyster was still in the dark six weeks later as to the terms of the treaty: "I have nothing more than the Kings Proclamation from Authority," he wrote on June 18, but "everything that is bad is spread through the Indian country." *Michigan Historical Collections,* XI, 368-369.

[6] Clarence M. Burton, "Ephraim Douglass and His Times. A Fragment of History," *Magazine of History,* III, Extra No. 10 (New York, 1910); Reginald Horsman, *Matthew Elliott, British Indian Agent* (Wayne University Press, 1964), pp. 41-43; *Michigan Historical Collections,* XI, 375, 378-379.

[7] Haldimand to George Washington, August 11, 1783, in *Michigan Historical Collections,* XX, 165-166; Haldimand to Lord North, August 6, 1783, in *ibid.,* XI, 378-379; Burt, *The United States, Great Britain, and British North America,* pp. 91-92. The Governor was still using this excuse a year later when William Hull was sent to Canada to ascertain the precise time when each of the posts occupied by British troops would be turned over to the Americans. Haldimand to Hull, July 13, 1784, in *Michigan Historical Collections,* XX, 238-239.

cluded Michilimackinac, Detroit, Sandusky, Presque Isle, Niagara, and Oswego.

Meanwhile, rumors of the peace terms had infiltrated the Indian villages and British officials at the various posts were beset with tribesmen wanting to know the truth. At Detroit a delegation of Wea and Kickapoo requested a meeting with De Peyster on June 28 in which they expressed their uneasiness over the rumors: "We are informed that instead of prosecuting the war, we are to give up our lands to the Enemy, . . . in endeavouring to assist you it seems we have wrought our own ruin," the Wea spokesman declared. Though their services were no longer needed, they expressed the hope that the British would continue to supply their wants. De Peyster wrote that "whole villages" of other nations were on their way to Detroit, "impatient to know what is to become of them and their lands" and to request a supply of goods. Without any instructions on how to answer the Indians and having no goods on hand to give them, the Detroit commandant feared trouble. He hoped that Sir John Johnson, who had been appointed superintendent of Indian affairs for Canada, would soon arrive and hold an Indian council. "The Hatchet must be buried in form, a ceremony not to be performed without expence," he wrote. General Maclean at Niagara told the Indians not to pay any attention to stories from "bad birds," only to listen to the messages delivered by the British. At present, the only message they had was that "Peace was made."[8] Representatives of the Six Nations went directly to the governor of Canada who assured them that the British had not deserted them; they would continue to supply them with presents and to trade with them, but they should come to terms with the

8 De Peyster to Haldimand, June 28, 1783, enclosing minutes of Indian Council, and De Peyster to Maclean, June 18, 1783, in *Michigan Historical Collections,* XI, 370-372; XX, 128; Maclean to De Peyster, June 26, 1783, in *ibid.,* XX, 130.

Americans and cease their raids against the settlements. If they desired they might come to Canada to live.[9]

Later in the summer, Johnson met with representatives of the Six Nations at Niagara and assured them that the King still considered them his faithful allies and his children; they were not to believe that the treaty would deprive them of the "right of soil" established in 1768 by the Treaty of Fort Stanwix (i.e., the Ohio River as the boundary between the settlers and the Indians); nor did he believe that the United States would try to deprive them of any part of their country under the pretense of having conquered it. He advised the Indians to bear their losses with fortitude, forgiving and forgetting what was past, and to look forward to the blessings of peace. Alexander McKee, deputy Indian agent, presented Johnson's message to the western Indians at Sandusky in a council held the last of August and first of September. In each instance the message was accompanied by the distribution of presents.[10]

The British interpretation of what the attitude of the United States would be toward the Indians proved to be wrong. On October 15, 1783, the Continental Congress adopted a report made by a special committee which had been studying the development of an Indian policy; the committee

---

9 Burt, *The United States, Great Britain, and British North America*, p. 88.

10 Transactions with Indians at Sandusky, August 26 to September 8, 1783, in *Michigan Historical Collections*, XX, 174-183; Alexander McKee's report to De Peyster on Sandusky Council, in *ibid.*, XI, 385-386; Burt, *The United States Great Britain, and British North America*, pp. 89-91. De Peyster was transferred to Niagara in the fall of 1783 and Jehu Hay was made commandant at Detroit. The latter had formerly served under Henry Hamilton at that place, had accompanied him to Vincennes in 1778 where he was taken prisoner, and returned to Canada in 1782. Due to various circumstances the change of commandants was not made until the summer of 1784. Hay immediately ran into difficulty over the distribution of presents to the Indians. John Johnson and his deputies were supposed to have the entire management of Indian affairs, but Hay contended this method was unsatisfactory. See his correspondence in *Michigan Historical Collections*, XI, 396-397, 399, 444-445; XXIV, 17-20.

took the position that the red men were a defeated nation, that they had no right to the soil on which they lived. Recognizing that it would be difficult to expel them completely from the area east of the Mississippi, they proposed that for the present they be allowed to remain west of a boundary formed by the Great Miami, Mad, and Maumee rivers, thus giving the United States the greater part of the present state of Ohio. Though the committee believed the Indians could have no "reasonable objections to the American government's appropriating these lands without payment, some compensation might be offered if it was deemed necessary to avoid the risk of renewing the war." In their unrealistic thinking, the Congressmen believed they could dictate the terms in one general treaty with all the tribes claiming land north of the Ohio. To them the land west of the mountains was a future source of income which would help the new government out of its dire financial straits; those portions not already pledged as a reward for military service could be sold to prospective settlers.[11]

Congress moved slowly to implement the report on Indian affairs and it was not until March 4, 1784, that five commissioners were appointed to negotiate with the tribes north of the Ohio. Then two of the original appointees declined to serve and others had to be appointed. The five who accepted were Richard Butler, George Rogers Clark, Benjamin Lincoln, Arthur Lee, and Oliver Wolcott; only three served at a time.

In the meantime, Congress reversed its plan of one treaty and directed the commissioners "to treat with the several nations of Indians collectively or at different times and places as they shall find most conducive to the Interest of the United

[11] Burt, *op. cit.*, pp. 85-87; Reginald Horsman, *Expansion and American Indian Policy, 1783-1812* (Michigan State University Press, 1967), pp. 10-15; Walter H. Mohr, *Federal Indian Relations, 1774-1788* (Philadelphia, 1933), pp. 100-104. The committee report is printed in *Journals of the Continental Congress,* XXV, 681-686. It dealt only with Indian affairs in the northern and middle departments.

States." The commissioners first met representatives of the Six Nations at Fort Stanwix, New York, in October, 1784, where terms of a treaty were dictated in which these nations ceded a small tract of land in western New York and all that part of Pennsylvania north and west of the Indian boundary established by the first Treaty of Fort Stanwix in 1768 (about one fourth the area of the state). They also relinquished their claim to land west and north of the Ohio River.[12]

Two of the commissioners, Arthur Lee and Richard Butler, then traveled to Fort McIntosh, on the Ohio below Fort Pitt, where they were joined by Clark for a meeting with representatives of the Wyandot, Delaware, Ottawa, and Chippewa tribes in January, 1785. Here again the claims of the Indians were brushed aside and a forced consent was obtained to lands in the southeastern part of the present state of Ohio, and to lands around the military and trading posts of Detroit and Sandusky in the Indian country.[13] The Indians were given the right to punish intruders settling on their lands. The Shawnee had refused to come to the conference table and before any security could be accorded to frontier settlements it would be necessary to negotiate with them. Representatives of this tribe and of the Wyandot, Miami, Chippewa, Ottawa, and those on the Wabash were invited to meet the treaty commissioners in the fall of 1785, but only representatives of the Shawnee gathered at Fort Finney at the mouth of the Great Miami in January, 1786.

---

[12] Butler, Lee, and Wolcott were the commissioners at Fort Stanwix. *Journals of the Continental Congress,* XXVI, 124-125, 238, 282; Horsman, *Expansion and American Indian Policy,* pp. 16-20; Mohr, *Federal Indian Relations,* pp. 108-110; Downes, *Council Fires on the Upper Ohio,* pp. 289-292; William L. Stone, *The Life of Joseph Brant—Thayendanegea, including the Border Wars of the American Revolution* . . . (2 volumes, New York, 1838), II, 243-247. For the text of the treaty, see Charles J. Kappler (ed.), *Indian Affairs. Laws and Treaties* (2 volumes, Washington, D. C., 1903), II, 3-4.

[13] Kappler (ed.), *Indian Affairs. Laws and Treaties,* II, 4-5; Horsman, *Expansion and American Indian Policy,* pp. 20-21; Downes, *Council Fires on the Upper Ohio,* pp. 292-295; Mohr, *Federal Indian Relations,* pp. 111-114.

William Clark, cousin of George Rogers, who was sent to invite the Wabash Indians to the treaty, held a council at Vincennes on September 23-24 with the chiefs of the Vincennes Piankashaw, the Vermilion Piankashaw, Kickapoo, Ouiatanon, and Picts or Miami. The Deaf Man, chief of the Vermilion Piankashaw, acting as spokesman for all those present, told Clark the lower Wabash tribes had listened to the French and Americans and had kept quiet, but above the Vermilion towns there were "some bad people whose Hearts he could not answer for." He promised to see that the invitation was delivered to them. Clark closed his official report of the council with some unofficial remarks to the effect that the Indians appeared careless and unconcerned about the invitation and complained that the lateness of the season and their hunting time coming on would make it impossible for them to attend the treaty.[14] George Rogers Clark was again one of the commissioners at the Fort Finney negotiations along with Butler and Samuel H. Parsons, who had replaced Lee. Their attitude toward the Indians was almost one of contempt, but in the end the Indians present signed a treaty giving up their claim to land east of the Great Miami.[15]

[14] The report is in the Papers of the Continental Congress, National Archives, Washington, D. C., and a copy is in the Indiana State Library. The message carried by Clark was probably the same as that sent by the treaty commissioners to the Potawatomi, Chippewa, Ottawa, and Wyandot, dated July 31 and August 3, 1785, printed in *Michigan Historical Collections*, XXIV, 21-22. These tribes held a council at Detroit on September 20 and sent word to the commissioners that they would not be ready to meet them before the following spring. *Ibid.*, XI, 465-467.

[15] Horsman, *Expansion and American Indian Policy*, pp. 21-23; Mohr, *Federal Indian Relations*, pp. 114-116; Bodley, *Clark*, pp. 268-275; Downes, *Council Fires on the Upper Ohio*, pp. 295-297; Kappler (ed.), *Indian Affairs. Laws and Treaties*, II, 12-13. Clark had led expeditions against the warlike Shawnee on more than one occasion, and they were implacable enemies. The following incident was reported at the treaty negotiations: after a particularly boisterous speech by a Shawnee spokesman, he threw a string of black and white wampum on the council table, signifying that they were prepared for either peace or war. Without moving, Clark took his cane and pushed the

Thus after two years of negotiations and three treaties, the United States commissioners felt that they had accomplished all that it was possible to accomplish through negotiation but were quick to point out that there was much hostility among certain tribes which could easily spread to those nations with whom the country had made peace.[16] In the first place the action of tribesmen who had signed the treaties was not acknowledged by their respective tribes; and, secondly, the coercive methods used to achieve the consent of those Indians who did come to the peace table aroused such a storm of protest and resentment that the Indians refused to recognize the treaties and wished to reopen the whole issue. The first steps toward forming a confederacy of the eastern and western tribes had been taken in 1785 under the leadership of Joseph Brant and efforts toward unity had continued the following year. A grand council was called to meet near Detroit in November-December, 1786, at which all the tribes northwest of the Ohio were represented. An address to Congress was agreed upon in which the Indians professed a desire for friendship and peace with the United States. The earlier treaties could not be accepted because they were not concluded with the confederacy as a whole; the Indians were willing to renew negotiations but only on the basis of the Ohio River being the boundary between themselves and the whites.[17]

wampum on the floor. Angered by this affront, the Indians sprang to their feet as if ready to attack, whereupon Clark calmly rose to his feet and after stomping on the wampum ordered the Indians from the hall. When they returned the next day, they were more docile. English, *Conquest of the Country Northwest of the River Ohio*, II, 791-794; "Military Journal of Major Ebenezer Denny," *Memoirs* of the Historical Society of Pennsylvania, VII (Philadelphia, 1860), 268-277.

[16] See the report of Commissioners Butler and Parsons to the Congress, June 19, 1786, which was used as a basis for the report of that body. Copy of former in Indiana State Library; the latter is in *Journals of the Continental Congress*, XXX, 349-350.

[17] Stone, *The Life of Joseph Brant*, II, 264 ff. The address is printed in *Michigan Historical Collections*, XI, 467-470, and in *American State Papers*.

In the meantime the Indians resumed their raids on Kentucky settlements and on immigrants traveling on the Ohio River. They were no doubt emboldened by the fact that the British were still holding their trading posts on the American side of the boundary. Their retention up to this time apparently was not altogether for economic reasons (a desire to keep the fur trade), but from a belief that the policy which the United States was pursuing toward the Indians was not going to work and sooner or later there would be war. After the failure to obtain in 1783 and again in 1784 any satisfaction from the Governor of Canada as to when the British posts would be evacuated, the discussion concerning them had been transferred to London in 1785 where John Adams, the American minister, had been instructed to press for the surrender of the posts. His efforts also proved fruitless, the British excuse being that the United States had failed to fulfill her treaty obligations in regard to the treatment of the Tories and the collection of prewar debts owed by Americans.[18]

Congress was sufficiently pleased with the results of the treaty negotiations with the Indians to dismiss the commissioners in July, 1786, and to set up a department of Indian

Indian Affairs (2 volumes, Washington, D. C., 1832), I, 8-9. It was not signed by individual chiefs but by the names of the nations. Brant was at the council and described the proceedings to Sir John Johnson. Although Brant's letter is not available, one facet of the British attitude toward the Indians is revealed in Johnson's reply: "Everything that is reasonable and consistent with the friendship that ought to be preserved between us, will be done for you all. Do not suffer an idea to hold a place in your mind, that it will be for your interests to sit still and see the Americans attempt [to take the] posts. It is for your sakes chiefly, if not entirely, that we hold them. . . ." A couple of months later, the new commandant at Detroit, Maj. Robert Mathews, wrote in a similar vein: "[His Lordship] cannot begin a war with the Americans . . . but they [the Indians] must see it is his Lordship's intention to defend the posts; and while these are preserved, the Indians must find greater security therefrom. . . ." Sir John Johnson to Brant, March 22, 1787, and Mathews to Brant, May 29, 1787, in Stone, *Joseph Brant,* pp. 267-268, 270-271.

[18] Horsman, *Expansion and American Indian Policy,* pp. 23-24, 30-31; Horsman, *Matthew Elliott,* pp. 51-55; Burt, *The United States, Great Britain, and British North America,* pp. 95-100.

affairs to handle all future problems that might arise. There was to be a north and south district divided by the Ohio River, each to have a superintendent responsible to the secretary at war. Trade regulations were set out: only United States citizens were to be allowed to reside among or trade with the Indians, and they must obtain a license from the superintendent of their respective district, giving $3,000 bond to insure their intention to obey any and all regulations. Richard Butler was appointed superintendent for the northern district. Congress hoped that the new measure would help obviate the threat of war.[19]

§

As an economy measure, the military strength of the United States had been cut to the bare minimum of less than one hundred after the Revolutionary War and then raised to seven hundred in 1784. At that time, Josiah Harmar, who had attained the rank of lieutenant colonel during the Revolution, was named the commanding officer. The troops were first based at Fort Pitt, but by the end of 1785 had moved down the Ohio, restoring Fort McIntosh and constructing Fort Steuben near the present Wheeling, Fort Harmar at

[19] Clarence E. Carter (ed.), *Territorial Papers of the United States* (Vols. 1- , Washington, D. C., 1934-   ), II, 19-22, 50n; Horsman, *Expansion and American Indian Policy*, pp. 32-33; Mohr, *Federal Indian Relations*, pp. 104-108. Despite the efforts of Congress to secure the Indian trade for the Americans, the British continued to dominate the trade in the area south of the Great Lakes until after the Treaty of Greenville. In addition to dominating the trade, some of the British traders were accused of meddling in Indian affairs and fomenting discord between the tribesmen and the United States. See Phillips and Smurr, *The Fur Trade*, II, 19-20, 68-78; *Michigan Historical Collections*, XXIV, 27, 99-100, 104, 105; Horsman, *Matthew Elliott*, pp. 54-55. For activities of British traders, see Phillips and Smurr, *op. cit.*, II, 15-35, 97-124; Milo M. Quaife (ed.), *The John Askin Papers* . . . (2 volumes, Detroit, 1928, 1931); Christopher B. Coleman (ed.), "Letters from Eighteenth Century Merchants," *Indiana Magazine of History*, V (1909), 137-159; Milo M. Quaife, *Fort Wayne in 1790* (Indiana Historical Society *Publications*, VII, No. 7, Indianapolis, 1921).

the mouth of the Muskingum, and Fort Finney at the mouth of the Great Miami.[20]

In June, 1786, Secretary at War Henry Knox had reported to Congress that the troops then in service were "utterly incompetent" to protect the frontiers. With the threat of a possible Indian war and the expectation of an expanding frontier, he recommended that the army be increased and additional posts established. The thought of the additional expense that this would entail caused Congress to delay action but the following October they voted to enlist an additional 1,340 men.[21]

§ §

While the Indians were being pressed to give up their land northwest of the Ohio, the states were being pressed to surrender their claims to western lands. As early as October, 1780, the Continental Congress had resolved that the lands that might be ceded to the national government should be "disposed of for the common benefit of the United States, and be settled and formed into distinct republican states, which shall become members of the federal union, and have the same rights of sovereignty, freedom and independence, as the other states. . . ." New York ceded her claims in 1781 and Virginia made a conditional offer that year which, however, was not accepted until it was revised three years

20 James Ripley Jacobs, *The Beginning of the U. S. Army, 1783-1812* (Princeton University Press, 1947), pp. 14-27; Francis P. Prucha, *The Sword of the Republic. The United States Army on the Frontier, 1783-1846* (London, 1969), pp. 3-11. The new troops were enlisted for only one year; it was hoped that many would re-enlist at the end of their term of service but very few were willing to do so. Congress was therefore under the necessity of recruiting additional troops in 1785 to bring the quota up to seven hundred; under the new act the term of enlistment was three years.

21 Jacobs, *Beginning of the U. S. Army*, pp. 34-35; Prucha, *Sword of the Republic*, pp. 11-13; Horsman, *Expansion and American Indian Policy*, pp.32-33. Only two artillery companies were raised under the new authorization.

later.[22] Five other states claiming western lands surrendered their claims at intervals over the next twenty years.

With Virginia's cession sufficient land had been ceded for Congress to proceed to determine the method of transferring the land to individuals. This joint ownership of the vast domain which eventually came into possession of the federal government would serve as a bond of union to hold the states together at a time when nationalism was weak; and the disposition which Congress would make of it would determine the future character of the American Union. Would the nation become a confederation of eastern states and their colonial possessions with the colonies deprived of self-government or equal rights, or would the rights of citizenship and self-government be held in trust for those who pioneered the

---

[22] *Journals of the Continental Congress,* XVIII, 915. Virginia's deed of cession is printed in Charles Kettleborough, *Constitution Making in Indiana* (3 vols. *Indiana Historical Collections,* I, II, XVII, Indianapolis, 1916, 1930), I, 11-15; Carter (ed.), *Territorial Papers,* II, 3-9; and Hubert H. Hawkins (comp.), *Indiana's Road to Statehood* (Indiana Sesquicentennial Commission, 1964), pp. 5-8, as well as in many other publications.

Conditions stipulated in the cession were that the state was to be reimbursed for her expenses in subduing the British posts and in maintaining forts and garrisons for the defense of the western territory; the French and Canadian inhabitants who professed themselves citizens of the United States should have their possessions and land titles confirmed; and the land granted to George Rogers Clark and his men should be reserved from the cession. Any future states formed out of the cession were to be "republican" and have the same rights of sovereignty, freedom, and independence as the original thirteen states. Jefferson, who was then representing his state in the Congress, was one of the signers of the document. For a discussion of the problems that arose in Congress in connection with Virginia's first offer, see Boyd (ed.), *Jefferson Papers,* VI, 571-575, 647-668; Thomas P. Abernethy, *Western Lands and the American Revolution* (New York and London, 1937), Chaps. XIX and XX; Bodley, *Clark,* pp. 153-156, 193-198, 254-255. The principal difficulty was over the claims of the land companies which Virginia insisted should be invalidated.

Virginia asked for approximately one million dollars as reimbursement for Clark's expeditions of 1778-79 and the defense of the northwest but received only half that amount. James (ed.), *Clark Papers, 1781-1784,* pp. 465-477; Temple Bodley, "George Rogers Clark's Relief Claims," Illinois State Historical Society *Journal,* XXIX (1936-37), 114-118; Randall, "George Rogers Clark's Service of Supply," *Mississippi Valley Historical Review,* VIII, 262-263.

West until such a time as they were numerous enough and of sufficient experience to carry on their own government? These were the questions that would be debated and resolved in the final years of the Confederation.

As soon as the provisional treaty of peace established the Mississippi River as the western boundary of the United States, plans for the settlement of the West began to be formulated. Among the leaders who were giving considerable thought to the question was Thomas Jefferson, and on the same day that Virginia ceded her claim to the western lands he presented to Congress, as a committee report, a plan for dividing the territory into future states and providing for a gradual assumption of representative government by the inhabitants. The plan provided that when any one of the proposed states acquired twenty thousand free inhabitants they should have authority to call a convention of representatives to establish a permanent constitution and government for themselves; at this stage they would elect a delegate to Congress with a right of debate but not of voting. When the population equalled that of the least populous of the older states, the new commonwealth should be admitted into the Union on an equal footing with the original states. A provision excluding slavery and involuntary servitude after the year 1800 was stricken out. The report was adopted on April 23, 1784. However, since this ordinance was drafted for all the western territory, both north and south of the Ohio, it was never put into operation, partly because all of the southern states had not yet ceded their claims to western lands.[23] Some of its features were later incorporated into the Ordinance of 1787.

[23] For the evolution of the Ordinance of 1784, see Boyd (ed.), *Jefferson Papers*, VI, 581-617n; Jay A. Barrett, *Evolution of the Ordinance of 1787* . . . (New York and London, 1891), pp. 17-32; Jacob P. Dunn, *Indiana. A Redemption from Slavery* (American Commonwealths Series, Revised edition, Boston and New York, 1905), pp. 177-187; Merrill Jensen, *The New Nation. A History of the United States During the Confederation, 1781-1789* (New York, 1950), pp. 350-354. Kettleborough, *Constitution Making in Indiana*, I, 15-21, has

The next step was to provide for the survey and sale of the lands. Here, too, Jefferson's influence was felt, but before the plan reached its final form he had been appointed minister to France and was out of the country until 1789. The ordinance which was adopted on May 20, 1785, established the future land policy of the United States.[24] Under its terms before any of the publicly owned land could be offered for sale the Indian claims had to be purchased by the government and the land surveyed by the system set forth in the ordinance. Thus all of the land in Indiana except the Vincennes Tract and Clark's Grant was set off by the Congressional or rectangular survey lines.[25]

The method of survey provided for the establishment of meridian and base lines starting at the point on the Ohio River where the western boundary of Pennsylvania touched that stream. The surveyors were first to mark a north-south line which was called a meridian and at right angles to it an east-west line which was called the geographer's or base line. Other north-south lines would be marked at intervals of six miles, the strip of land between these lines being called a range. East-west lines were also laid off at intervals of six miles from the base line to the Ohio River dividing the ranges into six-mile squares called townships. At the beginning alternate townships and later all of them were divided by additional north-south and east-west lines at intervals of one mile until the townships were surveyed into thirty-six one-mile squares. At first these sections, containing 640 acres, were the smallest pieces sold. The townships which were not divided were to be sold entire, but because this part of the system did not work it was soon abandoned. Both the sections and townships were first to be offered to the public at auction

---

both Jefferson's original report and the final form of the ordinance. For plans other than that of Jefferson, see Barrett, *op. cit.,* pp. 6-16.

[24] Carter (ed.), *Territorial Papers,* II, 12-18; *Indiana's Road to Statehood,* pp. 9-16.

[25] See below, pp. 341-342.

at a minimum price of $1.00 per acre. Any land that was not sold at auction could then be purchased at the minimum price. The ordinance also provided that section sixteen in each township should be reserved and the receipts therefrom used for educational purposes.

The system was so simple that anyone could see for himself where his land lay and its exact boundaries. Unlike Kentucky where boundaries were described by streams and trees and were so indefinite that two people might purchase the same tract or at least have overlapping boundaries, the purchaser of land north of the Ohio could be assured of a clear title if he met the purchase price.

Though the lands in the southeastern portion of what is now Ohio had been given up by the Treaty of Fort McIntosh in January, 1785, the appearance of the surveyors in the area in the fall of that year intensified the resentment of those Indians that had not acknowledged the treaty negotiations. Thomas Hutchins, official geographer of the United States, attempted to mark the first seven ranges which Congress was anxious to put on the market. By December, 1786, he had managed to complete only the first four.[26] It was hoped that the surveys would check the increasingly large number of persons who were squatting on the public lands. The soldiers sent to protect the surveyors had the disagreeable task of driving off many of these unauthorized settlers.

§ § §

Surveys were also going forward in an area still farther west, where land had been granted to George Rogers Clark and his men for their military service in the Illinois campaigns against the British during the Revolutionary War. At the time the Illinois campaign was inaugurated, Clark had received the assurance that "some further Reward in Lands . . . will be given to the Volunteers who shall engage in this

---

[26] Bond, *Foundations of Ohio*, pp. 248, 260-261.

Service in addition to the usual pay if they are so fortunate to Succeed."[27]

In fulfillment of this promise, the Virginia legislature adopted a resolution on January 2, 1781, providing that a quantity of land not exceeding 150,000 acres be allowed and granted to Clark's officers and men who marched with him on the original expedition and others later incorporated into the regiment. "The land was to be laid off in one tract . . . in such place on the northwest side of the Ohio as the majority of the officers shall choose." Then in 1783 an act was passed providing for appointment of a board of commissioners "for locating and surveying" the land and settling and determining the claims. The respective claimants were to present their claims on or before the first day of April, 1784, and those whose claims were allowed were to pay the commissioners $1.00 for each hundred acres, the money to be used to pay the cost of surveying and apportioning the land. One thousand acres was to be set aside for a town, and the remainder of the land divided into lots, with no lot exceeding five hundred acres. When Virginia ceded her western claims to the national government in 1784, she expressly provided that the above grant to Clark and his soldiers be excluded from the cession.[28]

The land selected was across the Ohio River from Louisville, in the present Indiana counties of Clark, Floyd, and Scott, but mainly in Clark. William Clark, a cousin of George Rogers Clark, was appointed principal surveyor of the grant, and when the work was completed Virginia issued a patent for the land on December 14, 1786. In the meantime, the commissioners had been meeting and determining the basis on which the lands should be allotted. In view of the manner in which the troops were raised, the irregularity of the terms

[27] Thomas Jefferson, George Wythe, and George Mason to Clark, January 3, 1778, in James (ed.), *Clark Papers, 1771-1781,* pp. 37-38.

[28] Hening (ed.), *Statutes of Virginia,* X, 26-27, 565; XI, 327-328, 335-336; Bodley, *Clark* pp. 353-357.

of service, the different campaigns, etc., it was a difficult and delicate matter to determine exactly who was entitled to share in the grant. Also, since some of the men had died, it became necessary to decide who were their legal heirs. Others had assigned any possible claims they might have; in such cases, the deeds were issued in the name of the persons then owning the claims.[29] Litigation over some of the claims was to continue down to the middle of the nineteenth century.

A town was platted in 1784 at the southwestern corner of the grant, opposite the lower part of the Falls, and named Clarksville. It was here that George Rogers Clark established his residence and built a saw- and gristmill nearby. Twenty or thirty families had moved into the town by the end of the year; additional lots were laid off the following year. The plat of the town as approved by the board of trustees in January, 1788, contained 135 lots; sales of lots continued to be held until all were sold.[30] Clarksville has the honor of being the first American town in the Old Northwest. Since most of the men of Clark's original army had been recruited on the Monongahela—Ohio River frontier, the inhabitants of Clark's Grant were largely from Virginia and Pennsylvania.

§　§　§　§

During 1786 the resentment of the northwestern tribes was building up against the United States and the dictated treaties

[29] A map of the grant, the Virginia patent, and the names of those who received land (or their assignees) are in English, *Conquest of the Country Northwest of the River Ohio*, II, 834-835, 839-850, 852-853, 1117-1119. The proceedings of the commissioners are printed in *ibid.*, II, 1068-1116. The last entry of the board was April 3, 1847. A copy of the minutes of the trustees of the town of Clarksville are in the Indiana Historical Society Library; the Society also has an abstract book of the grant, compiled by Thomas W. Gibson of Jeffersonville, giving plats and abstracts for each lot up to about 1849.

[30] English, *Conquest of the Country Northwest of the River Ohio,* II, 861, 863, 865, 1074. The town did not prosper, however, and the population in 1793 was still only forty. Carter (ed.), *Territorial Papers,* II, 470. An 1850 map of the town in the Indiana State Library, copied from an earlier one in the minutes of the board of trustees, shows 135 lots.

which certain of their leaders had been cajoled if not forced into signing. In the meantime, sporadic attacks on squatters north of the Ohio and against Kentuckians were stepped up; the Americans at Vincennes also were the object of Indian hatred.[31]

Conditions at that village had grown progressively worse in the five years since the principal inhabitants had complained of Clark's men in a memorial to the Governor of Virginia in 1781. John Filson, Kentucky's first historian, who visited the place in the early months of 1786 estimated it contained about three hundred houses, "most of which make a poor appearance but in general are Convenient and Clean within there is perhaps no people in the world more friendly and Cleanly than the french. . . ." Some seventy American families or individuals had been added to the French population, some of whom had been granted land by the court set up by John Todd while others were squatters on the public land in and around the village. In the cultivation of their fields, the Americans had introduced a new mode of life into the settlement and a new economy based on agriculture rather than the fur trade. Finding no market for their corn, they were prone to convert it into whiskey and trade it to the Indians. The French resented the Americans who disturbed their way of life, debauched the Indians, felled trees, and plowed the fields. On the other hand, the Americans considered the French as shiftless idlers. Of the Indians, Filson reported they were resentful of American encroachment on

31 Bodley, *Clark*, p. 276. Mr. Park, a British trader (probably William Park of the Detroit trading firm of Meldrum and Park) who was at Vincennes in April, 1786, described the fighting there between the Americans and the Indians; this terrorized the French, he said, and they were trying to act as arbitrators between the two hostile groups. Park found the Indians all along the Wabash in a hostile mood, while those at Miamis Town were described as being "in a wavering situation they are mostly all gone to war and when misfortune arrives to Indians they seldom pay little difference between Americans and English as they make mighty complaints against the English for having abandoned them after making them take up the ax." Letter of Park from Miamis, May 17, 1786, in *Michigan Historical Collections,* XXIV, 29-31.

their lands and were showing signs of organized resistance.[32]

At the request of the French and American inhabitants, Filson wrote a letter to George Rogers Clark on March 16, 1786, appealing for his aid against the probability of the "total depopulation" of American inhabitants by the "imperious savages."[33] They were also apprehensive about the validity of the deeds given by the court set up by Todd. On June 1 Filson drafted for the Americans at Vincennes a petition to Congress stating that French authority had broken down and the rising Indian menace exposed the inhabitants daily to danger and possible death. Congress was asked to establish a garrison of American soldiers at the town, create a land office for the settlement of land titles, and establish a civil government.[34] Chosen to carry the petition as far as Louisville, Filson set out that same day by way of the Wabash. At the mouth of White River, his canoe was attacked by Indians and two of the canoemen killed. Filson returned to Vincennes and set out again on June 12, this time by the overland route.[35]

John Small and Moses Henry took the opportunity of Filson's return to Vincennes to write again to Clark on June 12 regarding the hostile intentions of the Indians and attacks that had taken place. New arrivals from Miamis Town and Ouiatanon had brought word that both of those places were

[32] Beverley W. Bond, Jr. (ed.), "Two Westward Journeys of John Filson, 1785," *Mississippi Valley Historical Review*, IX (1922-23), 326-327; Leonard C. Helderman, "John Filson's Narrative of His Defeat on the Wabash, 1786," *Filson Club History Quarterly*, XII (1938), 187-199; Leonard C. Helderman, "The Northwest Expedition of George Rogers Clark, 1786," *Mississippi Valley Historical Review*, XXV (1938-39), 317-334.

[33] Leonard C. Helderman, "Danger on the Wabash," *Indiana Magazine of History*, XXXIV (1938), 456-457. The letter was signed by Filson, Moses Henry, John Small, Alexander Willson, James Johnson, John and Luke Decker.

[34] *Ibid.*, pp. 457-458. The petition was signed by seventy-one heads of families.

[35] Helderman, "John Filson's Narrative of His Defeat on the Wabash, 1786," *Filson Club History Quarterly*, XII, 187-189.

being evacuated due to the alarming movements of the Wabash tribes.[36]

Later in the month the Indians attacked a group of Americans outside the village and scalped one; in retaliation the Americans seized an Indian whom the French were trying to protect and put him to death. The French then ordered all the Americans to leave the village unless they could show the proper credentials. However, when an Indian war party moved down the Wabash in July, determined to destroy the Americans, the French rallied to their support and persuaded the Indians to depart, which they did after destroying crops and promising to return in the fall.[37]

The aversion of the people in the various counties of Kentucky to co-operate in their common defense had not changed in the years since Clark had experienced difficulty in raising volunteers in 1780 and 1782. Only when the danger was extended to their own area was there a general demand in 1786 for Clark to lead another expedition against the Indians. Clark hesitated, not sure that he could count on the united support of the people. An appeal to Congress for some of General Harmar's troops to lead the expedition was denied, whereupon Patrick Henry, who had again assumed the governorship of Virginia, sent instructions to the county lieutenants of Kentucky to draft men and supplies for an expedition against the Wabash Indians, estimated to number some fifteen hundred warriors. Discord became evident as the order was carried out and many evaded the call with the result that instead of the two thousand troops expected only twelve hundred appeared at Clarksville, the place of rendezvous, on September 12.[38]

---

[36] Helderman, "Danger on the Wabash," *Indiana Magazine of History,* XXXIV, 458-459.

[37] *Ibid.,* pp. 459-467.

[38] Bodley, *Clark,* pp. 277-284; Helderman, "The Northwest Expedition of George Rogers Clark, 1786," *Mississippi Valley Historical Review,* XXV, 324-327.

The Wabash tribes were aware of the proposed expedition against them and passed the word on to the Potawatomi at St. Joseph's who sought the aid of the British. This was not forthcoming inasmuch as British officials were bound by a policy of neutrality at this time. Though they could not furnish military assistance to the Indians, they were expected to keep them friendly.[39]

Clark, who had hoped for volunteers instead of drafted men, reluctantly accepted the command of the Kentucky troops and while Col. Benjamin Logan returned to Kentucky to recruit additional men, Clark proceeded to Vincennes with those at hand. It had been his wish to head directly for the Indian towns on the Wabash but he had been overruled and instead the supplies and provisions were sent with a portion of the men by boat while the remainder marched overland, taking seven days for a trip that could have been made in three. Discipline was so bad that the men were quartered across the river from Vincennes while Clark waited fifteen days for the arrival of the boats only to learn that the beef had spoiled en route and been thrown overboard. By this time the troops wanted to return home and only reluctantly took up the march northward. After two days' march and within a day's journey of the Indian towns, the majority mutinied, claiming an insufficiency of provisions, and set out for home.[40]

With those who remained faithful, Clark returned to Vincennes to plan the next move. Realizing that if the Indians learned the truth of the mutiny they would likely take advantage of the situation and attack either Vincennes or some other point, Clark determined to put up a bold front and camouflage

---

[39] Potawatomi Indian speech, September 19, 1786, and Lord Dorchester to Sir John Johnson, November 27, 1786, in *Michigan Historical Collections,* XXIV, 33, 39-40. Sir Guy Carleton, now Lord Dorchester, had again become governor of Canada. Reports concerning the approach of Clark's army continued to reach Detroit throughout October. *Michigan Historical Collections,* XXIV, 36, 38.

[40] Bodley, *Clark,* pp. 284-291; Helderman, "The Northwest Expedition of George Rogers Clark," *Mississippi Valley Historical Review,* XXV, 325-328.

the true situation of the troops as he had been forced to do in 1778 and 1779. Taking advantage of the friendly overtures that two of the Wabash chiefs had made earlier, Clark sent a speech addressed to the chiefs and warriors of the different nations on the Wabash, inviting them to a grand council at Clarksville on November 20; if they did not accept the invitation it would be understood that they preferred war to peace and he (Clark) would act accordingly. Clark's friend Le Gras not only endorsed the message but sent one of his own with it stating that the troops had returned from their march only at the earnest solicitation of himself and their other French friends and urging the Indians "to sit down and take again the hand of your Brothers, the Big Knives, who spare your blood."

While awaiting a reply Clark set in motion plans for the defense of Vincennes should the Indians spurn his offer and attack the town. Calling his officers together, it was agreed that 250 men be recruited to garrison the town, that a commissary be appointed, and that supplies sufficient for their support be obtained by impressment if not otherwise obtainable. About 140 men were enlisted (whether from the Vincennes citizenry or from the Kentucky troops the records do not indicate). Efforts to secure supplies in Illinois and Kentucky were not immediately successful and the citizens of Vincennes had little to offer. At this juncture three Spanish traders arrived at Vincennes with a cargo of merchandise for trading with the Indians, and when they could not produce the passports required of alien traders, Clark believed he was acting within his authority to impress their cargo for the use of the troops. What items they could not use would be auctioned and the proceeds applied to their support.

In the meantime, after waiting two weeks Clark began receiving replies from the various chiefs and warriors, indicating a desire for peace and a willingness to meet him, but instead of November 20 at Clarksville they proposed that a council be held at Vincennes the following April. Clark was happy to consent to the postponement for it would give time for preparation and lessen the probability of attack.[41]

Colonel Logan who had returned to Kentucky from the rendezvous at the Falls to try to recruit additional troops found his task comparatively easy when Clark directed that they should be used in an expedition against the Shawnee towns on the upper Miami. With some seven hundred men, mostly volunteers, Colonel Logan marched north in October and succeeded in surprising the Indians, killing some, taking a number of prisoners, burning several villages, and destroying crops. The warriors were mostly absent from the towns at the time of the attacks, but a number quickly assembled and pursued the Kentuckians.[42]

The need of a garrison at Vincennes having been resolved, Clark probably gave orders for the dispersion of the troops before he returned to his home at Clarksville in December. From there he made a report to the Governor of Virginia on the expedition against the Wabash tribes. Concerning the mutiny of a portion of the troops, he thought a court of inquiry should be appointed to investigate. Of his own actions, he wrote:

Serious Reflections convinced me that the State of our affairs would be wors than ever, if something was not done. I had a number of troops Recruited for one year, fortified myself in St. Vincens, and in the course of four weaks brought the whole of the Ouabache Indians to my own terms, Blinding the cause of the Retreat and eaven making

[41] Bodley, *Clark,* pp. 291-299; Helderman, "The Northwest Expedition of George Rogers Clark," *loc. cit.,* 328-332. Clark also impressed flour in the Illinois country after he failed to obtain it without the use of force. Alvord (ed.), *Kaskaskia Records, 1778-1790,* pp. 425-426. It is interesting to note that when Laurent Bazadone, one of the Spanish traders, sued Clark eleven years later in the Knox County Court of Common Pleas for $20,000 damages for the seizure the court ordered the action withdrawn and Clark reimbursed for his expenses in his defense. Minutes of the November Term, 1797, pp. 134-137, typed copy in Archives Division, Indiana State Library.

[42] Charles G. Talbert, "Kentucky Invades Ohio—1786," Kentucky Historical Society *Register,* LIV (1956), 203-213; Bodley, *Clark,* p. 286. Reports received by the British in Detroit regarding the expedition are in *Michigan Historical Collections,* XXIV, 34-39.

an advantage of it. The Grand Treaty would have been held this Fall if we had have known what articles to have agreed to.

He was leaving to others to determine the course of action to be taken in the spring, but he confidently expected the greatest number of Indians ever congregated at Vincennes to be present, and warned that the proceedings would need to be supported by men, money, and provisions. "The Different nations and my self have agreed to . . . rest Quiet untill that time, when it is Expected that a final peace will take place."[43]

Clark had once again demonstrated his skill in Indian diplomacy and thwarted the disastrous consequences that might have ensued from the mutiny of the undisciplined troops. The groundwork had been laid for a peaceful settlement, but other factors were at work which would not only delay the peace but would bring about Clark's own downfall. For when word reached Kentucky of his activities at Vincennes, it gave his enemies an opportunity to press charges against him, many of which were false. Government leaders in Virginia accepted the charges as true, and on February 28, 1787, the Virginia Council reprimanded him for acting without authority in recruiting troops and impressing supplies. Word was sent to Congress which in turn expressed its regrets for the incident to the Spanish minister.[44]

§   §   §   §   §

The United States was not only having trouble with Great Britain and the Indians but also with Spain and her colonial possessions in the south. Spain had joined France in the war against Great Britain in 1779 but had never recognized American independence and had rejected American efforts to negotiate a treaty of alliance and amity with her. The Span-

[43] *Calendar of Virginia State Papers,* IV, 213; Bodley, *Clark,* p. 304.
[44] See below, p. 263; Bodley, *Clark,* pp. 300-306, 310-329, 398-400; *Journals of the Council of the State of Virginia,* edited by H. R. McIlwaine *et al.* (4 volumes, Richmond, 1931-1967), IV, 46-47; *Journals of the Continental Congress,* XXXII, 190-199.

ish attitude was that the United States should be kept a weak and harmless nation, confined to the Atlantic seaboard.[45]

Great Britain had ceded East Florida to Spain at the end of the war and confirmed her retention of West Florida. No mention was made in that treaty of the right of the United States to navigate the Mississippi River, although this was guaranteed in Great Britain's treaty with the United States.[46] The stream of immigrants into Kentucky and Tennessee which had begun before the Revolution reached new heights after the war. To these people the Mississippi was the only practicable route whereby they might get their products to the outside world. From 1763 to 1776 the river had been open to them as British subjects and Spain had allowed the colonists to use it during the remainder of the war. Then in 1784 that part of the Mississippi which flowed through Spanish territory was closed to all but Spanish subjects. This was a severe blow to the hopes of the western settlers. If the weak government of the United States could not secure for them the free navigation of the Mississippi, then they might be influenced to separate from the eastern states and make their own arrangements with Spain.[47]

The Indian tribes south of the Ohio River constituted still another source of trouble for the new nation. The Cherokee numbered about two thousand warriors; the Creek, six thousand; Chickasaw, five hundred; and the Choctaw, five thousand. As in the North, the Indians refused to recognize the cession of their land to the United States and the presence

[45] John H. Latané and David W. Wainhouse, *A History of American Foreign Policy* (Second Revision, New York, 1940), p. 54; Samuel F. Bemis, *Pinckney's Treaty. A Study of America's Advantage from Europe's Distress, 1783-1800* (Baltimore, 1926), pp. 42, 44-46.

[46] Bemis, *Pinckney's Treaty*, pp. 42, 44-46; Albert P. Whitaker, *The Spanish-American Frontier, 1783-1795* . . . (Boston and New York, 1927), pp. 9-13.

[47] Whitaker, *The Spanish-American Frontier, 1783-1795*, pp. 4-9, 26-29; Bemis, *Pinckney's Treaty*, pp. 47-55.

among them of Spanish traders and agents hampered the efforts of the United States to come to terms with them.[48]

The United States desperately needed a trade agreement with Spain, and the eastern and middle states were willing to sacrifice the navigation of the Mississippi to obtain this. John Jay, secretary of foreign affairs, and Don Diego de Gardoqui, Spanish chargé d'affaires, spent four years, from 1785 to 1789, in fruitless negotiations without reaching any agreement on either a commercial treaty or the navigation of the Mississippi. A provisional agreement reached in 1786 whereby the United States would have given up the navigation of the Mississippi for twenty-five years in return for favorable commercial privileges was blocked by representatives of the southern states. Word of the possibility of such an agreement angered the western settlers and created in them the mood for rebellion.[49] A leader to voice their protests was found in the person of James Wilkinson, a former officer in the American Army, who arrived in Kentucky at this crucial moment and immediately penned two memorials to the Virginia legislature threatening separation from the mother state. When the expedition led by Clark against the Wabash Indians failed and the remnant of the army which stopped at Vincennes took over the property of a Spanish trader, thus endangering the negotiations with that country, a committee of Kentuckians, including Wilkinson, forwarded charges against Clark to the governor of Virginia insinuating that he had confiscated property of others for his private use, that his excessive drinking unfitted him for public business, and that the garrison at Vincennes was no more than a corps of banditti. An apology was sent to the King of Spain. Vir-

---

[48] Whitaker, *The Spanish-American Frontier, 1783-1795*, pp. 24-26; Bemis, *Pinckney's Treaty*, pp. 55-68; Horsman, *Expansion and American Indian Policy*, Chapters V and VIII, deal with the American government's relations with the southern Indians.

[49] Latané and Wainhouse, *History of American Foreign Policy*, pp. 55-56; Bemis, *Pinckney's Treaty*, pp. 71-123; Whitaker, *The Spanish American Frontier, 1783-1795*, pp. 68-77.

ginia resolved to disavow any further connection with the
expedition and directed the attorney general to bring criminal charges against Clark. However, these were never
pressed.[50]

Congress was apprised of the action taken by Virginia
against Clark, and that body in turn adopted a resolution on
April 24, 1787, to send a force under Lieutenant Colonel
Harmar to dispossess Clark's men who had in a "lawless and
unauthorized" manner taken possession of Post Vincennes.
During the previous summer, Harmar had been ordered to
place two companies at the Falls of the Ohio to aid in halting Indian raids against Kentucky settlements; they had specific instructions not to undertake any offensive operations
into the Indian country unless so ordered. These instructions
prevented them from joining with the militia on Clark's
expedition as he had requested. The troops built Fort Finney
opposite Louisville in the fall of 1786.[51]

Before receiving the orders to proceed to Vincennes, Colonel Harmar had spent a week at the new fort at the Falls
endeavoring to ascertain the feeling among the inhabitants
of Kentucky and to find out exactly what was taking place
at Vincennes. Regarding the latter, he learned that the militia
who had reportedly taken over the town had dispersed for
want of provisions. With respect to the treaty negotiations
which Clark had set up for April, Harmar judged that he had
no authority to proceed with them and sent Clark to so inform any Indians that assembled for that purpose.[52]

[50] Bemis, *Pinckney's Treaty*, pp. 124-164; Helderman, "The Northwest
expedition of George Rogers Clark," *Mississippi Valley Historical Review*,
XXV, 328-332.

[51] *Journals of the Continental Congress*, XXXII, 222, 231; Harmar to
Secretary at War, June 27, August 10, 1786, in *The St. Clair Papers. The
Life and Public Services of Arthur St. Clair* . . . , edited by William Henry
Smith (2 volumes, Cincinnati, 1882), II, 15n, 16-17; Dorothy Riker, "Fort
Finney," *Year Book* of the Society of Indiana Pioneers, 1944, pp. 15-20.

[52] Harmar to Secretary at War, May 14, 1787, in *St. Clair Papers*, II, 19-22.

Although the reported dispersal of the militia and the decision not to meet the Indians would seemingly have cancelled the need for the movement of troops to Vincennes, Harmar embarked for that place with some three hundred men the first of June, 1787, leaving only small garrisons at the different posts on the Ohio. Fortunately for Harmar, before the news of the dispersion of troops at Vincennes reached the Secretary at War, that official had reported to Congress on July 10 the need for a strong military post at Vincennes and the necessity for a treaty with the Shawnee and Wabash Indians. The latter he thought could be delegated to the commanding officer, and if peace could not be made with the Indians, he recommended that the troops should take forceful measures against them. In line with this report, Congress on July 21 authorized either the superintendent of Indian affairs or Harmar to proceed to Vincennes or some other convenient place to negotiate a treaty; also, in the disposition of the troops, three companies were to be stationed at Vincennes. Apparently in an effort to halt unauthorized retaliatory militia raids into the Indian country and prevent any more expeditions such as that in 1786, the resolution provided that henceforth the militia would be called into federal service and serve along with the regular Army troops.[53]

In the meantime, Colonel Harmar had arrived at Vincennes with a portion of his troops on July 17 and the remainder arrived by water on August 5. The French gave them a cordial welcome, feeling that at last Congress had taken notice of their many petitions; the Americans exhibited mixed feelings since they were fearful of losing the lands for which their title was somewhat tenuous. Harmar soon relieved their apprehensions on that score for he found the land claims far too involved to be settled during his brief

[53] *Journals of the Continental Congress,* XXXII, 370-376; XXXIII, 385-387; F. Clever Bald, "Colonel Francis Hamtramck," *Indiana Magazine of History,* XLIV (1948), 340.

visit; instead, he consented to forward to Congress petitions regarding their claims. After visiting Kaskaskia, Cahokia, and other Illinois towns and holding parleys with delegations of Piankashaw and Wea Indians, the Colonel decided on the site for a military post at Vincennes and ordered two companies to remain under the command of John Francis Hamtramck. Fort Knox was completed the following year. During the five years of Hamtramck's command, he was able to bring some degree of law and order to the town as well as carry on his military duties. Although he was able to maintain friendly relations with the Indians he could not prevent them from continuing their raids into Kentucky, and at least on one occasion he could not stop Kentuckians from making an unauthorized raid into the Indian country.[54]

§ § § § § §

The adoption of the Ordinance of 1784 for the government of the western territory did not end the debate in Congress on the subject. Thomas Jefferson who had largely been responsible for the Ordinance was appointed minister to France a couple of weeks after its adoption and James Monroe who assumed the leadership of the Virginia delegation had different ideas. Likewise, other members of the Congress were not satisfied with the Ordinance. Consequently, between

[54] Fort Knox was built a short distance up the Wabash from the earlier Fort Sackville built by the British, which was captured by Clark and renamed Fort Patrick Henry. For details on the establishment of the fort and the experiences of the garrison, see Gayle Thornbrough (ed.), *Outpost on the Wabash, 1787-1791. Letters of Brigadier General Josiah Harmar and Major John Francis Hamtramck* (Indiana Historical Society *Publications,* XIX, Indianapolis, 1957), and the article by F. Clever Bald in *Indiana Magazine of History,* XLIV, 335-354. Hamtramck revived the magistrates court at Vincennes that had been instituted by John Todd in 1781. Those elected to serve in May, 1788, were Jean Baptiste Miliet, Moses Henry, Nicholas Baillardjon (?), James Johnson, and Valentine Thomas Dalton. Thornbrough (ed.), *Outpost on the Wabash,* pp. 16, 79.

The Fort Knox Orderly Book for the period 1793-1797, kept by Capt. Thomas Pasteur, Hamtramck's successor, is printed in the *Indiana Magazine of History,* XXXII (1936), 137-169.

1784 and 1787 three variant proposals for the government of the western territory were submitted to the national legislative body. The last of these was under consideration in May of 1787 when an agent of the Ohio Company of Associates arrived in New York. Composed of former soldiers and officers, this company was negotiating for a large tract of land in the Ohio country and was therefore interested in the form of government that was to prevail. Some of the suggested changes outlined by their agent were incorporated in the plan under consideration which was enacted into law on July 13, 1787.[55] This, together with the land ordinance of 1785, was to provide for the orderly settlement and development of the area north of the Ohio River.

The new ordinance contained two parts: the first described the plan of government; the second part was a compact between the people of the original states and those who would immigrate to the new territory. As in the earlier plan, there were to be two stages of government. In the first stage, the people resident in the territory would be subject to a governor, secretary, and three judges until the free adult males equalled five thousand in number. These officials were to be appointed by the Congress of the Confederation until 1789 and then by the President with the consent of the Senate. Thus, in this first stage the people did not have a voice in their government. The executive and the judges were to exercise semilegislative authority by selecting from the stat-

[55] After making a trip down the Ohio River as far as Limestone, Kentucky, in the fall of 1785, Monroe recommended a reduction in the number of states to be formed in the western territory. "A great part of the territory is miserably poor," he wrote Jefferson, "especially that near lakes Michigan & Erie & that upon the Mississippi & the Illinois consists of extensive plains which have not had, from appearances, & will not have a single bush on them, for ages." He was of the opinion that the interests of the West would differ from those of the East and wished to insure the ascendancy of the latter. *The Writings of James Monroe* . . . , edited by S. M. Hamilton (7 volumes, New York, 1898-1903), I, 113, 117-118. For the variant proposals leading up to the Ordinance of 1787, see Barrett, *Evolution of the Ordinance of 1787,* pp. 33-80; Dunn, *Indiana,* pp. 187-218.

The Northwest Territory

utes already in force in the original states those which they thought were suitable for the Northwest Territory, the name that came to be applied to the region north of the Ohio River. The judges were also to exercise judicial authority. The secretary, in addition to keeping the official records, was to become acting governor if the governor resigned, was absent from the territory, or became disqualified.

When the free adult males in the territory should number five thousand, they were to be allowed representation in a territorial legislature. The members of the lower house were to be chosen by the adult males who owned at least fifty acres of land and the members themselves were required to own two hundred acres or more. The lower house was to meet and choose ten men, each of whom owned at least five hundred acres of land, and send their names to Congress, or after 1789 to the President; five of the ten were to be commissioned as councilors or members of the upper house. When the two houses met in regular session, they could legislate for the territory, but the governor by refusing to sign a bill was able to exercise an absolute veto. The assembly was also authorized to choose a delegate to Congress who could speak but not vote. The governor and judges were to continue during this second stage but without their legislative power.

The property of a person who died without leaving a will was to be divided equally according to the degree of relationship, a significant provision since Virginia had only recently abolished primogeniture or the giving of the inheritance to the eldest son.

The civil rights guaranteed in the six articles of compact, which comprised the latter half of the ordinance, were far in advance of their time. The first guaranteed freedom of religious belief and worship; the second the right of trial by jury, the benefits of the writ of habeas corpus, and the sanctity of private contracts, the last of these being the first appearance of such a guarantee in any charter of government. The third guarantee relating to education was also notable: "Religion, Morality and knowledge being necessary to good government and the happiness of mankind, Schools and the means of education shall forever be encouraged"; the fourth declared that the states that should be formed out of the territory should forever remain a part of the United States and be subject to its acts and ordinances; the navigable waters leading to the Mississippi and St. Lawrence were proclaimed common highways "forever free" to all citizens of the United States, a right we take for granted but one that is very essential to our everyday lives. The fifth article provided that no less than three nor more than five states should be formed out of the territory and the north-south boundaries of the three were fixed at approximately the present lines of Ohio, Indiana, and Illinois. Whenever any of the proposed states should have sixty thousand free inhabitants it should be admitted to the Union on an equal footing with the original states; the sixth and last article prohibited slavery and involuntary servitude in the territory. This provision was to be the subject of much controversy and various efforts would be made to repeal it, but it served as a strong safeguard for the cause of freedom during the territorial period and in the constitutional conventions that framed the charters of the states of the Old Northwest.[56]

The Ordinance of 1787 ranks with the Declaration of Independence and the Constitution of the United States as one of the great bulwarks of constitutional liberty. It did not, however, establish a democratic government for the territorial period. During the rule by the governor and judges, the government was not any more liberal than that in the royal colony of Virginia before the Revolution. Though this feature must have been disappointing to those frontiersmen who had already tasted of representative government in the original states, the promise of participation in elections of local officials and of representation in the territorial legislature at a future time made it tolerable. And beyond this second stage they could look forward to statehood. This guarantee (which was appropriated from the Ordinance of 1784) that men leaving their mother country to colonize elsewhere would not lose their full rights of citizenship but that these rights and those of self-government would be put in trust for them, was a new concept in the history of government.[57] Because of this planned advance in self-government, the Ordinance established

---

[56] For the text of the ordinance as submitted to Congress and the vote taken on July 13, 1787, see *Journals of the Continental Congress,* XXXII, 334-343. It contained a clause repealing the earlier ordinance of 1784.

[57] On the significance of the Ordinance of 1787, see Milo M. Quaife, "The Significance of the Ordinance of 1787," *Journal* of the Illinois State Historical Society, XXX (1938), 415-428; Theodore C. Pease, "The Ordinance of 1787," *Mississippi Valley Historical Review,* XXV (1938-39), 167-180.

a highly successful colonial policy, by means of which state after state entered the Union with a democratic government.

The period in Indiana's history between the end of the Revolution and the enactment of the Ordinance of 1787 was one of beginnings and of uncertainty. Conflict with the Indians over the possession of the land would continue, but in the vicinity of Vincennes and Clarksville events were transpiring which represented an advance of the frontier. Though small and relatively unimportant in the 1780s these beginnings would grow and become significant, while England's retention of the western posts and her influence over the Indians, and Spain's closure of the Mississippi, which were potentially very significant at this period, would recede before the development of the United States. Together the new nation and the new West would grow stronger as the West drew upon the power of the Congress in the solution of the problems of the frontier.

CHAPTER VIII

INDIANA: A PART OF THE NORTHWEST TERRITORY

Arthur St. Clair who was appointed governor of the Northwest Territory by the Congress of the Confederation arrived at the little village of Marietta on July 15, 1788, to inaugurate the government under the Ordinance of 1787. He was a native of Scotland, a resident of the Pennsylvania frontier, and had been a member and president of the Congress in 1786-87 while the Ordinance was under consideration. He had served as an officer in the armed forces during the Revolution and, although he had not established a brilliant record, was retired as a major general.[1]

The man chosen as secretary of the territory was Winthrop Sargent, a graduate of Harvard and a conscientious public servant but lacking frontier experience and the flexibility of mind to adapt himself to the West. St. Clair was not a popular governor, but the people were often glad to have him return after Sargent had been acting governor in his place.[2] The three original judges were Samuel H. Parsons, a New Englander and an officer in the Ohio Company; James M. Varnum, also a New Englander; and John Cleves Symmes,

1 St. Clair has not been the subject of an adequate, critical biography; for biographical material see the introductory chapters in the *St. Clair Papers,* I, 1-256. St. Clair had been appointed governor on October 5, 1787, and the contract with the Ohio Company for one and a half million acres of land for colonization purposes was signed on October 27. The first boatload of emigrants landed at the site of Marietta the following April. Bond, *Foundations of Ohio,* pp. 268-271.

2 There is no adequate biography of Sargent. See the sketch in *Dictionary of American Biography* (22 volumes, New York, 1928-59), XVI, 368-369, and B. H. Pershing, "Winthrop Sargent," *Ohio Archaeological and Historical Quarterly,* XXXV (1926), 583-601. There are Sargent Papers in the libraries of the Massachusetts Historical Society and the Ohio Historical Society.

a land speculator from New Jersey who was both impractical and overly optimistic, if not financially careless.[3]

The selection of three of the officials, St. Clair, Sargent, and Parsons, was due in part to the skillful lobbyist of the Ohio Company, the Rev. Manasseh Cutler. They were much better fitted to rule the homogeneous New England community which the Ohio Company established at Marietta than the usual settlements of frontiersmen. In a short time Rufus Putnam and George Turner replaced Parsons and Varnum. Putnam was a New Englander and an officer in the Ohio Company; like Symmes he had no legal qualifications for the judgeship, but did possess a fund of practical sense. Turner was born in England and no doubt owed his appointment to his friendship with President Washington. Though well educated, he had a quick temper and was considered a trouble-maker.[4] Under the first stage of territorial government which lasted for eleven years the territory was governed by these appointed officials in whose selection the people did not have a voice.

Detailed provisions for setting up county governments, organizing courts, and establishing the militia were made by the Governor and Judges at their first meeting in July-August, 1788. Washington County, created on July 27, 1778, remained the only county until early in 1790, when St. Clair, Sargent, and the Judges journeyed down the Ohio to Losantiville, where the Governor organized Hamilton County and changed the name of the village to Cincinnati. At Clarksville the population was not sufficient to support a county organization but the Governor appointed William Clark, cousin of George Rogers Clark and surveyor of Clark's Grant, as captain of the militia and justice of the peace. The party then

[3] Beverley W. Bond (ed.), *The Correspondence of John Cleves Symmes* . . . (New York, 1926), Introduction, pp. 1-24; Bond, *Foundations of Ohio,* p. 401.

[4] Rowena Buell (comp.), *The Memoirs of Rufus Putnam* (Boston, 1903); Bond, *Foundations of Ohio,* p. 401; Bond (ed.), *Correspondence of John Cleves Symmes,* pp. 291-292.

proceeded to the Illinois country where St. Clair County was established; from there the Governor was called back to Fort Washington because war with the Indians was imminent.[5]

Secretary Sargent, however, proceeded to Vincennes and organized Knox County on June 20, 1790, with the village on the Wabash as the county seat. On the east the county extended to the Great Miami River, on the north to Canada, on the south to the Ohio, and on the west to a line drawn north from Fort Massac to the Illinois River and along the river to the mouth of the Kankakee and thence north to the Canadian boundary.[6] Knox County alone was originally much larger than the present state of Indiana.

For county officials and militia officers of the new county Sargent chose from among the French families as well as from the Americans. Francis Vigo, the Sardinian who had befriended Clark, was named major of the militia. Of the county courts organized at Vincennes, the court of common pleas heard civil cases and the court of quarter sessions tried persons accused of petty crimes such as assault and battery, drunkenness, and gambling, and also acted as an administrative body. The judges of these courts were justices of the peace, appointed by the governor from various localities. Each justice held court in his own neighborhood in which very minor offenses were tried while persons accused of more serious crimes were bound over to the county court. Since persons qualified for the office of judge were scarce, the same men were often appointed to serve in both the court of quarter sessions and the court of common pleas. Important

---

[5] Beverley W. Bond, Jr., *The Civilization of the Old Northwest. A Study of Political, Social, and Economic Development, 1788-1812* (New York, 1934), pp. 61-64; Carter (ed.), *Territorial Papers*, III, 278-279, 294-295, 296, 301-303, 311.

[6] George Pence and Nellie C. Armstrong, *Indiana Boundaries. Territory, State, and County (Indiana Historical Collections*, XIX, Indianapolis, 1933), p. 514.

cases could be appealed to the circuit courts of the territory and, if very important, to the General Court; these were presided over by the territorial judges. There was also a probate judge in each county whose duties were similar to those performed by that officer today.[7]

The officials of the county included a sheriff, coroner, clerk, recorder, and treasurer (beginning in 1792), all of whom were appointed by the governor. Other local officials such as overseers of the poor and constables were appointed by the court of general quarter sessions, and by an act of 1795 this same court was to appoint three commissioners who together with the township assessors were to take care of the financial business of the county. The same act provided for the election of a township assessor by the free male inhabitants of each township.[8] Knox County had been divided into two town-

[7] Clyde F. Snider, "Indiana Counties and Townships," *Indiana Magazine of History,* XXXIII (1937), 119-126. The first judges of the court of common pleas were Pierre Gamelin, Louis Edeline, and James Johnson; of the court of general quarter sessions, Antoine and Paul Gamelin, Francis Bosseron; probate judge, Antoine Gamelin. Carter (ed), *Territorial Papers,* III, 316. The records of these early Knox County courts are preserved in the present courthouse at Vincennes. At the first session of the court of common pleas in July, 1790, Major Hamtramck's wife, the former Maria Edeline Perrot, was assured of her share of the estate of her late husband, Nicholas Perrot, according to the usages and customs of the French. At the second meeting of the court in January, 1791, twenty-seven cases were presented, for a number of which juries were called. The number of cases that came before the common pleas court continued to be prodigious, the majority being for the collection of debts. The proceedings reveal that the settlers (both American and French) were continuing to hunt and carry on a trade in beaver and deer skins. There were at least two gunsmiths, John Small and Daniel Pea; a blacksmith, Jacob Miner, and a distiller, John N. Seily. Proceedings of the Knox County Court of Common Pleas, 1790-1791, 1796-1799, typed copy in Archives Division, Indiana State Library.

[8] Theodore C. Pease (ed.), *The Laws of the Northwest Territory, 1788-1800 (Illinois Historical Collections,* XVII, Springfield, 1925), pp. 4-6, 8, 14, 18, 19, 20, 24-25, 38, 39, 68-69, 197-201, 201-216. The first persons appointed to fill the county offices were: sheriff, John Small; clerk, Samuel Baird; recorder, John Mills; coroner, Christopher Wyant; treasurer, Paul Gamelin; additional justices of the peace, James Johnson, Luke Decker. Carter (ed.), *Territorial Papers,* III, 313, 316, 384.

ships, Vincennes and Clarksville, in 1791 with the Blue River as the boundary between the two.[9]

A penal code had also been formulated by the Governor and Judges at their first meeting at Marietta in 1788.[10] Penalties which the law provided were very severe. Some counties did not have a jail, and those that were built were not strong enough to hold desperate criminals; for these reasons, punishments on the frontier were generally fines, whippings, and hangings. Three offenses—murder, treason, and arson (if death resulted)—were punished by hanging. Arson and perjury were punishable by the application of 39 stripes and then being placed in the pillory for two hours; burglary and larceny by whipping alone (39 stripes for the first and 31 for the second, if it was a first offense). If a child or servant was convicted of striking his parent or master he was to receive 10 stripes. Fines were the common punishment for lesser crimes.

In providing this comparatively elaborate machinery of local government and a penal code the Governor and Judges were clearly influenced by English precedents, some of which had been transferred to the colonies. Although they were instructed to confine their legislative activities to choosing from the codes of the original states such laws as seemed adaptable to the Northwest, in practice they disregarded this limitation. A Senate committee was appointed in January, 1799, to inquire how far the territorial laws were "authorized or expedient," but the committee never reported; by this time the Northwest Territory was about to pass into the second stage, and limitations on the legislative power of the Governor and Judges were no longer of practical importance.[11]

9 *History of Knox and Daviess Counties* . . . (Chicago, 1886), pp. 148, 172.

10 Pease (ed.), *Laws of the Northwest Territory*, pp. 13-21.

11 Snider, "Indiana Counties and Townships," *Indiana Magazine of History*, XXXIII, 124-126; Pease (ed.), *Laws of the Northwest Territory*, pp. xx-xxx, 4-10. Governor St. Clair made the comment in 1794 that the Judges did not have copies of the laws of the various states, and he had only those of Pennsylvania. Smith (ed.), *St. Clair Papers*, II, 334.

Judges Symmes and Turner and Acting Governor Sargent, sitting at Vincennes, adopted three laws pertaining particularly to the situation at that place. The first forbade the sale of liquor to the Indians and limited the trade with them to licensed citizens; the second prohibited the sale of liquor to and the receiving of military equipment from the soldiers stationed there; and the third forbade gambling and the indiscriminate discharge of firearms. Since the Judges could not agree on further legislation, Sargent issued proclamations of doubtful validity, one of which required the militiamen to be constantly ready for service and to notify the commanding officer at Fort Knox before leaving town, while another ordered foreigners to report to the same officer upon entering the county and forbade them to hunt within its boundaries.[12]

In addition to laying out the new county of Knox, organizing the militia, and appointing the necessary civil and military officers, Sargent was to execute the resolution of Congress of August 29, 1788, in which provision was made "for confirming in their possessions and titles the French & Canadian inhabitants and other settlers at post St. Vincents who on or before the year 1783 had settled there and had professed themselves citizens of the United States." By the same resolution a tract of four hundred acres was to be given to each head of family of this description.[13]

On July 31, 1790, after spending some six weeks in Vincennes, Sargent reported to the President that 143 persons had proved themselves as heads of families at Vincennes on or before 1783, and for these a tract of land had been laid out east of the village. Fifteen names were added to the list later. When it came to confirming the French and Canadians in their possessions, Sargent found that only one person in

---

[12] Pease (ed.), *Laws of the Northwest Territory*, pp. 26-34; Carter (ed.), *Territorial Papers*, III, 313-316; Bond, *Civilization of the Old Northwest*, pp. 64-66.

[13] Leonard Lux, *The Vincennes Donation Lands* (Indiana Historical Society *Publications*, XV, No. 4, Indianapolis, 1949), pp. 427, 441-448; Dillon, *History of Indiana*, p. 222.

twenty could produce a complete title. The problem of casual record keeping was compounded in some instances by fraud and forgery. After hearing oral testimonies and checking the written records available, he had confirmed 72 farms or fields to 60 claimants and 162 town lots to 128 individuals. The fields were located in the prairies surrounding Vincennes and were generally 2 or 4 arpents wide by 40 arpents deep, amounting to 66 or 136 English acres, depending on the width.[14]

American settlers who came to Vincennes after 1783 also wanted to share in the land grants. Fifty of them who were enrolled in the Knox County militia in 1790 drew up a petition which they presented to Sargent on July 19, 1790, beseeching him to make application on their behalf to the Congress to allow them each four hundred acres of land in "recompense for the many dangers they have encountered and losses they have sustained" since coming to Vincennes. The names of the petitioners and their dates of arrival are printed below.

NAME	DATE SETTLED IN KNOX CO.	NAME	DATE SETTLED IN KNOX CO.
John Martin	1785	Luke Decker	1784
Frederick Mathler	1785	Bastian Frederick	1785
Christian Barrachman	1785	Philip Catt	1785
Michael Thorn	1784	Jacob Pea	1785
Robert Day	1785	John Pea	1785
James Johnson	1784	Joseph Decker	1784
Godfrey Petters	1786	Henry Pea	1785
Peter Thorn	1784	Ralph Matson	1784

14 *American State Papers. Public Lands* (8 volumes, Washington, D. C., 1834-61), I, 9-12; VII, 675-727; Lux, *Vincennes Donation Lands,* pp. 448-449; Dillon, *History of Indiana,* pp. 233-234. The donations were confirmed by an act of Congress of March 3, 1791, which settled certain questions which Sargent had been unable to resolve. U. S. *Statutes at Large,* I, 221-222; Carter (ed.), *Territorial Papers,* II, 339-342. Proceedings regarding the claims and location of the grants continued for the next twenty years.

Name	Date Settled in Knox Co.	Name	Date Settled in Knox Co.
Thos. Jordan	1784	Isaac Decker	1784
Christopher Wyant	1785	Abraham Decker	1784
Jacob Thorn	1784	Moses Decker	1784
H. Vanderburgh	1787	Abraham Snapp	1784
Tobias Decker	1784	Lewis Frederick	1785
Allen Ramsey	1784	Abraham Barrachman	1785
John Decker	1784	Edw. Shoebrook	1784
Frederick Linden	1785	Jas. Johnson	1785
John Robins	1784	John Rice Jones	1785
Danl. Thorn	1784	Wm. Mayes	1784
John Lowe	1789	Jeremiah Mayes	1784
John Murphy	1789	Abraham Westfall	1785
Solomon Thorn	1784	John Harbin	1787
Daniel Smith	1785	Joshua Harbin	1787
Wm. Smith	1785	Daniel Meredeth	1780
Daniel Pea	1785	Hezekiah Holliday	1784
Charles Thorn	1784	Patrick Simpson	1785

Several of these men had fought in the Revolutionary War. The Deckers, Allen Ramsey, William and Jeremiah Mayes were all related and emigrated from western Pennsylvania, traveling in three skiffs down the Ohio and up the Wabash. One of the children in the party was captured by Indians the first night of their arrival at Vincennes. James Johnson, Michael Thorn, and Philip Catt had all served in the Revolution from western Pennsylvania. Congress acted favorably on their petition but reduced the extent of the land granted to one hundred acres.[15]

[15] The land grant to the militiamen was a part of the 1791 act and included the French as well as the Americans. The names of the 221 recipients are printed in *American State Papers. Public Lands,* VII, 682-685. In addition to asking for land for their own use, the American settlers asked for a plot of ground one fourth mile south of town that was being used as a graveyard, and sufficient additional land for the erection of "a house of worship." Both petitions are printed in the Vincennes *Western Sun,* May 21, 1859, from the original documents.

§

The most serious task of the territorial governor was the management of Indian affairs, in which the national officials had made an unfortunate beginning. By early 1787 the wisdom of the government's Indian policy of the past three years began to be questioned. Faced with the danger of a general Indian war and an empty treasury, Congress began to retreat from its highhanded attitude of the immediate postwar period. However, there could be no retreat from their objective of making the lands north of the Ohio available to those who wished to locate there. The Ordinance of 1787 committed the country to a policy of western expansion. The northwest tribes were equally adamant that the Ohio River should be the boundary between the United States and the Indian country. How to break this stalemate became the concern of committee after committee of the Congress. Out of these debates came a new concept of treating the Indians more on a footing of equality, of acknowledging their "right to the soil," and offering to purchase their lands instead of demanding them. This was a reversion to the policy to which the Indians had become accustomed with the British.

Instructions were given Governor St. Clair for negotiating a new treaty in which the Indians would be paid for the lands ceded by the treaties of 1784 and 1785. In the meantime, some of the Indians who had asked for a new treaty in December, 1786, were now drawing back and refused to meet the Governor. At last in December, 1788, some two hundred Iroquois, Wyandots, Delawares, Ottawa, Chippewa, and Potawatomi accepted the invitation to meet at Fort Harmar. The Governor stood firm against the Indian proposal to restore the Ohio River as the boundary between the Indians and white settlements and in the end negotiated two treaties, one with the western tribes which confirmed the western boundary established by the Fort McIntosh treaty of 1785 for an additional compensation of $6,000 in goods, and the other with the Six Nations which confirmed the boundaries set out in the Fort Stanwix treaty of 1784 for an additional compensation of $3,000; other provisions related to punishment for crimes and regulation of trade; both treaties were signed on January 9, 1789.[16] On the whole, the negotiations did not differ greatly from the earlier ones inasmuch as those Indians in attendance could not speak for their respective tribes and they were pressured into yielding more than they wished.

The Fort Harmar treaties were the culmination of the Indian policy of the Confederation. St. Clair hoped he had established peace and that the way was now open for settlement north of the Ohio; instead, Indian hostilities continued with little or no interruption.

With the inauguration of the federal government in 1789 a new effort was made to pacify the northwestern Indians. Henry Knox who had been in charge of Indian affairs under the Confederation was to continue in that capacity as secretary of war in the new administration. He now had the backing and support of President Washington in his efforts to negotiate with the Indians. A new concept of bringing civilization to the tribesmen began to be stressed.[17]

The Wabash and Illinois tribes were not represented in the Fort Harmar treaty and did not feel bound by it. In spite of the presence of American troops at Vincennes, these tribes continued their raids into Kentucky and Kentuckians on two occasions sent unauthorized expeditions into the Indian coun-

[16] Kappler (ed.), *Indian Affairs. Laws and Treaties,* II, 13-19; Downes, *Council Fires on the Upper Ohio,* pp. 299-309; Horsman, *Expansion and American Indian Policy,* pp. 44-49. An abstract of the treaty with the western tribes which appears among the papers in the Canadian Archives bears the notation: "The Indians do by no means consider this treaty as binding on them as a body as many of the principal chiefs were not only absent at this *Council-fire,* but absolutely declare they never will consent to such accession . . . The Hurons were the most forward to sign it . . . this nation is inconsiderable in number & influence & are seldom consulted on the general political affairs of the nations." *Michigan Historical Collections,* XXIV, 41-42. See also below, p. 297.

[17] Horsman, *Expansion and American Indian Policy,* pp. 53-59.

try.[18] In September, 1789, Congress authorized the President to call out the militia of Virginia and Pennsylvania if necessary to halt the depredations and bring the Indians to terms. Before resorting to force, Washington wished to make one more attempt at peace and wrote to Governor St. Clair on October 6, 1789, to ascertain whether or not the Wabash and Illinois Indians were "most inclined for war or peace." "If a peace can be established . . . on reasonable terms, the interests of the United States dictate that it should be effected as soon as possible." If the Governor should find the Indians determined on continuing hostilities, he was authorized to call out the militia as a last resort.[19] To carry out the President's orders, St. Clair wrote a long letter to the Indians on the Wabash and to the Miami, stating the desire of the United States for a general peace and cessation of hostilities. This was sent to Major Hamtramck at Vincennes who in turn chose Antoine Gamelin, a Frenchman well known to the Indians, to carry the message to the tribesmen. The Journal which Gamelin kept indicates the type of reception he received; most of the Wabash Indians were noncommittal, saying the decision for peace or war rested with the Miami. Some were critical because he had come empty-handed. On reaching the Miami village of Kekionga, Gamelin presented the message to an assemblage of Miami, Delawares, and Shawnee, and showed them the Fort Harmar treaty, which displeased them. The Shawnee reply was that they could give an answer to the message only after consulting the British commandant at Detroit and suggested that Gamelin go to see him. The Miami wished to consult the other tribes of the Indian confederacy as well as the British commandant. Gamelin refused to extend his journey any farther, whereupon the Shawnee and Miami promised to send an answer to Vincennes. On his return journey Gamelin found that the younger Indians from some of the villages had already taken to the

18 Thornbrough (ed.), *Outpost on the Wabash,* pp. 114-117, 175-177, 182-184.
19 Smith (ed.), *St. Clair Papers,* II, 125.

warpath. His report, which reached St. Clair while he was at Kaskaskia, convinced the Governor that there was not the least probability of making peace with the Indians. He departed immediately for Fort Washington, military headquarters for the western country, to make plans for a military expedition against the above tribes.[20]

The Governor called on Virginia, which at that time still included Kentucky, for one thousand militiamen and on Pennsylvania for five hundred. Three hundred of these were sent to Vincennes and the rest assembled at Fort Washington, from which General Harmar on September 30, 1790, led 320 regulars and 1,133 militiamen northward to the Indian country. The militia comprised many untrained, inexperienced, and unfit men; some had enlisted merely to get free transportation to the West and hoped they could avoid any fighting during the short time they would be in the service. There was no time for training because if frost came, the pack horses used for transportation would have no forage. The improvised soldiers would have to learn by experience. By October 17 the troops reached the Miami towns near the present Fort Wayne only to find that the Indians had fled into the forests. The villages that had not been destroyed by the departing tribesmen were burned and the stores plundered. On the nineteenth, Harmar sent 180 militia and 30 regulars under Col. John Hardin to reconnoiter. Near the St. Joseph

[20] Smith (ed.), *St. Clair Papers*, II, 130-132n; Thornbrough (ed.), *Outpost on the Wabash*, pp. 223-225. Gamelin's Journal is printed in *American State Papers. Indian Affairs*, I, 93-94; in Dillon, *History of Indiana*, pp. 226-232; and in *Readings in Indiana History*, pp. 58-65. Hamtramck first sent Pierre Gamelin with the message, but he returned to Vincennes after going only as far as the Vermilion River. Antoine was probably a brother of Pierre. Hamtramck apparently did not have much faith in the Governor's message for he wrote that the best treaty with the Miami would be "a good flogging." *Outpost on the Wabash*, p. 224n.

The object of this first expedition was not to establish a fortification in the Indian country, but to punish the Wabash tribes for their hostile depredations and their refusal to treat when invited to do so. Knox to St. Clair, September 12, 1790, in *American State Papers. Indian Affairs*, I, 100.

River they marched into an ambuscade in which 20 regulars and 40 militia died fighting; many of the latter fled without resisting. After the army had started its return march, Colonel Hardin asked to be sent back in hopes of surprising the Indians and redeeming his troops from their previous defeat. He marched on the night of October 21 with 300 militia and 60 regulars under Maj. John P. Wyllys. They reached one of the Indian villages on the Maumee a little after sunrise the next morning; while preparing to attack, one of the soldiers prematurely fired at a lone Indian thus alerting the others to their presence. As the Indians fled the militia broke ranks and scattered in pursuit. The regulars being thus deserted, the Indians came out of hiding and attacked; the Major and fifty regulars were killed. The total casualties, 180 killed and wounded. Believing that further offensive action was impossible, General Harmar decided to get out of the Indian country before the remainder of his army disintegrated and his transportation collapsed; one third of the pack horses had died or wandered off at night, and there was no longer any grazing for the remainder of the animals. On November 3, 1790, the troops reached Fort Washington. The expedition had the effect of advertising the incapacity of the American army and of stimulating the Indians to greater activity against the whites. On the credit side, some valuable lessons had been learned in fighting the Indians and in the matter of transportation and supply.[21]

21 Jacobs, *The Beginning of the United States Army,* pp. 52-62; Jack J. Gifford, The Northwest Indian War, 1784-1795 (Unpublished Ph.D. thesis in history, University of California at Los Angeles, 1964), Chap. III; Griswold, *Pictorial History of Fort Wayne,* I, 102-113. Personal accounts of Harmar's expedition include those of Maj. Ebenezer Denny in *Memoirs* of the Historical Society of Pennsylvania, VII, 343-355; of John Armstrong in Dillon, *History of Indiana,* pp. 245-248; of Thomas Irvin in *Ohio Archaeological and Historical Quarterly,* XIX (1910), 393-396; and letters of Harmar to Governor St. Clair, October 18 and 24, 1790, in the Indiana Historical Society Library.

St. Clair had sent a message to the commanding officer at Detroit assuring him that the expedition was aimed only at the red men and not against

In order to divert the attention of the Wabash tribes and keep them from joining the Miami in opposing Harmar's expedition, Major Hamtramck was instructed to lead an expedition up the Wabash and strike either the Vermilion, Wea, or Eel River towns. His force was drawn from the Fort Knox garrison, the French militia, and three hundred Kentucky militia; he was to move on September 25, before Harmer was scheduled to leave Fort Washington. Hamtramck estimated that he might have to meet a combined force of around 780 warriors (200 Vermilion Piankashaw; 330 Wea; 100 Kickapoo; 150 on Eel River), which would be greater than his own force. Supplies in the way of cartridges, flints, tents, and shoes for the men were ordered during the summer. Meanwhile, the Fort Knox commander reported the cattle and flour for his garrison were over six weeks late in arriving, many of his men were sick, and some of the officers were involved in speculating on the soldiers' pay and supplies.

The Kentucky militia did not arrive until September 29 and the following day Hamtramck set out with a force of 330, less than he had anticipated. He had sixteen thousand pounds of flour (but apparently lost a considerable amount because of improper storage) and twenty oxen (out of 96 intended for the expedition). After a march of eleven days the troops reached the Vermilion village where they found only empty

Detroit, and expressing his confidence that the British would not lend the Indians any assistance or encouragement. *Michigan Historical Collections,* XXIV, 99-100. Alexander McKee, British Indian agent, writing on October 18, 1790, did not think the Indians were strong enough "to make much opposition" to Harmar's forces. Before burning Miamis Town the Indians removed their women and children and helped the British traders take out their goods. Upwards of a thousand bushels of corn that could not be removed were lost in the fire. The Indians estimated that the Americans lost five hundred men in the two engagements. Correspondence of Alexander McKee, Matthew Elliott, and others in *Michigan Historical Collections,* XXIV, 105-109, 132-142 *passim.*

The court of inquiry appointed at Harmar's request to examine into the manner in which the expedition was conducted absolved him of any personal misconduct. *American State Papers. Military Affairs* (7 volumes, Washington, D. C., 1789-1838), I, 20-36.

houses, the Indians having departed several days earlier. To go on to the Wea or Kickapoo towns would take another nine days, it was estimated, yet they had provisions for only fourteen, not sufficient to get them back to Vincennes. Several of the Kentucky militia had already deserted and were not willing to accept half rations; the French were anxious to return to take care of their corn crop. Faced with these circumstances, the expedition returned to Vincennes without seemingly accomplishing anything. However, Hamtramck was later informed that six hundred warriors from the Wabash tribes had assembled to attack him had he moved farther up the Wabash; thus he felt that many tribesmen at least had been diverted from joining the Miami against Harmar.[22]

After the defeat of Harmar, the Indians turned increasingly to murder and plunder. They prophesied to General Putnam that "there should not remain a Smoak on the Ohio by the time the Leaves put out," i.e., by spring of 1791. When Congress met in December, 1790, they voted to increase the strength of the regular army by a single regiment of 912 men, and the President was granted discretionary power to raise two thousand militia for a period of six months' service. Governor St. Clair was appointed a major general on March 4, 1791, and placed in command of a new offensive operation against the western Indians.[23]

When word reached Quebec that the Americans were preparing another expedition against the Indians, Lord Dorchester warned the officer commanding the upper Canadian posts that he should place them "in a thorough state of defense," and that he should be "prepared to march forward should the turn of affairs render this absolutely necessary." The Governor also asked John Johnson, the superintendent of Indian affairs, what advanced stations should be occupied if the safety of the posts should require a forward movement.

<hr />

[22] Thornbrough (ed.), *Outpost on the Wabash,* pp. 236-237n, 242-243, 246, 248, 250, 258-259, 259-264, 266, 274n.

[23] Jacobs, *The Beginning of the United States Army,* pp. 67-71.

Johnson passed the inquiry on to his deputy, Alexander McKee, who replied on June 20 that the best location for a forward station would be at the foot of the Maumee rapids or in that vicinity, and that one hundred regulars plus fifty militia should be posted there. Dorchester thought this was a "judicious" suggestion, but shortly departed for England without making any effort to implement it.

At the same time that the Canadian governor was urging preparations for defense of the posts, he was also indicating his desire to play the role of mediator between the United States and the Indians. Johnson was asked to ascertain what peace terms would be acceptable to the Indians and again McKee was asked to provide the answer. He called a representative group of the chiefs together in July and secured from them a statement that they would accept as a boundary between the Indians and whites a line running up the Ohio River from the mouth of the Tennessee to the mouth of Muskingum, up that river to the portage across to the Cuyahoga, on to Venango, and thence north to Lake Erie along the line dividing the Six Nations from the western tribes. While in London Lord Dorchester proposed that a neutral barrier of exclusively Indian territory be set up between the United States and the neighboring British colonies, but this plan was never formally presented to the American government.[24] In the meantime, events had transpired in the Indian country which would make negotiations with the Indians more difficult.

§ §

To divert the Indians from continuing their raids on frontier settlements along the Ohio River and in western Virginia, the legislature of that state authorized the governor to organize offensive operations into the Indian country. Charles

24 Ernest A. Cruikshank (ed.), *The Correspondence of Lieut. Governor John Graves Simcoe* . . . (5 volumes, Toronto, 1923-31), I, 22-23, 25; *Michigan Historical Collections*, XXIV, 262-263, 280-281, 301; Burt, *The United States, Great Britain, and British North America*, pp. 116-121.

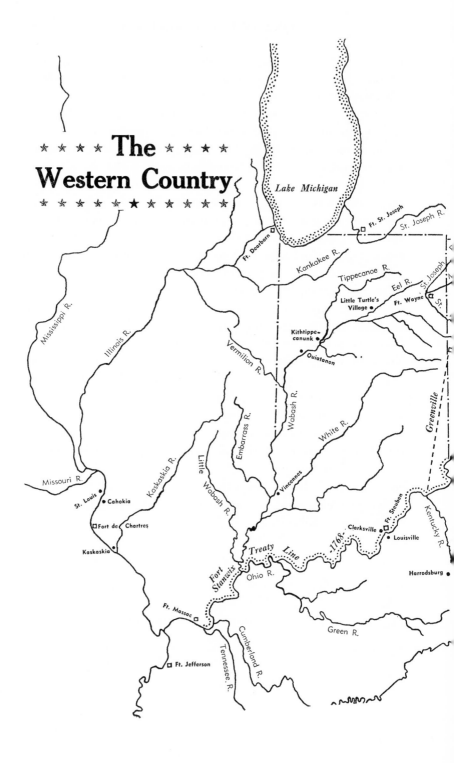

★ ★ ★ ★ The ★ ★ ★ ★
Western Country
★ ★ ★ ★ ★ ★ ★ ★ ★ ★

Lake Michigan

Ft. St. Joseph

St. Joseph R.

Ft. Dearborn

Kankakee R.

Tippecanoe R.

Eel R.

Little Turtle's Village •

Ft. Wayne

St. Joseph

Mississippi R.

Illinois R.

Vermilion R.

Kithtippe- canunk •

Ouiatanon •

Wabash R.

White R.

Greenville

Embarrass R.

Kaskaskia R.

Little Wabash R.

Vincennes •

Missouri R.

St. Louis • Cahokia

Fort de Chartres

Kaskaskia

Ft. Steuben

Clarksville • Louisville

Kentucky R.

1768

Treaty Line

Fort Stanwix

Ohio R.

Harrodsburg

Ft. Massac

Green R.

Cumberland R.

Ft. Jefferson

Tennessee R.

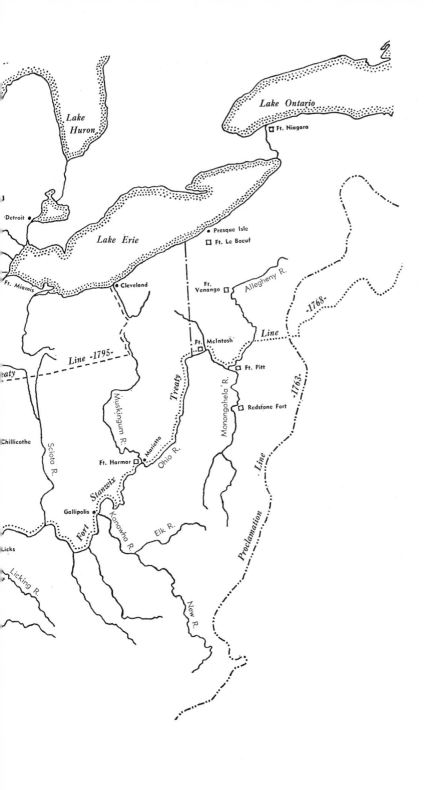

Scott was appointed brigadier general of the Kentucky militia with authority to enlist mounted volunteers; the services of these men were then offered to the Secretary of War and accepted. On May 23, 1791, General Scott with a force of about eight hundred mounted and armed men crossed the Ohio at the mouth of the Kentucky River and traveled in as near a direct line as possible toward Ouiatanon, crossing four branches of White River and many smaller streams that were flooded as a result of the spring rains that fell each day.

On the eighth day (June 1) as they reached the prairies south of the Wabash the troops were discovered by a lone Indian on horseback who escaped capture and rode away to warn the inhabitants of the Wea village of their approach. A few hours later the first of the Indian towns came into view on the left and a detachment under Col. John Hardin was sent to attack these towns of the Kickapoo, while the main body proceeded on to the main town on the Wabash where they caught the inhabitants trying to escape to the other side of the river. The troops fired on them and killed some. The Wabash could not be forded at this place, so one detachment was sent upstream to try to find a place to cross, while another group went downstream a short distance and crossed the river to reach a Kickapoo town which they found deserted.

In the meantime, General Scott received a request for additional help from Colonel Hardin's detachment which was attacking the Kickapoo towns, but before reinforcements arrived the Colonel's men had killed six warriors and taken fifty-two women and children prisoners.

Scott wished to press on to the town of Kithtippecanunk, eighteen miles farther north on the west side of the Wabash, but found the horses too crippled and exhausted. The following evening Col. James Wilkinson with 360 men crossed the Wabash and marched on foot to the above town which was near the mouth of the Tippecanoe, destroyed it, and returned to join Scott in twelve hours. He reported that many of the inhabitants of the village were French and lived in a state of civilization. "By the books, letters, and other documents found there . . . [it] was in close connection with, and dependent on, Detroit. A large quantity of corn, a variety of household goods, peltry, and other articles, were burned with this village, which consisted of about seventy houses, many of them well finished."

Having thus accomplished their objective of burning the Indian towns and taking a number of prisoners (which they hoped could be exchanged for white prisoners), the troops began the return trip on the fourth and arrived at the Falls of the Ohio ten days later where they delivered the captives to Captain Asheton of Fort Steuben. Scott had liberated sixteen prisoners too infirm for traveling and gave them a message to take back to their leaders urging them to make peace with the United States.[25]

A second expedition, which consisted of some five hundred Kentucky volunteers led by General Wilkinson, marched north in August from Cincinnati as though it was moving against the Miami villages at the site of Fort Wayne, but turned northwestward to the mouth of the Eel River of the north and demolished the Miami village of Little Turtle, and took 34 prisoners (mostly women and children). They then went on to Kithtippecanunk and Ouiatanon, the two Indian towns that had been destroyed in the spring, where they destroyed the crops that had been planted, and then took Scott's route back to the Falls of the Ohio. These expeditions demon-

[25] Scott to Secretary of War Knox, June 28, 1791, in *American State Papers. Indian Affairs*, I, 131-132; also in Dillon, *History of Indiana*, pp. 257-265, and in part in *Readings in Indiana History*, pp. 65-70. Another account of the expedition written by one of the soldiers is printed in George Imlay, *A Topographical Description of the Western Territory of North America* (London, 1793), and reprinted in Harlow Lindley (ed.), *Indiana as Seen by Early Travelers* (*Indiana Historical Collections*, III, Indianapolis, 1916), pp. 11-16. The report of the expedition that reached the British agent McKee is in *Michigan Historical Collections*, XXIV, 273. The goods of trader Jacques Godfroy amounting to five hundred pounds New York currency was reported destroyed.

strated the successful use of volunteers as against drafted militiamen, drew attention away from the main campaign in Ohio, and caused some of the Wabash tribesmen to seek peace.[26]

§ § §

While these expeditions were being conducted against the Indians, St. Clair was assembling a force at Fort Washington for the main effort against the enemy. He planned to build a chain of forts and mark the road to the headwaters of the Maumee, where a fort was to be constructed and garrisoned to keep the Miami and neighboring tribes at peace. He was promised three thousand men and was expected to strike a decisive blow against the tribesmen, but almost everything seemed to miscarry from the beginning. Just short of 2,700 men came to Fort Washington, most of them so late that again there was little or no time for training. Although the army was far from ready for active service, the troops began to move on September 17. St. Clair, now fifty-seven and afflicted with gout, was conscious of the shortcomings of his troops, but the original plans had called for the campaign to begin the first of July and any further delay would mean postponement until the following year. Fort Hamilton was built and garrisoned twenty-five miles north of the Ohio and forty-two miles farther north Fort Jefferson was constructed. It started raining on October 18 and continued for two or three days, then turned cold. Troops were ill clothed and had little protection from the weather. They were also hungry most of the time as it became increasingly difficult to bring in supplies for lack of pack horses. Under such conditions their morale became lower and lower and as their

[26] Wilkinson to St. Clair, August 24, 1791, in *St. Clair Papers,* II, 233-239; also in Dillon, *History of Indiana,* pp. 267-271. See also Robert B. Whitsett, Jr., "Snake-Fish Town, the Eighteenth Century Metropolis of Little Turtle's Eel River Miami," *Indiana History Bulletin,* XV (1938), 72-82; John Armstrong to Col. Francis Johnston, August 30, 1791, Armstrong Papers, Indiana Historical Society Library.

term of service expired they left; others deserted. The commander was obstinate and refused to turn back. The army
halted on the evening of November 3 and made camp close
to the east bank of the upper Wabash. The ground was low
and wet and the troops were exhausted and chilled to the
bone; no entrenchments or breastworks were thrown up; three
different officers were warned by scouts of an attack but still
nothing was done to prepare the troops. Early on the morning of November 4 the Indians, one thousand strong, attacked
the camp with great force. The militia fled, the artillery was
captured, and soon the entire army retreated in great confusion. The killed, wounded, and missing totaled approximately nine hundred. The Indians had administered a serious
defeat to the Americans and were ready to consider themselves invincible.[27]

President Washington was angered and disappointed at
the defeat of St. Clair's expedition. As a result, migration
to the West was checked, the Indians were determined to
continue their resistance to the expansion of the frontier, and
the British had hopes of a revision of the boundary between
the United States and Canada. St. Clair resigned his military
commission, and Washington and the Congress prepared for
a new and stronger campaign against the Indians. An act of
March 5, 1792, making more effectual provision for protection of the frontiers, provided for a complete reorganiza-

[27] Jacobs, *Beginning of the United States Army*, pp. 76-116; Bond, *Founda-
tions of Ohio*, pp. 324-328; Downes, *Council Fires on the Upper Ohio*, pp. 318-
320; Gifford, The Northwest Indian War, 1784-1795, Chaps. V-VI. For
personal accounts of the expedition, see "Winthrop Sargent's Diary," *Ohio
Archaeological and Historical Quarterly*, XXXIII (1924), 237-273; Diary of
Maj. Ebenezer Denny, in *Memoirs* of the Historical Society of Pennsylvania,
VII, 355-378, and in *St. Clair Papers*, II, 251-262; St. Clair's Journal in Dillon,
History of Indiana, pp. 276-277; letters of William Darke, a soldier, in *Mich-
igan Historical Collections*, XXIV, 331-334. See also St. Clair's report to the
Secretary of War in *St. Clair Papers*, II, 262-267, and in Dillon, *History of
Indiana*, pp. 278-282.

A committee of the Congress appointed to determine the causes of the failure
of the expedition placed the blame on the War Department for failing to
supply and properly equip the troops. *St. Clair Papers*, II, 286-301n.

tion of the army which now came to be known as the Legion of the United States. General Anthony Wayne, who bore from his Revolutionary service a reputation of being dashing and reckless, was named commander in chief. It was his task to mold into an effective fighting force this new military establishment which at the time existed only on paper.[28]

§ § § §

While "Mad Anthony" prepared for his coming expedition, the government once more endeavored to secure peace by negotiation. Two emissaries named Freeman and Gerrard who were sent by General Wilkinson from Fort Washington on April 7, 1792, with a speech to the Indians on the Maumee were captured and killed. On April 3 Capt. Alexander Trueman was sent by Secretary of War Knox with a message to the western Indians inviting them to send representatives to Philadelphia to negotiate a treaty of peace. He was joined at Fort Washington by Col. John Hardin with a similar message for the Wyandots. Both men were killed by Indians the last of May, about a week after they left the fort and before they had an opportunity to deliver their message.[29]

Gen. Rufus Putnam who was instructed to go to the Maumee and attend an Indian council in the summer of 1792 changed his mind when he learned the fate of Hardin and Trueman and went instead to Vincennes, where he called the Wabash tribes together on September 20. Six hundred and eighty-six Indians from the following tribes were present: Eel River Miami, Wea, Potawatomi, Kickapoo, Piankashaw, Mascoutens, and Kaskaskia. Interestingly enough it was a woman who spoke for the Wea, and apologized for her two sons who were too intoxicated to attend; she blamed the

[28] Richard C. Knopf (ed.), *Anthony Wayne, A Name in Arms. Soldier, Diplomat, Defender of Expansion Westward of a Nation* . . . (Pittsburgh, 1960), pp. 7-9, 13-15; Prucha, *Sword of the Republic,* pp. 28-36; Jacobs, *Beginning of the United States Army,* pp. 124-128.

[29] Dillon, *History of Indiana,* pp. 288-293; *American State Papers. Indian Affairs,* I, 229-230, 238; *Michigan Historical Collections,* XXIV, 390-393, 414-416, 420.

bad influence of the Miami for their condition. At the end of seven days, thirty-one Wabash and Illinois chiefs signed a treaty of peace and friendship with the United States which guaranteed to the Indians their lands without naming a definite boundary. Upon being submitted to the United States Senate, that body objected to Article IV which recognized that the land belonged to the Indians and that they had the right to sell or not to sell, but did not stipulate that the United States had the exclusive right of purchase. Upon coming to a vote on January 9, 1794, the Senate refused to ratify it.

Putnam was accompanied on his peace mission by the Moravian John Heckewelder. At Cincinnati they picked up the Indian captives taken by Generals Scott and Wilkinson on their expeditions the previous year and released them to the tribes assembled at Vincennes. Their release was received with joy by the Indians and no doubt created a favorable atmosphere in which to negotiate. The interpreter for the treaty negotiations was William Wells, a youth who had been captured by the Miami Indians from his home in Kentucky in 1774 and adopted into the family of Chief Little Turtle. He had fought with the Indians against Harmar and St. Clair after which it was agreed between himself and Little Turtle that he should join his own people. In subsequent years he served the United States in various capacities and in 1812 lost his life at the hands of the Indians.[30]

---

30 Putnam's correspondence with Secretary of War Knox and John Francis Hamtramck and the proceedings of the Indian council may be found in Buell (comp.), *The Memoirs of Rufus Putnam,* pp. 273-278, 280-282, 292-293, 296, 307-308, 320-324, 333-334, 335-336. Knox's instructions and the treaty are in *American State Papers. Indian Affairs,* I, 234-236, 338; the treaty is also in Dillon, *History of Indiana,* pp. 293-295n. Heckewelder described his experiences in "Narrative of John Heckewelder's Journey to the Wabash in 1792," *Pennsylvania Magazine of History and Biography,* XII (1888), 49, 167-172. Jacob P. Dunn's *True Indian Stories* (Indianapolis, 1909), pp. 113-130, presents a somewhat romantic portrayal of Wells.

§ § § § §

The council which Putnam was to have attended was held at the mouth of the Auglaize River from September 30 to October 9. It was an impressive gathering of representatives from the Six Nations and the western tribes. Among the chiefs who were present in all their splendor and regalia were the Delaware Buckongahelas and Chochenawaga of the Iroquois. The council had been suggested by John Graves Simcoe who had been appointed lieutenant governor of Upper Canada upon the division of the province in 1791, but it was not called by him. The disunity between the Six Nations and the western tribes in the Indian confederacy was demonstrated in the council, the former being anxious for a peace conference with the United States, while the latter were opposed. The western tribes finally agreed to a conference at Sandusky the following spring on the understanding that the negotiations would be based on the premise of the Ohio River as the boundary between the Indian country and the American states. This represented a change from the Muskingum-Venango boundary they were willing to accept in 1792; intoxicated by their victory over St. Clair, the Indians had advanced their price for peace.

The American government, however, was not aware of this stipulation and agreed to appoint commissioners to meet the Indians on June 1, 1793. They were instructed to obtain if possible confirmation of the boundaries established by the treaties made in the 1780s even if it meant paying an additional amount for the cessions; and if successful in this they were authorized to promise that the United States would confirm the right of the Indians to the remaining land north of the Ohio. Joseph Brant, the leader of the Six Nations, who apparently was responsible for the misunderstanding, hoped he could persuade the western tribes to modify their demands for the Ohio line before the two sides met.

When the American commissioners reached Niagara they were detained there by the British and again at the mouth of the Detroit River while the Indians were meeting in private council at the Maumee rapids in hopes of resolving their differences and presenting a united front to the commissioners. The western tribes won out in the end and a delegation from the council asked the commissioners if they were prepared to negotiate on the basis of the Ohio River as the boundary. This being beyond their instructions, they could only answer no. In their counterproposal, they pointed out (what the Indians already knew) that some of the land had been sold, cleared, and planted; homes had been built on it; if the Indians would confirm the cession made in the Fort Harmar treaty, the United States would give an additional sum of money at once and an annuity in addition. What was still more important, the commissioners acknowledged that the treaty of 1783 with Great Britain had not given the United States the title to the Indian land but merely the exclusive right to purchase it from the tribesmen. It had taken ten years of bitter experience to bring this admission; would it be accepted or was it too late?

While the commissioners waited impatiently at the mouth of the Detroit River, the Indian delegation returned to the council with the American proposal. Sixteen days later, on August 16, the Indian reply was received from the hands of two Wyandot messengers. It rehearsed the earlier negotiations and pointed out that the Indians who attended went to make peace but through fear they were obliged to sign whatever was laid before them, also that the treaty commissioners at Fort Harmar had been informed that no bargain or sale of any part of the Indian lands would be considered valid unless agreed to by a general council. Regarding the offer of additional payment, the Indians replied, "Money, to us, is of no value, and to most of us unknown"; they suggested that it be given to those who had settled on the land in order to get them to remove. "We want peace," they declared, "restore to us our country, and we shall be enemies no longer." They denied that the King of England had ever been given exclusive right to purchase Indian lands, therefore he could not have passed this right on to another country. "We consider ourselves free to make any bargain or cession of lands, whenever and to whomsoever we please." Thus the negotiations came to an impasse; the commissioners returned home without meeting the Indians in council. As soon as the news was received in Philadelphia of the failure to come to terms, Wayne was authorized to renew hostilities. Secretary of War Knox wrote on September 3: "Every effort has been made to obtain peace by milder terms than the sword—the efforts have failed under circumstances which leave nothing for us to expect but war." He warned Wayne not to move until his force was adequately trained "to make those audacious savages feel our superiority in Arms."[31]

The western tribes also believed that war was inevitable and were quick to inform Simcoe that now more than ever they were in need of British protection and friendship. Simcoe voiced his fears of an Indian war as well as a possible attack on the frontier posts being held by the British.[32] The follow-

[31] *American State Papers. Indian Affairs*, I, 340-360; Reginald Horsman, "The British Indian Department and the Abortive Treaty of Lower Sandusky, 1793," *Ohio History Quarterly*, LXX (1961), 189-213; Burt, *The United States, Great Britain, and British North America*, pp. 123-132; Samuel F. Bemis, *Jay's Treaty. A Study in Commerce and Diplomacy* (Revised edition, Yale University Press, 1962), pp. 218-228; Downes, *Council Fires on the Upper Ohio*, pp. 320-325; Dillon, *History of Indiana*, pp. 295-296; Knopf (ed.), *Anthony Wayne*, p. 271. For the minutes of the Indian council at the Auglaize in 1792, see Cruikshank (ed.), *Simcoe Correspondence*, I, 218-229. Americans blamed the British for the failure of the negotiations in 1793. Their agent, Alexander McKee, was present at the Indian council on the Maumee and although he claimed he had done his best to promote the acceptance by the western tribes of the Muskingum-Venango boundary line, William Wells, who was also present, claimed that McKee advised the Indians to hold out for the Ohio River as the boundary, and promised arms, ammunition, and provisions if they went to war. McKee to Simcoe, August 22, 1793, in *ibid.*, II, 34-35, and in *Michigan Historical Collections*, XXIV, 595; Dwight L. Smith, "William Wells and the Indian Council of 1793," *Indiana Magazine of History*, LVI (1960), 215-226. Wells, who was acting as a scout for General Wayne, estimated that 2,400 Indians had gathered for the council, 1,800 of whom were warriors.

[32] Speech of the chiefs of the western nations to Simcoe, and correspondence of Simcoe, in Cruikshank (ed.), *op. cit.*, II, 35-36, 40-44, 49-50, 59-63, and in

ing February Lord Dorchester, who only recently had returned to Quebec, told a delegation of Canadian Indians who had attended the 1793 Indian Council that he foresaw war between England and the United States during the year and that England's patience was almost exhausted by American encroachment on the lands of the Indians. A week later he ordered the construction of a fort on the Maumee, an act which was certain to encourage the Indians to believe that the English would aid them in their war with the Americans. For his inflammatory speech and for the order to build the fort, the Governor was censured both by the British secretary of state and by officers in Upper Canada. Although Simcoe delayed a month in carrying out the order, presumably because of the weather, by July, 1794, Fort Miamis had been constructed at the rapids of the Maumee and garrisoned by troops from Detroit. The Detroit commandant, who had sent most of his garrison to the new post, wrote on July 22 that he doubted if its construction would meet with the approval of the British ministry. "I don't believe they wish to provoke a war with the United States, and God knows this Country is by no means in a situation to commence hostilities. We don't see anything from home that justifies His Excellency's Speech to the Indians."[33] Before word reached Philadelphia of the fort's construction, John Jay was on his way to London to attempt to resolve the differences between his country and Great Britain.

Michigan Historical Collections, XXIV, 597-599 599-605, 607-609, 610-615. In a letter of September 30 to Henry Dundas, British Secretary of State, Simcoe wrote that withdrawal of the King's forces from the barrier posts "must take place sooner or later if the government of the United States hold their present language; unless it may be thought worth while to enter into a War for their preservation."

[33] Cruikshank (ed.), *Simcoe Correspondence,* II, 148-150, 154, 179, 211, 220-222, 334, 336; Burt, *The United States, Great Britain, and British North America,* pp. 133-137; Bemis, *Jay's Treaty,* pp. 123-133, 172-182, 218-247. For the correspondence that took place between the Secretary of State and the British minister to the United States regarding erection of the fort, see William R. Manning (ed.), *Diplomatic Correspondence of the United States: Canadian Relations, 1784-1860* . . . (3 volumes, Washington, D. C., 1940-43), I, 66-87 *passim,* 411-417, 447-450.

In the meantime, General Wayne had begun to collect and train his soldiers at a camp near Pittsburgh in the fall of 1792. He moved down the Ohio the next May and established his camp near Fort Washington. In October he advanced northward and built Fort Greenville, where he spent the winter, constantly training his men in alertness and in the methods of Indian warfare; to the Indians he came to be known as the chief who never sleeps. Fort Recovery had been erected at the scene of St. Clair's defeat during the winter and the army advanced to this outpost the last of June, 1794. On June 30 the Indians made a serious attack on the fort but were unable to capture it. Wayne believed the British had encouraged and aided the Indians in the attack, and this assumption was later proved to be true.[34]

Wayne left Fort Recovery in July and advanced to the mouth of the Auglaize where he built Fort Defiance in the heart of the Indian country. Again he offered peace to the tribesmen, but his offer was rejected. He then marched down the Maumee to the foot of the rapids and within two miles of the British fortification. On August 20 the Indians chose to challenge him on the banks of the river where a tornado had uprooted trees that formed natural breastworks and where new growth aided in concealing the warriors. The Indian forces were estimated at thirteen hundred warriors, principally from the Wyandot, Delaware, Shawnee, Miami, and Ottawa tribes; approximately nine hundred of these participated in the battle against about the same number of Wayne's troops. During these first three weeks in August the British Indian Department had been busy making sure that an

---

[34] Knopf (ed.), *Anthony Wayne*, pp. 297n, 345-349. The part played by the British in preparing the Indians against Wayne's expedition is related by Reginald Horsman in his article, "The British Indian Department and the Resistance to General Anthony Wayne, 1793-1795," *Mississippi Valley Historical Review*, XLIX (1962-63), 269-290. The Fort Recovery attack was considered a mistake by the British. Following it some of the tribesmen returned home, thus weakening Indian resistance.

effective Indian force would be available to resist the Americans; they also were supplied with provisions.[35]

Wayne attacked on the morning of August 20, sending mounted riflemen to outflank the Indian position while a charge of well-disciplined infantry overwhelmed the warriors. The action lasted about three hours and left the Indians in full retreat.[36]

Peace between England and the United States hung in the balance as Wayne marched to the very gates of the British fort. Lighted torches inside the fortification were ready to fire cannon trained on American troops who were flushed with victory and indignant at British occupation of the site. Although messages passed between Wayne and the English commander challenging each other's presence, fortunately neither fired on the other. While refusing to surrender the fort, the British made no effort to go to the aid of the retreating

[35] Jacobs, *The Beginning of the United States Army*, pp. 174-175; *American States Papers. Indian Affairs*, I, 491-495; Horsman, *Matthew Elliott*, pp. 102-103. Reports on the numbers of Indians and Americans actually engaged in the battle vary greatly depending on the source. Whether any warriors from the Wabash tribes were present is also debatable; Wayne thought there were a considerable number. A deputation from these tribes had appeared at the rapids on July 14 and requested a council with the chiefs of the Indian confederacy at which they expressed their sorrow for having listened to the Americans and begged to be received again into the confederacy. They were told they would be readmitted on condition that they return home, collect their warriors, and join the others who were preparing to fight. Knopf (ed.), *Anthony Wayne*, p. 357; McKee to Simcoe, July 26, 1794, in *Michigan Historical Collections*, XXIV, 697-698.

[36] For events leading up to the battle and the encounter, see Knopf (ed.), *Anthony Wayne*, pp. 351-355; Gifford, The Northwest Indian War, 1784-1795, Chap. X; Bond, *Foundations of Ohio*, pp. 342-347; Dillon, *History of Indiana*, pp. 345-355; Dwight L. Smith (ed.), *From Greene Ville to Fallen Timbers. A Journal of the Wayne Campaign . . . 1794* (Indiana Historical Society *Publications*, XVI, No. 3, Indianapolis, 1952). Another personal account of the expedition is that of John Boyer (Bowyer) published in *The American Pioneer* (Chillicothe, Ohio, 1842-43), I, 315-322, 351-357, and as a separate in 1866 under the title, *A Journal of Wayne's Campaign*. For British reports concerning the battle, see Cruikshank (ed.), *Simcoe Correspondence*, II, 395-419 *passim*, and *Michigan Historical Collections*, XX, 370-372; XXV, 14-15, 20-21, 22-24, 25-27.

Indians and refused to give them refuge. Neither the British commander nor General Wayne wished to provide the spark that might start a British-American war. Both men may have had some knowledge of negotiations that were going forward in London; these in time would result in the two powers settling their differences and signing a treaty of amity, commerce, and navigation.[37]

After destroying cornfields and stores of the Indians plus the storehouse and residence of Alexander McKee in the neighborhood of the fort, General Wayne marched his troops back up the Maumee to Fort Defiance where they halted two weeks to strengthen the fortification there, then opened a wagon road to the Miami villages at the junction of the St. Joseph and St. Marys rivers, where they arrived on September 17. Here he found nearly five hundred acres of fertile, cleared land and one of the largest Indian settlements in the area. The first object of Wayne's expedition had been to defeat the Indians; he was now ready to carry out the second objective, the establishment of a fort at the head of the Maumee. Equinoctial storms brought a deluge of rain which delayed the beginning of work until September 24 but during the following month officers and soldiers alike were pressed into the work of construction; even the rear wheels and axles of the wagons were utilized in hauling logs to the site. After four weeks of continuous labor, the fort was sufficiently finished for the dedication on October 22. Colonel Hamtramck, formerly at Fort Knox near Vincennes, was placed in command with a company of artillery and five companies of infantry. After firing fifteen rounds of cannon, the Colonel named the new establishment Fort Wayne in honor of the commander in chief. Wayne's troops left shortly thereafter

[37] Cruikshank (ed.), *Simcoe Correspondence,* II, 405-408; III, 5; Bemis, *Jay's Treaty,* pp. 240-250, 323-361; Dillon, *History of Indiana,* pp. 352-357. Campbell wrote the day following the battle that he was glad it had terminated "without bringing me into a scrape," and he professed ignorance of the whereabouts of the Indians. He seemed unaware that a number of Detroit militiamen had fought with the Indians.

for Greenville where they remained in camp while their leader prepared for his next objective, a treaty of peace with the Indians.[38]

§ § § § § §

For several months after the Battle of Fallen Timbers, the Indians were confused and uncertain whether to continue the contest with Wayne or to make peace; they were angry with the British for their failure to assist them, yet they were in danger of starvation and could only look to the British for food and ammunition, without which they could not hunt. The British officials in the Detroit area were very reluctant to accept the defeat as final, but were under instructions not to provoke war while negotiations were going on in London. Therefore, they could promise only to refer the Indians' request for aid to the King. Gradually, as the Indians realized that they could not secure military assistance, they began to approach Wayne's headquarters and indicate their desire for peace. As early as November 3, 1794, Indian delegations came to express their determination to "bury the hatchet"; June 15, 1795, was set as the date when the council should begin.[39] The tribes represented were the Wyandots, Delawares, Shawnee, Miami, Ottawa, Chippewa, Potawatomi, Kickapoo, Wea, Eel River Miami, Piankashaw, and Kaskaskia.

As usual, the Indians assembled very slowly and preliminary matters consumed much time. At last on July 15 the

[38] Knopf (ed.), *Anthony Wayne*, pp. 356, 358; Griswold, *Pictorial History of Fort Wayne*, I, 139-149. President Washington had given General Wayne instructions regarding construction of a fort at the headwaters of the Maumee shortly after naming him commander in chief in 1792. Wayne wrote that he was forced to make the fort smaller than the President had instructed because of the want of time as well as the lack of a force to garrison it. Even then he had difficulty in keeping the men at the task of construction.

[39] The relations between the British and the Indians following the battle may be traced in Cruikshank (ed.), *Simcoe Correspondence*, Volume III, and in *Michigan Historical Collections*, Volume XXV. They are summarized by Horsman in his article in the *Mississippi Valley Historical Review*, XLIX, 283-287, and in his biography of Matthew Elliott, pp. 105-112.

council was opened with an address by Wayne in which he declared that the Fort Harmar treaty should be the basis for the present negotiations. Little Turtle pleaded ignorance of the terms of that treaty and when informed of them said that those who agreed to the land cessions made at that time had no right to do so. On July 24 Wayne read to the chiefs and warriors portions of the Jay treaty which had been signed in London on November 19 of the previous year. The first article provided for a firm, inviolable and universal peace, and a true and sincere friendship between England and the United States; the second article began: "His Majesty will withdraw all His Troops and Garrisons from all Posts and Places within the Boundary Lines assigned by the Treaty of Peace [in 1783] to the United States." The transfer of the posts was to take place on or before June 1, 1796. This provision meant that the Indians need no longer expect military aid from the British, and without this aid there was little they could do but assent to an agreement with the United States. The treaty, known as the Treaty of Greenville, was signed on August 3, 1795.[40]

The Indians agreed to cease warring upon the American settlements and to accept a boundary which separated their lands from the area to be opened to settlement. This line was much farther north and west than the Indians had previously been willing to accept, but it was not as far as the Fort McIntosh line of 1785 which the government tried to get confirmed in 1789. Its acceptance was an indication of how thoroughly the Indians had been defeated. About two thirds of the future state of Ohio and a small portion of southeastern Indiana was thus freed of Indian claims plus sixteen small tracts at the portages and along the river

---

[40] The proceedings of the Greenville council and the treaty are in *American State Papers. Indian Affairs*, I, 562-582, and Wayne's correspondence leading up to and during the negotiations, in Knopf (ed.), *Anthony Wayne*, pp. 369-462. See also Dillon, *History of Indiana*, pp. 357-374; Frazer E. Wilson, *The Treaty of Greenville* . . . (Piqua, Ohio, 1894), pp. 81-99. For the text of Jay's Treaty see Bemis, *Jay's Treaty*, pp. 454-455.

View of Fort Finney at the Falls of Ohio, from the South East

View of Fort Finney at the Falls of Ohio, from the Main Gate

Fort Finney

Reproduced from originals in the Indiana Historical Society Library

Uniform of Infantry and Artillery Privates, 1802-1810

From *Uniform of the Army of the United States . . . prepared . . . by the Quartermaster General* (2 volumes, New York, 1885-1908), II, Plate 11

routes. In Indiana these included the Wabash-Maumee portage, Ouiatanon, Clark's Grant, and the Vincennes Tract around the village on the Wabash.

In consideration of the land cessions and relinquishments, the United States presented the tribes represented at the treaty with goods valued at $20,000; in addition they were to receive annually thereafter goods valued at $9,500, to be divided among the tribes as follows: Wyandots, Delawares, Shawnee, Miami, Ottawa, Chippewa, and Potawatomi, $1,000 each; Kickapoo, Wea, Eel River Miami, Piankashaw, and Kaskaskia, $500 each.[41]

As the time approached for occupying the British forts in accordance with the terms of Jay's treaty, Colonel Hamtramck with some three hundred men of the First Sub-Legion was ordered to descend the Maumee and be ready to take over Fort Miamis on that river and Fort Lernoult at Detroit. While Hamtramck waited above Fort Miamis, Capt. Moses Porter went on to Detroit with a detachment of sixty-five men. Thus the United States took possession of both forts on the same day, July 11, 1796. Oswego was transferred on July 15, Niagara on August 11, and Michilimackinac on September 1. Hamtramck arrived at Detroit on July 13 and took command until the arrival of General Wayne a month later. Acting Governor Sargent accompanied Wayne and established civil government under the provisions of the Ordinance of 1787. Wayne County was created by proclamation of August 15 with Detroit as the county seat. Its boundaries included almost all of the present state of Michigan plus a

41 Kappler (ed.), *Indian Affairs. Laws and Treaties,* II, 30-34. The treaty line began at the mouth of the Cuyahoga River, where the city of Cleveland was soon to be founded, followed that river to the portage, passed over the land route to the Tuscarawas River, along that stream to the crossing place above Fort Laurens, thence westwardly to a fork of Loramie Creek near the site of Loramie's trading post, northwestwardly to Fort Recovery, and finally southwardly to a point on the Ohio River opposite the mouth of the Kentucky River. The Indians gave up their claims to land south and east of this boundary.

strip of what is now northern Ohio and Indiana and a strip of eastern Illinois and Wisconsin.

Wayne remained in Detroit for three months during which time he disbanded the Legion in accordance with a new act of Congress and organized the army on a new basis. Many of the British citizens in the town moved across the boundary into Canada.[42]

§   §   §   §   §   §   §

During the Indian wars, the movement of people into the Old Northwest had been checked but not stopped. When St. Clair inaugurated the government of the Northwest Territory on July 15, 1788, the settlements in the territory included, in addition to the French villages, Clarksville and Marietta. Others were soon added. By the time the Governor arrived at the Symmes Purchase in the early spring of 1790, three little communities were in existence, Columbia, Losantiville, and North Bend, and in the vicinity the federal government built and garrisoned Fort Washington. About 2,400 persons, largely from New Jersey, were thought to be in the Symmes Purchase, comprising two million acres between the mouths of the Miami and Little Miami rivers. Approximately 430 settlers were on the lands of the Ohio Company at Marietta and Belle Pré by 1793. Three other villages had been started in other areas: Gallipolis was founded as a result of the activities of the Scioto Company; Manchester represented the beginning of settlement in the Virginia Military Tract, which had been reserved by Virginia for the land bounties promised her Revolutionary soldiers, and a few cabins

---

[42] Bald, *Michigan in Four Centuries,* pp. 95-103; Carter (ed.), *Territorial Papers,* II, 567-568; Bald, "Colonel John Francis Hamtramck," *Indiana Magazine of History,* XLIV, 350-351; Frank H. Severance, *Old Trails on the Niagara Frontier* (Cleveland, 1903), p. 129. Negotiations between the British and Americans leading up to the transfer of the posts may be followed in Vols. IV and V of Cruikshank (ed.), *Simcoe Correspondence;* they are reviewed briefly in Prucha, *Sword of the Republic,* pp. 38-40.

around the original Fort Steuben developed into the town of Steubenville.[43]

Following the victory at Fallen Timbers immigration into the Old Northwest increased. In 1796 Chillicothe was founded and very quickly became the home of the leaders of the Virginia group which challenged the control of St. Clair and the men he had drawn about him. At the mouth of the Cuyahoga on the shore of Lake Erie was established the little village that was to become the great city of Cleveland and a center of New England influence in the state of Ohio. Other towns appeared in the neighborhood, bringing the population of the Western Reserve to one thousand by 1800.[44] In Hamilton County, which included land purchased by Symmes, the population pushed inland along the two Miami rivers, and by 1798 ten thousand inhabitants were reported.[45]

The increase in population gave impetus to the growing dissatisfaction with the arbitrary rule of the Governor and Judges and to the desire to advance to the semirepresentative stage of government. Many of the earlier complaints had been rectified by the revision and codification of the territorial laws in 1795, but there still remained the fact that the people were without representation, a single one of the three Judges could hold the General Court, and the sessions of the Governor and Judges and of the General Court were held very infrequently. Perhaps one of the most irritating features of this stage of government was St. Clair's condescending attitude toward the people. One critic declared that they were in

[43] Bond, *Foundations of Ohio*, pp. 275-311; Carter (ed.), *Territorial Papers*, II, 470.

[44] Claude L. Shepard, "The Connecticut Land Company: A Study in the Beginnings of Colonization of the Western Reserve," Western Reserve Historical Society *Tract No. 96* (Cleveland, 1916), pp. 74-86; Bond, *Foundations of Ohio*, pp. 358-372; Harlan Hatcher, *The Western Reserve. The Story of New Connecticut in Ohio* (Indianapolis, 1949); Payson J. Treat, *The National Land System, 1785-1820* (New York, 1910), pp. 319-325.

[45] Carter (ed.), *Territorial Papers*, II, 648-649.

a much worse situation than the colonists under George III. The Governor made no attempt to ascertain whether the territory had the requisite population for the second stage until after Hamilton County proceeded to take a census of its inhabitants in 1798. He then ordered an enumeration of the free adult males in the entire territory, but before the complete results were known he proclaimed the advance to the semirepresentative stage on October 29, 1798. This brought an end to the first period during which the people had been subject for ten years to unrepresentative and arbitrary government.[46]

The advance to the second stage entitled the people to have a legislature of two houses. The lower house of twenty-two members (each of whom had to own at least two hundred acres of land) was elected by the adult free males who owned at least fifty acres. One of the twenty-two, John Small, was chosen from Knox County, one from each of the two Illinois counties, three from Wayne County, while sixteen came from counties within the bounds later established for the state of Ohio. In its first session the members of the Assembly chose from a list of residents of the territory who owned at least five hundred acres of land the names of ten which were sent to the President of the United States. The Chief Executive then appointed and commissioned five of the ten to be members of the upper house of the legislature or the legislative council. One of the five was Henry Vanderburgh, who then resided in Vincennes and who was chosen president of the council.[47]

---

[46] Criticism of the government is found scattered through the columns of the *Centinel of the North-Western Territory*, which began publication at Cincinnati in 1793. See also Randolph C. Downes, *Frontier Ohio, 1788-1803* (*Ohio Historical Collections,* III, Columbus, 1935), pp. 127-186; Bond, *Foundations of Ohio,* pp. 411-436.

[47] Rufus King, *Ohio. First Fruits of the Ordinance of 1787* (American Commonwealths Series, Boston and New York, 1888), pp. 269-270; Jacob Burnet, *Notes on the Early Settlement of the North-Western Territory* (Cincinnati, 1847), pp. 288-298.

The legislature which met at Cincinnati for its first session on September 24, 1799, and continued until December 19, brought together the representatives of the people and gave them an opportunity to organize and express their ideas publicly. On October 3 the Assembly elected William Henry Harrison, in preference to the Governor's son, as the first delegate to Congress from the Northwest Territory. The legislators passed forty-five bills, but the Governor vetoed several of them thus arousing considerable antagonism between himself and the legislative leaders. Among those who resented the Governor's veto power were Thomas Worthington, Nathaniel Massie, and Edward Tiffin, who concluded that the only way in which the people could escape arbitrary rule was to organize a state government.[48]

William Henry Harrison established a good record as delegate to Congress in the short time in which he served in this capacity. He sought to remedy at least two major difficulties: the inability of the settlers to buy land, and the failure of the judges of the General Court to render adequate judicial service. The conservative attitude of the East had prevented the government from selling land in small tracts to actual settlers at prices they could pay. The minimum tract of land which an individual could buy was 640 acres at a minimum price of $2.00 per acre, and the buyer had only one year in which to complete his payment.[49] Since settlers were required to own fifty acres in order to vote and two hundred acres to be

[48] *Journal of the House of Representatives of the Territory of the United States, North-west of the River Ohio . . . 1799* (Cincinnati, 1800); *Journal of the Legislative Council of the Territory of the United States, North-west of the River Ohio . . . One Thousand Seven Hundred and Ninety-nine* (Cincinnati, n.d.); Pease (ed.), *Laws of the Northwest Territory*, pp. xxx, 335-517; *St. Clair Papers*, II, 446-480; King, *First Fruits of the Ordinance*, pp. 270-272; Bond, *Foundation of Ohio*, pp. 437-448.

[49] U.S. *Statutes at Large*, I, 464-469; Treat, *The National Land System*, pp. 84-100; Dorothy B. Goebel, *William Henry Harrison. A Political Biography (Indiana Historical Collections*, XIV, Indianapolis, 1926), pp. 43-44; Benjamin H. Hibbard, *History of the Public Land Policies* (University of Wisconsin Press, 1965), pp. 67-69.

elected to the territorial Assembly, the land policy had political implications. Many people were moving to the territory who could not buy land and therefore could not take part in the government. A revision of the land laws in the interest of the settler was needed.

Harrison determined to change the act of 1796 in order to permit actual settlers to purchase smaller tracts direct from government land offices to be established at Marietta, Steubenville, Chillicothe, and Cincinnati. In order to assist those of limited resources he proposed to extend the use of credit. His effort resulted in the Land Act of 1800, often called the Harrison Act. It provided for the sale of land west of the Muskingum River in units as small as 320 acres at the same minimum price of $2.00 per acre. One fourth of the price had to be paid at the time of the purchase and the remainder in annual installments within four years. An additional year of grace, however, was allowed those who were delinquent in their payments. In theory it was assumed that the buyer would be able to raise sufficient crops on the land each year to enable him to meet the annual payment. The law was imperfect, the credit feature was abused and after twenty years was repealed; but much land was bought under its terms, and many of the actual settlers with small financial resources were able to acquire the farms they wanted so badly. When the land act was further liberalized in 1820, the settler could buy a farm of eighty acres for $100.[50]

The second problem which Harrison tried to remedy was occasioned by the inability of the territorial judges to hold court in every county of the vast territory each year. Some of the counties were without these courts for years; St. Clair County in the Illinois country did not have one until 1794. Harrison considered the possibility of increasing the number of judges, but another factor intervened. The differences be-

[50] U.S. *Statutes at Large,* II, 73-78; Goebel, *Harrison,* pp. 44-45; Hibbard, *History of the Public Land Policies,* pp. 69-100. The land act is reprinted in *Indiana's Road to Statehood,* pp. 27-36.

tween St. Clair and the Virginia group in the territorial legislature caused the latter to press for statehood. Both St. Clair and his opponents suggested the division of the territory, but St. Clair wanted to form three territories out of the one, which would have had the effect of delaying statehood and making the eastern state a Federalist state. Worthington, Massie, and Tiffin of the Virginia group wanted two territories, the eastern one large enough to become a state immediately, and they hoped a democratic republican state. Harrison, who had been elected by the latter group, favored their plans which did away with the need of additional judges.

The Congressional committee to which was referred the question of judicial reform withdrew their original bill and instead recommended on March 3, 1800, the division of the Northwest Territory into two distinct and separate governments. The report read, in part:

> That parts of said Territory are subject to several serious inconveniences, which require redress from the General Government; most of the evils which they at present experience are . . . to be imputed to the very great extent of country at present comprised under their imperfect government. The Territory Northwest of the Ohio, from southeast to northwest, [is] fifteen hundred miles, and the actual distance of travelling from the places of holding courts the most remote from each other, is thirteen hundred miles, and in a country so sparsely peopled, and so little reclaimed from its native wildness, this distance alone seems to present barriers almost insuperable against the exercise of the functions of government. . . .[51]

A bill to divide the Northwest Territory and to create Indiana Territory passed both houses of Congress and became a law on May 7, 1800. It provided

> That, from and after the fourth day of July next, all that part of the Territory of the United States Northwest of the Ohio river which lies to the westward of a line beginning at the Ohio, opposite to the mouth of Kentucky river, and running thence to Fort Recovery, and thence north until it shall intersect the territorial line between the

[51] *Annals of Congress,* 6 Congress, Appendix, p. 1320; Kettleborough, *Constitution Making in Indiana,* I, 39-40.

United States and Canada, shall, for the purposes of temporary government, constitute a separate territory, and be called Indiana Territory.[52]

When the eastern division should become a state, the permanent boundary between it and the Indiana Territory would be a line running due north from the mouth of the Great Miami.

The government of the new territory was to be in all respects similar to that provided for the Northwest Territory under the Ordinance of 1787. The inhabitants were to enjoy all of the "rights, privileges, and advantages, granted and secured to the people" by that document. One change was introduced regarding the advance to the second stage; instead of waiting until the population reached five thousand free adult male inhabitants, the second stage could be instituted whenever evidence was given the governor that a majority of the freeholders desired the advance. As a result of this provision the unrepresentative period of the governor and judges in Indiana lasted less than five years, while the same period in the Northwest Territory had exceeded ten years.

Harrison's record in securing the passage of the land act and the creation of Indiana Territory in his first and only year as delegate to Congress placed him in a position of leadership. That President John Adams should have regarded him as the most suitable person to be named governor of the new territory is not surprising.[53]

The remaining three years of the Northwest Territory are not without interest to Indiana. The division of the territory as provided in the act of 1800 was a defeat for Governor St. Clair and his followers who wished a threefold division of

[52] *Annals of Congress,* 6 Congress, Appendix, pp. 1498-1500; Kettleborough, *Constitution Making in Indiana,* I, 41-42; *Indiana's Road to Statehood,* pp. 24-26.

[53] Kettleborough, *Constitution Making in Indiana,* I, 42; Goebel, *William Henry Harrison,* pp. 47-52; "Letters of William H. Harrison to Thomas Worthington, 1799-1813," *Indiana Magazine of History,* XLVII (1951), 56-59. For a biographical sketch of Harrison, see below, pp. 315-316.

the territory in place of the twofold one that was adopted. A vigorous campaign for statehood was launched by the Chillicothe group, and Congress replied by passing an enabling act in 1802 which authorized the holding of a constitutional convention to form a state government. The majority of the delegates belonged to the group favoring statehood. Having lived for a time, at least, on the frontiers of Pennsylvania, Virginia, and Kentucky, the constitution which they formed was patterned upon those adopted by Tennessee, Pennsylvania, and Kentucky. It provided for an essentially democratic government, guaranteed and protected the basic civil rights of the citizens, granted the right to vote to adult males who were charged with a state or county tax, and prohibited slavery and involuntary servitude in the state. The new commonwealth came into existence on March 1, 1803. It was the first fruit of the Ordinance of 1787 and represented the desire of the frontiersmen to secure democratic self-government. When Indiana came to the same stage of development, its constitutional convention found much to emulate in the work of its sister commonwealth.[54]

[54] John D. Barnhart, "The Southern Influence in the Formation of Ohio," *Journal of Southern History*, III (1937), 28-42; Downes, *Frontier Ohio*, pp. 226-252; Bond, *Foundations of Ohio*, pp. 455-476; William T. Utter, *The Frontier State, 1803-1825* (*The History of the State of Ohio*, II, Columbus, 1942), pp. 3-31. As there was no formal admission of the state by Congress, the date of the beginning of state government in Ohio was a matter of dispute until in 1902 when by a joint resolution of the state legislature the date of the organization of the first General Assembly elected under the constitution, March 1, 1803, was declared to be the beginning of Ohio's statehood.

CHAPTER IX

THE RULE OF THE GOVERNOR
AND JUDGES

The people of Indiana Territory for sixteen years were subject to the provisions of the Ordinance of 1787 and the act of 1800 creating the territory. From time to time these provisions were modified by Congress in favor of a more democratic rule; for example, the extension of the right of suffrage and the popular election of the delegate to Congress and the members of the Legislative Council. Such changes were enacted by Congress in response to petitions of the legislature and of the people.

Indiana's territorial history, in which the rise of frontier democracy played an important part, can be divided into four short periods. First was the nonrepresentative stage which lasted from 1800 until 1804. The second period began with the Governor's proclamation of the advance to the second stage and the election of the territorial legislature, and continued down to the outbreak of Indian warfare in 1811; it was a period in which the people gained valuable experience in governing themselves. During this time the legislature gradually became the dominant branch of the government. The third period was one of Indian warfare, while the contest for statehood was the principal theme of the fourth and last period.

President John Adams appointed William Henry Harrison to be the first governor of Indiana Territory on May 13, 1800, next to the last day of the session of Congress in which Harrison was serving as a delegate from the Northwest Territory. Though appointed by President Adams, his first years as governor were to be under the direction of Thomas Jefferson who was inaugurated President on March

4, 1801. A native of Virginia, Harrison was born February 9, 1773, into an influential Virginia family. During his boyhood his father, Benjamin Harrison III, served as delegate to the Continental Congress, was one of the signers of the Declaration of Independence, a member of the Virginia legislature, and governor of that state. The family plantation, "Berkeley," on the banks of the James River, was in the same neighborhood as that of the Harrisons of "Brandon," and the Byrds of "Westover." Growing up in this environment, William Henry could scarcely have avoided the culture of the southern country gentleman.[1]

After attending Hampden-Sydney College in Virginia, young Harrison took up the study of medicine, first in Richmond and then in Philadelphia. Before he reached his nineteenth birthday, however, he abandoned his medical studies in favor of a career in the army, and in August, 1791, received a commission as ensign in the First Regiment of United States Infantry. Before the end of the year he was sent to Fort Washington, near the present Cincinnati, and participated in two expeditions to Fort Jefferson the following year. He served as aide-de-camp to Gen. Anthony Wayne in the campaign that led to the Battle of Fallen Timbers, for which he received a commendation from his commander. Harrison continued to serve under Wayne during the negotiations at Greenville in 1795, and in November of that year married a daughter of Judge John Cleves Symmes. Although advanced to the rank of captain in 1797, Harrison had by this time become disenchanted with the possibilities offered by a career in the army, and resigned shortly thereafter. In looking about for a civil appointment, he applied for the position of secretary of the Northwest Territory in place of Winthrop Sargent who had resigned, and received the appointment. He served in this capacity for a little over a year, making Cincinnati his residence, and then as noted above

---

[1] Goebel, *Harrison,* pp. 1-15. "Berkeley" is still standing and is open to the public on special occasions.

was elected by the territorial legislature as delegate to Congress. His work as a delegate in revising the land law and in legislation creating the new Indiana Territory made him the logical choice for appointment to the governorship of the new territory.[2]

A few days before the appointment was made, Harrison wrote to a friend in the Northwest Territory that he would not accept it even if it should be offered to him,[3] but friends prevailed on him to reconsider, pointing out that since he "was better acquainted with the wants and wishes of the people . . . than any other person" it would be easier for him "to make them Happy and satisfied with their government than a perfect stranger." They apparently reassured him, also, that his removal to Vincennes would not eliminate him from consideration if some better appointment turned up at a later time. With the entrance of Ohio into the Union, Harrison could well have had hopes of an office in the new state government that would have enabled him and his young wife to remain in the area where they had made many friends. On the other hand, the governorship of the new Indiana Territory must have presented a challenge to the young man who had only recently celebrated his twenty-seventh birthday. The decision to accept the appointment was made while he and his wife were visiting in Virginia, where they had gone after the adjournment of Congress.[4] Their third child was born there in September and Harrison delayed his departure to his new post until Mrs. Harrison was able to make the trip back to their home at North Bend and then on to Lexington, Kentucky, where she was to spend the winter with relatives. The new governor bade farewell to his family late in December and set out for Vincennes.[5]

[2] Goebel, *Harrison,* pp. 16-19, 25-52.

[3] William Henry Harrison, Philadelphia, to Thomas Worthington, Chillicothe, May 2, 1800, in *Indiana Magazine of History,* XLVII (1951), 58.

[4] Harrison, Richmond, to Worthington, July 13, 1800, in *loc. cit.,* 59-61; Goebel, *Harrison,* p. 52.

[5] Freeman Cleaves, *Old Tippecanoe. William Henry Harrison and His*

President Adams' choice for secretary of the Indiana Territory was John Gibson, a native of Pennsylvania, who had served in the frontier wars and in the Revolution, been captured by the Indians and adopted by them, and married a sister of Chief Logan. He had been a member of the Pennsylvania Constitutional Convention and a county judge in Allegheny County. He was sixty years of age.[6]

For territorial judges, President Adams chose William Clarke, then serving as attorney for the United States in Kentucky, Henry Vanderburgh, a New Yorker who had moved to Vincennes after the Revolution and married a daughter of one of the French families, and John Griffin of Virginia. Although their legal training was inferior to that of the judges of the Northwest Territory, this was compensated by the fact that they were acquainted with frontier conditions. Following Clarke's death on November 11, 1802, Thomas T. Davis of Kentucky was appointed in his place.[7] During the first period of nonrepresentative government, the Judges and the Governor adopted the laws that were deemed necessary.

Time (New York, 1939), p. 32. James A. Green in his biography of Harrison states that he rode horseback across country from Cincinnati with a single escort, but it seems more likely that he would have gone to Louisville, and then overland to Vincennes. *William Henry Harrison. His Life and Times* (Richmond, Va., 1941), pp. 86-88.

6 Francis S. Philbrick (ed.), *The Laws of Indiana Territory, 1801-1809* (*Illinois Historical Collections,* XXI, Springfield, 1930, reprinted by the Indiana Historical Bureau, 1931), pp. xiv-xv; William Wesley Woollen, *Biographical and Historical Sketches of Early Indiana* (Indianapolis, 1883), pp. 11-14.

7 Philbrick (ed.), *Laws of Indiana Territory,* pp. xv-xvi, ccxxxv-ccxxxvii; Clarence E. Carter, "William Clarke, First Chief Justice of Indiana Territory," *Indiana Magazine of History,* XXXIV (1938), 1-13. Harrison had a "strong interest" in the appointment of the Judges, especially Vanderburgh with whom he was acquainted. President Adams preferred to delay the appointments until Congress reconvened on November 17, 1800, so that the nominations could be presented to the Senate, but under the urging of the new Governor made interim appointments in September which were later confirmed by the Senate. See correspondence between the President and Secretary of State in Carter (ed.), *Territorial Papers,* VII, 18-23.

Gibson was the first of the new officials to arrive at Vincennes, on July 22, 1800, and proceeded to organize the new government and appoint the necessary civil and militia officers in the three counties of St. Clair, Randolph, and Knox that then constituted the Indiana Territory. In a large clothbound volume which he had brought with him from Pennsylvania, Gibson recorded the first entries in what was to constitute the "Journal of the Proceedings of the Executive Government of the Indiana Territory."[8]

The federal census taken in 1800 gave the Governor and Judges some idea of the area over which they had jurisdiction. Residents of the town of Vincennes numbered 714, of whom 216 were children under ten, while another 103 were between ten and sixteen; 147 were women; eight were slaves. In the neighborhood of Vincennes the census taker recorded 819, of whom 278 were children under ten, 115 others were between ten and sixteen, 158 were women, and 15 were slaves.[9] The Indians were not included in the census. In 1787 it had been estimated that over two thirds of the population of Vincennes was French,[10] but by 1800 the percentage of Americans had no doubt increased considerably.

In Clark's Grant where many of the men were former soldiers who had served under George Rogers Clark, the population was 929 in 1800. In the Illinois portion of the Indiana Territory, where the proportion of French was no doubt larger than at Vincennes, there were a number of scat-

---

[8] The Journal has been preserved and is in the Archives Division, Indiana State Library. It was printed in 1900 as Volume III, No. 3 of the Indiana Historical Society *Publications*. Many of the appointees had held these same offices under the Northwest Territory, only now there were more Americans and fewer French.

[9] The census figures are given in Carter (ed.) *Territorial Papers*, VII, 24-25, and in *Executive Journal of Indiana Territory, 1800-1816*, edited by William Wesley Woollen, Daniel Wait Howe, and Jacob Piatt Dunn (Indiana Historical Society *Publications*, III, No. 3, Indianapolis, 1900), p. 83, hereafter cited as Territorial *Executive Journal*.

[10] General Josiah Harmar estimated the number of French as 900 and Americans as 400 in 1787. Thor▚▚▚h (ed.), *Outpost on the Wabash*, p. 36.

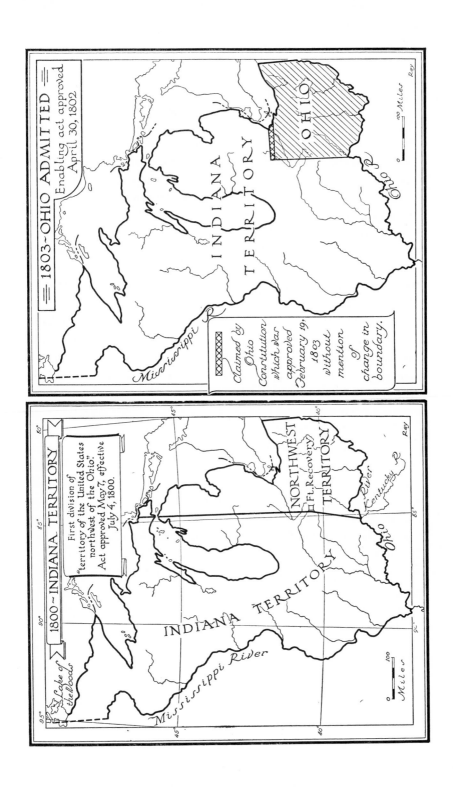

tered settlements including Fort Massac on the Ohio, Kaskaskia, Prairie du Rocher, and Cahokia on the Mississippi, Bellefontaine (an American settlement), and Peoria on the Illinois River. The total population of the counties of Randolph and St. Clair was 2,358, including 107 slaves; Prairie du Chien, not counted in St. Clair County, had 65, and in addition there were 55 traders on the Wabash. To the north, the census taker counted 251 at Michilimackinac, 50 at Green Bay, and 300 "boatmen from Canada, &c." The total white population of Indiana Territory was 5,641. Detroit and the area surrounding it remained a part of the Northwest Territory until Ohio became a state in 1803 as did the Whitewater Valley, east of the Greenville treaty line.

Except for Clark's Grant, the area around Vincennes known as the Vincennes Tract, the land around Fort Wayne, Ouiatanon, Fort Massac, and the French villages in the Illinois country,[11] the area comprising Indiana Territory was still in the hands of the various Indian tribes—the Miami and Potawatomi, Sauk, Fox, Shawnee, Piankashaw, and others.

Moses Austin who was at Vincennes in January of 1797 reported there were about two hundred houses, generally one story and "badly finished," but that only about three fourths of the houses were occupied, the occupants of the others having moved to farms in the neighborhood. Austin predicted that if the Indians remained peaceful the town would soon become a place of some consequence because of its natural advantages and the beauty of the country thereabouts.[12] Other travelers likewise remarked on the beauty of

11 These were ceded in the Treaty of Greenville or acknowledged in it as previous cessions. Kappler (ed.), *Indian Affairs. Laws and Treaties,* II, 30-34.

12 "A Memorandum of M. Austin's Journey from the Lead Mines in . . . Virginia to the Lead Mines in . . . Louisiana," *American Historical Review,* V (1899-1900), 527-531. C. F. Volney, who visited Vincennes in 1796, gave the number of houses as about fifty. "Each house, as is customary in Canada, stands alone, and is surrounded by a court and garden, fenced with poles." C. F. Volney, *A View of the Soil and Climate of the United States of America* (Philadelphia, 1804), pp. 332-337, reprinted in Lindley (ed.), *Indiana as Seen by Early Travelers,* pp. 19-24.

the landscape around the village and what a welcome sight it was after a two- or three-day journey through the woods from Clarksville. Seven years later, in 1804, a visitor reported only one hundred dwellings in the town so that the exodus to the farms must have continued.[13] Nevertheless, it still remained the only settlement of any consequence.

One of the leading citizens of Vincennes was Francis Vigo, the Sardinian who had aided George Rogers Clark. Now engaged in the fur trade and owner of considerable land, he had recently built a new home and generously offered it to Governor Harrison for his residence. The latter declined to take over the house but did gratefully accept the privilege of occupying one of the rooms on the ground floor until he could build a home of his own.[14]

Society at Vincennes in the early 1800s was diversified. At the top were the Governor and other public officials and professional men, traders, and merchants; at the bottom were the French, poor and uneducated, plus an element of poor, ignorant, ruffian Americans. In between were American farmers and shopkeepers.[15] John Badollet, who took up his residence in the town in 1805, described the French as ignorant, harmless, and indolent, exhibiting a combination of French and Indian manners. "Their former opulence having disappeared with the Indian trade by which they subsisted," they were living cooped up in town, for the most part in poverty, hauling their firewood from a distance of three or

13 Edward Hempstead, Vincennes, July 30, 1804, to Jared Mansfield, in *Bulletin* of the Chicago Historical Society, March, 1936, pp. 25-26. Governor Harrison wrote soon after his arrival at Vincennes, "The country about this place is I think the most beautiful in the world—& it now begins to flourish." Harrison to Thomas Worthington, September 9, 1801, in *Indiana Magazine of History*, XLVII, 62.

14 Cleaves, *Old Tippecanoe*, p. 33; Lee Burns, *Early Architects and Builders of Indiana* (Indiana Historical Society *Publications*, XI, No. 3, Indianapolis, 1935), p. 183.

15 Gayle Thornbrough (ed.), *Correspondence of John Badollet and Albert Gallatin, 1804-1836* (Indiana Historical Society *Publications*, XXII, Indianapolis, 1963), pp. 20-21.

four miles, raising a little corn in the neighborhood, and following boating for employment. Among the Americans, Badollet found a want of activity, although he thought those who had emigrated from the northern states were more enterprising than those from the South. Volney wrote of the language barrier between the French and Americans: the former with a few exceptions not understanding English, and the Americans for the most part not understanding French.[16]

Despite their poverty, the French people were characterized as hospitable, easy going, and pleasure loving. The original church of St. Francis Xavier built before the Revolutionary War had been replaced by a second log structure in 1785. In response to pleas for a resident priest, Bishop John Carroll of Baltimore had sent Father Benedict Joseph Flaget to Vincennes in 1792. Upon his arrival he found the log church in bad condition and the people largely indifferent to religion. In the nearly two and a half years he remained there he not only did his best to care for the spiritual and physical needs of his parishioners, but tried to encourage the French to engage in farming and the domestic arts. Father Flaget was followed by Father John Francis Rivet who arrived in May, 1795, with a commission from the United States government as missionary to the Indians, this being a part of the new program to civilize the tribesmen. He also took on the additional duties of priest to the villagers. As long as the Indians had access to liquor, Rivet found it almost impossible to improve their condition, but he did conduct a school for the Indian and French children until his death in 1804. For the next twelve years Vincennes was without a resident priest but received occasional visits by priests from Kentucky and the Illinois country.[17]

16 *Ibid.*, pp. 57-58; C. F. Volney in Lindley (ed.), *Indiana as Seen by Early Travelers*, pp. 19-24.

17 Thomas T. McAvoy, *The Catholic Church in Indiana, 1789-1834* (New York, 1940), pp. 64-69, 76-106.

§

The law which created Indiana Territory re-established the same nonrepresentative type of government which existed in the first stage of the Northwest Territory. Governor Harrison had gained experience by his service as secretary and delegate to Congress for the Northwest Territory, and apparently tried to avoid many of the arbitrary acts which had made Governor St. Clair and Secretary Sargent unpopular. Nevertheless, his policies and appointments were to attract to him many of the more conservative leaders and antagonize a few vigorous men and a growing number of the newer settlers. From the beginning much interest was taken by the people in the acts of government, and neither the efforts of the people to make the government more democratic nor the Governor's critics were suppressed. An almost immediate and continuous movement was begun to make the government not only responsible to the wishes and needs of the people, but also to place it in their hands. The appearance at Vincennes in 1804 of the first newspaper in the Territory, the *Indiana Gazette* published by Elihu Stout, offered a convenient vehicle for the expression of public opinion. The printing plant was destroyed by fire in 1806, but a year later Stout began publication of *The Western Sun*.[18]

Harrison did not arrive at Vincennes until January 10, 1801, and two days later met with the Judges in their legislative capacity. During the session which lasted two weeks, seven laws and three resolutions were adopted, some of which were intended to smooth the transition from the government of the Northwest Territory to that of Indiana Territory. Of the two laws adopted from the Pennsylvania code, one concerned the listing of taxable property and the other provided for a more simple court system. A third law, taken from the Kentucky code, authorized the Governor to appoint a territorial treasurer. One of the resolutions adopted

[18] Elizabeth M. Denehie, "Indiana's First Newspaper," *Indiana Magazine of History*, XXXI (1935), 125-130.

(these did not have to be taken from the codes of other states) authorized the Governor to declare by proclamation what ferries should be established, and a second repealed the one-year residence requirement for the practice of law so far as it concerned Indiana Territory.[19] Lawyers were scarce on the frontier and the year's residence seemed unnecessary.

Having taken care of his legislative duties and made the appointments that would enable the General Court, presided over by the territorial Judges, to function,[20] the Governor exercised his executive power by creating a new county named Clark out of the eastern half of Knox County, and altering the boundaries of St. Clair and Randolph.[21] Judges and other local officials were appointed for the new county.[22] Harrison then turned his attention to still another facet of

[19] Logan Esarey (ed.), *Governors Messages and Letters. Messages and Letters of William Henry Harrison* (2 volumes, *Indiana Historical Collections*, VII, IX, Indianapolis, 1922), I, 20-21; Philbrick (ed.), *Laws of Indiana Territory, 1801-1809*, pp. 1-20. One of the first persons to take advantage of the second resolution was Benjamin Parke, a recent arrival from Kentucky, who had studied law with Henry Clay. He was admitted to the practice of law by the Knox County Court of Common Pleas on May 5, 1801. Transcript of Court Minutes, 1801-1806, p. 21, in Archives Division, Indiana State Library. Parke became one of the territory's most influential leaders.

[20] The Governor appointed Henry Hurst clerk of the General Court and John Rice Jones attorney general of the territory on January 14 and 29 respectively. Territorial *Executive Journal,* p. 95. The latter was a federal officer yet the earlier incumbents were appointed by the governors. He represented the United States in cases before the General Court. The two Order Books of the General Court for the territorial period are in the Archives Division, Indiana State Library. At the first session on March 3, 1801, a grand jury was selected, rules of the court were formulated, and a date set for the examination of Robert Hamilton, General Washington Johnston, Gabriel Jones Johnston, and John Rice Jones as counselors at law. The grand jury brought two indictments, one for murder and the other for assault and battery.

[21] Territorial *Executive Journal,* pp. 97-100. Following the creation of Clark County, the court of general quarter sessions of Knox County divided Vincennes Township into three townships: Vincennes, Harrison, and Palmyra. Microfilm of Court Minutes, February term, 1801, p. 4, in Archives Division, Indiana State Library; *History of Knox and Daviess Counties,* pp. 148-149.

[22] Territorial *Executive Journal,* pp. 100-101.

the governorship, that of superintendent of Indian affairs, which he would find demanding more and more of his time. In his first report to Secretary of War Henry Dearborn on July 15, 1801, the Governor wrote that he had been receiving visits from the Chiefs for the past ten or twelve weeks and listening to their complaints. "They say that their people have been killed—their lands settled on—their game wontonly destroyed—& their young men made drunk & cheated of the peltries. . . ."

While acknowledging the validity of their complaints, the Governor pointed out to the Secretary of War the difficulty of keeping the whites from encroaching on the Indian lands since the boundary between the United States and the Indian tribes was not marked; also how difficult it was to obtain sufficient information and evidence to find and prosecute those whites who had committed murder. He had already issued on May 9 a proclamation forbidding whites from settling, hunting, or surveying on any of the Indian lands.[23] Harrison felt that the British influence over the Indians still persisted, citing as evidence the large quantity of goods they continued to give them.[24] In order to keep better control over the Indians, the Governor suggested that United States troops again be sent to Vincennes.[25]

[23] Esarey (ed.), *Harrison's Messages and Letters,* I, 24, 25-31. In reply to this part of Harrison's letter, the President requested that a "handsome" reward be offered for apprehension of any one committing murder on any Indians. Carter (ed.), *Territorial Papers,* VII, 37. Yet apparently no white person was ever convicted of the murder of an Indian during the territorial period. Harrison wrote that his "utmost efforts" to bring murderers to punishment were in every instance unavailing. Philbrick (ed.), *Laws of Indiana Territory, 1801-1809,* pp. clxxxiv-clxxvn; Harrison to War Department, November 25, 1815, in Indiana Historical Society Library.

[24] In a later letter, Harrison repeated that the British were spreading such lies as that the high price of American goods was intended to impoverish the Indians, and that the Americans intended to destroy the Indians by smallpox. Harrison to Secretary of War, February 19, 1802, in Esarey (ed.), *Harrison's Messages and Letters,* I, 37-39.

[25] *Ibid.,* I, 25-28. After Hamtramck's successor at Fort Knox, Capt. Thomas Pasteur, left in 1798 the fort apparently remained unoccupied until 1801. Three

On the other hand the Governor had little sympathy for the drunken and dirty Indians who frequented Vincennes daily, breaking into homes and attacking both whites and other Indians, nor for the traders who supplied them with liquor. To halt such traffic he issued a proclamation forbidding traders to sell spirituous liquor to tribesmen within a mile of the town. Another proclamation regulated the Indian trade. Traders must be licensed and should restrict their trading to the Indian towns.[26]

Following enactment in 1802 of a law by Congress authorizing the President to take such measures as were deemed expedient to prevent the introduction of ardent spirits amongst the Indians, and having received authority from the President to suppress the sale of the same within the Indiana Territory, the Governor issued a new proclamation suppressing the sale of ardent spirits to any Indians whatsoever.[27] Little Turtle of the Miami and Five Medals of the Potawatomi tribe both requested such action.[28] The law, however, proved ineffectual because its operation was construed to extend exclusively to the sale of liquor in the

months after making a request for troops, Harrison wrote that a company commanded by Capt. Francis Johnston of the Fourth Regiment was at Vincennes. "Fort Knox Orderly Book, 1793-1797," edited by Milo M. Quaife, *Indiana Magazine of History*, XXXII, 137-169; Harrison to James Findlay, October 15, 1801, in Esarey (ed.), *Harrison's Messages and Letters*, I, 35. They were replaced sometime during the next year by a detachment of the First Infantry Regiment under the command of Cornelius Lyman. The latter built a new Fort Knox, three miles up the Wabash from Vincennes. Esarey (ed.), *op. cit.*, I, 57; Secretary of War to Lyman, August 4, 1803, in Carter (ed.), *Territorial Papers*, VII, 117.

[26] Esarey (ed.), *Harrison's Messages and Letters*, I, 27-29, 31-32. For a list of thirty-eight traders licensed by Harrison in 1801-1802 and the towns where they were to trade, see *Indiana Magazine of History*, II (1906), 5-7. Some of the traders were Frenchmen and some were Americans.

[27] Proclamation dated October 24, 1802, in Esarey (ed.), *Harrison's Messages and Letters*, I, 59-60.

[28] See the addresses of the chiefs and the memorial to Congress prepared by the Society of Friends, in Gerard T. Hopkins, *A Mission to the Indians, from the Indian Committee of Baltimore Yearly Meeting, to Fort Wayne, in 1804* (Philadelphia, 1862), pp. 158-176.

Indian country and did not apply to territory purchased from the Indians even though still occupied by them.[29]

To the credit of the Indians, the Governor was happy to report in his letter of July, 1801, that the Delawares on White River were attempting to become agriculturists under the supervision of Moravian missionaries who had come to live with them; also, the Kaskaskia, Piankashaw, and Potawatomi had asked for farm implements and animals.[30] Little Turtle invited the Quakers to aid his tribe in learning how to till the soil.[31]

During the summer of 1802 Harrison made preparations for his first Indian council at Vincennes, the purpose of which was to obtain consent to the running of the boundaries of the Vincennes Tract. The cession of this tract had been agreed upon at the Treaty of Greenville, but its exact extent was left undefined.[32] Its history dated back to 1742 at which time the French inhabitants of Vincennes claimed that the Indians of the Wabash River had ceded to them all the land along that stream from Point Coupee (four miles below the present Merom) to the mouth of White River, and subsequently had extended it forty leagues west of the Wabash and thirty leagues east. This cession had been recognized by the Piankashaw in 1775 in their sale of adjoining land to the Wabash Land Company. Congress had refused to confirm the latter sale, but claimed that the grant

29 Esarey (ed.), *Harrison's Messages and Letters*, I, 153-154; Carter (ed.), *Territorial Papers*, VII, 49n-50n.

30 Esarey (ed.), *Harrison's Messages and Letters*, I, 30. The experiences of the Moravians are recorded in Lawrence H. Gipson (ed.), *The Moravian Indian Mission on White River—Diaries and Letters, May 5, 1799, to November 12, 1806* (*Indiana Historical Collections*, XXIII, Indianapolis, 1938).

31 Hopkins, *A Mission to the Indians*, pp. 4-5.

32 Secretary of War to Harrison, January 22, June 17, and August 5, 1802, in Carter (ed.), *Territorial Papers*, VII, 46-47, 53-54, 63-64; President Jefferson to Secretary of War, August 12, 1802, in *ibid.*, VII, 67-70; Kappler (ed.), *Indian Affairs. Laws and Treaties*, II, 32. Harrison was instructed to press for the inclusion in the tract of all the land possible without angering the Indians to the point that future negotiations would be imperiled.

made to the French inhabitants would have been made in fact to the French government and therefore had since passed to the United States.[33]

Chiefs of the Kaskaskia, Piankashaw, Potawatomi, Wea, Kickapoo, and Eel River Miami were invited to the council which began on August 12 and continued until the 17th of September when the chiefs signed a provisional agreement which was to be confirmed by a formal treaty the following year. Some five hundred Indians (men, women, and children) attended the council. Harrison had hoped to have some United States Army uniforms and some medals to distribute to the chiefs, but, in the event they should not arrive in time, the Governor was authorized to expend $1,500 to obtain other gifts. The chiefs at first were adamant against acknowledging any claim of the United States to land around Vincennes, saying only a small tract extending to the high lands around the town had been lent to the French, but not sold nor given to them; and any grant made by the Piankashaw would not be binding, as that tribe owned very little land. It took considerable skill on the part of the Governor, assisted by the interpreter William Wells, to bring them to the point of authorizing Miami chiefs Little Turtle and John B. Richardville and Potawatomi chiefs Topenebee and Winamac to make over to the United States the following year a rectangular tract of land beginning at the mouth of the Wabash below Vincennes, thence west 12 miles, northeast 37 miles, southeast 72 miles, southwest 37 miles and west to the place of beginning.[34]

33 George R. Wilson, "The First Public Land Surveys in Indiana: Freeman's Lines," *Indiana Magazine of History,* XII (1916), 1-7; George R. Wilson, *Early Indiana Trails and Surveys* (Indiana Historical Society *Publications,* VI, No. 3, Indianapolis, 1919), pp. 395, 410 ff.

34 Secretary of War to Harrison, August 5 and 6, 1802, in Carter (ed.), *Territorial Papers,* VII, 63-64, 65; Minutes of the Council, September 17, 1802, in Esarey (ed.), *Harrison's Messages and Letters,* I, 56-57; Moses Dawson, *A Historical Narrative of the Civil and Military Services of Major-General William H. Harrison* . . . (Cincinnati, 1824), pp. 21-28; Lexington (Kentucky) *Gazette,* October 1 and 19, 1802.

On the eve of the assembly, the Illinois Potawatomi killed two Americans north of the village of Cahokia, thus creating a tension that was difficult to dispel. Harrison termed it a breach of the peace between that tribe and the United States rather than an act of war and the Secretary of War ordered that the tribe's annual annuity be withheld until they made full and ample restitution, which apparently meant turning the murderers over to the United States or putting them to death themselves.[35] In opening the council, Harrison reproved the Indians for their conduct and urged them henceforth to aim their "arrows at the buffaloe, the bear, and the deer . . . but spare your brother man."[36]

Judging from his correspondence, President Jefferson was greatly interested in the Indian affairs of the territory, and although most of his comments and instructions were communicated to Harrison through his Secretary of War, on occasion he wrote personally to the Governor. Such was the case when he explained in detail on February 27, 1803, the government's policy towards the Indians in order that Harrison might better know how to fulfill his part in unison with that policy.

"Our system," the President wrote, "is to live in perpetual peace with the Indians, to cultivate an affectionate attachment from them, by every thing just & liberal which we can [do] for them within the bounds of reason, and by giving them effectual protection against wrongs from our own people. the decrease of game rendering their subsistence by

[35] President Jefferson to the Secretary of War, August 30, 1802, and the Secretary of War to Harrison, September 3, 1802, in Carter (ed.), *Territorial Papers*, VII, 71-72, 73-74.

[36] Address to the Council, August 12, 1802, in *Harrison's Messages and Letters*, I, 52-55. Following the Council, Harrison sent a letter to his brother-in-law in Cincinnati by the hand of William Wells, saying the latter could give him information about the "late negotiations with the Indians." Harrison mentioned that his three children had been very ill and that his wife had given birth to a fourth child on September 6. Harrison to James Findlay, September 23, 1802, in Indiana Historical Society Library; Cleaves, *Old Tippecanoe*, p. 37.

hunting insufficient, we wish to draw them to agriculture, to spinning & weaving. . . ." At the same time the government was working for the advancement of the Indians, Jefferson saw no contradiction or equivocation in trying to reduce the amount of land they held. "When they withdraw themselves to the culture of a small piece of land, they will percieve how useless to them are their extensive forests, and will be willing to pare them off from time to time in exchange for necessaries for their farms & families." To promote this disposition to exchange lands for necessaries, the President proposed to establish trading houses in the Indian country, then when the Indians ran into debt beyond what they could pay, they would "become willing to lop th[em off] by a cession of lands." In this way, too, they would get rid of the traders for the government could afford to sell the merchandise at a lower cost than private individuals could.[37]

Jefferson also disclosed to Harrison in his letter of February 27, 1803, the expected transfer of Louisiana to France, and the effect this might have on the Indians. Spain had retroceded Louisiana to France by the Treaty of San Ildefonso, on October 1, 1800, but the latter had not yet taken possession of the colony. With the occupation of New Orleans by the French now imminent it was believed the Indians would stiffen their resistance to any land cessions and look to the French

[37] President Jefferson to Harrison, February 27, 1803, in Carter (ed.), *Territorial Papers,* VII, 90-91. The President wrote in a similar vein to Benjamin Hawkins, superintendent of the southern tribes, on February 18, 1803. Paul Leicester Ford (ed.), *The Works of Thomas Jefferson* (12 volumes, New York, 1904-1905), IX, 446-448.

Harrison was probably referring to this letter when he wrote later that President Jefferson had recommended, as the means of softening the obstinacy of the Indians toward land cessions, that he acquire their confidence "by an attention to their wants by treating them always with justice & [hu]manity— by securing them from imposition in their dealings with the whites & by liberal presents to the chiefs & influential men." Harrison to George Graham, chief clerk of War Department, November 25, 1815, in Indiana Historical Society Library.

for protection. In urging the purchase of the Illinois land from the Kaskaskia and other tribes who held claims there, Jefferson wrote, "whatever can now be obtained [in the way of cessions] must be obtained quickly."

Napoleon's plans for the colony, however, went awry and by the spring of 1803 his pressing need of money caused him to offer to sell Louisiana to the United States. The sale was consummated on April 30, 1803, for the sum of $11,250,000.[38]

With the boundaries of Indiana Territory about to be enlarged by the addition of that part of the Northwest Territory not included in the new state of Ohio, Governor Harrison on January 24, 1803, announced that whenever Ohio's statehood should go into effect, Wayne County, Northwest Territory, should become a part of Indiana Territory, and the officers holding commissions under the former government should continue to carry out their duties. Since the citizens of that county were preparing a petition asking for the creation of Michigan Territory out of this area, the Governor apparently considered the appointment of new officials unnecessary, but not so in another section about to be added to Indiana Territory. The area known as "the Gore," between the Indian boundary line of 1795 and a line drawn north from the mouth of the Great Miami River was temporarily attached to Clark County until he could learn "who were the proper persons . . . to be appointed to the several offices" in the new county which he intended to establish. He asked Samuel C. Vance to assemble the people in order that they might recommend "such characters for the several appointments as were most likely to fill them with ability," and also to name the place they desired for the seat of justice. Harrison presumably acted upon these recommendations when he proclaimed the formation of Dearborn County

38 Jefferson to Harrison, February 27, 1803, in Carter (ed.), *Territorial Papers*, VII, 92; *Dictionary of American History*, III, 305, 307-308.

on March 7, 1803, with Lawrenceburg as the county seat, and appointed the various county officials.[39]

Harrison's first term as governor was due to expire in May, 1803, and he apparently had some apprehension about his reappointment and wished to visit Washington to press his case in person; also, the trip would give him the opportunity to urge upon Congress the necessity of certain legislation that was needed for the benefit of the territory. Though the President granted him permission to make the trip, there is no evidence that he did so. The President was apparently satisfied with Harrison's administration of affairs and reappointed him on February 8, 1803, three months before his first commission was due to expire.[40] On the same day he was given a commission to treat with the Indian tribes northwest of the Ohio River "with full power to conclude and sign any Treaty or Treaties, which may be found necessary."[41]

Foreseeing that considerable sums of public money would likely pass through his hands in carrying out this responsi-

[39] Territorial *Executive Journal,* pp. 114-116, 116-117; Harrison to Vance, January 31, 1803, in Indiana Historical Society Library. This represents one of many instances in which Governor Harrison sought the advice of the residents of a county or district before exercising his power of appointment. Louis A. Ewbank and Dorothy Riker (eds.), *The Laws of Indiana Territory, 1809-1816* (*Indiana Historical Collections,* XX, Indianapolis, 1934), pp. 27-28.

[40] Secretary of War to Harrison, November 2, 1802, in Carter (ed.), *Territorial Papers,* VII, 75; Harrison to Thomas Worthington, Chillicothe, June 11, 1802, in *Indiana Magazine of History,* XLVII, 64-65; Harrison to Senator Jonathon Dayton, Washington, January 12, 1803, quoted in Cleaves, *Old Tippecanoe,* p. 37, from *Henkel's Catalogue of Autograph MSS,* No. 663, p. 58, in New York Public Library. The commission is in Carter (ed.), *Territorial Papers,* VII, 113. Harrison delayed beginning the construction of a home in Vincennes until after he was assured of a second term. Built on the style of the family home in Virginia, the house has been restored by the Francis Vigo Chapter of the Daughters of the American Revolution, its present owner, and is open to the public. Burns, *Early Architects and Builders of Indiana,* pp. 183-184.

[41] Carter (ed.), *Territorial Papers,* VII, 84-85; it was by the authority of the latter commission that Harrison in succeeding years made some thirteen treaties with various Indian tribes.

bility, Harrison explained later how he tried to guard against any charges of peculation by adopting the following rules of conduct: (1) that all councils with the Indians be held in public and attended by the most respectable citizens within reach; (2) that all goods and money to be paid to the Indians be delivered in the presence of as many respectable persons as could be collected, and instead of attesting only to the signing of the receipts by the chiefs, the witnesses should certify that they had examined the money and goods they saw delivered; (3) that separate bills be drawn for every account so that the account, the receipt for payment, and the draft for the amount would appear on the same paper and could be so presented to the War Department. In handling the current expenses of the Indian department, he explained that to acquire the confidence of the Indians, he treated those who were found daily about Vincennes as children, admitting them to his house and table, caring for them when they were sick, burying at public expense those who died, and stifling any complaints of injustice with small presents, all of which expense he estimated did not usually amount to more than $1,200 annually, or $2,000 at the most. His efforts in thus securing the friendship of the Indians he felt had paid off.[42]

Before Harrison could do anything further to consummate the cession of the Vincennes Tract it was necessary that the boundaries as consented to by the council of September, 1802, be surveyed. Thomas Freeman, an experienced surveyor, was chosen by the Surveyor General's Office and began tracing the boundary of the Tract in the fall of 1802 and com-

---

[42] Harrison to the War Department, November 25, 1815, in Indiana Historical Society Library; Dawson, *Harrison*, pp. 51-52. In spite of the precautions taken in the handling of public funds, Harrison's political enemies on more than one occasion charged him with using these funds to his own advantage. The above letter was written in response to a resolution of Congress to investigate his purchases of goods for and presents given to the Indians while serving as superintendent of Indian affairs. Cleaves, *Old Tippecanoe*, pp. 234-235; *Annals of Congress*, 14 Congress, 1 session, col. 1273. Congress took no further action on the resolution.

pleted it the following spring.[43] In the meantime, the Governor turned his attention from Indian affairs to other problems of his administration.

§ §

Before the formation of Indiana Territory, petitions for the admission of slavery into the Northwest Territory were sent to Congress from the Illinois country. And before Harrison arrived at Vincennes, another petition, containing 270 names and requesting a limited type of slavery, was forwarded from the same region. Other petitions and letters were sent or presented to the Governor, largely from the Illinois counties, advocating an advance to the second or semirepresentative stage of government. Harrison opposed the last request, calling attention to the increased costs which the people would have to bear. As a result this phase of the agitation was temporarily halted.[44]

The next year, 1802, the slavery phase of the movement was resumed, and the Governor was requested to call a convention to consider the propriety of repealing the antislavery article of the Ordinance of 1787. Professing to believe that a majority of the people in the territory favored slavery in some form, he acceded to the petitioners and called for an election of twelve delegates from the four counties to meet at Vincennes on December 20, 1802.[45] On Christmas Day

[43] Wilson, *Early Indiana Trails and Surveys*, p. 411. The north line of the Indiana portion of the Tract ran from Point Coupee on the Wabash to the present town of Orleans, then slightly southwest to a point in the present Perry County, then west to the mouth of White River; the Tract extended west of the Wabash approximately fifteen miles and comprised in all some 1,600,000 acres, probably far more than the Indians intended when they confirmed the cession in 1795. *Ibid.,* pp. 410-412, 418, 420-422; Wilson, "The First Public Land Surveys in Indiana," *Indiana Magazine of History,* XII, 8-20. See map, p. 377.

[44] Philbrick (ed.), *Laws of Indiana Territory, 1801-1809,* pp. xx-xxiii; Jacob Piatt Dunn (ed.), *Slavery Petitions and Papers* (Indiana Historical Society *Publications,* II, No. 12, Indianapolis, 1894), pp. 447-461.

[45] Territorial *Executive Journal,* pp. 113-114. Harrison, Vigo, William Prince, and Luke Decker represented Knox County, James N. Wood and

the convention adopted a resolution in favor of a ten-year suspension of Article VI of the Ordinance. A petition to Congress dated December 28 requested the suspension on the grounds that desirable settlers were forced to move west of the Mississippi because they could not bring their slaves into Indiana Territory. It was also requested that the slaves and their children that would be brought into the territory during the proposed suspension should remain slaves after the ten years had passed.

In addition to the request regarding slavery the petition also asked the government to clear the Indian title to the southern part of the territory, to sell the public land in smaller quantities and at a lower price, to grant pre-emption to the squatters who were waiting the opportunity to buy the land on which they were living, and to grant lands to encourage the building of roads and the establishment of educational institutions. Looking ahead to the time when the territory would have a general assembly, they petitioned that the right to vote for members of the lower house be extended to all free adult males of the age of twenty-one and over. All these requests had the same objective, the attraction of settlers. Legalization of slavery was expected to attract the wealthy while the poorer settlers would be attracted by the opportunity to buy land in smaller quantities and at lower prices and to have a voice in the government. The convention itself was a step in the direction of self-government.[46]

Charles Beggs, Clark County. Dunn, *Indiana,* pp. 303-305; certificate of election, Clark County, December 8, 1802, in English Collection, Indiana Historical Society Library. At least one of the Clark County delegates, and perhaps both, opposed the introduction of slavery into the territory.

[46] Esarey (ed.), *Harrison's Messages and Letters,* I, 60-67; Dunn (ed.), *Slavery Petitions and Papers,* pp. 461-470; Dunn, *Indiana,* pp. 302-307. Harrison was charged with undue influence in bringing the convention into existence. See "The Letters of Decius," edited by John D. Barnhart, *Indiana Magazine of History,* XLIII (1947), 271, 278-279, 292-293; and "A Freeholder of Knox County," in Vincennes *Indiana Gazette,* August 7, 1804.

Benjamin Parke carried the petition to Washington, presenting a copy to the President as well as one to the Speaker of the House of Representatives.[47]

When Congress failed to act favorably on any of the requests of the Vincennes Convention, the Governor and Judges decided to take matters in their own hands and permit a form of slavery in the territory by an official evasion of the Ordinance of 1787. In their legislative capacity they adopted in 1803 a law concerning servants which was taken from the Virginia code. It provided that Negroes and mulattoes brought into the territory must perform the service due their masters and that contracts between master and servants were assignable.[48]

At the same session the lawmakers endeavored to meet the need for additional county revenue by improving the method of collecting taxes and listing a long series of fees that were to be charged for various services. The courts of general quarter sessions were authorized to enter into contracts for the building or repairing of courthouses, jails, pillories and whipping posts, and bridges. Another act provided for taxing various law processes, the revenue from which would go to the territory.[49]

One possible source of revenue which the Governor and Judges could not touch without permission from Congress was the levying of a tax on licenses issued to Indian traders. Harrison had written as early as 1802 suggesting that such a tax might produce as much as $1,000 a year for territorial expenses. A petition to Congress requesting permission to levy such a tax was turned down in 1804.[50]

47 President Jefferson to Harrison, February 28, 1803, in Carter (ed.), *Territorial Papers*, VII, 93.

48 Philbrick (ed.), *Laws of Indiana Territory, 1801-1809*, pp. 42-46.

49 *Ibid.*, pp. 46-63, 68-81, 81-83. The first jail in Knox County was completed in 1803; the contract for a courthouse was let in 1808. Henry Vanderburgh had erected a pillory and stocks during the early days of the Northwest Territory. *History of Knox and Daviess Counties*, pp. 152, 172, 177.

50 Esarey (ed.), *Harrison's Messages and Letters*, I, 88-89; Carter (ed.),

William Henry Harrison

From a Painting attributed to Rembrandt Peale. The
original is in the Harrison House at Vincennes

Harrison and Tecumseh in Council at Vincennes

From a Painting by Stanley M. Arthurs

As early as 1803 petitions from both the Illinois counties and from Detroit were sent to Congress pleading for a separation of their areas from the Indiana Territory. Their great distance from Vincennes was cited as one of the reasons, while a political motive was also present in the case of the Illinois counties. The 1803 memorial from the citizens of Detroit and the northern area was favorably received by the United States Senate and a bill was introduced and passed by that body creating a new territory north of a line running through the southern extreme of Lake Michigan. The bill failed to pass the House at that session, but a second bill introduced in December, 1804, creating the Michigan Territory, passed both houses and was approved on January 11, 1805, effective June 30. Whereas the first bill would have made the Mississippi River the western boundary of the new territory, the second made the western boundary a line running north from the "southerly bend, or extreme, of Lake Michigan" to the northern boundary of the United States, and east from the same point to Lake Erie.[51] Separation of the Illinois counties was postponed for four more years.

§ § §

Harrison ascended the Wabash in the spring of 1803 as soon as the ice permitted and invited the Miami, Shawnee, Delaware, Potawatomi, and Kickapoo chiefs to meet him at Fort Wayne. The party, which included Secretary Gibson, Attorney General John Rice Jones, Surveyor Thomas Freeman, two army officers, and twelve rank and file soldiers, traveled by barge to the headwaters of the Wabash where

---

Territorial Papers, VII, 47. When the General Assembly passed a bill in 1805 to tax Indian traders, Harrison returned it to the House with the notation that Congress had exclusive jurisdiction in regulating trade with the Indians. Harrison to House of Representatives, August 22, 1805, in English Collection, Indiana Historical Society Library.

[51] Pence and Armstrong, *Indiana Boundaries,* pp. 7, 142-143; the petitions from Detroit are in Carter (ed.), *Territorial Papers,* VII, 99-106, 118-123, 227-231, 240-242.

the soldiers remained with the boat while the others went on to Fort Wayne. Harrison continued on to Detroit where he obtained supplies for the treaty negotiations and the annuity payment which would follow. While there he attended a ball given in his honor.[52]

On his return to Fort Wayne from Detroit, Harrison was disappointed to find that only a few of the Indians had responded to his invitation. The Owl or Long Beard prevented the main body of Miami from attending, and the Delawares likewise apparently stayed away. Both of these tribes were angry about the agreement made at the Vincennes Council the previous year. The Governor obtained the consent of the Indians who were present to the boundary of the Vincennes Tract as run by Thomas Freeman, and to the cession of the valuable salt spring near the present Shawneetown; the treaty was signed on June 7, 1803. Richardville and Little Turtle signed for the Miami, Topenebee and Winamac for the Potawatomi, and all four for the Eel Rivers, Wea, Piankashaw, and Kaskaskia, "whom they represent." Two Kickapoo and two Shawnee chiefs also signed the treaty, and four Delawares from White River. A couple of days later some one hundred to one hundred and fifty Miami appeared, whereupon Harrison tried to call the others back into council, but on the day appointed for the reconvening neither the Miami nor Delawares appeared. When they came in a few days later, they reported they had been in a council of their own in which the Miami had recognized the title of the Delawares to the land between the White River and the Ohio. Harrison by this time had become impatient with the delaying tactics of the Indians and being in a hurry to get back to the point where the boat was waiting for him (the water was falling rapidly and soon would be too low to use the boat), he turned the task of explaining the treaty and distributing the annuity over to William Wells, the Indian agent.[53]

Later that year the Governor had a much easier time in negotiating with the Kaskaskia, the remnant of a once flourishing confederacy of five Illinois tribes. War with the Sauk had reduced their numbers, whiskey and disease had weakened them, and the Potawatomi were threatening their extirpation. They were now anxious to come under the protection of the United States, and Harrison was successful in obtaining almost all their land, reserving two tracts for tribal use and hunting rights in the ceded territory, in exchange for protection against all possible enemies and a small increase in their annuities. The extent of the cession was between seven and eight million acres.[54]

A year later, in November, 1804, the Sauk and Foxes ceded their claims to land in the Illinois country and west of the Mississippi. They, too, were taken under the protection of the United States.[55]

In August of that same year Harrison met the Delaware chiefs at Vincennes and in return for $800 in goods, an additional annuity of $300 for ten years, and a further sum of $300 for the next five years to be spent in teaching them agricultural and domestic arts, obtained from them their right and title to the land between the Ohio and Wabash rivers and south of the Vincennes Tract and the road leading to Clarksville. By a separate treaty the Piankashaw relinquished their claim to the above land.[56] By another article of the

<hr />

[53] Harrison to Secretary of War, March 3, 1803 [1805], in Esarey (ed.), *Harrison's Messages and Letters,* I, 82-83; U. S. *Statutes at Large,* VII, 74-76; Dawson, *Harrison,* pp. 47-50. Though the Miami and the Delawares allegedly settled their respective claims to land in southern Indiana at this time, as a matter of fact these conflicting claims remained a thorny problem in future negotiations until finally resolved by the treaty of Vincennes in 1805.

[54] Esarey (ed.), *Harrison's Messages and Letters,* I, 100-101, 114-115; II, 635; Carter (ed.), *Territorial Papers,* VII, 190-191; Kappler (ed.), *Indian Affairs. Laws and Treaties,* II, 49-50.

[55] Kappler (ed.), *Indian Affairs. Laws and Treaties,* II, 54-56.

[56] *Ibid.,* II, 51-53.

treaty with the Delawares, the United States agreed to recognize that tribe as being the sole owner of another tract extending east from the Vincennes Tract to the Ohio boundary. This last provision aroused the anger of the Miami, who claimed they owned the tract and had only allowed the Delawares to occupy it. To settle the controversy Harrison called another council in August, 1805, at which the Miami, Eel River Miami, Wea, Delawares, and Potawatomi were all present. By the promise of additional annuities the Governor was able not only to get the Delawares to relinquish their claim, but succeeded in purchasing the Miami claim to the tract. That tribe and the Potawatomi then acknowledged the right of the Delawares to cede the land south of the Vincennes Tract in 1804. In addition to increasing their annuities, the Governor distributed $4,000 at the time of the 1805 treaty— $1,000 each to the Delawares, Miami, and Potawatomi, and $500 each to the Eel River Miami and Wea.[57]

Harrison was pleased with the results of the conference and wrote to the President that it had had a most beneficial effect—"every improper prejudice has been removed from their minds and that all the chiefs have . . . expressed the warmest attachment to the United States and their Willingness to follow their advice in every instance. One of their orators . . . assured me in the name of the rest that they would in future look upon the United States in the same light that they had formerly done their fathers the French—An unexpected Compliment and one which I never supposed I should hear from an Indian."[58] This warm attachment, however, would prove to be of brief duration.

Thus by the fall of 1805 the Indian title had been cleared to the southern fourth of the future state of Indiana, but this was only the first step in opening it for sale to settlers;

[57] *Ibid.*, II, 58-60. For correspondence relating to the 1805 treaty, see Esarey (ed.), *Harrison's Messages and Letters*, I, 76-84, 117-118, 121-123, 125-126, 132-134, 137-140, 141-147, 161-165, and Carter (ed.), *Territorial Papers*, VII, 287-288, 293-294, 301-302.

[58] Harrison to the President, August 29, 1805, in Carter (ed.), *Territorial Papers*, VII, 301-302.

the next step was to have it surveyed. Surveyors of the area around Vincennes and other French settlements were confronted with the diagonal lines of the donations to the French and early American settlers which were entirely different from the rectangular surveying method adopted by the United States. In addition, the boundaries and ownership of some of the donation lands had never been definitely determined. An extensive correspondence ensued between the Secretary of the Treasury, the United States Surveyor General, Governor Harrison, and others regarding the problems involved. The procedure to be followed was set out in an act of Congress of March 26, 1804, which provided for a re-examination and a resurvey of the former donation claims, the survey of the land to which the Indian title had been extinguished, and the establishment of land offices at Vincennes and Kaskaskia. The registers and receivers of the land offices were to serve as commissioners to examine and determine the claims to the donation lands in their particular districts.[59]

John Badollet, a native of Switzerland and a close friend of Albert Gallatin, secretary of the treasury, was appointed register of the Vincennes Land Office and arrived in September, 1804, to take up his duties. He was joined by Nathaniel Ewing of Pennsylvania, the receiver. Nine months had been allowed them for the task of settling the land claims, but so intricate was the work that it required two years. Their reports showed that only a small portion of the tracts were still in the hands of the original claimants or their heirs; Americans had bought up most of the French claims, thus defeating the purpose of Congress in compensating the French for their long suffering during the period of American conquest and their subsequent neglect by the American government.[60]

59 U. S. *Statutes at Large,* II, 277-283.
60 Lux, *Vincennes Donation Lands,* pp. 464-477. The reports of the commissioners are printed in *American State Papers. Public Lands,* I, 288-303, 558-581.

After settlement of the claims to the donation tracts, they were resurveyed in the years between 1807 and 1810 and fitted into the rectangular surveys of the other land to which the Indian title had been extinguished.[61]

While not immediately concerned in the settlement of the donation claims, Governor Harrison was an interested observer inasmuch as he had purchased some of the land from earlier claimants; he was at times accused of speculating in the same to the detriment of actual settlers.[62]

Jared Mansfield had been appointed surveyor general of the public lands in 1803 and the following year was instructed to supervise the surveys in the Indiana Territory under the act of March 26, beginning with the Vincennes Tract which it was hoped could be completed in twelve months and the land placed on sale in April or May, 1805. However, various problems arose to delay the progress of the surveyors and the land was not offered for sale until two years later. Both the base line and the second meridian had to be laid down before the township and section lines could be run.[63]

§   §   §   §

Governor Harrison was given still another responsibility in 1804-1805, that of administering the government of the United States in Upper Louisiana. Capt. Amos Stoddard from the military post at Kaskaskia took possession of the country for the United States on March 9, 1804, in a cere-

61 Lux, *Vincennes Donation Lands,* pp. 477-484.

62 For charges leveled against the register, receiver, and Governor and their defense, see Thornbrough (ed.), *Correspondence of Badollet and Gallatin,* pp. 68-89; Vincennes *Western Sun,* August 22 and September 19, 1807.

63 For Mansfield's correspondence, see Carter (ed.), *Territorial Papers,* VII, Index; for the names of some of the surveyors and the methods of survey, see Wilson, "The First Public Land Surveys," *Indiana Magazine of History,* XII, 9-14; R. Carlyle Buley, *The Old Northwest. Pioneer Period, 1815-1840* (2 volumes, Indiana Historical Society, 1950), I, 118-122. The small hand-made notebooks of the surveyors, about 3 x 6 inches in size, and sometimes bound in buckskin, are in the Archives Division, Indiana State Library.

mony in which the French flag was raised for a moment in witness of its transfer to France in 1800, and then it was lowered and the American flag raised. The country was under the control of the military until October 1, when the law of Congress providing for the institution of civil government went into effect. By this act the territory was divided and that part north of the 33d parallel was attached to Indiana Territory for administrative purposes. Harrison's executive power was thus extended over the district and together with the Judges he enacted such laws as were necessary. Early in October, 1804, the Governor and Judges, Francis Vigo, William Prince, and Joseph Barron, with an escort of mounted regulars, set out for St. Louis where on October 12 Captain Stoddard yielded control of the province to civil authorities. During the next five weeks Harrison reorganized the courts and the militia, appointed the necessary officials, took up the question of land claims, and held the treaty with the Sauk and Foxes mentioned above. His authoritative manner of assuming control naturally aroused the enmity of some of the residents. His fear of British and Spanish intrigue may have led him to assume this firm attitude, for he wrote on his return to Vincennes that the people of Louisiana were much more attached to the United States than he had expected them to be. The following year, by an act of March 3, effective July 4, the Territory of Louisiana was created with a government of its own. At the close of Harrison's brief administration over the region, the citizens thanked him and the Judges for their "assiduity, attention, and disinterested punctuality," and for their "just and impartial administration."[64]

[64] U. S. *Statutes at Large,* II, 283-289, 331-332; Carter (ed.), *Territorial Papers,* XIII, 4-5, 8, 76, 148-149; Harrison, St. Louis, to Senator Jonathan Dayton, October 9, 1804, in Indiana Historical Society Library; Harrison, Vincennes, to Thomas Worthington, Chillicothe, December 25, 1804, in *Indiana Magazine of History,* XLVII, 69-70; Louis Houck, *A History of Missouri . . .* (3 volumes, Chicago, 1908), II, 356-363, 369-382.

The Governor and Judges had met on September 22, 1804, for the last time as a legislative body for Indiana Territory and passed three resolutions. In the four sessions they had held since January, 1801, they had adopted sixteen laws from the codes of other states, principally from Virginia, and passed eleven resolutions. Inasmuch as the laws adopted for the Northwest Territory remained in force in the Indiana Territory unless specifically repealed, the task of the Governor and Judges of the latter had been far less than that of their predecessors, nor did their legislation raise the storm of protest produced by the earlier laws.[65] While the period of nonrepresentative government had lasted for eleven years in the Northwest Territory, the younger territory was about to enter the second stage at the end of four years.

[65] Philbrick (ed.), *Laws of Indiana Territory, 1801-1809*, pp. cii-cxv.

CHAPTER X

THE GROWTH OF DEMOCRACY

The first period of territorial government came to an end in 1804 when Governor Harrison reversed his position on the advisability of passing into the second or semirepresentative stage. In the three years that had elapsed since he had refused to consider the proposal considerable progress had been made in clearing Indian claims to the land and opening it for settlement. When he called for a vote to be taken on the question on September 11, 1804, the majority of those voting favored the change.[1]

The Governor then issued a proclamation on December 5, declaring the territory to have passed into the second grade and calling for an election on January 3, 1805, of nine representatives—three from the county of Wayne, two from Knox, and one each from St. Clair, Randolph, Clark, and Dearborn. The representatives were to meet on February 1, 1805, to nominate members for the Legislative Council.[2]

[1] Vincennes *Indiana Gazette,* August 7, 1804; Esarey (ed.), *Harrison's Messages and Letters,* I, 106-107, 112-113; Territorial *Executive Journal,* pp. 124, 125-126. The election apparently was not well publicized outside of Knox County for out of the four hundred votes cast, 175 were from that county. Wayne County did not receive word in time to vote; the 26 votes in Dearborn County were all opposed. The results showed a majority of 138 in favor.

[2] The creation of Michigan Territory by act of Congress on January 11, 1805, made necessary a change in the apportionment and the Governor issued another proclamation on April 18 giving St. Clair County two representatives instead of one and calling for a new election in that county on May 20. Philbrick (ed.), *Laws of Indiana Territory, 1801-1809,* pp. xxvi-xxixn; Dunn, *Indiana,* pp. 323-324; Territorial *Executive Journal,* pp. 125-127. This made the total representation seven, still within the stipulation of the act of 1800 organizing Indiana Territory. Those elected were: Jesse B. Thomas, Dearborn County; Davis Floyd, Clark County; Benjamin Parke and John Johnson, Knox County; Shadrach Bond, William Biggs, St. Clair County; George Fisher, Randolph County. *Journals of the General Assembly of Indiana Terri-*

The Governor's proclamation incited a violent newspaper controversy in which Harrison's critics soon made known their opposition, asserting that the advance should have come spontaneously and not have been forced by the Governor; it would be expensive; and sufficient able men could not be found to serve in the legislative Assembly.[3] Actually, the gains in democratic government that came with the transition were slight. The Governor still retained his appointive power and his general executive authority; he could convene and dissolve the Assembly at his will and could veto any legislative measure that they might pass. He was subject to no control but that of public opinion.

The method of choosing the members of the first upper house or Legislative Council contributed to the Governor's influence over the legislative branch for the immediate future. The House of Representatives met the first week in February, 1805, and chose the names of ten men to be sent to the President, who was to choose five of the ten. Instead, President Jefferson returned the list to Harrison and asked him to make the choice, admonishing him to pick only honest men who were not Federalists or land jobbers. Those nominated were Jean Francois Perrey and John Hay of St. Clair County; Pierre Menard of Randolph County; John Rice Jones and Jacob Kuykendall of Knox County; Samuel Gwathmey and Marston G. Clark of Clark County; Benjamin Chambers of Dearborn County; and James May and James Henry of Wayne County. From these Harrison chose Hay, Menard, Jones, Gwathmey, and Chambers. Hay declined to serve and the nomination of Shadrach Bond, Sr., as his successor was approved by the United States Senate on January

tory, 1805-1815, edited by Gayle Thornbrough and Dorothy Riker (*Indiana Historical Collections*, XXXII, Indianapolis, 1950), pp. 28, 30. Biographical sketches of all those who served in the territorial Assembly from the Indiana counties, may be found in *ibid.*, pp. 958-1018.

[3] See especially the issues of the Vincennes *Indiana Gazette* for August 7, 14, 21, 28, September 11, 18, 1804, and "Letters of Decius," *Indiana Magazine of History*, XLIII, 268-272.

9, 1806. This left a vacancy in the House which was filled by Bond's nephew of the same name.[4] Wayne County having become a part of Michigan Territory, the nominations from that county were dropped.

Another victory for the Governor was the election by the Assembly of his friend Benjamin Parke as delegate to Congress.[5]

The first session of the General Assembly met on July 29, 1805, and continued until August 26.[6] After adopting rules of procedure based on those of the legislative assemblies of the Northwest Territory, the two houses met in joint session to hear a message from the Governor in which he urged them to strive to accomplish the wishes of the friends of representative government and to disappoint its enemies. The legislation which they enacted disproved the allegations of those who claimed that there was not a sufficient number of men of talent in the territory to fill the legislative positions. Among the thirty-three laws enacted were those for the simplification of the county court system, creation of a court of chancery, appointment of a committee to codify the laws, prohibiting the giving or selling of intoxicating liquors to the Indians, relief of persons imprisoned for debt, modification of the act for levying and collecting the taxes on land, regulating the fees charged by ferries, mills, and taverns, and establishing a standard of weights and measures.[7]

The pro-slavery element succeeded in passing a bill allowing any person owning or purchasing slaves outside the territory to bring them into Indiana and bind them to service. If the slaves were over fifteen years of age, the owner could make a contract for service with them for any term of years. The indenture was to be recorded with the county clerk within

---

[4] *Journals of the General Assembly,* pp. 21-23, 109; Esarey (ed.), *Harrison's Messages and Letters,* I, 126-127.

[5] Dunn, *Indiana,* pp. 328-329.

[6] *Journals of the General Assembly,* pp. 28-95.

[7] Philbrick (ed.), *Laws of Indiana Territory, 1801-1809,* pp. 91, 97-98, 99-103, 108-112, 114-118, 133-136, 147-153.

thirty days after the arrival of the slave into the territory, and if the slave refused the terms offered him, the master could have him taken out of the territory within sixty days without losing his title. Slaves under the age of fifteen were to be registered and required to serve until the age of thirty-five if they were males, thirty-two if females. Children born to the slaves after they were brought into the territory were to serve the master of the parent until they reached the age of thirty for males, or twenty-eight for females.[8]

This was clearly an attempt to evade Article VI of the Ordinance of 1787 prohibiting slavery and involuntary servitude in the territory. Negroes brought into Indiana under the terms of the law had a choice of binding themselves for a term of years fixed by their master (which might extend beyond their life expectancy), or of being sent out of the territory and sold for life. Books kept by the county clerks of Knox and Clark counties in which indentures under the law were recorded reveal that two indentures called for a term of service of 99 years, others for 90, 70, 60, and 50; the most common were 40 or 20 years, and the shortest was 10 years. Thirty-six persons were indentured in Clark County during the five years the law remained in effect while in Knox County fifty persons were indentured during the first three years. Many of the prominent men in the territory held Negroes under the indenture law, including Governor Harrison.[9]

Some of the same members that passed the indenture bill also sponsored a memorial to Congress urging revocation of Article VI of the Ordinance; however, it failed of adoption by the General Assembly because it also contained a protest against the separation of the Illinois counties and a proposal that the Indiana Territory be admitted immediately to state-

8 Philbrick (ed.), *Laws of Indiana Territory, 1801-1809,* pp. 136-139.

9 Emma Lou Thornbrough, *The Negro in Indiana. A Study of a Minority* (*Indiana Historical Collections,* XXXVII, Indianapolis, 1957), pp. 8-12. Miss Thornbrough's figures are based on a study of the two registers. The Indiana State Library has a microfilm copy of the Knox County book and the original of the one kept in Clark County.

hood. The members from St. Clair and Clark counties joined in opposing the memorial, the former because they were pushing for separation and the latter because they opposed slavery. It was signed by those from Randolph, Knox, and Dearborn and sent to Congress.[10] The Congressional committee to whom the memorial was referred, along with a petition from the Illinois counties favoring separation and one from Dearborn County opposing slavery, reported in favor of the revocation of Article VI but against separation.[11] The indenture act was denounced by newspapers in both Cincinnati and Washington.[12]

The legislators took time out from their deliberations to attend the treaty negotiations then in progress with the Indians and a number of them were present and witnessed the signing of the treaty on August 21, 1805.

Harrison's second term as governor of Indiana Territory was due to expire in May, 1806, and although, as he wrote to Senator Worthington, "I have every reason to believe that the President entirely approves of my administration," he did not propose to "neglect any honourable means of securing a reappointment," and ended by soliciting the Senator's aid.[13] Charges against the Governor had been sent to the Secretary of State by an anonymous correspondent, later identified as Isaac Darneille, with a request that they be presented to the President and the Senate. The charges included par-

[10] *Journals of the General Assembly*, pp. 101-108; Dunn (ed.), *Slavery Petitions and Papers*, pp. 476-482.

[11] Dunn, *Indiana*, pp. 336-337, 341-347; Dunn (ed.), *Slavery Petitions and Papers*, pp. 494-497; Esarey (ed.), *Harrison's Messages and Letters*, I, 187-190. Thomas T. Davis, judge of the General Court, wrote the attorney general of the United States: "If you have any influence for God's sake dont let Congress introduce Slavery among us. I dispise the Colour & Situation & if Congress will let us alone we will in Two years become a State. But if they Humor the St Vincennes party they will have the whole Territory in Confusion. Let us alone and we will do well." Davis to John Breckinridge, January 26, 1806, in Carter (ed.), *Territorial Papers*, VII, 335.

[12] Dunn, *Indiana*, pp. 330-334.

[13] Harrison to Thomas Worthington, November 23, 1805, in *Indiana Magazine of History*, XLVII (1951), 72.

tiality in making appointments and in the matter of land claims, the use of federal troops for his private use, fraud in distribution of annuities, interference in judicial proceedings, neglect of duty in connection with the district of Louisiana, and interference in the right of petition. The Governor forwarded a refutation of the charges the following year after he had received his reappointment.[14]

At the opening of the second session of the First Assembly, which convened on November 3, 1806, the Governor congratulated the members upon the semirepresentative government under which they were then living and pointed to statehood as a goal. Until that time arrived the Governor assured them it would be his practice in all his public acts to consult not only the interests but as far as possible the wishes of the people.[15]

The legislation of this session showed little evidence on the part of the representatives of a desire to secure self-government in advance of the plan embodied in the Ordinance. A bill was passed permitting the time of service of Negroes and mulattoes bound under the 1805 act to be sold as part of a personal estate,[16] and the members united this time in passing and sending to Congress a resolution asking a suspension of Article VI prohibiting slavery.[17] Again the Congressional committee made a favorable report on the resolution, but no further action was taken.[18]

14 "Letters of Decius," *Indiana Magazine of History*, XLIII, 265-266, 280-284; Esarey (ed.), *Harrison's Messages and Letters*, I, 194-195. The Senate adjourned on April 21, 1806, without acting on the reappointment, whereupon Jefferson made an interim appointment to run until the end of the next session of the Senate. The President submitted Harrison's name to that body on December 15, 1806, and the nomination was confirmed two days later. The new commission, dated January 16, 1807, was to run for three years from that date. Carter (ed.), *Territorial Papers*, VII, 359, 419; U. S. Senate, *Executive Journal*, II, 44, 45, 130.

15 *Journals of the General Assembly*, pp. 110-118.

16 Philbrick (ed.), *Laws of Indiana Territory, 1801-1809,* p. 189.

17 Dunn (ed.), *Slavery Petitions and Papers*, pp. 507-509.

18 *Ibid.*, pp. 509-510.

The terms of the representatives to the First Assembly being due to expire, an election for their successors was held on February 2, 1807. James Beggs replaced Davis Floyd for Clark County and two new representatives—General Washington Johnston and Luke Decker—were elected in Knox County; otherwise the membership remained the same.[19] The Second Assembly, in session from August 17 to September 19, 1807, continued to work in co-operation with the Governor during its first session as had the previous Assembly, but there was evidence of a growing difference between them. Benjamin Parke was re-elected as the territorial delegate to Congress, and another resolution was passed favoring the suspension of Article VI.[20] The revision of the laws provided by the First Assembly was adopted. This was the work of John Johnson and John Rice Jones and amounted to little more than a compilation of earlier acts.[21] The members of the Council from Randolph and St. Clair counties resigned during or at the close of the session and members of the House were recommended and appointed by the President to the vacancies. In the elections to fill the House seats a contest arose between those favoring division of the territory and those opposing, which was won by the divisionists.[22]

[19] *Journals of the General Assembly,* p. 125, See *ibid.,* pp. 125-157 for documents pertaining to the 1807 session; the Journals have not been found. Floyd had become involved with Aaron Burr and his plot to establish a colony on Spanish territory. He was indicted and found guilty by the territorial court at a session held in Clark County in June, 1807, for "aiding in setting on foot a military expedition against . . . the King of Spain, with whom the United States was then at peace." However, the sentence was light—three hours in jail and a fine of $10. The affair did not prevent him from being elected clerk of the House of Representatives the following month. Microfilm copy of record of courts held in Clark County by federal judges, 1802-1813, in Indiana State Library. For criticism and defense of his election as clerk, see Vincennes *Western Sun,* November 25, 1807, January 6, 1808; Carter (ed.), *Territorial Papers,* VII, 511-514.

[20] *Journals of the General Assembly,* pp. 149, 154-156.

[21] The Revised Laws and the original acts of the 1807 session are printed in Philbrick (ed.), *Laws of Indiana Territory, 1801-1809,* pp. 221-642.

[22] *Journals of the General Assembly,* pp. 147, 153-154. Shadrach Bond, Jr. and Thomas Todd were nominated to replace Shadrach Bond, Sr.; George

This was not propitious for the Governor since he continued to oppose the separation of the Illinois counties.

Following the session the antislavery people held a large mass meeting in Clark County on October 10, 1807, to take action against the pro-slavery resolutions of the past two sessions. A memorial, probably the work of James Beggs, was prepared and sent to Congress. Its wording is significant in that it declared for the first time the doctrine of squatter sovereignty—that Congress should withhold any legislation on the slavery question until the inhabitants of Indiana should have the right to adopt such a constitution as would "comport with the wishes of the majority of the citizens."[23]

One petition opposing slavery had already been sent to Congress from Dearborn County in 1805, but a second one was prepared in 1807 expressing the disapprobation of the residents with the action of the legislature and asking Congress to allow their county to be annexed to Ohio, a free state.[24] The Senate committee to which the resolution of the legislature and the memorial from Clark County were referred, reported it inexpedient to suspend Article VI of the Ordinance; no action was taken on the Dearborn County petition.[25]

The divergence between the Governor and the legislature widened during the second session of the Second Assembly in 1808. The opponents of Harrison were in control of the House and only three members of the Council attended, one of whom was unfriendly to the Governor. The most important action of the session was the election of Jesse B.

Fisher and James Finney to replace Pierre Menard. The President chose Bond and Fisher as legislative councilors. The new representatives elected were John Messinger and Rice Jones, son of John Rice Jones.

[23] Dunn (ed.), *Slavery Petitions and Papers,* pp. 518-520; Dunn, *Indiana,* pp. 358-359.

[24] *Annals of Congress,* 10 Congress, 1 session, col. 1331; Dunn, *Indiana,* p. 360. Apparently no copy of the petition has been preserved.

[25] *Annals of Congress,* 10 Congress, 1 session, cols. 23-27, 816, 920; Dunn, *Indiana,* pp. 362-363. The House took no action on the resolution and petitions.

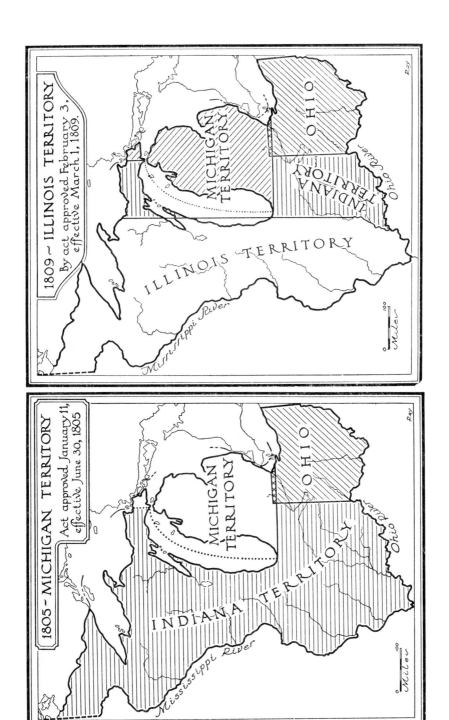

1809 ~ ILLINOIS TERRITORY
By act approved February 3, effective March 1, 1809.

OHIO

MICHIGAN TERRITORY

INDIANA TERRITORY

ILLINOIS TERRITORY

Mississippi River

Ohio River

0 100
Miles

1805 ~ MICHIGAN TERRITORY
Act approved January 11, effective June 30, 1805.

OHIO

MICHIGAN TERRITORY

INDIANA TERRITORY

Mississippi River

Ohio River

0 100
Miles

Thomas of Dearborn County as delegate to Congress after he had agreed to work for the division of the territory.[26] A second important development was the report delivered in the House by General Washington Johnston on the subject of slavery, in which he declared that the practice of bringing slaves into the territory and of holding them in slavery until they agreed to a contract of indenture was a violation of the Ordinance of 1787 and that the admission of slavery would be a "retrograde step into barbarism." The report was accompanied by a bill to repeal the 1805 indenture act which the House immediately passed. However, when the bill came up five days later in the Legislative Council it failed to pass second reading.[27]

The House also went against the wishes of the Governor in declaring Samuel Gwathmey, one of the Governor's original appointees to the Council, ineligible to the office because he had accepted an appointment by President Jefferson as register of the land office at Jeffersonville. The House also petitioned Congress to take from the Governor the power to veto acts of the legislature and to prorogue and dissolve its sessions.[28] However, when it came to naming the new county formed at this session out of Knox and Clark counties it was called Harrison in honor of the Governor.

26 Dunn, *Indiana,* pp. 367-369, 376-377; *Journals of the General Assembly,* pp. 248-249n.

27 *Journals of the General Assembly,* pp. 232-238, 301; Dunn, *Indiana,* pp. 370-376. The report given by Johnston may have been the work of John Badollet. See Thornbrough (ed.), *The Correspondence of John Badollet and Albert Gallatin,* pp. 104-105n. Dunn described the report as one of the ablest, if not the ablest, of state papers ever produced in Indiana.

28 *Journals of the General Assembly,* pp. 190, 191, 214-215. A resolution was introduced in the United States House of Representatives on November 15, 1808, by the delegate from Mississippi Territory to appoint a committee to inquire into the expediency of repealing that part of the Ordinance of 1787 which authorized the territorial governors to prorogue and dissolve the territorial assemblies and a bill was subsequently introduced and debated before being postponed. The same delegate brought the question up again at the next session but no action was taken. *Annals of Congress,* 10 Congress, 2 session, cols. 487, 492-494, 501-510; 11 Congress, 1 session, cols. 218-219.

§

The petitions of the residents in the western part of the territory for separation from Indiana Territory were finally granted by Congress by an act of February 3, 1809. The eastern boundary of the new Illinois Territory was to be the Wabash River from its mouth to Vincennes and thence from a line drawn due north to the boundary of the United States.[29] In answer to other petitions and resolutions, the Congress in 1808 extended the right to vote to owners of town lots valued at one hundred dollars and to landowners who had made the initial payment on fifty acres of land. A year later the Congress provided for the future election by the people of the delegate to Congress and the members of the Legislative Council; also the Assembly was given the authority to apportion the members of the lower house.[30]

These measures were certain to change the political situation significantly. With the separation of the Illinois counties, the eastern portion of the territory, populated largely by settlers from eastern states and by those from the southern states who had emigrated because of their dislike of slavery, had an increased representation.

Harrison's third term as governor was due to expire January 10, 1810. If he wrote to friends in Washington asking them to work in behalf of his reappointment, the correspondence has not been found. However, he was accused of soliciting the aid of friends in the territory as he traveled across country to the Fort Wayne treaty ground and of influencing members of the legislature by taking care of their lodging during the 1809 session. Recommendations for reappointment were sent to the President and the Senate by the Knox County militia, by residents of Harrison County, and

29 Pence and Armstrong, *Indiana Boundaries,* pp. 8-9, 144-145. The act is published in Ewbank (ed.), *Laws of Indiana Territory, 1809-1816,* pp. 102-103; in Kettleborough, *Constitution Making in Indiana,* I, 54-56; and in *Indiana's Road to Statehood,* pp. 48-50. See map, p. 353.

30 Kettleborough, *Constitution Making in Indiana,* I, 48, 56-57.

by the legislature. Clark County residents sent an adverse petition as did a group from Harrison County.[31]

Before word was received of the division of the territory an election had been held on April 3, 1809, for members of the House of Representatives; since only four of those elected were from the Indiana counties, a reapportionment was necessary and another election was called for May 22 to choose four additional representatives. The territory was also apportioned for the election of the five councilors on the same date. The new county of Harrison which had been formed out of Knox and Clark counties by an act of October 11, 1808, effective December 1, was given one representative, Knox County three, Clark and Dearborn each two; for the Legislative Council, Harrison, Clark, and Dearborn counties were each to elect one, and Knox County two.[32]

The editor of the Vincennes *Western Sun* had written prior to the election of April 3 that there had never been an election in Knox County in which "more anxiety or stir had been made," and now with another contest scheduled for the selection of a third representative, two councilors, plus a delegate to Congress, political fever reached a high pitch. John Johnson and General Washington Johnston had led the ballot on April 3 over three other candidates—John Hadden, Thomas Randolph, and Daniel Sullivan. Slavery was a prominent issue in the earlier campaign as well as in the second one in which John Hadden, "an admirer of the Harrison regime,"

[31] Thornbrough (ed.), *The Correspondence of John Badollet and Albert Gallatin,* pp. 131-132, 133-137; Carter (ed.), *Territorial Papers,* VII, 678, 703-704, 705-707, 710-711; Esarey (ed.), *Harrison's Messages and Letters,* I, 385-387, 391-392; Ewbank (ed.), *Laws of Indiana Territory, 1809-1816,* pp. 770-771. Harrison was reappointed to the office by President Madison on December 19, 1809, and confirmed by the Senate the following day. U. S. Senate, *Executive Journal,* II, 130-131; *Journals of the General Assembly,* pp. 326, 330, 338-339n, 341-342.

[32] Territorial *Executive Journal,* pp. 154-155; *Journals of the General Assembly,* pp. 11, 315n; Kettleborough, *Constitution Making in Indiana,* I, 57.

easily won the seat in the lower house over his opponent William Bruce, while William Prince and Luke Decker, also friendly to the Governor, won the Council seats. Prince's connection with Aaron Burr was called into question but apparently was explained to the satisfaction of the voters.[33]

The campaign for delegate to Congress created the most excitement and set a precedent for future political campaigns in the Hoosier state. Thomas Randolph, who only recently had arrived in the territory from Virginia and been appointed attorney general, was Governor Harrison's choice. Thirty-eight years of age, a cousin of Thomas Jefferson, with a background of experience in the Virginia Assembly, he was apparently well qualified for the position. In spite of his qualifications, to the growing number of residents who opposed the Governor he was anathema—aristocratic, proslavery, and above all a friend of the Governor.

Randolph's principal opponent was Jonathan Jennings who was also fairly new in the territory. Twenty-five years of age, a native (probably) of New Jersey who had grown up in western Pennsylvania, he had studied law, and been admitted to practice at Vincennes in 1807. During his brief stay in that town he had displayed an eagerness to get ahead in the world, both politically and financially, and on a number of occasions had clashed with Harrison and his friends. In 1808 he changed his residence to Clark County, believing that it offered more professional and political opportunities for a young lawyer. When word reached the territory that a delegate to Congress was to be elected, Jennings offered himself as the candidate of the anti-Harrison and antislavery factions.

John Johnson, the third candidate, had already been elected to a seat in the House of Representatives from Knox County. He claimed a residence in the territory of twenty-three years

[33] Vincennes *Western Sun,* March 25, April 15, May 27, 1809.

but admitted that his law practice and his farm had kept him from getting acquainted outside his home county. Politically, he was proslavery but anti-Harrison.[34]

In announcing his candidacy, Randolph had indicated that although personally in favor of slavery, he would submit to the will of the people and if elected would not make any attempt to introduce slavery into the territory unless so instructed by a decided majority of his constituents. In fact, he thought the slavery issue should be put to sleep. With the indenture law still in force in the territory, this last statement in particular aroused the ire of the antislavery group and during the next few weeks the editor of the *Western Sun* was flooded with anonymous communications both assailing and defending Randolph.[35]

Jennings toured the central and eastern counties but apparently left it up to his friends to campaign for him in Knox. Among Randolph's friends outside of Knox County who were supporting his candidacy were Waller Taylor in Jeffersonville, John George Pfrimmer, John Boone, and John Smith in Corydon, James Dill and Samuel C. Vance in Lawrenceburg. Randolph himself apparently did some campaigning in the eastern part of the territory for the story is told of one occasion when he came upon a log rolling on the farm of David Reese and waited in the house for the men to finish their work before talking "politics," while Jennings on a similar occasion pitched in and helped roll logs before talking to the men. When the votes of the four counties were tallied, Jennings had 428, Randolph 402, and Johnson 81. Randolph announced his intention to contest the election, alleging irregularities in the voting in Dearborn County which had given Jennings a majority.[36]

[34] See sketch of Randolph in Woollen, *Biographical and Historical Sketches of Early Indiana*, pp. 391-399; of Jennings in *Indiana Magazine of History*, XXVIII (1932), 223-230; and of Johnson in *Journals of the General Assembly*, pp. 985-987.

[35] See the issues of April 15 through May 27, 1809.

[36] Vincennes *Western Sun*, July 1, 1809; Carter (ed.), *Territorial Papers,*

Two weeks after the election and while the results were still in doubt, Randolph demanded that the editor of the Vincennes paper reveal the name of the author or authors of the communications that had appeared against him. When told it was Elias McNamee, Randolph sent a challenge to meet him "on the other side of the Wabash" for a duel. The latter did not accept (presumably because of his Quaker background) and instead swore out a warrant against Randolph, alleging that he was planning to kill him. Randolph then countered by calling McNamee a "treacherous rascal, who ought to be branded with infamy." "I sincerely lament, instead of treating him with the respect due to a gentleman, I had not striped him with a cow hide, the merited reward of a cowardly slanderer." He promised to continue the fight on paper but the editor apparently decided his readers had had enough.[37]

Both Jennings and Randolph made the trip to Washington for the opening of Congress on November 27; Jennings produced his certification of election signed by John Gibson and was seated pending an examination of his credentials by the House committee on elections to which Randolph's petition was also referred. The committee reported back to the House that in their opinion the entire election was illegal and Jennings' seat should be vacated; however, after two days of debate on the matter, the House refused to accept the report and Jennings was permitted to retain his seat.[38]

Meanwhile, the members of the General Assembly elected on May 22 had met on October 16, but because the Governor's reapportionment did not give the territory the required number of representatives, the House dissolved itself after five days in the belief that it could not be legally organized.

VII, 651-655, 680, 694-695, 696-702. The election returns as certified by Secretary John Gibson were: Jennings, 421; Randolph, 382. *Ibid.,* VII, 655.

37 Vincennes *Western Sun,* June 10 and 24, July 1, 1809.

38 *Annals of Congress,* 11 Congress, 2 session, cols. 682, 683, 844-848, 1172-1173, 1199. In the election for delegate in 1811, Jennings again defeated Randolph. Dunn, *Indiana,* pp. 406-410.

An appeal was sent to Congress to straighten out the difficulty and in reply the Governor was authorized to make a
new apportionment which was done and a new election held
on April 2, 1810.[39] When the new Assembly convened in
November of that year a significant change was noted: the
initiative in governmental affairs had now passed from the
Governor to the legislature, and the majority of that body
was opposed to the Governor's program. The 1805 act concerning the indenture of Negroes and mulattoes was repealed
as well as the first section of the 1803 law of the Governor
and Judges requiring servants of color brought into the territory to fulfill their contracts.[40] As a further blow to the
Harrison forces, plans were made for the removal of the
capital from Vincennes to a more central location.[41] The
formation of three additional counties at this session—Jefferson, Franklin, and Wayne—was evidence of the growing
population in the Whitewater Valley and in the area between
Clark and Dearborn counties.[42]

Not satisfied with the democratization of the government
which had already been achieved, the 1810 legislature petitioned Congress to remove completely the land ownership
qualification for voting and make the office of sheriff elective
rather than appointive.[43] Congress responded by extending
the franchise to all free adult males who paid a county or
territorial tax and had resided in the territory for a year;

[39] *Journals of the General Assembly,* pp. 315-316n, 327-329, 332-338, 340-
344, 345; Territorial *Executive Journal,* pp. 158-159. The federal act of
February 27, 1809, making the offices of delegate and legislative councilor
elective, granted to the General Assembly the power of apportioning the representatives and stipulated there should not be less than nine nor more than
twelve. Since there was no legislature in existence at that time, the Governor
had made the apportionment. Under the supplemental act of December 15, 1809,
the Governor was given the power to make a temporary apportionment in
order that a legislature might be formed. U. S. *Statutes at Large,* II, 525-526,
554-555.

[40] Ewbank (ed.), *Laws of Indiana Territory, 1809-1816,* pp. 138-139.

[41] *Ibid.,* pp. 153-157.

[42] *Ibid.,* pp. 104-105, 108-110, 190.

[43] *Ibid.,* pp. 772, 780-783.

they also made ineligible to membership in the Assembly any officer under appointment by the Governor except justices of the peace and officers of the militia.[44]

The next session of the Assembly was called to meet the first Monday of October in 1811 but was twice postponed because of the imminence of an Indian war and finally convened on November 11.[45]

§ §

By the time the decennial census of 1810 was taken Indiana Territory had lost the Illinois portion of Knox County and gained the area that became Dearborn County, which was added in 1803 when Ohio became a state. Compared with Knox County's 2,517 inhabitants in 1800, there were now four counties with a population of 24,520. Dearborn had 7,310, Clark, 5,670, Harrison, 3,595, and Knox, 7,945. The act creating Jefferson, Franklin, and Wayne counties did not become effective until January 1, 1811; the residents of these counties were counted in Dearborn and Clark. Almost half of the slaves, 108, were in Palmyra Township, Knox County, which lay between the two forks of White River and north of the base line. The total number of slaves had increased from 135 to 237.[46]

Broken down by age and sex, the 1810 census reveals that the male population as a whole outnumbered the female; approximately four fifths of the men were under the age of forty-five while the percentage of women in that bracket was slightly larger; the number of women over forty-five was considerably less than the number of men, indicating that the hardships of pioneer life had taken their toll. Children under ten represented the largest group. Without any census data to indicate the place of birth of these early residents,

[44] Kettleborough, *Constitution Making in Indiana*, I, 58-59; *Indiana's Road to Statehood*, pp. 55-56.

[45] *Journals of the General Assembly*, p. 367n.

[46] Territorial *Executive Journal*, pp. 83-85.

one must depend on less accurate data for their origin. It has generally been conceded that most came from the Upper South—Kentucky, Tennessee, North Carolina, and Virginia, with lesser representation from the Middle Atlantic states, New England, and Europe.

Dearborn County now ranked next to Knox in population. Freed from Indian claims by the Treaty of Greenville in 1795, its settlement began almost immediately by squatters who located along the northern bank of the Ohio. Secretary Sargent estimated in 1797 that there were a thousand of these intruders west of the Miami River. Farther north in the Whitewater Valley, settlement was in part an expansion from the Miami Valley.[47]

Indiana Territory was only a few years old when the migration of Quakers to the upper Whitewater began. Dissatisfied with the spread of slavery into the Piedmont area of North Carolina, large numbers migrated north into Ohio and thence into eastern Indiana. They were a serious and sturdy people with democratic principles and a prejudice against slavery; their migration to the upper Whitewater was an important factor in the political development of that area.[48]

Farther north, the military post of Fort Wayne was garrisoned by United States soldiers until 1819; surrounding the fort were the homes of the traders who carried on a flourishing trade with the Indians.

West of the Whitewater Valley, Clark's Grant and Vincennes constituted the main areas of settlement in Indiana

[47] Pence and Armstrong, *Indiana Boundaries*, pp. 4-5, 22, 308; Winthrop Sargent to Secretary of State, January 20, 1797, in Carter (ed.), *Territorial Papers*, II, 587; Ezra Ferris, *The Early Settlement of the Miami Country* (Indiana Historical Society *Publications*, I, No. 9, Indianapolis, 1897); Chelsea L. Lawlis, "Settlement of the Whitewater Valley," *Indiana Magazine of History*, XLIII (1947), 23-40. Because of its original triangular shape, the area which became Dearborn County was known as "the Gore."

[48] Bernhard Knollenberg, *Pioneer Sketches of the Upper Whitewater Valley, Quaker Stronghold of the West* (Indiana Historical Society *Publications*, XV, No. 1, Indianapolis, 1945).

Territory, and these were soon joined by trails through the forests and by the expansion of settlement along the Ohio and along the streams and traces which led into the interior. The most important of the early traces was the Buffalo Trace which ran from Clarksville to Vincennes, where it connected with the trace to the Illinois country. It was used first by soldiers, then by settlers and travelers; its various names epitomize its history for it was also called the Old Indian Trail, the Governor's Road, and the Kentucky Road. The Rome, Yellow Banks, and Red Banks traces extended from points farther down the Ohio River north into the interior.[49]

The need for roads was so keenly felt that the legislative Assembly of 1807 enacted a comprehensive law for locating, opening, and keeping in repair roads in the various counties. All the men between the ages of twenty-one and fifty who had resided in a township for thirty days were required to work as much as twelve days a year on the roads if it should be deemed necessary. The bridging of the smaller streams was also to be performed by the local citizens, while the longer spans were to be erected and paid for by the county. Federal funds were used in attempting to cut a route from Vincennes east to Cincinnati.[50]

[49] Wilson, *Early Indiana Trails and Surveys*, pp. 349, 352-355, 359-360, 364-380, 384-387, 392-395; George R. Wilson and Gayle Thornbrough, *The Buffalo Trace* (Indiana Historical Society *Publications*, XV, No. 2, Indianapolis, 1946).

Jonathan Anthony, operator of the ferry across the Ohio River at Red Banks (now Henderson, Ky.), made a proposal to the Knox County Court of Common Pleas in 1806, to which they agreed, that he would open a good wagon road, at least twelve feet wide, from the Ohio to where Mr. Soverns lives on the Patoka River and keep it in good repair for three years on condition that the court would allow him to charge fifty instead of twenty-five cents for each man and horse ferried across the Ohio. Transcript of Court Minutes, 1801-1806, pp. 245-246. The Yellow Banks Trace started at Rockport, ran north to the forks of White River, and on to Vincennes; the Rome Trace started at the town of that name in the present Perry County and joined the Yellow Banks Trace near the present Selvin in Warrick County.

[50] Philbrick (ed.), *Laws of Indiana Territory, 1801-1809*, pp. 427-439; Carter (ed.), *Territorial Papers*, VII, 614-617, 623-624; John Badollet, register

Southeastern Indiana, between Clark's Grant and the Gore, was settled slowly but in 1806 settlers coming down the Ohio or crossing the Ohio from Kentucky settled the area around Madison. Four years earlier a colony of Swiss immigrants entered 2,500 acres of land in the present Switzerland County and shortly began the cultivation of grapes.[51] On down the Ohio, settlements were started by 1810 in all the area bordering the river as well as farther north.

When the land sales were opened at Cincinnati in 1801, Vincennes in 1807, and Jeffersonville in 1808, purchasers made the first payment on the land they had chosen, hoping that industry and good fortune would enable them to meet the succeeding payments. Though there were some large landowners and land speculation was rife, in the main the immigrants bought the minimum amount permissible, 160 acres.[52]

For means of travel the early settlers had the canoe, the pirogue, the Kentucky boat (or ark as it was called), the keelboat, the flatboat, and after 1812 the steamboat; and on land the sled, cart, or wagon used by the farmer, the stagecoach, the horse and saddle, and occasionally a carriage or chaise. The houses of the early inhabitants were in nearly all cases of wood—mostly log cabins; a few were of brick. Greased paper served for window panes instead of glass. Doors were made heavy, with the latch string so it could be pulled inside in case of danger from the Indians; some-

of the Vincennes Land Office, who let the contracts for surveying and opening federal roads, had considerable difficulty with the contractors. Thornbrough (ed.), *Correspondence of John Badollet and Albert Gallatin,* pp. 74-75n, 100-102, 103-104n.

[51] "The Pioneers of Jefferson County," *Indiana Magazine of History,* XII (1916), 214-231; Perret Dufour, *Swiss Settlement of Switzerland County, Indiana (Indiana Historical Collections,* XIII, Indianapolis, 1925), Introduction, pp. xiii-xviii.

[52] Margaret R. Waters has compiled one volume of the land entries that were made at the Vincennes Land Office during the years it was in existence; there is also a similar volume for the Indiana entries in the Cincinnati Office. Mimeograph copies are in the Genealogy Division, Indiana State Library.

times there were holes through which the occupants could fire. The furniture was homemade and often crude.[53]

Clothing was mostly made in the home. Here the wool or flax was prepared and spun and woven, then cut into garments and sewed by hand. Hides were tanned and shoes made by the head of the household or by an itinerant cobbler. The chief industries were those which processed products of the field and forest into marketable goods. The census of arts and manufactures for 1810 listed in Indiana Territory 1,350 spinning wheels, 1,256 looms, one cotton factory, 33 gristmills, 14 sawmills, 18 tanneries, and 28 distilleries. The value of manufactured goods was as follows: cloth, $159,052; nails, $4,000; tanned leather, $9,300; distillery products, $16,230; gunpowder, $1,800; wine, $6,000; maple sugar produced, 50,000 pounds.[54]

An article signed "P" which appeared in the Vincennes *Western Sun* of March 25, 1809, noted the apathy which pervaded the country, and advocated the growing of cotton and hemp for domestic manufacture and export as well as the more common tobacco, wheat, and corn. Pointing to the income produced from the sale of horses in Kentucky, "P" thought something similar could be done north of the Ohio. The following year the Society for the Encouragement of Agriculture and the Useful Arts was organized and Governor Harrison was chosen as its first president. Premiums were offered by the Society in 1811 for (1) the finest and best piece of cotton cloth used for sheeting; (2) the best

[53] Rolla M. Hogue, "Life in Indiana, 1800-1820," *Indiana Magazine of History*, IX (1913), 87-90.

[54] *A Statement of the Arts and Manufactures of the United States of America, for the Year 1810* (Philadelphia, 1814), pp. 162-163. The statistics are also given in *American State Papers. Finance* (5 volumes, Washington, D. C., 1834), II, 810. The census indicated that a considerable quantity of cotton goods was being manufactured in Indiana in 1810. The cotton factory may have been in Jeffersonville since it was reported by George F. Pope, one of the assistant marshals. Pope was a resident of Harrison County but his district may have included Clark County.

piece of woolen cloth for men's apparel; (3) same for linen
shirting; (4) the largest quantity of hemp seed which may
be raised.[55]

§   §   §

In addition to the Catholic church at Vincennes, which
dated back to 1749, some progress had been made by 1810
in establishing Protestant congregations in Indiana; but with
the population being widely scattered probably most of the
settlers were without organized religious services. Those
who were affiliated with a church were likely to be either
Baptists and Methodists for both of these denominations
had become well established in the South a generation before
Indiana was opened to settlement. Also, they both provided
lay preachers in contrast to the Presbyterians who usually
had to depend on eastern congregations to send out pastors.
Lay preachers crossed the Ohio into Clark County shortly
before the turn of the century and established congregations,
the Baptists in 1798 and the Methodists a year later. The
former had the distinction of building the first Protestant
structure for religious worship in 1803, the Silver Creek
Church.[56]

Baptist and Methodist preachers from Ohio came into
Dearborn County early in the 1800s and established congregations; in the Whitewater Valley, the Little Cedar Baptist congregation was organized in 1806 and six years later
erected a brick church three miles southeast of Brookville
at a time when most settlers on the frontier were retreating
because of the Indian raids. It has been restored in recent
years and is believed to be the oldest Protestant church in
Indiana still standing on its original site.[57] In Wayne County

55 Vincennes *Western Sun,* May 26, 1810. The prizes were to be awarded
in April, 1811; unfortunately there are no issues of the paper for that month.

56 It was first known as the Fourteen Mile or Owens Creek Church. The
first record book, beginning in 1798, is among the manuscripts in the Indiana
Division, Indiana State Library.

57 The early records of this church are also in the Indiana State Library.

the Society of Friends established their first monthy meeting in 1809 as an offshoot of one in Ohio.[58]

Farther west, the Baptists started congregations in Jefferson County in 1806-1807 and built a meeting house near North Madison in the latter year. They were in Harrison County about the same time and erected Old Goshen Church, south of Corydon, by 1813.[59]

Only in Knox County did the Presbyterians take the lead. Missionaries from the Transylvania (Ky.) Presbytery visited the area in 1805 and the following year the Indiana Church was organized by Samuel B. Robertson of Kentucky. The Reverend Samuel T. Scott became pastor of the church in 1808, and the first resident Presbyterian minister in Indiana Territory. That same year the Reverend Peter Cartwright of the Methodist Church answered a call to preach in the Busseron settlement in the northern part of the county and before he left instituted a Methodist society in that area. The following year the Vincennes Circuit was organized with William Winans in charge. The first Baptist church in the county was the one on Maria Creek, organized in 1809, of which Isaac McCoy served as pastor prior to beginning his missionary work among the Indians.[60]

The opportunities for attending school in Indiana Territory before 1810 were also very limited. Congress had appropriated in 1806 a township of land for the use and sup-

[58] The minutes of this Meeting, including births, deaths, and marriages, have been published by the Indiana Historical Society as *Part One. Abstracts of the Records of the Society of Friends in Indiana,* edited by Willard Heiss (Indiana Historical Society, 1962).

[59] "The History of Madison," *Indiana Magazine of History,* XVI (1920), 325; Frederick P. Griffin, "Old Goshen Church and Cemetery," *Indiana Magazine of History,* XXXIX (1943), 315-319.

[60] J. H. Barnard, "Sketch of Early Presbyterian Church in Indiana," *Indiana Magazine of History,* XXI, 300-302; mimeographed copy of the Minutes of the Indiana Church, 1812-1873, in Indiana Division, Indiana State Library; Fernandez C. Holliday, *Indiana Methodism* . . . (Cincinnati, 1873), pp. 24-26, 28-29; Ben. F. Keith, *History of Maria Creek Church* . . . (Vincennes, 1889), pp. 5-23.

port of a university in the Vincennes land district, and that same year the territorial Assembly incorporated and appointed trustees for the school. The preamble of the incorporation act reveals the need and desire of the citizens for educational institutions:[61]

Whereas the independence, happiness and energy of every republic depends . . . upon the wisdom, virtue, talents and energy, of its citizens and rulers. And whereas, science, literature, and the liberal arts, contribute in an eminent degree to improve those qualities and acquirements. And whereas, learning hath ever been found the ablest advocate of genuine liberty, the best supporter of rational religion, and the source of the only solid and imperishable glory, which nations can acquire. . . . And considering that in a commonwealth, where the humblest citizen may be elected to the highest public office, and where the Heaven born prerogative of the right to elect, and to reject, is retained, and secured to the citizens, the knowledge which is requisite for a magistrate and elector, should be widely diffused, Be it therefore enacted. . . .

The first efforts of the trustees were directed toward a preparatory or "grammar" school but even here they were unsuccessful until 1811 when Samuel Scott, the Presbyterian minister, agreed to open such a school.

The land ordinance of 1785 had provided that section 16 in each township should not be sold but reserved to the states for the maintenance of public schools; this was implemented by the territorial Assembly in 1808 when provision was made for leasing the sections. Though the revenue from this source was to be of help later in establishing township schools, it was of little or no help during the territorial period. Other than the Vincennes school, those that were in existence were of a private nature, in which some schoolmaster gathered about him the children of the neighborhood, or were connected with a church. The Society of Friends accepted the responsibility of starting schools as a duty; this is borne out in Wayne County where the Whitewater Monthly Meeting

---

61 Philbrick (ed.), *Laws of Indiana Territory, 1801-1809*, pp. 178-184. For the early history of the University, see the article by Howard Burnett in *Indiana Magazine of History*, XXIX (1933), 114-121.

had a school by 1811 and perhaps even earlier. Friends who settled in Washington and Orange counties were also leaders in establishing schools in those counties.

Plans for the first circulating library in the territory were made at a meeting of the citizens of Vincennes on July 20, 1806, with Governor Harrison presiding. A company was formed and a constitution adopted. Within three years the library had obtained 245 volumes, the selections being largely of an informative and educational nature rather than entertaining.[62]

Although the admission of slavery appears to have been the leading issue in the first decade of territorial history, it was not the only one; separation of the northern and western portions of the territory, dissatisfaction with the lack of self-government, and criticism of Governor Harrison were subjects of numerous petitions to Congress. The slavery issue was practically dead after 1810; the separation of Michigan and Illinois was resolved in 1805 and 1809 and continuous progress was being made in the democratization of the government. Criticism of the Governor would continue, though as he became stripped of much of his power this was no longer as important an issue as in the early years of the decade.

[62] The library was incorporated by an act of the territorial Assembly. Philbrick (ed.), *Laws of Indiana Territory, 1801-1809*, pp. 202-203. The Minutes of the Library Company are printed in the *Indiana Magazine of History,* Vols. LXI-LXIII (1965-1967).

CHAPTER XI

CONFLICT WITH THE INDIANS

During the same period in which great strides were made in the achievement of a more democratic government, the relations with the Indians had been worsening. The "warm attachment" to the United States professed by one of the Indian spokesmen at the conclusion of the 1805 council at Vincennes was soon disavowed through the influence of two new Indian leaders whose purpose was to unite all the northwest tribes into a grand confederacy and halt any further advance of the whites. Tecumseh and his brother the Prophet, Shawnees, were presumably born in the 1760s at the Shawnee town of Piqua, Ohio. Their enmity toward the United States dated back to 1774 when their father was killed in the battle of Point Pleasant, and continued as they became old enough to take up arms against the Americans. The Treaty of Greenville, which gave most of the Ohio country to the whites and threw the Shawnee and other Ohio tribes westward into what became Indiana without any land of their own, added to their resentment and caused them to advance the theory that the land belonged to all the tribes in common. Yet, Governor Harrison had not invited these tribes to the treaty negotiations of 1804 and 1805 nor did they receive a share of the goods and money distributed at that time.

While Tecumseh was the statesman of the two, the Prophet assumed the role of moral leader that his name indicated. Claiming that he received his teachings from the Great Spirit, he advocated complete separation from the whites and all their ways and customs and condemned drinking of spirituous liquor, witchcraft, lying, and stealing. His presence among the Delawares on White River in 1806 made them "extremely restless and uneasy" and led to the burning of one of their chiefs and a Christian Indian, both of whom were suspected of witchcraft. Upon learning of these murders Governor Harrison sent a message to the Delawares by William Prince reprimanding them for their actions and urging them to drive the Prophet from their midst. To the Kickapoo, who had been committing depredations on settlers in the Illinois country, he also sent a message warning them not to "follow the advice of those who would lead . . . [them] to destruction."[1]

The following year, after an attack by a band of Delawares on a family traveling from Clarksville to Vincennes, the southern part of the territory was divided into three sections and the militia of each section was organized for ranger and scouting service. At the same time settlers in isolated areas built blockhouses for the protection of their families in case of attack.[2]

During the summer of 1807 the Prophet invited all the Indians of the Northwest to assemble at Greenville in Ohio, and William Wells, Indian agent at Fort Wayne, wrote that nothing could be done to prevent them from doing so. "The Indians are religiously *mad* and beleaves all the Shawnese says to them," he wrote the Secretary of War; "and it is much feared that his ententions are not friendly to peace." Wells expected two thousand to heed the Prophet's call.[3]

Governor Harrison wrote to the Shawnee in August and repeated the warnings he had made earlier to the Delawares and again asked that the imposter be driven away; he "speaks not the words of the Great Spirit but those of the devil, and

[1] Esarey (ed.), *Harrison's Messages and Letters,* I, 191-194, 195; Gipson (ed.), *Moravian Indian Mission on White River,* pp. 415-416, 421-422n. The most recent biography of Tecumseh was published in 1956, entitled *Tecumseh. Vision of Glory,* by Glenn Tucker.

[2] The correspondence between John Gibson and William Hargrove, commander of the western section, is printed in William M. Cockrum, *Pioneer History of Indiana . . .* (Oakland City, Ind., 1907), pp. 202-229, and reprinted in Esarey (ed.), *Harrison's Messages and Letters,* Vol. I.

[3] Wells to Secretary of War, July 14, 1807, in Carter (ed.), *Territorial Papers,* VII, 465.

of the British agents." The Prophet denied that he was an instrument of the British and said the Indians were gathering of their own accord, "to listen and hear the words of the Great Spirit."

In September the governor of Ohio became alarmed and sent two representatives to Greenville to learn the object of the large body of tribesmen who had assembled; they too were told it was purely for religious purposes, that the Prophet might convince them of the error of their ways and persuade them to change their lives and serve the Great Spirit. President Jefferson had learned of the Indian council and sent a message on September 27 to the Indians in the vicinity of Detroit, which was delivered by William Hull, governor of Michigan Territory, warning them of the consequences if they failed to keep the peace.[4]

Most American officials in the West were confident that the British were responsible for the ever-increasing anti-American feeling. At this particular time the relations between Great Britain and America were close to the breaking point because of the attack in June on the American ship "Chesapeake" by the British ship "Leopard" and the impressment of three American seamen from the former. This incident was part of the larger struggle going on between France and Great Britain for control of international trade. Public opinion in America was greatly aroused but British offers to make reparations enabled President Jefferson to avert war at this time. The belief that there was a connection between the "Chesapeake" incident and the renewal of Indian disturbances in the West was expressed by the President in his message to Congress in October, 1807. The correspondence of the American officials at Detroit and British officials at Amherstburg reveals that in the event of a

---

4 Esarey (ed.), *Harrison's Messages and Letters,* I, 249-251; E. O. Randall, "Tecumseh, the Shawnee Chief," *Ohio Archaeological and Historical Quarterly,* XV (1906), 464-465; *American State Papers. Indian Affairs,* I, 745-746.

war between the two countries, the British wished to insure Indian support.[5]

In the spring of 1808 the Prophet moved his headquarters to a site on the upper Wabash, above Ouiatanon, and invited the Sauk, Fox, Iowa, and Winnebago tribes to meet him there for the purpose, according to Wells, of putting the "tomahack in their hands."[6] However, the Shawnee leader declared his peaceful intentions to Governor Harrison and asked for corn to feed the women and children until a crop could be harvested. The Governor was willing to admit there was some merit in his teaching and promised not to interfere as long as his intentions remained "peaceful."[7]

After meeting him in person at Vincennes in August, the Governor wrote, "He is rather possessed of considerable talents and the art and address with which he manages the Indians is really astonishing." The Governor hoped that this influence could be used advantageously for the United States.[8] As for his followers, they appeared to Harrison as a "miserable set of Starved wretches." He gave them a few provisions and got rid of them as soon as possible.[9]

Before leaving office President Jefferson spoke to delegations of Miami and Delawares who were visiting Washington, reminding them of the beneficent attitude of the United States toward them as compared with the British policy which "has worn you down." Though he still spoke of the Indians turning to agriculture and the domestic arts, in reality little

[5] *Dictionary of American History,* I, 354-355; Vincennes *Western Sun,* September 12, 1807; Horsman, *Matthew Elliott,* pp. 157-158; Burt, *The United States, Great Britain, and British North America,* pp. 246-254; *Michigan Historical Collections,* XV, 44-45, 47-48, 49-50, 53; XL, 253-254; Carter (ed.), *Territorial Papers,* X, 101-102n, 134-136.

[6] Wells to Secretary of War, March 6, 1808, in Carter (ed.), *Territorial Papers,* VII, 531-532.

[7] The Prophet to Harrison, June 24, 1808, and Harrison to The Prophet, no date, in Esarey (ed.), *Harrison's Messages and Letters,* I, 291-295.

[8] Harrison to Secretary of War, September 1, 1808, in *ibid.,* I, 302.

[9] Harrison to Secretary of War, February 14, 1809, in Carter (ed.), *Territorial Papers,* VII, 640-641.

had been accomplished along that line in the Indiana Territory. When he left office in March, 1809, Jefferson could look back on the tremendous gains made in freeing the land of Indian control and opening it up for settlement in the territories both north and south of the Ohio River, but his program of civilization for the Indians had been much less successful, especially with the northwest tribes.[10]

During the winter months of 1808-9, as in other years, the Indians were engaged in hunting and there was little evidence of hostility, but with the coming of spring rumors began reaching Harrison from all directions that the Prophet and his followers were planning an attack on the frontier settlements. The Governor believed the danger real enough to warrant organizing and equipping two companies of militia for protection of the frontiers, but after a few weeks he allowed the men to return to their homes to take care of their crops. Anyone who reads the Governor's correspondence during the summer of 1809 will realize the difficulty he was having in learning the truth about the Prophet's intentions. Although he had a French trader acting as a spy at Prophet's Town, he secured little information of value from him.

The Prophet again visited Vincennes in July, 1809, but even then Harrison could not be sure of his intentions, and wrote, "I must confess that my suspicions of his guilt have been rather strengthened than diminished in every interview I have had with him since his arrival." In one of his more optimistic letters, the Governor expressed a desire to proceed with the negotiations for an additional land purchase and permission was granted. The compensation for the land was not to exceed the rate heretofore given, and he was particularly instructed to treat with the chiefs of *all* the nations who have or think they have a right to the proposed land cession.[11] It

10 Esarey (ed.), *Harrison's Messages and Letters,* I, 322-323; Horsman, *Expansion and American Indian Policy,* pp. 156-157.

11 Harrison to Secretary of War, May 16 and July 5, 1809; Secretary of

is surprising that neither Harrison, the Secretary of War, nor President Madison seemed to realize the effect such a negotiation would have on the already strained relations between the Indians and whites or the opportunity it would give the Prophet to fan the flames of resentment against the latter.

To effect the new cession of land, Harrison left Vincennes on September 1, accompanied by Peter Jones and Joseph Barron, secretary and interpreter, a Frenchman as guide, a personal servant, and two Indians. They proceeded over the new road that had been laid out to North Bend, Ohio, and then north to Fort Wayne, where they arrived on the fifteenth. A few Delawares and their interpreter, John Conner, joined the party for the last part of the journey. John Johnston, who had replaced Wells as Indian agent and was in charge of the government store at that place, had been instructed to assemble the Eel River and the main branch of the Miami tribe and the Delawares and Potawatomi. As usual the Indians were slow in assembling. Barron was sent to persuade Jean B. Richardville (who was soon to replace Little Turtle as chief) to attend, but he pleaded illness as an excuse for absenting himself. Before calling a full council of all the tribes, Harrison visited each tribe individually at their separate camps. It was estimated that nearly fourteen hundred Indians finally gathered for the treaty negotiations.

The Potawatomi and Delawares indicated their willingness to cede additional land, but the Miami, who considered themselves as the sole owners of the proposed cession, refused. After three days of repeated conferences, they still refused; the following day a portion of the tribe gave in to Harrison's demands, but not the Mississinewa branch, who demanded to know why the Governor was dealing with other tribes when they were the sole owners of the land. Finally, after two

War to Harrison, July 15, 1809, in Esarey (ed.), *Harrison's Messages and Letters,* I, 346-347, 349-350, 356-357.

more days of pleading and haranguing, the Miami agreed to cede a strip twelve miles wide west of the Greenville Treaty line, and a strip thirty miles or more wide north of the Vincennes Tract. The Wea and Kickapoo would have to agree to the latter cession before that part of the treaty could become effective. To satisfy the Miami, the document was to be so worded that the Potawatomi and Delawares would be considered only as allies and not as owners of the land. The treaty was finally signed on September 30. Payment of annuities, delivery of promised goods, and the settlement of claims consumed the next two days. The Potawatomi were so dissatisfied with the portion they received, that Harrison had to advance them $500 of their next year's annuity.[12]

It had been a strenuous two weeks for Governor Harrison and he was no doubt glad when it was over. On reaching the Wea towns, Harrison invited that tribe to visit him at Vincennes the following week. Upon their arrival, the Governor explained the terms of the treaty made at Fort Wayne and how they would be benefited by locating higher up the Wabash with the other branches of their tribe. A treaty was signed and goods delivered to them on October 26 and 27. The Kickapoo likewise consented to the cession north of the Vincennes Tract and in addition agreed to give up another small tract west of the Wabash.[13] The total extent of the ceded tracts was first estimated at 2,600,000 acres but later it was found to be closer to 2,900,000 acres. John Johnston reported that the tracts contained some of the finest land in

[12] The text of the treaty and the proceedings leading up to it are printed in *ibid.*, I, 349-362, 362-378. Rations issued during the negotiations comprised 16,428 rations of beef, 21,973 of bread and flour, 506 quarts of salt, and 3,026 gills of whiskey, the last presumably issued at the close of the deliberations. Gayle Thornbrough (ed.), *Letter Book of the Indian Agency at Fort Wayne, 1809-1815* (Indiana Historical Society *Publications*, XXI, Indianapolis, 1961), pp. 66-69.

[13] Proceedings of treaty negotiations in Esarey (ed.), *Harrison's Messages and Letters*, I, 376-378.

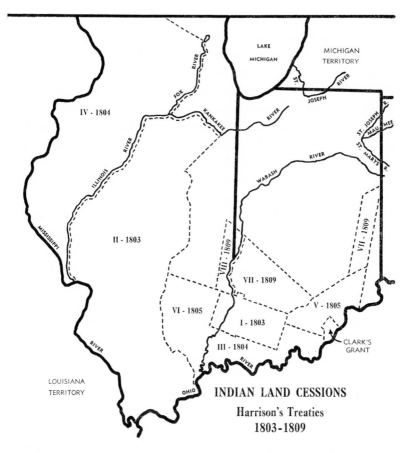

INDIAN LAND CESSIONS

Harrison's Treaties

1803-1809

I. June 7, 1803, at Fort Wayne, with the Delawares, Shawnee, Potawatomi, Miami, Eel Rivers, Wea, Kickapoo, Piankashaw, and Kaskaskia.

II. August 13, 1803, at Vincennes, with the Kaskaskia.

III. August 18 and 27, 1804, at Vincennes, with the Delawares and Piankashaw.

IV. November 3, 1804, at St. Louis, with the Sauk and Foxes.

V. August 21, 1805, at Grouseland, with the Delawares, Potawatomi, Miami, Eel Rivers, and Wea.

VI. December 30, 1805, at Vincennes, with the Piankashaw.

VII. September 30, 1809, at Fort Wayne, with the Delawares, Potawatomi, Miami, Eel Rivers, and Wea.

VIII. December 9, 1809, at Vincennes, with the Kickapoo.

the United States; Harrison believed they included two or three salt springs.[14]

As might have been expected, news of the Treaty of Fort Wayne increased the tension already existing between the Indians and the whites. The former could envision their land being whittled away by cession after cession until there would be none left east of the Mississippi. Those Indians who had gathered around the Prophet believed the government had already gone too far, and that the recent cessions must be invalidated and the land returned to the tribes. They were determined to halt any efforts to survey it. Though Harrison tended to place the blame for Indian hostility on the activities of British agents, the basic cause could be traced to the continued determination of the federal government to gain control of the Indian land and open it for settlement. Instead of inciting the Indians to hostile action in 1810, it appears that the British officials of Upper Canada were instructed to restrain them because the home government did not want war at this time. They were, however, to retain the friendship of the Indians in case their help was needed in the future.[15]

Harrison's agents among the Indians continued to give discouraging reports. The Prophet's followers were estimated to be as high as three thousand. Toussaint Dubois who interviewed the Shawnee leader said his anger stemmed from the fact that the Indians had been cheated out of their lands; he held that no cession was valid unless agreed to by all the tribes. He would not go to see the Governor because he felt he had been ill-treated on previous visits. When Joseph Barron attempted to deliver a communication from the Governor to the Prophet, he was denounced as a spy and his

[14] Harrison to Secretary of War, November 15, 1809, in *ibid.*, I, 392-393; Johnston to Editors of Cincinnati *Liberty Hall*, October 3, 1809, in Thornbrough (ed.), *Letter Book of the Indian Agency at Fort Wayne*, pp. 65-66.

[15] See correspondence of Harrison in Esarey (ed.), *Harrison's Messages and Letters*, I, 417-459 *passim*; Burt, *The United States, Great Britain, and British North America*, pp. 287-288, 302-309 *passim*.

life threatened. Up to this time Tecumseh, the Prophet's brother, had played a minor role but he now intervened and assured Barron he was in no danger. He received no definite answer to the Governor's letter but was told Tecumseh would visit Vincennes in a few days and meet with the Governor.

In Tecumseh's opinion it was not possible to remain friends with the United States unless it was willing to abandon the idea of extending its settlements and acknowledge the principle that all lands in the western country were the common property of all the tribes. Harrison had not seen Tecumseh since the Treaty of Greenville, but in reporting Barron's interview, the Governor wrote, it was he who was "really the efficient man—the Moses of the family. . . . He is described by all as a bold, active, sensible man daring in the extreme and capable of any undertaking."[16]

The Governor's reports to the Secretary of War on the warlike attitude of the Prophet's followers and the increased number of depredations, resulted in federal troops being sent to Vincennes. With their help Harrison hoped to establish a fort on the Wabash above Vincennes. In the meantime he played host to Tecumseh who arrived on August 12, accompanied by a large body of Indians. The council was held in the walnut grove to the south of Harrison's home and continued for some eight days. During the first two days Tecumseh's remarks followed the theme that he and his brother had formed a combination of the tribes to establish the principle that Indian lands should be considered common property and none should be sold without the consent of all. He further stated that it was their intention to put to death all the chiefs who were parties to the late treaty, and in the future no village chiefs should be allowed to manage the affairs, but that everything was to be placed into the hands of the warriors. Every instance of injustice and injury which

16 Harrison to Secretary of War, June 14-19, July 4, 18, August 6, 1810, in Esarey (ed.), *Harrison's Messages and Letters*, I, 422-430, 438-440, 446-447, 456-459; Dillon, *History of Indiana*, pp. 441-442.

had been committed by the Americans upon the Indians since the commencement of the Revolution was brought forward and exaggerated. When Harrison attempted to answer, he was contradicted by Tecumseh. At this point Secretary John Gibson, fearing violence on the part of the Indians, requested that a guard of soldiers be stationed by the Governor for his safety, whereupon the latter ordered an end to the council and refused to reconvene it until particularly requested to do so by Tecumseh.

During the remaining days of the council, the Shawnee leader was less arrogant but nothing was accomplished toward a peaceful settlement of differences. But whereas previous information on the designs of the Prophet had been vague and contradictory, the Governor felt he now had something definite on which to base his future actions. "I am far from believing that an Indian war is inevitable," he wrote, "but I believe the avoiding it will depend upon our showing an ability to punish the first aggression." A few days later he made the observation that the savage mind was so constructed that it could not be at rest; while not occupied with the chase, war was the only stimulus that was sufficiently strong to fill up the gap. "If he hunts in the winter he must go to war in the summer."[17]

Lacking authorization to build the fort north of Vincennes, Harrison abandoned the project in October due to the lateness of the season. The following month he received word that the President deemed it inexpedient to establish the post or survey the boundary line of the recent treaty at the present time. In addition to the lateness of the season, the existing state of things in West Florida might require all of the disposable force on the western waters. For the

---

[17] Harrison to Secretary of War, August 22 and 28, 1810, in Esarey (ed.), *Harrison's Messages and Letters,* I, 459-463, 470-471; Tecumseh's speech in *ibid.,* I, 463-469.

present, preservation of peace with the Indians should be considered the prime object with the Governor.[18]

Harrison also received word that the Miami and Wea Indians had refused to accept their annuities for 1810 because of their dissatisfaction with the Fort Wayne treaty, but Johnston finally persuaded all but the Mississinewa band to take them. At Vincennes the Governor had refused to pay the annuities to the Kickapoo because only a few appeared; until a majority of the tribe should attend and formally renounce the Prophet he wrote that he would continue to withhold the sum due that tribe.[19]

§

Harrison gave a full account of Indian affairs in his message to the legislature on November 12, 1810. The tribes who were parties to the Fort Wayne treaty of 1809 were satisfied with it, the Governor reported, until the Prophet convinced them they had been forced to sign it. The Shawnee leader's assertion that the Indian lands were the common property of all the tribes was termed "extremely absurd," and if acknowledged by the government would prevent any further purchase of land. Harrison admitted that at first he had been misled in believing there was some merit in the Prophet's teachings, but was now convinced of his hostile intentions. He believed him to be the tool of the British who, out of fear and avarice, wished to form a combination of Indians which would assist them in case of war or be

18 Harrison to Secretary of War, October 17 and 24, 1810, and Secretary of War to Harrison, October 26, 1810, in Esarey (ed.), *Harrison's Messages and Letters,* I, 480-481, 482-483. The inhabitants of that part of West Florida nearest the Mississippi River had revolted against Spain and requested annexation to the United States. By proclamation of October 27, 1810, President Madison asserted claim to the area by virtue of the Louisiana Purchase and ordered Louisiana's territorial governor to extend authority over the district. Great Britain protested this action.

19 John Johnston, Fort Wayne, to Harrison, October 14, 1810, and Harrison to Secretary of War, November 7, 1810, in Esarey (ed.), *Harrison's Messages and Letters,* I, 476-480, 483-484.

the means of keeping back American settlements and thus securing to themselves a continuance of the valuable fur trade.[20]

As usual, warm weather brought a resumption of friction between the Indians and the whites. With increasing frequency Harrison reported the theft of horses and the murder of frontiersmen; similar reports were sent by Governor Ninian Edwards of Illinois Territory and Gen. William Clark of St. Louis as well as by various agents in the Indian country. On June 24, 1811, Harrison sent a sharp warning to Tecumseh by special messenger:[21]

> . . . This is the third year that all the white people in this country have been alarmed at your proceedings, you threaten us with war, you invite all the tribes to the north and west of you to join against us. . . .
>
> . . . I have . . . received the speech that you sent to the Potawatamies and others, to join you for that purpose. . . .
>
> . . . Do you really think that the handful of men that you have about you are able to contend with the power of the Seventeen Fires [states]. . . .
>
> . . . I am myself of the long knife fire; as soon as they hear my voice, you will see them pouring forth their swarms of hunting-shirt men, as numerous as the musquitoes on the shores of the Wabash. . . .

Tecumseh replied that he would come to see Harrison in eighteen days and "wash away all these bad stories." On learning of the proposed visit, the Governor sent word that the Indian leader should not bring a large force with him as on the previous occasion, and warned that there could be no discussion of the Fort Wayne treaty. The Shawnee chief agreed to bring only a few men, but Harrison dispatched scouts to keep a watch lest the chief be followed by his warriors. While awaiting Tecumseh's arrival, the Governor wrote the Secretary of War that "unless some decisive and energetic measure is adopted to break up the combination formed by the Prophet we shall soon have every Indian tribe

---

[20] *Journals of the General Assembly,* pp. 348-355.
[21] Esarey (ed.), *Harrison's Messages and Letters,* I, 522-524.

in this quarter united against us and you may depend on it that it will be attended with much trouble and expence and loss of blood to subdue them."[22] Before receiving this urgent message, the Secretary had ordered the Fourth Regiment from Pittsburgh to Newport, Kentucky, placed them under Harrison's orders, authorized the Governor to call out the militia, and to attack the Prophet if he commenced hostilities. Three days later, the Secretary wrote that the President hoped that hostilities could be avoided and that the federal troops would be available for another assignment.[23]

In the meantime Harrison was awaiting the appearance of the Indians, who arrived at Vincennes on July 27. Three days earlier the Governor's scouts sent word of Tecumseh's approach with 120 warriors, not counting the Wea who were coming on behind him. By the time the whole party got together there were close to three hundred Indians, notwithstanding the promise to bring only a few. The Governor responded with a show of his own forces and held a review of some seven or eight hundred militiamen on the day the Indians arrived; this apparently discouraged any attack the Indians may have contemplated at this time.

Harrison opened the council by telling of the great alarm the Indians were causing. He assured them he was willing to listen to their complaints, but that any negotiation about the Treaty of Fort Wayne would have to be conducted by the President. He asked for an explanation of the seizure of salt which he had sent up the Wabash to the various tribes and demanded the surrender of the Indians who had murdered some of the whites. Tecumseh answered that he intended only peace and requested that things remain as they were until the next spring when he would return from the South, where he hoped to unite all the tribes in the bonds

---

[22] Tecumseh to Harrison, July 4, 1811, and Harrison to Secretary of War, July 10, 1811, in *ibid.*, I, 529, 532-535.

[23] Secretary of War to Harrison, July 17 and 20, 1811, in *ibid.*, I, 535-537.

of peace. He promised to send out runners to order all the Indians to stop doing any more mischief to the whites; no disposition was shown to punish the murderers or make restitution of the salt. At the close of the conference, Tecumseh sent his warriors up the Wabash to Prophet's Town while he departed with twenty of his followers down the river.[24]

Even though the danger of war seemed to be increasing every day, Harrison wrote at the end of December that a further extinguishment of the Indian title was necessary to satisfy the needs of the settlers. He feared that delay would permit the Prophet to unify all the tribes in opposition to further land cessions. The President and the Secretary of War, however, rejected the Governor's request and suggested instead that it might be expedient to quiet the Indians by making some "arrangement" about the last treaty. From this time on Harrison seemed more aggressive than the national administration. He may have been launched on the program of buying land by President Jefferson when the latter learned of Napoleon's interest in the province of Louisiana and when there was need of a large white population to protect the western border, but in 1810 President Madison was more interested in the southern border and wanted peace in the Northwest.[25]

Two days after Tecumseh left Vincennes, Harrison wrote to the Secretary of War, "His absence affords a most favorable opportunity for breaking up his Confederacy." The evaluation which he placed upon the Shawnee brothers indicates the change which had occurred in the leadership of the movement which the Prophet had initiated.

The implicit obedience and respect which the followers of Tecumseh pay to him is really astonishing and more than any other circumstance

[24] Harrison to Secretary of War, August 6, 1811, in Esarey (ed.), *Harrison's Messages and Letters,* I, 542-546; Vincennes *Western Sun,* June 22 and August 3, 1811.

[25] Harrison to Secretary of War, December 24, 1810, in Esarey (ed.), *Harrison's Messages and Letters,* I, 496-500; Secretary of War to Harrison, March 7, 1811, in Carter (ed.), *Territorial Papers,* VIII, 113-114.

bespeaks him one of those uncommon geniuses, which spring up occasionally to produce revolutions and overturn the established order
of things. If it were not for the vicinity of the United States, he
would perhaps be the founder of an Empire that would rival in glory
that of Mexico or Peru. No difficulties deter him. His activity and
industry supply the want of letters. For four years he has been in
constant motion. You see him today on the Wabash and in a short
time you hear of him on the shores of Lake Erie or Michigan, or on
the banks of the Mississippi and wherever he goes he makes an impression favorable to his purposes.

He is now upon the last round to put a finishing stroke to his work.
I hope, however, before his return that that part of the fabrick, which
he considered complete will be demolished and even its foundations
rooted up. Altho the greater part of his followers are attached to him
from principle and affection, there are many others who follow him
through fear and he was scarcely a mile from the Town, before they
indulged in the most virulent invectives against him. The Prophet is
imprudent and audacious but is deficient in judgment talents and
firmness.[26]

Harrison might have added that he had no faith in Tecumseh's protestation of peaceful intentions; he was only seeking
to deceive the whites while he organized the tribesmen and
perfected his plans. That he should have expected the Governor to believe his promises of peace and to remain inactive
while he attempted to secure the co-operation of the southern
Indians indicates a naiveté which qualifies the estimate that
Harrison made of his greatness.

In Tecumseh's absence Harrison proposed to call upon the
tribes to deliver those of their number who had murdered
American citizens, to require that they give information on
and stop any parties passing through their territory with hostile intentions, and to require those parties who had joined
the Prophet to return to their respective tribes or forfeit the
protection of the United States. He wanted the Miami to
repudiate the Prophet. If any tribe dared to "take up the
Tomhawk," they could expect to be exterminated or driven

[26] Harrison to Secretary of War, August 7, 1811, in Esarey (ed.), *Harrison's Messages and Letters,* I, 548-551.

beyond the Mississippi. Realizing that these demands would need to be backed up by military force, Harrison proposed to move about the middle of September with United States troops and militia to the northern border of the recent purchase on the Wabash.[27]

The Secretary of War sent Harrison's letter to the President with the comment that the movement up the Wabash appeared to be advisable. The Fourth Regiment plus the two companies of regulars already at Vincennes and two troops of cavalry or mounted riflemen he thought should assure "a peaceable march" to the extremity of the recent purchase. Without waiting for the approbation of the President, he directed Harrison to go ahead with the above troops; he expressed the hope that the Fourth Regiment would be able to return to Newport before winter set in.[28] In the West it was believed that the success or failure of the campaign depended upon the strength of the army which Harrison was attempting to put together; to insure success the Governor decided to increase the militia forces beyond the number advised by the Secretary of War.[29]

While making his final preparations for the expedition, the Governor was visited by a deputation from the Prophet's Town who on learning of the proposed march came to profess their peaceful intentions and a willingness to comply with the Governor's demands. Any change of plans which this gesture might have prompted, however, was canceled

27 Harrison to Secretary of War, August 7, 1811, in *ibid.*

28 Secretary of War to Madison, no date, Madison Papers, Library of Congress; Secretary of War to Harrison, August 22, 1811, in Carter (ed.), *Territorial Papers,* VIII, 130-131. In another letter of August 29, the Secretary acknowledged the necessity of employing additional militia to make up for those of the Fourth Regiment who were ill. Esarey (ed.), *Harrison's Messages and Letters,* I, 560-561.

29 Capt. W. Piatt, Louisville, to the Secretary of War, August 24 and September 7, 1811, in War Department correspondence, National Archives; Harrison to Secretary of War, September 3 and 17, 1811, and Benjamin Parke and Waller Taylor to Harrison, September 13 and 15, 1811, in Esarey (ed.), *Harrison's Messages and Letters,* I, 563-564, 565-566, 568-569, 570-575.

when word arrived of horses having been stolen from the Busseron settlement and from the army contractor. After trailing the Indians and recovering the horses, the search party was fired on and had to take refuge in a swamp. In reporting the incident to the Secretary of War, Harrison wrote that he had resolved after erecting a fort on the Wabash to make a demonstration towards the Prophet's Town.[30]

The Fourth Regiment arrived at Vincennes on September 19. Sandbars and a swift current made poling the flatboats up the Wabash a laborious task. The men attracted a lot of attention with their colorful uniforms which contrasted with the rough caps, hunting shirts, and breeches of the militia.[31] Harrison had hoped the expedition could be on its way by September 20, but found it necessary to wait another six days for needed supplies.[32]

On the morning of the 26th the signal was given and the army numbering about one thousand commenced its march northward. The heavy supplies were sent by boat, the lighter ones in wagons. The men marched in two columns with guards well out on both sides and in front, while the mounted troops led the advance and brought up the rear. The order of encampment would depend on the camp sites.[33]

[30] Esarey (ed.), *Harrison's Messages and Letters,* I, 590-592.

[31] Jacobs, *The Beginning of the United States Army,* p. 358. Harrison met Col. John P. Boyd, commander of the Fourth Regiment, at the Falls of the Ohio and the two rode overland to Vincennes.

[32] Harrison to Secretary of War, September 25, 1811, in Esarey (ed.), *Harrison's Messages and Letters,* I, 589-590.

[33] General Orders in Esarey (ed.), *Harrison's Messages and Letters,* I, 592-594. The field report of October 12 listed 1,225 men in the various units, but absentees, men on specific assignments, and the sick reduced the effective fighting force and officers to less than one thousand. Of these, 345 belonged to the Fourth Regiment, 415 to the Indiana militia, 120 to the dragoons or mounted militia, 84 mounted riflemen, and 13 scouts and spies. Among the mounted militia and riflemen were a number of Kentucky volunteers. *Ibid.,* I, 597-598. The rosters of the various companies and detachments are printed in Reed Beard, *The Battle of Tippecanoe* (Fourth edition, Chicago, 1911), pp. 102-121, and in Alfred Pirtle, *The Battle of Tippecanoe* (Filson Club *Publi-*

John Tipton, who later became a United States Senator from Indiana, was a volunteer militiaman during the campaign and the author of a picturesque diary. His spelling was phonetic and if he knew any rules of grammar he must have discarded them for the duration. His diary gives an interesting picture of the experiences of the ordinary soldier during the campaign. For example, he met a Delaware chief who spoke good English and played cards with the soldiers. He went to "tare hott" [Terre Haute], a location but not a settlement, with an Indian on October 15 to look for hostile tribesmen. His companion "got Drunk," but since they started with whiskey, stopped twice to drink, and lost their horses each time, it may well be that they were both in that condition. Almost a month after he left home he wrote: "I Staid in Camp washd my Clothes for the first time." Between Vincennes and Prophet's Town, Tipton mentions the killing of a pheasant, two each of pigeon, turkey, raccoon, and squirrel, and eleven deer. They found and cut eight bee trees, got from nine to ten gallons of honey from three of them, but neglected to cut five others. At another time he caught two fish. This game must have been a very welcome addition to army rations.[34]

Sixty-five miles north of Vincennes the army halted and spent almost a month in building a fort with three blockhouses which was named Fort Harrison. During this interim, Harrison brought the Secretary of War up to date not only on the progress of the expedition but on the state of Indian affairs. Reports of new depredations by the Indians made

cations No. 15, Louisville, 1900), pp. 111-131. Photostatic copies of the pay rolls of the Indiana militia engaged in the campaign are in the Genealogy Division, Indiana State Library.

34 The small handmade notebook in which Tipton recorded his daily experiences is preserved among the Tipton Papers in the Indiana State Library. It is printed in the *Indiana Magazine of History,* II (1906), 170-184, and in *The John Tipton Papers,* edited by Nellie A. Robertson and Dorothy Riker (3 volumes, *Indiana Historical Collections,* XXIV-XXVI, Indianapolis, 1942), I, 62-83.

the commander in chief want to move immediately to the Prophet's Town. A week later authorization was received from the Secretary of War to proceed: "You will approach and order him [the Prophet] to disperse, which he may be permitted to do, on condition of satisfactory assurances that in the future he shall not assemble or attempt to assemble any number of Indians, armed or in a hostile attitude. If he neglects or refuses to disperse he will be attacked and compelled to it by the force under your command." Regarding the British, the Secretary added that, "in the present delicate posture of our relations with that nation, it is peculiarly desirable that no act should be committed, which may be construed into an aggression on our part."[35]

While the army was at Fort Harrison, the Governor learned that the Delaware chiefs who had gone to Prophet's Town on a peace mission had been badly received, abused and dismissed. The killing of a sentinel indicated that the army was under Indian surveillance. Friction had developed between the militia and the regulars, and the nonperformance by an army contractor made a reduction in the flour ration necessary. These and other developments led the Governor to request that additional companies of mounted riflemen and militia be sent from Kentucky. One bit of good news received was that the Wea, Miami, and part of the Potawatomi had deserted the Prophet.[36]

The army took up its march again on October 29, and two days later crossed to the west side of the Wabash. At this

[35] Secretary of War to Harrison, September 18, 1811, in Carter (ed.), *Territorial Papers,* VIII, 133-134.

[36] Harrison to Secretary of War, October 13 and 29, 1811, in Esarey (ed.), *Harrison's Messages and Letters,* I, 599-603, 604-605; Col. John Boyd to Secretary of War, October 18, 1811, in War Dept. correspondence, National Archives; Harrison to Governor Charles Scott, October 25, 1811, in Washington (D.C.) *National Intelligencer,* November 21, 1811. Fourth Regiment Orderly Book and Notes collected by John G. Biel, chairman of the Harrison Trail Commission, in Indiana Historical Society Library. At least some of the additional troops requested from Kentucky arrived in time to take part in the battle.

point Harrison built a blockhouse for the protection of the provisions and boats to be left there. Continuing on the troops came into sight of Prophet's Town on November 6. Some of the officers advised an immediate attack but Harrison abided by his instructions and accepted the proposal of two or more chiefs who came out from the Indian town and asked that a council between the Indians and the commander in chief be held the following morning.[37] Harrison then asked concerning a good camping place, and after the Indians gave rather general and indefinite directions, officers went to examine the area above and below the town. The raised ground northwest of the town, extending from the hills into a low prairie along Burnetts Creek, was chosen.

Before daylight the next morning, probably about 4:30, before the men had been awakened, the Indians attacked. Apparently they were crawling up to the American camp through the long grass when one of the sentinels saw some-

[37] Isaac Naylor, a member of one of the rifle companies, wrote in later years: "When the army arrived in view of the Prophet's town, an Indian was seen coming toward General Harrison with a white flag suspended on a pole. Here the army halted, and a parley was had between General Harrison and an Indian delegation, who assured the General that they desired peace, and solemnly promised to meet him next day in council, to settle the terms of peace and friendship between them and the United States." *Indiana Magazine of History,* II (1906), 164.

Tipton said the army surrounded the Indian town, after which the Indian delegation came out and "Pled for Peace." *Ibid.,* II, 180. Harrison in his official report stated that he halted the troops a mile and a half from the town and sent Toussaint Dubois, leader of the spies, to request a conference with the Prophet but the Indians prevented him from carrying out the mission. Then while the officers were looking for a suitable place to camp three Indians approached the advanced guard and signified a wish to speak to Harrison, and on meeting with him expressed their surprise at the army's approach, stating they had sent word two days earlier that they would meet him a day or so journey from their village. Apparently the messengers had taken a different route. Upon learning that Harrison had no intention of attacking them until they had a chance to comply with his demands, they seemed pleased and likewise promised no hostile action. Later in the day some hostility was shown as the troops tramped through the Indian cornfields in search of a place to camp. Harrison to Secretary of War, November 18, 1811, in Esarey (ed.), *Harrison's Messages and Letters,* I, 618-620.

thing move and fired a shot. Learning they had been discovered, the Indians began the attack with a great yell. A
small number penetrated behind the American lines but were
soon killed. The troops took their positions quickly (they
had slept on their arms) and Harrison said most were in
line before attacked, which may well have been true since
the entire line was not immediately involved.

The first assault came at the north, and the troops at the
northwest angle were forced back. Harrison quickly strengthened this point with other troops from the center of the line.
The left end of the front line was next threatened, but Maj.
Joseph Hamilton Daveiss, a Kentucky volunteer, reinforced
it with his dragoons.

The Indians waged a desperate battle for two hours, then
withdrew with the coming of daylight, leaving almost a
fifth of Harrison's force killed or wounded. The Indians
left twenty-five to thirty-five dead on the battlefield, but
others were discovered later in the town; the total number
of Indians engaged varied from one hundred to six hundred
according to whether the Indians or the Americans were making the estimate.[38] Though the American casualties were

[38] Harrison estimated the number of Indians in the battle as at least six
hundred; his men found 36 to 40 of their dead on the battlefield and other
bodies were discovered in the Indian town. Harrison to Secretary of War,
November 18, 1811, in Esarey (ed.), *Harrison's Messages and Letters*, I, 628,
630. According to accounts given by various Indians, the number engaged and
the number of casualties were much lower. For example, a Kickapoo chief reported to Matthew Elliott, the British agent, that about one hundred were
engaged and twenty-five killed; John Johnston, Indian agent at Fort Wayne,
was told that only 28 Indians were killed out of 350 engaged in the battle—
principally Kickapoo, Winnebago, some Shawnee and Potawatomi, and a small
number of Wyandot—"a collection of all the vagabond Indians he [the
Prophet] could find." Elliott to Maj. Gen. Isaac Brock, January 12, 1812,
in *Michigan Historical Collections*, XV, 66-68; Johnston to the Secretary of
War, November 28, 1811, National Archives; Johnston to Cincinnati *Liberty
Hall*, November 30, 1811, in Vincennes *Western Sun*, January 11, 1812. In a
later letter Harrison raised his estimate to seven hundred. Letter to Secretary
of War, January 14, 1812, in Esarey (ed.), *Harrison's Messages and Letters*,
II, 12-13.

large, they were not so numerous as the losses of Harmar or St. Clair.

The troops remained on the battleground throughout the day, erected barricades for protection, cared for the wounded, and buried the dead. The food supplies were inadequate as the livestock had been driven away during the battle. The soldiers lay through a cold, wet night at their breastworks without fire. Obviously they feared and expected another attack. On the next day, November 8, after spies found Prophet's Town abandoned, men were sent to salvage the corn that was found and to set the town on fire. After another night on the battlefield, the wounded were loaded in wagons, excess baggage destroyed, and the army marched eight miles towards home. The wounded suffered greatly from the jolting over the rough terrain until they reached the blockhouse where as many as could be accommodated were transferred to boats. The route for the others was the same as that taken on the way to the Indian town. Vincennes was reached without incident on November 18.

§   §

The legislative session which had been twice postponed finally convened on November 11, but did little business until Harrison returned to Vincennes, other than to pass a resolution congratulating him and his troops on their victory over the Indians. In his brief message to the Assembly, delivered on the twentieth, the Governor termed the expedition "a complete victory over the hostile combination of Indians . . . formed by the Shawny prophet."[39] But the citizens as a whole did not extend to the Governor the welcome customarily accorded a returning hero. All were shocked at the sight of the wounded, maimed, and disabled soldiers as they returned from the battlefield, many of whom were their friends and neighbors, and everyone no doubt joined in the memorial serv-

---

[39] *Journals of the General Assembly*, pp. 367, 379-380, 381, 383.

ices for those who did not return. Some questioned whether the Governor had sacrificed the men to satisfy his own personal ambitions. John Badollet was one who believed that if Harrison had been satisfied to build a fort in the tract ceded by the Treaty of Fort Wayne, the Indians would not have objected; instead, by invading the Indian country and marching to their town with a large military force, the Indians had been convinced that their destruction was intended.[40]

In addition, the bad feeling and rivalry between the militia and United States troops which had shown itself during the campaign now became more intense, with the latter maintaining that they had saved the militia from complete destruction. This controversy extended to the legislative halls where the friends of Harrison succeeded in blocking passage of a joint resolution of thanks to Colonel Boyd and his men. Finally on December 4, almost a month after the battle, the House finally extended its thanks for the aid rendered by the men of the regular army.[41]

Criticism of Harrison was not limited to Indiana Territory, but extended into Kentucky which had lost some of its prominent citizens in the battle; to New England, whence the men of the Fourth Regiment had come; and into the halls of Congress where Jonathan Jennings, the territorial delegate, was quick to make capital of any criticism of his political enemy.

The first accounts of the battle published in Kentucky conveyed the idea that the army had been thrown into confusion by a surprise attack. Harrison was accused by residents of that state of ordering Colonel Daveiss to make the attack

[40] Thornbrough (ed.), *The Correspondence of John Badollet and Albert Gallatin*, pp. 208-210, 214-220.

[41] *Journals of the General Assembly*, pp. 392-393, 400-401, 409-410, 416, 421, 426, 427-428. Colonel Boyd sent his own version of the expedition to the Secretary of War and to a friend in Congress. Boyd to Eustis, November 20, 1811, in Philadelphia *Aurora*, January 4, 1812; Boyd and Prescott to Eustis, December 11, 1811, in Vincennes *Western Sun*, February 8, 1812; Boyd to Richard Cutts, December 16, 1811, Indiana Historical Society Library.

that led to his death, and of being responsible for Col. Abraham Owen's death because he was mounted on the Governor's white horse. In New England (where an aggressive Indian policy was very unpopular) the Boston *Columbian Sentinel* of December 7 reported that Harrison had been "gulled" by an old Indian trick and allowed his troops to be surprised.[42] The following year the Congressional committee on Indian affairs, after inquiring into the orders by which the campaign was authorized and carried out, reported that in their opinion the use of the militia and federal troops was justified in order to protect the frontiers from the attacks with which they were threatened.[43]

Some of the Governor's critics thought he should have attacked the Indians immediately upon his arrival at the Indian town, but as he pointed out his orders forbade this.[44] William Clark at St. Louis, after learning of the battle, presumed that the Prophet's party would be pursued "in every direction, caught and punished,"[45] yet with nearly one fifth of his men dead or wounded, and destitute of provisions Harrison was in no position to pursue an enemy that had scattered in various directions. Seldom was condemnation directed against the Fort Wayne treaty, because it was popular in the West, yet it was the basis of the disaffection around which the Prophet and Tecumseh had rallied the tribesmen.

[42] For answers to these and other charges, see the correspondence of Harrison and others in Esarey (ed.), *Harrison's Messages and Letters,* I, 612-614, 629, 666-672, 683-685, 686-692; II, 3-12.

[43] Extracts from letters of the governors of Michigan, Indiana, and Illinois territories from 1807 through 1811 were submitted to the Congressional committee as well as Harrison's letters regarding the campaign. The committee was concerned not only with the Tippecanoe expedition but with the extent to which the British had encouraged the Indians. *American State Papers. Indian Affairs,* I, 776-780, 797-811.

[44] Harrison to Governor Charles Scott, December 13, 1811, in Esarey (ed.), *Harrison's Messages and Letters,* I, 669.

[45] Clark to Secretary of War, November 23, 1811, in War Dept. correspondence, National Archives.

The November 1811 term of the Knox County Court of Common Pleas was postponed for three weeks because of the Battle of Tippecanoe, and when finally convened most of the term was spent in the administration of the estates of those who had lost their lives in the conflict. This form of business continued to occupy the judges during the next year, and as late as the November term of 1812, they appointed administrators and accepted proof of wills of twenty-four different individuals. Though not all these deaths were battle casualties, a considerable number occurred as the result of it.[46]

§   §   §

President Madison was so optimistic that the Battle of Tippecanoe and the dispersion of the Prophet's followers would bring a cessation of the murders and depredations on the frontier that he suggested that Harrison invite the leaders of the hitherto hostile tribes, including the Prophet and Tecumseh, to visit Washington. Harrison broadened the invitation to include also the leaders of the tribes that had been faithful to the United States, but it was declined.[47] With the coming of spring the Indians resumed their raids on the frontier settlements in both the Indiana and Illinois territories. By the middle of April Harrison was forced to admit that the hopes he had entertained for peace were "entirely dissipated."[48] A few days later the Indians came

[46] Transcripts of Minutes of the Knox County Court of Common Pleas, November term 1811 through November term 1812, Archives Division, Indiana State Library.

[47] *American State Papers. Indian Affairs,* I, 776; Secretary of War to Harrison, January 17, 1812, in Esarey (ed.), *Harrison's Messages and Letters,* II, 14-15; Harrison to Secretary of War, February 19, 1812, in *ibid.,* II, 25-26; Thornbrough (ed.), *Letter Book of the Indian Agency at Fort Wayne,* pp. 103-105, 108-110, 114.

[48] Harrison to Secretary of War, April 14, 1812, in Esarey (ed.), *Harrison's Messages and Letters,* II, 32. For reports of depredations, see *ibid.,* II, 30-59; Thornbrough (ed.), *The Correspondence of John Badollet and Albert Gallatin,* pp. 226-240; Thornbrough (ed.), *Letter Book of Indian Agency at Fort Wayne,* pp. 112-113, 116-119.

within a few miles of Vincennes to make a vicious attack on a family of seven and leave them all dead. The territorial capital became an armed camp and settlers all along the frontier from the western to the eastern borders either fled southward or moved into blockhouses and forts. From Lawrenceburg James Dill wrote, "The people are flying from the back parts of this county . . . and we shall soon be completely a desert"; from Vincennes Harrison commented, "Families, abandoning their homes and flying they know not whither and many of them without any means of support, are seen in every direction."[49]

What protection could be offered? One of the six companies of Rangers authorized by the act of Congress of January 2, 1812, was assigned to Indiana Territory; when organized, they were to be ready to march on short notice wherever they might be needed. But with the vast expanse of frontier to be covered, how could they prevent small parties of Indians from penetrating the settlements and doing mischief? Members of the territorial militia were also to be placed in a state of readiness awaiting a possible call, but as the Governor pointed out those on the frontier were needed for the protection of their own families, and only those from Ohio River counties could be counted on. Since the militiamen had not yet received any compensation for their service in the Tippecanoe campaign, it would work a real hardship for them again to leave their homes.[50]

Fort Harrison, which had been built and garrisoned to keep a watch over Indian movements, was also vulnerable.

[49] Dill to Return J. Meigs, May 11, 1812, in Richard C. Knopf (ed.), *Document Transcriptions of the War of 1812 in the Northwest* (6 volumes, Columbus, Ohio, 1957-59), II, 4; Harrison to Secretary of War, April 29, 1812, in Esarey (ed.), *Harrison's Messages and Letters,* II, 42.

[50] Secretary of War to Harrison, February 28, 1812, in Carter (ed.), *Territorial Papers,* VIII, 168-169; Harrison's correspondence in Esarey (ed.), *Harrison's Messages and Letters,* II, 35, 43, 48. For defense measures taken in Franklin County, see Caroline Dunn, "Defense in Pioneer Days: Col. James Noble's Franklin County Militia," *Year Book* of the Society of Indiana Pioneers, 1953, pp. 5-13.

One of the officers stationed there wrote on May 3, "We hourly look for an attack . . . and so sure as it is made, so sure are we all killed."[51] Capt. Josiah Snelling of the Fourth Regiment, commanding at Fort Harrison, had performed valiant service in keeping Harrison informed, but in March he and his men were ordered to rejoin their regiment for a new assignment. They were to be replaced by a company of the Seventh Regiment under Capt. Zachary Taylor. When the latter arrived in July, he found the fort "destitute of protection."[52] The few settlers who had moved into the neighborhood in the belief that the Indian war was over had either departed or moved into the fort.

An Indian council was held on the Mississinewa River in May, 1812, at which representatives of twelve different tribes were present. The Indian agent at Fort Wayne reported that the tribesmen had agreed to consider themselves as one nation for the purpose of making peace; also that large numbers continued to pass through that place on their way to visit the British at Malden.[53] One last effort was made by the United States government in June to establish peace with the Indians by inviting them to a grand council at Piqua, Ohio,[54] but by the time the invitation was extended by the various territorial governors and agents, war had been declared by the United States on Great Britain. This was the eventuality for which the British officials of Upper Canada had been preparing; their cultivation of the Indians over the past five years was now rewarded and a majority chose to fight on the side of the British. The United States govern-

[51] Extract of letter in Washington (D.C.) *National Intelligencer,* June 6, 1812.

[52] Secretary of War to Harrison, March 7, 1812, in Carter (ed.), *Territorial Papers,* VIII, 170; Taylor to Secretary of War, July 16, 1812, in War Dept. correspondence, National Archives.

[53] Thornbrough (ed.), *Letter Book of the Indian Agency at Fort Wayne,* pp. 106n, 126-129, 139, 144-146; Esarey (ed.), *Harrison's Messages and Letters,* II, 50-56.

[54] Thornbrough (ed.), *Letter Book of the Indian Agency at Fort Wayne,* pp. 147-148n, 153, 155-156, 162, 166, 167, 168, 169-170n.

ment promised protection to those tribes who remained faithful.[55]

Although the decision of Congress on June 18 to declare war seemed to have been made suddenly, it was the culmination of years of friction between the two nations. And although the conflict has been regarded as useless and perhaps could have been avoided, the United States did not go to war without serious provocation. After the Revolution the British government chose to ignore the United States. It had refused to surrender the northwest posts until 1796, to make a treaty of commerce, or to try seriously to settle the points at issue between the two nations. As early as Washington's administration, English sea captains began to impress American sailors into British service, claiming that they were English deserters; in some instances they were, but the greater number were Americans. England also began to search neutral vessels for French goods and to seize the ships carrying such goods; this particularly affected American ships engaged in carrying products of the French West Indies to Europe. The issues of impressment as well as the search and seizure of ships and cargoes reached a crisis in 1807 and war was narrowly avoided at that time. In December of that year Congress passed the Embargo Act to keep American ships at home, but this hurt the United States more than it did England and was responsible for much dissatisfaction, especially in New England.[56]

The blockades and the embargo also destroyed the markets for the surplus agricultural products of the West and South and brought hard times to these sections.[57] The frontiersmen

[55] Ibid., pp. 181-183n, 187n; Charles N. Thompson, Sons of the Wilderness. John and William Conner (Indiana Historical Society Publications, XII, Indianapolis, 1937), pp. 65-67.

[56] Burt, The United States, Great Britain, and British North America, Chaps. XII and XIII; Reginald Horsman, The War of 1812 (New York, 1969), Chap. I. Harry L. Coles, The War of 1812 (Chicago, 1965), pp. 2-37, summarizes the position taken by various historians on the causes of the war.

[57] George R. Taylor, "Agrarian Discontent in the Mississippi Valley Pre-

blamed England for their economic predicament; they also believed that the British traders and Indian agents were responsible for the Indian warfare. With the inauguration of a new president, the Embargo Act was replaced by the Non-intercourse Act of 1809 which opened up commerce with all the world except France and England. The President was authorized to suspend the operations of the act in favor of either belligerent that repealed its restrictions on American trade. This was modified by another act the following year which permitted the United States to resume trade with France.

Far to the south, the frontiersmen saw in Spain another enemy because she controlled the mouths of the rivers which flowed across Florida and because she supplied the southern Indians with goods and ammunition. There was also an upsurge of nationalism; a new generation of leaders had arisen, men who were too young to know the sufferings and hardships of the Revolution. Convinced of the inadequacy of the administration's dependence upon economic warfare with its unfortunate results, a group of young "war hawks" took control of Congress and swept the nation into a war for which it was ill prepared. The renewal of Indian warfare in Indiana and Illinois territories also affected the decision of some western Congressmen to declare war, though the delegates of these territories could not vote.

To provide for the eventuality of war, Congress had voted in January, 1812, to increase the size of the army and appoint additional officers. Although two new brigadier generals were chosen from the West, Governor Harrison was passed over in favor of William Hull and James Winchester. Hull,

ceding the War of 1812," *Journal of Political Economy,* XXXIX (1931), 471-505; and by the same author, "Prices in the Mississippi Valley Preceding the War of 1812," *Journal of Economic and Business History,* III (1930-31), 148-163; Cecil K. Byrd, The War of 1812 in the Old Northwest: First Phase (Unpublished Ph. D. Thesis, Department of History, Indiana University, 1942), pp. 21-84.

who was governor of Michigan Territory, was to command the Northwestern army and draw his troops from Ohio, while Winchester, a Tennessean, was to recruit another army in Kentucky and go to Hull's aid if needed. Hull received the official notice of the declaration of war on July 2, as he and his troops reached Frenchtown, the present Monroe, Michigan. The British at Fort Malden received the word at the same time or earlier and were able to capture valuable papers and supplies which Hull had sent by boat from the rapids of the Maumee to Detroit. They also alerted the British garrison on St. Joseph Island, in the channel between Lakes Superior and Huron, and they were able to organize an expedition and take Fort Michilimackinac on July 17, before the American commandant knew of the declaration of war.[58] When the news reached Detroit of the loss of this northern fort, Hull ordered Capt. Nathan Heald, commander at Fort Dearborn on Lake Michigan, to evacuate that post and take his troops (54 officers and soldiers) to Fort Wayne or Detroit. The commanding officer at Fort Wayne was asked to inform William Wells and the Indian agent of the order and to advise Heald as to the best route. They thought the safest route would be by way of Fort Wayne and Wells volunteered to recruit some of the Miami to escort the troops and their families. Meanwhile, Captain Heald had been warned by Chief Winamac not to attempt to leave because of the hostile disposition of the Indians in the neighborhood, and Wells apparently was of the same opinion by the time he reached the fort. However, it was too late to change the plans made for the evacuation on August 15. After marching about a mile and a half the soldiers and their families were attacked by some four hundred Indians, mostly Potawatomi, and half of the garrison, plus two women, twelve children, and ten other civilians were massacred; the remainder were taken prisoner. Wells was also slain; Indian cannibals removed his heart

[58] Coles, *War of 1812*, pp. 45-50.

Monument at Tippecanoe Battlefield

William Henry Harrison House at Vincennes

Erected 1803-1804; restored to its original appearance
by the Francis Vigo Chapter, D.A.R.

Vincennes Capitol, 1805-1813

and ate it with the thought that his courage would be thus transmitted to them.[59]

Although General Hull had protested that his supply lines were unsafe as long as the British controlled Lake Erie, he advanced to Detroit on July 5 and after a brief pause marched into Canada. Gen. Isaac Brock, who commanded the British forces in Upper Canada, forced the Americans to return to Detroit and attacked that place on August 16. Hull surrendered without offering any resistance. He was later court-martialed and sentenced to death but was pardoned by the President.[60] The easy victories at Michilimackinac and Detroit convinced the Indians that the British were going to win and those who had been hesitating now joined the British.

War now broke with fury in Indiana. Penetrating almost to the Ohio River, as if to discourage the militia from aiding those on the frontier, the Indians attacked an unprotected little settlement called Pigeon Roost in present Scott County and killed twenty-four men, women, and children on September 3. The following day they set fire to one of the blockhouses at Fort Harrison. Despite the illness of part of his small force, Capt. Zachary Taylor and his men were able to keep the fire from spreading to the remainder of the fort. A temporary breastwork was erected across the opening created by the destruction of the blockhouse and after several hours of cross firing the Indians departed.[61]

[59] Eyewitness accounts of the massacre and discussion of the same are in Milo M. Quaife, *Chicago and the Old Northwest, 1673-1835* (Chicago, 1913), pp. 378-408, 415-421; letter of Walter Jordan in *Indiana Magazine of History,* XLI (1945), 187-199; Robert B. McAfee, *History of the Late War in the Western Country* (Lexington, Ky., 1816), pp. 98-101. See also Thomas Forsyth to the Governor of Louisiana Territory, September 7, 1812, in Carter (ed.), *Territorial Papers,* XVI, 261-263. Forsyth arrived at Chicago the day after the massacre.

[60] Coles, *The War of 1812,* pp. 47-57; Horsman, *The War of 1812,* pp. 34-41.

[61] Accounts of Pigeon Roost massacre, in Indiana Historical Society *Publications,* II, No. 4, pp. 128-134; Zachary Taylor to Harrison, September 10, 1812, in Esarey (ed.), *Harrison's Messages and Letters,* II, 124-128;

Fort Wayne was the next to suffer attack. Indians began to assemble about it on August 28, but not until September 5 did they open fire. A direct assault was made during the night of the sixth, but the garrison repulsed it. The siege was continued and on the eleventh another assault was made and turned back. In the meantime, word of the siege had reached army officials in Ohio and reinforcements were on their way.

§   §   §   §

Although Governor Harrison had been temporarily passed over by the national administration in its preparations for defense, he was not willing to accept this as final. During the latter part of June he had left Vincennes to visit friends in Kentucky and review some of the militia regiments there. After expressing to Governor Charles Scott his dissatisfaction at seeing the military appointments go to others, his Kentucky friends began to bombard the President and other influential persons to secure a commission for him. In the meantime he was brevetted major general of the Kentucky militia. Armed with this commission, General Harrison went on to Cincinnati where he took over the command of the Kentucky troops in Winchester's army and persuaded that officer to assign to him the regiment of regulars over which he certainly had no authority. When Winchester received orders to advance to the relief of Hull, Harrison prepared to carry out the order, but when word arrived of Hull's surrender and Fort Wayne being besieged, he marched with the army to that place after telling Winchester he would yield

Dillon, *History of Indiana*, pp. 488-491, 492-493. William Plasket writing from Clark County six days after the Pigeon Roost raid, said twenty-one persons were killed, one wounded, and six houses burned. "The alarm was so great the people flew in every direction." After the attack the Indians fled so precipitously that the volunteers who assembled were unable to find them, but the next evening a party of Rangers caught up with them and killed two, and rescued three horses loaded with the plunder they had taken from the settlement. John Armstrong Papers, Indiana Historical Society Library.

the command when the siege of Fort Wayne had been lifted.[62] Finding on his arrival at that place that the Indians had fled, he proceeded to destroy the Indian villages in the vicinity together with their food supplies. Following this movement into Indiana Territory, Harrison returned the troops to Winchester's command since dispatches from Washington had made it clear that the Indiana governor was to act in a subordinate capacity. Later in the month (September), however, Harrison received word that he had been appointed to command the Northwestern army and that he should prepare to retake Detroit and invade Canada.[63] Before proceeding north Harrison made arrangements for the protection of the frontiers in Indiana Territory, and during September and October Vincennes became the headquarters for various military activities.

Col. William Russell who had been placed in command of the regular troops in the Indiana Territory plus the five companies of Rangers raised in the territory and adjoining states, arrived at Vincennes about September 10 with twelve hundred men en route to the Illinois Territory. On hearing of the attack on Fort Harrison, he immediately marched his troops to the aid of Captain Taylor. Finding that the Indians had departed, Russell left the company of Kentucky Rangers as a reinforcement at the fort while he and the remainder of the troops went on to aid the Illinois territorial governor in an expedition against the Kickapoo.[64]

A week or so later Samuel Hopkins, major general of the Kentucky militia, arrived at Vincennes to take charge of some

[62] Goebel, *Harrison,* pp. 133-139; Cleaves, *Old Tippecanoe,* pp. 112-117.

[63] See Harrison's correspondence in Esarey (ed.), *Harrison's Messages and Letters,* II, 103-104, 108-110, 117-118, 136-138, 143-147; Goebel, *Harrison,* pp. 139-142; Griswold, *Pictorial History of Fort Wayne,* I, 198-213.

[64] Gibson to Harrison, September 10, 1812, Indiana Historical Society Library; Gibson to Secretary of War, same date, and Russell to Secretary of War, September 23, 1812, in Knopf (ed.), *Document Transcriptions of the War of 1812 in the Northwest,* VI, Pt. 3, pp. 157, 186; Vincennes *Western Sun,* September 15 and 22, 1812; Logan Esarey, *A History of Indiana . . .* (2 volumes, Third edition, Fort Wayne, 1924), I, 221-222.

two thousand mounted riflemen raised in response to a request of Acting Governor John Gibson. They were unorganized and had been arriving in small groups over a period of eight or ten days. With the addition of Indiana militia, the expedition marched north from Vincennes to Fort Harrison, expecting to "clear out all the Indian tribes" along the Wabash and Illinois rivers. They proceeded north of the fort on October 15, but by the end of the fourth day the commander had lost control of his army and was forced to return to Vincennes without fighting a battle or seeing an Indian. As Hopkins discharged his men, he appealed for volunteers to go back and destroy Prophet's Town, which had been rebuilt following its destruction the year before. In command of some twelve hundred militia and a small force of regulars under Captain Taylor, he left Fort Harrison on November 11 and marched up the Wabash. His men demolished a large Kickapoo village, Prophet's Town, and a large Winnebago town as well as the food supplies therein. The Indians offered no resistance, but on succeeding days two small engagements were fought with bands of Indians. Sharp cold weather interrupted the campaign at this point and Hopkins led his men back to Vincennes.[65]

The final campaign of the year on Indiana soil was conducted against the Miami Indians by Col. John B. Campbell in December, 1812. He was sent by General Harrison from western Ohio with six hundred men, including United States troops, militia, mounted dragoons, and infantry. Both the men and horses suffered from the bitter cold weather. After they had destroyed three Indian villages on the Mississinewa River, the Indians made a surprise attack on their camp early in the morning of December 17. When daylight permitted

[65] Gibson to Secretary of War, October 14, 1812, in Carter (ed.), *Territorial Papers*, VIII, 209; Hopkins' correspondence in Esarey (ed.), *Harrison's Messages and Letters*, II, 162-163, 231-234; letters of Capt. Robert Hamilton in *Indiana Magazine of History*, XLIII (1947), 393-402; Dillon, *History of Indiana*, pp. 496-505; Vincennes *Western Sun*, September 29, October 6, 20, November 3, 1812.

his men to see their adversaries, the attack was repulsed with the loss of eight killed and forty-two wounded, some of whom later died. After the battle Campbell marched his forces slowly back to Ohio on account of the condition of the wounded men and the poor condition of others, some three hundred of whom were rendered unfit for duty by being frostbitten.[66]

With the arrival of spring, the Indians resumed their killing of isolated individuals and families, the theft of livestock, and the destruction of property. But no major massacres or campaigns occurred on the soil of Indiana in 1813. The Rangers were kept busy trying to prevent the Indians from raiding the settlements, or chasing them if they succeeded. Col. Joseph Bartholomew, commander in chief of the Indiana militia, led three companies of Rangers to the Delaware towns on the West Fork of White River in June, 1813. Col. William Russell at the head of some five hundred Rangers and volunteer militia, conducted a larger raid on the Mississinewa Indian towns, the Eel River village, Winamac's village, Prophet's Town, and the Winnebago town nearby on Wild Cat Creek, and returned by way of Fort Harrison. He did not see a single Indian on the campaign; the Indians had moved their families out of the territory while the warriors had followed Tecumseh to Canada to aid the British.[67]

Harrison resigned the governorship of Indiana Territory in a letter of December 28, 1812, to Secretary of State Mon-

[66] Dillon, *History of Indiana,* pp. 508-516; Esarey, *History of Indiana,* I, 223-224. The military units that participated in the battle and muster rolls of the same are in *Indiana History Bulletin,* XLV (1968), 152-166. A participant, William B. Northcutt, wrote an interesting account of the campaign, in "War of 1812 Diary, Part II," Kentucky Historical Society *Register,* LVI (1958), pp. 256-262.

[67] Cockrum, *Pioneer History of Indiana,* pp. 371-375; Dillon, *History of Indiana,* pp. 524-527; Esarey, *History of Indiana,* I, 227-228; reminiscences of John Ketcham in Esarey (ed.), *Harrison's Messages and Letters,* II, 274-284; Russell to Posey, July 25 and August 4, 1813, in *ibid.,* II, 497-499, 509-510.

roe.[68] He had been away from Vincennes for over six months during which time Secretary Gibson had been acting governor. Thomas Posey was appointed governor on March 3, 1813, and took over the office the following month.

As 1812 drew to a close, Harrison with the Northwestern army was struggling northward toward Detroit but got bogged down in the mud and swamps of northwestern Ohio. Winchester with one division spent the early part of the winter at the rapids of the Maumee. The people of Frenchtown (modern Monroe, Mich.) on the River Raisin appealed to him for protection against the Indians, and on January 14, 1813, he sent six hundred and fifty Kentucky militia to drive away the British forces. When this was accomplished with ease, he advanced with three hundred additional men and foolishly established his own headquarters some distance from the camp. Within easy striking distance were the British at Fort Malden. On January 22 the English stormed the American camp and took Winchester prisoner. The Indians massacred scores of the wounded Americans, and henceforth "Remember the River Raisin" became a battle cry. Realizing that he could not reach Detroit before spring, Harrison settled down in winter quarters at the rapids of the Maumee where he built Fort Meigs. Part of his troops were located at Forts Stephenson and Seneca on the Sandusky River. The British carried the war farther into American territory when they attacked Fort Meigs from April 28 to May 7, 1813, and Fort Stephenson at the end of July. They were repulsed, however, in both instances.[69]

68 Ewbank (ed.), *Laws of Indiana Territory, 1809-1816,* p. 819. The letter appeared in Cincinnati *Liberty Hall,* January 12, 1813, and in at least four other Ohio newspapers as well as in the Vincennes *Western Sun* of January 30, 1813, but it apparently was never received in Washington. Ewbank (ed.), *op. cit.,* 819n; Carter (ed.), *Territorial Papers,* VIII, 227n.

69 Correspondence of Harrison and others in Esarey (ed.), *Harrison's Messages and Letters,* II, 319-338, 431-444; Goebel, *Harrison,* pp. 155-161; Cleaves, *Old Tippecanoe,* pp. 132-171; Utter, *The Frontier State,* pp. 96-105; Prucha, *Sword of the Republic,* pp. 108-110.

Harrison was busy during the spring and summer raising and equipping an army which would be adequate for the invasion of Canada, for many of his troops of the previous year had returned home when their terms expired. At the eastern end of Lake Erie, Oliver Hazard Perry was building a little fleet with which he hoped to gain control of the lake. At Put-in-Bay on September 10 he met and defeated the small British fleet. Together Perry and Harrison ferried the latter's army across the lake to the vicinity of Fort Malden. Governor Isaac Shelby of Kentucky arrived with twelve mounted regiments to join the invasion. The British forces evacuated Detroit and Malden and fled eastward. Harrison overtook them on October 5 on the banks of the Thames. A Kentucky mounted regiment rode through the thin lines of the redcoats and then attacked the Indians under Tecumseh. Resistance of the tribesmen ceased when their famous leader was killed. Harrison had carried the war out of the United States and finally by defeating the British and their Indian allies in western Canada had brought peace to the northwestern frontier.[70]

The formality of negotiating a treaty of peace with the Indians was delegated to Harrison and Lewis Cass, the recently appointed governor of Michigan Territory, who were to meet the Indians at Greenville the first of July. The first instructions prepared for the treaty commissioners called for the attainment of a sincere and lasting peace, an alliance for the further prosecution of the war, and an additional land cession, but the last was dropped by President Madison after Harrison had convinced him that it would not be opportune to ask for a cession at this time. Also, the assistance of the Indians in the further prosecution of the war was to be obligatory only if specifically requested.

[70] Esarey (ed.), *Harrison's Messages and Letters,* II, 525-526, 539, 540-541, 557-565; Goebel, *Harrison,* pp. 178-183; Esarey, *History of Indiana,* I, 228-229; Prucha, *Sword of the Republic,* pp. 110-112.

As usual the Indians were slow in making their appearance, but finally some four thousand men, women, and children from eight tribes were assembled. On their arrival Harrison renewed his acquaintance with many of them whom he had not seen since 1811. When the council was finally opened on July 8, Harrison lighted the peace pipe and passed it around. A message from the President acknowledged the faithful war services of the Wyandots, Seneca, Delawares, and Shawnee, and four silver pipes were presented to the leading chiefs. In his opening address to the council, Harrison reviewed the events leading up to Tecumseh's confederacy; the Fort Wayne treaty was defended as open and just. The object of the present council, he said, was to bury the hatchet with those tribes who had been fighting with the British. The chiefs of these tribes were given an opportunity to recite their grievances, but when the Miami chief Charley said the Americans had drawn the first blood, both John Johnston and Cass interposed, and the Indians made no further rebuttal. After the chiefs of the Potawatomi, Wyandot, Miami, Wea, Kickapoo, and Ottawa had declared they would take up the American war hatchet, the council was ended and a war post erected around which the Indians conducted their war dances.[71]

The war in the West was only a small part of the larger conflict. While the Americans were experiencing defeat at Michilimackinac and Detroit in 1812, they were also suffering military reverses in the East. Gen. Henry Dearborn led an army of five thousand men along Lake Champlain toward Montreal in November only to have the militia refuse to cross the international boundary. In a campaign against Niagara in October the militia crossed into Canada to lay siege to Queenstown, and this time the regulars under Brig.

71 Goebel, *Harrison*, pp. 207-209; Cleaves, *Old Tippecanoe*, pp. 224-228; *American State Papers. Indian Affairs*, I, 827-836; Kappler (ed.), *Indian Affairs. Laws and Treaties*, II, 76. According to Goebel, the government never employed the northwestern Indians in offensive measures with any great success. The treaty was therefore largely an expression of good intentions.

Gen. Alexander Smyth refused to co-operate. The militia was driven back and forced to surrender. Similar efforts along the New York-Canadian border were unsuccessful except that General Dearborn seized York (Toronto) early in 1813, where some of his men unfortunately set fire to the government buildings. Only in the South was victory attained when Andrew Jackson in command of five thousand Tennessee militia advanced into the Alabama River Valley where he destroyed the towns of the Creek Indians and on March 27, 1814, administered a serious defeat to the Creeks at Horseshoe Bend.

More success was achieved in 1814 at Chippewa and Lundy's Lane on the Niagara front and on Lake Champlain where Capt. Thomas MacDonough's naval victory turned back an invading army of eleven thousand British. In the Chesapeake Bay region, however, disaster overtook the still unprepared American forces. A British army seized Washington on August 24 and burned the federal buildings. Far to the south an English expedition landed below New Orleans and on January 8, 1815, attacked the position of Gen. Andrew Jackson who had placed his forces between the enemy and the city. The British were repulsed with heavy losses; not until after the battle was it learned a treaty of peace had already been signed by representatives of Great Britain and the United States.

The Treaty of Ghent, signed on December 24, 1814, did not mention the maritime causes which earlier had stirred up a warlike fervor in the United States; with the close of the wars in Europe, these matters were relatively unimportant. Fighting was stopped, the conquests were returned, and a commission was provided to settle the disputed Canadian border; each nation was to make peace with the Indian tribes with whom they were at war.

It was in fulfillment of this last provision that the United States government in June, 1815, appointed William Henry Harrison, John Graham of the State Department, and Gen.

Duncan McArthur of Ohio as commissioners to meet the Indians and offer them a treaty of peace, at the same time obtaining a confirmation of all former treaties. Before receiving the formal instructions, Harrison feared the government would expect a land cession, in which case he anticipated a difficult time for a spirit of irritation and hostility still persisted between the whites and the red people. Among the former, he wrote, "scarcely anything is spoken of but a war of extermination even of those tribes who have remained faithful," while the Indians were "not in any disposition to grant anything that they can withhold."[72]

Representatives of the Chippewa, Ottawa, and Potawatomi, and of certain bands of Wyandot, Delaware, Seneca, Shawnee, and Miami were requested to meet the commissioners at Spring Wells near Detroit on August 25. Harrison had suggested Fort Wayne as the proper place for the treaty, but because of the difficulty of transporting supplies and provisions to that place the other site was chosen. When Harrison found that some of the chiefs had not arrived at the appointed place on the date set, he accused the British of detaining them at Amherstburg; however, the council was opened on August 31 and the treaty signed on September 8.

Inasmuch as many individuals belonging to the friendly tribes had taken up arms against the United States and because these tribes wished and expected to be made a party to the treaty, the commissioners decided to include them as well as the tribes that had been hostile. Harrison wrote that the commissioners had no difficulty in prevailing on the tribes to renew and confirm their former treaties with the United States and to acknowledge themselves once more under the protection of that government. Although the Shawnee Prophet and his followers left the council and retired to British territory before the treaty was signed, Harrison re-

---

[72] Harrison to A. J. Dallas, acting secretary of war, June 26 and July 14, 1815, in Indiana Historical Society Library.

ported they had professed a willingness to adhere to any treaty that was made. The wisdom of not pressing for a land cession at this time was borne out, for once peace was established it was only two years before a treaty at the Maumee rapids brought a cession of Ohio lands.[73]

For the West, the significance of the war lies in the defeat of the Indians which removed the last barrier to frontier expansion and in the rise of American nationalism, which brought a new interest in the West. The United States— and Indiana—were now free of European alliances; free to work out their own destinies.

[73] *American State Papers. Indian Affairs,* II, 13-25; Kappler (ed.), *Indian Affairs. Laws and Treaties,* II, 83. Other treaties of peace were negotiated with the Potawatomi, Kickapoo, Piankashaw, and other western tribes in 1815 and 1816 by William Clark, Ninian Edwards, and Auguste Chouteau, and one with the Wea and Kickapoo by Thomas Posey and Benjamin Parke in 1816. Kappler (ed.), *op. cit.,* II, 79-82, 90-91, 100-108; Esarey (ed.), *Harrison's Messages and Letters,* II, 732-733, 738-743.

CHAPTER XII

PREPARATION FOR STATEHOOD

The advances made toward democratization of the government during the first decade of the Indiana Territory were continued in the second decade and even during the war years. In response to petitions, Congress in 1809 had made the legislative councilors and delegate to Congress elective by the people. Then two years later property qualifications for voting were dropped and the franchise was extended to all free white adult males who had paid any kind of a territorial or county tax, and had resided in the territory for one year.[1]

The second session of the Third General Assembly (November 11-December 19, 1811) supplemented the above acts by passing two of its own which served to increase the number of voters still further. The first provided that all single men above the age of twenty-one without taxable property should be subject to a poll tax; and the second, regulating general elections, transferred the supervision of elections from the sheriffs to the judges of the court of common pleas and provided that a polling place should be opened in each township instead of having one in each county. The latter also changed the method of voting from oral to written ballot.[2] Undoubtedly, the increase in the number of polling places increased the number of voters.

---

[1] Kettleborough, *Constitution Making in Indiana,* I, 56, 58.

[2] Ewbank (ed.), *Laws of Indiana Territory, 1809-1816,* pp. 225-236, 278. The members of the House of Representatives in the 1811 session were: Thomas Downs, Clark County; James Dill, Dearborn County; John Templeton, Franklin County; William McFarland, Jefferson County; John Caldwell, Peter Jones, General Washington Johnston, Knox County; Richard Rue, Wayne County. William Hoggatt's election in Harrison County was contested by Dennis Pen-

Though the power exercised by the territorial legislature had gradually grown in the years since 1805, the Governor could still block legislation with his veto, and this Harrison exercised to prevent the removal of the capital to Madison and to prevent the creation of a new county out of Knox.[3]

A new tax law in 1811 provided for the appointment by the courts of common pleas of listers who were required to set down the name of each landowner, the number of acres owned, and whether they were first, second, or third rate. The tax rate to be set by the territorial auditor was not to exceed one cent an acre on first-rate land, three-fourths cent on second-rate, and one-half cent on third-rate.[4] Previously, taxes were based on the value of the land.

The law regarding taxes collected for county purposes was also changed at this session. For the first time billiard tables were to be taxed at thirty dollars each; persons selling imported merchandise were required to obtain a license; and the tax on mansion houses (country houses valued at over $200) was repealed and in its place a land tax was levied equal to one half of that levied for territorial purposes.[5]

On December 11, 1811, the House adopted, by a vote of four to three, a memorial to Congress asking for permission for the citizens of Indiana Territory to form a state constitution and be admitted to the Union. The dissenting votes were cast by Peter Jones of Knox County, James Dill of Dearborn, and Richard Rue of Wayne; a protest signed by the first two of these men was forwarded to Congress along with the memorial. Their principal objections were that the territory was too small, the population scattered, and expenditures under a state government would increase fourfold,

nington; the House decided that neither was entitled to a seat. *Journals of the General Assembly*, pp. 367n, 377-378. The members of the Legislative Council remained the same as in 1810 session.

[3] Ewbank (ed.), *Laws of Indiana Territory, 1809-1816*, p. 25; *Journals of the General Assembly*, pp. 450, 469-471.

[4] Ewbank (ed.), *op. cit.*, pp. 254-264.

[5] *Ibid.*, pp. 273-278.

adding to the woes of an already depleted treasury. The Congressional committee to whom the memorial and protest were referred reported in favor of admitting the territory to statehood when the population reached 35,000.[6] By the time the next Assembly met the territory was in such a dire financial condition that a reduction of taxes was called for. As a result the movement for statehood was temporarily shelved.

One of the subjects of conversation among the lawmakers was the arrival at Louisville on October 28 of the first steamboat to navigate the Ohio River. Built by Robert Fulton and his associates, the boat waited for high water to be able to pass over the Falls and then went on to New Orleans; not until four years later was a steamboat able to come up the Mississippi and Ohio rivers.[7] Another event that caused considerable conversation during the last days of the session was the earthquake that was felt in Vincennes and elsewhere in Indiana over several successive days.[8]

During the summer of 1812 the election for delegate to the Thirteenth Congress was held. Jennings' opponent this time was Waller Taylor, a Virginian whom Harrison had appointed chancellor of the territory in 1807. In announcing his candidacy, Taylor said he had never been an advocate of slavery other than to say it would be a present benefit but a future evil. Knowing that an immense majority of the residents of the territory opposed it, he pledged not only to refrain from taking any steps in favor of its introduction, but to oppose any measure brought forward by others. He promised to seek an amelioration of the land act, and said he favored the advance of the territory to statehood.[9] Jennings was again successful in his bid for re-election.

[6] *Journals of the General Assembly,* pp. 442-444n; Carter (ed.), *Territorial Papers,* VIII, 147-148.

[7] Ewbank (ed.), *Laws of Indiana Territory, 1809-1816,* p. 30; Archer B. Hulbert, *The Ohio River. A Course of Empire* (New York and London, 1906), pp. 331-334.

[8] Vincennes *Western Sun,* December 21, 1811, January 11 and 25, February 8, 15, and 22, 1812.

[9] Vincennes *Western Sun,* June 23, 1812.

In the election for the lower house of the territorial Assembly, held at the same time, only two members from the previous session, James Dill and William McFarland, were re-elected. New members were James Scott, Clark County; James Noble, Franklin County; David Robb, Daniel McClure, and Robert M. Evans, Knox County; and James Brown, Wayne County. Dennis Pennington, who had served in the 1810 session, was re-elected from Harrison. Members of the Legislative Council remained the same except John Johnson was elected to succeed William Jones of Knox, who had resigned.

In the absence of Governor Harrison, Acting Governor Gibson issued a proclamation on December 18, 1812, calling the first session of the Fourth General Assembly to meet the first day of February, 1813. By the time the legislature met, Governor Harrison had resigned but no successor had yet been appointed. In his brief address to the Assembly, Gibson referred to conditions created by the war: "Our former frontiers are now wilds and our inner Settlements have become frontiers." Of complaints concerning the militia law, Gibson felt the difficulty lay in the execution of the law rather than in the law itself; too many unqualified men were seeking commissions.[10]

Much of the legislation of the 1813 session reflected the financial plight caused by the war. There was a general bill for the relief of sheriffs and collectors as well as individual relief bills for these officials; there was also a memorial praying for an extension of time for land purchasers to make payments. The reports of the auditor and treasurer revealed that many tax collectors had been unable to collect the amounts due from taxpayers; no doubt some of them had left the territory. The balance in the treasury had reached a low of $2.47. A new tax measure was passed, combining into one the several acts establishing a permanent revenue. This made some changes in the tax levies. For example, the

10 *Journals of the General Assembly,* pp. 492-494.

land tax was reduced to 75 cents for one hundred acres of first-rate land and 50 cents and 25 cents, respectively, for second and third rate. On some items the tax was raised; for example, that on slaves or servants of color was doubled from $1.00 to $2.00, the tax on billiard tables was raised from $30 to $50, and that on horses could be as high as 37½ cents. County listers were replaced by township tax commissioners appointed by the court. Retail stores were to be taxed at $20, town lots at 50 cents on every $100 of their value, taverns not more than $20, and ferries not more than $10. The law of 1811 making it necessary to obtain a license to vend any articles manufactured outside the territory was repealed.

Various sites were discussed for a new capital, with Corydon in Harrison County being the final choice; two new counties (Gibson and Warrick) were formed out of Knox County.[11] The antislavery forces sponsored a bill more effectually to prevent the immigration of Negroes into the territory, but this was vetoed by Gibson.[12]

During the deliberations word was received of the defeat on January 23 of the Northwestern army at the River Raisin. Waves of fear swept over Indiana and legislators made plans for organizing new militia companies and of building new forts or repairing those erected earlier.[13] Gibson acted on this advice and ordered into immediate service sixteen com-

[11] Ewbank (ed.), *Laws of Indiana Territory, 1809-1816,* pp. 310, 329-330, 335-338, 339, 345-347, 348-350; *Journals of the General Assembly,* pp. 522-524. Corydon was to be the capital from and after May 1, 1813. The refusal of any public officer to remove the public records and papers in his charge was made punishable by a fine of not more than $1,200. Both the territorial auditor and treasurer, who were residents of Knox County, resigned their offices rather than remove to Corydon. A supplementary resolution allowed the governor and secretary to reside anywhere they chose within the bounds of the territory.

[12] *Journals of the General Assembly,* p. 592. A similar bill introduced at the following session failed of passage.

[13] *Ibid.,* pp. 512n-513n, 603-604n; Esarey (ed.), *Harrison's Messages and Letters,* II, 354-355.

panies of militia to be stationed in a line of blockhouses from one extreme of the territory to the other.[14]

To succeed William Henry Harrison as governor, President Madison appointed on March 3, 1813, Thomas Posey, a Virginian who had served in the American Revolution, lived for a time in Kentucky, then moved to Louisiana where in 1812 he was appointed to the United States Senate to fill a vacancy. He arrived at Jeffersonville on April 7. In a letter to Gibson, written from Washington a few days after his appointment, Posey said he understood there was some opposition to him in the Indiana Territory because he was from a slave state, and he wished to assure the people that he was opposed to slavery and had emancipated the few slaves that he had owned, and added: "I am sure I shall never sanction a law for slavery or any modification of it." He promised to attend strictly to his duties and "endeavor to make the people as happy as I am capable [of doing], paying strict attention to the general welfare of the Territory." He said he had not applied for the job and did not know of his appointment until it was confirmed by the Senate.[15]

Governor Posey's message to the second session of the Fourth General Assembly which met at Corydon on December 6, 1813, and continued until January 6, 1814, dealt mostly with the war in which recent British victories had wiped out American gains of the summer and fall. The Governor apparently had no misgivings of the eventual victory

[14] Gibson to Secretary of War, February 17, 1813, in Esarey (ed.), *op. cit.,* II, 362-363. Congress also made provision for the organization of four more companies of Rangers in the territory. *Ibid.,* II, 376-377. These probably replaced the militia as the short terms for which they were called out expired.

[15] Carter (ed.), *Territorial Papers,* VIII, 253-254; Posey to Secretary of War, March [May] 4, 1813, in Esarey (ed.), *Harrison's Messages and Letters,* II, 377; Posey to Gibson, March 13, 1813, English Collection, Indiana Historical Society Library. The territorial legislature had adopted a resolution requesting Congress not to appoint as governor anyone who favored slavery. Ewbank (ed.), *Laws of Indiana Territory, 1809-1816,* pp. 795-796.

of the United States for he suggested that that country should take and keep possession of both Upper and Lower Canada. In the way of legislation, he recommended revising both the militia and the judicial systems, and pointed out the need of better roads and the establishment of public schools.[16]

The first two of these recommendations occupied most of the time of the legislators. The inadequacies of the militia system as revealed during the past two years were remedied by a very comprehensive act. When the annual return of the militia in 1814 showed a total of 5,017 enrolled, the Governor recommended forming three divisions, six brigades, and twelve regiments. A major general for each division and a brigadier general for each brigade were to be appointed by the President and confirmed by the United States Senate after nomination by the governor. Heretofore the Indiana militia had served under Kentucky officers, which had been a source of complaint. However, when Governor Posey forwarded to the Secretary of War recommendations for the three major generals and six brigadier generals, he was informed that only one of the former and two of the latter would be appointed, and this was not done until 1816.[17] In addition to the militia law two memorials were sent to Congress regarding pay for the militia and Rangers who had served in the defense of the territory during the war.[18]

An attempt was made to improve the court system by creating circuit courts and requiring the territorial judges (appointed by the President) to serve as president judges of

[16] *Journals of the General Assembly,* pp. 690-693. There were four new members of the House at this session to replace those who had resigned: Isaac Dunn for James Dill of Dearborn; John Douthitt for James Scott of Clark; William Hendricks for William McFarland of Jefferson; and Isaac Montgomery for Robert M. Evans of Knox, Gibson, and Warrick. There were no changes in the Legislative Council.

[17] Ewbank (ed.), *Laws of Indiana Territory, 1809-1816,* pp. 60-63, 373-429; Esarey (ed.), *Harrison's Messages and Letters,* II, 630, 648-649, 685; U. S. Senate, *Executive Journal,* III, 23, 24.

[18] Ewbank (ed.), *Laws of Indiana Territory, 1809-1816,* pp. 797-798, 798-801.

these courts. The measure apparently was aimed at raising the caliber of the judiciary without increasing the financial burden of the territory. Congress was petitioned to pass an act requiring the federal judges to perform the duties which the territorial Assembly had assigned, but it did not comply and the courts were unable to function.[19]

The caliber of the judges was not the only handicap under which the courts were operating. In many instances court-houses had not yet been built and the courts had to meet in private homes or in some public building other than a court-house. Records also were kept in the homes of various officials and were sometimes lost or destroyed by fire, as in the case of Knox County deed records destroyed in 1814 while housed in the recorder's home. The lack of or the inadequacy of county jails often hindered the carrying out of the orders of the courts. The Knox County sheriff in 1813 protested that the want of a jail prevented him from executing the process directed to him; he had only one room in which both criminals and debtors were confined. In Wayne County the jail at Salisbury had neither chimney, stove, nor bed. If Dr. David F. Sackett of the town had not provided hot bricks, extra bedclothing, and hot coffee during extremely cold weather, some of the inmates might not have survived.[20]

[19] Jonathan Jennings, the territorial delegate, worked hard to obtain Congressional approval of the measure but it was judged by Congress to be unconstitutional. Benjamin Parke, who would have been president judge of the first circuit, gave as his reason for not complying that the territorial judges derived their jurisdiction and power from the federal government and therefore could not be controlled in the exercise of their duties by persons under the authority of the territorial government. Both the May and August terms of the Knox County courts were adjourned by the county sheriff, while in Washington County the associate judges alone held court in March, April, and May, 1814. Ewbank (ed.), *Laws of Indiana Territory, 1809-1816*, pp. 65-66n, 474-481, 801-802; *Journals of the General Assembly*, pp. 14, 617-618n; transcripts of records of the Knox and Washington County Circuit Courts, Archives Division, Indiana State Library.

[20] Minutes of the Knox County Court of Common Pleas, 1811-1813, p. 88; Knollenberg, *Pioneer Sketches of the Upper Whitewater Valley*, p. 41.

The Harrison County sheriff wrote to Governor Posey on February 9, 1814, that the jail in that county was such as to endanger the health of his prisoner in case he was held there until the meeting of the General Court. "If I furnish him with fire it must be done in a kettle and I then must have a guard (which will be expensive to County) for fear he might burn out" (the prisoner being charged with arson). The Franklin County sheriff reported in 1813 that the county jail was insufficient in point of strength and had no separate rooms for men and women.[21]

The beginnings of town government are depicted by acts passed at the 1813-14 session regulating the towns of Brookville, Charlestown, and Jeffersonville. The last two towns had been incorporated in 1807 and 1810, respectively; in the case of Jeffersonville the new act gave the trustees power to enact such bylaws and ordinances as were deemed necessary for the government of the town. By the 1810 act the members of the board of trustees of Charlestown were allowed to perpetuate themselves; this was apparently considered undemocratic and the new act named as trustees five persons different from the original trustees.[22] The act regulating the town of Brookville was very comprehensive, providing for a board of five trustees to serve until an election was held in 1815, and giving them power to levy and collect taxes (not exceeding $1.50 per annum on any one citizen), power to lay out and repair streets, remove nuisances and obstructions, erect a market house, and keep the public well in repair.[23]

Brookville had been platted in 1808, but because of legal difficulties over the ownership of the land the first lots were not sold until three years later. By that time it had become the county seat of the new county of Franklin which boasted

---

[21] Ewbank (ed.), *Laws of Indiana Territory, 1809-1816,* p. 32n.

[22] *Ibid.,* pp. 140-142, 463-466, 473-474; Philbrick (ed.), *Laws of Indiana Territory, 1801-1809,* pp. 564-566.

[23] Ewbank (ed.), *op. cit.,* pp. 437-442.

467 taxpayers in 1811. During the War of 1812 the population of the town and county had declined but with the end of the war settlers once more flocked into the Whitewater Valley. By 1815 the county had a population of 7,370 and 1,430 voters; Brookville being the only town would have had a fair share of these.[24] Repeated attempts were made at this session to remove the capital from Corydon but to no avail. Madison, Charlestown, Salem, Vincennes, Jeffersonville, and Columbia (the present Patoka) were all mentioned as possible locations.[25]

The financial condition of the territory had not improved any over the previous session, but the committee to which the reports of the auditor and treasurer were referred blamed part of it on the former auditor, William Prince, who had not collected the taxes from two counties. A resolution was passed requiring him to come forward and straighten out the accounts before the following June or suit would be brought against him and his securities.[26]

The growing population in the area north of Corydon led to the formation on December 21 of the new county of Washington out of Clark, Harrison, and Jefferson counties; com-

[24] August J. Reifel, *History of Franklin County, Indiana* . . . (Indianapolis, 1915), pp. 97-101; Kettleborough, *Constitution Making in Indiana,* I, 69.

[25] See Index to *Journals of the General Assembly* under names of these towns. The retention of the capital at Corydon no doubt depended in part upon the ability and willingness of Harrison County citizens to furnish suitable quarters for the territorial officers and meetings of the General Assembly. A courthouse had not yet been built and the legislators were apparently using the same temporary building that the court was using on lot 12. In May, 1814, the Harrison County Court appointed trustees to let out the building of a stone or brick courthouse on the public square. Dennis Pennington, a member of the House of Representatives, received the contract for the stone work, and John Smith the contract for the wood and carpenter work; the total cost of the building was nearly $3,000. The building continued to be used by the state until the removal of the capital to Indianapolis at the end of 1824; its original features have been restored and it is now a state memorial. *The Corydon State Capitol. A State Memorial* (Indiana Department of Conservation, n.d.).

[26] *Journals of the General Assembly,* pp. 684-685; Ewbank (ed.), *Laws of Indiana Territory, 1809-1816,* pp. 508-509.

missioners appointed to designate the county seat chose the town of Salem. A revision of the 1811 act regulating elections provided for additional safeguards against fraud and for the restoration of oral voting.[27]

The bill that was introduced to prevent dueling was no doubt prompted by two recent duels in which Parmenas Beckes, sheriff of Knox County, and Lieut. Thomas H. Richardson of the United States Army were killed. As enacted the bill required all civil and military officers, members of the legislature, and attorneys, to take an oath that they had not participated in a duel after February 1, 1814, nor carried a challenge to any person to engage in one.[28]

There had been no reapportionment of the Legislative Council since 1809 when Knox County had been given two members, Harrison, Clark, and Dearborn each one. Since then the counties of Gibson, Warrick, Washington, Jefferson, Franklin, and Wayne had been organized and unless a reapportionment was made prior to the election of councilors in August, 1814, half of the territory would be unrepresented in the Council. Governor Posey, believing that the federal law of 1809 under which Governor Harrison had divided the territory into five districts for the election of councilors permitted him to do likewise, made a reapportionment. The Legislative Council protested his action in a resolution to Congress and the committee appointed to consider the matter reported that the law of 1809 was a special act and could not apply after once used. It was the opinion of the committee that the House of Representatives should redistrict the territory and a bill to that effect was introduced and passed. Governor

27 Ewbank (ed.), *op. cit.,* pp. 446-448, 488-494.

28 *Ibid.,* pp. 442-445. Beckes was challenged by Dr. Edward Scull and Richardson by Irwin Wallace. Vincennes *Western Sun,* July 10, 1816. An earlier bill to prevent dueling passed both houses of the legislature at the 1811 session but apparently the Governor did not sign it. *Journals of the General Assembly,* pp. 383, 387-388, 391, 407, 409, 414. As a result of the new law, Elliott Herndon was fined $50 at the May 1814 term of the Franklin County Circuit Court for challenging James Noble to fight a duel. Minute Book, August, 1813–October, 1814, p. 69. Noble was serving as prosecuting attorney during that term.

Posey then called the House to meet in special session on June 1, 1814, at which time the ten counties were grouped into five districts as follows: Knox and Washington, Harrison and Clark, Gibson and Warrick, Franklin and Wayne, and Dearborn and Jefferson. The legislature had reapportioned the House at the 1813-14 session, each of the ten counties to have one representative.[29]

In addition to members of the General Assembly, a delegate to Congress was also to be elected on August 1, 1814. Jennings again announced his candidacy and won an easy victory over Elijah Sparks of Dearborn County who had been serving as attorney for the United States in the territory during the past year. Apparently there were no particular issues involved: Sparks stated only that his ambition was "to assist in raising up & establishing the equal rights of man—of all men, above the iron grasp of tyranny, the yoak of despotism, and the drudgery of oppression," while Jennings pointed to his record of service during his four and a half years as delegate.[30]

The failure of Congress to act favorably upon the petition asking that the territorial judges be required to submit to the authority of the legislature and the consequent breakdown of the local judiciary system caused Governor Posey to call the legislature back into session on August 15, 1814, instead of the first Monday in December as provided at the previous session.[31] A bill establishing circuit courts was introduced

[29] *Journals of the General Assembly*, pp. 743-753n; Ewbank (ed.), *Laws of Indiana Territory, 1809-1816*, pp. 454-456. Members of the House elected in August, 1814, were: Alexander Buckner, Ezra Ferris, James Noble, James Smith, Dennis Pennington, William Hendricks, William Polke, Ratliff Boon, Marston G. Clark, and James Brown; for the Legislative Council: Jesse L. Holman, John Test, David Robb, John Harbison, and John Johnson. Buckner's election was contested by Charles Beggs; the House declared the seat vacant and in a new election, Beggs was successful. *Journals of the General Assembly*, pp. 754, 759-760n.

[30] Vincennes *Western Sun*, June 11 and July 23, 1814; Dunn, *Indiana*, p. 418.

[31] Posey issued his proclamation from Jeffersonville on July 16; the election for the General Assembly was August 1, giving the members little time to prepare for the session. Esarey (ed.), *Harrison's Messages and Letters*, II, 657.

immediately and fifteen days later was enacted into law. This divided the territory into three circuits, each to be presided over by a circuit judge appointed and commissioned by the governor to hold office during good behavior, at a salary of $700 per year. In each county two associate judges, to be appointed in the same manner for like terms, were to assist in holding court. The new courts were given much more extensive criminal jurisdiction than that possessed by the courts of common pleas. Whereas the latter had no cognizance over offenses where the punishment extended to life, limb, or imprisonment for more than a year, the circuit courts were given jurisdiction "over all crimes and misdemeanors of whatsoever nature or kind" that might be committed in the territory.[32]

Supplementary acts passed at this session concerned the method of transferring business from the former courts of common pleas to the new courts, and the time of holding the circuit courts and regulating practice in them. The 1807 act creating a chancery court was now repealed and its business transferred to the circuit courts.[33]

To do away with the confessed "collision and jarring" between the Assembly and the judiciary, Congress was asked to define more specifically the powers and jurisdiction of the judges of the General Court. It was pointed out that under the existing law one of the judges was competent to hold a court and decide a principle or point of law, but at the next term, if the other two judges were present they might reverse the decision of the first judge, thus creating confusion. No federal provision had ever been made as to where and when courts were to be held, or in what manner they were to conduct their business. In response to the memorial, the Congress passed an act setting the time for the meeting of the

---

[32] Ewbank (ed.), *Laws of Indiana Territory, 1809-1816,* pp. 517-522; statement of Isaac Blackford in Vincennes *Western Sun,* June 24, 1815.

[33] Ewbank (ed.), *op. cit.,* pp. 523-525, 557-559, 567-573, 573-585.

General Court and providing that it be composed of at least two judges.[34]

On September 14, 1814, Governor Posey appointed Isaac Blackford, Jesse L. Holman, and Elijah Sparks as presiding judges of the first, second, and third circuits, respectively. Following Sparks's death early in 1815, James Noble was appointed in his place. In speaking to the grand jury at the opening of the circuit court at Vincennes on June 5, 1815, Blackford reminded them that possessed with such great authority over the lives and liberties of their fellow men, the court should "act with great circumspection—with no other object, but the distribution of impartial justice—with no other zeal, but for the promotion of virtue, by the punishment of vice." Referring to recent disorderly meetings held in Vincennes, Blackford told the grand jury, "their suppression depends in a great degree upon the vigilance & firmness of the conservators of the peace; if these officers do their duty, and are protected and supported by the people, we shall seldom hear of riots & unlawful assemblies." He went on to say:

Where are the advantages of the most regular and best organized governments, if the peace and good order of society cannot be preserved?— Where are the benefits of the most excellent and perfect laws, if obedience to them cannot be enforced? In vain will peace officers use their exertions in protecting the rights of the community, if that community will not assist in their protection. . . . They have a difficult and unprofitable, a dangerous & unthankful task to perform. . . . Hence it is the bounden duty of every person to fly to the assistance of a peace officer when required, and it is the bounden duty of a grand jury to indict those who refuse or neglect the summons. . . .[35]

Three more counties were created by the legislature in 1814—Posey, Perry, and Switzerland—indicating a continued growth in population. The number of days that any person might be compelled to work on the highways (except in

34 *Ibid.*, pp. 808-810; Kettleborough, *Constitution Making in Indiana*, I, 60.
35 Vincennes *Western Sun*, June 24, 1815.

payment of a "land tax") was now reduced from twelve days per year to five "unless a new road is to be opened," when one might have to work ten days.[36]

Private acts passed at this session included those organizing banks at Vincennes and Madison, and incorporating the borough of Vincennes, the Corydon Seminary, and the Literary Society of Vevay. The Bank of Vincennes and the Farmers' and Mechanics' Bank of Madison were each to have a capital stock of $500,000; in the Vincennes Bank this was divided into 5,000 shares at $100 each and in the Madison bank, 10,000 shares at $50 each. The amount of debts contracted was not to exceed double the amount of money deposited. Shares to the amount of $125,000 were to be reserved for the territory, to be subscribed at such times as the legislature might direct, and in turn the territory could draw on the banks for loans or the payment of salaries. However, on the same day that Governor Posey signed the two bank acts, he signed a joint resolution to suspend the subscription for any shares in the two banks until further requested by the legislature, and providing that the treasurer not call for any loans from the banks until ordered to do so by the governor.[37] No further action was taken concerning the banks at the next session; Article X of the Constitution of 1816 provided for their continuation under the new state government.

A memorial to Congress asked a further extension of time in which to make payments on land purchased since 1810 due to conditions created by the war. Congress was also requested to subdivide the quarter sections or reduce the price of those of inferior quality. This latter request was not granted but Congress did extend the time for making payments on lands purchased between April, 1810 and April, 1811.[38]

---

[36] Ewbank (ed.), *Laws of Indiana Territory*, pp. 529-533, 538-542, 566-567.

[37] *Ibid.*, pp. 729-731, 732-734, 735-737, 747-763, 805-806.

[38] *Ibid.*, pp. 806-808; *Journals of the General Assembly*, p. 766n.

There was little or no opposition to a joint resolution requiring the listers of taxable property in the several counties
to make a list of the free inhabitants as well as a list of
the free males above the age of twenty-one. These results
were to be transmitted to the following Assembly, and paved
the way for the advance to statehood. The certified statement of the census as submitted to the Assembly was as
follows:[39]

Counties	White Males of 21 and upwards	Total Number
Wayne	1,225	6,407
Franklin	1,430	7,370
Dearborn	902	4,424
Switzerland	377	1,832
Jefferson	874	4,270
Clark	1,387	7,150
Washington	1,420	7,317
Harrison	1,056	6,975
Knox	1,391	8,068
Gibson	1,100	5,330
Posey	320	1,619
Warrick	280	1,415
Perry	350	1,720*
	12,081	63,897

The organization of a theatrical society by the young men
of Vincennes in the fall of 1814 indicates at least a measure
of relaxation from the war which had demanded their attention for several years; two dancing schools were also adver-

* No record received from lister of Perry County, but the representative of
that county says he had the number above stated from good authority.

39 Ewbank (ed.), op. cit., pp. 587-588. The results of the census are taken
from Kettleborough, Constitution Making in Indiana, I, 69. The following
variant figures are given in a document in the English Papers, Indiana
Historical Society Library: Jefferson County, 873; Clark, 1,357; total for
Harrison, 5,775. The Journals of the General Assembly, pp. 838, 839, 848,
893, give 4,286 as the total for Jefferson County, 7,315 for Washington, and
1,308 for Warrick, and total number of white males, 12,111. The document in
the English Collection gives the total number of inhabitants as 62,697.

tised. The first performance of the former was held on November 21, 1814, at Mr. Withers' Inn when the comedy, "She Stoops to Conquer," plus a farce "Miss In Her Teens" were given. Curtain time was 6:00 P.M.; the price per seat, $1.00. After four performances over a period of five months, the society listed their expenditures and receipts showing a deficit of $2.58. Apparently interest was dwindling, leaving members no alternative but to bid goodby to acting. Perhaps one of the reasons for the society's failure was the refusal to give the young ladies of the town any of the roles. Another form of diversion for a limited number of the male population of Vincennes would have been the meetings of the Masonic Lodge. General Washington Johnston had been instrumental in getting a charter for the local group in 1809 from the Grand Lodge of Kentucky.[40]

The last session of the territorial Assembly met from December 4 through 28, 1815, including Christmas Day. New members of the House elected since the last session were David Mount, Franklin County; Christopher Harrison, Jefferson; Joseph Holman, Wayne; Elisha Golay, Switzerland; and Peter Wilkinson, Posey and Perry; the last two men were from counties newly organized. In the Legislative Council, Solomon Manwaring replaced Jesse L. Holman and James Noble replaced John Test. For the first time the Governor did not appear in person to present his message but had it read. He congratulated the members on the termination of the war which in turn was bringing a new tide of immigration into the state. He recommended that these newcomers be taxed moderately because of the expense to which they had been subject by the change of residence. With the return to peaceful pursuits, the Governor thought it a favorable time for the legislators to turn their attention to the

---

[40] Vincennes *Western Sun,* September 3, October 15, November 19, 1814; January 7, April 1, and 8, 1815; George R. Wilson, "General Washington Johnston," *Indiana Magazine of History,* XX (1924), 145, 149, 150.

promotion of education and the improvement of roads and highways.[41]

Regarding the taxing of immigrants, the House committee to which the recommendation was referred resolved that it was neither just nor expedient to make any distinction between early and late immigrants.[42] A supplementary act was passed for opening and repairing roads which further reduced the period of compulsory work on roads to two days except on new roads which required an additional two days. For the upkeep of roads, a tax equal to one half of the territorial tax was to be levied upon lands, stores, and other objects of taxation. Persons might work out their road tax if they preferred.[43]

Several additional acts were passed incorporating and regulating towns; these included Vincennes, Salisbury, Vevay, Centerville, Lexington, and Lawrenceburg. The act concerning the last town was the only one which committed to a vote of the inhabitants all questions concerning the town's government, including the question of incorporation, thus reflecting the New England background of some of its residents. The borough of Vincennes was empowered to levy and collect additional taxes of not more than $5.00 on each four-wheeled, and $2.00 on each two-wheeled "Pleasure Carriage"; $1.00 on each deck of cards; $15 on billiard tables; 50 cents on swine running at large; $1.00 on each dog; $5.00 on each horse race; $5.00 on each ball alley, and $10 on each retail store.[44] Two more counties were organized at this session, Jackson and Orange, which brought the total number of territorial counties to fifteen.

The measure in which the majority of the legislators as well as a majority of the citizens was most interested was the memorial to Congress praying that an election be ordered

---

[41] *Journals of the General Assembly*, pp. 839-841.

[42] *Ibid.*, p. 845.

[43] Ewbank (ed.), *Laws of Indiana Territory, 1809-1816*, pp. 608-616.

[44] *Ibid.*, pp. 79-80, 82.

to choose delegates to a convention, which could proceed with the formation of a state constitution if the majority so agreed. Since the returns of the recent census showed that the population of the territory exceeded sixty thousand, the number stipulated in the Ordinance of 1787 as requisite for statehood, that part of the memorial was almost certain to be granted. But the legislators also asked that certain land grants be accorded the state for educational purposes and for a future state capital, that all coal mines and salt licks be reserved, and that 7 per cent of all moneys received from the sale of public lands after April 1, 1816, be returned to the state, to be used "in such way as may be judged most conducive to the General welfare."[45]

Following the adjournment, Governor Posey wrote a personal letter to the Secretary of State in opposition to the petition for statehood, claiming that at least two thirds or perhaps three fourths of the people could contribute but little to the support of a state government and that there would be a great scarcity of men of talent to fill the necessary offices. However, since Posey was at the same time soliciting a reappointment as territorial governor for another three years, it is understandable that he would prefer that the territorial government continue.[46]

In response to the memorial for statehood, Congress passed an Enabling Act on April 19, 1816, providing for an election on the second Monday in May of delegates who were to meet a month later to determine whether or not a majority of them were in favor of statehood; if it were so agreed, they were authorized to form a constitution. Congress further complied with the memorial by granting a township of

[45] Ibid., pp. 812-814; Kettleborough, Constitution Making in Indiana, I, 68-72.

[46] Carter (ed.), Territorial Papers, VIII, 380. Posey was reappointed governor on February 15, 1816, for a new three-year term, but this was cut short on November 7, 1816, with the inauguration of Jonathan Jennings as governor of the new state. For other objections to statehood see Donald F. Carmony, "Fiscal Objection to Statehood," Indiana Magazine of History, XLII (1946), 317-320.

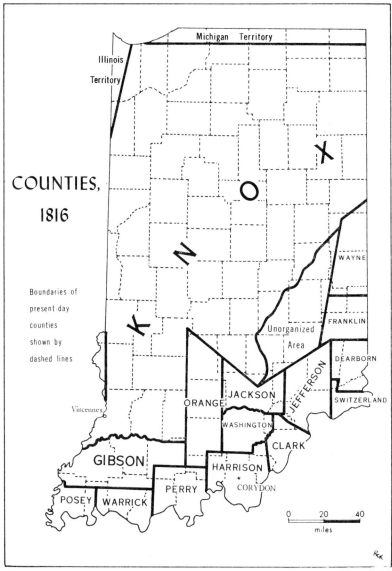

COUNTIES, 1816

Michigan Territory

Illinois Territory

K N O X

WAYNE

Boundaries of present-day counties shown by dashed lines

FRANKLIN

Unorganized Area

DEARBORN

JEFFERSON

Vincennes

ORANGE

JACKSON

SWITZERLAND

WASHINGTON

CLARK

GIBSON

HARRISON

CORYDON

PERRY

POSEY WARRICK

0   20   40
miles

Kingsbury, *An Atlas of Indiana* (1970)

land for a college, in addition to the one previously granted for an academy, by reserving section 16 in each township for the use of schools, by granting four sections for a state capital, and by reserving the salt springs; instead of the 7 per cent of the net proceeds from the sale of lands only 3 per cent was granted to the state, and this was to be used for public roads and canals. An additional 2 per cent was to be used by the federal government on roads leading to the state. One gain, not requested in the memorial, was the moving of the northern boundary of the territory to a point ten miles north of a line running through the southerly extreme of Lake Michigan. All of the grants were made on the condition that the state should not tax for five years any land sold within its bounds after December 1, 1816.[47]

Those who objected to statehood for fiscal reasons had a valid point for the federal government had been bearing over half the expenses of the territorial government.[48] During the first or nonrepresentative stage, territorial costs averaged about $5,700 annually with all but $200 being provided by the federal government. This sum represented the salaries of the governor ($2,000), secretary ($750), three judges ($800 each), and a contingent fund of $350 which covered in part the costs of postage, rent, printing, and legal processes. The salary of judges was increased to $1,200 in 1807 and a year later that of the secretary to $1,000. Legislative expenses increased the cost of territorial government to about $10,000 annually, but this increase was borne by the territorial treasury. The total costs for the fifteen-plus years of territorial government would have been less than $100,000,

[47] Kettleborough, *Constitution Making in Indiana,* I, 72-77; *Indiana's Road to Statehood,* pp. 64-67. The original bill as reported by Jennings, the territorial delegate, designated the northern boundary of the proposed state to be a line running east and west through the extreme southern tip of Lake Michigan. At what stage of the bill's process the change was made is not known. For a discussion of the subject, see Mrs. Frank J. Sheehan, *The Northern Boundary of Indiana* (Indiana Historical Society *Publications,* VIII, No. 6, Indianapolis, 1928), pp. 293-301.

[48] For a detailed study of territorial expenditures, see Donald F. Carmony, "Indiana Territorial Expenditures, 1800-1816," *Indiana Magazine of History,* XXXIX (1943), 237-262.

John Gibson
Secretary, 1800-1816

Thomas Posey
Governor, 1813-1816

Corydon Capitol, 1815-1825

not counting the sums appropriated for treaty negotiations, Indian annuities, and federal troops stationed in the territory.

On the credit side of the ledger, the sale of public lands through the Vincennes and Jeffersonville land offices during the territorial period netted approximately $2,400,000; this does not take into account the lands in the southeastern part of the state that were sold through the Cincinnati Land Office.[49] Under the credit system of land purchases, five years were allowed in which to complete payments. During the war years, many settlers found themselves unable to make their payments and their land reverted to the government. During the year 1812-13 in the Vincennes Land Office District, the number of acres that reverted exceeded the amount sold.[50]

The chief attraction for immigrants following the war was the Harrison land purchase of 1809 consisting of over two million acres lying north of Vincennes and intersected by the Wabash and the two branches of the White River. The surveying of this land had been halted by the refusal of the Indians to allow the surveyors to enter the purchase and then by the war, but with the close of hostilities settlers began moving in before the land was ready for sale. When finally put on the market there was a big rush at the Vincennes and Jeffersonville offices.[51] Half of the area of the new counties of Orange and Jackson, organized in December, 1815, lay within the Harrison purchase of 1809.

Beginning in 1814, the federal government collected internal duties or excise taxes in the Indiana Territory in the form of licenses for stills and boilers used in distilling spir-

[49] See Reports of the Commissioner of the General Land Office, 1806-1816, in *American State Papers. Finance,* Vols. II and III; Malcolm J. Rohrbough, *The Land Office Business . . . 1789-1837* (New York, 1968), pp. 130-131.

[50] *American State Papers. Finance,* II, 657.

[51] Rohrbough, *The Land Office Business,* p. 131. At the sale of lots at Terre Haute in November, 1816, lots valued at $21,000 were sold the first day. Vincennes *Western Sun,* November 9, 1816.

ituous liquors and on licenses to retailers of the same. These amounted to about $11,200 for the period from 1814 to 1816. Then beginning in 1815, taxes were also levied on the manufacture of such items as hats, leather and leather goods, saddles and bridles, tobacco and snuff, and spirituous liquors. These should have brought in an additional revenue of about $7,000, but not all of it could be collected.[52]

The establishment of towns in Indiana Territory would make an interesting study which can only be touched on here. Richard C. Wade, urban historian, believes that many settlers migrated West in search of promising towns rather than good land, and town proprietors competed for these migrants by advertising in glowing colors the opportunities offered by their particular village.[53] Most of the West's young cities owed their initial success to commerce and since the Ohio River was the chief artery of trade and travel, Cincinnati and Louisville became early trading centers; in Indiana Territory the founders of Lawrenceburg, Vevay, Madison, Jeffersonville, and New Albany chose sites on that stream. As these commercial centers grew, some inhabitants turned to manufacturing. Other towns came in existence as sites for county seats, for example, Brookville, Salisbury, Centerville, Salem, Corydon, Charlestown, Princeton, and Troy. In some instances towns grew up around mills.

[52] See the revenue acts of 1813 and 1814 in U. S. *Statutes at Large,* III, 82-84, 180-186; and Reports of the Secretary of the Treasury, in *American State Papers. Finance,* II, 361-365; III, 44-51, 210, 216-217. Allan D. Thom was appointed collector of internal revenue in December, 1813, and inserted a notice in the Vincennes *Western Sun* of January 1, 1814, regarding the federal duties. The manuscript volume in which he kept the record of the amounts collected and by whom paid has been preserved and is in the Archives Division, Indiana State Library.

[53] Richard C. Wade, "Urban Life in Western America, 1790-1830," *American Historical Review,* LXIV (1958), 14-30. See advertisements of towns in Vincennes *Western Sun,* March 12, 1814 (Princeton), July 2 (Evansville), September 24 (Darlington); July 1, 1815 (Busseron), and July 29 (New London); in Armstrong Papers, Indiana Historical Society Library, November 1, 1815 (Bethlehem).

Life in these towns differed but little from that in the country. They consisted of groups of houses sprawling at intervals along a road or street that was full of stumps and seasonal mud holes, weeds, dust, and garbage. Most of the houses were log, but there were some unpainted frame houses and a few painted ones. Only a very few early settlers were able to build brick homes.[54]

Towns founded by special groups for a specific purpose were the Shaker community on Busseron Creek in northern Knox County and the Rappite community in Posey County. The beginning of the Shaker movement dates back to 1756 when a young English woman named Ann Lee made her deep beliefs and convictions known to others. A group of her followers came to New York on the eve of the Revolution and from there spread into Ohio and Kentucky; the Indiana settlement founded in 1805 was an offshoot of one in Ohio. During the War of 1812 the members left the state, then returned after the war and remained until 1827. At its peak, membership of the community numbered approximately two hundred. Because of their beliefs in celibacy and communal living they were regarded as queer but in time they came to be respected for their art of building and their abilities in agriculture and in the crafts. The products of their saw- and gristmills, their orchards, and especially their furniture came to be known throughout the settled portion of the state. Shaker-made chests and tables are much sought after even today.[55]

[54] Buley, *The Old Northwest,* I, 235-239. In addition to the Harrison Mansion at Vincennes, Isaac White, a friend of Governor Harrison, was in the process of building a brick home on his farm several miles from Vincennes at the time of the Tippecanoe campaign; he enlisted and lost his life in the battle. The house was still standing in 1935, though badly in need of repair. George Rapp built a brick home for himself at Harmony in 1815 and another was the two-story brick built by Jacob Conrad at the edge of Corydon in 1809 which was used as a tavern. Burns, *Early Architects and Builders of Indiana,* pp. 184-185, 188, 189-190.

[55] Marcia Sue Hodges, "The Shakers," copy of typed MS in Indiana State Library.

The Harmony Society, commonly called Rappites, sold their original settlement in Harmony, Pennsylvania, and purchased nearly 25,000 acres of land in what is now Posey County, Indiana, in 1814, with the entire community moving to the location in 1815. The settlement, numbering between seven and eight hundred persons, was led by George Rapp, a native of Germany. The Society believed "it was their destiny to set an . . . example of the harmony of human relations, the natural coöperative economy of the community of goods, and the peaceful reign of Christian fellowship under such conditions; so that other communities observing this marvel of communal life, would gradually be led to adopt a similar policy." The members followed the custom of celibacy; however, marriage was not disdained for those members who did not favor the celibate way of life.

The thrifty, industrious people quickly created a thriving agricultural and industrial community, along with the construction of numerous substantial homes and public buildings, some of which still stand. In 1824 the Society decided to move again to a new site in Pennsylvania at the present Economy. Harmony, Indiana, was sold to Robert Owen, who renamed it New Harmony.[56]

The first post office established in Indiana Territory was at Vincennes in 1800; the trace between there and Louisville had been approved as a postal route that year which meant there would be a regular weekly service between the two points, the charge would be at a fixed rate according to the distance, and the government would share the responsibility of keeping up the road over which the mail was carried. In the first year of service the entire postage received by the government was $85.49, while the cost to the government

[56] George B. Lockwood, *The New Harmony Communities* (Marion, Ind., 1902), pp. 19-57; Don Blair, *Harmonist Construction* (Indiana Historical Society *Publications*, XXIII, No. 2, Indianapolis, 1964), pp. 46. 81. The Indiana Historical Society is planning to publish in the near future a Documentary History of the Harmony Society, Indiana Decade, 1814-1824, compiled and edited by Dr. Karl J. R. Arndt.

was $600. The route was extended to Kaskaskia the following year.

In 1803 a second post office was opened at Jeffersonville and a third at Corydon in 1809. Between 1812 and 1816 a number of additional postal routes were established and mail service was opened as far north as Salisbury in Wayne County, Vallonia and Brownstown in Jackson County, and White Oak Springs in Pike. Bad weather, accidents, Indian attacks, illness, drunkenness, and willful neglect by post riders frequently upset the schedules and brought complaints of poor service.[57]

Other than the *Indiana Gazette*, published from 1804 to 1806, and its successor, the Vincennes *Western Sun* which began publication in 1807, there were no other newspapers in the territory until the summer of 1813 when the *Western Eagle* was begun at Madison by Seth M. Levenworth and William Hendricks. After about four months this partnership was dissolved and the paper was issued by Hendricks and Camron. Then in April, 1814, Jacob Rhoads and William Camron appear as publishers. During the last half of 1815 it was published at Lexington. The last issue to appear was on January 6, 1816.[58] The *Cornucopia of the West* was published for a few months during the summer of 1816 at Lexington by D. T. Madox, but no issues have survived. The earliest paper at Brookville was the *Plain Dealer*, apparently begun during the fall of 1816. Its third number is dated November 5 of that year, printed by Benjamin Ogle, Jr., for Bethuel F. Morris. Although Corydon became the territorial capital in 1813, it did not have a newspaper until 1815 or possibly 1816; this was the short-lived *Indiana Herald* published by a Mr. Cox and Reuben E. Nelson. It was succeeded by the *Indiana Gazette* which was started appar-

[57] Howard Peckham, "Mail Service in Indiana Territory," *Indiana Magazine of History*, XLVII (1951), 155-164.

[58] The Indiana Historical Society Library has an incomplete file of the *Western Eagle*.

ently in November, 1816, by Armstrong Brandon and John Lodge. The only other territorial newspaper was the Vevay *Indiana Register* established by William C. Keen, the first issue probably being June 17, 1816.[59]

In the brief span of ten years during which the Indiana Territory was under a semirepresentative type of government, great strides had been made in liberalizing the provisions of the Ordinance of 1787 to allow more participation by the people. The territorial legislature had asserted its rights to be heard and soon was dominated by the group that was critical of the actions of the governor and in time became the dominant branch of government. The efforts of the governor and his friends to circumvent Article VI of the Ordinance of 1787 and to legalize slave or semislave labor in order to attract settlers from the planter class of Kentucky and other southern states was also defeated, thus assuring that Indiana would enter the Union as a free state.

[59] Donald F. Carmony, "The Pioneer Press in Indiana," *Indiana History Bulletin,* XXXI (1954), 185-210; Clarence S. Brigham, "Bibliography of American Newspapers, 1690-1920," American Antiquarian Society *Proceedings,* XXIII (1913), 398-403.

CHAPTER XIII

THE CONSTITUTIONAL CONVENTION

Though there was some opposition among the citizens of Indiana Territory to the formation of a state government in 1816, it was minor. The advance to statehood was considered as the normal procedure, the capstone of the territorial structure; the only question was whether the people were ready for it at this particular time. Statehood promised to bring to a victorious conclusion the long struggle of the anti-Harrison or Jennings party to democratize the territorial government and to do away with slavery. Citizens of the new state would be able to elect their highest officials rather than have them appointed by the federal government; they would make their own laws without the possibility of an absolute veto by a governor they did not choose. In addition to local self-government, they would be able to participate in national affairs, and they were very conscious at this time of the importance of national policies respecting the Indians, defense, and the disposal of the public lands. And considering the situation realistically, as politicians are wont to do, it would mean more offices to be filled.

News of the passage of the Enabling Act by Congress on April 19 reached Vincennes on May 2 and was published in the Vincennes *Western Sun* two days later. This left only nine days before the date stipulated in the act for the election of delegates to the convention. However, since passage of an enabling act in some form was almost a foregone conclusion, those interested in becoming delegates had no doubt communicated orally, if not in writing, their willingness to serve. Jennings wrote from Washington as early as February 7 that he "should be gratified to be in the convention," and about the same time William Hendricks was writing in

Indiana that in his opinion "no country ever presented more candidates for its population, than does Indiana, to lay the foundation of our proposed State fabrick."[1]

A letter from "A Citizen of Gibson," which appeared in the *Western Sun* on March 2, attempted to prepare the voters for the selection of delegates, describing it as "one of the most important duties that freemen were ever called on to discharge. . . . A State Constitution is, properly speaking, the will of a people, clearly expressed and publicly proclaimed, . . . marking out for themselves and for their posterity a certain rule of conduct, which shall govern on all general and important subjects." The writer went on to emphasize the necessity of the people instructing their delegates and the duty of the latter to adhere to their instructions. He considered the position of delegate different from that of a representative in the legislature, inasmuch as the latter was not "bound implicitly to adhere to the wishes of his particular constituents . . . independent of that light and knowledge which he might obtain by a full discussion of the subject" with other representatives. The writer's final admonition to the voters was to "lay aside . . . all party bickerings, all local considerations, all personal prejudices or prepossessions, and vote independently for the men that are most capable . . . —select men of talents and integrity, if such can be found, and all is well."

Another correspondent blamed Jennings for so regulating the time of the election as to allow less than two weeks in which to choose delegates for a responsibility "the most important that ever has, or ever may again, occur to us. And . . . the gentlemen whom we may select should have only a few weeks to collect the sense of the Territory, and fit themselves to conform with it." Considering the extensive country and the scattered population, he considered it well

[1] Jennings to John F. Ross, February 7, 1816, and Hendricks to Jennings, quoted in Jennings to Jesse L. Holman, February 19, 1816, in *Indiana Magazine of History*, XXXIX (1943), 290-291.

nigh impossible for the people to come to the polls "prepared."[2]

In spite of the importance of the coming convention, most of the discussion in the Vincennes *Western Sun* during the early months of 1816 centered around a proclamation warning "uninformed and evil disposed persons" off the public land and the status of the Negro in the event the territory should become a state. From the eastern part of the territory came warnings against accepting slavery, even partially in the new government, while from the neighborhood of Vincennes there were those in favor of it.[3]

Between the election and the time of meeting of the convention, "Republican" addressed "The Citizens of Indiana," apparently in hopes of influencing the delegates to decide against framing a constitution. His arguments were confined largely to the fiscal issue. Indianans were urged to attend for a while longer to "the opening, clearing, and cultivation of their farms, have a surplus produce for market, invite emigrants, & then we shall be able to pay our state revenue without the sheriff's taking our children's bread." The immediate assumption of statehood, he reminded them, would result in the tax exemption of all lands sold by the federal government within the state for five years from the date of sale, thus depriving the state of a portion of its main source of revenue at the same time that its governmental expenses would be greatly increased.[4]

The Enabling Act had apportioned the delegates according to the suggestion made by the territorial Assembly in its memorial to Congress, except Harrison County was given five instead of four delegates.[5] The total number was forty-three

2 Vincennes *Western Sun,* May 4, 1816.

3 *Ibid.,* January 20, 27, February 3, 10, 17, 24, March 2, 30, April 20, May 4, 1816. The memorial to Congress was printed in the issue of January 27, 1816.

4 Vincennes *Western Sun,* June 1, 1816, a supplement to the regular issue.

5 Harrison County's population was first reported as 5,775 instead of 6,975; the earlier figure was probably used in the apportionment made by the territorial Assembly. See above, p. 427.

apportioned among the thirteen counties in existence prior to the 1815 General Assembly. Clark, Franklin, Harrison, Knox, and Washington County each had five; Gibson and Wayne, four; Dearborn and Jefferson, three; and Perry, Posey, Switzerland, and Warrick, one each.

The following persons were elected delegates:

From the county of Clark	Thomas Carr
	John K. Graham
	Jonathan Jennings
	James Lemon
	James Scott
From the county of Dearborn	James Dill
	Ezra Ferris
	Solomon Manwaring
From the county of Franklin	James Brownlee
	William H. Eads
	Robert Hanna
	Enoch McCarty
	James Noble
From the county of Gibson	Alexander Devin
	Frederick Rapp
	David Robb
	James Smith
From the county of Harrison	John Boone
	Davis Floyd
	Daniel C. Lane
	Dennis Pennington
	Patrick Shields
From the county of Jefferson	Nathaniel Hunt
	David H. Maxwell
	Samuel Smock
From the county of Knox	John Badollet
	John Benefiel
	John Johnson
	William Polke
	Benjamin Parke

From the county of Perry	Charles Polke
From the county of Posey	Dann Lynn
From the county of Switzerland	William Cotton
From the county of Warrick	Daniel Grass
From the county of Washington	John DePauw
	William Graham
	William Lowe
	Samuel Milroy
	Robert McIntire
From the county of Wayne	Patrick Beard
	Jeremiah Cox
	Hugh Cull
	Joseph Holman

Eleven, or possibly twelve, of the delegates were born in Virginia, seven in Pennsylvania, six in Kentucky, five in Maryland, two each in New Jersey and Connecticut, one each in North and South Carolina and Delaware, four in Ireland, and one each in Switzerland and Germany. Although only six were natives of Kentucky, twenty-seven had lived there prior to coming to Indiana.[6] Only nine of the members had not lived previously below the Mason-Dixon line.

The youngest member was twenty-eight, the oldest fifty-eight; sixteen were in their thirties, twenty-one in their forties, and five were in their fifties. Eleven of the delegates had served in the territorial legislature; two were judges of the General Court; thirteen had served as county judges, three as prosecuting attorneys, three as sheriffs, and at least half had been justices of the peace; over half had some legal training. Eight were field officers in the militia; five had been on the Tippecanoe campaign. Three were Baptist preachers, one a Methodist preacher, and two were physicians.[7]

6 John D. Barnhart, *Valley of Democracy. The Frontier versus the Plantation in the Ohio Valley, 1775-1818* (Indiana University Press, Bloomington, 1953), pp. 184-185; John D. Barnhart, "The Southern Influence in the Formation of Indiana," *Indiana Magazine of History*, XXXIII (1937), 265-271.

7 Logan Esarey (ed.), *Messages and Papers of Jonathan Jennings, Ratliff*

Historian John B. Dillon described the convention as composed

mainly of clear-minded, unpretending men of common sense, whose patriotism was unquestionable and whose morals were fair. Their familiarity with the Declaration of American Independence—their territorial experience under the provisions of the Ordinance of 1787 —and their knowledge of the principles of the Constitution of the United States, were sufficient, when combined, to lighten materially their labors in the great work of forming a Constitution for a new State.

Another student of the convention wrote, "None of them [the delegates] were truly great men; many of them men of limited education, and very few of them learned men. Nearly all . . . were frontier farmers, having a general idea of what they wanted, but willing that the more learned members should put it in shape."[8]

When the convention assembled at Corydon on June 10, 1816, Jennings was chosen as president and William Hendricks, who was not a delegate, as secretary.

The Journal of the convention does not include any record of debates, speeches, or discussions, but the recorded votes make possible to some extent a division of the members into a majority and a minority group.[9] The independent voting of some of the members, however, makes the division at some points rather uncertain. The opposition or minority

Boon and William Hendricks, 1816-1825 (*Indiana Historical Collections*, XII, Indianapolis, 1924), pp. 8-10; Leander J. Monks, Logan Esarey, and Ernest V. Shockley (eds.), *Courts and Lawyers of Indiana* (3 volumes, Indianapolis, 1916), I, 51.

[8] Dillon, *History of Indiana*, p. 559; W. W. Thornton, *Constitutional Convention of 1816* (A paper read before the State Bar Association in 1912), p. 26.

[9] Barnhart, "The Southern Influence in the Formation of Indiana," *Indiana Magazine of History*, XXXIII, 272-273; Barnhart, *Valley of Democracy*, pp. 185-190. The Journal was reprinted in the *Indiana Magazine of History*, LXI (1965), 87-155, from the original printing at Louisville in 1816. The constitution is printed in Kettleborough, *Constitution Making in Indiana*, I, 83-125, and in *Indiana's Road to Statehood*, pp. 70-94. Two manuscript copies of the constitution are known to be in existence; one is in the State Library and the other in the Indiana Historical Society Library. The manuscript copy of the Journal apparently has not survived.

seems to have had less cohesion than the majority, but the latter sometimes separated into two divisions which may be called regulars and independents. Generally speaking, the majority group led by Jennings agreed upon the main issues and disagreed only on minor points. The leaders of the opposition were Benjamin Parke, David Robb, and James Dill, all friends of Governor Harrison. Parke, a native of New Jersey, had served as attorney general of Indiana Territory, representative in the General Assembly and delegate to Congress, and, since 1808, a judge of the General Court. In addition he was active in the militia and a leader in the civic and educational life of Vincennes. He was probably the most able and experienced member of the convention.[10]

David Robb, representing Gibson County, was another of Harrison's friends who had held various offices including that of representative in the territorial legislature. He was born in Ireland and settled below Vincennes in 1800 after brief residences in Pennsylvania and Kentucky. He had advanced to the rank of major in the militia; his business enterprises included a grist- and sawmill. James Dill, from Dearborn County, was a friend and son-in-law of Governor Arthur St. Clair and an unwavering champion of Harrison, by whom he was frequently appointed to office. He, too, was born in Ireland and was a former resident of Kentucky and Ohio. He has been described as a gentleman of the old school, wore a queue, and appeared in court with knee breeches decorated with silver buckles. At the end of the first week of the convention, he wrote to a friend, "My own prospects in the arrangement of the future state are such as will be pleasing to myself and gratifying to my friends—The Truth

[10] For biographical material on the delegates, see Barnhart, "The Southern Influence in the Formation of Indiana," *Indiana Magazine of History,* XXXIII, 265-271, and the William H. English Collection, Indiana Historical Society Library. Appendix II of the *Journals of the General Assembly* has information on those who served in the territorial legislature.

is Talents are most damnably lacking here—and he who has but a moderate share is looked upon as a great man."[11]

Two other Knox County delegates, John Johnson and John Badollet, who had been friends of Harrison but had drifted away from him, now joined Parke and a fourth delegate, William Polke, in voting with the minority in the convention. In contrast, not a single delegate from the eastern part of the territory, except Dill, co-operated with the opposition. John Benefiel, the fifth member of the Knox County delegation, was from Busseron in the northern part of the county, and voted with the Jennings group. Badollet, who was a native of Switzerland, and lived in Pennsylvania before coming to Vincennes, characterized the convention as containing "several thinking men," but the majority he described as "empty bablers, democratic to madness, having incessantly the *people* in their mouths and their dear selves in their eyes, who resist every effort to avoid those defects which are so justly chargeable to our constitution."[12]

Some of the delegates from the central counties occasionally voted with the minority. Aside from Jennings, the leader of the Clark County delegation was James Scott, a judge of the General Court. He has been described as "a stout, rugged and burly man, plain spoken with a vein of humor and pleasantry." He had held himself aloof from political disputes and seemed to have the respect of both factions. John K. Graham, another delegate from Clark County, was a personal friend of Jennings and was likely encouraged by him to emigrate from Pennsylvania to Indiana Territory; he was a surveyor by profession.

Samuel Milroy, delegate from Washington County, was also a native of Pennsylvania. He had first come to the territory in 1812 as a member of a volunteer militia company

---

11 Dill to Samuel C. Vance, June 16, 1816, in Vance Collection, Indiana Historical Society Library.

12 Thornbrough (ed.), *Correspondence of John Badollet and Albert Gallatin,* pp. 261-263.

from Kentucky, and returned two years later to make it his home. He was a carpenter and joiner. David H. Maxwell, delegate from Jefferson County, was a physician; he moved to Monroe County in 1819 where be became active in the location and development of the state seminary.

Dennis Pennington and Davis Floyd were the best known of the Harrison County delegation. Pennington has been described as a man of little culture, but of a strong mind; he had built the courthouse in which the convention was meeting, and was a personal friend of Henry Clay. Floyd was portrayed as a bold, daring man, full of fun and anecdotes, always ready for anything that promised excitement and adventure. This last trait probably caused him to become involved with Aaron Burr in 1806-07, but during the War of 1812 he had an opportunity to prove his attachment and fidelity to his country.

The Jennings group was strongest in the east and southeast, but did not boast any prominent leaders with the exception of James Noble. A Virginian by birth, Noble had represented Franklin County in the territorial legislature and served as prosecuting attorney. He has been described as an outstanding speaker upon the "hustings" and before a jury; no other lawyer "equalled him in swaying the masses upon the stump and influencing juries in the box." He was also proficient as a militia officer. With Noble from Franklin County came a native of each of the four states of Pennsylvania, Maryland, Virginia, and South Carolina. Robert Hanna, the South Carolinian, had "an innate prejudice against slavery and slaveholders," as did Patrick Beard and Jeremiah Cox, the two Quakers from Wayne County. Joseph Holman, also from Wayne County, was the youngest member of the convention, while Hugh Cull, the fourth member of the delegation was a local Methodist preacher, and next to the oldest member. The other two delegates from Dearborn, in addition to Dill, were Ezra Ferris and Solomon Manwaring;

they were natives of Connecticut and Delaware respectively and voted with the majority.

The first order of business after the selection of a presiding officer and secretary was the adoption of the rules for governing the convention. That its work was to be conducted in a businesslike fashion is indicated by Rule XI, "Whilst the president is putting a question, or addressing the convention, none shall walk across the room; nor when a member is speaking enter on private discourse, or pass between him and the chair," and Rule XVII, "Every member shall particularly forbear personal reflections, nor shall any member name another in argument or debate." Rule XXII would seem to disprove the accusation that the constitution was pushed through the convention without time for debate: "No resolution, section or article, in the constitution, shall be finally agreed upon until the same shall have been read on three several days, unless a majority of two-thirds may think it necessary to dispense with this rule." The convention sat as a committee of the whole a short time each day, and in regular session another brief period. The remainder of the time was spent by the various committees in their work. There is no evidence of any long speeches being made, but there was ample time for discussion.

Following the adoption of rules and the report of the committee on the credentials of the delegates, the convention adopted on June 11, by a vote of thirty-four to eight, a resolution in favor of going into a state government. Those who opposed were Johnson and Polke of Knox County, Robb and Rapp of Gibson, Boone of Harrison, and the entire delegation of Jefferson. Benjamin Parke had not yet arrived.

On the third day the following committees were appointed by President Jennings to prepare and report the various portions of the projected constitution:

1. Preamble and bill of rights
2. Distribution of powers
3. Legislative department

4. Executive department
5. Judicial department
6. Impeachments
7. General provisions outside the foregoing
8. Revision of constitution
9. Changeover from territorial to state government
10. Education
11. Militia
12. Elective franchise and elections
13. Printing
14. Prisons

Committees on state banks and on revision and phraseology were appointed later. On most of the committees, Jennings' friends were in the majority, but seven of the twelve most important ones were headed by and three contained a majority of members of the opposition. The committee on revision and phraseology was appointed entirely from the minority group. Undoubtedly the ability of the older and experienced leaders was responsible for these appointments and for the prominent part played by the territorial officials in the convention. The majority, however, scrutinized the work of this group and on occasion defeated their proposals. For example, when James Dill reported a rule that called for two thirds of the members to form a quorum, it was replaced with one that called for only a simple majority. If the first rule had been adopted, the opposition might have been able to prevent the convention from proceeding to business. In the middle of the second week, three successive motions made by John Johnson in respect to the method of amendment were rejected. A little later David Robb was administered a triple defeat concerning judicial provisions.

A large part of Indiana's first constitution was taken from the earlier Ohio Valley constitutions.[13] The portions that

13 For the provenience of the various articles, see John D. Barnhart, "Sources of Indiana's First Constitution," *Indiana Magazine of History*, XXXIX (1943), 55-94.

were not so copied constitute less than 10 per cent of the entire document. The process involved, however, was not simply copying the constitutional law of another state, but was a matter of selection. As a general rule, entire articles were not lifted from a single constitution; instead, the delegates seem to have searched through several constitutions to find the sections which embodied the provisions they considered preferable for the government of the new state. Occasionally they wrote a new section when a suitable one was not found in the older documents.

No attempt will be made here to trace in detail the wording of the various articles from the time they were reported by the committees until they reached their final form; only the more important changes will be noted.[14]

John Badollet was chairman of the committee that drafted the Preamble and Article I, which were taken largely from the Ohio constitution. The original draft was reported by the committee on June 14, and referred to the committee of the whole, where it was taken up on the 19th and minor changes made. On June 22 it was read a second time and was passed on third reading on June 27 without a roll call vote.

The Preamble asserted the right of admission of Indiana as a member of the Union consistent with the Constitution of the United States, the Northwest Ordinance, and the Enabling Act, and on an equal footing with the original states. The Bill of Rights, which constituted the first article and which may have been placed in a primary position as a recognition of its importance, protected and guaranteed those priceless civil liberties and fundamental rights of the citizen which are so often assumed rather than appreciated. Freedom of religion, of speech and the press, the right of trial by jury, assembly, petition, of altering and reforming the government

14 The changes in wording are shown in detail in the footnotes to the constitution as printed in Kettleborough, *Constitution Making in Indiana*, I, 83-125, and in Ruth E. Brayton, The Constitution of 1816 (Unpublished M.A. thesis, Indiana University, 1929), pp. 44 ff.

as they think proper, were some of the privileges promised by this article. The citizen could read its several sections with the conviction that they protected him from tyranny and oppression.

John Johnson, who was considered the best lawyer among the delegates, was chosen to head the committee on the distribution of power between the three branches of government—legislative, executive, and judicial. In searching through the constitutions at hand for an expression of their ideas, they took the Kentucky constitution as a model but amplified and strengthened its provisions. The government was to be divided into three separate and independent departments, and no person in any one of the departments could exercise any power that belonged to either of the others (Art. II). It was intended to prevent too much power falling into the hands of one man or set of men who might thereby be enabled to oppress the people.

Article III dealing with the legislative branch was drafted by a committee headed by James Noble. The draft, reported on the morning following the committee's appointment, was drawn largely from the Ohio constitution. Among the significant changes made by the convention were: the reduction of the age requirement of representatives and senators from thirty years to twenty-one and twenty-five respectively; the reduction in the residence requirement of representatives from two years to one; the biennial election of senators to triennial. An attempt was made to omit the requirement that a representative should have paid a state or county tax, but it failed to pass.

An amendment to Section 20 permitted members of the first General Assembly to accept offices created by the Indiana constitution or the constitution of the United States.

The legislature was given sufficient powers and responsibilities to make it the dominant branch of state government, but was held in restraint by the division of power and the system of checks and balances. It was to consist of a senate and a house of representatives possessed of all the authority usually exercised by such bodies. Representation was to be apportioned on the basis of an enumeration of adult white males which was to be made every five years. The representatives were to be elected annually. The senators were to serve for three years, but their terms were to be so arranged that one third of the body would be elected every year. The two houses possessed powers of legislation, appropriation, impeachment, some power of appointment, and control of their own members and procedure.

The provisions regarding the executive branch of government (Art. IV) were drafted by a committee of which John K. Graham was chairman. In the state governments which came into existence during and immediately after the Revolution, the provisions regarding the executive reflected a reaction against arbitrary authority; such executives were almost powerless and only gradually did they gain in stature. This process was well under way at the time Indiana framed her first constitution. The Indiana article was drawn largely from the Kentucky constitution. The governor and lieutenant governor were to be elected for three-year terms and were eligible for re-election but could hold the office for only six of any nine years. The governor was to be the commander in chief of the military and naval forces of the state; he was given limited appointive powers, had authority to remit fines and forfeitures and grant reprieves and pardons, could call the legislature into special session, and could veto bills which he did not approve. If a majority of the members of each house repassed a bill over his veto it became law. This veto was therefore weaker than many state executives exercise today. A secretary of state, a treasurer, and an auditor were to be elected by joint ballot of both houses of the legislature and their duties were to be fixed by law. At one point in the debate an amendment was offered to make the office of the secretary of state appointive by the governor with the advice and consent of the Senate, but it was defeated.

Seven of the nine men chosen to draft the provisions regarding the judicial branch of the government (Art. V) were lawyers; James Scott was chairman and other members included John Johnson, James Noble, Benjamin Parke, and James Dill. They were all familiar with the defects of the territorial court system and sought to avoid them. Free use was made of the Kentucky and Ohio constitutions in writing the original draft, but after it was considered by the convention as a whole the article was referred to a select committee of six of which Parke was named chairman and both Scott and Johnson were omitted. In their redrafting of the article, it was made to conform more with the Ohio constitution. Among the changes made by the new committee were: the term of office of all the judges was changed from "during good behaviour" to a definite term of seven years; instead of the president judges being appointed by the governor with the consent of the Senate, they were to be elected by joint ballot of the two houses of the legislature; and only two of the three judges of the Supreme Court were needed to form a quorum, while in Scott's draft a full court was required. Also, under the Scott plan, the clerks of the circuit courts were to hold office at the pleasure of the courts, but under the new draft they were limited to a seven-year term. A twelfth section was added, on motion of James Noble, which provided for the election of a competent number of justices of the peace to serve for five-year terms. Their powers and duties were to be regulated and defined by law.

In its final form Article V vested the judiciary power of the state in a Supreme Court, circuit courts, and such other inferior courts as the General Assembly might from time to time establish. The Supreme Court was to exercise only appellate jurisdiction and was comprised of three judges to be appointed by the governor with the advice and consent of the Senate. The circuit courts were to consist of a president judge and two associates, the president to serve a whole circuit, of which there were to be three, the two associates a single county. They were to have common law, chancery, and criminal jurisdiction. Additional circuits could be created by the General Assembly as they were needed. The new system was simple and clear cut, and eliminated the conflicting powers, duplicate or concurrent jurisdictions, and uncertainty of sittings that had been a feature of the territorial system. As a co-ordinate branch of the government, the judiciary seemed rather weak, but the intelligent and dignified performance of its duties, particularly that of judicial review, caused its significance to be fully recognized in time.

Article VI dealing with the elective franchise was drafted by a committee headed by Ezra Ferris, using a similar article in the Ohio constitution as a model. The convention changed the residence requirement of six months for voters, as reported by the committee, to one year. Most of the discussion on the article centered around the method of voting, whether it should be by ballot or *viva voce*. The latter was the choice of the committee, but this was amended to read "by ballot" with the proviso that the General Assembly in 1821 could change the method to *viva voce,* after which it should remain unalterable. The franchise was granted to every white male citizen of the United States of the age of twenty-one years and upwards who had resided in the state one year immediately preceding the election. This represented the ultimate in democracy in that day when woman suffrage was scarcely thought of and when few considered the Negro qualified to vote. Elections were to be quite frequent because of the different classes of officials to be elected and the varied terms of office.

In 1816 the militia was an important organization for the protection of the frontier. Although the defeat of the Indians in the War of 1812 had lessened the need for it, this was not yet evident at the time the constitution was being written. Article VII, which was drafted by a committee headed by James Dill, provided that all able-bodied male persons between the ages of eighteen and forty-five except Negroes, mulattoes, and Indians should be enrolled in the militia. Conscientious objectors were to be fined but not forced to bear arms. All officers below the rank of brigadier general should be elected by those subject to militia duty; the brigadier and major generals were to be chosen by the commissioned officers of their units. The adjutant general and quartermaster general were to be appointed by the governor. If the committee used any state constitution as a model it was that of Ohio, but the Indiana article was more democratic and more specific. One significant change made by the convention in the original draft was the substitution of the word "persons" in place of "citizens" in Section 1. A proposed amendment to permit the governor to appoint the general officers was voted down.

The convention failed to devise a workable plan for amending the constitution. It provided in Article VIII that a vote be taken every twelve years on the desirability of a new convention to revise or amend the constitution. If a majority of the voters were in favor of a revision, the governor was to inform the General Assembly, which should then provide for calling a convention if two thirds of the members agreed. In the original draft a poll was to be taken every three years, during the gubernatorial elections. As amended it was not clear whether the question of revision had to be submitted to the voters at least once every twelve years but could be submitted sooner and oftener, or whether the question could be voted on only once in every twelve-year period. Proponents of the first theory were in the majority in the General Assembly of 1822-23 when a bill was passed authorizing the first referendum to be held the following August. The second and third referendums were held in 1828 and 1840 in accordance with the twelve-year intervals; the fourth in 1846 and fifth in 1849 were provided for by special legislation. The first three referendums showed decided majorities against calling a convention.[15] The convention added to the original draft

[15] Kettleborough, *Constitution Making in Indiana*, I, xxxiii-lxxxiii, 144-145, 148-151, 158-159, 160-162, 163-164, 165-167, 171-183, 184-217.

the proviso that the constitution could never be changed so as to admit slavery.

A most unusual portion of the constitution was Article IX which committed the state to the encouragement of learning on the grounds that the general diffusion of knowledge and the advantages of education were essential to the preservation of free government. "As soon as circumstances will permit," the legislature was to provide "for a general system of education, ascending in a regular gradation, from township schools to a state university, wherein tuition shall be gratis, and equally open to all." Unfortunately the qualification at the beginning of the section enabled the legislature to avoid its responsibility in this matter until after a new constitution was adopted in 1851. It was a noble vision, the attainment of which was prevented by the lack of wealth and the indifference of the people until the frontier period was past. The fines collected for breaches of the penal law and the fees paid for exemption from militia duty were to be devoted to the support of county seminaries. Ten per cent of the proceeds of the sale of lots in county-seat towns was to be set aside for the use of public libraries. A penal code was to be formed on the principles of reformation and not of vindictive justice. The legislature was to found one or more farms as asylums for the aged, infirm, and unfortunate. On the whole the article embodies a rare recognition (in a frontier state) of the public's social responsibilities.

Although James Scott was chairman of the committee appointed to draft the article on education, John Badollet, writing seven years later, said he was responsible for the last four sections of the article, which were original, while Section 1, which he called the preamble, was the work of another member of the committee. A comparison with other constitutions shows it was drawn in part from that of New Hampshire. Badollet did not think it fit the other portions but said he hesitated to try to change it for fear the result might be something worse. In drafting the other sections, he said he was "convinced that to change and better the manner of a people, moral causes operate more effectually than prohibitory enactments & the disgusting repetition of penal statutes."[16]

A committee on banks and banking companies was appointed on June 20 with James Noble as chairman. The article which they drafted was original. There were two chartered banks and several private ones operating in the territory; inasmuch as a system had developed whereby the banks were issuing their own bills of credit, some form of regulation was needed.[17] Article X, Section 1, provided that there should not be established in the state any bank or banking company for the purpose of issuing bills of credit or bills payable to order or to bearer. This was not to be construed as preventing the General Assembly from establishing a state bank and branches at some future date. The Bank at Vincennes and the Farmers' and Mechanics' Bank of Madison were to continue under their original charters and either might be designated as the state bank and the other as a branch.

Article XI was reported by the committee on general provisions, David Maxwell, chairman. Its most important provision concerned slavery, and was taken largely from the Ohio constitution. One of the most difficult problems before the convention concerned the status of the Negro. No disposition was shown to question the rejection of slavery which had been decided in the territorial legislature. This was now reaffirmed in Section 7, "there shall be neither slavery nor involuntary servitude in this state, otherwise than for the punishment of crimes, whereof the party shall have been duly convicted. Nor shall any indenture of any Negro or mulatto hereafter made, and executed out of the bounds of this state be of any validity within the state."

[16] Badollet to Gallatin, September 10, 1823, in Thornbrough (ed.), *Correspondence of John Badollet and Albert Gallatin,* pp. 261-263. There is a gap in the correspondence between the two men from 1816 to 1823 while Gallatin was serving as minister to France.

[17] Logan Esarey, "The First Indiana Banks," *Indiana Magazine of History,* VI (1910), 145-146.

The first mention of slavery in the convention came during debate on Article VIII dealing with amending the constitution. As adopted the article provided a double lock against the admission of slavery: "But, as the holding any part of the human Creation in slavery, or involuntary servitude, can only originate in usurpation and tyranny, no alteration of this constitution shall ever take place so as to introduce slavery or involuntary servitude."

An important compromise was adopted, however, in respect to indentured servitude. The original form of Section 7, Article XI, would have prohibited indentured servitude of adults except when entered into willingly, and declared illegal the indentures of Negroes or mulattoes whether made within or without the state except apprenticeships. In the committee of the whole this was reduced to a simple declaration that no "indenture of any Negro or mulatto hereafter made, and executed out of the bounds of this state [shall] be of any validity within the state." Though definitely settling the question of future importations, the effect of this provision on pre-existent slavery and servitude was left open to various interpretations. In the eastern counties it was generally considered that slaves and servants were emancipated and their masters acted on that theory. In the western counties a few masters removed their slaves from the state, and some of these were afterwards released by the courts of southern states. The great majority, however, simply continued to hold their slaves, believing that property in slaves was a vested right secured by the Ordinance of 1787, and could not be impaired.[18] Nor was strict regard paid to the rights of indentured servants.

The census of 1820 showed 190 slaves in the state, only 47 less than in 1810. The larger portion of these, 118, were in Knox County, while Gibson had 30, Posey, 11, Vander-

---

[18] The Ordinance preserved to the French and Canadian inhabitants and other settlers of Kaskaskia and Vincennes, "who have heretofore professed themselves citizens of Virginia, their laws and customs now in force among them relative to the descent and conveyance of property."

burgh, 10, and the remainder scattered over Owen, Perry, Pike, Scott, Spencer, Sullivan, and Warrick counties. Male slaves outnumbered females 98 to 92, while classification by age revealed 83 were under the age of fourteen, 58 were between fourteen and twenty-six, 32 were between twenty-six and forty-five, and 17 were over forty-five.

Desiring to make a test case of the provision in the constitution, a group of attorneys in 1820 arranged for Polly, a slave of Hyacinth Lasselle of Vincennes, to sue her master for her freedom. The case was decided in favor of Lasselle in the Knox County Circuit Court, but when an appeal was taken to the Indiana Supreme Court, the decision was reversed and Polly was set free. His attorneys wished to appeal the case to the United States Supreme Court, but Lasselle refused to let the case go any farther. This decision brought to an end the slavery question in Indiana so far as any legal right was concerned; however, Negroes continued to be held as slaves for many years. A local census of Vincennes taken in 1830 showed 32 slaves; the federal census of the same year makes no mention of these but it did list one each in Orange, Decatur, and Warrick counties. Ten years later there were two listed in Rush County and one in Putnam.[19]

In addition to the two provisions concerning Negroes mentioned above, there were three other references affecting them in the constitution. Article VII, Section 1, excluded Negroes, mulattoes and Indians from the militia. Article VI, Section 1, restricted the franchise to white adult male citizens of the United States, and representation in the General Assembly was to be apportioned according to the number of white adult male inhabitants (Art. III, Sec. 2).

Section 11 of Article XI provided that Corydon should be the seat of government until 1825, and Section 12 stated that in laying off any new county the General Assembly should not reduce the old county to less than four hundred square miles.

[19] Dunn, *Indiana,* pp. 430-442; Thornbrough, *The Negro in Indiana,* pp. 23-30.

Section 16 established the salaries of judges and state officials
and stipulated that they could not be increased prior to 1819.
Section 17 established the boundaries of the state.

By a resolution formally adopted on June 29, the convention accepted the five contingent Congressional propositions set
out in the Enabling Act.[20] The constitution was not submitted
to the electors for ratification but became operative on June
29, the day on which the convention completed its labors and
the delegates affixed their signatures.

The work of the convention was completed in nineteen
days, at a total cost of $3,076.21.[21] Each member was al-
lowed $2.00 per day for each day's attendance plus $2.00 for
each twenty-five miles traveled to and from the seat of government. The secretary and assistant secretaries received
$3.50 per day; doorkeeper and assistant doorkeeper $2.00
per day. Mann Butler of Louisville was allowed $200 for
printing and stitching the constitution and journal; $41.50
for books, stationery, etc.; $27.50 for tables, benches, etc.;
and $40 for overseeing the printing, stitching, and distribu-
tion of the constitution and journal.[22]

Transition from the old to the new government was provided in Article XII and was relatively simple, at least on
paper. The President of the convention was directed to issue
writs to the county sheriffs calling for an election to be held
under territorial laws on August 5, 1816, to choose a governor, lieutenant governor, a representative in Congress, members of the General Assembly, sheriffs, and coroners. The
Enabling Act had stipulated that Indiana was to have one
representative in Congress until after the census was taken in
1820, while Section 9, Article XII of the constitution had
outlined the first apportionment of members of the Assembly

20 Kettleborough, *Constitution Making in Indiana,* I, 82-83.
21 Auditor's report, December 8, 1817, in Indiana *Senate Journal,* 1817-18,
p. 19.
22 *Laws of Indiana,* 1816-17, pp. 171-172, 239-241.

among the counties of the state. There were to be twenty-nine representatives and ten senators.

The time between the close of the convention and the election was only five weeks. Printing presses were available by this time not only at Vincennes, but at Brookville, Lexington, Corydon, and Vevay, and possibly elsewhere. Fourth of July gatherings would have offered opportunities also for prospective candidates to make themselves known. A spirited campaign for the governorship was waged between Jonathan Jennings and Thomas Posey, with the former receiving 5,211 votes as against 3,934 for Posey. In the race for lieutenant governor only 7,474 votes were cast, of which Christopher Harrison of Salem received 6,570, and the remaining votes were divided between John Vawter, Abel Findley, John Johnson, Davis Floyd, and Amos Lane. For representative in Congress William Hendricks defeated Allan D. Thom and George R. C. Sullivan by a decisive majority. Sullivan withdrew from the contest two days before the poll in the hope of throwing his support to Thom but the announcement did not reach most of the counties until after the election.[23]

Looking at the returns for the General Assembly, it will be noted that one third of the successful candidates had served in the constitutional convention, while eleven of the thirty-nine had served in the territorial legislature. In the returns for sheriffs, in seven counties those who had been holding the office under appointment from the territorial governor were elected.

The first General Assembly under the state government met on November 4, the governor and lieutenant governor were inaugurated on November 7 and the following day the Assembly elected James Noble and Waller Taylor as members of the United States Senate. Hendricks was sworn into

---

[23] *Indiana Election Returns, 1816-1851,* compiled by Dorothy Riker and Gayle Thornbrough (*Indiana Historical Collections,* XL, Indianapolis, 1960), pp. 71, 137, 159, 183-184n; Esarey (ed.), *Messages and Papers of Jonathan Jennings, Ratliff Boon, William Hendricks,* pp. 15-16.

office and seated in Congress on December 2 and the two senators on December 12. A resolution admitting Indiana to the Union "on an equal footing with the original States in all respects whatever" was adopted by Congress and approved by President Madison on December 11, 1816. This date has generally been regarded as marking the birthday of the state although the federal laws were not formally extended to the new commonwealth until March 3, 1817.[24]

No provision had been made in the Enabling Act or in the constitution whereby the Indiana electorate could participate in the presidential election of 1816. The General Assembly therefore chose three presidential electors on November 16, and they met shortly thereafter and cast their votes for James Monroe for president and Daniel Tompkins for vice-president. When the two houses of Congress met the following February to count the electoral votes, the question was raised whether or not Indiana's votes should be counted since they had been cast prior to her admission into the Union. After Representative Hendricks made a forceful presentation of the case for his state, the decision was made to include Indiana's three votes.[25]

Judging from the meager contemporary literature on the subject, the constitution was received with general satisfaction. Some few of its provisions, because of obscurities and imperfections, aroused adverse criticism for a number of years following its adoption. Those that were special targets included: fixing the seat of government at Corydon for a period of nine years; the provision for amendment; prohibiting any increase in the salaries of public officers until 1819; limiting the term of judges; and failure to provide for an attorney general or prosecuting attorney. Critics pointed out that the establishment or removal of the state capital belonged to the General Assembly as did the limiting of the

24 *Annals of Congress,* 14 Congress, 2 session, cols. 21, 31, 230, 1337-1338, 1348.

25 *Ibid.,* cols. 943-950; *Indiana Election Returns,* p. xii.

salaries of public officials. By making these provisions a part of the constitution it was feared they could be altered only by amending that document and not by a legislative body. The arguments employed prior to and during the year 1816 in opposing statehood were also used retrospectively for some time after the adoption of the constitution. The document was described as "premature," and there were those who professed to fear that Indiana would resemble "a puny child, taken from nurse too soon." As late as 1821 the constitution was described as "miserable, objectionable and disjointed."[26]

The framing of the constitution under which Indiana began its existence as a state was the culmination of the struggle of the pioneers to escape the undemocratic government of the territorial period. The men who took the initiative from Governor Harrison and who successfully struggled to liberalize the Northwest Ordinance continued to labor for self-government until they had formed a democratic state. As a part of this contest they reiterated the prohibition of slavery and halted the further introduction of indentured servitude. White manhood suffrage and the equal apportionment of representation, unchecked by a strong gubernatorial veto, placed the power in the hands of popularly chosen representatives.

The true significance of the constitution is seen when it is compared with the early fundamental law of the southern states with their property qualifications for office holding and voting, unequal representation, and protection of slavery, which tended to produce an aristocratic social structure. From these states came most of Indiana's pioneers, but when in their turn they founded a state government they took the opportunity to eliminate the undemocratic features of these older documents.

[26] Vincennes *Western Sun,* June 30, July 21, 27, Aug. 4, 1816; July 14, 1821; Kettleborough, *Constitution Making in Indiana,* I, xxii-xxvii.

BIBLIOGRAPHY

Compiled by Dorothy Riker

This bibliography is not exhaustive. The compiler has attempted to list the most significant materials that are available for the study of this early period of Indiana history even though some of these have been little used in the preparation of the present volume. Likewise, not all items cited in the footnotes are included. Much of the materials in the French archives that relate to North America are now available through photocopies and others may be found in the Public Archives of Canada. The manuscripts in the British archives have been utilized by historians more than those in France, but their possibilities have not been exhausted. The general reader may be unaware of the substantial amount of French and British material that has appeared in printed form; citations have been made to printed sources when these were available. For the period of the American Revolution and the critical years that followed, the authors have used both British and American sources. Not until we come to the periods of the Northwest and Indiana Territories is there any appreciable amount of original manuscript material in Indiana libraries. An examination of the secondary works will show the fields in which most of the research has been done.

It has seemed best to divide the bibliography by periods—Prehistoric, French, British, American Revolution, Post Revolution and Northwest Territory, and Indiana Territory—listing under each period the manuscript material, printed sources, and secondary writings that are most useful. This has meant some duplication but on the whole it seemed the best method of presentation. General secondary works that have been useful for all periods are listed first.

General Works

Anson, Bert, *The Miami Indians* (University of Oklahoma Press, 1970).

Barnhart, John D., and Carmony, Donald F., *Indiana. From Frontier to Industrial Commonwealth* (5 vols. [3-5 biographical], New York, 1954).

Dillon, John B., *A History of Indiana from Its Earliest Exploration by Europeans to . . . 1816 . . .* (Indianapolis, 1859).

Donaldson, Thomas, *The Public Domain . . .* (Washington, D. C., 1884).

Dunn, Jacob P., *Indiana. A Redemption from Slavery* (American Commonwealths Series, Revised edition, Boston and New York, 1905).

——, *Indiana and Indianans. A History of Aboriginal and Territorial Indiana and the Century of Statehood* (5 vols. [vols. 3-5 biographical], Chicago and New York, 1919).

Esarey, Logan, *A History of Indiana* . . . (2 vols., Third edition, Fort Wayne, 1924).

Hodge, Frederick W. (ed.), *Handbook of American Indians North of Mexico* (2 vols., U. S. Bureau of American Ethnology, *Bulletin 30,* Washington, D. C., 1906, 1910).

Kappler, Charles J. (ed.), *Indian Affairs. Laws and Treaties* (2 vols., Washington, D. C., 1903).

Lindley, Harlow (ed.), *Indiana as Seen by Early Travelers* (*Indiana Historical Collections,* III, Indianapolis, 1916).

McCord, Shirley S. (comp.), *Travel Accounts of Indiana, 1679-1961* (*Indiana Historical Collections,* XLVII, Indianapolis, 1970).

Malloy, William (comp.), *Treaties, Conventions, International Acts . . . between the United States of America and Other Powers, 1776-1909* (2 vols., Washington, D. C., 1910).

Malott, Clyde A., "The Physiography of Indiana," *Handbook of Indiana Geology* (Indiana Department of Conservation, *Publication No. 21,* Indianapolis, 1922), Pt. 2, pp. 59-256.

Schneider, Allan F. (ed.), *Natural Features of Indiana* (Indiana Academy of Science, 1966).

Thornbrough, Gayle, and Riker, Dorothy (eds.), *Readings in Indiana History* (*Indiana Historical Collections,* XXXVI, Indianapolis, 1956).

Voegelin, Erminie W., "Indians of Indiana," Indiana Academy of Science, *Proceedings,* L (1941), 27-32.

PREHISTORIC PERIOD

Black, Glenn A., *Angel Site. An Archaeological, Historical and Ethnological Study* (Indiana Historical Society, Indianapolis, 1967).

Lilly, Eli, *Prehistoric Antiquities of Indiana* (Indiana Historical Society, Indianapolis, 1937).

Quimby, George I., *Indian Life in the Upper Great Lakes, 11,000 B.C. to A.D. 1800* (University of Chicago Press, 1960).

Silverberg, Robert, *Mound Builders of Ancient America: The Archaeology of a Myth* (New York Graphic Society, 1968).

Willey, Gordon R., *An Introduction to American Archaeology. Volume I* (New York, 1966).

Winters, Howard, *An Archaeological Survey of the Wabash Valley in Illinois* (Illinois State Museum, *Reports of Investigations,* 1963).

The volumes of the *Prehistory Research Series* published by the Indiana Historical Society, occasional publications of the Indiana Historical Bureau, archaeological publications of Ball State University, and the *Proceedings* of the Indiana Academy of Science contain reports of archaeological work done in Indiana. For a recent bibliography, see Ronald L. Michael, *Bibliography of*

Literature on Indiana Archaeology (Archaeology Reports, No. 5, Ball State University, 1969).

THE FRENCH PERIOD

Manuscripts

Most of the original material on the French period in Indiana is in the French achives in Paris, but fortunately much of the relevant material has been copied and is available both in the Public Archives of Canada and in the Library of Congress. French records left at Kaskaskia when the British took control there, consisting largely of notarial instruments and court records, ultimately reached either the Chicago Historical Society or the Illinois State Historical Library.

Mr. Douglas Brymner, archivist of the Province of Canada, began in 1873 the collection of archival material relating to its early history in the Archives Nationales des Colonies in Paris and in the British Museum and government offices in London. The work of copying records in Paris was begun by Abbé Hospice Verreau in the above year, and was continued by Joseph Marmette, Edouard Richard, and H. P. Biggar. This being before the era of copying machines, the transcribing was all done by hand. Summaries of the more important documents were published from time to time in the *Reports* of the Canadian archives. Those for 1885-1887 contain summaries of the greater portion of the C 11 series, consisting of correspondence received from Canada. The volumes of C 11 A deal particularly with activities in the region of the Great Lakes and southward. The Supplement to the *Report* for 1899, Appendix K of the *Report* for 1904, and Volume I, Part VI of the *Report* for 1905 contain a calendar of the more important documents in Series B, consisting of letters and orders sent from government officials in France to the colonial officials. Some work was also done in copying Series C 13 relating to the colony of Louisiana.

The 1899 Supplement and Volume I of the 1905 *Report* also have calendars of the important Moreau St. Méry Collection consisting of original documents and transcripts from the archives of the Minister of the Marine that were collected with the idea of writing a history, and later purchased from the St. Méry family by the French government. Some of the original documents from which the transcripts were made are no longer available. This collection covers both the colonies of Canada and Louisiana and has some Indiana material.

With the advent of modern methods of photocopying, the Library of Congress has obtained photocopies and microfilm of the B and C series and the St. Méry Collection directly from the French archives. The Indiana Historical Society Library and various libraries in Illinois, Michigan, and Wisconsin have photocopies or microfilms of selected documents from the above series.

For more detailed information regarding the manuscript sources for the French period, the following bibliographies are among those available: Waldo G. Leland *et al., Guide to Materials for American History in the Libraries and Archives of Paris* (2 vols., Carnegie Institution of Washington, D. C.,

1933, 1943) ; Henry P. Beers, *The French in North America. A Bibliographical Guide to French Archives, Reproductions, and Research Missions* (Louisiana State University Press, 1957) ; Nancy M. Surrey, *Calendar of Manuscripts in Paris Archives and Libraries Relating to the History of the Mississippi Valley to 1803* (2 vols., Carnegie Institution of Washington, D. C., 1926, 1928) ; David W. Parker, *Guide to the Materials for United States History in Canadian Archives* (Carnegie Institution of Washington, D. C., 1913) ; Henry P. Beers, *The French & British in the Old Northwest. A Bibliographical Guide to Archive and Manuscript Sources* (Wayne State University Press, Detroit, 1964). The last contains a discussion of judicial, notarial, and land records as well as administrative records. For those who can read French, there is Joseph-Edmond Roy, *Rapport sur les Archives de France Relative à l'Histoire du Canada* (Ottawa, 1911).

Published Sources

Various historical agencies have been active in translating and publishing documentary material relating to the French period in the Old Northwest. The following have been the most useful in the preparation of the present volume.

Bossu, Jean-Bernard, *Travels in the Interior of North America, 1751-1762,* translated and edited by Seymour Feiler (University of Oklahoma Press, 1962).

Burton, Clarence M. (ed.), "The Cadillac Papers," *Michigan Pioneer and Historical Collections,* XXXIII (1903), 36-715; XXXIV (1904), 11-214.

Dunn, Caroline and Eleanor (trans.), *Indiana's First War* (Indiana Historical Society *Publications,* VIII, No. 2, Indianapolis, 1924). Documents on Chickasaw War.

Dunn, Jacob P., *The Mission to the Ouabache* (Indiana Historical Society *Publications,* III, No. 4, Indianapolis, 1902). Most of documentary material concerns Post Vincennes and its founder; facsimile letters of Sieur de Vincennes of March 7 and 21, 1733.

French, B. F., *Historical Collections of Louisiana . . .* (3 vols., New York, 1846-51).

Krauskopf, Frances (ed.), *Ouiatanon Documents* (Indiana Historical Society *Publications,* XVIII, No. 2, Indianapolis, 1955).

Lambing, A. A. (ed.), "Journals of Céloron de Blainville and Father Joseph Pierre de Bonnécamps," Ohio Archaeological and Historical Society *Quarterly,* XXIX (1920), 335-396, 397-423.

Margry, Pierre (ed.), *Découvertes et Établissements des Français dans L'Ouest et dans Le Sud de L'Amérique Septentrionale (1614-1754)* (6 vols., Paris, 1879-1888).

Massicotte, E. Z., "Congés et permis déposés ou enregistrés à Montréal sous la régime français," *Rapport* de L'Archiviste de la Province de Quebec, 1921-22, pp. 189-223; 1922-23, pp. 192-265; 1932-33, pp. 245-304. Covers the years 1720-30, 1739-52, and 1758.

Mullett, Charles F., "Military Intelligence on Forts and Indians in the Ohio Valley, 1756-1757," *William and Mary Quarterly* (3d series, Williamsburg, Va., 1944-   ), III, 398-410.

O'Callaghan, Edmund B., and Fernow, B. (eds.), *Documents Relative to the Colonial History of the State of New-York* . . . (15 vols., Albany, 1853-87). Vols. IX and X contain Paris documents.

Pease, Theodore C. (ed.), *Anglo-French Boundary Disputes in the West, 1749-1763* (*Illinois Historical Collections,* XXVII, Springfield, 1936).

Pease, Theodore C., and Jenison, Ernestine (eds.), *Illinois on the Eve of the Seven Years' War, 1747-1755* (*Illinois Historical Collections,* XXIX, Springfield, 1940).

Pease, Theodore C., and Werner, Raymond C. (eds.), *The French Foundations, 1680-1693* (*Illinois Historical Collections,* XXIII, Springfield, 1934).

Riddell, William R., "Last Official French Report on the Western Posts," *Journal* of the Illinois State Historical Society, XXIV (1931-32), 578-587.

Rowland, Dunbar, and Sanders, A. G. (eds.), *Mississippi Provincial Archives, 1701-1743* (3 vols., Jackson, 1927-32).

Roy, Pierre-Georges, *Sieur de Vincennes Identified* (Indiana Historical Society *Publications,* VII, No. 1, Indianapolis [1919]). Documents and narrative.

St. Francis Xavier Parish Records, 1749-1773, in American Catholic Historical Society *Records,* XII (1901), 41-60, 193-211, 322-336. The original records are in the parish library, Vincennes, Indiana. The Genealogy Division, Indiana State Library has photostatic copies covering the period 1749-1838.

Thwaites, Reuben G. (ed.), "The French Régime in Wisconsin," 1634-1727, in *Wisconsin Historical Collections,* XVI (1902), 1-477; 1727-1748, in *ibid.,* XVII (1906), 1-518; 1743-1760, in *ibid.,* XVIII (1908), 1-222.

———— (ed.), *The Jesuit Relations, and Allied Documents* . . . (73 vols., Cleveland, 1896-1901). Dablon's Journal of Marquette's trip around Lake Michigan is in Vol. LIX.

Secondary Sources

Among the general accounts of French exploration and colonization, the following may be noted: John B. Brebner, *The Explorers of North America, 1492-1806* (New York, 1933); Louise P. Kellogg, *The French Régime in Wisconsin and the Northwest* (Madison, Wis., 1925); Gustave Lanctot, *A History of Canada* . . . (2 vols., Harvard University Press, 1963, 1964); John D. Shea, *Discovery and Exploration of the Mississippi Valley* (Redfield, N. Y., 1852); George M. Wrong, *The Rise and Fall of New France* (2 vols., New York, 1928).

For general biographical information on French families, see *Dictionnaire National des Canadiens Français, 1608-1760* (3 vols., Institut Généalogique Drouin, Montreal, 1965), and Cyprien Tanguay, *Dictionnaire Généalogique des familles canadiennes depuis la fondation de la colonie jusqu' à nos jours* (7 vols., Montreal, 1871-90), while for particular individuals there are the following: Paul Chesnel, *History of Cavelier de La Salle, 1643-1687* . . . (New York and London, 1932); Jean Delanglez, "A Calendar of La Salle's Travels,

1643-1683," *Mid-America,* XXII (1940), 278-305; Frances Krauskopf, "The Documentary Basis for La Salle's Supposed Discovery of the Ohio River," *Indiana Magazine of History,* XLVII (1951), 143-153; William P. McCarthy, "The Chevalier Macarty Mactigue," *Journal* of the Illinois State Historical Society, LXI (1968), 41-57; Reuben G. Thwaites, *Father Marquette* (New York, 1902); Howard N. Eavenson, *Map Maker & Indian Traders. An Account of John Patten, Trader* . . . (University of Pittsburgh Press, 1949); Walter B. Douglas, "The Sieurs de St. Ange," Illinois State Historical Society *Transactions,* 1909, pp. 135-146; and Yves F. Zoltvany, "The Frontier Policy of Philippe de Rigaud de Vaudreuil, 1713-1725," *Canadian Historical Review,* XLVIII (1967), 227-250.

Volumes relating particularly to the colony of Louisiana are Alcée Fortier, *A History of Louisiana* (4 vols., New York, 1904), and N. M. Miller Surrey, *The Commerce of Louisiana during the French Régime, 1699-1763* (Columbia University *Studies in History, Economics and Public Law,* LXXI, No. 1, 1916). Much of the literature on the period carries some references to the fur trade, but the following deal specifically with it: Harold A. Innis, *The Fur Trade in Canada. An Introduction to Canadian Economic History* (Yale University Press, 1962); Paul C. Phillips and John W. Smurr, *The Fur Trade* (2 vols., Norman, Okla., 1961), Vol. I; R. M. Saunders, "Coureur de Bois: A Definition," *Canadian Historical Review,* XXI (1940), 123-131.

For government and life in the Illinois country under the French régime, see Clarence W. Alvord, *The Illinois Country, 1673-1818* (Springfield, Ill., 1920); Natalie Belting, *Kaskaskia under the French Regime* (*Illinois Studies in the Social Sciences,* XXIX, No. 3, Urbana, 1948); Norman W. Caldwell, *The French in the Mississippi Valley, 1740-1750* (*Illinois Studies in the Social Sciences,* XXVI, No. 3, Urbana, 1941); Edward G. Mason, "Kaskaskia and Its Parish Records," *Fergus Historical Series,* No. 12 (Chicago, 1881); Wayne C. Temple, *Indian Villages of the Illinois Country. Historic Tribes* (Illinois State Museum, *Scientific Papers,* II, Pt. 2, Springfield, 1958); Joseph J. Thompson, "Catholic Statesmen of Illinois," *Illinois Catholic Historical Review,* III (1920-21), 196-216.

The following publications deal particularly with the Indian tribes and French posts in the Indiana area: Bert Anson, *The Miami Indians* (University of Oklahoma, 1970); Wallace A. Brice, *History of Fort Wayne* . . . (Fort Wayne, 1868); Oscar J. Craig, *Ouiatanon, a Study in Indiana History* (Indiana Historical Society *Publications,* II, No. 8, Indianapolis, 1893); Bert J. Griswold, *The Pictorial History of Fort Wayne, Indiana* (2 vols., Chicago, 1917), Vol. I, Chaps. III-VI; James H. Kellar, "In Search of Ouiatanon," *Indiana History Bulletin,* XLVII (1970), 123-133; Frances Krauskopf, The French in Indiana, 1700-1760. A Political History (Unpublished Ph. D. thesis, Indiana University, 1953); Edmond Mallet, *Sieur de Vincennes, the Founder of Indiana's Oldest Town* (Indiana Historical Society *Publications,* II, No. 2, Indianapolis, 1897); Paul C. Phillips, "Vincennes in its Relation to French Colonial Policy," *Indiana Magazine of History,* XVII (1921), 311-337; Pierre-Georges Roy, *Sieur de Vincennes Identified* (Indiana Historical Society *Publications,* VII, No. 1, Indianapolis [1919]); Erminie W. Voegelin,

"Indians of Indiana," Indiana Academy of Science, *Proceedings,* L (1941), 27-32; Paul W. Woehrmann, *At the Headwaters of the Maumee. A History of the Forts of Fort Wayne* (Indiana Historical Society *Publications,* XXIV, Indianapolis, 1971).

Fort St. Joseph, north of the present Indiana state line, is dealt with in Dunning Idle, The Post of the St. Joseph River during the French Regime, 1679-1761 (Unpublished Ph.D. thesis, University of Illinois, 1946), and in Daniel McCoy, "Old Fort St. Joseph," *Michigan Pioneer and Historical Collections,* XXXV (1907), 545-552.

For the rivalry between the English and the French and the final struggle for control of the area south of the Great Lakes, see Beverley W. Bond, Jr., *The Foundations of Ohio* (*The History of the State of Ohio,* Vol. I, Columbus, 1941); Randolph C. Downes, *Council Fires on the Upper Ohio . . .* (University of Pittsburgh Press, 1940); Catherine E. Gregory, The Miami Revolt, 1748-1752 (Unpublished M.A. thesis in history, University of Illinois, 1936); C. A. Hanna, *The Wilderness Trail or the Ventures and Adventures of the Pennsylvania Traders on the Allegheny Path . . .* (2 vols., New York, 1911); Wilbur R. Jacobs, "Presents to Indians along the French Frontiers in the Old Northwest, 1748-1763," *Indiana Magazine of History,* XLIV (1948), 245-256; Donald H. Kent, *The French Invasion of Western Pennsylvania* (Harrisburg, Pa., 1954); R. W. McFarland, "Forts Loramie and Pickawillany," Ohio Archaeological and Historical Society *Quarterly,* VIII (1900), 479-486; Ronald D. Martin, "Confrontation at the Monongahela: Climax of the French Drive into the Upper Ohio Region," *Pennsylvania History,* XXXVII (1970), 133-150.

The founding of the St. Francis Xavier Parish at Vincennes in 1749 and its subsequent history are related in Gilbert J. Garraghan, "Vincennes: A Chapter in the Ecclesiastical History of the West," *Mid-America,* II, No. 4 (April, 1931).

THE BRITISH PERIOD

Manuscripts

Except for a brief occupation of the French posts of Miamis and Ouiatanon the Indiana area had no resident British officials during the British regime in the Old Northwest, but was under the jurisdiction of officials at Fort de Chartres, Detroit, and Fort Pitt. The Indian trade was under the direction of Sir William Johnson, superintendent of the northern department of Indian affairs. There are no original manuscripts for the British period in Indiana libraries but some transcripts and microfilm copies are available. The largest collection of original sources and transcripts is in the Public Archives of Canada.

At the same time that the Canadian archivist Douglas Brymner began his search for archival material in Paris, he also instituted a search of the British archives in London. During the years that he held the post of archivist he had copies made of the papers of Henry Bouquet and Frederick Haldimand in the British Museum (Series A and B) and Series Q and part of M of the Colonial Office correspondence in the Public Record Office. Bouquet came to America in 1756 as an officer in the Royal American Regiment; his correspondence centers around the Seven Years' War and Pontiac's conspiracy. A calendar of his papers was printed as a supplement to the *Report* of the Canadian Archives for 1889. That part of Haldimand's correspondence which concerns Indiana is for the period 1773-74 when he was in charge of the British forces in America, and the period of the American Revolution when he was serving as governor of the Province of Quebec. His entire correspondence was calendared by Dr. Brymner and occupies a large portion of the *Reports* of the Canadian Archives for 1882 and 1884-89 inclusive. The Library of Congress has acquired in recent years photocopies (negatives) of the Bouquet and Haldimand Papers from the British Museum; the Indiana Historical Society has transcripts of the former.

Transcripts from the Public Record Office, Series Q, include correspondence of the colonial officials with the Colonial Office in London. The calendars of these in the *Reports* of the Canadian Archives for 1890 and 1891 cover the period prior to 1800.

Although the above series were the principal ones used in the preparation of the present volume, the Canadian Archives has transcripts of much additional material relating to the United States, especially Series C dealing with military affairs and Series S dealing with Indian affairs.

The William L. Clements Library has the papers of Maj. Gen. Jeffrey Amherst, British commander in chief when the French posts were taken over by the British, and the papers of Gen. Thomas Gage, who succeeded Amherst and served as commander in chief until 1773, and again in 1774-75.

The papers of the trading firm of Baynton, Wharton and Morgan which was active in the Illinois country during the British period are in the library of the Pennsylvania Historical Commission at Harrisburg. The Indiana Historical Society Library has a microfilm of these.

For additional information regarding sources for the British period, see Henry P. Beers, *The French & British in the Old Northwest. A Bibliographical Guide to Archive and Manuscript Sources* (Wayne State University Press, Detroit, 1964), Chaps. III-IV; and by the same author, "The Papers of the British Commanders in Chief in North America, 1754-1783," *Military Affairs,* XIII (1949), 79-94. See also Grace Gardner Griffin (comp.), *A Guide to Manuscripts Relating to American History in British Depositories Reproduced for the Division of Manuscripts of the Library of Congress* (Washington, D. C., 1946); David W. Parker, *Guide to Materials for United States History in Canadian Archives* (Carnegie Institution of Washington, D. C., 1913); and Howard H. Peckham (comp.), *Guide to the Manuscript Collections in the William L. Clements Library* (Ann Arbor, Mich., 1942).

Published Sources

Account of the Proceedings of the Illinois and Ouabache Land Companies (Philadelphia, 1796).

Alvord, Clarence W., and Carter, Clarence E. (eds.), *The Critical Period, 1763-1765 (Illinois Historical Collections,* X, Springfield, 1915).

Alvord, Clarence W., and Carter, Clarence E. (eds.), *The New Régime, 1765-1767* (*Illinois Historical Collections,* XI, Springfield, 1916).

Alvord, Clarence W., and Carter, Clarence E. (eds.), *Trade and Politics, 1767-1769* (*Illinois Historical Collections,* XVI, Springfield, 1921).

Bond, Beverley W., Jr. (ed.), *The Courses of the Ohio River Taken by Lt. T. Hutchins . . .* (Cincinnati, 1942).

Henry Bouquet Papers, in *Michigan Pioneer and Historical Collections,* XIX (1892), 27-295.

Carter, Clarence E. (ed.), *The Correspondence of General Thomas Gage with the Secretaries of State . . . , 1763-1775* (2 vols., Yale University Press, 1931, 1933).

—— (ed.), "Documents relating to the Occupation of the Illinois Country by the British," Illinois State Historical Society *Transactions,* 1907, pp. 202-221.

Dunn, Jacob P. (ed.), *Documents Relating to the French Settlements on the Wabash* (Indiana Historical Society *Publications,* II, No. 11, Indianapolis, 1894). The Indiana Historical Society Library has Xerox copies of the documents in this volume.

"The Gladwin Manuscripts," in *Michigan Pioneer and Historical Collections,* XXVII (1896), 605-680.

Frederick Haldimand Papers, in *Michigan Pioneer and Historical Collections,* X (1886), XI (1887), XIX (1892), and XX (1892).

The Papers of Sir William Johnson (13 vols. + Index, State University of New York, Albany, 1921-62).

O'Callaghan, Edmund B., and Fernow, B. (eds.), *Documents Relative to the Colonial History of the State of New York . . .* (15 vols., Albany, 1853-87), Vols. VII and VIII.

Peckham, Howard H. (ed.), "The Journal of Capt. Thomas Morris, 1764," *Old Fort News,* VI, No. 1 (Allen County—Fort Wayne Historical Society, 1941).

—— (ed.), *George Croghan's Journal of His Trip to Detroit in 1767 . . .* (Ann Arbor, Mich., 1939).

Journal of Major Robert Rogers . . . (London, 1765).

Shortt, Adam S., and Doughty, Arthur G. (eds.), *Documents Relating to the Constitutional History of Canada, 1759-1791* (2 vols., Ottawa, 1918).

Stevens, Sylvester K., and Kent, Donald H. (eds.), *The Papers of Col. Henry Bouquet* (17 vols., mimeograph, Pennsylvania Historical Commission, 1940-43).

Thwaites, Reuben G., "British Regime in Wisconsin, 1760-1800," *Wisconsin Historical Collections,* XVIII (1908), 223-468.

—— (ed.), Journals of George Croghan in *Early Western Travels, 1748-1846* (32 vols., Cleveland, 1904-1907), Vol. I.

Watts, Florence G. (ed.), "Some Vincennes Documents of 1772," *Indiana Magazine of History,* XXXIV (1938), 199-212.

Secondary Sources

Among the publications dealing with the British regime in the area south of the Great Lakes are: Clarence W. Alvord, *The Mississippi Valley in British Politics. A Study of the Trade, Land Speculations, and Experiments in Imperialism Culminating in the American Revolution* (2 vols., New York, 1959); Clarence E. Carter, *Great Britain and the Illinois Country, 1763-1774* (American Historical Association, 1910); Lawrence H. Gipson, *The British Empire before the American Revolution* ... (13 vols., Caldwell, Idaho, 1936-67), Vols. IX and XI; and Jack M. Sosin, *Whitehall and the Wilderness. The Middle West in British Colonial Policy, 1760-1775* (University of Nebraska Press, Lincoln, 1961).

The best account of Pontiac's conspiracy is Howard Peckham, *Pontiac and the Indian Uprising* (Princeton University Press, 1947). Two other volumes dealing with Indian affairs are Randolph C. Downes, *Council Fires on the Upper Ohio* ... (University of Pittsburgh Press, 1940), Chaps. V and VI, and *Historical Account of Bouquet's Expedition against the Ohio Indians, in 1764* (Cincinnati, 1868). The activities of the British Indian agent George Croghan are treated by his two biographers Albert T. Volwiler and Nicholas B. Wainwright.

Secondary accounts dealing particularly with the Indian trade are Paul C. Phillips and John W. Smurr, *The Fur Trade* (2 vols., Norman, Okla., 1961), I, Chaps. 27-29; Max Savelle, *George Morgan, Colony Builder* (Columbia University Press, New York, 1932), Chaps. II and III, and Wayne E. Stevens, *The Northwest Fur Trade, 1763-1800* (University of Illinois, *Studies in the Social Sciences*, XIV, No. 3, Urbana, 1928). For a brief account, see Charles M. Thomas, "Successful and Unsuccessful Merchants in the Illinois Country," *Journal* of the Illinois State Historical Society, XXX (1937-38), 429-440.

THE AMERICAN REVOLUTION

Manuscripts

Transcripts of the correspondence of Edward Abbott who served briefly as lieutenant governor at Vincennes in 1777-78 are in the Public Archives of Canada, Series Q, copied from the Public Record Office in London. The Indiana Division, Indiana State Library, has a microfilm of the transcripts. Some of the letters have been published.

The two most important British officers in the West during the American Revolution were Col. Henry Hamilton, lieutenant governor at Detroit from 1775 until his surrender at Vincennes in February, 1779, and Col. Arent S. de Peyster, lieutenant governor at Michilimackinac, 1775-79, and at Detroit, 1779-83. Fortunately the administrations of both men are well documented. Hamilton's correspondence may be found in the Haldimand Papers in the British Museum and in the Gen. Thomas Gage and Lord George Germain Papers in the William L. Clements Library, University of Michigan. Hamilton's Report, 1776-81, is also in the British Museum. The Canadian Archives has transcripts of the Hamilton Papers in the British Museum, about one third of which have been published. The Indiana State Library has a microfilm of those relating to the Vincennes expedition. The Indiana Historical Society Library has a copy of Hamilton's Report. Hamilton's Journal for 1778-79 is in the Houghton Library, Harvard University, and has been printed. De Peyster's correspondence may also be found in the Haldimand Papers, with transcripts in the Canadian Archives, and in the Daniel Claus Papers, the originals of which are in the Canadian Archives. Much of it is available in printed form.

On the American side, George Rogers Clark is the outstanding figure of the American Revolution in the West. Others, in addition to Clark's officers, were John Todd, Francis Vigo, Pierre Gibault, Francis Bosseron, and J. M. P. Le Gras. Clark's movements in the West were directed first by Patrick Henry and then by Thomas Jefferson until 1781. The principal depositories for the papers of George Rogers Clark are the Draper Collection, Wisconsin State Historical Society, the Virginia State Library, and the Virginia State Archives. Many of them have been published. Patrick Henry's letter of secret instructions to Clark is in the Indiana Historical Society Library. A great deal of correspondence on the western expeditions that is in the Jefferson Papers in the Library of Congress is printed in the Julian P. Boyd edition of his *Papers*.

The Francis Vigo Papers, 1751-1841, comprising 483 items, are in the Indiana Historical Society Library; many of these deal with land and the fur trade. The Gibault Papers are in the Archdiocesan Archives in Quebec; John Todd's Journal and Papers for 1779-80 when he was lieutenant of the Illinois County of Virginia are in the Chicago Historical Society and have been printed. The account book of Francis Bosseron is in the Lasselle Papers, Indiana Division, Indiana State Library; a Clark letter of 1780 to Bosseron is also in the Indiana Division.

Published Sources

Much of the Henry Hamilton and Arent S. de Peyster correspondence and two Abbott letters are printed in *Michigan Pioneer and Historical Collections,* Vols. IX-XI and XIX-XX; other Hamilton letters and some of Edward Abbott and of Rocheblave, British agent at Kaskaskia, are printed in *Illinois Historical Collections,* Vol. I, edited by Hiram W. Beckwith, and in Edward G. Mason (ed.), *Early Chicago and Illinois* (*Chicago Historical Society's Collection,* IV, Chicago, 1890). Hamilton's Journal is in John D. Barnhart, *Henry Hamilton and George Rogers Clark in the American Revolution with the Unpublished Journal of Lieut. Gov. Henry Hamilton* (Crawfordsville, Ind., 1951). Other De Peyster correspondence is in *Miscellanies by an Officer, . . . ,* edited by J. Watts de Peyster (2 parts, New York, 1888).

The account of the British surrender of Fort Sackville written by Jacob Schieffelin, one of Hamilton's officers, was printed in the New York *Royal Gazette,* July 17, 1780; the Indiana State Library has a photostatic copy.

Two volumes of *George Rogers Clark Papers,* edited by James A. James, are printed as *Illinois Historical Collections,* Vols. VIII and XIX (Springfield, 1912 and 1926). Other correspondence of Clark with his officers as well as other material on the Revolution in the West appears in the two volumes edited by Clarence W. Alvord, entitled *Cahokia Records, 1778-1790* and *Kaskaskia Records, 1778-1790* (*Illinois Historical Collections,* II and V, Springfield, 1907, 1909), and in Milo M. Quaife (ed.), *The Capture of Old Vincennes. The Original Narratives of . . . Clark and . . . Hamilton* (Indianapolis, 1927). Clark's proclamation to the citizens of Vincennes and the names of those who signed the oath of allegiance to the American government is in *Transactions* of the Illinois State Historical Society, 1907, pp. 265-276.

John Todd's Record Book and Papers relating to his administration of the County of Illinois are in Mason (ed.), *Early Chicago and Illinois*; the Account Book kept by Francis Bosseron of Vincennes during the Revolution was edited by Janet P. Shaw and printed in *Indiana Magazine of History,* XXV (1929), 212-241.

Julian P. Boyd (ed.), *The Papers of Thomas Jefferson . . .*, Vols. II, III, and IV (Princeton University Press, 1950-51) cover the war years while he was governor of Virginia.

Five volumes edited by Louise Kellogg and Reuben G. Thwaites and published by the Wisconsin State Historical Society concern the events that were transpiring on the Upper Ohio immediately preceding and during the Revolution. They are *Documentary History of Dunmore's War, 1774* (1905); *The Revolution on the Upper Ohio, 1775-1777* (1908); *Frontier Defense on the Upper Ohio, 1777-1778* (1912); *Frontier Advance on the Upper Ohio, 1778-1779* (1916), and *Frontier Retreat on the Upper Ohio, 1779-1781* (1917). The contents of these were drawn largely from the Draper Collection.

Francis Vigo's claim against the government for services rendered Clark is outlined in a petition filed in the U. S. Court of Claims by Vigo's heirs, a printed copy of which is in the Indiana Division, Indiana State Library. See also U. S. *House Reports,* 30 Congress, 1 session, No. 216 (1848). Letters of Father Pierre Gibault to Bishop Briand are printed in American Catholic Historical Society *Records,* XX (1909), 406-430.

The Rayneval Memorandum prepared in 1782 by the private secretary of Count de Vergennes, French minister of foreign affairs, for use in the treaty negotiations was edited by Florence G. Watts and printed in the *Indiana Magazine of History,* XXXVIII (1942), 167-207. The original is in the William L. Clements Library, University of Michigan.

Secondary Sources

Biographies. George Rogers Clark has been the subject of several biographies, those of Temple Bodley and James A. James (published in 1926 and 1928) being perhaps the best known. Others are by John Bakeless (1957), Frederick Palmer (1929), Lowell Thomas (1929). Especially suitable for young people are those by Walter Havighurst (1952), Ross Lockridge (1927), and William E. Wilson (1940). William H. English's *Conquest of the Country Northwest of the River Ohio, 1778-1783 and Life of Gen. George Rogers Clark* (2 vols., Indianapolis, 1897) contains biographical material not only on Clark but also on the men he drew around him.

Oliver Pollock, the unofficial agent of Virginia in New Orleans, who obtained much needed funds and supplies for the American cause, is the subject of a full length biography by Clark's biographer, James A. James. Francis Bosseron and Francis Vigo are treated in articles in the *Indiana Magazine of History*, XXV (1929), 204-211, and XXVI (1930), 12-24, by Janet P. Shaw and Dorothy Riker respectively. One of Clark's most trusted soldiers, Leonard Helm, is the subject of an article by Bessie T. Conkwright in the *Indiana History Bulletin*, X (1932-33), 407-434, and the story of Godefroy Linctot, a French trader who espoused the American cause and aided Clark in winning the Indians to his side, is told by George Brennan in the *Journal* of the Illinois State Historical Society, X (1917-18), 323-366.

Other volumes and articles on Clark's Illinois expedition are: Consul W. Butterfield, *History of George Rogers Clark's Conquest of the Illinois and the Wabash Towns 1778-1779* (Columbus, Ohio, 1904); Theodore C. Pease and Marguerite Jenison Pease, *George Rogers Clark and the Revolution in Illinois, 1763-1787* (Springfield, Ill., 1929); James G. Randall, "George Rogers Clark's Service of Supply," *Mississippi Valley Historical Review*, VIII (1921-22), 250-263; R. C. Ballard Thruston, "Colors of the Illinois Campaign under George Rogers Clark," *Indiana History Bulletin*, IX (1931-32), 230-239; and F. M. Woolard, "Route of Colonel George Rogers Clark and his Army from Kaskaskia to Vincennes, 1779," *Transactions* of the Illinois State Historical Society, 1907, pp. 48-63.

On the British side neither Henry Hamilton nor Arent S. de Peyster are the subjects of full length biographies, but the Mohawk chief, Joseph Brant, who aided the British during the Revolution and afterwards, is treated in William L. Stone, *The Life of Joseph Brant—Thayendanegea, including the Border Wars of the American Revolution* . . . (2 vols., New York, 1838). British and American relations with the Indians are discussed in Louise Phelps Kellogg, "Indian Diplomacy during the Revolution in the West," Illinois State Historical Society *Transactions*, 1929, pp. 47-57.

Alexander Scott Withers' *Chronicles of Border Warfare* (Clarksburg, Va., 1831) is one of many publications that recount the story of Indian raids on American settlements; Charles Martindale tells of Lochry's (Loughery's) Defeat in Indiana Historical Society *Publications*, II, No. 4, (Indianapolis, 1888), pp. 97-127; and Mrs. Maude W. Lafferty writes of one Kentucky raid in "Destruction of Ruddle's and Martin's Forts in the Revolutionary War," Kentucky Historical Society *Register*, LIV (1956), 297-338. American raids into the Ohio country in retaliation for Indian raids on Kentucky settlements are related by Charles G. Talbert, "Kentucky Invades Ohio," Kentucky Historical Society *Register*, LI-LIV (1953-56).

Bernardo de Galvez, the Spanish governor who aided the American cause during the early days of the Revolution, is the subject of a biography by John W. Caughey. Other volumes and articles on the part played by Spain are: Lawrence Kinnaird, *Spain in the Mississippi Valley, 1765-1794* (American Historical Association, *Annual Report*, 1945); the same author's article, "The Spanish Expedition against Fort St. Joseph in 1781. A New Interpretation," *Mississippi Valley Historical Review*, XIX (1932-33), 173-191; and

A. P. Nasatir, "The Anglo-Spanish Frontier in the Illinois Country during the American Revolution, 1779-1783," *Journal* of the Illinois State Historical Society, XXI (1928-29), 291-358.

The diplomacy of the American Revolution is treated in Samuel Flagg Bemis, *The Diplomacy of the American Revolution* (New York, 1935) and in Paul C. Phillips, *The West in the Diplomacy of the American Revolution* (University of Illinois *Studies in the Social Sciences,* II, Nos. 2 and 3, Urbana, 1913). The importance of Clark's Illinois expeditions and his subsequent control of the Illinois country in relation to the treaty negotiations at the close of the war are dealt with in many of the above volumes as well as in Clarence W. Alvord, "Virginia and the West," *Mississippi Valley Historical Review,* III (1916-17), 19-38, and in James A. James, "The Northwest: Gift or Conquest?" *Indiana Magazine of History,* XXX (1934), 1-15.

POST REVOLUTION AND NORTHWEST TERRITORY

Manuscripts

Indiana Division, Indiana State Library

Lyman C. Draper Collection, microfilm of originals in Wisconsin State Historical Society. Draper collected in the middle 1800s a vast amount of material relating to the trans-Allegheny region and the Ohio and upper Mississippi valleys, about one third of it original manuscripts. Upon his death in 1891, the collection was given to the Wisconsin State Historical Society where it was arranged by Reuben G. Thwaites into 486 volumes. In recent years the collection has been microfilmed and made available to other libraries; the State Library has microfilms of the greater part of the collection. Of particular interest to Indiana historians are the George Rogers Clark Papers, the Kentucky Papers, and those on the Frontier Wars.

Hyacinth and Charles B. Lasselle Collection, 1713-1904. 6,000 items; 91 account books. Contains materials on Fort Wayne and Vincennes; trade with Indians; militia; account books of Francis Bosseron and Hyacinth Lasselle.

Continental Congress Papers concerning Indian affairs, 1785-86. Photostats from National Archives. Letter of William Clark, messenger to Wabash Indians, and letter of treaty commissioners to Congress.

Archives Division, Indiana State Library

Records of Knox County courts of common pleas, general quarter sessions, orphans, and probate courts between 1790 and 1800. Microfilm and some transcripts.

Plat Book and Minutes of Board of Commissioners for Clark's Grant, 1785-1820.

Indiana Historical Society Library

John Armstrong Papers, 1775-1867. Approximately 5,000 items, about half of them for the period before 1816. Those for 1775-99 are calendared and indexed. Armstrong served in the Revolutionary War from Pennsylvania, was in the U. S. Army until 1793, then was a resident of Hamilton County, Ohio, and Clark County, Indiana Territory, until his death in 1816. The collection contains letters of such army officers as Hamtramck, Harmar, St. Clair, Wayne, and Wilkinson.

John Francis Hamtramck correspondence, microfilm and prints from Harmar Papers in William L. Clements Library, University of Michigan. About 200 pages.

Josiah Harmar letters, 1784-1792, transcripts in William Henry Smith Collection.

Diary of David Jones, chaplain in Wayne's army, 1794-1797. Microfilm of original in American Baptist Historical Society, Rochester, New York; also typed transcript.

Orderly book of John Mills, adjutant general of the Legion of the United States, April 8, 1794—January 18, 1795 (2 vols.).

Northwest Territory Collection. Approximately 400 items. Includes letters of Clark, Harmar, Knox, St. Clair, Wayne, and the Spanish governor of Upper Louisiana.

James O'Hara order books, 1792-93, and letter book, 1792-94. O'Hara was a contractor for the U. S. Army during the St. Clair and Wayne expeditions.

Arthur St. Clair Papers, 1771-1819, transcripts in William Henry Smith Collection. Also microcards for St. Clair Papers, 1788-1815, in Ohio State Library, including index.

Francis Vigo Papers, 1751-1841. Approximately 500 items, about half of them for the period 1782-1800. Fur trade, land, etc.

Lilly Library, Indiana University

Charles Willing Byrd Papers, 1784-1802. Byrd succeeded William Henry Harrison as secretary of the Northwest Territory in 1799.

John G. Jackson Letters and Papers, 1781-1832. Jackson was appointed surveyor of public lands in Ohio in 1793, and later served in Congress from Virginia.

John Wilkins Papers, 1797-1801. Wilkins was quartermaster of the U. S. Army during this period.

Published Sources

Of the official federal papers for the period 1783-1800, there are: Worthington C. Ford *et al.* (eds.), *Journals of the Continental Congress, 1774-1789* . . . (Library of Congress edition, 34 vols., Washington, D. C., 1904-37); William R. Manning (ed.), *Diplomatic Correspondence of the United States: Canadian Relations, 1784-1860* . . . (3 vols., Washington, D. C., 1940-43); *American State Papers. Indian Affairs* (2 vols., Washington, D. C., 1832, 1834); *Military Affairs* (7 vols., Washington, D. C., 1789-1838); *Public Lands* (8 vols., Washington, D. C., 1834-61).

For the Northwest Territory there are: Clarence E. Carter (ed.), *The Territorial Papers of the United States* (Vols. 1-26, Washington, D. C., 1934-62), Vols. II and III; *Journal of the House of Representatives . . . 1799* (Cincinnati, 1800); *Journal of the Legislative Council . . .* [1799] (Cincinnati,

n. d.) ; and Theodore C. Pease (ed.), *The Laws of the Northwest Territory, 1788-1800 (Illinois Historical Collections,* XVII, Springfield, 1925).

Important Congressional documents relating to the Northwest Territory are reprinted in Charles Kettleborough, *Constitution Making in Indiana. Volume I* (Indiana Historical Commission, Indianapolis, 1916) and in Hubert H. Hawkins (comp.), *Indiana's Road to Statehood* (Indiana Sesquicentennial Commission, 1964).

The papers of a number of army officers and persons holding public office have been printed and throw light on events of the period. Among these should be noted: *The Writings of James Monroe,* . . . edited by S. M. Hamilton (7 vols., New York, 1898-1903) ; *The Writings of George Washington . . . 1745-1799,* edited by John C. Fitzpatrick (39 vols., Washington, D. C., 1931-44) ; *The St. Clair Papers. The Life and Public Services of Arthur St. Clair* . . ., edited by William Henry Smith (2 vols., Cincinnati, 1882) ; "Military Journal of Major Ebenezer Denny . . .," *Memoirs* of the Historical Society of Pennsylvania, VII (Philadelphia, 1860), 205-492; Gayle Thornbrough (ed.), *Outpost on the Wabash, 1787-1791. Letters of Brigadier General Josiah Harmar and Major John Francis Hamtramck . . .* (Indiana Historical Society *Publications,* XIX, Indianapolis, 1957) ; Rowena Buell (comp.), *The Memoirs of Rufus Putnam* (Boston, 1903) ; Beverley W. Bond, Jr. (ed.), *The Correspondence of John Cleves Symmes . . .* (New York, 1926) ; "Winthrop Sargent's Diary while with General Arthur St. Clair's Expedition against the Indians," Ohio Archaeological and Historical Society *Quarterly,* XXXIII (1924), 237-273; Milo M. Quaife (ed.), "General James Wilkinson's Narrative of the Battle of Fallen Timbers," *Mississippi Valley Historical Review,* XVI (1926-27), 81-90; Richard C. Knopf (ed.), *Anthony Wayne. A Name in Arms . . . Wayne-Knox-Pickering-McHenry Correspondence* (Pittsburgh, 1960). Wayne's Orderly Books are printed in *Michigan Pioneer and Historical Collections,* XXXIV (1904), 341-733.

On the British side there is *The Correspondence of Lieut. Governor John Graves Simcoe . . .,* edited by Ernest Cruikshank (5 vols., Toronto, 1923-31), Vols. II and III. The *Michigan Pioneer and Historical Collections,* Vols. X-XII, XX, and XXIII-XXV contain documents and correspondence from the Haldimand Papers and from the British Public Record Office regarding the British government's relations with the Indians and with the United States following the Treaty of Paris in 1783.

Three other personal accounts of soldiers in General Wayne's army are those of John Bowyer (or Boyer) in *The American Pioneer* (Chillicothe, Ohio, 1842-43) ; "William Clark's Journal of General Wayne's Campaign," *Mississippi Valley Historical Review,* I (1914-15), 418-444; and *From Greene Ville to Fallen Timbers. A Journal of the Wayne Campaign . . . 1794,* by an unidentified soldier (Indiana Historical Society *Publications,* XVI, No. 3, Indianapolis, 1952). The original journal of the last soldier is in the Indiana Historical Society Library.

John Filson's experiences on an unofficial mission to Vincennes in 1785-86 are recorded in Beverley W. Bond, Jr. (ed.), "Two Westward Journeys of John Filson, 1785," *Mississippi Valley Historical Review,* IX (1922-23), 320-

330, and in Leonard C. Helderman, "John Filson's Narrative of His Defeat on the Wabash, 1786," *Filson Club History Quarterly,* XII (1938), 187-199. Letters of Vincennes residents at this critical time are in Helderman, "Danger on the Wabash. Vincennes Letters of 1786," *Indiana Magazine of History,* XXXIV (1938), 455-467, taken from the Draper Collection, State Historical Society of Wisconsin. The Moravian John Heckewelder accompanied Gen. Rufus Putnam on a peace mission to Vincennes in 1792 and left an account which is printed in *Pennsylvania Magazine of History and Biography,* XI (1887), 466-475, and XII (1888), 165-184.

Information on the fur trade during this period may be found in Milo M. Quaife (ed.), *The John Askin Papers,* 1747-1795, 1796-1820 (2 vols., Detroit, 1928, 1931), and in Christopher B. Coleman (ed.), "Letters from Eighteenth Century Indiana Merchants," *Indiana Magazine of History,* V (1909), 137-159. A visitor to Fort Wayne, believed to be Henry Hay, described his experiences in Milo M. Quaife (ed.), *Fort Wayne in 1790* (Indiana Historical Society *Publications,* VII, No. 7, Indianapolis, 1921). Other travelers who visited Indiana before 1800 and described what they saw were Moses Austin, "A Memorandum of M. Austin's Journey from the Lead Mines in . . . Virginia to the Lead Mines in . . . Louisiana," 1796-97, *American Historical Review,* V (1899-1900), 518-542; George Imlay, *A Topographical Description of the Western Territory of North America* (London, 1793), reprinted in part in Harlow Lindley (ed.), *Indiana as Seen by Early Travelers* (*Indiana Historical Collections,* III, Indianapolis, 1916), pp. 9-16; and C. F. Volney, A *View of the Soil and Climate of the United States of America* (Philadelphia, 1804), reprinted in part in *Indiana as Seen by Early Travelers,* pp. 17-24. *Travel Accounts of Indiana, 1679-1961* (*Indiana Historical Collections,* XLVII, Indianapolis, 1970), pp. 30-49, has excerpts from the writings of several other travelers.

Secondary Sources

There are a number of general histories for the period of the Confederation. One of the most recent is Merrill Jensen, *The New Nation. A History of the United States during the Confederation, 1781-1789* (New York, 1950).

Trouble with the Indians which in turn involved the United States with the British officials in Canada dominated much of the period. Four of the best studies dealing with these problems are Alfred L. Burt, *The United States, Great Britain, and British North America from the Revolution to . . . 1812* (Yale University Press, 1940); Reginald Horsman, *Expansion and American Indian Policy, 1783-1812* (Michigan State University Press, Lansing, 1967); Walter H. Mohr, *Federal Indian Relations, 1774-1788* (Philadelphia, 1933); and Francis Paul Prucha, *American Indian Policy in the Formative Years: The Indian Trade and Intercourse Acts, 1770-1834* (Harvard University Press, 1962). Others include Clarence M. Burton, "Ephraim Douglass and His Times," *Magazine of History,* III, Extra No. 10 (New York, 1910); Jack J. Gifford, The Northwest Indian War, 1784-1795 (Unpublished Ph.D.

thesis, University of California, 1964); Leonard C. Helderman, "The Northwest Expedition of George Rogers Clark, 1786," *Mississippi Valley Historical Review,* XXV (1938-39), 317-334; Reginald Horsman, *Matthew Elliott, British Indian Agent* (Wayne State University Press, Detroit, 1964); and the same author's two studies on "The British Indian Department and the Abortive Treaty of . . . 1793," *Ohio Historical Quarterly,* LXX (1961), 189-213, and "The British Indian Department and the Resistance to General Anthony Wayne, 1793-1795," *Mississippi Valley Historical Review,* XLIX (1962-63), 269-290; Thomas Irvin, "Harmar's Campaign," Ohio Archaeological and Historical Society *Quarterly,* XIX (1940), 393-396; Dwight L. Smith, "William Wells and the Indian Council of 1793," *Indiana Magazine of History,* LVI (1960), 215-226; Paul W. Wehr, Treaty of Fort Finney, 1786: Prelude to the Indian Wars (Unpublished M.A. thesis, Miami University, Oxford, Ohio, 1958); Robert B. Whitsett, "Snake-Fish Town, the Eighteenth Century Metropolis of Little Turtle's Eel River Miami," *Indiana History Bulletin,* XV (1938), 72-82; and Frazer E. Wilson, *The Treaty of Greenville . . .* (Piqua, Ohio, 1894).

On the development of the army, army posts, and biographies of military figures, see F. Clever Bald, "Colonel Francis Hamtramck," *Indiana Magazine of History,* XLIV (1948), 335-354; James R. Jacobs, *The Beginning of the U. S. Army, 1783-1812* (Princeton University Press, 1947); Francis Paul Prucha, *The Sword of the Republic. The United States Army on the Frontier, 1783-1846* (Toronto and London, 1969); Dorothy Riker, "Fort Finney," *Year Book* of the Society of Indiana Pioneers, 1944, pp. 15-20; Gayle Thornbrough, *Outpost on the Wabash . . .* (Indiana Historical Society *Publications,* XIX, Indianapolis, 1957), Introduction; Harry E. Wildes, *Anthony Wayne, Trouble Shooter of the American Revolution* (New York, 1941); Paul W. Woehrmann, *At the Headwaters of the Maumee. A History of the Forts of Fort Wayne* (Indiana Historical Society *Publications,* XXIV, 1971).

Diplomatic relations with Great Britain and Spain may be traced in Samuel F. Bemis, *Jay's Treaty. A Study in Commerce and Diplomacy* (Revised edition, Yale University Press, 1962), and the same author's *Pinckney's Treaty. A Study of America's Advantage from Europe's Distress, 1783-1800* (Baltimore, 1926); Lawrence Kinnaird, *Spain in the Mississippi Valley, 1765-1794* (American Historical Association, *Annual Report,* 1945); Albert P. Whitaker, *The Spanish-American Frontier, 1783-1795. The Westward Movement and the Spanish Retreat in the Mississippi Valley* (Boston and New York, 1927); and by the same author, *The Spanish-American Frontier, and the Mississippi Question, 1795-1803* (New York and London, 1934).

The work of an unofficial agent of the Illinois settlers in their dealings with Congress, is related in Howard C. Rice, *Barthélemi Tardiveau, a French Trader in the West . . .* (Baltimore, 1938). Phillips and Smurr, *The Fur Trade,* is valuable for this period as well as for the French and British periods. See Vol. II, Chaps. 31-32, 34-36.

Formulating a government for the area west of the Appalachians and its settlement hinged upon how the country settled its difficulties with the Indians, Great Britain, and Spain. The land question is particularly dealt with in

Thomas P. Abernethy, *Western Lands and the American Revolution* (New York and London, 1937); Benjamin H. Hibbard, *A History of the Public Land Policies* (University of Wisconsin Press, 1965); Leonard Lux, *The Vincennes Donation Lands* (Indiana Historical Society *Publications,* XV, No. 4, Indianapolis, 1949); Claude L. Shepard, "The Connecticut Land Company . . .," Western Reserve Historical Society, *Tract No. 96* (Cleveland, 1916); and Payson J. Treat, *The National Land System, 1785-1820* (New York, 1910). William H. English, *Conquest of the Country Northwest of the River Ohio . . .* (2 vols., Indianapolis, 1897), Vol. II, 1068-1121, deals with the distribution of the land in Clark's Grant.

Biographies of Governor St. Clair and Judge Rufus Putnam may be found in the Introduction to *The St. Clair Papers* and in *The Memoirs of Rufus Putnam,* mentioned above under Printed Sources; a brief sketch of Secretary Winthrop Sargent is in the Ohio Archaeological and Historical Society *Quarterly,* XXXV (1926), 583-601.

The important task of developing a government for the Northwest Territory is discussed in Jay A. Barrett, *Evolution of the Ordinance of 1787, with an Account of the Earlier Plans for the Government of the Northwest Territory* (New York, 1891), and in Edward Coles, *History of the Ordinance of 1787* (Historical Society of Pennsylvania, 1856). On the occasion of the sesquicentennial of the Ordinance, its significance is assessed by two historians of the Middle West, Theodore C. Pease, in *Mississippi Valley Historical Review,* XXV (1938-39), 167-180; and Milo M. Quaife, in *Journal* of the Illinois State Historical Society, XXX (1938), 415-428.

The settlement of the Northwest Territory and particularly the Ohio portion, is related in Beverley W. Bond, Jr., *The Civilization of the Old Northwest. A Study of Political, Social, and Economic Development, 1788-1812* (New York, 1934); Jacob Burnet, *Notes on the Early Settlement of the North-Western Territory* (Cincinnati, 1847); Randolph C. Downes, *Frontier Ohio, 1788-1803* (*Ohio Historical Collections,* III, Columbus, 1935); and Rufus King, *First Fruits of the Ordinance of 1787* (American Commonwealths Series, Boston and New York, 1888).

INDIANA TERRITORY

Manuscripts

For the territorial period, 1800-1816, there is an abundance of original manuscript material in the Indiana State Library, the Indiana Historical Society Library, and the Lilly Library at Indiana University.

Archives Division, Indiana State Library

Journal of the Proceedings of the Executive Government of the Indiana Territory, 1800-1816. Records civil and militia appointments, proclamations, pardons and remissions of fines, ferry licenses, writs for elections, etc. It has been printed.

Governors' papers. Miscellaneous correspondence regarding appointments and other official business, about 80 items; also bonds of public officials.

Journals of the House of Representatives for the sessions of 1805 (incomplete), 1808, Rump Session 1809, 1811, 1813, 1813-14, Special Session 1814, Regular Session 1814, and 1815.

Journals of the Legislative Council for the session of 1813-14.

Enrolled bills. Most of these are preserved in the Archives Division; a few are in the Indiana Historical Society Library.

Order Books of the General Court of Indiana Territory, 1801-1810, 1811-1816 (2 vols.). Some of the original papers in the cases have also been preserved.

Treasurer's Account Book, 1806-1813.

Constitution of 1816 (one of two original copies).

In addition to the records of state agencies, the Archives Division has the following original and microfilm records of federal agencies:

Record book of Allan D. Thom, collector of internal revenue, 1814-1816.

Notebooks of surveyors, plat books, and records of sale of land in Vincennes and Jeffersonville Land Offices; plat books for that portion of the territory which lay in the Cincinnati Land District.

Records of militia companies called into U. S. service during the War of 1812; these companies manned blockhouses on the frontier. Photostats from National Archives.

Correspondence of War Department and General Land Office. Microfilm from National Archives.

The Archives Division has some original county records, mostly for the circuit courts, for the counties of Harrison, Jefferson, Perry, Switzerland, and Wayne. They have microfilm copies of court, deed, marriage, probate, and will records for the counties of Clark, Franklin, Gibson, Harrison, Jefferson, Knox, Perry, Posey, Warrick, and Washington. The original Clark County Register of Negroes, 1805-10, and a microfilm of the Knox County Register of Negro Slaves, 1805-1807, are in the Archives Division.

Genealogy Division, Indiana State Library

Muster, Pay and Receipt Rolls of Indiana Territory, Volunteers or Militia, War of 1812 (4 vols.). Photostats from National Archives.

Pay Rolls of Militia in the Battle of Tippecanoe. Photostats from National Archives.

Vincennes. St. Francis Xavier Parish Records, 1749-1838 (6 vols.). Photostats.

Indiana Division, Indiana State Library

Joseph Bailly Papers, 1794-1836. 42 ledgers and daybooks on fur trade. Bailly's trading activities were centered first around Michilimackinac and then in northwestern Indiana.

Church records. Indiana Church (Presbyterian), Knox County, Minutes of the Session, 1812-42 (typed MS); Little Cedar Grove Baptist, Franklin County, Minute Book, 1806-30 (microfilm); Records of Owens (or Silver) Creek Baptist, Clark County, 1798-1837 (2 vols.).

Dufour Collection, 1801-1836. Articles and original papers dealing with the early history of Switzerland County.

Franklin County. Estray Record of cattle and livestock, 1811-1814; Record of marks and brands, 1811-1839. Microfilm.

Jonathan Jennings Papers, 1806-1832, 60 items. Photostats of personal and official correspondence from William H. English Collection, University of Chicago; also some original documents.

Lasselle Collection, see above, p. 478.

William Prince Papers, 1809-1834, 20 items. Prince was a resident of Vincennes, served in General Assembly, as auditor, Indian agent, and militia officer.

Hosea Smith Papers, 1810-1823, 23 items, photocopies. Letters written from White Oak Springs to relatives in North Carolina.

Waller Taylor Papers, 1812-1815. Photocopies from originals in Library of Congress.

John Tipton's Journal of Tippecanoe expedition and correspondence regarding militia, in Tipton Papers, 1806-1858.

Vincennes Papers, 1772-1827, 21 items. Microfilm of letters and documents in possession of Thomas Emison, Vincennes.

Miscellaneous papers and documents relating to removal of capital, elections, impeachment or removal of Governor Harrison, militia, etc.

Indiana Historical Society Library

John G. Biel Notes, 1808-1820, on 5 x 8-inch cards. Chronological account of events leading to Battle of Tippecanoe and subsequent material relating to Fort Harrison as abstracted from known correspondence and newspaper accounts.

John Badollet Papers, 1768-1901, 171 items. Microfilm from originals in Vincennes University Library.

William H. English Collection, 1777-1896. About 100 items for territorial period including correspondence of Governors Harrison and Posey and Secretary Gibson; election returns for 1809 and 1812 from certain counties; biographical sketches of members of the territorial Assembly, judges, and other officials.

Thomas W. Gibson abstract record of Clark's Grant (1 vol.). Plats and abstracts of each lot down to about 1849.

Christian Graeter Account Books. Graeter operated a tavern in Vincennes during the teritorial period and early statehood. Three daybooks, three records of billiard games, and two lists of debtors, etc. for the territorial period.

John Kennedy Graham Papers, 1786-1921. 427 items, about 80 of which are for period prior to 1816. Graham was a surveyor, a resident of Clark and Floyd counties.

William Henry Harrison Miscellaneous Papers, 1793-1864. About 300 items for the territorial period. Includes both official and personal correspondence, miscellaneous material relating to the period and the War of 1812.

William Henry Harrison Papers, 1734-1932. 3 reels microfilm from originals in Library of Congress. Reels 1 and 2 and part of 3 are for period before 1816.

Indiana Constitution, 1816. One of two original copies.

Isaac McCoy Papers, 1808-1874. 13 reels microfilm from originals in Kansas State Historical Society. Includes correspondence while McCoy was pastor of Maria Creek Church, Knox County, 1815-17.

James Miller Papers, 1811-1812. Photostats from B. J. Lossing Collection, Detroit Public Library. Miller was a member of Fourth Regiment; letters to his wife written from Vincennes and Fort Harrison.

Arthur G. Mitten Collection, 1474 items. Includes manuscripts on Northwest Territory, Battle of Tippecanoe, War of 1812, Indiana governors, James Taylor and Samuel Hodgdon Papers.

Records of the Moravian Missions among the Indians of North America. 40 reels microfilm from originals in Archives of Moravian Church, Bethlehem, Pa. Reel 21 contains diaries and letters of founders of White River Mission.

Orderly Book, U. S. Infantry, Fourth Regiment, under Col. John P. Boyd, 1808-12.

Samuel C. Vance Papers, 1797-1868. About 350 items prior to 1816. Calendared and indexed. Vance was deputy paymaster of U. S. Army, 1799-1802, with headquarters at Fort Washington; later resident of Lawrenceburg.

Francis Vigo Papers, see above, p. 479.

Lilly Library, Indiana University

William Henry Harrison Letters and Papers, Group II. The papers are for the period 1794-98 and pertain to Harrison's service in the U. S. Army; the letters are for the period 1803-34.

Harrison Township, Knox County. Official records, 1808-88, and other material covering the period, 1796-1874.

Jones and Stockwell store, Princeton. Daybooks for period 1815-67.

Hyacinth Lasselle Papers. Family papers dating back to 13th century.

David H. Maxwell Papers, 1811-1852. Maxwell was a physician and a member of Constitutional Convention.

William Polke Letters and Papers, 1809-69. Polke was a territorial legislator and member of Constitutional Convention.

Rappite Manuscripts, 1814-1889.

War of 1812 Manuscripts. These relate to all phases of the war including campaigns in the West. Includes letters of Generals William Henry Harrison, William Hull, Andrew Jackson; of Secretary of War James Monroe; and of James Taylor, quartermaster general of Northwest army.

Glenn A. Black Laboratory of Archaeology, Indiana University

Special mention should be made of the material collected on the Indians by the Great Lakes—Ohio Valley Ethnohistory Project under the direction of Mrs. Erminie Wheeler-Voegelin which has become available for research as the present volume goes to press. It is separated into three main divisions: (1) a microfilm collection, which includes films of the Indian material in the National Archives, films of the entire Draper Collection at the Wisconsin State Historical Society, and of other manuscripts containing Indian material; (2) excerpts relating to Indians, collected from all known sources and arranged by Indian tribes and then by year; (3) reports submitted to the Department of Justice by the Project in connection with Indian claims for compensation. Persons interested in using the material should write to Dr. James H. Kellar at the Glenn A. Black Laboratory.

Printed Sources

Federal

American State Papers. Finance (5 vols., Washington, D. C., 1832). For the volumes on Indian Affairs, Military Affairs, and Public Lands see p. 479.

Annals of Congress, 10 Congress, 2 session; 11 Congress, 1 and 2 sessions.

Carter, Clarence E. (ed.), *The Territorial Papers of the United States* (Vols. 1-26, Washington, 1934-62), Vols. VII and VIII.

U. S. Census. *A Statement of the Arts and Manufactures of the United States of America, for the Year 1810* (Philadelphia, 1814).

————, Population figures for 1800 and 1810 are printed in *Executive Journal of Indiana Territory, 1800-1816,* pp. 83-85.

U. S. Senate, *Executive Journal,* Vols. I-III. Federal appointments.

U. S. *Statutes at Large,* Vols. II and III (1799-1823).

State

Esarey, Logan (ed.), *Governors Messages and Letters. Messages and Letters of William Henry Harrison* (2 vols., *Indiana Historical Collections,* VII, IX, Indianapolis, 1922). Includes messages and letters of Thomas Posey.

Ewbank, Louis B. (ed.), *The Laws of Indiana Territory, 1809-1816* (*Indiana Historical Collections,* XX, Indianapolis, 1934).

Executive Journal of Indiana Territory, 1800-1816, edited by William Wesley Woollen, Daniel Wait Howe, and Jacob Piatt Dunn (Indiana Historical Society *Publications,* III, No. 3, Indianapolis, 1900).

Journal of the Convention of Indiana Territory . . . (Louisville, 1816), reprinted in *Indiana Magazine of History,* LXI (1965), 87-155.

Journals of the General Assembly of Indiana Territory, 1805-1815, edited by Gayle Thornbrough and Dorothy Riker (*Indiana Historical Collections,* XXXII, Indianapolis, 1950).

Kettleborough, Charles, *Constitution Making in Indiana* (3 vols., *Indiana Historical Collections,* I, II, XVII, Indianapolis, 1916, 1930). Vol. I.

Philbrick, Francis S. (ed.), *The Laws of Indiana Territory, 1801-1809* (*Illinois Historical Collections,* XXI, Springfield, 1930, reprinted by Indiana Historical Bureau, 1931).

Thornbrough, Gayle (ed.), *Letter Book of the Indian Agency at Fort Wayne, 1809-1815* (Indiana Historical Society *Publications,* XXI, Indianapolis, 1961).

The following unofficial papers throw light on the period:

Barnhart, John D. (ed.), "Letters of William H. Harrison to Thomas Worthington, 1799-1813," *Indiana Magazine of History,* XLVII (1951), 53-84.

—— (ed.), "The Letters of Decius," *Indiana Magazine of History*, XLIII (1947), 263-296. Criticism of Harrison's administration.

Constantine, J. Robert (ed.), "Minutes of the Vincennes Library Company, 1806-1883," *Indiana Magazine of History*, LXI-LXIII (1965-67).

"Documents Relating to Detroit and Vicinity, 1805-1813," *Michigan Pioneer and Historical Collections*, XL (1929).

Dunn, Jacob Piatt (ed.), *Slavery Petitions and Papers* (Indiana Historical Society *Publications*, II, No. 12, Indianapolis, 1894). Petitions to Congress from the legislature and unofficial groups.

Gipson, Lawrence H. (ed.), *The Moravian Indian Mission on White River— Diaries and Letters, May 5, 1799, to November 12, 1806* (*Indiana Historical Collections*, XXIII, Indianapolis, 1938).

Hopkins, Gerard T., *A Mission to the Indians, from the Indian Committee of Baltimore Yearly Meeting, to Fort Wayne, in 1804* (Philadelphia, 1862).

Riker, Dorothy (ed.), *Unofficial Letters of Jonathan Jennings* (Indiana Historical Society *Publications*, X, No. 4, Indianapolis, 1932).

"Some Additional Jennings Letters," *Indiana Magazine of History*, XXXIX (1943), 279-295.

Robertson, Nellie A., and Riker, Dorothy (eds.), *The John Tipton Papers* (3 vols., *Indiana Historical Collections*, XXIV-XXVI, Indianapolis, 1942). Vol. I.

Thornbrough, Gayle (ed.), *Correspondence of John Badollet and Albert Gallatin, 1804-1836* (Indiana Historical Society *Publications*, XXII, Indianapolis, 1963).

Additional sources relating to the Battle of Tippecanoe and the War of 1812 include:

"Mrs. Lydia B. Bacon's Journal, 1811-1812," *Indiana Magazine of History*, XL (1944), 367-386; XLI (1945), 59-79. Mrs. Bacon's husband was an officer in the Fourth Regiment; she accompanied her husband to Indiana Territory.

Hamilton, Capt. Robert, "The Expeditions of Major-General Samuel Hopkins," *Indiana Magazine of History*, XLIII (1947), 393-402. Letters by one of Hopkins' soldiers.

Jordan, Walter K., letter describing Fort Dearborn Massacre, in *Indiana Magazine of History*, XLI (1945), 187-199.

Naylor, Isaac, "Account of Battle of Tippecanoe," *Indiana Magazine of History*, II (1906), 163-169.

Relations of the British government with the United States preliminary to and during the War of 1812, in *Michigan Pioneer and Historical Collections*, XV (1889). Papers from the Canadian Archives. See also Vol. XL containing the correspondence of American officials with the United States government.

"War of 1812 Diary of William B. Northcutt," Kentucky Historical Society *Register*, LVI (1958), 256-262. Northcutt was a member of the Mississinewa expedition.

War of 1812 in the Northwest. Document Transcriptions of, compiled by Richard C. Knopf (10 vols. + Index, Ohio Historical Society, 1957-62). Official and unofficial correspondence and documents.

Secondary Sources

For general accounts of the territorial period, see *"Territorial Days in Indiana 1800-1816" (Indiana History Bulletin,* XXVII, No. 5, May, 1950); Rolla M. Hogue, "Life in Indiana, 1800-1820," *Indiana Magazine of History,* IX (1913), 83-92; Donald F. Carmony, "Indiana Territorial Expenditures, 1800-1816," *Indiana Magazine of History,* XXXIX (1943), 237-262. R. Carlyle Buley, *The Old Northwest. Pioneer Period, 1815-1840* (2 vols., Indiana Historical Society, Indianapolis, 1950), deals more particularly with the period after 1816, but it is also valuable for the territorial period.

There are a number of biographies of William Henry Harrison, the principal figure in the territorial period, including: Freeman Cleaves, *Old Tippecanoe. William Henry Harrison and His Time* (New York, 1939); Moses Dawson, *A Historical Narrative of the Civil and Military Services of Major-General William H. Harrison . . .* (Cincinnati, 1824); Dorothy Burne Goebel, *William Henry Harrison. A Political Biography (Indiana Historical Collections,* XIV, Indianapolis, 1926); James A. Green, *William Henry Harrison. His Life and Times* (Richmond, Va., 1941).

There is no adequate biography of Thomas Posey; the sketch in the *Dictionary of American Biography* gives the main points in his career. Sketches and biographies of other figures of the period include: Clarence E. Carter, "William Clarke, First Chief Justice of Indiana Territory," *Indiana Magazine of History,* XXXIV (1938), 1-13; Charles N. Thompson, *Sons of the Wilderness. John and William Conner* (Indiana Historical Society *Publications,* XII, Indianapolis, 1937); Dorothy Riker, "Jonathan Jennings," *Indiana Magazine of History,* XXVIII (1932), 223-239; George R. Wilson, "General Washington Johnston," *Indiana Magazine of History,* XX (1924), 123-154; E. O. Randall, "Tecumseh, the Shawnee Chief," Ohio Archaeological and Historical Society *Quarterly,* XV (1906), 419-498; Glenn Tucker, *Tecumseh, Vision of Glory* (Indianapolis, 1956). Biographies of William Hendricks and Waller Taylor are in the process of preparation by Frederick D. Hill and Donald E. Baker. For other sketches, see William Wesley Woollen, *Biographical and Historical Sketches of Early Indiana* (Indianapolis, 1883), and "Roster and Sketches of Members of the Territorial General Assembly," in *Journals of the General Assembly of Indiana Territory,* Appendix II, pp. 953-1018.

For land surveys and sales and early roads, there are the following: Charles J. Bayard, The Development of the Public Land Policy, 1783-1820 (Unpublished Ph.D. thesis, Indiana University, 1956), Chaps. VII-IX; Leonard Lux, *The Vincennes Donation Lands* (Indiana Historical Society *Publications,* XV, No. 4, Indianapolis, 1949); Malcolm J. Rohrbaugh, *The Land Office Business. The Settlement and Administration of American Public Lands, 1789-1837* (New York, 1969); George R. Wilson, *Early Indiana Trails and Surveys* (Indiana Historical Society *Publications,* VI, No. 3, Indianapolis, 1919), and by the same author, "The First Public Land Surveys in Indiana: Freeman's Lines,"

Indiana Magazine of History, XII (1916), 1-7; George R. Wilson and Gayle Thornbrough, *The Buffalo Trace* (Indiana Historical Society *Publications,* XV, No. 2, Indianapolis, 1946).

The boundaries of the territory and state and of various counties are adequately treated in George Pence and Nellie C. Armstrong, *Indiana Boundaries. Territory, State, and County (Indiana Historical Collections,* XIX, Indianapolis, 1933) and Mrs. Frank J. Sheehan, *The Northern Boundary of Indiana* (Indiana Historical Society *Publications,* VIII, No. 6, Indianapolis, 1928).

In addition to Indian and military material in the printed sources and in the Harrison biographies, the following should be mentioned: Accounts of Pigeon Roost Massacre, in Indiana Historical Society *Publications,* II, No. 4 (Indianapolis, 1888); William H. Cockrum, *Pioneer History of Indiana . . .* (Oakland City, Ind., 1907); Reed Beard, *The Battle of Tippecanoe* (Fourth edition, Chicago, 1911); Alfred Pirtle, *The Battle of Tippecanoe (Filson Club Publications* No. 15, Louisville, 1900); Murray Holliday, "The Battle on the Mississinewa," *Indiana History Bulletin,* XLV (1968), 152-166. Rosters of troops are included in the last three items.

Indian land cessions are discussed in Dwight L. Smith, Indian Land Cessions in the Old Northwest, 1795-1809 (Unpublished Ph.D. thesis, Indiana University, 1949). Various other developments are treated in Howard Burnett, "History of Vincennes University," *Indiana Magazine of History,* XXIX (1933), 114-121; Lee Burns, *Early Architects and Builders of Indiana* (Indiana Historical Society *Publications,* XI, No. 3, Indianapolis, 1935); Donald F. Carmony, "The Pioneer Press in Indiana," *Indiana History Bulletin,* XXXI, No. 10 (October, 1954); Logan Esarey, "The First Indiana Banks," *Indiana Magazine of History,* VI (1910), 144-158; Logan Esarey, *State Banking in Indiana, 1814-1873 (Indiana University Studies,* No. 15, Bloomington, 1912); Thomas T. McAvoy, *The Catholic Church in Indiana, 1789-1834* (New York, 1940); Howard H. Peckham, "Mail Service in Indiana Territory," *Indiana Magazine of History,* XLVII (1951), 155-164; and Emma Lou Thornbrough, *The Negro in Indiana . . . (Indiana Historical Collections,* XXXVII, Indianapolis, 1957).

The following accounts of the War of 1812 have been useful in following the western phases of the war: Cecil K. Byrd, The War of 1812 in the Old Northwest: First Phase (Unpublished Ph.D. thesis, Indiana University, 1942); Harry L. Coles, *The War of 1812* (Chicago, 1965); Reginald Horsman, *The War of 1812* (New York, 1969); Robert B. McAfee, *History of the Late War in the Western Country* (Lexington, Ky., 1816).

The preparation for statehood and the Constitutional Convention are treated in the following: John D. Barnhart, "The Southern Influence in the Formation of Indiana," "Sources of Indiana's First Constitution," *Indiana Magazine of History,* XXXIII, 261-276, XXXIX, 55-94; and *Valley of Democracy. The Frontier versus the Plantation in the Ohio Valley, 1775-1818* (Indiana University Press, Bloomington, 1953), Chaps. 11-12; Ruth E. Brayton, The Constitution of 1816 (Unpublished Master's thesis, Indiana University, 1929); Donald F. Carmony, "Fiscal Objection to Statehood in Indiana," *Indiana Magazine of History,* XLII (1946), 311-321; W. W. Thornton, *Constitutional Convention of*

1816 (a paper read before the State Bar Association, 1912). The 1816 Constitution is printed in Kettleborough, *Constitution Making in Indiana,* I, 83-125, with editorial notes tracing the preparation of the various articles from their original to final form. It is reprinted in the pamphlet, *Indiana's Road to Statehood* (Indiana Sesquicentennial Commission, 1964).

Newspapers

The files of the Vincennes *Indiana Gazette,* August 7, 1804-April 12, 1806, and its successor, the Vincennes *Western Sun,* July 11, 1807 through the year 1816 are invaluable in the preparation of any history of the territorial period. The editor, Elihu Stout, sometimes had to suspend publication for weeks at a time because of lack of paper or other reasons, and unfortunately this often happened at a crucial time when a newspaper account would have been especially helpful. The Archives Division, Indiana State Library, has photostatic copies of the *Indiana Gazette* for the above period and a complete file of original issues of the *Western Sun* that are known to exist.

The Archives Division and the Indiana Historical Society Library together have most of the issues of the *Western Eagle* that were published at Madison and Lexington between the summer of 1813 and January 6, 1816. The first issue that has been found is Volume I, No. 10, dated August 6, 1813. The 1813-14 issues in the Historical Society Library are photostats of originals in the American Antiquarian Society Library, Wooster, Massachusetts. By the time other papers were started at Brookville, Corydon, and Vevay the territorial period was practically at an end.

The Cincinnati *Liberty Hall,* which began publication on December 4, 1804, is also useful, especially for events transpiring in the southeastern counties. Photostats of the issues through December 26, 1810, are in the Archives Division.

INDEX

Abbott, Edward, lieutenant governor at Vincennes, 175-176, 178-179, 184-190.

Adams, John, President, 312, 314, 317.

Adena culture, 32-35.

Agriculture, climate favorable for, 11; in colony of Louisiana, 65; at Ouiatanon, 67; at Vincennes, 123n, 164, 255.

Agriculture, Society for the Encouragement of, 365-366.

Albany Congress, 119.

Aliens, 277.

Alvord, Clarence W., 234.

Amherst, Sir Jeffrey, receives capitulation of Canada, 132; charged with administration of British colonial policy, 134, 139, 147, 176; and Pontiac conspiracy, 142, 143-144.

Andrew the Huron, 161.

Angel Mounds, 49-51.

Anthony, Jonathan, 363n.

Archaeological sites, Dearborn Co., 33-34; Hamilton Co., 25; Henry Co., 41-42; Madison Co., 40-41; Marion Co., 48-49; Perry Co., 21; Posey Co., 39-40; Shelby Co., 34-35; Spencer Co., 28; Sullivan Co., 45; Vanderburgh Co., 49-51; Warrick Co., 31, 38, 47-48.

Archaeology, see Prehistory.

Artifacts, Indian, bannerstones, 23; birdstones, 26-27; found with burials, 24, 26-27, 34, 35, 36, 39, 40, 41, 42, 45. See also Pottery; Projectile points.

Asheton, Capt. Joseph, 291.

Augé, François, 86.

Austin, Moses, 320.

Badollet, John, appointed register Vincennes Land Office, 341; lets contracts for federal roads, 363n-364n; criticizes Harrison, 393; in Constitutional Convention, 442, 446, 450, 456-457; quoted on Vincennes residents, 321-322.

Bailey (Bayley), John, 207, 211, 229-230.

Baillardjon (?), Nicholas, 266n.

Baird, Samuel, 275n.

Banks, private, chartered, 426; provisions regarding, in 1816 Constitution, 457.

Baptist congregations, 366-367.

Baptiste, John, 230n.

Barrachman, Abraham, 279.

Barrachman, Christian, 278.

Barron, Joseph, 343, 375, 378-379.

Bartholomew, Col. Joseph, 405.

Baumer, ————, notary, 174.

Bayeul, Camet, 122.

Baynton, Wharton and Morgan, trading firm, 158, 162n, 163, 166-167n.

Bazadone, Laurent, 259, 260n.

Beard, Patrick, 443, 447.

Beaubien, Charles, British agent at Miamis Town, 181, 190, 199, 204, 223n, 238.

Beauharnois, Charles de la Boische, Marquis de, governor of Canada, receives instructions, 77-78; aids Louisiana governor, 81, 82; instructs Noyelle re Miami, 84; laments scarcity of trade goods, 94-95.

Beckes, Parmenas, 422.

Becquet brothers, 185.

Beggs, Charles, 423n.

Beggs, James, 351, 352.